LAS CASAS

LAS CASAS

IN SEARCH OF THE POOR
OF JESUS CHRIST

Gustavo Gutiérrez

Translated by Robert R. Barr

ORBIS BOOKS
Maryknoll, New York 10545

Originally published as *En Busca de los Pobres de Jesucristo,* copyright © 1992 by the Instituto Bartolomé de las Casas-Rimac, Ricardo Bentín 763, Apartado 3090, Lima 25, Peru, and the Centro de Estudios y Publicaciones (CEP), Lampa 808, Of. 601, Apartado 6118, Lima, Peru.

English translation copyright © 1993 by Orbis Books
Published in the United States by Orbis Books, Maryknoll, NY 10545
Manufactured in the United States of America

Library of Congress Cataloging-in-Publication Data
Gutiérrez, Gustavo, 1928–
    [En busca de los pobres de Jesucristo. English]
    Las Casas : in search of the poor of Jesus Christ / Gustavo
Gutiérrez ; translated by Robert R. Barr.
      p. cm.
    Includes bibliographical references and index.
    ISBN 0-88344-838-6
    1. Casas, Bartolomé de las, 1474–1566. 2. Indians, Treatment of—
Latin America. 3. Missions—Latin America—History. 4. Spain—
Colonies—Latin America. 5. Liberation theology. I. Title.
F1411.G97913   1993
282'.092—dc20   93-42517
                                              CIP

To Vicente Hondarza,
to Ignacio Ellacuría and his companions,
and in them to all those who, born in Spain,
have come to live and to die in the Indies,
in search of the poor of Jesus Christ.

Contents

Preface to the English Edition

There are figures in history — few, to be sure — who leap the barriers of time to become the contemporaries of all ages. These are people who immerse themselves so deeply in their own age that they remain relevant long after historical anecdotes and others of their own time are simple memories of the past. In their lives they combine a commitment to the immediate present with vision of the future, achievement and failure, intense action and original reflection, covenants and protests that transcend death.

One of these figures is Bartolomé de Las Casas. The study of his life and his works, therefore, breaks the mold of narrow specialization and demands a much broader and richer approach. Lewis Hanke, a great North American historian who died recently, dared to say that Las Casas was too great to leave to the Las Casas scholars.[1] The comment comes, let us note, from one of the great Las Casas scholars of this century; indeed, it was Hanke who revived studies on Las Casas some sixty years ago with his famous work *La lucha por la justicia en la conquista de América*.[2]

The contribution of Las Casas is not limited to the debate — still quite heated until just a few years ago — regarding the colonization and the defense of the inhabitants of the continent that today we call America. His contribution has been decisive in the arenas of human rights, religious freedom, democratic institutions, and the effort to understand the "other" of Western civilization.

On the other hand, he was a man of profound faith, and his theological reflection is of capital importance. Las Casas was not at all

---

1. We owe a great deal to this learned scholar and gracious friend. His work marks a step of greatest importance in works on Las Casas; these lines are in homage to his extraordinary work.

2. This book was based on his thesis at Harvard; he restudied and continued to deepen his understanding of this subject throughout his life. In relation to his works, or independently of them, important North American scholars have made decisive contributions regarding the life and thought of Las Casas and have translated some of his works into English. Among them I want to mention Henry R. Wagner, Helen Rand Parish, Stafford Poole, Benjamin Keen, and Francis Sullivan.

what many studies would have him to be, namely, a good friar and activist who did nothing more than apply the theology elaborated by the masters of Salamanca. We are in the presence of a man who thinks for himself, imbued, indeed, with his experience in the Indies, an experience of evangelization and, in a certain way, of politics.

He spoke in a loud voice, but a reasonable one. He prophetically denounced the injustices that he witnessed, but he spent his life proposing concrete solutions. He had very strong opinions, but his thought evolved and he always learned from both people and events. He defended the Indians, but above all he respected their human dignity and their right to be different. He believed in the importance of evangelization, but he refused to accept that Europeans had the right to be in the Indies without the free consent of the inhabitants. He loved his country, but he demanded that it be faithful to the faith that it was so proud of. He wanted the Indians to become Christians, but not if the cost was a violation of their personal freedom. He was a man of action, but on the basis of action he charted new theoretical courses. He had historical perspective and political vision, but the driving force of his life was faith in Christ, whom he encountered in the afflicted and crucified Indians.

In a world that some would level into a facile homogeneity, Las Casas reminds us of the human value of difference. In a situation marked by the growing gap between rich countries and poor countries, Las Casas is a witness to basic human rights: to life and liberty. For a humankind increasingly more interdependent, the figure of this man, situated between the Indies (America) and Europe, is a bracing challenge.

To present the radical unity of a tumultuous life and multifaceted thought is the purpose — the challenge — of this book.

Acknowledgments

This book was begun some twenty years ago. Several times, and for long periods, the writing was interrupted, for this period has been a very difficult one for our country; recently I have resumed the work again with determination.* During this process I have received the help of many friends, so my thanks are also many. I want to mention especially Pilar Arroyo, whose dedication and capacity for work have been crucial in the preparation of this book, as well as Laura Elias for her valued and continuous contribution.

My profound thanks also to those who in so many ways have made this book possible through their support: Luzmila Acuña, Rolando Arotinco, Blanca Cayo, Carlos Corzo, Jesús Cosamalón, Pedro de Guchteneere, Consuleo de Prado, Juan Bautista Lassègue, Carmen Lora, Alberto Maguiña, Francisco Moreno, Irene Pujazón, Pablo Thai-Hop, Cecilia Tovar, and Suasana Villarán. My most sincere thanks also to Catalina Romero and María Rosa Lorbes, directors of the Instituto Bartolomé de Las Casas, and to all the friends of the Institute and of the Centro de Estudios y Publicaciones, which enabled and supported this work.

I am also indebted to those who welcomed me in friendship at the University of Michigan, Boston College, Cambridge University, and the University of California (Berkeley). The Dominican Convent of Alcobendas and the Consejo Superior de Investigaciones Cientifi-cas, both in Madrid, gave me access to important documentation. In those places I also had the opportunity for fruitful conversations with David Brading, Francesca Cantù, Lewis Hanke, Helen R. Parish, Isacio Pérez Fernández, and Vidal Abril Castelló.

The translation and publication of this work in English were a daunting challenge for all involved. I would like to thank editor-in-chief of Orbis Books Robert Ellsberg and translator Robert R. Barr, as well as Hank Schlau and John Eagleson, who edited the text. Finally, I

---

*Several articles and especially the book *Dios o el oro en las Indias* (Lima: IBC-CEP, 1989) represented excerpts of the work in progress.

would like to thank my friend James B. Nickoloff, who painstakingly reviewed the translation and offered many comments and corrections.

During the initial stages of this work I shared concerns and reflections with two friends who are no longer with us: Hugo Echegaray and Enrique Ruiz Maldonado. I remember them with grateful affection.

Chronology

1543	Las Casas is named bishop of Chiapa
1543	*Memorial* to Emperor Charles V
1544	*Carta al Consejo de Indias* (Letter to the Council of the Indies)
1546 (?)	*Quaestio Theologalis* (*De Exemptione sive Damnatione*)
1547	Las Casas returns permanently to Spain
1550–51	Debate with Juan Ginés de Sepúlveda in Valladolid
1550–51	*Apología*
1552	Publication in Seville of eight tracts: *El octavo remedio, Aquí se contiene una disputa, Sobre los indios que se han hecho esclavos, Confesionario, Brevísima, Treinta proposiciones muy jurídicas, Principia quaedam, Tratado comprobatorio*
1555	*Carta a Carranza* (Letter to Bartolomé Carranza)
1560	*Memorial* to the Council of the Indies (with Domingo de Santo Tomás)
1563–64 (or 1552)	*De imperatoria vel regia potestate*
1563	*De Thesauris*
1564	*Tratado de las doce dudas* (Tract on twelve doubts)
1564	Testamento
1564	*Carta a los dominicos de Chiapa y Guatemala* (Letter to the Dominicans of Chiapa and Guatemala)
1566	Petition to His Holiness Pius V
1566	*Memorial* to the Council of the Indies
1566	Death of Bartolomé de Las Casas in Madrid (July 18)

Abbreviations Used in Text and Notes

A.H.	*Apologética historia* (Las Casas)
Apología (GS)	*Apología* of J. G. Sepúlveda
CHP	Corpus Hispanorum de Pace; in reference to Vitoria's works, see n. 6, ch. 5, below
DII	*Colección de documentos inéditos relativos al descubrimiento, conquista y organización de las antiguas posesiones españolas de América y Oceanía, sacados de los archivos del reino y muy especialmente del de Indias.* 42 vols. Madrid, 1864–84

Franciscans' and Dominicans' Letter
Written by a group of Franciscan and Dominican friars; in *DII* 7; see n. 11, ch. 1, below, for details

H.I.	*Historia de las Indias* (Las Casas)
Latin Letter	Written by Dominican and Franciscan missioners working in Hispaniola to Cardinal Cisneros and Adrian of Utrecht; May 27, 1517; in Medina, *Comunidad al servicio del indio*

Letter of the Dominicans
Written by Pedro de Córdoba; undated; in *DII* 11; see n. 51, ch. 1, below

Letter to the King
Written by Pedro de Córdoba to King Charles, May 28, 1517; in *DII* 11

O.E.	*Obras escogidas* (Las Casas)

Providence version

> Version of the *Doce dudas* found in the John Carter Brown Library (Providence, R.I.)

Yucay

> For discussion of the document, see nn. 1 and 2, ch. 14, below

Upstream to the Source

In the prologue of his *History of the Indies,* citing an ancient author, Bartolomé de Las Casas reminds us that history is the "teacher of life" and the "life of our memories" (*H.I., O.E.* 1:6a).[1] This is especially the case with the testimony of Bartolomé himself. With Bartolomé, deeds and commitments are inseparable. Each sheds light on, and sustains, the other. To study them is to infuse with life the memory of his reflections. He was a witness of his time — of that fact that, in this "Indian world, I have seen suffering," as he said (*H.I., O.E.* 1:10a). He speaks to us from an era whose pace had accelerated at the sight of a widening of the then-known world.

His long life prevented him from simply remaining under the impact of the first events of the Indies. He was able to get beyond this stage and conceive, as far as possible, a complete, integral notion of his era. "I am perhaps the oldest and, of those alive today, the most experienced" in these matters, he declares, not without a touch of pride, "with the possible exception of one or two others in all of these West Indies" (*H.I., O.E.* 1:17a). In this ample period of time, he always learned from reality; he conceived a thousand projects, was on the mark with some of them and missed it with others, fought with impressive tenacity, knew how to analyze situations with great lucidity, survived numerous attacks, achieved many of his objectives, evolved in his thinking.

But above all Bartolomé was moved by "the charity of Jesus Christ, which knows neither measure nor rest as long as it is a pilgrim on this earth" (*Carta al Consejo,* 1531, *O.E.* 5:43a). Indeed, neither did Las Casas rest. He was always moved by "the sight of the faith of Jesus Christ being so vituperated, affronted, and brought low in this New World," its inhabitants being the victims of such rapacity (ibid., *O.E.* 5:43b). Therefore — he says at the close of his life — he has walked "in dedication to the task of acquiring a remedy for the native folk of what we call the Indies," in order that "the havoc and massacre com-

1

mitted there, counter to all reason and justice," might cease (*Memorial al Consejo*, 1565, *O.E.* 5:536a).

This is the living context of his reflections. He never ceased revising and deepening those reflections with a view to a better understanding of what was occurring in his time in the Indies and in Europe. Conscious of the sixty-one years that had elapsed since he had seen "these tyrannies begin," and the forty-eight he had labored "to inquire and study and bring the truth out into the open," Las Casas says, in a delicate moment of his life, writing to the Dominican friars of Chiapa and Guatemala: "I believe, if I am not deceived, that I have plumbed the depths of these things and managed to reach the headwaters" (1563, *O.E.* 5:470b). Upstream to the source. Las Casas always sought the waters that would write *finis* to the sterility and suffering of the Indies he knew. These deep waters are the material of this book. Like him, we too shall have to travel upstream, to the headwaters, for we seek the source of his own writings and testimony. In traveling up this stream, we shall attempt to make his historical journey of the past a challenge and "teacher of life" for us today.

Facing the Truth

We are currently celebrating the fifth centenary of an occurrence of capital importance in the history of humanity. The event to which we refer changed the life of Bartolomé de Las Casas as well. We mean the encounter (or collision), unexpected on both sides, not only between the peoples of the territory today called America and those who lived in Europe, but including Africa, as well — a third continent promptly and violently incorporated into the process of which we speak. This event is regarded as a *discovery* by those who see history from the old continent (as they themselves call it). A *covering*, others call it — referring to a history written in blatant disregard of the viewpoint of the inhabitants of the so-called New World. The "Conquista," it was dubbed in the old history books; "invasion," some prefer to call it today.

One thing is certain: the matter is a complex one, and one that we have not yet adequately interpreted. Individuals of a number of different spiritual families devote attention to it. As might be expected, diverse, even opposed, focuses come into confrontation, for we are dealing with the historical course of a reality whose wounds are old and still open. The fifth centenary has endowed with renewed vitality polemics that have basically never ceased to smolder. A further contributing factor, doubtless, is the better understanding we have today, thanks to a great deal of research, of the manner in which the Indian peoples themselves have always read this same history.[2]

The controversy kindles mighty passions and produces towering indignation. And with good reason. Let us take just one fact: whatever calculation we accept of the original population of America, the decline in population over the seventy or eighty years following the arrival of Columbus can be regarded only as an authentic demographic collapse.[3] Add to this the disappearance of cultures that for one reason or another were unable to offer resistance to the invaders, along with so many other, similar factors.

The very mention of these matters is deeply distasteful to many in certain European nations: Spain and Portugal, present at the beginning and constituting the principal European presence ever since; France, England, and Holland, which later arrived on the scene; Germany, with its episodic financial investments and presence in the Indies; and Italy, through the presence and influence of certain personages. All of these countries are proud of what they have accomplished in the Indies, and actually regard it as civilizing and evangelizing. It is important, however, to remember that Spain alone had the courage to hold a comprehensive debate on the ethics and morality of the European presence in the Indies. In the other countries of the old world, the right to occupy these lands was regarded as too obvious to be questioned.

True, the discussion could be overwhelmed today by a flood of data and documents. We could be trapped in a fog of emotions, or hand down judgments that would be anachronistic in the face of history's advance and the presence of irreversible situations. A consideration of what happened from the sixteenth century onward must not be transformed into an invitation to turn back the clock of history.[4] History cannot be remade. This is simple realism. But this must not prevent us — on the contrary, it should stimulate us — to see the meaning for us today of an honest interpretation of the events that have occurred since that time. That time, to quote Las Casas, was "altogether new, and unlike any other." Now is a crucial moment, therefore, for a realistic understanding of our present, and of the promise that present holds for the future.

The question becomes more urgent — and more difficult — when we take account of the fact that, in this controversial encounter, the gospel of Jesus, too, came to these lands. What are we to think of the enormous human cost to which the evangelization of the Indies has de facto been linked? How are we to understand the role of the church in these events? In what way do these occurrences mark the current situation of Christian community on this continent? What can we learn today from Christians' first reactions to the demands on, contempt for, and death of the Indian populations? To what extent ought the protests, reflections, and engagements of so many missionaries of the sixteenth century in the face of the Indians' suffering be guidelines for our own days?

With the most profound respect for the historical coordinates of the past, we necessarily address that past out of our present concerns and anxieties. The effort will require courage and honesty. Only by looking historical truth full in the face shall we be able to embark upon the times to come with responsibility and efficacy.[5]

We do not seek solely an understanding of history and of the society in which we live. Also at stake is the *intellectus fidei* — the "intelligence" or understanding of Christian faith. After all, it is impossible to divorce the experience of faith and reflection on that experience from the history of peoples. A hope for and welcome of the Reign of life must necessarily call in question, and radically, a political reality of oppression and injustice. Las Casas said that the Indians were being "stripped of their lives before their time" and thus despoiled of "space for their conversion" (*H.I.*, bk. 3, ch. 128, *O.E.* 2:484b).

Unfortunately, something of the same must be said of the poor of today in Latin America, who continue to suffer a premature, unjust death. From the outset, the so-called controversy of the Indies had an important theological dimension. It could not have been otherwise in an age and a country like that of the Spain of that time, where the Christian element weighed so heavily in the balance. At a distance of several centuries, something of the sort is occurring today. Today once more, in these same lands of the Indies, the process of a reflection upon faith has been leading rapidly to an effective commitment in an awareness of the situation of poverty and injustice in which the majority of the population of Latin America live and under the inspiration that should animate the quest for a liberation that takes account of the complexity of the human person. It is for these reasons that we find the testimony of Bartolomé de Las Casas so meaningful today. Here was someone driven to proclaim the Reign of God in a fitting manner, through a defense of the life and freedom of persons in whom his faith enabled him to perceive Christ himself.

Center of a Tradition

In this book we shall focus our interest on reflections that emerged from the turbulent, combat-fraught life of Bartolomé de Las Casas, part of which — as Las Casas says in his last testament — was spent "going and coming from the Indies to Castile, and from Castile to the Indies, many times" (*O.E.* 5:539b). To follow the course and development of his thinking, we must endeavor to assimilate — as far as possible — the chronological data and the events of his life. This becomes all the more urgent in view of our author's constant reworking, rewriting, and revision of his texts. On occasions, certain drafts of early date are incorporated into later works. Las Casas uses scissors along with a pen. This sometimes makes a correct understanding of what he is writing rather elusive on first approach. Dates, consequently, are a valuable element for an understanding of his thought.[6] Therefore, although we shall not make the biographical aspects of the Lascasian odyssey a special concern of our investigations, we do need to attend to the more recent historical studies in their regard.[7]

While the life and work of Bartolomé de Las Casas clearly constitute a key factor in the sixteenth-century battle for the rights of the Indians, it would not be true to history to see him as an isolated figure in the Indies — rather like a stubborn, solitary, idealistic person fighting against everything and everyone. The truth is that not only did he achieve a great influence in his own time (as even his adversaries acknowledge), but, besides, all through his life he had many allies (missionaries, bishops, theologians, and even certain royal officials, including members of the Council of the Indies) in his task of a defense of the natives.[8] In fact, some of these had preceded him in that effort.[9]

Let us make it clear that Bartolomé's coincidence with the ideas of such persons (if sometimes only a temporary one, and not on all points) is owing to the fact that they all experienced the same reality — the oppression of the Indian — and felt impelled by the same gospel, the good news of Jesus Christ. They constituted an active minority daringly doing battle for justice. Las Casas was perhaps the one who drilled the deepest into what was occurring in the Indies and best articulated a theological reflection on the basis of those events, but he was only *primus inter pares.* Accordingly, in commenting on his writings, we shall have to attend as well to all those who, before and during his own long life, embarked on the same combat.[10] Many years ago, J. M. Chacón y Calvo observed incisively: "Las Casas is not an isolated figure. . . . He is at the center of tradition, yes. But he is not the whole tradition."[11]

That Las Casas was a person of action is beyond question. His theoretical abilities, on the other hand, have been disputed: we allude not only to the Sevillian's stubborn detractors, who obviously could not acknowledge such abilities in him, but to those as well who show a certain sympathy for him. For some of these latter, Las Casas is the missioner and ardent defender of the Indians who puts in practice the theses of the theologians of Salamanca. Their purpose is to justify

Bartolomé's activity by supporting it with a theology they regard as serious and academic.[12] And when, in the best of cases, his theoretical contributions are indeed appreciated, they are situated mainly in the area of law and political philosophy.[13]

However, the discovery of certain hitherto unknown Lascasian texts, and the publication of others that had long lain in manuscript, as well as the appearance of recent scholarly monographs on him, afford us a better understanding of his thinking today.[14] Gradually, despite the resistance of old prejudices, an interest has been awakened in the theological dimension of Bartolomé's intellectual production. For our part, we believe that Las Casas presents a discourse upon faith that emerges with a profile of its own against the background of sixteenth-century theology. His enormous erudition — acknowledged by all, although with varying appraisals of its value[15] — never smothers the creativity that comes to him from a great sensitivity to the challenges of the situation of the Indian nations and from a deep spirituality. We are dealing with a genuine theology, which, on more than one occasion, blazes innovative, unexpected trails.

A continuous interaction takes place, in Las Casas's work, between reflection and concrete commitment — theory and practice. His is a thinking that not only *refers* to practice, but is developed by someone *engaged* in practice. This does not diminish the intellectual, even academic (in the sense of scientific rigor), caliber of his contributions. On the contrary, in many instances this engagement actually enhances the theoretical quality of his work. Faith — trust in God and acceptance of God's message — sheds light on a discourse that seeks to plumb human experience. The "intelligence of the faith" deals with a revealed truth that is accepted by concrete persons. A certain philosophical and theological perspective might incline us to think that, the more a reflection takes its distance from the hodgepodge of the everyday and from the ambiguity of action, the more authentic and serious it is. However, this is not the oldest and most traditional Christian concept of theology. From the first Christian centuries onward, theology was done in intimate, constant interconnection with Christian existence and the mission of the church, which it challenged and questioned with a view to contributing to a greater fidelity to revelation and to giving witness to salvation in Jesus Christ.

This is Las Casas's perspective. In order for him to be able to judge what is transpiring among the numberless folk of these lands and in order for the word of God to be the all-consuming criterion of that judgment, Bartolomé has a need to know the complex reality of the Indies. "Law and right...arise from and have their origin in the truth-relation of the facts" (*H.I., O.E.* 1:14b), he repeatedly says. Otherwise there would be no way for changing things. Bartolomé welds faith to what we today would call social analysis. This enabled him to unmask the "social sin" of his time. That, doubtless, was his forte — and also the difference between him and the great majority of those in Spain who were concerned with the affairs of the Indies.[16] The situation — the stormy, conflict-ridden situation — he has before his eyes is a decisive, pressing motive for his work, indeed for his life. Those who had not seen the abuse and contempt to which the Indians were subjected, those who had not suffered in their own flesh the aggression of the mighty ones of the Indies, those who had not counted dead bodies, had other priorities in theology.

In the intelligence of the faith that Las Casas forged, not only are the *authors* of religious discourse important, but the *actors,* as well, in the living drama of the Indies. The latter are the motivation of his reading and citations of the former. Las Casas does not write to "express his ideas," as we like to say; his works are not written to mark stages in his personal intellectual development. Rather they are milestones in his battle for the rights of the Indians. For him, his writings are manifestations of a concrete solidarity with others. Therefore they have immediate social and political contexts without which it is impossible to understand them.[17] Bartolomé worked without thought for what would be said of him later, but within a quest for concrete "remedies" (and not bandages, as he will say on one occasion) that it was urgent to secure. His was an extraordinary capacity to learn and to perceive new corollaries of an old argument, as well as to draw unexpected conclusions from old elements of Christian tradition.

At the same time, he was endowed with an enormous power of persuasion, which made him a redoubtable adversary for anyone upholding a doctrine he sought to attack. Agile with pen and print, he used them both to defend the Indians and fight the powerful. All of this has led some to think that, in the Indians' defense, he accommodates theoretical principles to the needs of the moment. If this criticism is intended to insinuate a lack of interest in the actual postulates in question — an all but exclusive concern for practical problems — it seems to us to be a mistaken interpretation. It will not be difficult to demonstrate that Las Casas always remained faithful to his great source intuitions. They fed his reflection his whole life long. His was a fidelity bordering on stubbornness.

This led him constantly to present projects for changing very specific situations. Nor was he afraid of making mistakes along the way. This is a risk that has to be taken by those who have made a commitment to their age and to actual, living persons. True, we are dealing with a flexible intelligence, one attentive to the challenges emerging from reality and to the objections raised by opponents. What we see is a reflection that refuses to sever its ties with concrete, personal experience and becomes sufficiently sure of itself only as it evolves. Had Bartolomé wafted above what was happening in the Indies, he would not have made certain errors in his proposals and vacillations in his arguments. But then perhaps he would not have left us the witness that is engraved on our memories today.

These and Other Indies

Let us dispel one misconception from the outset. It is frequently said that Bartolomé de Las Casas was "ahead of his time" and that he employs a kind of modern language, one more familiar to us today, when he speaks of the right of the Indian nations to be different, when he defends what we call civil liberties, or when he manifests his sensitivity to the concrete, historical dimensions of faith. The intent, of course, is to eulogize a person of the sixteenth century — calling him modern because he thought in his time as we do today. But in the course of the eulogy, innocently or disingenuously, the criterion of discernment invoked consists in today's categories — those of our present understanding of the Christian message. This mentality is an outgrowth of the arrogance of the modern spirit, which regards itself as the final stage of history and which distorts past reality accordingly. Furthermore, these persons argue as if only now has the gospel finally come to present us with its urgent requirements of justice. The actual case is that these requirements are writ large in the biblical message itself, as well as on the hearts of all who have kept that message alive, despite — often enough — mistrust and hostility, throughout the history of Christian community.

On the other hand, to dub Las Casas a "liberation theologian" may have the interest of calling attention to certain important aspects of his thought and the permanent liberative dimension of Christian faith. We understand and appreciate what is meant by those who express themselves in this way. Still, we prefer not to do so. It does not seem to us to be appropriate, or even necessary, for an expression of our appreciation of his theological work and his witness. That work and witness transpired in a context very different from today's, at the social level as at the theological. The conceptual tools and the language are different too. Their depth accrues to them from their gospel roots and from the way in which Las Casas managed to live his fidelity to the Lord. We cannot ask him to speak after the fashion of a person of the twentieth century. The question we must ask when it comes to Las Casas is this one: How, in his time, under particular conditions and with specific opportunities, was he able to proclaim the gospel of Jesus? An attempt to answer this question will be stimulating and instructive.

To approach this witness to God's love in the Indies means respecting Las Casas in his world, in his era, in his sources. It calls for lucidity with regard to his limitations. Far from distancing us from his production, this attitude will move us closer to it, without our pretending to identify his approach with the way in which we today defend causes that are, we readily grant, of the same general kind. The liberative vectors of faith are there: they can be found by anyone willing to proclaim the good news amid the sufferings and hopes of the poor.

Persons like Bartolomé de Las Casas have a special talent for recalling those dimensions of faith to people's memories — amid evasion, dissimulation, lies, and the efforts of power and the bureaucracy of his time to domesticate the biblical message. But it needs to be emphasized that the Sevillian was one of those who, on the basis of their faith in the God of the Reign, denounced the poverty and plundering of which the oppressed of history were the victims. Nor were the abuses they decried the acts of individuals alone. They were rooted in the profound injustice of the economic and social system being implanted in the Indies at that time.

In recalling the facts, these writers have left us with testimonials of realities that they strove to change, many of which we would not know without their having told us of them. It was a difficult enterprise, in the face of the ideological enthrallment of prevailing views regarding the events of the age, but it ought to be evaluated and appreciated — with its limitations and ambiguities — within the historical framework in which it was situated. These persons risked, and lost, their lives in their undertaking: for example, Bishop Antonio Valdivieso in Nicaragua. They also exposed their reputations: they were representatives of the best of Spain, but those who, then as now, seem so stiffly opposed to a reexamination of the history of the era regarded them (and still regard them) as champions of "extremist" positions and enemies of their native country. In reality, the only sin of these persons was to have ripped the mask from the face of those whose behavior actually did defame their native land and who made the Christian faith they claimed as their own a laughingstock.

A perceptive remark of J. A. Maravall deserves to be cited here. According to this historian, Las Casas "wrote not only to defend the Indians.... If he wrote so harshly against the persons of the old world ... if he excoriates them, it is in order to move them to start off down the road to utopia — in order to move them to reform their conduct."[18] The observation is absolutely correct. In his carefully pondered introduction to the *Historia de las Indias,* Bartolomé asserts that one of the reasons for writing this work is "the good and utility of all Spain." He intends, he says, to deliver "my Spanish nation" from its error concerning the way in which the Indian nations ought to be treated (*H.I., O.E.* 1:15a–b). The reforming zeal of this evangelizer actually embraces the natives of the old world, as well — however little they may have appreciated it! This is one of the reasons why the figure of Las Casas is of such striking universality: here we have someone who, still today, issues a challenge to persons of various corners of the planet. This broad human compass impelled one of the greatest Lascasists, Lewis Hanke, to make the following provocative statement: "Las Casas is too important to be left to the Lascasists."[19]

Surely a better knowledge of the social mechanisms and structural causes of poverty makes us more attentive today to aspects of poverty that had lain hidden. Our aim is sharpened today; it concentrates on the right targets. However, it will not be forcing things if we assert that our friar's task, simple as it may seem to say so, consists above all in letting it be known in the Indies that there is a God, and that that God is the God of Abraham, Isaac, Jacob, and Jesus. And for a believer, nothing will inspire a more profound refusal to tolerate misery and social oppression than the will to love and justice of God.

Indeed, justice, which is an expression of love, is a Christian demand of the first importance. According to the Bible, to establish "justice and right" among the Hebrew people means prolonging, extending, the liberative act of God that withdrew that people from the oppression under which it suffered in Egypt. The establishment of justice and right is fidelity to the Covenant struck by believers with God and must lead to fullness of life. From this perspective, the word "justice," while referring to the bonds established among persons living in society, denotes the nexus of human beings with God as well. The first meaning is not erased. It is only assumed into a connotation so important and rich, in Scripture, that it comes to be equivalent to salvation — that is, to total communion with God and others. St. Paul, for example, speaks of salvation as justification. For the same reason, the word "just," in the Bible, becomes a synonym for "holy."

When Las Casas links salvation and justice, then, he is only responding to this biblical focus, which constitutes, furthermore, a permanent facet of Christian tradition. Precisely because Bartolomé de Las Casas regards it as the proper characteristic of the follower of Jesus to proclaim and bear witness to the salvific will of God, to "establish justice and right" in the Indies becomes an imperative for him. It is a condition for attaining the face-to-face vision of God — to use the Pauline expression — which John of the Cross, prevented from journeying to these lands, exquisitely denotes as those "other, better Indies."[20] Bartolomé always sought to bring it about that something of those better Indies (fullness of love and friendship) become history and flesh (justice) in the Indies that it was his lot to know.

For Bartolomé as a member of the church, that "rule and measure of our believing," as he calls it in his testament (*O.E.* 5:539b), it is faith and the consequent task of evangelization that are the mainspring of his commitment. The "better Indies" function as a utopia to move history. They ought to transform, radically, the here and now of the reality of the Indies that Las Casas knew as no one else in his time. This utopia of love, justice, and peace remains in force today.

The same utopia is the food and drink of the controversial Peruvian Indian, Felipe Guamán Poma de Ayala (d. 1615?) as well, who, early in the seventeenth century, wrote a book, in an epistolary style, which he addressed to Philip III, king of Spain.[21] Here he recounts that, his youth spent, he undertook a long journey through the lands of the ancient Tawantinsuyu. In a beautiful formula inspired by the gospel, he tells us of the motive that impelled him to do so: he "walked through the world *in search of Christ's poor.*"[22] He went forth to learn firsthand of the situation of dispossession and contempt in which the Indians, his racial siblings, now lived. "In order to testify to this," he declares, he "must write as an eyewitness."[23] This he does with a moral purpose: "for the emendation of life of Christians and unbelievers."[24] For both alike.[25]

In search of Christ's poor: here was the life of Bartolomé de Las Casas as well. For those poor he fought, and from out of their midst he announced the gospel in a society being established on a foundation of plunder and injustice. This is why his proclamation of the Christian message is invested with characteristics of prophetic denunciation that maintain all their validity today. The situation in the Indies in the sixteenth and seventeenth centuries was the occasion of some persons' rediscovery of the very fonts of faith. In the "afflicted, scourged" inhabitants of these lands, Bartolomé was able to see the presence of Christ himself. From this evangelical outlook springs a reflection upon Jesus Christ, a christology, that becomes flesh and history in the Indies and the backbone of his thought.

The outrages perpetrated upon the Indian nations by those who "go by the name of Christian," as Las Casas repeatedly describes them, will awaken consciences and decide destinies. Guamán Poma and Las Casas were two of those who, from a starting point in a faith in the God of life, refused to tolerate the unjust, premature death of the Indians. They belonged to culturally different worlds, and they lived in different years; but they had this in common, that they both saw an autochthonous population living a life of contempt and abuse at the hands of others. They communed as well in their determination to test this situation in the crucible of the exigencies of Christian faith, an effort that, naturally, had different accents in each of the two writers. Both, in their different ways, set off down the road of solidarity with the outcast and oppressed — with "Christ's poor," to use Guamán Poma's words.

Plan of the Book

The variety of challenges he faces moves Las Casas to appeal to many different aspects of the thought of his time. He works and reworks his points. He does battle with adversaries from various sides of the intellectual world. Often enough he repeats his ideas tiresomely, which can be deceiving when, as sometimes happens, under the guise of mere reiteration his insistence gives rise to new outlooks, decisive nuances in his argumentation. All of this endows his reflections with a very great complexity. A presentation of them will necessarily require entering upon discussions that, in their outward trappings, are no longer our own, but that, at their core, are still alive. Compare the citation today of works of theologians, philosophers, or jurists that are indeed old but that bear witness to permanent human and Christian values. It will also require us to bring in texts from across the whole, broad gamut of his writings — without, to be sure, any claim to exhaustiveness in our examination of a literary corpus that calls for many approaches by different specialists. It is a vast task, which some have undertaken, and most courageously. If, as J.-B. Lassègue says, Las Casas's life was "a long journey,"[26] so too will be the study of his witness, which is inscribed in a framework of the sorrowful, yet hope-filled, process of the integral liberation of a people. This book is intended as one more milepost along that itinerary.

Each of the five parts of this work begins with an introduction presenting the topics to be set forth in the three chapters that compose it. Each part, furthermore, ends with a conclusion in the form of a brief summary of its contents. This will dispense us from entering into detail here as to the content of the five parts. Let us merely explain a few strokes of the general outline.

The topics of Bartolomé's reflection are closely determined by the problems arising in his missionary practice and Christian awareness. They are questions arising from the sequence of the events that was triggered by the arrival of the Europeans. Basically, they are: the *wars,* and the ensuing *domination* revolving around the *encomienda.* It is Las Casas's perception of these facts, repeated numberless times, that will guide us in our presentation. Naturally, it is only a general orientation, with a view to putting order into the points treated. In the concrete, indeed, all of these questions intersect. The events Bartolomé recalls pose severe challenges to human sensitivity, to justice, and to Christian faith. Bartolomé examines and criticizes the reality around him from a point of departure of faith in Jesus Christ. The celebrated question of the right of the citizens of European countries to travel to and remain in the lands that had begun to be called the West Indies is dealt with by Las Casas — long before the intervention of the school of Salamanca — on the basis of the facts he has before his eyes. Thus, a presentation of his reflections on what he regards as the two steps of the Iberian entry into the Indies will enable us to grasp his intuitions at their source, and accordingly to follow his development more closely.

But first, in *Part One,* we shall attempt to sketch Las Casas's central ideas — the wellspring of the waters that flow through all his work. Here is the source of his evangelizing concern and of his commitment to the aboriginal populations. Here are perspectives that, besides being initial, are abiding. For this reason, we must follow closely here the chronology of the Lascasian writings and activities, from his first interventions to his last. Las Casas's faithfulness to his germinal intuitions is no obstacle to a continual evolution in a thought that sought ever to respond to the new situations it had to confront. The Sevillian lives and thinks amid the cruel death of the Indians, their death "before their time." Thus, the question of justice is posed with urgency. It was not only a preliminary question. It framed his whole existence. In the Indians dying prematurely and unjustly he sees Christ. There is a christological focus, then, at the root of his reflection. To proclaim Christ — the sole legitimate reason for the presence of the Europeans in these lands — in this context of death means announcing the gift of life and liberty. Las Casas's way of approaching matters of the Indies, his methodology, is of supreme importance. Indeed, it constitutes a trait of the Lascasian spirituality: adopting the viewpoint of the other, the Indian.

In *Parts Two and Three,* we shall study the questions of the war and its challenges. Spontaneously, the newcomers thought the native peoples had nothing better to do than accept European culture and religion. These were boons for them, and worthy of being imposed by force if need be. This is what the theology of the age, despite certain nuances, maintained. Bartolomé champions dialogue and persuasion, instead, as the "only means" of evangelization, following the guidelines of Jesus, who came to announce the Reign of God in full respect for persons. This leads him to posit bold theses on the subject of religious freedom — a matter that the question of human sacrifice will turn into even more of a burning question. The content of the gospel is salvation in Jesus Christ. Las Casas reminds his compatriots that their condition as Christians is not a lifelong guarantee of their salvation — which they will reach only if they practice justice toward the Indians and among the Spaniards themselves. Thus, our author faces the question of God's salvific will from a standpoint amid the situation of the Indian nations. Not without difficulty does he find fertile pathways for his reflection here.

Part Four bears on the regime being established with the commencement of the Conquista. The centerpiece of that regime is the *encomienda*. Bartolomé will battle it lifelong, and it is impossible to say what additional corruption it would have caused had Las Casas not combated it so doggedly. His opposition to the *encomienda* justifies his biting criticism of the Burgos Laws, which confirmed it, and his decisive influence, thirty years later, on the New Laws, which sought to limit it. Las Casas clearly perceives that the injustices affecting the native peoples are not rooted solely in personal excesses or abuses. That would be the easy, more comfortable explanation, of course, since it involves a refusal to look at reality and therefore change it. The main cause of the evils being perpetrated lies in the socioeconomic system — in structural elements, we would say today. And that system is justified through an appeal to the postulate of the Indian's human inferiority. The fight against this notion was another of Las Casas's great battles. The papal bull *Sublimis Deus* constituted an important support for his position in the matter. The controversial — but actually unambiguous — Lascasian position with regard to black slavery will confirm for us one of Bartolomé's core theses: that Indians and blacks are the poor in the gospel sense of the word. This view provides him with new light for an understanding of the liberative work of Christ. It is an intuition that imposes a particular course and direction on his theology, which is different from that presented by the Salamancans — among them, and in the forefront, Francisco de Vitoria — with whom he also maintains broad areas of agreement.

Part Five extends the foregoing considerations on the colonial regime, with the accent on what was occurring in Peru, which was the Dominican friar's great concern in his last years. Las Casas not only champions the rights of the Indians, but indicates the social and economic causes of their misery. The Peruvian situation leads him to tighten his theses and to synthesize his thought concerning the right of the Indian nations to free themselves from the yoke to which they are subjected. Bartolomé follows the Dominicans of Hispaniola into the breach they have made in the seamless ideology of the colonizers and demands for these nations the restitution of what has been stolen from them. Otherwise the way will be open for a legitimate defense of their rights even by the use of force. Little by little, Bartolomé arrives at another core notion: without the consent of the native peoples, the presence of the Europeans is illegitimate. Drawing an unusual conclusion, for the time, from the principle of restitution, he asserts that the authentic descendants of the Incas ought to be restored to the throne of Peru. Nor does he stop there, but shows as well that, beneath Christians' behavior, which is motivated by greed for gold, an idolatrous conduct lurks: gold de facto replaces God. In opposition to what a later document, written in Peru, would assert (the *Yucay Opinion*), Las Casas maintains that the sole mediator between God and the Indians is Jesus Christ. Guamán Poma will likewise criticize the Christians' idolatrous conduct, and will resume, in a way very much his own, the Lascasian proposal for Peru.

•

In his battle for justice, Las Casas constantly appeals to an "intelligence of the faith" marked by his personal meditation on the figure of Christ. It is this meditation that enables him to practice discernment amid the whirlwind of events, to convince his interlocutors, and to perceive the exigencies of the good news of the gospel in the concrete time and place in which he lived. Only thus could he proclaim the love of the God of his faith and his hope. What we have is a theological reflection — vigorous at some moments, hesitating at others, but always in progress — at the service of the proclamation of God's love for each and every person, and especially for the poor of his time. This is the material of the pages to follow.

We propose to delve into Bartolomé's life and thought by following the advice he gave for arriving at a correct understanding of the human and Christian values at stake in his time in the Indies and in Europe. One can reach such an understanding, Las Casas stated and advised, "by commending oneself earnestly to God, and by piercing very deeply — until one finds the foundations" (*Confesionario*, 1552, O.E. 5:239b). This is what he did. A profound, fecund spirituality runs between the lines of his pages, even the most convoluted. In that spirituality is expressed, with the inevitable seal peculiar to his era and temperament, the deepest heart of the Dominican soul: to transmit to others the fruit of one's prayer (*contemplata aliis tradere*). At the same time, we find in his writings an insatiable desire to know the facts and a firm commitment to see them in the light of the fonts of the Christian message and the universal requirements of the human being. At the service of this enterprise he placed his readings, his logical reasoning, and his ability to persuade.

But none of this should make us forget that the grand theme of his life was the God of Jesus Christ, the God who dwells in history. That is the ultimate foundation of his acute sense of the value of persons (of their life and their freedom), and of his particular sensitivity to the most forgotten. Frequently, in order to maintain this witness, he had to "pass through the lake of infamy and tribulation" (*Carta al Consejo,* 1534, *O.E.* 5:63b).[27]

Accordingly, the voice of this witness of "a greater Church and a surer God," as Pedro Casaldáliga puts it,[28] continues to challenge us, and to teach us to evangelize.

Part One _____

The Wellspring

✠ Around 1549, Las Casas writes to his friend Domingo de Soto, confessor of King Charles V, a letter full of rich reflections. Alluding to the position held by the great theologian, he says that God has placed the latter "at the wellspring [*fontano lugar*] whence must flow the dew and consolation of revelation and of liberation from so great a loss of bodies and souls."[1] The expression "wellspring" can be applied to Las Casas's basic intuitions. Those intuitions constitute a whole that we may regard as the wellspring of the vital impulse of all his work, which, as we know, was devoted to the liberation of the Indians. In Part One we should like to draw a sketch of this wellspring of the Lascasian adventure.[2] We need to have the framework of these central ideas clear before seeing the manner in which they are taken up to confront the various challenges that present themselves in the Indies. An initial synthetic overview may provide us with a useful frame of reference and help us achieve greater clarity in our presentation. It is this synthetic view that we propose to set forth in Part One.

Arriving in the Indies very early — only ten years after Columbus — Las Casas has an in-depth, firsthand knowledge of something that will mark his life and lead him to definitive options. That something is the untimely and unjust death of the dwellers of these lands. It sets him directly before a terrible dilemma, which shows him what is at stake in these regions.

"The entire [papal] concession," he writes, "to the monarchs of Spain, its motivation, and the sovereignty they have over these lands and people, was and is for the *life* of the latter, and for the *salvation* and conversion of their souls. Yet it has become a very quick and miserable *death*, and final *perdition*" (*Carta a un personaje de la corte*, 1535, O.E. 5:62a; emphasis added). Here we have a capital text. It is found in a letter written in Nicaragua, after an unsuccessful attempt to sail to Peru.[3] Life and salvation, or death and perdition: this is what is at

17

stake. Life and salvation are inseparable for Las Casas. Each demands the other. He has a clear awareness that the Lord came to bring life, and life in abundance (see John 10:10).

The disjunction Las Casas presents is reminiscent of the one in Deuteronomy: "Here, then, I have today set before you life and prosperity, death and doom" (Deut. 30:15). "Choose life," Yahweh says, a few verses further on (Deut. 30:19). In the Indies, death has been selected instead, and ultimately the "perdition" of souls. Las Casas himself participated for a time in the system that fostered these things. The reversal that his experience, his contact with the first Dominican missioners, and his reading of Scripture effect in his existence leads him to an option for life, which wars against the situation in course. He must swim against the current. To the wellspring.

This point of departure, for Las Casas, is the conviction that in the Indian, as the poor and oppressed one, Christ is present, buffeted and scourged. The evangelical inspiration of this perception is evident. It will indelibly mark Bartolomé's spirituality and theology. This intuition will endow his thinking and the positions he has taken with energy and consistency. It also endows his thought with universality: he begins with Indian reality, but he reaches to every person, and most concretely, any poor and abused person. From this intuition flows the dew that must wash away the hard, dry clay of oppression.

Las Casas's overwhelming concern was the proclamation of the gospel. The real accomplishment of that objective is his major criterion for discerning and judging what is happening in the Indies. The situation of death prevailing in the Indies deprives of the last shred of credibility the proclamation of God's love to which some missionaries are committed. He writes in his last work: "When we preach to the Indians the humility and poverty of Jesus Christ, and how he suffered for us, and *how God rejoices in the poor* and in those the world despises, they think that we are lying to them" (*Doce dudas*, 1564, *O.E.* 5:512b; emphasis ours).[4] Here is the God of Jesus Christ, whose promise and humility we have the obligation of manifesting. The God of the Reign is glad, is pleased, with the poor, as Las Casas says so delicately and perceptively. The poor are God's favorites because they find themselves in a situation altogether contrary to the divine design, which is a design of life. For God, the despised of this world come first. They must come first as well for those who call themselves believers. The practice of these latter must bestow credibility on the proclamation of the God who is love.

The right of the poor to life and liberty will be one of Las Casas's great claims. His theology of grace is a theology of life, a life that embraces the temporal and the spiritual alike. It is also a theology of freedom as the indispensable condition of a worthy human existence and an authentic Christian faith. Life and salvation.

One of the key elements of Las Casas's work and thought is his historical perspective on all of the above. His commitment to "those the world despises" goes very far indeed. His life is an immense effort to make the outlook of the Indian his own. This presupposes, of course, that he recognize the dwellers of the Indies as persons different from Westerners. They must not only be respected in their otherness, but listened to as well and understood in their way of seeing things. Perhaps it is because he tried to do this that Las Casas has been seen as an aberration — crass error! — throughout the centuries by some of his compatriots. His adoption of the native view of things distanced him from his fellows — from those he had close at hand. But it enabled him to draw near the remote nations of the Indies. And become their neighbor.

Dying before Their Time

The causes were many, but the reality was one, and very harsh. In the years following the arrival of Columbus, the inhabitants of the islands that had just been named the Antilles saw their world fall to pieces. Types of labor were imposed that they had never known. Military expeditions were undertaken to obtain their total submission. There were lethal food shortages. The natives were abused and harassed. New diseases were pandemic. Depopulation, social disorder, violent protests, and frequently even the disappearance of any desire to go on living increased dramatically. Here was a totally new state of affairs for the peoples of the islands.

The foreign invaders — which is how they were regarded by the natives — also found it very difficult to comprehend what they were seeing. True, the Spaniards had had the experience of the reconquest of their homeland. Some of them had come to America with direct or indirect experience of action in Africa or the Canaries. But none of this was of much help when it came to appreciating the human value of peoples so different from Europeans.

To Indian eyes, the attitude of some of the newcomers — that of a minority — seemed more moderate, or even simply different, from that of the rest. True, these few as well found it difficult to appreciate the native world, especially its religious customs. But their behavior was frequently of a different cast from that of their compatriots. We are thinking of the missionaries (or persons like Cristóbal Rodríguez, Pedro de Lumbreras, and Pedro de Rentería, all of whom we shall speak of later, or Pedro de Isla; see *H.I.*, bk. 1, ch. 45, *O.E.* 2:112a, where Las Casas mentions them appreciatively), who had been arriving, a handful at a time, over the first few decades. It is mainly owing to them that we know the horrors of the Antilles. Conquistadors and civil functionaries had every reason to conceal their atrocities — which, even today, some would like to deny ever happened (in the face of utterly reliable, unequivocal testimony that they did).

It would be far better to face up to reality. Let us go in serene quest

of the truth and not fear the incomprehension and indignation that
our search will arouse in the minds of some. Unless we have a good
sketch of the reality to which we refer, we shall find ourselves incapable of appreciating the scope and tenacity of the protest of the friars
who, relatively early, arrived on the island soon to be known as Hispaniola. These missionaries' loyalty to the gospel, their efforts to draw
near the Indians, and the valor of their denunciation are as a light in
the dark of night. Not that the denunciation had a great deal of effect. The perpetrators of these depravities refused to be enlightened.
But without hearing the missionaries, we should surely fail to recognize the proclamation of the Reign of God, the Reign of love, heard by
America over the course of these first years of colonization. Nor did
the friars escape a long, painful struggle for justice (as historian Lewis
Hanke put it) — a justice that, in the minds of the first missionaries,
could come only by way of the liberation of the Indian.

1. *From Haiti and Quisqueya to Hispaniola*

In 1509, Diego Colón — son of the first Columbus — saw his lengthy
and laborious machinations come to fruition in his appointment as
governor, succeeding Ovando, of the island (or at least of a goodly part
of it) the natives called Haiti and Quisqueya and the newcomers had
christened Hispaniola: today's Dominican Republic and Haiti.[1] Colón
had been instructed to redistribute the Indian populations. The actual
execution of the task, however, fell mainly to the sinister Spanish treasurer general, Miguel de Pasamonte. King Ferdinand had never much
trusted the younger admiral, and preferred to deal directly with Pasamonte.[2] It was a difficult moment on the island — especially, of course,
for the surviving natives. It was difficult as well for their neighbors on
outlying islands.

Seed of All Abuse

At Santa Fe, in April of 1492, Christopher Columbus had struck an
agreement with Ferdinand and Isabella whereby he was granted,
along with certain honors and privileges, a tenth part of the "pearls,
precious stones, gold, silver, spices, and other things and merchandise
whatsoever, of whatever sort," to be found in the lands that "should be
discovered or gained."[3] Giménez Fernández puts it baldly: For Columbus as for King Ferdinand, the enterprise in question was "purely and
simply economic. It had nothing to do with looking for souls to save,
or finding a route to follow to rescue the Holy Places, as political
necessities later constrained the king and his viceroy to proclaim."[4]

Indeed, in his diary and other texts Columbus leaves abundant testimony to his obsession with the gold he hoped to find in the lands
to which he had come.[5] Even in his last years, for example in 1503,
in a letter to the king and queen of Spain, he writes: "The gold is
most excellent, and he who fills his coffers with it will be able to
do whatever he likes in the world, including flinging souls to Paradise."[6] But Columbus was surely a complex personality.[7] There was
also within him a burning thirst for glory, together with a certain
confused, rapturous kind of mysticism.[8]

The first contact of Columbus and his men with the natives of the
Antilles was peaceful. The Europeans were well received by the natives, and at first the expeditionaries, whose quest was for wealth,
exchanged trinkets for gold and other valuables.[9] Once they had
landed, however, the newcomers unfurled before the astonished eyes
of the Lucay Indians the banners of the Spanish king and queen, claiming possession of the islands (in the presence of a notary, naturally)
without their indigenous inhabitants so much as grasping what was
taking place. Then Columbus decided to take a few of the natives
along with him as prisoners, that they might learn "our speech." And
he adds, in his letter to his royal retainers, that such is his intent "unless Your Highnesses should desire that they all be brought to Castile,
or else held captive on the island itself — since," he confidently sub-
joins, "with fifty men you shall have them all in subjection, and be
able to do with them anything you desire."[10] Las Casas, who saw
no justification for this display of dominion and sway, observes incisively that it was thus that "the seed and the poisonous germ of
the destruction of the Indies" was sown very early (*H.I.*, bk. 1, ch. 41,
O.E. 1:145a). And so, despite the initial welcome, when Columbus returned to Hispaniola some years later on his second voyage, he found
that a confrontation had arisen between the Indians and the Spaniards, provoked by abuses on the part of the latter.[11] The situation now
grew tense, and measures of a military nature were taken. Columbus pursued his explorations, and continued to assert his policy of
enslavement of the natives.

Failing to discover the expected quantities of gold, the Admiral now offered the sovereigns another source of wealth: the sale
of slaves.[12] In 1494, in the course of a military action, he captured
more than a thousand natives, of whom he sent some five hundred
to Spain to be sold (1495). Initially, the sovereigns approved the idea.[13]
But they very promptly withdrew their consent,[14] pending the verdict of a commission of theologians and jurists appointed to render
an opinion as to the ethics and legality of the sale. Finally, in 1500,
the sovereigns decided to have the traffic suspended and ordered the
release of the Indians sent over by Columbus.[15] This last royal order

has come in for considerable praise, and indeed with some reason. But it must not be forgotten that it was only issued five years after the arrival of the Indians and the sale or transfer of many of them to do labor. Some were then taken back to Hispaniola, others (a lesser number) voluntarily remained in Spain, while the fate of the rest is unknown. And in any case, one is struck by the length of time (during which Columbus continued to send Indian slaves to Spain) it took the scholars of the royal commission to hand down their decision (whose text, if there ever was one, is no longer extant), as well as by the scant sense of urgency manifested by the Crown to have it in hand.[16]

Columbus continued to carry out certain military expeditions, "waging cruel war on all of the kings and peoples who failed to obey him" (*H.I.,* bk. 1, ch. 105, *O.E.* 1:291a). Thereupon he at once subjected the Indians to hard labor, placing them at the disposition of the Spaniards in residence on the island. Columbus always held the Indians in low regard. Las Casas transcribes a part of a letter Columbus sent to the Spanish sovereigns in which he tells them that these lands are "Yours as is Castile," and that their inhabitants are a very primitive people: "They have no weapons, they all go naked, [they are] very cowardly, . . . and thus are ideal for menial labor — to be sent out to cultivate the fields, or anything else that might be needful." As a result, Friar Bartolomé, who, despite his liking for Columbus personally (and for his family), did not spare his criticism, made a very serious reproach: "And surely here the Admiral has overreached himself in his speech, and this thing that he has conceived and produced by his mouth has been the origin of the mistreatment that [the natives] have later had to suffer" (*H.I.,* bk. 1, ch. 54, *O.E.* 1:184b–185a).[17]

As he brings his "history of the first Admiral," in his *History of the Indies,* to a conclusion, Las Casas draws up a balance sheet of Columbus's accomplishments. While well aware of Columbus's complexities and ambivalences, he hands down a severe judgment. He admires the daring, the spirit of adventure, and the navigational skills that had sent Columbus in search of a new route to the East. But, reflecting on Columbus's pitiable last years and on the mistreatment that he was receiving at the end of his life, he declares the wrongs the Indians had suffered to have been by the "perpetration and consent of the Admiral, absurdly and inordinately, in the absence of any jurisdiction over them whatsoever, or any just cause, and himself being rather their subject, as he was in their lands, kingdoms, and estates, where they had natural jurisdiction, and were using and administering the same." Perhaps he had deserved his own misfortune. Therefore "without great difficulty, nor indeed with any unwarranted temerity, we may recommend he feel that all of this misfortune and adversity, anguish and penalization, has only been the just requital and punishment of those offenses."

He concludes with a perspicacious, but very critical, analysis:

> None of us who have always been familiar with his affairs could have denied his good and simple intention, or his loyalty to the Sovereigns to the point that, in order to serve them, as he personally confessed and swore in a letter that he wrote them from Cádiz when he was about to embark on his last voyage, he exercised more diligence in serving them than in gaining Paradise. And thus it appears that, by God's permission, they have requited him aright. And I know for certain that this extravagant concern and desire to serve his Sovereigns, and to seek to please them with gold and wealth, as well as his great ignorance, has been the mightiest cause of his having erred, in all that he has done against these people. (*H.I.,* bk. 2, ch. 38, *O.E.* 2:95a–96b)

Columbus's intent to serve his royal patrons, or what he sought to obtain from them through that service, meant more to him than his obligations either to the defenseless Indians or, ultimately, to God.[18]

Free but "Pressured"

In addition to everything that we have described, the Indians also suffered repercussions of the Europeans' own intestine strife. The close of the Columbian period (in 1500) brought no improvement here. On the contrary, during Bobadilla's brief tenure things only became more difficult for the aboriginal population. The appointment of Nicolás de Ovando (in 1501) as governor signaled the commencement of a period of stability, but it also meant a consolidation and even intensification of native servitude. With Ovando had come 2,500 other Europeans, bringing a radical change to the physiognomy of the island. Now life was even more painful for the Indians than before.

The Spanish colonists, old and new, eagerly made the most of the measures dictated by the Crown in the course of these years. In instructions dated March 20 and 29, 1503, Ovando was ordered "not to permit or allow the Christians who are in the said Indies to take possession of the said Indians' wives or sons or daughters, or do them any harm or injury in either their person or their goods, or consent to their making use of them as they have done up until now, except when the said Indians have so undertaken *of their own will,* and on condition of their receiving such *just wages* as our said Governor will have stipulated."[19] What was forbidden, and rightly, was of course what actually occurred on the island.

But a few months later, on December 20 of the same year, another royal order declared that the sovereigns had been informed "that, on account of the *excessive freedom* of which the said Indians dispose, they flee and shun intercourse and communication with Christians, in such wise that, even though the latter are willing to pay them wages, they do not wish to work, and wander about aimlessly." This had made the Christianization of the Indians more difficult, and consequently Ovando was ordered "henceforward to *impel and pressure* the said Indians to have dealings with the Christians of the said Island, and to labor in the construction of their buildings, in gathering and extracting gold and other metals, and in providing farm labor and sustenance to their Christian neighbors dwelling on the said island." And so impelling and pressuring is now authorized by the Crown. To add to the confusion, in the very next line of the same text we read that the Indians are to "do and perform this as the *free* persons that they are, and not as bondservants."[20] In actual fact, this disposition legalized the *encomienda*, as all historians acknowledge.[21]

Las Casas perceives the difficulty of this last decretal, especially as it came from the hand of Queen Isabella, whom he held in high esteem and whose testament he frequently cites in defense of the Indians. Many years later, in his *Eighth Remedy* (also known as *Among the Remedies*),[22] he transcribes its text, with his customary fidelity, and supplies a lengthy commentary upon it. First he essays a benevolent interpretation. For example, he takes the expression, "you shall impel and pressure," in the sense of "as free persons are urged and driven." Otherwise, he says, there would be a contradiction: "Your Highness would be commanding them to do something freely."

Surely the contradictions present in the text itself afford an adequate margin for Bartolomé's exegesis. But the document's context — the concrete situation in which it was read — was incompatible with the interpretation he championed. Las Casas finally had to admit that the order was a mistake — based, surely, on incorrect information in the hands of the queen, who could not have intended, our friar continued to maintain, the Indians' destruction. The good will of his sovereign — not her text — is clear to Las Casas. After all:

> Had Her Highness known the quality of the land, the frailty, poverty, meekness, and goodness of the Indians, the nature of the harsh and heavy labors which they must perform, the difficulty of mining gold, the unhappy, desperate life that has befallen them, and finally, the impossibility of their going on living, and not perishing, as they have perished, with neither faith nor sacraments — she would never have dispatched such a commission. (*O.E.* 5:101b–102a)[23]

Bartolomé's pained analysis of the document continues, with a reaffirmation of his rejection of the document and his censure of the inexact communications that must have been received by the queen (see *O.E.* 5:106b).

However, it seems that there was more involved than false information supplied to the Crown. The benign royal order of Zaragoza (of March 1503), which we have cited, was actually accompanied by certain secret instructions (dictated on the same dates) of which Las Casas was ignorant. They show that the published text was not as favorable to the natives as might be supposed. Its dispositions "are of such a quality that they can and must be published, while there are other things in our interest," the new norms specify, "which it will be appropriate to keep secret, and known to you alone." The supplementary indications have a distinct finality: increased profit from the labor of the Indians. For example, the secret instructions say: "Endeavor that some of the Indian villages that you order built be constructed near the said mines where the gold lies, that more of it may be obtained."[24] Thus, the intention was not, or at least not exclusively, that the Indians be better protected.

The upshot of it all was a catastrophic demographic plunge.[25] This condition of death and desolation, of which Las Casas was the intimate witness, marks his entire work.[26] It pervades not only his reflections themselves, but the style and tone in which he presents them. The protest mounted by the Dominicans would enable him to perceive things differently.

2. *A Right with Roots in the Bible*

In 1510 a little group of Dominican friars, headed by Pedro de Córdoba, arrived in Hispaniola.[27] This remarkable religious would have great influence on Las Casas. Indeed, Bartolomé would come to regard him as something of a spiritual mentor.[28] It is worth noting that the Dominican missionary community had been dispatched from the Convent of St. Stephen in Salamanca, one of the centers of the order's internal reform, which was based on a return to the original sources of Dominican spirituality with its accent on contemplation and poverty. The friars' intervention in behalf of the Indians would inaugurate what has been called the "controversy of the Indies."[29]

Preaching the Gospel Truth

It had been nineteen years now since the inhabitants of the so-called Indies had begun to suffer foreign occupation, with its attendant abuse, exploitation, and death at the hands of the "discoverers" (from the European viewpoint) of these lands. The natives were treated "as if they had been useless animals," and the colonists "mourned their deaths only for reason of the inconvenience that now they would no longer be able to work the gold mines and plantations for them," since the Europeans only sought "to grow rich on the blood of those wretches."[30] Sorrowfully the friars asked: "How can so very many people that there had been on this island, according to what we have been told, in such a brief time, a space of fifteen or sixteen years, have so cruelly perished?" The allusion is to the horrible decimation of the population of the island, which we have seen.

A consideration of the "sorrowful life and awful captivity suffered by the native people of this island" now led the Dominican religious of Hispaniola to "set the facts of the case over against the principles of justice and right" — *juntar el derecho con el hecho,* as they put it. That is, it moved them to submit their knowledge of the situation to an ethical reflection and to confront the oppression they saw before them with the "law of Christ" (*H.I.,* bk. 3, ch. 3, *O.E.* 2:174a–b). On that law is based the right which Las Casas says "must be proclaimed." After all, he goes on, "Are we not obliged to preach the law of Christ to them, and to labor with all diligence to convert them?" (ibid.).

Nor was this act of *juntar el derecho con el hecho* to be a mere speculative enterprise on the Dominicans' part. It would move them to make a decision, "after commending themselves to God," to "preach in the public pulpits, and to declare, the state in which our sinful compatriots have held and oppressed these people." Thus they would be performing their function as preachers. Las Casas then makes the ironic observation that it was necessary to call the oppressors' attention to the fact that, by dying in this sin, "as the crown of their inhumanities and greed, they were assuring themselves of their reward." Las Casas remarks the role played in this decision by a former conquistador, Juan Garcés. Garcés had repented his crimes and after passing through a number of personal difficulties had became a "lay friar" of the Dominicans. To the wonder and admiration of the religious, he straightforwardly recounted the "execrable cruelties" that he and others had committed against the Indians (*H.I.,* bk. 3, ch. 3, *O.E.* 2:174b–175a).[31]

The Dominicans ("spiritual individuals," Bartolomé calls them, "and very much the friends of God"; ibid., *O.E.* 2:174b), aware of the gravity of the matter, composed, and all signed, the sermon to be delivered by Friar Antón Montesino (as Las Casas writes the name), whom he calls a great preacher and "most severe in the reprehension of vices."[32] They selected the Fourth Sunday of Advent and took as their text John the Baptist's cry, "I am a 'voice in the desert...'" (John

1:23). They invited all of the notables of the island, among them Admiral Diego Colón, to sit and listen (ibid., *O.E.* 2:175).[33] The content of the sermon is known to us only in Las Casas's version, which — even if he has placed, decades later, something of his own there — is basically authentic, as reactions to the sermon, which we know from other sources as well, credibly attest.[34]

The text is familiar enough, but in view of its historical importance, and especially its influence on our friar's thought, it will be worth our while to examine it here. Las Casas reports that, in keeping with the spirit of the gospel reading for that Sunday, the preacher began with an observation on the "sterility of the desert of the consciences" of those present. Montesino then claims to be the voice crying on that bleak and barren plain.

Let us reproduce verbatim what Friar Bartolomé reports:

> You are all in mortal sin! You live in it and you die in it! Why? Because of the cruelty and tyranny you use with these innocent people. Tell me, with what right, with what justice, do you hold these Indians in such cruel and horrible servitude? On what authority have you waged such detestable wars on these people, in their mild, peaceful lands, where you have consumed such infinitudes of them, wreaking upon them this death and unheard-of havoc? How is it that you hold them so crushed and exhausted, giving them nothing to eat, nor any treatment for their diseases, which you cause them to be infected with through the surfeit of their toils, so that they "die on you" [as you say] — you mean, you kill them — mining gold for you day after day? And what care do you take that anyone catechize them, so that they may come to know their God and Creator, be baptized, hear Mass, observe Sundays and Holy Days? Are they not human beings? Have they no rational souls? Are you not obligated to love them as you love yourselves? Do you not understand this? Do you not grasp this? How is it that you sleep so soundly, so lethargically? Know for a certainty that in the state in which you are you can no more be saved than Moors or Turks who have not, nor wish to have, the faith of Jesus Christ. (*H.I.*, bk. 3, ch. 4, *O.E.* 2:176)

Many of the burning questions that would be debated over the next half-century and more are present in seed here. The first fact that provokes the friars' indignation is the oppression of the Indian, of which they themselves are direct and daily witnesses. The natives are subjected to a "horrible servitude," and a lethal one, as they toil in the mines "for gold, day after day." The tragic relationship between *greed* and *death* thus makes its appearance in the very first denunciation. Second, this deadly exploitation — this murder — has only been a prolongation of the initial injustice: that of the "detestable wars" that had been waged against the Indians, for no just reason whatever. Third, Montesino ridicules the official pretext for the *encomiendas:* What genuine concern is there, he scoffs, on the part of the oppressors for the Christian life of their native victims?

The friars go even further. To these three denunciations they add, speaking through the mouth of Montesino, a consideration that will become the material of a distinct tractate. After all, the Indians are persons, and consequently have all the rights of persons. "Are they not human beings? Have they no rational souls?" The preacher's premise is destined to be an important one in the great dispute launched by his sermon. But for Montesino, this humanistic proposition is only a stepping stone to an exigency of the gospel: "Are you not then obliged to love them as yourselves?" This radical Christian requirement, which supposes equality ("as yourselves") between Spaniards and Indians before God, goes beyond the duties of justice, which has been so treacherously violated. It transfers the problem to new ground: that of love, which knows no juridical or philosophic limits.

This evangelical perspective, it seems to us, is the key to an understanding of the Dominicans' mighty challenge. The elaborate theology of law being developed at about this same time by Vitoria, Domingo de Soto, and others, based on the thought of Thomas Aquinas, has recently occasioned a retrospective interpretation of the missionaries' theological stance in the light of the *jus gentium,* or Law of Nations — if not indeed of natural law and its theological implications. This is what occurs, it seems to us, in the case of V. Carro, author of a classic work on the sixteenth-century theologians of law. Carro builds his exegesis of the sermon on the pertinent questions — "Are they not human beings? Have they no rational souls?" — and asserts that the friars have indicated the route "the theology of law will take, from that point onward, to give life to the best elements of the Laws of the Indies, the route that theologians like Vitoria and de Soto will develop and broaden. . . . These expressions will give rise to the theories that legal theology will posit for the protection of the rights inherent in human personhood. Very precisely, Montesino reflects the correct teaching, one having its roots in the principles of St. Thomas."[35]

But Carro fails to go on to the next question, which recalls human siblingship along such demanding evangelical lines: "Are you not obliged to love them as yourselves?" Shortly before quoting the text of Montesino's sermon, in a reference to the moment at which the friars decided to denounce "the deeds that the Spaniards were perpetrating upon the Indians," Las Casas sets forth some of the concepts that will be contained in that sermon. In the face of the "ugliness and enormity of such unheard-of injustice," he says, surely we shall have to ask: " 'Are these not humans? Need not the precepts of *charity* and justice be kept in our dealings with them?' " (*H.I.*, bk. 3, ch. 3, *O.E.* 2:174b; emphasis added). And indeed, uppermost in the Dominicans' mind is the ever new commandment of love.

We are not attempting to set up a facile opposition between the theologico-juridical foundations and the exigencies of the gospel. But we do think it important to call attention to the difference in their quality and extension. After all, without the gospel, the foundations of a theology of law lack their proper, vital context. The various questions of Montesino's homily are interconnected, of course. But the one that recalls the Indian's quality as "neighbor" to the Spaniards, which the missioners see as entailing a duty to love, is the furthest-reaching question, and the one that gives meaning to the others.

In a penetrating and frequently cited passage, Chacón y Calvo asserts, apropos of the sermon upon which we are commenting: "At this solemn moment, in the humble residence of a few courageous friars, a new system of law sprang into being, a law with deep theological roots."[36] And a law with deep biblical roots, let us add, since the power of the cry of Hispaniola is truly rooted in the Bible.

New Teaching

Bartolomé de Las Casas comments that the sermon aroused a variety of reactions, ranging from astonishment to compunction. But, he adds, it left "no one, so far as I have heard, converted" (*H.I.*, bk. 3, ch. 4, *O.E.* 2:176b). Montesino stepped down from the pulpit, his head erect, amid the indignant murmurs of the congregation, who all but prevented him from finishing the Mass. But the meaning of the homily was clearly understood, as is evinced by the angry reactions of the "second Admiral," Diego Colón, and the other royal officials who now gathered at the latter's residence. There it was decided to "go and give that preacher and his confreres a good dressing-down, even punish him as a scandal-monger and sower of a new, unheard-of teaching, condemned by all — someone who has spoken against the king and his sovereignty over these Indies with the claim that he had no right to own Indians" (ibid., *O.E.* 2:177a). And indeed Ferdinand V will himself interpret Friar Antón's intervention as an assault on his rights. He considers the friar as someone who defends new and unheard-of ideas.

Unperturbed and unintimidated, Pedro de Córdoba, the Dominican superior, confronted the complainers. They demanded to see Friar Antón. At their insistence that Montesino retract his statements, since he had "preached something so new" (ibid.), de Córdoba responded that the sermon had been the responsibility of the entire community.

The superior agreed to summon Montesino, "who came down all in a tither," smiles Las Casas sarcastically (ibid., *O.E.* 2:177b). The preacher at once explicitly stated the intent of the controversial sermon. After mature deliberation, he explained, the friars "had determined to preach *the gospel truth* necessary for the salvation of all the Spaniards of this island, as well as of the Indians, whom they saw perishing by the day without the former having any more concern for them than if they had been beasts of the field" (ibid.; emphasis added). At stake indeed was the "gospel truth," as we have observed, and the principal concern of the sermon was for the salvation of the Spaniards, on account of the oppression to which they were subjecting the Indians. (Thus, they are named before the Indians in the passage from Las Casas just cited. Furthermore, they were the direct auditors of Montesino's celebrated homily.)

Las Casas always considered that, in the Indies, after Montesino's sermon, there was no possibility of invincible ignorance as to the injustice with which the Spaniards had proceeded. He states it altogether clearly in his last work: "At least since the year 1510, now that, by God's grace, we are in the year 1564, there has never been, nor is there today, a person in all the Indies who has ever had good faith" (*Doce dudas*, 1564, *O.E.* 5:498b).

The missioners would persist in what the notables of Hispaniola called "new doctrine" and would do so despite the latter's request for a retraction "to satisfy the people, who had been, and were still, grandly scandalized" (ibid., *O.E.* 2:178a). "People," as we may expect, meant the Admiral and his friends. Las Casas comments ironically that "the novelty" of the Dominicans' sermon "consisted in asserting that killing Indians was worse than killing insects" (*H.I.*, bk. 3, ch. 3, *O.E.* 2:175a).[37] It was this that had scandalized the "people."

On the following Sunday, in an atmosphere of tension, Montesino again mounted the pulpit and repeated the same notions, pointedly omitting the requested retractation. He adduced "with further arguments and an appeal to authority what he had declared, namely, that it was unjustly and tyrannically that they held those people in oppression and exhaustion." The preacher recalled that in that state they could not be saved, and furthermore threatened to refuse them sacramental absolution should they persist in their attitude (see *H.I.*, bk. 3, ch. 5, *O.E.* 2:178b). With this the Dominicans provoked another protest on the part of the island's notables; but this time the complaint was promptly lodged not with the local religious superior, but beyond the seas, before the friars themselves had had any opportunity to explain their position to their superiors there.[38]

The indictment had reached Spain, then, and from Spain the friars were showered with the reprimands of the king as well as of their own religious superior. All officialdom saw — quite rightly — that what the missioners had done was tantamount to an interdict on the authority and rights of the Crown over the Indies, as well as on the privileges of the *encomenderos* and functionaries.[39] Here was a dangerous, unexpected germ of subversion, which threatened to give a whole new direction to the social order that was beginning to be implanted. It must be nipped in the bud.

In a royal order of March 20, 1512, addressed to Diego Colón by way of a response to his new complaint, Ferdinand V speaks of the presence of Diego Velázquez in Cuba (the first mention of this island in official documents) and refers to Montesino's intervention. "I have likewise seen," the king writes, "to my exceeding wonderment, the sermon that you say a Dominican friar called Friar Antón de Montesinos has delivered. Truly he has no solid foundation in theology, the canons, or civil laws, according to the opinion of scholars and in my own belief." He then cites "the rights of the Crown and the solid theological and canonical foundation of the servitude that the Indians perform for Christians," and, accordingly, the aberration of the missionaries in calling these rights into question. He invokes "the grace and donation that our Holy Father Alexander VI has made to us of all of these islands and lands."

It can only come as a surprise, then, and as an act of insubordination, that the friars should lay down as a condition for sacramental absolution that the *encomenderos* set the Indians free. And the king states that, if there is any burden of conscience, "which there is not, it is mine," thereby assuming responsibility for the Indians' servitude, "and that of those who have counseled us to ordain what is ordained; and not of those who hold the Indians." The refusal of absolution to those who fail to comply with the elementary demands of justice will be a means that Las Casas — who suffered it himself when he had had charge of an *encomienda* — will counsel later in his well-known *Instructions and Rules for Confessors* (hereafter *Confesionario*), the only book of his to be confiscated by Spanish political authorities during his lifetime.[40]

Ferdinand was uneasy about repercussions from the Dominicans' sermon and anticipated great inconvenience should the Indians themselves come to "believe that the case was as they had represented it." He is well aware that the opinion at issue — as Las Casas, too, maintains — is that of an entire group of friars, and not of one person only. Along with the members of his Council, he regards it as a "thing of such novelty, and so lacking in foundation," as to merit some exemplary punishment. As we know, for a conservative mentality (one that would keep things as they are), the adjective "new" is always synonymous with "false."[41] The Dominicans' words, accordingly, could surely be explained "by a want of information concerning any of the causes that have moved me and the Queen to ordain the distribution of the Indians." Indeed, as we have recalled, the *encomienda* had been legal since 1503.

The missioners' are likewise ignorant of the "right that We have to all of these islands, as well as . . . the justifications there have been not only of having these Indians serve as they do serve, but even to hold them in harder servitude." The rights of the king would legitimate even a service more lowly still, which, however, the royal benignity forbears to impose. Wherefore the king commands — as Charles V will later do in the case of the Dominicans of Salamanca, including Vitoria — that they be ordered that neither "they nor other friars of their Order speak upon this matter or others similar, in the pulpit or away from it, in public or in private." The prohibition was total. The friars might touch on the theme again only to retract what they had said. In case they persisted in their attitude, despite Ferdinand's "great devotion to this Order," he ordains that "they be sent here, to their Superior, that he may punish them, in the first available vessel." Time was of the essence, "since every hour they spend on that island maintaining this accursed opinion will do a great deal of harm to all things there."[42] The matter was urgent.

Carro cites this letter and comments optimistically: "We shall soon see him placated. He will change his mind and side with the Dominicans."[43] Actually this did not occur. Pedro de Córdoba, arriving in Spain shortly after the Burgos Laws had been decreed, seems not to have had a pleasant memory of his initiatives at Court. When cleric Las Casas was on the point of leaving for Spain for the first time, "to seek complete redress in behalf of these unfortunates, whom we thus see perishing," as he put it to his friend Rentería (*H.I.*, bk. 3, ch. 80, *O.E.* 2:360a), de Córdoba perspicaciously cautioned the enthusiastic voyager, not without a certain amount of skepticism: "Father, it will never be labor lost, for God will keep a good account of it. But know that, as long as the King is alive, you shall achieve nothing of what you and we desire." Bartolomé recounts that these words impressed him, but that they did not deter him from his purpose, and he only asked Friar Pedro "to commend him to God, and always have him commended" to God (*H.I.*, bk. 3, ch. 83, *O.E.* 2:336b). De Córdoba's evaluation with respect to what might be accomplished under Ferdinand's reign[44] must be the reason why he declined the king's offer of a position entailing certain civil responsibilities in the Indies (see *H.I.*, bk. 3, ch. 17, *O.E.* 2:212a).

Thus, King Ferdinand fully endorsed the reaction of Colón, Pasamonte, and the ranking officials of Hispaniola. Furthermore, he charged them with the implementation of his dispositions. Finally, in the same letter to Colón, the king says he has summoned the Dominican provincial to complain of the conduct of his religious. The provincial, Alonso de Loaysa, accepted the royal admonition, and he too pronounced against the turn of events in Hispaniola. We have the text of three letters addressed by Loaysa to his friars. The contrast between their content, on the one hand, and the evangelical inspiration of Montesino's sermon and Pedro de Córdoba's dignified comportment, on the other, leaves the reader with a painful impression.

Alonso de Loaysa — who has no real knowledge of what is occurring in the Indies and whom the affair has caught by surprise — adopts the position of the governor and the king. In a first dispatch to Pedro de Córdoba, he maintains that any preaching on the matters addressed by the friars creates an "obstacle to the attainment of the desirable end for which you so magnanimously undertook the labor of traveling to those parts, which is the conversion of the infidels to faith in Jesus Christ." In other words, any denunciation of the exploitation of the Indians, any questioning of the right of the Spaniards to oppress the natives of these regions, not only is unconnected with salvation in Jesus Christ, but actually runs counter to it. This was the first time such a thing had been said in the Indies — although far from the last, nor do we refer to the sixteenth century alone. If anything defines the attitude of the defenders of the Indians, it is that these persons thought precisely the contrary. The salvation the Lord has come to bring and proclaim must necessarily have repercussions on temporal history. As we see, the polemics are of ancient date.

Loaysa consequently forbids de Córdoba to preach any further on these matters.[45] But precisely what the Dominicans living in the Indies had perceived is that the proclamation of salvation implies a demand for justice. In fact, from a point of departure in what today is sometimes called the other side of the coin of the missionary endeavor, their understanding was that they were to secure not only the conversion of the infidels, but that of the Christians themselves. Las Casas would later develop this intuition in breadth and depth. The friars persisted in their attitude and made it clear to what purpose they had come to the Indies — more clear than it had been to themselves on their departure from Spain: to proclaim *integral* salvation in Christ. And this remains the most urgent demand on ourselves in our own time.

Mere days later, the father provincial returned to the subject and declared the teachings of his brothers in religion "scandalous." He is alarmed, he says. "Were [these teachings] to be observed, no Christian would remain" in these regions. The notorious sermon was having repercussions in Spain, he tells his subjects. "Where you think to help, you harm, on both sides of the sea. You are surely doing us little good here" in the mother country. And so he serves warning: "I shall give no friar permission to go there until the Lord Governor writes to me of the amends you will have made in the matter of this scandal, which has had such loud echoes here."[46] This last sentence shows that none of the implications of the Hispaniola affair were lost on the Crown. It also reveals the pressure being exerted on the Dominican order to obtain a retraction from Pedro de Córdoba's annoying friars.

In a third text, Alonso de Loaysa returns to the same charge, and this time decides to furnish his position with a theological basis. He begins by informing his addressees — the entire group of friars now, and no longer just Pedro de Córdoba — that "all India, as a result of your preaching, is on the point of rebellion, and neither ourselves nor any Christian layman may enter there." The "rebellion" (obviously the danger is being exaggerated for effect) could only have been one mounted by the Indians themselves. The fear was that, in their case, the voice of Montesino would be no mere voice crying in the desert, as it had been with the Spaniards. Thus, the Dominicans would have been responsible for a most difficult situation. They would have caused "harm to our religion." A number of times in the course of the sixteenth century — as even today, under the pens of some historians of these events — the argument would be invoked that, if what the defenders of the poor and oppressed asked were to be granted, no European would be left in the Indies, because no Indians would toil for the newcomers, and consequently the latter would have no interest in remaining in these lands. This argument would be used, for example, to obtain the abrogation of the New Laws of 1542 — a request to which, as we shall see, Charles V will accede. But Las Casas's answer always was: the end does not justify the means.

The provincial then launches a theological assault. He cannot attribute the friars' outrageous conduct merely to the propensity to sin introduced into history with Satan's seduction of Adam. His brethren seem actually to have fallen into the captivity and snares of the Devil. After all, as is clear to everyone, "these islands have been acquired by His Highness *jure belli,* by right of war, and His Holiness has made to our Lord King a donation of the same, wherefore the servitude [of the Indians] is meet and just." In this way, Loaysa adds the right of conquest to the argument employed by the king in his letter to Colón (that based on the papal donation). Both considerations justify the Indian servitude so imprudently questioned by the Dominicans. The truth of the matter, of course, is that, if anyone was ill-informed, it was the provincial. Upon the arrival of the Spaniards in these islands, not even the staunchest partisans of their right of dominion could seriously adduce the principles of the old just-war doctrine to justify the domination and enslavement of the Indians.

The political repercussions of the events continued to be of concern to Loaysa. Thus, he states that even if his theological reasons appeared to them to be insufficient, they must not again preach on the matter at issue without consulting, "first, here, the members of His Highness's Council, as well as the council their own Governor maintains there. All must agree, and say what is most pacific and profitable to all." In fact, he orders — under pain of mortal sin and excommunication, nothing less — that "none dare to preach upon this matter any further." Here is a very different attitude from the evangelical freedom with which the friars of Hispaniola had acted. Not to do anything that might run counter to political authority, indeed to consult that authority before preaching the Good News, becomes a guarantee of doctrinal orthodoxy and "religious obedience."[47] While the historical and social context here is different from our own, we can only regard Loaysa's demand (and not the friars' preaching!) as an expression of the "captivity" of the Christian message. This, like many bishops and missioners in the Indies, Las Casas could not accept. Instead, the missionaries upheld the validity of the demands of the gospel. Furthermore, their testimony demonstrates that any attempt to justify this attitude of submission to political power with an appeal to the customs of the age clearly falls short as a criterion of legitimacy.[48]

When all is said and done, neither Diego Colón nor Ferdinand V nor the Dominican provincial was entertaining false fears. The cry of Hispaniola was more than a protest against the way in which the Indians were being treated. It attacked the specious foundations and radical injustice of the war, indeed of the oppressive system itself.[49] Ultimately, this denunciation issues from a basic exigency of the gospel: the love of neighbor. We are very far from the scandalous use that Sarmiento of Gamboa will make of this commandment of the Lord in order to justify wars against the Indians and a consequent oppression of the natives.[50] From the very outset of the controversy of the Indies, the Dominican friars of Hispaniola stand the gospel upright.

3. *Liberation of the Indian*

Despite these reactions, the group of Dominican friars under de Córdoba's leadership would go on with its battle in defense of the Indian.[51] Not only would they continue it, they would intensify it. Montesino had sketched out a criticism of the economic, social, and religious causes of the oppression suffered by the Indians. To criticize their servitude, as well as the legal and Christian considerations being brought forward in its justification, was surely an important task. But it was also necessary, and urgent, to knock away the underpinnings of the specious justification of the social system then being established in the Indies. Not satisfied with the Burgos Laws, to the promulgation of which they had contributed,[52] or with other measures undertaken by the Crown, the Dominicans only become more explicit in the matter. In a letter to King Charles of May 28, 1517, for example, Pedro de Córdoba writes, alluding to Las Casas and his interviews with Ferdinand V in Spain: "And he returned here with what remedy he could, although neither he, nor indeed we, are satisfied."[53]

In various texts, the missionaries demonstrate that nothing has changed in the Indies since Montesino's sermon. The Burgos Laws have only supplied the oppression suffered by the Indians with further specious legitimacy. And the reform imposed on the Hieronymite fathers by Cardinal Cisneros had been a debacle. Dominican and Franciscan missioners working in Hispaniola wrote to Cisneros and to Adrian of Utrecht apropos of the Indians subjected to forced labor: "Since the arrival of the Hieronymites they die just as before — indeed, more rapidly still."[54] A year later, discouraged, Pedro de Córdoba wrote to Antón Montesino, who was visiting Spain: "The affairs of these lands are going as you might expect from the letters that I have written to you. I am quite discontent. Ask God to help all He can."[55]

Painted Corpses

The friars straightforwardly attack the regime of the *encomienda*. They consider it to be "against divine, natural, and human law." They regard this as demonstrable in many ways. But a more telling proof than any argument, it seems to them, is a massive fact: "All of these Indians have been destroyed, soul and body, even in their posterity, and all the land is wasted and parched. Thus, they can neither be Christians, nor even remain alive."[56] Here we have a premise for argumentation in behalf of the Indian that we often find with Bartolomé de Las Casas, and one frequently invoked by all of those who take their position from the perspective of the oppressed: the *fact* (*hecho*) of the untimely, unjust death of the poor contradicts the *right* (*derecho*) that they have to life. The very choice of vocabulary is significant, and Las Casas will make it his own. It is a matter of the *destruction of persons*.[57] The denunciation is lodged at a basic level: that of concrete life and death. And it disqualifies any ideological disquisition calculated to mask the raw reality of an economic and social system based on the destruction and death, slow or violent, of the oppressed.[58]

The facts speak for themselves, and no authentically Christian conscience could remain indifferent. The Franciscans of Hispaniola would now join the Dominicans of that island in their denunciation of the entry of Christians into the land "like ravenous wolves amid gentle sheep." And the letter signed by the religious of both orders continues:

> As the people of Castile who embarked upon this deed were not God-fearing, but altogether greedy and crazed for money, as well as filled with other filthy passions, they commenced to crush and destroy the land in such varied and horrible ways that not only pen, but tongue itself must fail in an attempt to recount them. In such wise, of a number of people that could be reckoned at one *cuento* [million] one hundred thousand persons, all have been destroyed and scattered, so that not twelve thousand souls remain, counting children and adults, old and young, healthy and sick.[59]

The missioners illustrate this assertion with a long and frightful list of cases "from the infinitudes [of such cases] that could be recounted."[60] In conclusion, they state, graphically enough, that the destruction of Hispaniola is such that the few thousand Indians who remain on the island "have the appearance rather of painted corpses than of living human beings."[61] The pitiful sparks of life that remain in the faces of these "painted corpses" denounce the reality of death that has made an end of the natives of these lands. Unless something is done quickly, "there will be no avoiding the imminent catastrophe: all will be utterly destroyed."[62]

The occasion of this lethal situation, as we have indicated in one of the texts that we have just cited, is greed for gold. The Indians, under the working conditions imposed by the Spaniards, "if they must mine gold, must necessarily perish."[63] There is no alternative. Indeed, those who hold the Indians *encomendados* (committed, bestowed) "have exercised great care and diligence that they mine gold and work the soil all the day long,...keeping them in far worse conditions than those in which beasts are customarily maintained, as the latter are cared for, while the former are not."[64] The subhuman treatment of the Indians moves Pedro de Córdoba to tell the king that Christians have created a situation "to be wept for."[65] The colonists have not populated this land, but have "depopulated" it.[66] The destruction being wrought in the Indies is such that "not Pharaoh and the Egyptians themselves committed such cruelties."[67] The reference to the biblical paradigm of the oppression of Egypt is classic in a theological approach to the plunder and oppression of the poor.

And the Dominicans petition for the liberation of the Indians. "Therefore our opinion is that they ought to be withdrawn from the power of the Christians and set at liberty."[68] This is the only remedy. The missionaries are not in a position to propose concrete means to the attainment of this end; but they are convinced of the need for measures to be taken to "prevent the Indians from vanishing."[69] They are forthright: unless appropriate means can be taken against the exploitation to which the Indians are subjected on the *encomiendas,* it would be better that these unfortunates should return to their primitive condition. This is clear for two reasons. First, "though they were to gain nothing in their souls, at least they would gain in their lives, and temporal multiplication, which would be a lesser evil than that they should lose everything."[70] Here is a persistent notion among these missionaries. To their minds, toils and sufferings "have destroyed and banished the natural power of generation of these poor people, who neither engender nor multiply, nor can engender or multiply, or have posterity, which is a thing of great sorrow."[71]

It is a bold proposition, as Bartolomé de Las Casas would later remark, and is tantamount to saying that the freedom and corporeal health of infidels is better than their captivity as Christians destined for death. The "materialism" of this opinion — or rather, its sense of the value of life — escapes no one. But in their great spiritual liberty these friars feel themselves more compelled by the gospel and by the horrors they behold in the Indies than by conceptual distinctions and hierarchies established by ivory-tower theologians.

The second reason why the missioners regard it as more desirable that the Indians should return to their primitive condition is no less meaningful. "It is a lesser evil," the Dominicans write, "that the Indians be in their lands as they are than that the name of Christ be blasphemed as it is blasphemed among the infidels."[72] This is the attitude that Las Casas will adopt. This second consideration may appear more "religious" than the first, but it is no less fraught with immediate consequences, because those who exploit the Indians to the death also blaspheme the name of Christ. Indeed, they scandalize them "with the bad example that they have given them, with their lust, violence, blasphemies, and cruelties of every sort."[73]

As Las Casas began to do in these same years, the Dominicans lay bare the reality of the *encomienda.* "Christians have had [the Indians] divided up among themselves allegedly to teach them the things of the faith, but actually these things have not been taught to them."[74] For that matter, "how will they teach the Christian faith to the Indians entrusted [*encomendados*] to them when they themselves know it not, and what is worse, practice it not?"[75]

Not to practice the faith is, in a way, worse than not knowing it. More precisely, not to practice the faith is to be ignorant of the meaning and demands of the faith. This gives the lie, and radically, to any pretense to instruct someone in a faith that fails to inspire the instructor's own behavior, so that, when all is said and done, the instructor is actually rejecting it. To exploit the poor is to reject faith in Jesus Christ.

The perspective of the insignificant and oppressed ("whom we see") always withdraws us from the world of abstract principles — from a false pretense of loving "the God we have not seen" — and stands us willy-nilly on the flinty terrain of evangelical practice and truth (see 1 John 4:20).

Right of the Poor

The missioners do not fear the conclusions that may have to be drawn from their accusations and arguments. They propose — in the area of their proper competency — certain concrete measures. These measures have their roots in the right of the poor to life and to faith.

Inasmuch as the goods acquired by the *encomenderos* are the fruit of an unjust, oppressive regime based on the Indians' labor, that acquisition, in moral terms, is theft and robbery. The Dominicans then apply a traditional principle of moral and sacramental theology: the obligation to make *restitution* of what has been unjustly taken, as a condition for sacramental absolution from the sin that has been committed. "In recent days," writes Pedro de Córdoba, "we have preached straight out against the [culprits], declaring to them the state of damnation in which they live and the obligation they have of making restitution, not only for what they have acquired in the way of temporal goods, but also for the harm they have caused in the course of that acquisition."[76] The observation is a sophisticated, precise one. The obligation of restitution is not limited to the material thing taken. It includes the harm caused to the persons from whom it has been taken — including any harm in the moral and spiritual dimension of their lives.

The second measure the friars propose would have radically transformed the situation in the Indies. Little convinced — after the experience of the Burgos legislation — that new laws or dispositions could change anything, they consider it better to hack to the root of the evils of these lands. Thus, one must "stop Christians from coming to the Islands and the Continent, since they are a fire, consuming everything in their path. First of all, it should be considered whether *preachers alone* might be sent at first, in order to introduce the faith here." Sending "preachers alone" would suffice to enable the king to fulfill the obligation imposed on him by the pope in giving him "title and sovereignty over these lands."[77] Preachers alone: Las Casas will return to this proposition, after hard experience.

The motivation of the missioners' recommendation is a concern for the proclamation of the gospel. Christian comportment in the Indies, contrary to what these people argue to justify there, is the greatest obstacle to this undertaking. If the missionaries were alone — without the company of soldiers and would-be *encomenderos* — current relations with the Indian nations would be different.[78] Here is the utopia that, in witnesses of the gospel, everlastingly accompanies their hope. The missioners base their optimism and zeal on what they regard as the Indians' excellent human dispositions for receiving the Christian message. These dispositions foster in the friars the hope of being able to build something similar to the primitive Christian community. The primitive church represents the model that inspires the work of evangelization among these sixteenth-century missionaries. In this era, Las Casas and the Dominicans share ideals and projects that will abide in the future Dominican's heart all the days of his life.

The matter of the aptitude of the Indians for receiving the gospel has another implication as well. One of the reasons adduced for holding them "in trust" (*en encomienda*) was the notion that the inhabitants of these lands were somehow inferior beings. This was the conviction of those who used the Indians — the Franciscans and Dominicans write — "as if they were brute beasts," on the pretext that they are "fit neither for marriage nor for receiving the faith." The authors of the letter demonstrate that greed for gold is the reason for that position. "The Christians say all this," they write, "that it may be thought that the Indians are good for nothing but mining gold — in which," they add ironically, "and not in what pertains to the faith, Christians have taught them subtleties indeed."[79] Christians may not know the faith, but they certainly know gold-mining. Obviously the conviction of the colonists regarding the human inferiority of the Indians is one of the causes of the exploitation and death the Indians had to suffer.

The Dominicans, on the other hand, stubbornly emphasize the equality of all human beings. We find this thesis in Montesino's sermon itself. It is implied, the preacher shows, in the evangelical injunction to "love one's neighbor as oneself." Later, Pedro de Córdoba will expatiate on it in his *Christian Doctrine*, a book that takes a catechetical approach and is addressed to the Indians.[80] There we read: "And observe well that God has sent us to you to give you to understand who is the true God, as well as to know why God has made you, as well as ourselves." The equality of nature among human beings derives from the fact that God has willed that we all be descended from "one father and mother, Adam and Eve."[81]

The Dominicans make a third suggestion, one more relative to procedure, but pregnant with consequences. The situation in the Indies is such that they think that the pope ought to be brought up to date on what is occurring there. It is important, they say, to find a way for "the Supreme Pontiff to be informed of everything that has happened on these Islands since their occupation." Given the complexity and extent of the information to be conveyed, however, they doubt that it would be "sufficient to give it in writing. There would be need of one or two persons who have had long experience of matters here,... that they may inform His Holiness *viva voce,* and answer any questions His Holiness may ask in the matter."[82]

The idea is that, once the pope were abreast of things, he would take measures to remedy matters. It is a daring proposal, since, in conformity with the mentality of the age, the citizens of a country could address the pope only through their civil rulers. What the Dominicans seem to be asking is direct contact with the Holy Father. Not only they, but others, later, will make this recommendation, through Fray Bernardo Minaya, who will carry to Paul III certain documents — among them, according to Parish, the manuscript of Las Casas's first book, *De Unico Modo* ("The Only Way").[83] And at the end of his life, Las Casas will take a similar initiative, turning directly to Pope Pius V (see *O.E.* 5:541b–42a).

Pedro de Córdoba was not afraid to "burden the king's conscience," as it used to be put in those days, with the information in question. If His Highness has not been informed until now, or if he has received misinformation, now he knows what is happening in the Antilles.[84] Consequently, he ought to begin to act. And the Friar Pedro warns:

> After all, from the spiritual viewpoint, Your Highness's conscience cannot rest secure unless, after having come to know of such great evils, although it has been impossible to report the majority of them here, he were to apply all diligence and care that these sorrowing people receive remedy: that they be set free, and that Your Highness's wicked Christian vassals be known and held for what they are.[85]

The responsibility does not rest, then, with subordinate functionaries alone. Inescapably, it is a matter of the conscience of the king. A personal account of all this will be required of him by God. Free the Indians and punish the oppressors: this is what the king must do if he would have a clear conscience.[86]

It is likely that Las Casas had a hand in these reflections and proposals. He was already active, in these years (1516–19), among the dogged little group of Dominicans. His earliest known writings in defense of the Indians are from this same period, and they express similar ideas. In the years to follow, he will develop these perspectives in all their implications.

However the case may be with Las Casas's collaboration with the Dominicans in this matter, the fact is that the noble and valiant Pedro de Córdoba considers him one of his group and puts in a good word for him with the king. "In these parts," he writes, "God our Lord has stirred the spirit of a cleric called Bartolomé de Las Casas,... a person of virtue, and one who has long been in these lands and is acquainted with all matters here." Although he has just begun his mission, our cleric has spent more time in the Antilles than the Dominicans have and is deserving of all confidence by reason of his virtue and his knowledge of the Indies. "Your Highness can justly credit him," de Córdoba goes on, "in all that he might say. He is a true minister of God, and I believe that the hand of God is upon him, to the end that he may work at tearing up all of these evils by the roots."[87] Time will prove the justice of this judgment on the part of Pedro de Córdoba (and the other friars). The uprooting of the mistreatment of the Indians, because this is the will of God, will be Las Casas's lifelong purpose. The "letter of introduction" to the king is the Dominicans' most important move in their struggle on behalf of those whom they regard as their brothers and sisters in Christ, the Indians.

●

The friars' protest and commitment surely implies an assertion of the basic equality of all human beings, and this authorizes us to understand their attitude and defense of the Indian as a demand for the observance of a human and natural law. But underlying their approach, and even more basic to it, is a perception of the Indian — or more precisely, the Indian nation — as an oppressed neighbor: as the poor one, as the neighbor par excellence, whom one is under an obligation to love. Bartolomé de Las Casas will make this viewpoint even more explicit; but it is already conspicuous in the texts that we have cited. Henríquez Ureña's remark, then, it seems to us, is correct: By way of the Indians, "the preachers restored Christianity to its ancient role as a religion of the oppressed."[88] That is the question, indeed.

In other words: human rights, to be sure. But not in a laissez-faire, liberal, merely formally egalitarian perspective; rather, along the lines of the rights of the poor, who are condemned to death and destruction by the oppressor whose quest is for gold. In our own day, we have heard of the rights of the poor at the Bishops' Conference of Medellín.[89] We are dealing with a distinct set of rights, then, whose roots — as we have observed — are not only theological, but profoundly biblical. A declaration of the rights of the poor does not overlook the universality of human rights, as some seem to fear. On the contrary, a proclamation of the rights of the poor bestows on human rights in general an authentic universality — through enhanced historical concretion and evangelical realism, which are the foundation of all authentic prophecy.

Chapter 2

Scourged Christs of the Indies

The battle waged by the Dominican friars, which we have just sketched, is the immediate context of the meaning with which secular priest Bartolomé de Las Casas will invest his new life from 1514 onward — the year of his call to serve Christ in the poor of the Indies. The little band of Dominicans on Hispaniola was proposing ideas that we find shortly afterwards in Bartolomé himself. Furthermore, Las Casas has a clear awareness that fighting for the rights of the Indian means, in the concrete, associating himself with the actions of this group of missionaries. And this he does, with the accumulated experience of someone who has spent more than a decade in the Indies.

The profound change that now takes place in Bartolomé's life is stamped with his experience of the untimely, unjust deaths of the Indians, which he has known in Hispaniola and which he has seen with his own eyes, most traumatically in the course of the first steps of his activities of evangelization in Cuba. The Caonao massacre, which he has personally witnessed, has marked him with an indelible scar. He mentions it repeatedly in his writings. He also perceives that in some way he belongs to an enterprise and social order that have brought these deeds about. This experience has led him to the heart of his spirituality and theology: the recognition of Jesus of Nazareth, the Christ, in the tortured, scourged natives of the Indies.

1. A Prophet Is Called[1]

In 1514, with the ever-expanding "harvest of human beings, apace with the increase of greed, so that more and more of them were perishing" (*H.I.*, bk. 3, ch. 76, *O.E.* 2:356a), secular priest Las Casas was an *encomendero* in Cuba. Greed and death — the first being the cause of the second — score the moment of the turning point in Las Casas's mentality. All the rest of his life he will remember the crucial impor-

45

tance of that tragic relationship between greed — the true idolatry, as he will call it, taking his cue from St. Paul — and the death of the Indians.

Blood of the Poor

According to his own version, Las Casas was a good *encomendero,* diligent in his business affairs and yet humane and fatherly with the Indians who worked for him. He was little concerned, however, despite his priestly state,[2] with the "obligation he had to give them doctrine, and bring them to the bosom of the Church of Christ" (*H.I.,* bk. 3, ch. 71, *O.E.* 2:356a). Some time before, while still in Hispaniola, he had been refused sacramental absolution by a Dominican friar precisely on account of this neglect of his duties to the Indians that he had had in his service on Hispaniola as well (ibid., *O.E.* 2:356b). It is possible that the Dominican who had refused him absolution was Pedro de Córdoba himself, for whom Las Casas always maintained a great admiration.[3] In any case, in discussion with Friar Pedro, the cleric finally came to realize "how much reverence and honor he owed him, as . . . a venerable person and far better instructed than the secular Father [i.e., himself]. But as to giving up the Indians, he was not healed of his opinion" (ibid.). This episode constitutes an important step in the process that will lead Las Casas to his transformation into a defender of the Indians.[4]

In Cuba, Bartolome's *encomienda* had been given him in return for his part in the "pacification of the island."[5] He had served as a chaplain in the campaign conducted by Captain Narváez.[6] In his *History of the Indies,* Fray Bartolomé has left us a shattering account of the Caonao massacre of 1513 (see *H.I.,* bk. 3, ch. 29, *O.E.* 2:244–48). Although at the moment his repudiation of these events was not as radical as it would be when he recalled it many years later, even then they filled him with repugnance. He regarded them as unjust and contrary to God's will, since, as he would later say, "No greater harm can be done than to take someone's life" (*De Unico,* 202v; *The Only Way,* 168).[7] What is more, this experience disposed him to comprehend that participation in the colonial system implied approval of that system.

Bartolomé de Las Casas himself has left us a sketch, written several decades later, of the enlightenment of his conscience. It includes details of the more personal aspects of his experience of which we have no other testimonials. Fidelity to detail, however, is of little importance here for our own immediate purposes. What is of interest to us is the meaning we are to gather from his narrative as a whole — a meaning the later Las Casas unambiguously endorses and confirms in the texts that we have from him dated in the years immediately following the change he experienced in his life at this time. All of this ensures the profound historical authenticity of the account.[8]

Preparing to celebrate Mass and preach to the Spaniards on Pentecost, and setting himself to studying the "sermons that he had preached to them that Easter [or: 'the previous Pentecost'] and others from around that same time, he began to consider within himself some of the declarations of Sacred Scripture; and, if I remember rightly, first and foremost Ecclesiasticus 34." Let us reproduce, as Bartolomé de Las Casas himself does, the passage to which he refers, inasmuch as the exact terms it employs have great importance:

> Tainted his gifts who offers in sacrifice ill-gotten goods!
>   Mock presents from the lawless win not God's favor.[9]
> The Most High approves not the gifts of the godless.
>   [Nor for their many sacrifices does he forgive their sins.][10]
> Like the man who slays a son in his father's presence
>   is he who offers sacrifice from the possessions of the poor.
> The bread of charity is life itself for the needy,
>   he who withholds it is a person of blood.
> He slays his neighbor who deprives him of his living;
>   he sheds blood who denies the laborer his wages.
>   (Sirach 34:18–22; in the Vulgate, 34:21–27)

The text is clear and stern, which is typical of Ben Sirach, a writer ever concerned for the purity of public worship. Only now, however, after having seen the crimes denounced by Scripture actually committed in the Indies — indeed, having helped commit them, by way of insufficient protest — Bartolomé suffers pangs of conscience. He has now meditated upon the classic prophetic theme of the mutual exigencies of prayer or public worship, and the practice of justice. But this time he underscores the fact that the absence of the second entails the death of the poor. In fact, he presents it as bloodshed. The crust of bread — symbol of human nourishment, as its minimal expression — is the life of the poor. To deprive them of that is to kill them. Worse, we are dealing with a murder perpetrated by someone who dares to attempt to use the stolen thing to honor God. The comparison the text makes is freighted with consequences: it is like killing children before their parents' eyes.[11] God is the Parent of all and has a predilection for the neediest. Deuteronomy, in a text reminiscent of Las Casas's passage from Ecclesiasticus, accords the mistreated the right to call upon the Lord for redress (see Deut. 24:14–15).

Las Casas allows himself to be challenged by the biblical passage, which calls in question his position in the nascent colonial system. This rereading was the occasion for him to "consider the misery and servitude that those people suffer" owing to a greed for gold on the part of others. That is, a "consideration" of Scripture from a starting point in his experience in the Indies leads him to a new "consideration" of the reality unfolding before him. Scripture and reality are mutually illuminating. They reinforce one another, and this relationship produces Las Casas's transformation. He was also aided by "what he had heard on this island of Hispaniola to have been said and experienced by the religious of St. Dominic in their preaching" (*H.I.*, bk. 3, ch. 79, *O.E.* 2:356b).

He spent several days in this meditation, he tells us, writing in the third person (as he always does in the *History of the Indies*), and became convinced of this truth: "That everything perpetrated upon the Indians in these Indies was unjust and tyrannical." From the moment he "commenced to cast out the darkness of that ignorance" of his, the tack of his readings changed, and the interpretation he now made of them came to be enlightened by a growing awareness of the injustice being committed against the Indian. "Never," he writes, "have I read a book, in Latin or Romance, all these interminable forty-four years, in which some argument or authority was not adduced to prove and corroborate the justice of these Indian peoples and to condemn the injustices and evils and harm done to them" (*H.I.*, bk. 3, ch. 79, *O.E.* 2:356–57).

Let us be precise. Las Casas does not change from being a cruel *encomendero*, personally aggressive toward the Indians, into being their defender. His transformation is more subtle, and, in a way, more demanding. He forsakes his condition as a member of an oppressive system, whose contrariety to all justice and to God's will he has not until now perceived. What he abandons is this blindness. Thus, he will be very sensitive, in the time to come, not only to the misdeeds of those who exploit the dwellers of the Indies, but also to sins of omission — sins similar to those he himself committed — that is, to the misdeeds of those who, without being directly responsible for acts of oppression, enjoy the privileges of the resulting state of affairs, which they fail to question. That is why he denounces so often the "blindness" of those who proceed this way. They too have a grave responsibility.[12] In that Pentecost, the feast that recalls the presence of the Holy Spirit, Las Casas recognized his own responsibility.

Las Casas makes another important reference to this same text from Ecclesiasticus. In connection with the incursions of the Portuguese into Africa just before Columbus's voyage to the Indies, Las Casas manifests his sympathy for the inhabitants of those lands, who have been so cruelly abused by the Europeans. Bartolomé recounts that, on their return from an expedition in Africa, Portuguese navigators brought back a certain number of Africans to be sold as slaves. Two of them, Muslims, were placed at the service of the church, before a fifth of the entire number were handed over to the Infante, Don Henrique, and the rest sold. "Thus," Las Casas comments, with sorrow and indignation, "it is as if they sought to render to God His part of the blood that had been shed and of the unjust, abominable captivity of those innocent beings — as if God were a violent and wicked tyrant who would be pleased by these tyrannies, and rendered benign toward those offering Him His part. Those wretches knew not what is written..." And Las Casas goes on to cite the text from Ecclesiasticus (34:19–20) that had played such an important role in his new way of looking at things. This time, besides the Latin text, he provides us with a Spanish translation, which brings out his personal concerns: "God does not approve the gifts of those who, with their sins, and the harm they do their neighbors, offer to God in sacrifice a part of their plundered, ill-gotten goods. The sacrifice with which they express their reverence is as if, to do honor and service to a father, they were to hack his child to pieces before his very eyes" (*H.I.*, bk. 1, ch. 24, *O.E.* 1:92b–93a). Las Casas's translation is not very literal, but it shows us, by its reinforcement of certain expressions in the original, his own understanding of the text: to "ill-gotten" he adds "plundered," and the "slaying" of a child becomes a hacking to pieces.

Here, owing to the context, Bartolomé cites only the first verses of the text, which refer to God's rejection of offerings seen as robberies and murders of innocent persons. Las Casas regards the offering of this kind of present to God (by offering it to the church) as blasphemous, as it makes God equivalent to a "violent and wicked tyrant." He denounces the Infante's claim that these incursions have been undertaken "out of zeal to serve God," since "in my view, he surely offended, rather than served, God: he slandered his faith and held up the Christian religion as a thing of horror in the eyes of those infidels" (*H.I.*, bk. 1, ch. 24, *O.E.* 1:91a).[13] Once again, it is a matter of defending the God of biblical revelation, who refuses to tolerate the murder and unjust treatment of the defenseless. What Las Casas has learned with regard to the Indians now helps him perceive the tremendous injustice being committed against the Africans. This will lead him to an unequivocal rejection of black slavery.[14] It is interesting and significant that, in order to denounce the injustice shown to the blacks, he appeals to the passage from Ecclesiasticus that changed his mind in 1514, which suggests that here, too, a radical change may have occurred in his way of thinking.

Just as eloquently, he goes back to this same text when he protests the incursions of the Portuguese into the Canary Islands and the abuse to which, under pretext of Christianizing them, the Iberians had subjected the Guanches, the inhabitants of these islands. This time Las Casas's citation is only implicit, but it is very clear. The people of the

Canaries are not only harassed physically, but are forced to submit to baptism and to accept the Christian faith. "And thereby," he writes, "the Infante and the Portuguese thought that God would not regard it as a sin when they offered Him a sacrifice steeped in human blood" (*H.I.*, bk. 1, ch. 18, *O.E.* 1:68b). Religious sacrifice and homicide are incompatible.

Once more in the *History of the Indies* he appeals to the biblical passage in question to expose so-called Christian behavior. He relates how "Bachelor Anciso" (Martín Fernández de Enciso) "and those with him" (including Vasco Núñez de Balboa and Francisco Pizarro) arrived at a native village in the region of Darién. Before attacking the Indians, they commended themselves to God and made a vow "to Our Lady, or Nuestra Señora del Antigua, as she is called in Seville, . . . that, would she grant them victory, they would name the first church and town to be built in this region Santa María del Antigua," and furthermore that they would send to Seville "jewels of gold and silver." Having made these prayers and promises, they launched an assault against the Indians, killing a large number of them, and then sacked their village. Las Casas says that deeds of this nature should not be overlooked, and that there ought to be "some consideration for Christendom." This "consideration" will focus on God's rejection, according to the passage from Ecclesiasticus, of offerings stained with blood. Bartolomé quotes only verses 21 and 22 of chapter 34, but they are precisely the verses expressing God's displeasure with the gifts of the wicked (*H.I.*, bk. 3, ch. 64, *O.E.* 2:154–56).

In the *Apología* he once more cites this biblical text in a significant framework. With reference to those who justify their wars against the Indians on the pretext of coming to the rescue of the victims of human sacrifice, Las Casas objects that the deaths these wars produce are offered on the altar of the great god gold, and asks, "Will *our* sacrifices be pleasing in the eyes of the divine mercy?" They are only an immolation of victims such as is reproached in the Indians — but this time offered by persons calling themselves Christians. Doubtless these sacrifices will be just as acceptable "as the offering of a 'man who slays a son in his father's presence' (Eccl. 34)." Bartolomé adds: "These things are foreign to the teaching of Christ and the example of the apostles and are pleasing only to cruel and inhumane brigands or certain foolish enemies of the teaching of Christ, who by their conduct make Sodom look just" (169; emphasis added).

Indians, blacks, and Canarians are all innocent victims. One may not offer worship to the God of life at the price of their death and their blood unjustly spilled.

There is one other mention of the text of Ecclesiasticus; it is found in his last work and demonstrates his constant recourse to this text.

The fifth doubt posed for him about what happened in Peru concerns the obligation of those who have received money from the *encomenderos.* In one of his responses the bishop of Chiapa refers to the religious and ecclesiastics who have received from the *encomenderos* "any offerings or gifts of any kind" for church buildings or for the altar. Las Casas believes that if they do not return this money to the Indians "they sin mortally." His argument is based on Alexander of Hales (d. 1245) and the text of Ecclesiasticus: the bread of the poor is their life. And this is certainly the case for the Indians who have died of hunger (*Doce dudas*, 1564, O.E. 5:519b–520a-b).[15]

"They Must Be Dreaming"

A clearer view of the situation in the Indies leads not to flight or retreat, but to a commitment to alter that situation. And so our cleric "made up his mind to preach this" (*H.I.*, bk. 3, ch. 79, O.E. 2:357a). The Dominicans had shown him the path. Las Casas takes that path, with his long experience in the Indies (which the friars lacked) and his enormous vigor. In order to execute this enterprise, it was necessary to undo any attachment to the system that exploits and plunders the poor. As an *encomendero,* Las Casas owned Indians. At the same time, he had before him "the reprobation of their sermons" — the Dominicans' condemnation of the servitude and oppression that the Indians were suffering in the newborn colonial society. In this conflict, the cleric "agreed to condemn openly the distributions or *encomiendas* as unjust and tyrannical, and then to release [his own] Indians" (ibid.).

For him, a commitment to the poor involves abandoning his position of privilege and rending the fabric of social relations that is its vehicle. This descent from his social class is the condition of the authenticity of a transformation that he does not wish to remain, all too idealistically, on a purely interior and "spiritual" level. To continue holding his *encomienda* would be to deny in practice what he proposed to preach in theory. Las Casas tries to conform his life to the example left us by Christ. The Lord, as the cleric will say in his first book, "did first, then said what he wanted the fundamental way of preaching the gospel to be. He took his own advice, he obeyed his own command" ("Nam fecit quod monuit, ostendit quod jussit," *De Unico,* 158v). This consistency is actually the central characteristic of Jesus' witness: his most severe criticisms of those who "strain out the gnat and swallow the camel" (Matt. 23:24) are provoked by the fact that they speak in one way and act in another. And so the Gospel of Matthew, which, as we know, focuses on the theme of discipleship, presents hypocrisy as the greatest of dangers for a disciple of Jesus Christ.

Las Casas is faced with a concrete decision, not with the enunciation of a principle. The matter is a complex one. The Indians in his power are caught in a wicked, unjust system. On a personal level, however, they are well treated by him and would surely be even better cared for in the future ("as a father might do for his children," he says). In these circumstances, to place them in the hands of Diego Velázquez, the chief official of the island, and his like would mean "handing them over to those who would oppress them, and use them up, to the very death." And Las Casas ends, in great distress, with: "...as indeed they did kill them." What was he to do then? Las Casas abides by his decision, painful as it is for him. Otherwise he would be easy prey for the calumnies of those who resisted any radical change in the system of the *encomienda,* as now they would have an additional pretext for their attitude. To keep his Indians for such plausible motives would also, and especially, be to forget so many other victims of a social order that simply must be attacked at its root. It is a harsh dilemma. It presents itself in various forms, but it is always present in the battle to be waged against the structural causes of a situation of exploitation and injustice and is of immediate concern to the persons who suffer that situation. This was surely one of the most difficult decisions that Bartolomé ever had to make in his life.

In the absence of his friend Pedro de Rentería, with whom he held his *encomienda,* his distribution of Indians,[16] and desiring to "preach what he felt obliged to preach," Las Casas communicated to Velázquez his decision to break with his situation as *encomendero.* The latter reacted as anyone might be expected to do who does not want his or her conscience disturbed: he called the cleric's decision a "thing so new and, as it were, monstrous." It was new that a cleric involved in the things of the world "should be of the opinion of the Dominican friars who had first attempted this and should dare to bring it out into the open." And it was "monstrous," because Las Casas had been on the way to "becoming wealthy in a short time," thanks to his diligence with regard to his "farms and mines." Las Casas comments that Velázquez seemed not to perceive "the danger in which he himself lived, as chief and captain of the tyranny being perpetrated upon the Indians on that island."

For the beneficiaries of a given social order, that social order is always the best possible one, at least of those humanly available. Anything that calls it into question is new, unheard of, and utopian. As we have seen, this had been the reaction of King Ferdinand and the Spanish Dominican provincial to Montesino's sermon. The gospel will invariably be "new" when read from the standpoint of the poor.

Velázquez refused to accept Las Casas's renunciation and gave him a fortnight to "reconsider." But Bartolomé rejected any such cooling-off period and went ahead with his "novelty," making it public on

Assumption Day in a sermon on the gospel for that feast (the story of Mary and Martha) dealing with the "contemplative life and the active." Apropos of "works of charity," the cleric spoke to those present of the "obligation that they must meet and perform among these peoples, of whom they had made such cruel use," and criticized "the omission, neglect, and oblivion of them in which they lived." This led him to "declare to them their blindness, injustices, and tyrannies — the cruelty they were committing against those innocent, meek people, and how they could not be saved if they continued to hold them, neither they nor those who had distributed them to them." The responsibility was that of the *encomenderos*, then, but it was also that of the authorities who supported them. The cleric also spoke to his congregation of the "obligation to restitution by which they were bound and explained that he himself, knowing the danger in which he lived, had released [his] Indians."

His congregation was "in wonderment, even fear, ... and some thought they must be dreaming." What "unaccustomed things" to be hearing! That it was "sinful to hold the Indians in their service"! Las Casas concludes his account incisively: to the ears of his auditors, it was "as if they had been told that they were not permitted to use the beasts of the field" (*H.I.,* bk. 3, ch. 29, *O.E.* 2:358a–b). What Las Casas preached that day — a message rooted in the good news of the Reign of God — would constitute the core of his prophetic message. And it is a novelty still.

In the subsequent chapters of his *History,* Las Casas speaks of his continual sermons to the same effect and of the support that he received from the Dominicans arriving in Cuba. The *encomenderos,* however, as our cleric notes a number of times, did not change their attitude. And so Las Casas finally decided to go to the king, despite the warning he received from his venerable friend Pedro de Córdoba: "As long as the King is alive, you shall achieve nothing of what you and we desire." The influence of Fonseca, bishop of Burgos, and of Secretary Lope Conchillos at the royal Court was very great (*H.I.,* bk. 3, ch. 83, *O.E.* 2:36b). With Antón Montesino, Las Casas set sail for Spain in September 1515.

Chosen for a Ministry

On three important occasions, Las Casas refers to the material of the account that we have just reported. These texts confirm and complete the meaning he assigns to the facts cited.

We find the first in the *History of the Indies* itself, in a summary of the author's December 1519 presentation to King Charles in Barcelona. The context is polemical. Juan Cabedo, bishop of Darién, in Panama, maintains the Indians' conditions as slaves *a natura,* from their very nature. He is the first to speak before the king. Then it is Las Casas's turn. Bartolomé begins with the situation of death that reigned in the Antilles, a situation occasioned by a "greed, thirst, and insatiable hunger for the gold of the dead" — that is, for the precious objects buried with the Indians when they died. Next he sets forth the manner in which this occurs, positing to this end a distinction to which he ascribes a great deal of importance. It is found countless times in his *History,* and we shall return to it later, in order to show the plan he follows in that work.

The Indians, he says, perish in the following two ways. (Elsewhere he calls them two "entryways.")

> The one, by way of the unjust, utterly cruel wars [waged] on those Indians, who had been dwelling in all security in their homes and on their lands, harming no one, where the individuals, peoples, and nations who have died are numberless. The other: after having slain the natural rulers and principal persons, they place [the rest of the people] in servitude, distribute them among themselves by hundreds or by fifties, and cast them into the mines, where finally, under the burden of the incredible toils they suffer in mining gold, they all die.[17]

That was the reality he left behind him in his journey to see the king. This, he says, alluding to the events of 1514, is what has stirred him to enter the lists in defense of the dwellers of the Indies. "Seeing all this," he says, "I was moved, not because I was a better Christian than anyone else, but by a natural, most pitiful compassion for people who had never deserved this from us, suffering such terrible wrongs and injustices" (*H.I.,* bk. 3, chs. 148–49, *O.E.* 2:534–35). In our next chapter we will see the importance that Las Casas attributes to the feeling of compassion when it comes to his commitment and reflection.

The second reference is less precise regarding this moment of his life, but Bartolomé makes the allusion, and it is of particular interest to us because it is coupled with a fertile concept for the comprehension of its meaning. Let us situate the text in its context. From 1516 to 1518, Las Casas presents projects that would bring about changes in the Indies (and we shall speak of these in the following chapter). After laborious initiatives, he receives a land grant in Cumaná (Venezuela). In the course of his visit to the royal Court with this particular proposal, the incident takes place that we shall recount a few pages further on and that has given us a beautiful text on the scourged Christs of the Indies. The Cumaná project was intended as the realization of something the cleric had been seeking for quite some time: a peaceful colonization and evangelization, with Indians and Spanish peasants sharing a common life. In the petition to the grand chancellor for a land grant, he asserts that God has given him a desire for this undertaking "because God loses much fruit, daily, which He hopes will ripen there for His Church" (*O.E.* 5:40a).

The enterprise eventually concludes in heartbreaking defeat.[18] The cleric now becomes a Dominican friar (1522) — the step frequently referred to as his "second conversion." He withdraws, for a time, from the heat of the fray. (To the rejoicing of many, he tells us: some, the friars, "at the boon of the conversion of one they loved with a holy love; others, in the world, because the one who had been harassing them about their thefts was as good as dead and buried.")

For some years, Las Casas maintains something of a low profile. Not that he is unnoticed in Hispaniola, where he now lives; still, there is surely a great difference between these years and those preceding the Cumaná experiment. The trouble was, says the new Dominican humorously, "I rose again — by the will of God, it could have been thought... — to cause some more trouble" (*H.I.*, bk. 3, ch. 160, *O.E.* 2:556b–67a).

But in 1531 we find him once more in the thick of the fight. Reappearing on the public stage,[19] he addresses a letter to the Council of the Indies. His basic ideas are the same as before, but their formulation reflects his years of silence and study. In his reappearance on the scene, he addresses a judicial body in whose presence he has spent a great deal of time, he recalls — "some six continuous years." Some of the current members of the Council are the same.

The former secular cleric, now a Dominican friar, propounds his motive for this new initiative: on the one hand, "the charity of Jesus Christ, which knows no measure nor seeks any rest while on this pilgrimage"; and on the other, "the distress and endless misery which, in these lands, although unknown, these unfortunate infidel peoples here have suffered for so long a time now, without a day of rest, respite, or relief, but with more agony still" — and with these people, he adds, expressing an extremely interesting notion, "the whole mystical body of concern to ourselves [*que a nuestra parte toca*]." We are dealing with a clause within a long sentence, which could of course mean that the entire church, the "mystical" or Pauline "body of Christ," is affected by the predicament of the Indians — the church as a whole, then, and not only those who for one reason or another personally react to these injustices. After all, the indefatigable charity of Jesus Christ is not present exclusively in them; it informs the entire Christian community.

But a second interpretation of the text is possible and would be even more interesting: the Indians, even in their condition as unbelievers, are members of the Pauline body of Christ. Therefore when they, who are a part, suffer, the entire body suffers. In this case we should be witnessing the early appearance of a concept that we shall consider later in this chapter (in speaking of Las Casas's central intuition, the presence of Christ in the Indian), a concept explicitly stated in one of his treatises of 1552 (see *Tratado comprobatorio*).

In 1563–64, fifty years after the change in his attitude that takes place in Cuba, Las Casas writes two important texts. It is an appropriate moment for a "rereading" of one's entire life. The first is the dedication of the *Doce dudas* (Twelve doubts) to Philip II.[20] The affairs of the Indies, he says, he knows with his "own eyes and from very long experience." From the beginning he was aware of the difficulty of the problems, but he was sustained by his faith in God: "During the last fifty years, from the year fourteen when I became a cleric and then later as a friar and then as bishop for another thirteen years," he adds, "in which I have seen what happened, I have not ceased tirelessly to inquire how, according to God and natural reason, divine and human justice, we should relate to those peoples." This was the point of his whole life: to clarify what rights Spain had over these lands. It was not just a theoretical concern. It pointed up the doctrinal foundation of his struggle; faced with "the calamities of those people" he was "obliged to denounce them and insist on a remedy" for them. This is what he did, and, conscious of his age, he says with a certain charm: "And since by divine mercy God has given me such a long life, there has been time for everything" — time to deal with the issue theoretically and time to enter the daily fray proposing "remedies."

The other writing, his testament, opens with the obligatory exordium, a profession of faith in the Triune God and protestation that the testator hopes to "die, and to live as long as may befall to him to live," in that same faith. Then Bartolomé goes on to speak of the mission that has constituted the meaning of his life. He considers that through God's goodness and mercy God has chosen him "as His minister, without any merit of my own, in order to champion and defend all those tribes of what we call the Indies,...[in view of] the outrages, evils, and harm" that "they have received against all reason and justice, and in order to restore them to their pristine liberty, of which they have been unjustly stripped, and to deliver them from the violent death that they continue to suffer, and perish, as they have perished,...many of them in my presence."

Here are the great themes that have sustained his struggle of half a century. God's call, which is the expression of a gratuitous love, is at the root of everything: the obligation of indemnification to be made to those who have suffered such unjust wars and domination; an insistence upon the original freedom of these people whose human dignity cannot be questioned and to whom that of which they have been dispossessed must be restored; the liberation of persons who suffer a premature, unjust death, as they still do, all of this based on his own experience: " . . . in my presence," as he puts it. Apart from his years in Hispaniola and Cuba, first, and then in other lands of the Indies, Bartolomé's battle is incomprehensible.

He sets forth in his last will and testament what it was that, in 1514, impelled him to abandon the station he had held up until then in the nascent colonial society, and to commit himself to those whom he regards as the favorites of the God who has called him. He has acted "for some fifty years, since the year one thousand five hundred fourteen, for God alone, and by compassion at the sight of such multitudes of rational human beings perishing." Only God and a sensitivity for the poor, God and the death of the Indians, are the motives of his engagement. Nor does he see this — in his rereading — as a purely personal commitment. "I believe and deem," he writes, "that thus the Holy Roman Church will have it, that standard and rule of our believing: that everything perpetrated by the Spaniards against those people — robbery and death and the usurpation of the estates and domains of their natural kings and lords, their lands and kingdom, and other goods without limit, with such damnable cruelty — has been contrary to the most righteous, immaculate law of Jesus Christ, and contrary to all natural reason" (*O.E.* 5:539b–540a).

His years of struggle have enabled him to understand, interiorly and viscerally, that none of this is a mere matter of the personal position of an individual Christian. It is something that involves the entire church. What is at stake is not someone's delicacy of conscience, but an objective violation of the law of Christ. Bartolomé's effort has been part of an action that is incumbent on the church as a whole.[21] He will have no heirs of his own to whom to bequeath the task, in this, his last will and testament. But he has no need of such. That task falls to all of Jesus' followers, wherever they are found, in whatever era they may live. Las Casas has done what he has done as a disciple of the Lord, and others will follow. The law of Jesus Christ, the "perfect law of liberty" (James 1:25), is theirs as well, just as it is ours today.[22]

2. *Beginning of a Journey*

The account that we have cited is the story of Las Casas's breach with his former life and a new departure for his activity. His practice in behalf of the Indians begins very early. As for his theories, they will have some catching up to do. Bataillon has shown the remnants of a colonial mentality in our cleric, in the first years of his new life, when it comes to his manner of conceiving the presence of the Spaniards in the Indies.[23]

Bartolomé will manage a systematic presentation of perspectives of his own only after a time of maturation, as is surely to be expected. However, this process will materialize largely on the basis of intuitions he has had early in his life, coexisting with the vestiges of which we have spoken. We should like to emphasize two of these initial intuitions or ideas. We refer to the terrible relationship established from the outset in the Indies between gold and death. This leads him to a definitive, incisive perception of what is occurring in the Indies. There it is not the God of Jesus Christ who is worshiped. Instead, gold has been transformed into the idol to which those who call themselves Christians render homage and which they serve. As we now address these themes, we shall see the content and scope of the prophetic call that Bartolomé experienced in 1514.

A Greedy, Marauding People

The causal relationship between the quest for *gold* and the *death* of the Indians smites the conscience of our cleric-*encomendero* in function of his reading of the Bible. That tie is vociferously denied by many of those who call themselves Jesus' followers. But it is also ideologically disguised — as in the *Yucay Opinion*, for example — under the postulate that without gold there would be no gospel in the Indies.[24]

Las Casas's position is different. For him, the great majority of those who have come to the Indies, "vaunting the name of Christian,"[25] have done so "with the sole concern of making money" (*Memorial de remedios*, 1516, O.E. 5:27b).[26] These persons are utterly unconcerned with any proclamation of the gospel — or with the death of the Indians, the price to be paid for obtaining the gold.[27]

In the presence of the lust for gold, the life of these "inferior creatures" is worth next to naught. The Franciscans' and Dominicans' Letter, cited above, declares forthrightly and eloquently:

> The original causes, Most High Lord Chamberlain, for the murder of such a great number of people, have been these: first, the belief of all who have come here that, inasmuch as these people are without the faith, they may be casually killed, taken captive, robbed of their lands, possessions, and domains and chattels, and that it is not a matter of conscience; second, the meek, peaceful disposition of these unarmed people. Along with these two reasons, there is the fact that those who came here, or the ma-

jority of them, are the dross of Spain — a greedy, marauding people.[28]

This "greedy, marauding people" has created a situation that Las Casas will decry in terms of a key expression of his — one that he will therefore use all through his works: *destruction*.[29] In a rather extensive, but precise and expressive, text, Las Casas explains the concrete meaning of this word — which, as we have seen, was used by the first missionaries of Hispaniola as well — as the term is applied to the Indies:

> And whenever Your Majesty hears us speak of so many realms having been "destroyed," and still being "destroyed," let Your Majesty not understand any exaggeration, as if by "destruction" we meant what is commonly meant [by this expression] in Europe, such as when some realm has been or is being "destroyed" in the sense of not having any more money, or of the affliction of not having managed to bring its wars to a successful conclusion, or of some need or dearth that might come upon a polity and its ruler. This, Most Exalted Lord, is not what we mean to convey here. Rather, when we say that seven realms of Your Majesty's, each greater than Spain, have been "destroyed," we mean that we have seen them as filled with people as a hive is filled with bees, and that now they are all devastated, the Spaniards having in the ways described above slain all of their native inhabitants and dwellers, so that nothing is left of the villages but stark walls, as if all of Spain stood devastated, with only the walls of the cities, villas, and localities left, and all the people having died. (*Octavo remedio*, 1542, 108a)[30]

This is what Las Casas means by "destruction." It is not a use of the literary or rhetorical device known as hyperbole. It is not "a way of raising the ante." Nor is it a way of calling attention to the crisis that a polity may be passing through.[31] "Destruction" here means principally the premature, unjust death of the Indians and the depopulation of entire localities — in a word, the brutal ruin of a people. But it also implies the annihilation of autochthonous cultures and the laying waste of the world of nature. The defense of life, on these three levels — which, as it happens, are interdependent — constitutes one of the great motivations of Bartolomé's struggle.

The Conquistadors' Deep Aspiration

Gold and death, greed and destruction, are correlative pairs, expressive of a state of affairs that Las Casas tirelessly challenges. A central point in his indictment will be a denunciation of the cause: ambition for gold. It is this that snuffs out "lives before their time" (*H.I.,* bk. 3, ch. 38, *O.E.* 2:484b). Those who have come to these lands to grow wealthy are the "insidious enemies and manifest destroyers of the lives of the Indians, and capital enemies, called *hostes,* in Latin, of all their generation" (*Octavo remedio,* 1542, *O.E.* 5:80a–81b). They are a people, Bartolomé says graphically, who have not cleansed "their understanding of the cataract of dung that is their greed" (*H.I.,* bk. 3, ch. 152, *O.E.* 2:542b). The facts show the incompatibility of the quest for gold and the life of the Indians.

The problem will not go away. Native consciousness was deeply marked by the invaders' eagerness for wealth. Here we have an unusual witness, as he welds his native view to the Christian perspective. We refer to Guamán Poma, who, a number of decades later, writes: "Even until now that desire for gold and silver perdures, and the Spaniards slay one another and flay the peoples of the Indian poor for gold and silver." Of those who have come to the Indies, Guamán says in his telegraphic style: "They have been unwilling to bring anything but weapons and pistols, and a greed for gold and silver, to the Indies, Pirú. None has escaped this desire of gold: filled with covetousness, very many priests and Spaniards and ladies, merchants, embarked for Pirú. Everything was Pirú, Indies and more Indies, gold and silver, gold and silver in Pirú." Here is the conquistadors' solitary passion. Nor need we read much further to find the reproach it merits: "With greed for good and silver," says Guamán, "they go to hell."[32]

Las Casas presents us with numerous examples of this in his *History of the Indies.* Let us recall one, from Cuba, involving a well-known personage: Hernán Cortés. Cortés, for Bartolomé, is a typical conquistador, unscrupulous, an exploiter of Indians, elevated to noble rank by the Crown and much admired by Ginés de Sepúlveda, the theologian who strove to justify the wars against the Indians. "Cortés made all haste," Bartolomé writes, "and employed all diligence, that the Indians distributed to him by Diego Velázquez should mine for him a great quantity of gold, which was everyone's keen desire. And thus they mined for him two or three thousand pounds of gold, which was great wealth in those times. As for those who died mining it for him, God will have tallied them better than I" (*H.I.,* bk. 3, ch. 27, *O.E.* 2:240b).[33]

Reporting his experiences in Cuba during the wars of "pacification," Las Casas tells us that in Caonao there had been an effort to "obstruct the death" of the Indians at the hands of the conquistadors, but that it had not been very successful (*H.I.,* bk. 3, ch. 29, *O.E.* 2:245a), and that when a few human lives had indeed been spared — he adds with frustration — it was only so that "they might kill them little by little in the mines and other works, as they finally did kill them" (*H.I.*, bk. 3, ch. 30, *O.E.* 2:248a).

The text of Ecclesiasticus had reminded Las Casas of a classic prophetic theme: An offering made to God without the practice of justice is a gift stained with the blood of the poor. It is of no use, in Las Casas's mind, to pretend that one believes in the God of the Bible when one "lives...on the blood of the Indians" (1516, *O.E.* 5:10b). For Bartolomé, to defend the life and temporal welfare of the Indian will be from this point forward to affirm the living God proclaimed to us by Jesus Christ. This outlook is central for an understanding of Bartolomé's theology and missionary activity alike.

3. *Christ in the Indian*

From the very beginning of his battle, Las Casas begins to gain a clear consciousness that the oppression of the Indian is contrary to the "intention of Jesus Christ and to the whole of Scripture," that what God wishes instead is the "liberation of the oppressed."

The Poor, Preferred by God

This conviction takes such deep root in him that it motivates the struggle he will wage all the rest of his life. The poor are beloved of God with a love of predilection because: "God has a very fresh and living memory of the smallest and most forgotten" (*Carta al Consejo*, 1531, *O.E.* 5:44b). This preference, then, ought to be a norm of life for the Christian. And Fray Bartolomé, reminding us that those who exploit and murder the Indian "have gold as their actual, principal end," will deny them the name of Christian, stating, in a text we have already cited: "Christ did not come into the world to die for gold" (*Octavo remedio*, 1542, *O.E.* 5:88b).[34] No, it will be ambition for riches and capital that will kill Christ, in the murder of the Indians. Indeed, in one of the most profound, beautiful, and evangelical passages of all of his writing, the Dominican friar will identify these "Indian oppressed" with Christ himself.

In his *History of the Indies*, Las Casas recounts how, in his endeavor to "protect these miserable people and prevent their perishing," he embarked on the difficult — and actually questionable — enterprise of a peaceful colony in the lands of today's Venezuela, an undertaking we have already mentioned. To this purpose, he offered the king a sum of money in exchange for the concession of these lands and of other faculties. A raw realism induced him, at that moment, "in virtue of the great experience he has had, to establish upon this negotiation all of the Indians' good, freedom, and conversion — on the purely temporal interest of those whose help was necessary to attain this" (*H.I.*, bk. 3, ch. 131, *O.E.* 2:490a, b).[35]

This manner of "negotiation" scandalized a certain individual who held cleric Las Casas in high esteem and who now expressed his perplexity and disapproval. Bartolomé favored this personal friend with an explanation. In that reply he has given us one of the most impressive passages anywhere in his works, and it will be worthwhile to transcribe it in its entirety:

> The cleric learned of this, and said: "Supposing, Sir, that you were to see Our Lord Jesus Christ abused — someone laying hands on him, afflicting him, and insulting him with all manner of vituperation — would you not beg with the greatest urgency and with all your strength that he be handed over to you instead, that you might worship and serve and please him and do everything with him that, as a true Christian, you ought to do?"
>
> "I surely would," replied the other.
>
> "And supposing they would not simply give him to you, would you not purchase him?"
>
> "That I would do indeed," said the other. "Of course I would purchase him."
>
> Then the cleric added: "Indeed, Sir, I have but acted in that very manner. For *I leave, in the Indies, Jesus Christ,* our God, scourged and afflicted and buffeted and crucified, *not once but millions of times,* on the part of all the Spaniards who ruin and destroy these people and deprive them of the space they require for their conversion and repentance, *depriving them of life before their time,* so that they die without faith and without the sacraments. Many times have I besought the King's Council to provide them with a remedy and remove the impediments to their salvation, which consist in the Spaniards holding in captivity those whom they already have, and where they still do not, to send Spaniards to go to a certain part of the continent where religious, servants of God, have commenced to preach the gospel. The Spaniards who traverse that land with their violence and wicked example prevent them from doing so and make the name of Christ into a blasphemy. They have replied that there is no room there, that is, if the friars were to occupy the land, the King would have no income from it. The moment I saw that they were asking me to sell the gospel, and consequently Christ, and that they scourged him and beat him and crucified him, I agreed to purchase him, offering many goods, much income, and temporal wealth, to in-

demnify the King, in the manner in which Your Mercy will have heard." (*H.I.*, bk. 3, ch. 138, *O.E.* 2:511b; emphasis added)

After this paradoxical "sale of the gospel and of Christ" and his own ambivalent, reformist attempt at peaceful colonization in Venezuela, Las Casas is seized with a passion: his love for the living Jesus Christ, scourged, buffeted, crucified, and murdered in the "captive poor" of the Indies "not once, but thousands of times." He assimilates the conviction that a love of Christ must necessarily impel a person to try to achieve the liberation of the Indians and to prevent the "untimely" looting of their lives by way of the regime of the *encomienda*. Once more, and in this case he identifies Christ and the poor, we find a fine perception of the poor and their material, concrete, and temporal lives. Their spoliation, exploitation, and murder is "blasphemy of the name of Christ." We have already encountered this attitude on the part of the Dominicans of Hispaniola. The reasons are the same. The name of Christ is offended, say the Dominicans, in the counter-testimony given by way of the prevention of the "life and temporal multiplication" of the Indians.

There are echoes of this central text in another work by Fray Bartolomé de Las Casas. Apropos of the link obtaining between the love of God and the love of neighbor, Las Casas writes: "The one who loves God does not hate the brethren, does not prefer material to spiritual wealth, but always behaves generously." As usual, Las Casas will prove his proposition with an appeal to "authorities": Augustine and Chrysostom will be among his favorites. But the definitive argument is to be found in the gospel: among the numerous texts he cites, the first will be from Matthew 25, ever suggestive, that reminds us of the one who has said, " 'Whoever helps one of the helpless, helps me' (Matt. 25:40). That one thinks that his ministry makes him a servant alongside God," and knows that God regards a service rendered a fellow servant as rendered to God (*De Unico*, 167v; *The Only Way*, 136).

God is at the center of any relationship of charity and justice and is absent from any contempt for neighbor. It is the same with the divine salvific grace. In a concrete relationship with the other, the final destiny of all human existence is at stake: God "regards as done to Himself" any deed addressed to our neighbor.[36] An act addressed to the poor always reaches the God present in the poor. We must be aware of this, Las Casas says.

Two annotations apropos of the same Matthean text show what an exigency this has become for him. In a commentary on the expressions, "You fed me nothing.... You gave me no water ... " (Matt. 25:41–42), Bartolomé insists: "They are damned, not for doing evil, but for not doing good" (*De Unico*, 169; *The Only Way*, 138). Abstention from acting is impossible. To neglect to do something for a person in need is to fail to do one's duty of helping that person. It constitutes a sin of omission. Concretely, in the Indies, no one can take a position with regard to history at a kind of "dead center" and just watch it roll by.

A few pages further on, Bartolomé returns to this gospel passage, recalling a penetrating question posed by Augustine of Hippo: "If someone is damned to hellfire by Christ saying to him or her, 'I was naked and you did not clothe me,' to what hellfire will they be damned to whom He says, 'I was clothed and you stripped me!'" (*De Unico*, 196; *The Only Way*, 162). That, of course, is what is actually going on in the Indies. Not only are the naked not clothed, but, perversely, the poor of those lands are violently unclothed: the Indians are despoiled of their legitimate possessions. The poor are robbed and, in them, Christ himself.

Exhuming the Truth

Years later, after a great deal of study and reading, Las Casas will plumb this same intuition to greater depth in a treatise that has a very special place among his works: the *Tratado comprobatorio*.[37] In order to identify the nature of papal authority and consequently the scope of the grant made to the Spanish sovereigns by Alexander VI, Las Casas discusses the authority of Christ. This leads him to considerations of interest to us here.[38]

"The salvation of persons belongs to Christ," he begins. "Christ performs this deed in his quality as head of all persons" — even of unbelievers. Unbelievers, of course, do not belong to the church *in actu*, as do the baptized. But they do belong to it *in potentia*: that is, "they can enter and become part of" the church. This potentiality is based on two principles: the grace of Christ, and the freedom of any persons "drawn to a knowledge of the faith."

Up to this point, Las Casas has followed Thomas Aquinas almost verbatim, in a text from the *Summa Theologiae* that he explicitly cites (bk. 3, ques. 8, art. 3). But now he goes a step further. He holds that in some sense it can also be said that "Christ [is] head of unbelievers *in actu*," since his grace operates interiorly also in non-Christians, withdrawing them from evil and disposing them "to hear the teaching of the faith and to receive it." Las Casas concludes plainly: "Christ, then, is the head of unbelievers" (*O.E.* 5:353a–b).[39]

For our purposes, it is important to note that the doctrinal context to which Bartolomé refers here enriches his intuition of the encounter with Christ in the Indian. The Indian, who is the unbeliever Las Casas has in mind in the texts, is a member of the body of Christ.

On the road to Damascus, the Lord asks Saul, who was harrying Christians: "Saul, Saul, why do you persecute me?" (Acts 9:3). Thus, Jesus identifies himself with his followers. Doubtless this experience plays a role in the later development of the notion of the Pauline body of Christ. Las Casas has learned the lesson: in the mistreatment of the Indian, who is part of the body of Christ, Jesus himself is being tortured. And let us observe, without setting more store by it than it may warrant, that, despite the fact that his principal source, Thomas Aquinas, speaks of a "mystical" body of Christ, Las Casas does not use the adjective (not here; he does so elsewhere). He conforms his terminology to that of Ephesians 4:15 (which he also cites), which does not speak of a "mystical" body of Christ — an expression from the patristic era — but only of a body of Christ.[40] The overall sense will be unaffected by the use or omission of this adjective, but Bartolomé's Pauline realism is worth noting.

Enmity toward the Indians, or worse, their actual maltreatment, is enmity toward or maltreatment of the body of the Lord, that is, it is abuse of Christ himself. The biblical roots of Bartolomé's proposition are clear, and the demands of his outlook very great.

Matthew 25:31–45, Las Casas's inspiration here (along with the text from Ephesians), has the same repercussions, and powerful ones, on Felipe Guamán Poma de Ayala. In both cases — with both Las Casas and Guamán — a keen biblical sense enables a believer to read what is at stake for those who genuinely believe in Christ and see him present in the suffering of the Indians.

It is impossible, of course, to arrive at this outlook if one regards the Indians as belonging to a naturally inferior race, as does Ginés de Sepúlveda, Las Casas's great adversary — or his more sophisticated followers of today. Nor, indeed, can one come to this conclusion merely in a defense, even a laudably strenuous one, of the Indians as human beings with rights formally èqual to those of all others, as with Francisco de Vitoria. One reaches this pinnacle of spirituality only if one perceives in the Indian, as did Bartolomé de Las Casas, the poor of the gospel. Lassègue is correct: "This admirable text, in all its simplicity, expresses a high point in the spirituality of the sixteenth century, as of all the Christian centuries — the identification of Christ with the martyred Indian."[41]

Surely the dwellers of the Indies are persons, with all of the rights appertaining to them as such. But more than anything else they are "our siblings, and Christ has given his life for them" (*Apología* 252v), to the point of identifying himself with these "Indian oppressed." This will be a capital point in the theological thought of Bartolomé de Las Casas, which has such deep evangelical and spiritual roots. It is a point to which the practice of solidarity with the poor invariably leads. This outlook will crisply and definitively distinguish Las Casas from the great Spanish theologians of the sixteenth century who will simply remain on the level of philosophy and of the theology of law. Many of them, nobly enough, sought to be attentive to the hard facts of the Indies. But it was natural for the New World to be, for them, a distant world. The consequences of these differences are many. The differences help us to acquire a more adequate perspective on the Lascasian contribution, which took shape in the light of the gospel and in the face of a reality contrary to the demands of that gospel.

Las Casas was always troubled with the misinformation that reached the Court from the Indies. On one occasion he denounces it: "How unfortunate those realms, to receive misinformation concerning the evils here, and how the truth is suppressed and buried, lest it sound and breathe!" (*H.I.*, bk. 1, ch. 5, *O.E.* 1:179b). To exhume the truth of the Indies will be Bartolomé's life purpose. The hidden truth, hidden deeper than the mines worked by the Indians, is this: in these abused and despised beings, Christ is present. To oppress and bury the dwellers of the Indies is to oppress and bury Christ himself, who is "truth and life" and also "the way" to take (John 14:6) in order that that truth might resound and breathe: the preferential option for the poor.

Chapter 3 _____

If We Were Indians

==

An early death for the Indians, and sin on the part of those who oppress them. It is the context in which Bartolomé receives the call to denounce these conditions, and to proclaim the Reign of life in its stead. The liberation of the "Indian oppressed" looms before his eyes as a colossal exigency. In the Indians, he sees Christ himself, humiliated and scourged.

It is within this christological perspective that Bartolomé reaches the great intuitions of his life. The first and last reason for the presence of the Christians in these lands, of whose discovery they boast, is to communicate the gospel to their inhabitants. This is the distinguishing characteristic of those who believe in the God of Jesus and the importance of friendship with that God, which Christians know as salvation. How shall Bartolomé speak of the gospel of life to those he refers to, with sensitivity and accuracy, as the "natural dwellers of those lands" (*Doce dudas*, 1564, *O.E.* 5:478a)? Here is his great anxiety and solicitude. We are in the new order of grace. No corner of human life is ever beyond the reach of God's grace, not even social organization, let alone that now coming into existence in the Indies. On the contrary, these lands present a historic opportunity to build a church that will be in genuine conformity with the gospel. Here is the dream that will pursue Las Casas and so many other missionaries — the Franciscans in Mexico, for example.

It is in the light of this evangelizing purpose that the deeds and events springing from the European presence must be judged. The missionary task constitutes the great concern of this human being who took his condition as Christian, priest, religious, and bishop so seriously. The enlightenment of his conscience that we have recorded in the foregoing chapter shows him that, in the Indies, what he regards as the two fundamental human rights are being violated: the right to life and the right to liberty. All of his work turns upon the defense of these two basic claims. Both will appear in his eyes as more and more demanding, throughout his life, but they are with him from the beginning.

It is not a mere matter of defending the right to life and liberty. Bartolomé's intuition goes deeper. We are dealing with rights of concrete persons, and what is more, persons whose human worth colonial society refuses to accept. Persons who are "different" are not acknowledged in their otherness. Their vital and mental world, so different from what the West is accustomed to, seems to the newcomers to these lands to be simply nonexistent. This is where Las Casas will develop an approach of his own, whose focus we might call methodological. He strives to understand the events of which he is the witness by seeking to take on the viewpoint of the Indians themselves.

The demand of evangelization, the right to life and freedom, and the adoption of the perspective of the native, constitute, it seems to us, Las Casas's basic intuitions. At their root is the Christ of his faith, present historically in persons who suffer violent dispossession and unjust death.

1. The First and Last Aim

From the very outset of his combat in defense of the Indian, Las Casas believes that the only possible justification for the presence of the Christians in the Indies is the proclamation of the gospel of Jesus Christ. This is a persistent theme in his writings and one from which he never ceases to deduce urgent demands on the responsibility of the Iberians, including the responsibility involved in the dominion over these lands exercised by the king and queen of Spain. This is how he interprets, for example, the controversial bulls of Alexander VI with regard to the New World. But actually, as we shall see, we meet with Bartolomé's concern for evangelization before he mentions and comments on those papal documents. Step by step, Las Casas forges a position of his own, which enables him to respond to this immense new reality, these Indies that captivated his heart and mind lifelong.

With Evangelization in Mind

In September 1515 (one year after having publicly declared that he was abandoning his *encomienda*), secular priest Las Casas leaves for Spain, along with Antón Montesino. In December he has an audience with King Ferdinand. In the new year he presents Cardinal Cisneros with an important *Memorial de remedios,* the first text which we have directly from his hand.[1]

In this document, he coins a thesis to which he will remain faithful throughout his life. It expresses the meaning of his life and of his own presence in the Indies. In these lands, "the principal end for which all that has been ordained, or might be ordained, is accomplished, and for this we are to strive and aim, is the salvation of the Indians, to be effected through the Christian doctrine that His Highness commands be imparted to them" (*O.E.* 5:20a).

The expression "principal end" will flow from his pen constantly, all through his life. He does not exclude, at this particular time, the legitimacy of other motives for the Spanish presence in the Indies. But these will all have to be judged in the light of evangelization as the primary purpose. Soon the principal end becomes the exclusive one. None other will matter. The Europeans must seek the salvation of the dwellers of the lands to which they have come — that is, full and final friendship with God. By "final" we do not mean only in the next life. Salvation must become present this very moment: this is a central point of Las Casas's theology of grace. Hence his well-known insistence on an appreciation of the temporal aspects of the human condition. The message of salvation must be announced in words and witness, he will say so often. This is what it is to transmit Christian doctrine. The author regards it in large measure as the responsibility of the king: in this text he does not indicate how or why, but the duty is recorded. Years later, Bartolomé will plumb the point in depth and extract demanding consequences from it.

The last words of the same memorandum summarize the matter, and with a polemical bite. "I beseech your most reverend lordship," he writes, "that you consider, as I know you will, that the first and last aim that must motivate us in a remedy for those sad souls must be God, and to attract them to heaven; because he did not redeem them nor discover them so that they might be cast into hell [by our Spaniards], with no thought but acquiring money. And thus this does not seem unreasonable, let alone an enormous burden" (*O.E.* 5:27a–b). The author's refinements of the earlier text are important. Now God is found at the beginning and end of the entire matter. Only if you begin with God can you find a remedy for such abuse and injustice. It is this *theocentrism* that puts teeth in Las Casas's analyses, denunciations, and proposals. It was also what made him so fearsome for his adversaries. The rights of the Indians, which he defends, are actually the rights of God.[2] Here is the reason for the "stubbornness" with which Bartolomé has so frequently been, depending on the case, either credited or reproached. The ultimate motive of a believer's action ought to be that person's faith in God. This is what made Bartolomé such a tireless seeker of "remedies," solutions, for the problems of the Indies and the sufferings of the dwellers of these lands.

Out of the deepest heart of his faith and his reading of the gospel, an urgent relationship springs: that between love of neighbor and love of God. This relationship is of particular importance when it is a matter of persons who suffer, "sad souls" who have not been redeemed — nor even been permitted by God to be found by Christians ("nor discovered") — to their woe, either today or later ("would cast them into hell"). And these self-styled Christians are concerned only with the getting of wealth. The matter is urgent, concludes the cleric. It may not be postponed. It is too serious. There is too much pain and injustice to put off our response.

In a firm hand, therefore, Las Casas sketches the outline of what for him is the only way in which the presence of the peninsulars in the territory of the Indians can be understood and justified. Let us observe that he does not mention the Alexandrine bull, to which he will appeal so frequently in later years, nor even the Testament of Isabella, whom he always held in such high esteem. His position springs from his faith, from his contact with Scripture, from his already broad experience of the uses and abuses of Hispaniola and Cuba alike, from the witness of the missionary friars, his friends, and from the change he experienced in his life a mere two years before. This is the attitude with which he opposes those who aim at what, for all practical purposes, is their "ultimate aim, which is to acquire gold, and to swell themselves with riches" (*Devastation*, 1542, 41; *O.E.* 5:137b). His awareness of the authentic purpose of the Spanish presence — the evangelization of the Indies — sharpens his attention to what is happening in these lands instead.

We cannot utterly exclude the possibility that the papal and royal texts mentioned were already known to him and that he was thinking of them when he redacted this *Memorial*. What is certain is that he does not yet refer to them. His conviction seems to flow ultimately from a more distant source — or rather a nearer one: what he has seen and reflected on in his experience in the Antilles. True, an appeal to these important edicts will give further solidity to this intuition and outlook. That will not be lost on Las Casas, although in this first manifestation of the "first and last aim" of the European presence in the Indies he does not cite these documents. Eventually he will appeal to them profusely.

A writing chronologically close to the one just considered, but of disputed authorship, is the *Memorial de denuncias* (1516).[3] If authentically from Bartolomé's pen, it would be the first Lascasian text to cite the celebrated Testament of Isabella.[4] The queen, too, takes a firm stand, on the basis of the bull of Alexander VI, in line with the missionary outlook of the papal concession, which is that of "inducing and attracting their peoples, converting them to our Catholic faith, and sending to those islands and Continent, prelates, religious, clerics, and other learned, God-fearing persons, in order to instruct the inhabitants and dwellers of the same in the Catholic Faith." Isabella beseeches and enjoins King Ferdinand, his daughter, and the Prince her spouse, that they "thus do and observe, and that this be the principal end" (*O.E.* 5:27a).

This document will become one of Bartolomé's war horses, and understandably. It supports his position that the purpose of the colonization is evangelization. In the *Memorial de denuncias* the commentary on the text is brief. The author thinks that the queen's assertions call for a change in the way the colonists behave with the Indians, and that up until now they have ignored their sovereigns' intentions. He briefly alludes to the obligation of "training" the Indians "in the things of the faith" (*O.E.* 5:27b), but especially insists on the lamentable consequences entailed for the Antilles by disregard of this end.

The Alexandrine bull is not directly cited or commented on in the *Memorial de denuncias.* For now, it is mentioned only in citations from Isabella's Testament. Perhaps indeed it has been by way of the latter that Bartolomé has come to perceive the advantage of an appeal to the papal document. Las Casas had certainly sought a number of bases of support for the conviction he had acquired in order to render it more persuasive and telling, perhaps even before he read these documents. There is no other reason for being in these lands that belong to the Indians than to communicate to them the Christian message. The principle will abide. But as for the practical conclusions to be drawn from that presence, Las Casas's thinking will constantly evolve, in step with his wins and losses in the combat on behalf of the Indians.

The *Memorial de remedios* of 1516, which we have analyzed above, was one of the sources of Cardinal Cisneros's project for the Indies, to be implemented by the Hieronymite mission.[5] As we know, that undertaking did not succeed. Indeed, for Las Casas it actually began badly.[6] In the first years of the cardinal's enterprise, the Sevillian cleric continued to denounce atrocities and propose solutions for the relief of the Indians. He resorted to the expedient of offering rewards to the governors in exchange for a more humane treatment of the native population. He did not see, at this time, any other means of obtaining a substantial transformation of what was happening. It is probable as well that he had a bad taste in his mouth from his past experience as a colonist. In terms of this outlook, there are two other memoranda, the *Memoriales de remedios* of 1518 and 1519. At the beginning of the first there is a mention of the king's responsibility before God "to save such numberless souls now being lost" (*O.E.* 5:31a). In the second there is a brief reference to the conversion of the Indians "to our faith" (*O.E.* 5:36a). These are echoes of the "principal end," although the latter does not come in for explicit treatment in these texts.

The Major Responsibility

As we know, upon taking cognizance of the bull *Inter Caetera* of 1493 Las Casas ordered it printed.[7] He found it a strong endorsement of his thesis of evangelization as the first and last legitimate aim of the presence of Christians in the Indies. However, the *first* Lascasian writing in which this bull is cited is the Letter to the Council (1531),[8] whose doctrinal wealth we have already seen.

Bartolomé begins by establishing his position: "The first thing I place before Your Lordships and Mercies, . . . that is, to secure the glory of God and the salvation of souls in these regions, ordering their governance in such wise as not to present impediments to the preaching of the faith." Their obligation flows not only from their being Christians, but is also "incumbent upon them as rulers" of this new world. This is their major responsibility in these lands. This, and nothing else, is the task that they must delegate to their subordinates. The pope's mandate is to "preach to and convert these people," and it is he who in turn enjoins this obligation upon the sovereigns and upon the members of the Council — "under mortal sin, unless they do it with great vigilance and care, preferring it to all temporal interests, the interests of the world" (*O.E.* 5:44a).

This is the precept given you, he writes, by the vicar of Christ, Alexander VI. Thereupon he quotes the substantial paragraphs of the bull and wonders: "Why is that bread from heaven that is the Christian faith so niggardly, neglectfully, and cruelly given to the hungering?" (*O.E.* 5:47b–48a). The "true end" is perverted in the Indies. It is replaced by a lust for wealth. He tells the dignitaries who are his addressees: "If the first and principal thing to be secured among the people to whom preaching is directed is the glory of God and the propagation of the divine worship, then how is it, My Lords, that the first and principal thing claimed to provide a legitimate title for coming to these lands is how the King will acquire enormous treasures?" (*O.E.* 5:49b). The very servants of the king turn their backs on the purpose of the presence of Christians in the Indies. The quest for riches replaces the proclamation of the gospel.[9]

The papal precept goes hand in hand with the command of Queen Isabella. Lest the addressees of his letter have any "excuse before the judgment of God" on the day of their death, the new Dominican reproduces the apposite material of the Isabelline text. Once more he contrasts what Isabella holds regarding the "principal end" with what is happening in the Indies: the practice of Christians there — with no appropriate measures being taken on the part of the members of the Council to prevent it — flies in the face of the injunctions of both Alexander VI and the queen (*O.E.* 5:50a–b).

Four years later, he repeats what he has so earnestly at heart: the implications of faith in God. "The footing, or doorway," he declares, "whereby the jurisdiction of the King is to enter, is the preaching of the faith, that they may first receive their God." But this is not the way things actually are for the Indians. "On the contrary, they are made to blaspheme and curse their God," owing to the wars and oppression of which they are the victims (*Carta a un personaje,* 1535, *O.E.* 5:62a; a little further on he will quote the papal text). This contradicts the sole justification for the Hispanic presence. Again we see the importance of the primacy of God, which we have already noted.

It would not be to our purpose to follow in detail the presence of this initial intuition (the place of the proclamation of the gospel) in Las Casas's later writings. His thesis is contained in them with all the clarity that one could wish. Bartolomé's central notion does not change. But the scope of their application does: the Dominican friar draws different conclusions in the different stages of his work and of his view of the problem of the Indies. The theme is present even in his last works. In the *De Thesauris,* which in his unpublished dedication of the *Doce dudas* to Philip II he calls "my last testament,"[10] he asserts that it was the preaching of the faith that was the mission entrusted to the sovereigns of Spain, so that that preaching and that faith constituted the only authentic criterion for a discernment of what was right and just in the Hispanic presence there (see, for example, 22 and 30v–31v).

It is the same with the *Doce dudas* itself, in whose dedication to Philip II he says he regards it "somewhat as a codicil"[11] to the work he calls his testament. In the *Doce dudas,* apropos of the problems posed by the conquest of Peru, he incisively reiterates his viewpoint:

> The sole final cause of the Apostolic See's grant of supreme governance and imperial sovereignty over the Indies to the Sovereigns of Castile and León was the preaching of the gospel, the spread of the Christian faith and religion, and the conversion of the native peoples of those lands — and not that they themselves might become greater sovereigns or wealthier princes than they already were. (*Doce dudas,* 1564, *O.E.* 5:491a)

Only the former consideration might justify the European presence in these lands. It is the latter, however, that seemed actually to carry the day.

But more than thirty years elapse between the texts under our examination here (*Carta a un personaje* and *Doce dudas*), and although the nucleus of their interpretation remains the same, there are important nuances and variations peculiar to each as to their scope and practical consequences (for example, "the supreme principate" spoken of in the *Doce dudas*). It is not our task, in this study, to enter into the tangle of debate occasioned by the task of interpreting the Alexandrine bulls.[12] Our only interest is to gain some purchase, after the fact, on Las Casas's understanding of these papal documents.[13] And we shall return to this matter.

For the moment, let us limit our considerations to the following brief reflection. It has many times been said that, on this topic, the Lascasian thinking corresponds to a medieval, theocratic mentality that sixteenth-century theologians (along with some of their predecessors, of course) sought to overcome.[14] The matter appears to us to be more complex than that. We believe that Las Casas reaches a position of his own in this matter, and one that defies the framework of familiar classifications. Let us make one thing clear from the start: Las Casas is the first to assert that the Alexandrine bull has meaning only in terms of evangelization. The bull lays a charge on certain rulers to carry out the task of evangelization. Later on, Vitoria, Soto, and others will say this, and say it very well. (Their interventions on these themes come later than the Lascasian letter of 1531, as well as other writings of Bartolomé's of the time. And as we already know, the concept is present in his first writings, as well.)[15] Neither must we forget that Bartolomé's reference to the proclamation of the gospel as the sole reason for the European presence in the Indies *precedes* his mention and interpretation of the papal text.

It is more meaningful to perceive what leads Las Casas to this focus. To posit the proclamation of the gospel as the only legitimate reason for the European presence is to assert that the concrete manner of that presence must be judged in the light of its evangelizing purpose. Bartolomé insists on this from his first quotation of *Inter Caetera* onward: "And does it still seem to you," he asks, "that, when this utterance of the Queen, with the letter from the Pope, is read forth on the Day of Judgment before you and those who have lived in the time when this world has been destroyed, you will wish to have been born, and that you will have a reply, or any excuse?" (*O.E.* 5:50b–51a). This is the important thing. On that last day, all will be transparent. The lives of those responsible for what is happening in the Indies will be read in the light of these texts. Then let that light begin to chase the shadows even today.

An immediate, urgent expression of the proclamation of the gospel is a defense of the life and freedom of those who are to receive it. This is what we are now about to see.

2. *Exorcising the Hell of the Indies*

Toward the end of his most controversial book, the *Brevísima relación,* or *The Devastation of the Indies: A Brief Account,*[16] Las Casas presents himself as someone who goes about seeking "to bring about the ending of [seeking to *echar,* to cast out] that inferno in the Indies." He does so, he says, for love of the Indians "redeemed by the blood of Jesus Christ," and for "my native land, Castile" (*Devastation,* 1542, 139; *O.E.* 5:175b–176a). Two loves — for the Indians and for his own country — move him to denounce what is occurring in the Indies. That inferno, that hell (for example, "the hell of Peru," *H.I.,* bk. 3, ch. 90, *O.E.* 2:387b), has been created by the unjust death and the oppression of the dwellers of the New World. They suffer *"servitude,* than which, except for *death,* there is no greater evil" (*Octavo remedio,* 1542, *O.E.* 5:95a; emphasis added).

His personal experience of this hell, this daily hell all around him, stamps Bartolomé with an indelible seal. In the face of this situation, the gospel places him on the road to an assertion of *life* and *freedom.* These are the fundamental rights of the human being, and they are of a piece. Concretely, it is a matter of the actual suffering of the Indians. Refusing to accept their subjection to slavery, the Sevillian cleric maintains that "men's *liberty,* after *life,* [is] the most precious and admirable thing they have" (*Tratado sobre los indios que se han hecho esclavos,* 1552, *O.E.* 5:270a; emphasis added).[17] Freedom and life are opposed to the servitude and death to which Bartolomé alludes in the text we have cited just above.

Placing Obstacles in Death's Way

Repeatedly Las Casas tells us that, since his rereading of the text of Ecclesiasticus, his effort has been to "obstruct" the continued violent, unjust death of the Indians.

In the *Representación a los regentes* (1516), the first Lascasian text that we have (by way of a secretary's summary), twenty items are listed for denunciation. It is a list of events occurring in the Antilles. In sixteen of them, the words "death," "die," or a synonym recur almost like a litany. The other four speak of other abuses inflicted on the Indians. The text is a chain of deaths, and it leaves a deep impression of desolation, or "destruction," as the text says. The last point in the text makes a terrible declaration — to be taken up again later in the form of an anecdote — in a cold, bureaucratic style: "He says that the name of Christian is so abhorrent that they would rather go to hell, reasoning that there will be no Christians to associate with there, than to paradise, where they would have to be with them" (*O.E.* 5:5b). As always with Las Casas, the memorandum is not limited to the description of a situation. Its causes are indicated and a corrective sought.[18]

To this last task Bartolomé devotes his *Memorial de remedios* of 1516, to which we have referred in the foregoing section. In this document the cleric presents what has been called a "community schema." He recommends a project for the establishment, in mutual respect, of free communities of Indians on the one hand, and villages of Spanish peasants on the other, which would maintain relationships of peaceful coexistence and mutual assistance.[19] Furthermore, he considers that the races themselves ought to mix: "the sons of the ones with the daughters of the others, etc." (*O.E.* 5:7b).[20] The plan is presented in detail. It stipulates the size of the villages. It specifies the officials to be put in charge of constituting these human groups. It describes the government of the Indians by their native chiefs and the special care that will have to be taken of the children of a vanishing population. It indicates the distances between the settlements, the hours of the working day (with a four-hour break each day), the suitability of a sand clock in each community lest the Indians "work too long." It determines how the Indians are to receive Christian instruction and insists on the opportunity for young natives to become "clerics or friars" if they so desire.[21] It declares the need for physicians, pharmacists, and schoolteachers.[22]

The proposal is dominated — and this is what is of interest for our purposes — by the notion of defending the life and freedom of the natives. In various places Las Casas underscores the contrast between these and the death and servitude so far prevailing. Only if they are alive, obviously, will the Indians be in a condition to hear the Christian message. "This community," he writes, "materializing under the requisite conditions about to be set forth, will no longer be responsible for the accidental death of the Indians that has been occurring until now. *Living,* [the Indians] will have an opportunity to be instructed in the faith and to be saved, *instead of dying*" (*O.E.* 5:7a; emphasis added). After all, faith can only be accepted freely. The basic point is the transformation of the conditions of existence of the Indians. But the proposal will benefit the Spaniards too. Until now, they have lived "on the blood of the Indians." They have shed a "great quantity of blood" (*O.E.* 5:14b). This must change.[23] In any case, it is an exigency flowing from the duty of proclaiming the gospel. This teaching should lead one to defend life, and not — as today, he says — to "give the Indians death for doctrine" (*O.E.* 5:14b).

Bartolomé's concern for life is very concrete. Here it is even expressed in considerations that might appear superfluous and unnecessarily detailed, but that actually reflect great anguish and profound sensitivity. The first thing to be done is to suspend the Indians' hard labor, which leads to their "killing and death in a brief space" (*O.E.* 5:5a–b). This and other rights must be heralded in "languages of the land to all the Indians" (5:8a), that is, in Indian tongues (and not simply cried aloud in Spanish, as the *Requerimiento,* or Notification, was "proclaimed" to the Indians). In this way the inhabitants of these lands will know of the measures taken and be able to defend them. Las Casas is anxious for the Indians' "souls' salvation and bodies' health" (5:12a). Thus, they, who have a right to recover their strength, "will at least to some extent recover their health" (5:5b). The importance of the point for Las Casas is meaningful. He mentions it twice more: that the Indians "may have relief and where they may recover their strength and bodily substance" (5:12a), and that they be "able to refresh themselves and recover their health" (5:12a) and be "healthy and fat and out of danger" (5:13a). To this end, they must "eat very well" (5:22b). Indeed, in "sufficiency [of nourishment] is their life, and in the lack thereof has been their death" (5:18b). If they rest as they should, they "will multiply, and in a short time the said island will be restored and repeopled" (5:11b). The life in question is the one we are accustomed to call material or temporal. But it, too, is an expression of salvation, and salvation is the content of the evangelizing proclamation. Salvation must be manifested in history, in the everyday. Las Casas never lost sight of this dimension. As we have remarked, this is part of his theology of grace. This is what happens in the heart of someone on familiar terms with the starvation, disease, mistreatment, and death of the poor.

This is the first of a number of projects mapped out by our cleric. Bartolomé sought to deliver the Indians from the oppression to which they were subjected, and which had almost exterminated them. He will resume many points of this proposal in later plans. The "community schema" has a germinal role in all the Lascasian reflection. Its architect will undergo a great evolution with respect to these initial ideas. He will even painfully repent of some of them (his approval of the so-called legal slavery of the Africans, for example). But he will return repeatedly to the core intuitions expressed in his *Memorial.*

The Lascasian project has been called utopian, and it has been noted that, curiously, Thomas More's *Utopia* was published the same year as the *Memorial de remedios,* 1516. An interesting and suggestive recent work attempts to show that this was no sheer coincidence. Its author, Víctor N. Baptiste, hypothesizes that a first, Latin draft of the "community schema" was sent to Flanders, where King Charles was sojourning late in 1515. By way of Erasmus, recently appointed to the Royal Council, the Lascasian document could then have reached Thomas More (as may be suggested by a remark of More's), and thus have served as inspiration for the latter's celebrated famous work.

Furthermore, in a close comparison of the two texts, Baptiste shows a surprising and fascinating similarity of ideas, right down to details like Utopia's resemblance to Cuba in More's map,[24] the size of the villages in the two books, the distance between the villages, the length of the working day, the local chiefs, More's use of neologisms corresponding to words used by Las Casas in the language of the natives, and the help of slaves in doing work (despite the atmosphere of freedom that animates both writings), and so on.[25]

However the case may be with Baptiste's theory, what we wish to set in relief is that Bartolomé's proposal for free native communities was an expression of the sole reason for which the Europeans might legitimately find themselves in these lands at all: the proclamation of the gospel. This orientation necessarily excludes all manner of oppression and calls for respect for the Indians' life and freedom, their political rulers, and their customs. The proposition that God is the first and last end of all things leads immediately to the conclusion that a people on the brink of extinction ought to be treated decently. Or in biblical terms: God cannot be separated from a tormented, plundered people. The Lascasian schema, in its concrete aspects, represents only the inaugural — and rudimentary — stage of Bartolomé's thought, but the evangelizing and theocentric intuition is already there.

In other writings, while reiterating his emphasis on the persistent, cruel death occasioned by war and oppression more directly, Las Casas also points to deaths occurring for reason of a want of the will to live. Indians were hanging themselves (see *H.I.,* bk. 3, ch. 82, *O.E.* 2:364b), taking poison, or simply "pining away and dying" (*Octavo remedio,* 1542, 5:97a). Mothers were killing their own children lest they leave them to live under "so hard a yoke" (*Carta al Consejo,* 1531, *O.E.* 5:49; *Carta a un personaje,* 1535, *O.E.* 5:62a). In the face of this situation, Bartolomé challenges the members of the Council to devote their own lives to the prevention of a situation this cruel to the natives and invites them to a life in Jesus Christ.

Let us say one last thing about Las Casas's defense of the right to life. Attention has frequently been called to the seduction and enchantment that the native Indian universe held for him. And indeed he has left us very beautiful pages evincing the attraction he felt for this world. What we are seeing is an expression of his utopian perspective (a utopia calculated to move history), provoked by the awareness (and the astonishment) of finding himself before a new world charged with all of this potential. Let us attend here to one point alone: for Las Casas, the defense of the life of the Indians involves the defense of the nature around them, the protection of their entire vital medium. Each individual's life supposes a context. If he or she is deprived of that context, especially if this is done violently, the individual perishes.

The human being is like a plant: to stay alive, the human being, too, needs to sink his or her roots in the earth. Today we call it ecological balance.

Wrenched from their natural ambience, the Indians die. "This," he writes, "has been the infallible, universal rule, that with the removal of these people from where they have been born and bred to some other place, however nearby, they take sick, and few are they who escape death" (*H.I.,* bk. 3, ch. 13, *O.E.* 2:203a).[26] This is only one of many texts expressing Bartolomé's strong, so frequently reiterated conviction: what is dying here is a world, with all that it contains. After all, he writes, "who has the right to sentence to a death so cruel, uncivil, and unnatural, a world so utterly blameless, without [this world] being heard, or defended, or formally convicted, but absent from the pronouncement of its death sentence, from which such evil and harm ensues?" (*Octavo remedio,* 1542, *O.E.* 5:97b). To defend life is not merely to salvage persons one by one. The natural universe, social relationships, the story of a people — all of these are part and parcel of human life itself.

Las Casas will see no substantial changes in any of this. The Conquista rolls southward, bringing more death still. The situation only worsens. Frequently, for example, Bartolomé will refer to "that unfortunate land of Peru" to which he wished to journey (see *Carta a un personaje,* 1535, *O.E.* 5:60b, 59b). In his last work he describes very particularly a constant reality: "Countless beyond belief are the women in the Indies today who have been widowed by their husbands going off to seek the wherewithal to pay tribute to the tyrant *encomendero* and not returning" (*O.E.* 5:513a). Indeed the situation was becoming traumatic. Undeniably, these were decades of wholesale demographic collapse. (See our Appendix, p. 461 below.) This fact bestows flesh — wounded flesh — on Las Casas's defense of life.

This is the context in which, moved by his evangelizing concern, Las Casas asserts the right of the Indians to life and liberty. In his *Memorial a Carlos V* (1543), he denounces the plunder of their possessions, family members, and finally "life and freedom, to the point of doing away with them" (*O.E.* 5:191b). In another *Memorial,* addressed to Philip II in 1556, protesting the perpetuity of the *encomienda,* he asserts that the king cannot wish to condemn someone "all of whose *freedom* will be lost, [along with] his status, if he is a ruler, and his very *life* (as must all be lost by those people if Your Majesty sells them)" (*O.E.* 5:455b; emphasis added).

The texts could be multiplied. Of interest here is that, for Bartolomé, life is the natural right of every human being, but it is also a gift of God, and so a believer ought to respect and defend it. Las Casas constantly links these two aspects. The ultimate root of this stubborn conviction is his faith in Jesus Christ, in whom all has been created and all has been redeemed.

Pristine Freedom

It has often been said that human freedom plays a capital role in Las Casas's writings.[27] Indeed his statements about it are so frequent, extensive, and emphatic as scarcely to leave us in any doubt. It will be to our purpose to recall this here, in function of the points that we have just set forth.

Here again the intuition is present from the start. The topic of death (and bloodshed) figured in the passage from Sirach that stimulated and endorsed the change Bartolomé has made in his life, as it is present in his denunciations of the oppression of the *encomiendas* and his call for the liberation of the Indians. Throughout his life, he will have recourse to a Thomistic philosophy and theology in order to formulate these themes. Indeed, he will go very far in the democratic demands implied in human beings' freedom. But, we repeat, the ultimate source is his personal experience: the message of the gospel, on one side, and, on the other, his experience among the Indians — plus, doubtless, what he saw and knew of the Castile of his time.[28]

Let us look once more at his first writings. In the *Memorial de remedios* (1516), he declares that the Indians are "free human beings, and ought to be treated as human beings and free" (*O.E.* 5:10a).[29] The entire "community schema" is thought out precisely with a view to the defense and enhancement of the life and liberty of the Indians. Again, in the document read aloud by Friar Reginaldo Montesino (1517), in which Las Casas probably had a hand, three things are presupposed: "The first," it is firmly stated, is "that the Indians are free," and we find an appeal here to the meeting of theologians and lawyers that took place in Valladolid.[30]

These assertions do not yet have the scope they will acquire in Las Casas later. But already they decry a situation of oppression against which Las Casas will struggle all of his life, as he seeks to remedy what he has before his eyes. In his *History of the Indies* he relates that very shortly after the change he made in his life, certain Dominican friars dispatched by Pedro de Córdoba arrived in Cuba, and that they were very happy to see that he "was trying to defend the freedom of the Indians and criticize the servitude and tyranny they suffered" (*H.I.*, bk. 3, ch. 81, *O.E.* 2:361a). The reasons given to justify that subjection will challenge his mind and oblige him to more precision in his position.

In the final chapters of the same work, Bartolomé tells us of the discussions that he has held at Court with the champions of the subjugation of the Indians. Here we have his first mention of the Aristotelian thesis that some human beings are born to be slaves (they are "slaves by nature"), and he contradicts this with all his might.[31] The effort will help him to see that human freedom and the equality of persons go hand in hand. One thing is emerging with great clarity in his mind: A defense of the liberty of the Indians means a commitment to their liberation from the servitude they suffer today. The intuition is a product of his initial utopian projects, his discussions, and even his failure in Cumaná.

In that other germinal text (the first is the *Memorial de remedios* of 1516), that is, his *Carta al Consejo* (1531), he continues to speak from his experiences. But he also expresses himself more competently (after his studies) in "law" and in doctrine. The liberation of the oppressed is more than a matter of the social order that is to prevail. It is based on the God of Jesus Christ. He places his addressees before that God: "By all of which they shall know and appreciate the great value attached by our mighty God and merciful Father to the deliverance of the oppressed, the succor of the anguished, and the salvation and redemption of souls, for whose remedy the Son of God came upon earth, fasted and hungered here, took his repose and preached, and at the last, died, together with the other merciful exploits he accomplished" (*O.E.* 5:46a). Once again the Lascasian theocentrism, to which we have already called attention, founds a position to be taken. What God wills is the liberation of the mistreated. This is part of the mission, the sending, of the Son. The behavior of that Son draws the guidelines for those who seek to walk in his footsteps as his disciples.

The *Octavo remedio* (Eighth remedy, 1542) is a treatise on the *encomienda* — the concrete way in which the servitude of the Indians is maintained. Precisely for this reason it is a treatise on freedom. The importance and significance of freedom comes in for particular emphasis in "reason the ninth" (*O.E.* 5:93b–98a).[32] Bartolomé begins by laying down a principle: "Those peoples of all of that order are free," and he specifies: "They do not lose that freedom in accepting and holding Your Majesty as universal lord."[33] This text advances propositions that we shall find once more in the *Tratado comprobatorio*, which we have seen. The lofty lordship of the king of Spain in the Indies is conceived by Las Casas as first and foremost a sovereignty of service to the Indians and their nations. To establish this, he takes as his basis documents of the Crown itself, which, to a large extent under pressure from the missionary friars and himself, have asserted the liberty of the Indians. Las Casas knew very well that these were merely declarations for formality's sake, having little or no repercussion in the Indies. But they were there, in black and white, and they provide support for his demands.

On the supposition of this truth and in light of the fact that the Spanish king and queen had no rights in these lands, the natives could not be *encomendados,* entrusted, handed over. This is all the more the case in view of the fact that the sole justification for the Spanish presence in the Indies is the task imposed by the papal bull *Inter Caetera* of announcing the gospel. The sovereigns had committed themselves to that charge "of their own free initiative." Now, without acknowledgment of, and respect for, the liberty of the dwellers of the Indies, evangelization will be impossible: "After all, in order to receive our holy faith, there must be in those who are to accept and receive it a ready freedom of will, because God left it in the hand and choice of each one whether to receive it or not." We are back to basics. Unless the aboriginal population lives in freedom, there is no reason for the Europeans to remain in the Indies. Indeed, "the end for which God strives in all of this business," which is evangelization, is "based on the voluntary wish of these people." Without free acceptance there is no genuine faith. Anything that militates against freedom militates against faith.

It is God's plan itself that is at stake — God's "rule and gospel and commandment." Consequently, says Bartolomé, forcefully: "No power on earth is competent to curtail or cripple the status of the free, as long as the key of justice is maintained, for freedom is the most precious and paramount of all the goods of this temporal world and so beloved and befriended by all creatures sentient and nonsentient, and especially by rational ones."[34] Freedom is a condition for the due proposal of the gospel.[35] Otherwise "the first and last end" lose their viability. The bond between evangelization and freedom makes the argument more compelling.

To be sure, Las Casas reasons expertly and easily in the area of natural law. But he does not remain there. The root of his position is that, for him, "the law of Jesus Christ [is] the law of supreme freedom": to hear and understand that law, one must be free (*O.E.* 5:75a). Here is an echo of a classic Pauline theme and an almost verbatim citation of the Letter of James, which speaks of "freedom's ideal law" (James 1:25). Under that law we shall also be judged as to our respect for the rights of others.

Human beings are free because God has "fashioned them to his image and likeness, and made them thus free, with dominion over their actions and themselves, endowing them with free choice and an utterly free will, which cannot be forced by any constraint or [in any other] way" (*Tratado comprobatorio,* 357b–358a). The immediate context of these considerations is a defense of religious freedom, a point which we shall develop later.[36] This is one of the first aspects to be perceived by Las Casas in the area of liberty. His concern for evangelization and for the means employed to carry it out made him particularly sensitive on this point. But from these premises he deduces implications — ever more radical and demanding — in the political field.

To deliver the Indian oppressed is to restore them to what Las Casas calls, countless times, their "pristine and natural freedom" (*H.I.,* bk. 3, ch. 86, *O.E.* 2:371b). On one occasion he asks the king to do justice to those in unjust captivity, "by Your Majesty's restoring them to their pristine and natural freedom" (*Memorial,* 1543, *O.E.* 5:193b). The bishops of the Indies should "beat on the King's door" for the Indians to be "restored to their pristine freedom," even, "were it necessary, at the risk of your lives" (*Tratado sobre los indios,* 1552, *O.E.* 5:281b). It was not that, before the coming of the Europeans, this "pristine freedom" had necessarily been fully respected among the Indians nations; but it was there, with all its exigencies, as an expression of the natives' human condition.

On the other side, as with life itself (as we have seen in the foregoing point), it was their relationship with the natural world of the Indies that provided the framework in which these "most free and innocent" Indians lived and developed (*Representación al Consejo,* 1549, *O.E.* 5:291a). Furthermore, the individual's bodily condition influences the exercise of the dispositions of the soul, and one of these dispositions is freedom. In the *Apologética historia,* Las Casas devotes page after page to these considerations as applied to the case of the native population (see chaps. 33–39). Today his discourse is called "anthropological," as it describes persons in their cultural and cosmic context, and it has been most highly praised for its novelty and its attention to concrete details.

In the same connection, it will be in order to point out that Las Casas viewed freedom as an attribute of persons not only as individuals, but as living in society as well. Therefore he speaks of a "liberty of peoples" (*H.I.,* bk. 3, ch. 55, *O.E.* 2:303b), which, as we have already had occasion to observe, ought to be respected by any supreme and universal sovereignty to be exercised by the rulers of Spain. But this respect is not accorded in the Indies. Bartolomé transcribes the verdict of the king's preachers, with whom he has met to deal with matters of the Indies: "I know not where to find this freedom of the Indians. It is only written in laws; it is not executed in those who should have enjoyed it" (ibid., bk. 3, ch. 135, *O.E.* 2:502b).[37] The goal ought to be real freedom, not its formal proclamation. Besides, only free persons can constitute a nation. The Indian peoples, therefore, must be kept free: "That is, the people [must] live in social and popular unity, and for this purpose they must be free. Otherwise they cannot be part of a people" (*Octavo remedio,* 1542, *O.E.* 5:74b).

Gradually, Bartolomé will come to require the consent of a people for their legitimate government by their political authorities. He arrives at his conclusion over the course of a long process. He advances and he retreats. But in the end, in his *De Regia Potestate,* his position is unambiguous. In order to deal adequately with this topic we shall have to include other elements, which are beyond the purview of our present pages. We have alluded to the subject in speaking of the Alexandrine bulls, and we are doing so now in connection with the theme of freedom. We shall return to it later.[38]

By way of a final observation: Las Casas likes to repeat the juridical axiom, "In cases of doubt, pronouncement and sentence must be on the side of freedom" (*Tratado comprobatorio,* 1552, O.E. 5:278b; see also ibid., O.E. 5:270b–271a; as well as earlier, in *Octavo remedio,* 1542, O.E. 5:95a). "On the side of freedom" will mean, for Las Casas concretely, on the side of the weaker, who are so often the victims of those in power. Freedom is a property of human persons. Bartolomé is thinking especially of the Indians, and he does so throughout his life and work. He strives to take the side of the freedom of those who are losing it, along with their lives, through the servitude to which they are being subjected. He wished for the Indians (and indeed for everyone else as well), what, he says, farm workers of Berlanga, in Castile, told him with Castilian pride on their departure for the Indies. They were not going there for gold, they said. "We're going in order to leave our children in a *free and royal land*" (*H.I.,* bk. 3, ch. 105, O.E. 2:427a; emphasis added). They were looking for a land of liberty. "Royal" is to be understood in the context of the time: the farmers were expressing their opposition to and rejection of the oppression to which they were subjected by their local rulers. Doubtless this reminded the secular cleric of the *encomiendas* of the Indies. In some fashion this call for freedom on the part of the Castilian peasants linked them with the natives of the New World. Here is what the Indies should be: a territory whose inhabitants are "aware of their freedom" (*H.I.,* bk. 3, ch. 1, O.E. 2:7b), where their lives and liberty are respected (indeed, restored, he will say, since they had been robbed of it). And reflecting on how matters actually stood, he will say: "It is enormously prejudicial to the freedom and life of the peoples to have many rulers over them" (*Octavo remedio,* 1542, O.E. 5:95b).

Las Casas's defense of freedom issues from his experience in the Indies and from his Christian sensitivity. Very soon he will make a connection with (or become more aware of) the libertarian tradition of the Castilian *comuneros* and will draw on juridical and theological vectors that were winning greater currency in his age. Throughout the course of his efforts to remedy the situation of the Indies and through all the disputes in which he becomes enmeshed on that account, he sees ever more clearly that to deny the freedom of these persons is to eviscerate the proclamation of the gospel, which can only be accepted voluntarily. Accordingly, it is tantamount to abandoning the reasons for which the Spanish Crown remains in the Indies. Las Casas will continue to delve to the depths of the Indian's right to liberty and will arrive at a position that we have not yet seen him take: a remarkably democratic conception of society.

An appreciation of his defense of life and liberty, then, is an important key to an understanding of Las Casas's thinking. But we still have another key to examine — a methodological one.

3. The Other History

To pronounce in favor of liberty, we have been saying, is, in the concrete, to make an option for the very weakest. Las Casas employs an old axiom of law to express a perspective he has taken up very early: to focus things from the viewpoint of the victims of history — those whom he is watching die unjustly and suffer the deprivation of their liberty.

What he is engaged in at this point is not mere intellectual hairsplitting, the fine-tuning of an abstract principle, with a view to applying that principle to reality and to reflection upon reality. It is far more than this. Direct contact with persons who were suffering endowed Bartolomé's perspective with a vital content. Here is an outlook that has room for emotion and tenderness. Las Casas practiced what Pascal would preach a century later: "Le coeur a ses raisons que la raison ne connaît point" — the heart has "reasons" unknown to the mind. The adoption of the viewpoint of others became for Las Casas a matter of Christian spirituality and theological methodology alike.

From the Viewpoint of the Indian

If Las Casas's approach to matters of the Indies seems so different from others of the time, it is because its champion did not follow the beaten path, but took a way that, in his time, was unheard of. He tried to understand things from a point of departure in the Indian, poor and oppressed. He began with those in whom, says Las Casas with an acute psychological observation, "so much inner pain, so much anguish and sorrow," was joined to the massacres they suffered in the wars of conquest and the servitude in which they lived (*H.I.*, bk. 1, ch. 106, *O.E.* 1:293b). This way of looking at things could only be very different from that of his compatriots.

This perspective is based on Bartolomé's knowledge of the reality of the Indies. What lends prophetic force — and theological insight —

to Las Casas's task as a missionary and a thinker is that he speaks from experience. His theory comes from practice. His discourse on the faith is rooted in his own evangelizing activity. His love of God is translated into solidarity with persons stripped of their rights. Thus, the two aspects are inseparable in his work.

His contact with the world of the Indies took place very promptly. Returning from his first voyage, Columbus put in at Seville (April 1493). He had some Indians with him, whom he intended to take ("show" might be a better word) to the Spanish sovereigns. There were seven of them, Bartolomé recalls, "and I saw them that day in Seville. They had been put alongside the Arch of the Images, at San Nicolás" (*H.I.*, bk. 1, ch. 58, *O.E.* 1:233a). The reporter's memory is a good one. He had been only nine years old. At that tender age, then, he saw for the first time, with innocent curiosity and astonishment, those to whom — and this time it was they who would be astonished — he would later devote his life. There would be no point in our trying to penetrate what went though this child's head at the sight he beheld at the Arch of the Images. But we may surely think that the grown man recounting this scene is rereading that first experience, and, in retrospect, feels that it was by God's will that it occurred symbolically in his native city, with which he would always feel such close ties.

The friar from Seville is fully aware of the crucial role of personal experience and will refer to it in a thousand ways all his life long. In his letter to the Royal Council of 1531, for instance, he says he speaks of deeds "not read in made-up tales, or told by chattering tongues, but seen with our own eyes, in the presence of our persons" (*O.E.* 5:48b). Four years later he confesses that he is an "eyewitness" of what happened in the Indies in those decades (*Carta a un personaje*, 1535, *O.E.* 5:59a). In the Prologue of his *History of the Indies* he insists that he has seen and studied what he writes "for very few days short of seventy-three years (immense thanks to God, who has granted me so long a life): I have seen and traversed these Indies since about the year 1500, and *I know what I write.*" This permits him to assert, not without a certain legitimate pride: "By the divine mercy, I am perhaps the oldest and, of those alive today, the *most experienced*, with the possible exception of one or two others in all of these West Indies" (1:16b, 17a; emphasis added). Since 1502, to be exact.

Experience is the key — "experience most lengthy," that "teacher of everything," as he calls it in his letter to Pope Pius V, one of his last writings (*O.E.* 5:541b). This is the support of his positions and reflections. His knowledge of the facts he relates comes to him not "by long ways" (1:15a), but by direct contact with reality. This is a deep conviction in our author. Responding to the argumentation of John Major (d. 1550),[39] who was attempting to justify the wars against the Indians,

Las Casas maintains that that theologian "shows himself to be utterly ignorant in the area of law and when he rushes into the facts, losing his bearings completely." The Spanish Dominican argues from a point of departure in the situation of the Indies and concludes his allegation incisively and boldly: "...a fact that we know not only theoretically, but that we have experienced in practice" (*Apología*, 236, 237). What we have here, then, is something Bartolomé regards as an authentically methodological outlook, and it will stamp his entire approach to the various questions to which the reality of the Indies will lead him.

But let us also note that, for Las Casas, it is not a mere question of the importance of a *direct knowledge* of a particular state of affairs. It is also a matter of adopting the *perspective of others,* other persons, in order to experience and understand from within the situations and events in which those persons are caught up. And he gives us an example, in the form of a whole program of approach to the realities of the Indies. This example, this program, will enable us to explain what we mean. Of the same John Major he says, with biting irony, that if the Scots theologian "were an Indian," he would see the "gross impiety" of the situation he is attempting to justify. Here is Las Casas's text: "I in no way think that John Major himself would tolerate a situation so impious and brutal *if he were an Indian* ['si Indus esset']" (ibid., 229; emphasis added).

Bartolomé presents his hypothesis in depth, and with it the outlook he proposes (still referring to John Major):

> If the Hungarians or Bohemians, of whose language he is ignorant, were to despoil him of his dignity and his realm, were he a king, in the first moment of contact with him, sowing uproar everywhere and terrorizing his provinces with the tumult of war, however they might feel themselves to be motivated by a "good cause" — by any chance would John Major graciously and joyfully accept this "good cause"? By any chance would he [willingly] defray the costs thereby occasioned, when in the course of time all might come to understand one another in both languages?

The supposition of this *ad hominem* argument corresponds, point for point, to the situation and responds to the most subtle of the pretexts advanced for the occupation of the Indies. Las Casas emphatically answers his own question. "I think not" (ibid.), he says.

His three-word reply ("si Indus esset") is more than just a phrase in passing, or even a cry in the heat of the polemics. We are dealing with something demanding and basic for Bartolomé de Las Casas. We shall find expressions of this kind in his writings over and over. For example, apropos of the task of proclaiming faith and salvation, he compares the ancestors of the Spaniards with the Indians of his day (an equivalency that must have given his audience a considerable case of indigestion). He asserts that the Indians are not heathen who "resist the faith, nor hold nor seize what is another's, nor pursue us in order to slay us, but are *what we were* in Spain before St. James's disciples converted us — indeed, are far better disposed for conversion, and better fitted to receive the faith, than we were then" (*Carta a un personaje*, 1535, *O.E.* 5:65a; emphasis added). "They are what we have been" again expresses the perspective of the other. But there is a difference: The Indians are better! Along these same lines he asks: "Which of our forebears would have been saved, or which of us would have been left alive, if before having the faith preached to them they had been punished for idolatry and other sins committed in their unbelief?" (*Octavo remedio*, 1542, *O.E.* 5:82a).

We find another example of this focus in the next-to-last work that Las Casas wrote. Apropos of the right to engage in commerce (proclaimed by Vitoria, who is not cited here), he wonders (after a favorable mention of Domingo de Soto): "By some chance would our most stern King Philip patiently tolerate, and this in the kingdom of Castile, that the king of France, or the French of that king's realm, come to ours, entering it without permission and reaching the silver mines of Guadalcanal and other places, and there recovering [from the earth] silver, gold, or other precious objects?" And he adds incisively: "And if they indeed entered, would this not be a violent act of theft or robbery? Furthermore, would they not be harming and disturbing the Kingdom of Spain?" And carrying his argumentation to its ultimate consequences, he concludes: "Finally, would the King of Spain, in this case, sleep with folded hands?" (*De Thesauris*, 132v).

An interesting article by Saint-Lu provides a fine illustration of what we are saying. The author establishes a revealing parallel between the way in which the Indians relate, in their oldest texts, the massacres they have suffered at the hands of the invaders and the versions that Las Casas offers of them.[40] The similarity is impressive, and this says a good deal about the viewpoint adopted by the Dominican. Saint-Lu concludes his study:

> What must be especially emphasized, above all, in this agreement of the two testimonies, is that the viewpoint of Las Casas, a Spaniard, intimately takes on that of the indigenous people, as if he also had undergone their physical sufferings and their sorrow. But to the desperate pain of the martyred people there is added, in the defender of the Indians, the vehement denunciation of so many cruelties, judged as detestable crimes and deeds. The indigenous accounts constitute a pathetic lamentation; those

of Las Casas, also heart-rending but full of indignation, are a cry of anguish and rebellion.[41]

In his attempt to see things "as if he were an Indian," Las Casas seeks to assume what today is called "the viewpoint of the defeated," since defeat was the concrete outcome of the historical events reported.[42]

For the same reason, he asserts that he himself, a Spanish Christian, would now wish to have the attitude of the natives who had just received the faith, of which so many of his compatriots considered them unworthy. His reference, as always, is living experience — in this case, to what we should call today his pastoral practice. "I went to confession and communion," he writes, "and I found myself with some of them when they died, after they had been baptized and instructed, and I say that I beseech our Lord God that *he give me the devotion* and the tears and contrition for my sins when I receive his body and blood at the time of my end and death such as it seemed to me that I felt and experienced in them" (*H.I.*, bk. 2, ch. 45, *O.E.* 2:113a; emphasis added). Let us note that the Indians here are the Lucay — islanders who were particularly despised and abused, inhabitants of the "useless islands." Besides this, it is a matter here of the Christian behavior — their relationship with God — of the dwellers of these lands.

The matter can go far indeed. In his twelfth reply to Sepúlveda, in the Valladolid disputation, he responds to his adversary's positions on the wars waged on the Indians for the purpose of evangelization. Confronted with Bartolomé's absolute pacifism, the Cordovan recalls that this position led to the death of Dominican missionaries in Florida. Among them had been one very close to Las Casas, Luis Cáncer. The argument was therefore incisive and painful for Bartolomé. Nevertheless, he did not change his opinion. Sepúlveda had gained precious little ground, and Las Casas says energetically: "Though they had slain all the friars of Santo Domingo, and St. Paul along with them, not a single point of law would have accrued beyond those already possessed — which was none — against the Indians" (*O.E.* 5:346b). The strict right of the Indians to use force to defend themselves against the harassments of which they are the object is not called into question by a painful and lamentable event such as the one recalled. And lest there be any doubt, Las Casas specifies that, were they to kill the great missionary St. Paul himself, this would not change the situation. To be able to maintain something like this, one must perceive things from another angle — that of the heathen who were to be attracted to Christianity. And not just see things from this other angle — as if the subject were one for reflection alone — but feel them as well.

Here we have two dimensions of solidarity with scorned and abused persons.

Another expression of this attitude is the concern Las Casas always had for learning the language of the Indians. (We have given an example of this a few pages above, with reference to his community schema of 1516.) For him, this was important, if one desired to proclaim the gospel to them. It was important in his Verapaz experiment,[43] and he insists on it in a very significant text, his petition to Pius V. There he speaks of requiring bishops appointed for the Indies to learn the native languages "with all diligence" (*O.E.* 5:542a). This is also a manifestation of his defense of life. A language is an element of the culture of a people. And culture is life, as the anthropologists like to say.[44]

Adopting the perspective of the natives of the Indies was one of the great efforts of Bartolomé's life,[45] and the principal source of his pastoral and theological creativity. Therefore when he makes the viewpoint of the "Indian oppressed" his own, his reflections acquire a new, liberated tone, and he is able to see in the message of the gospel what was otherwise hidden from him and many of his contemporaries.

We shall have occasion, over the course of these pages, to cite numerous examples of what we have just been saying. One of the most remarkable will be the matter of human sacrifice.

Breasts That Tremble with Fear

Making the viewpoint of the Indian one's own requires actually approaching, drawing near, concrete persons. Las Casas has left us a testimonial of his sensitivity to the Indians' condition, and of the impression that that condition produced on him. He does more than merely adopt the viewpoint of another. That would have been too abstract for him. He regards that other as a brother or sister in the gospel sense of the word, the neighbor we are to love. Unless we are willing to go this far, we shall not understand Las Casas's sense of what we call "otherness" today — sensitivity for a person's right to be different.

We have already mentioned the impact of the massacre at Caonao, in Cuba, on Las Casas while he was still a secular cleric. His terrible experience there exerted an important influence on the change he experienced in his life. "Seeing the wounds on many of the dead," he recounts, "and on others who were still dying, was a thing of horror and terror." A certain episode in the panorama of the massacre taking place was one that he was never to forget. Among the wounded was someone who seemed to be a brother "of the king or lord of that province." His right shoulder had been cut off, and he was left lying there for an entire week, without food, until the Spaniards left, and Las Casas with them. Bartolomé was haunted all his life by the specter of his not having done everything necessary to save this person. Forty years later, he writes, with profound feeling: "The cleric harbored much regret for not having treated him, as he had so many others, with a certain pomade of tortoise shell that would have cauterized his wounds and healed him from them in a week. Meanwhile, the [others] who had no stab wounds had practically recovered — but not this one, for his wound was so strange and mortal." Had he known how to act, the fate of that person could have been different. "He thought that if he had replaced the bone in its socket, binding up his whole side with a large needle or darning spike, in the otherwise fine condition he seemed to be in, perhaps he would have got well." The matter rankled in his mind like a task unfinished, like an open wound. "Finally," he says, painfully, "no more was known of him. It does not seem possible that he could have survived" (*H.I.*, bk. 3, ch. 29, *O.E.* 2:246a).

It could be said — with, shall we say, borderline cynicism — that very little is represented by one case when the dead in these events were thousands. But Bartolomé's vivid recollection recalls to our minds the fact that every person is, in some sense, an absolute. It tells us a great deal as well about how Las Casas experienced these events.[46] What is happening is something very simple. For Bartolomé — unlike the others to whom Velázquez had "distributed" Indians — the inhabitants of Cuba were "people of flesh and blood" (*H.I.*, bk. 2, ch. 17, *O.E.* 2:355a). This is what had been forgotten in the Indies. But it was something Bartolomé always held present, perhaps even before the prophetic call that changed his life.

Against those who attempted to justify the wars against the dwellers of the Indies, the Sevillian argues theologically. He reflects that, were these persons to "consider that war and death for these timid people go on not for just a day, or a hundred days, but for ten, twenty years," perhaps they would change their mind. This is no passing attitude. Bartolomé's statement gives us the very meaning and purview of his *Apología.* He goes on:

> The extent of the natives' destruction is unbelievable, and they wander about, hiding in woods and forests, scattered, unarmed, naked, and bereft of all human aid, are quartered by the Spaniards, stripped of their fortunes, reduced to wretchedness and landlessness. They stumble about aghast and terrified by incredible fear at the sight of the monstrous crimes perpetrated against them by those tyrants.

And he concludes, with tender emotion: "If those who say such things would consider that the breasts of those wretched people tremble with such great fear that they seek to cast themselves into the deepest crevices of the earth in order to escape the hands of those bandits, I am certain that they would speak more carefully and prudently" (*Apología*, 13).

Our text gives us a full-length portrait of Bartolomé de Las Casas. The concrete meaning of persons pervades his inferences and his reasoning. It is not a taste for intellectual polemics, a pleasure in the erudite citation or intricate proof, that matters most to him. These are (legitimate) weapons of self-defense. When Bartolomé writes, he has before his very eyes the reality he has just painted for us — the trembling breasts of these people who simply could not understand what was happening to them ("aghast and terrified"). These events gripped his heart and motivated him to defend the Indians with all the means within his grasp. That is why he recalls this situation at the beginning of one of his most polemical works, precisely before throwing himself into a rigorous intellectual exercise (one of the most successful of his extensive work). He also does it because he believes that nothing will convince his opponents more than direct contact with the situation prevailing in the Indies. That, more than the arguments he will adduce, may perhaps lead them to speak more "carefully and prudently," and consequently to cause less harm to the native population. Ignorance of what is occurring in the Indies is the greatest reason for theoretically erroneous lucubrations that, in the long run, are so damaging to these persons.

It is a matter of a deep, ongoing sentiment on the part of the Dominican. Describing elsewhere the capture of the Lucay Indians for the purpose of transporting them as slaves to the island of Hispaniola, he says: "To see them just sitting there, along that shore or river bank, thrown on the ground on land they might have no longer, two, three days and nights, in the sun and the rain, while they were divided up, filled with terror and every sorrow, was one of the greatest miseries and calamities that could be seen. It would have broken any heart not of stone or marble" (*H.I.*, bk. 3, ch. 156, *O.E.* 2:581a–b).[47] But the Indians would be crushed to earth by those hearts of stone.

What is happening in the Indies is something that "can scarcely be reported without tears" (*Apología*, 237). Also with regard to the Lucay, Las Casas asks, from his experience, "Who with a heart of flesh and human entrails could abide such inhuman cruelty? What memory must there be of that precept of charity, 'You shall love your neighbor as yourself,' among persons so oblivious of being Christians, or even human, that they have dealt thus with humanity in these human beings?" (*H.I.*, bk. 2, ch. 43, *O.E.* 2:108b). Neighbors in the gospel sense indeed. One can only love them "as thyself" (*Doce dudas,* 1564, *O.E.* 5:489a).

The Indian is a human person, the subject of rights that are constantly being violated. On the basis of this humanistic principle, and with implacable logic, Bartolomé deduces demanding corollaries. But if we delve deeper into his reflection we shall find that, for him, the Indian is first and foremost what we have just said: the evangelical neighbor. We have noted this perspective in Montesino's sermon itself. Therefore that person is someone to whom love is owed, over and above all rights and deserts. In this same line, concluding his *Apología,* he asserts, with the firm conviction of someone conscious of driving home a point with a final argument: "The Indians are our siblings, and Christ has given his life for them. Why do we persecute them with such inhuman cruelty when they do not deserve such treatment?" (252v–253).[48] Here is that love of one's brother or sister without which — and this is key for Las Casas — there is no love of God. We have been placed before a basic evangelical datum. Our friar's entire merit consists in recalling that datum, in a context of this precise moment of the Christian experience in the Indies. "Love of God," he maintains, "cannot exist without love of neighbor, love of neighbor without love of God. 'Love of God, love of neighbor, simultaneous loves!' says Chrysostom" (*De Unico,* 167v; *The Only Way,* 136). This is the commandment, ever new, left us by the Lord. New, and in the Indies, particularly urgent.

To proclaim God, then, is not enough. Solidarity with others is required as well, especially with the very poorest and most helpless. No, let us put this in a better way. It is not merely insufficient to announce the truth; to limit oneself to this — without attending to its implications — is actually to lie, and to deny the God of Jesus Christ. "Just think," he declares, "how God was so concerned to have people love one another with a mutual charity that through Scripture He showed how the whole law was contained in loving one's neighbor, that alone. Even though there are two precepts, even though the one can be understood in the other, nonetheless the two are made into one, compressed: 'Love your neighbor as yourself,' as in Galatians 5:14: 'The whole law is contained in one statement: Love your neighbor as yourself' " (*De Unico,* 168; *The Only Way,* 137).

Fullness of the law, and of justice as well. The latter is a capital demand, according to Las Casas. This is what the situation in the Indies will ultimately lead to. It must not be forgotten, however, that for Bartolomé, as for any believer, love does not soften the demand for justice. On the contrary, it charges it with a more radical exigency, at the same time as giving it a more comprehensive context — a context of limitless demands.

Las Casas, this "Christian, friar, bishop, and Spaniard" (in that order), as he says in the letter to Philip II in which he presents his project (*Apología*, 9v–10), believes in a God who "appraises all things with ineffable charity" (*Apología*, 12v). So also he seeks to regard the situation in the Indies with charity and tenderness, and wishes to reason from a point of departure in the "breasts of those wretched people, which tremble with such great fear."[49] Here is a reflection that supposes what Luke, in the parable of the Good Samaritan, calls a wrenching of the bowels (Luke 10:33), often translated as "compassion."[50] We should take the expression literally. "Compassion" is a "suffering with" another, a sharing of the sufferings of others.

Las Casas's idyllic descriptions of the natural world of the Indies correspond to the same kind of attitude. His poetic enthusiasm for the very physical makeup of these lands has sometimes been criticized. But, notwithstanding an occasional bit of imprecision,[51] it reveals the fondness he has conceived for these places, implying a profound communion with those who live here. Of Nicaragua, a land he always praised to the skies, he says, beautifully, that it is "the marrow and loins of all the Indies" — their very heart (*Carta a un personaje*, 1535, *O.E.* 5:60b).[52] His description of the Gran Vega, the Great Plain of Hispaniola, that island he so loved, is classic. As it is surely one of the loveliest passages in all his writings, it is difficult to resist the temptation to quote it. He begins by asking: "Who will not acknowledge that the joy, gladness, consolation, and rejoicing inspired by the sight are inestimable and beyond compare?" That is what he himself experiences: "I say truly: many — more than many, countless — are the times I have gazed upon this Plain, from the mountain ranges and other heights from which a great part of it can be surveyed, and, considering it peacefully and at length, I have found myself so renewed and have so admired and rejoiced in it, as if it had been the first time I had seen it and begun to regard it."

Merely to know "the beauty and gladness and loveliness of this Plain" makes the voyage from Castile worthwhile. Philosophers and Christians would do very well to visit those dwelling places — "the philosopher, to be delighted by a work of nature so signal in beauty; and the Christian, to contemplate the power and goodness of God who in this visible world has created a thing so worthy, lovely, and delightful." The contemplation of God in creation is a classic theme among mystics. Their contemplative experience feeds on this natural loveliness. Those who admire it have a true foretaste of what heaven is. Indeed, by it they can "rise, in contemplation, to a knowledge of what the invisible lodgings of heaven will be, which God has prepared for those who have had the divine faith and have fulfilled the divine will." The face-to-face vision of God draws near. We shall know in what "lodgings" we shall live, in that case, and shall be able to "gather from this a motive for the dissolution of all things in lauds and praises of the One who has created it all" (*A.H.*, ch. 8, *O.E.* 3:31b–32a). And the passage ends with an act of thanksgiving.

The Indies are the place of a painful encounter with scourged Christs and with their untimely, unjust death. But they are also the place of a joyous experience of God revealed in natural beauty and in the human dignity of their inhabitants. Any attempt to comprehend Las Casas's life and work in terms of the former aspect alone would be a flawed one. In fact, that aspect appears in all of its cruelty when it is contrasted with the will to life and gladness of the God proclaimed by Jesus — a God so present in this remarkable friar.

Conclusion to Part One

Let us briefly summarize what we have seen in Part One. The nucleus of the missionary and theological perspective of Bartolomé de Las Casas is to perceive the Indian as the poor person according to the gospel and, as a consequence, to know that any gesture made toward the Indian is made toward Christ himself. To will "the preservation and liberty of [our] neighbors the Indians" is to put into practice the "divine precept that commands us to love the neighbor" (*Confesionario*, 1552, *O.E.* 5:240a). Otherwise we also refuse to love the Son of God made one of us. *Christ is the Indian.* This mystical and evangelical intuition — also present in Guamán Poma — is the root of his spirituality, that is to say, of his manner of being Christian, of being a follower of Jesus. It characterizes a discourse on faith that finds its main support in christology.

The experience of the massive, premature, and unjust death of the inhabitants of the Indies moved him profoundly. He had been blind, but once he became aware of this fact it was always before his eyes. This was a situation contrary to the will of God and therefore opposed to the core of the gospel message: the gift of the Reign of life and liberty. The only justification for Christians' presence in these lands is to proclaim this message. If "the prosperity and temporal growth and the conversion and spiritual salvation of these peoples" (*H.I.*, bk. 1, ch. 106, *O.E.*, 1:294a) are not sought, and if "the ability and the liberty to be able to live on their own are never given to them" (*H.I.*, bk. 3, ch. 18, *O.E.* 2:215a), it makes no sense to remain in these lands. Indeed life and liberty are fundamental elements of the gospel.

This way of understanding the message of Jesus can be found in the first works of Bartolomé to the last. This was his prophecy, that is — according to the Hebrew meaning of the word — his speaking "in the name of God." On this basis he forged his utopia that moves history, a utopia that he detailed tirelessly in the many projects he proposed and carried out with varied success. They reveal the evolution of his understanding of the Spanish and Indian realities — a historical and believing intelligence. One thing remains: the facts are read and reread from the standpoint of the poor of these lands ("as if we were Indians") in whom Christ is present. It is not only a question of theological methodology; it is a question of the path toward the God of life.

What Does the Gospel Have to Do with Guns?

✝ In defending the native peoples of the Indies, Las Casas seeks to be clear and incisive in his arguments. This concern for his argumentation, as well as his experience in the Indies, lead him to make a distinction to which he will remain faithful all his life, and which will put order into many of his reflections. We refer to what he calls the "two entries" or "two feet" of the Iberians in the Indies: the wars of the Conquista, and the *encomiendas*. He writes, for example:

> *One* [entry consists in] the most unjust and cruel *wars* being waged on these Indians, who have harmed no one but have only dwelt in the safety of their homes and fields, where now countless individuals, peoples, and nations have died. The *other* [entry is that by which], having murdered their natural lords and leaders and placed them in *servitude,* [the Spaniards] have divided them among themselves, a hundred at a time, or fifty, and flung them into the mines, where at the last, owing to the unbelievable labors they must undergo in extracting the gold, they all die. (*H.I.,* bk. 3, ch. 149, *O.E.* 2:535a; emphasis added)

The same idea, but this time accompanied by a concrete ethical judgment on the European presence in the Indies, appears in another text:

> The *first entry* of the Spaniards into the Indies, and each province and part thereof, from their discovery in the year 1492 until today inclusively, January 1564,[1] was wicked and tyrannical. So was the *progress and disorder* of the government established throughout that world. (*Doce dudas,* 1564, *O.E.* 5:496a; emphasis added)[2]

The preceding chapters afforded us an opportunity to sketch an overview of the great Lascasian themes. In Part Two (as in Part Three), we shall be concerned only with the challenges presented to a discourse on faith by the "first entry" — the matter of the *ingressus* (the wars of conquest), and consequently the meaning of these wars when it comes to evangelization, which is the proclamation of salvation. We shall leave a consideration of the "second entry," the *progressus* (the colonization and the regime of the *encomienda*), for Parts Four and Five. Theological reflection on these two stages will intersect, of course. But the stages themselves are differentiated, and as Las Casas so frequently distinguishes between them, we shall regard this as authorization to adopt the same distinction as the guideline of our presentation.

Bartolomé's first question is charged with indignation. "What does the gospel have to do with guns [*cum bombardis*]? What do preachers of the gospel have in common with armed thieves?" (*Apología*, 117). The use of instruments of death and soldiers under arms — in other words, war — means a violation of the right to life and the right to make free decisions without which there is no authentic reception of the gift of Christian faith.[3] Again with reference to this absurd fashion of proclaiming the gospel, elsewhere Bartolomé maintains: "Our people began not with words, but with tortures" (*De Thesauris*, 106v).[4] In no case does Las Casas approve the wars of conquest. His rejection is not directed against possible excesses, but against these acts of war themselves — whatever reason may be advanced to justify them in the Indies.

In a first step, we shall see the fact of the wars of conquest, which were so frequently waged under the pretext of evangelization. And we shall see that, very promptly, a theology will arise — intimately linked to the juridical doctrines of the day — calculated to bestow legitimacy on the situation in question, or at least to justify its toleration. Las Casas rejects what he deems to be an aberration and underscores its antievangelical nature: its profound incompatibility with the gratuity of faith and with human freedom.

Christian tradition, it is true, emphatically asserts the freedom of the act of faith. But we shall have to place that claim in its historical context and process of development. This will show us that it is not the product of a homogeneous process. On the contrary, the various positions in which the church has found itself vis-à-vis political society lead to different emphases, and the shifts in those accents entail important changes of meaning. The perspective of a church linked to political power is the backdrop against which the dominant theology in Las Casas's time develops. This will be the topic of our chapter 5.

Finally, challenged by the reality of the Indies, Bartolomé grafts his thinking onto the most ancient Christian tradition and concludes that the only way to evangelize is by way of persuasion and dialogue. He distances himself, then, on this point from the theology just mentioned, in its Thomist version — which, as we might expect, had originally been his own. In doing so, he rediscovers certain intuitions that prevailed in the first Christian centuries and that asserted with utmost clarity every individual's right to practice the religion of his or her choice. Las Casas arrives at this position thanks to his effort to understand the difficult matter of human sacrifice and cannibalism.

Chapter 4

Evangelization at Gunpoint

In a reference to the incursions of the Portuguese into Africa in the mid-fifteenth century, especially those directed by the Infante, Don Henrique, son of King John of Portugal, Las Casas mentions the following fact: "Another vessel arrived, dispatched by the Infante for the same purpose. Out they leapt on land by night, with a great cry, 'Portogal and St. James!' Presently they came upon a certain number of Moors, killed three, captured ten," and — Bartolomé comments with pained irony — "returned to their vessels in glory and triumph, offering thanks to God that they had *preached them the gospel at the point of a spear*" (*H.I.*, bk. 1, ch. 23, *O.E.* 1:89b; emphasis added).[1]

Let us observe that our friar rejects this manner of behaving with the Moors, even though, good Spaniard of his time that he is, he does not usually use very kind language when speaking of those people.[2] What has happened is that, in terms of his evangelizing concern, his sensitivity and perceptivity have been sharpened, and they overcome his historical and cultural conditioning. Furthermore, we observe that, contrary to the stubborn thesis to the effect that Bartolomé hated everything Spanish, here the culprits are the Portuguese. The whole context of the paragraph cited denounces the injustices committed by these Christians against the blacks and Moors of Africa, whose rights he defends.[3]

Actually, as we have repeatedly stated, this inconvenient missionary's dominant concern is the perspective of the poor. It is from this point of departure that all oppression is rejected — all the more so when an attempt is made to justify it on the pretext of evangelization, whether it be of Indians, blacks, Arabs, or even Spaniards, as we shall have the occasion to see below. There is no justification, either legal or ethical, for the wars, and no "damned Notifications [*requerimientos*]" made of the dwellers of the Indies can afford them one. Las Casas will lay a solid theological foundation for a peaceful evangelization in his *Del único modo de atraer a todos los pueblos a la verdadera religión* (The only way to attract all peoples to the true religion).[4]

1. Baptizing the Wars

Formally, at least, all were in agreement in the sixteenth century as to the duty to proclaim the gospel in the Indies and to make Christians of the persons living there. Sepúlveda, of course, was no exception. Where Christians disagreed, it was with respect to *how* this enterprise was to be furthered. Here missionaries and theologians, civil officials and bishops, expressed different opinions. If we go to the heart of the matter, however, it is clear that this disagreement did not turn simply on the means to be employed in order to obtain the same end. We should be missing the point if this is what we were to gather here. What Las Casas perceives so clearly is that, in the question of method, what is at stake is the very meaning and content of the faith — of that which we are proposing when we announce the gospel.

The *hecho y derecho* of the wars — the fact of the wars, and their justification — are both rejected by Bartolomé. It is in order to examine how the question was posed from the outset. Situations will continue to be cited and arguments in favor of violent methods will later be repeated with the stubbornness of weeds.

A Question of Fact

Some missioners and theologians defended, or at least accepted, the use of force in order first to subject the Indians — at the cost that we have seen — and then to Christianize them. We find holding this position all those who, while asking moderation in the wars or placing certain juridical conditions on them, ultimately for one reason or another approve the wars as a means of evangelization. Indeed, on this precise point there is no middle ground, especially in the concrete situation of the Indies.[5] Murder may not be used as a means of announcing the Reign of Life. Las Casas defended this point with all his might and always emphasized it with crystal clarity. If we keep in mind the "just war" theory, sometimes appealed to in those days (but which Las Casas rejects in the case of the Indies), we should have to say that, in the mentality of the time, a war could be just as a means of last resort. But it will not be just as a means of evangelization. Why, then, Las Casas will ask trenchantly, in one of his first letters to the Council of the Indies, "do you send ravenous, tyrannical, cruel wolves, to tear, destroy, scandalize, and scatter the sheep?" (1531, *O.E.* 5:49a). And years later, in his polemic with Sepúlveda, he will say that the Indians "will never be under obligation to lend credence to any preacher of our holy faith, as long as that preacher is accompanied by tyrannical persons, men of war, plunderers and murderers such as the Doctor would like to introduce" (*Aquí se contiene*, 1552, *O.E.* 5:334a).

For some, however, this was the right means to use in the concrete situation of the Indies — due, it was asserted, to the savagery, ferocity, and violations of the natural law of the dwellers of these lands. Besides, this would preclude, it was said, the mistreatment and even murder of missionaries and other Spaniards who had moved to the Indies. To speak of war as an instrument in the service of the task of evangelization may shock a modern mentality. It was in these terms, however, that the question was long posed with regard to the Indies (and the Philippines). But are we so far from this attitude even today? For example, we have the defense, in recent times on our continent, of "Western Christian civilization" through repression, murder, torture, and imprisonment. These measures, furthermore, have been championed by rulers who, like the conquistadors and *encomenderos*, call themselves Christian. According to them, it was a matter of defending the old values — and, they asserted, the virtues as well — of our peoples: religious and cultural values that (again, according to them and those around them) are the heart and soul of the fatherland.

Curiously, violence inflicted from a position of power and strength is said to be a necessary means for human beings' peaceful coexistence and for Christian life. Let us not play games and simply cry "foolishness" or "scandal" when examining these sixteenth-century discussions. The "modern mentality" only rends its garments at the sight of this crude attitude because the persons of that time talked about it coarsely and frankly. But, indeed, our contemporaries have only invented more subtle — but no less cruel — ways of defending their interests and plundering the poor.

There were not lacking at this time, it is important to recall, preachers and thinkers (a minority, but in increasing numbers thanks to the activity of the Dominicans and others) who considered that evangelization, in order to be such, must use peaceful means, solely and exclusively. Accordingly, all use of force ought to be proscribed as contrary to the gospel and prejudicial to human freedom. In both cases, argumentation proceeded with an appeal to the theology and major theologians of the time.

But we should be deceiving ourselves were we to think that we are dealing with theological positions being prepared to be put in practice as doctrinal discussions have come to a close. This was not to be. As the theoretical collation of these opposing viewpoints begins, we *already* have the practice of the wars against the Indians. "Preaching the gospel by force of arms" (*Apología*, 154v) was what many had been doing since the Europeans first arrived, or since the beginning of the destruction of the Indies, to use Las Casas's expression.[6]

Thus, Gómara — elevating to the status of doctrine the practice of his protector Hernán Cortés — writes in his *Historia* (as Las Casas recounts): "War, and men under arms, is the authentic path to the removal of idols, sacrifices, and other sins from the Indians, and hereby, he says, the more easily and more quickly and better for them to receive and hear the preachers and take the gospel and baptism of their own pleasure and will." In response to this strange way of understanding human freedom, Las Casas reasserts the scandalous nature of this so-called means of evangelization and recalls "the state of eternal damnation in which they abide who secure, order, or counsel what Gómara says" (*H.I.*, bk. 3, ch. 117, *O.E.* 2:456a).

This is only a pretext. Graphically, Las Casas calls it "baptizing" the wars. Appealing to this sort of reasoning, "Diego Velázquez and the other tyrants have baptized their execrable tyrannies, ambitions, and acts of greed" committed in Cuba (*H.I.*, bk. 3, ch. 93, *O.E.* 2:393a).[7] And so Bartolomé speaks ironically of "our Spanish saints" who perpetrate such crimes against the Indians.[8] In the same vein, Las Casas writes of the people of Peru, "whom Pizarro and his holy disciples have extirpated by the law of robbery, in which they believe," storming through that land, "preaching and sowing [their word] so earnestly...that the land is still not secured, and is now devastated and destroyed" (*Carta a un personaje*, 1535, *O.E.* 5:61a–b).

Elsewhere, again on the authority of Portuguese historian João de Barros, Bartolomé relates that, around 1500, King Manuel of Portugal sent an expedition to India. "The principal instructions carried by the captain of the armada, one Pedro Alvares Cabral, were, first, that Moors and idolaters be put to the material, secular sword by way of a war to be waged on them, leaving it to the religious and priests to make use of their spiritual one, which was to proclaim the gospel with admonishments and Notifications [*requerimientos*]." The king and his men, Las Casas comments, "thought that these peoples must receive the faith under a rain of blows" — just as, he continues with realism, it was also under a rain of blows that they were obliged to do business: "Whether they liked it or not, they had to engage in commerce and trade their things for other people's, [even] if they had no need of the latter" (*H.I.*, bk. 1, ch. 172, *O.E.* 1:460a–b).[9] Faith, like merchandise, was imposed by force. In fact, the faith served as a pretext to acquire economic benefit. On this occasion the place is Asia. On another it will be the land of the "Moors." But Western behavior is the same, whatever the place, and Las Casas denounces its injustice.

Here is what is behind this so-called evangelization. "I fear," says the Dominican, "that the Portuguese were seeking a pretext, under color of spreading the Christian religion, to despoil India of gold and silver, any spices it had, and other wealth, and usurp the native rulers' domains and liberty, as we Castilians have found for extirpating and ruining our Indies." The Spaniards are no better than the Portuguese.

Mockingly, Las Casas points out that, in this task of "evangelization," the Portuguese work "elegant miracles . . . confirming the doctrine that the religious had preached: robbing [the Indians], taking them captive, burning them alive and cutting them to pieces. It would be well to ask the Portuguese," he concludes, "whether they [themselves] had been called to the faith by this route, and under threat of these perils" (ibid., 1:460b–461a). This is another application of the principle, "If we were Indians. . . ." But the viewpoint of the Indians — the addressees of that so-called proclamation — was precisely what was of least interest to those assiduous "evangelizers."[10]

We have cited these texts on the Portuguese incursions into Africa and Asia for a purpose. As we see, Las Casas's judgment and denunciation are not restricted — as some think (or thought, now that his work is becoming better known) — to the Spaniards and the Indies. No, in comparable situations, his reaction is the same. He denounces the outrages committed against *Muslim* Africans and Asians or against *Indian* peoples, whoever the perpetrator.

Amid Swords and Spears

Accordingly, let us not forget, to defend a proclamation of the gospel by peaceful means was to swim against the current of *an existing situation*. It meant denouncing what was already being done in the Indies, with all of the interests that this created. It meant taking a courageous stance in the midst of the battlefield, and — literally — reflecting on the faith from there. But not wafting idyllically amid swords and spears, as someone has put it — rather incompletely, as it happens, since, among other things, he forgets the horses, harquebuses, and dogs — with reference to the missionary labors of that era. This would be a false neutrality, a mask for injustice — scarcely the style of Bartolomé de Las Casas. His activity and reflection invoke no disguises: they brand the swords of the invaders and oppressors for what they are, for it is these that provoke the Indians to lift their poor spears in defense of their violated rights. Without justice, there can be no authentic peace. In other words, it was a matter of ripping the mask from the face of a use of force for a so-called *evangelization*, showing that the war had been undertaken only out of *greed for gold*, as Fray Bartolomé tirelessly repeats.

The proper venue for this discussion, then, is not a university lecture hall in Salamanca or a debate by theologians in Burgos or Valladolid, as some scholars seem to believe. Not that academic discussions are useless or these halls the wrong place to hold them. Only this was not the urgent terrain on which matters stood. Unless we keep that in mind, we shall not understand Las Casas's sense of urgency or the vigorous tone he adopts in these polemics. Nor shall we understand his proposals — not always above criticism themselves — as the means he regards as necessary to bring about changes in a situation that was beginning to strike permanent root. The matter at issue is not whether force and war may be used for these ends, but how to prevent them from being so used.

The concrete historical context, the acts of war on the part of the new settlers in these lands, the conflicts of interest between the Crown and the *encomenderos*, the death of the Indians and the defense of that death made by many a missionary, deprive of all romanticism or merely academic interest these discussions of a possible justification for the wars of conquest. This excruciating reality, as Fray Bartolomé will say, ultimately undermines any legitimacy of the Crown's conditional "just titles" to these lands, which Francisco de Vitoria proclaimed.

Let no one think that war on the pretext of evangelizing — as some like to say who seek to soften the facts — was limited to the first years of the occupation of the Indies. For various reasons (some of which we shall treat later on), these deeds were repeated all through the sixteenth and early seventeenth centuries (when the situation in the Indies finally began to present a face of its own) — both in the Indies and in the Philippines. Furthermore, the mentality underlying this behavior will abide and to a certain extent be taken for granted.

Thus we confront a spectrum of positions. On the one extreme are the cynical declarations of Fernández de Oviedo: "Satan has now been exiled from this island [Hispaniola]: it is all over now, with the end and finish of the lives of most of the Indians"; and elsewhere: "Who can doubt that gunpowder against heathen is incense for the Lord?"[11] At the other extreme is the combat waged by Fray Bartolomé, who rejected even the use of the word "conquest." He says: "This term or name, 'conquest,' used with regard to all of the lands and realms of the Indies discovered and to be discovered, is a tyrannical, Mahometan, abusive, improper, and hellish term."[12] What we ought to change it to, he continues, is " 'preaching of the gospel of Christ,' 'expansion of the Christian religion,' and 'conversion of souls,' for which there is no need of conquest by arms, but only of persuasion by sweet, divine words, and the example of works of a holy life." Accordingly, "the damned Notifications [*requerimientos*] that have heretofore been made are unnecessary, and this undertaking ought to be called not 'conquest,' but 'preaching of the faith,' and 'conversion' and 'salvation' of these unbelievers" (*Memorial de remedios*, 1542, O.E. 5:121–22).[13]

Neither side was without its partisans. And between the two, inevitably, some tried to find a "middle ground." One of these "middle" positions, really rather a grotesque one, is represented by the "requirements" to which Las Casas alludes. Another of these insufficient or failed approaches is expressed in the Burgos Laws, with which we shall be concerned below. Both attempts, a result of the indictment lodged by Montesino and the friars of Hispaniola, will be harshly attacked by Bartolomé de Las Casas, who does not permit himself to be deceived by appearances and formalities.[14]

The presence of the Iberians in the Isles of the Antilles was consolidated early in the second decade of the sixteenth century. At that same time, word began to spread of the wonderful wealth of the kingdoms on the American continent itself. The moment had arrived to conduct an expedition of greater enterprise, in accordance with this news and these facts. "Enthusiasm for the affair grew," writes Las Casas, "in the mind of the King, the Bishop of Burgos, and the rest of their Council, [all of whom conceived] the purpose of dispatching a more considerable armada than the one of which they had been thinking" (*H.I.*, bk. 3, ch. 43, *O.E.* 2:299b). To this purpose, Pedro Arias de Avila, better known as Pedrarias, seemed to be the man of the hour. The year was 1513.[15]

But the controversy of the Indies was already under way, thanks to the Dominicans of Hispaniola, and the debate had reached the mother country. Colonists, alarmed at the prospect of repercussions from these denunciations, dispatched a representative to defend their interests in Spain: Franciscan superior Alonso del Espinal, who had been in the islands for some years now.[16] The Dominicans had already decided that Antón Montesino himself should go to Castile. The bishop of Palencia (and later of Burgos), Juan Rodríguez Fonseca, and Secretary Lope Conchillos, personages currently wielding great influence at Court, received the Franciscan with reverence and the Dominican with hostility. The magnitude of the expedition about to be undertaken by Pedrarias lent extreme interest to the ensuing discussions. A commission of theologians and jurists was appointed by the king to study the matter, and an order was issued postponing the departure of the expeditionaries. A year later, the Burgos Conference had been held, on the basis of which legislation on the Indies was promulgated.

In the following pages, we shall be concerned with the astonishing document known as the *Requerimiento,* or Notification (1513). Later we shall speak of the Burgos Conference (in our chapter 10). It will not be easy to separate the two. The questions they involve crisscross, in their theoretical stage as well as in the chronology of the historical facts of the time. Nevertheless, even at the price of a certain amount of unavoidable repetition, we shall maintain the distinction, with a view to greater expository clarity.

Theocratism Plus Royalism

Through the mouth of Antón Montesino, the Dominican friars of Hispaniola had presented the colonists a penetrating question: "With what authority have you waged such execrable wars upon these people?" King Ferdinand had rightly felt his own authority to be questioned here. The subject will be examined by the lawyers and theologians appointed to work with the king's Council. These persons will be charged with establishing the necessary justifications and, if necessary, with suggesting improvements in the treatment of the Indians. Las Casas will have to deal with these first efforts at justifying the wars and the subjection of the Indians. These efforts constitute the theological framework of the Notification.

In the execution of their task, the royal councilors have recourse principally to two eminent medieval canonists: Pope Innocent IV (d. 1254), and Enrique de Susa (d. 1271), cardinal of Ostia (hence, "the Ostian").[17] Both are dogged partisans of pontifical authority in temporal affairs. Basically, we are dealing with a theory of hoary vintage, but one which really came into its own only with the actual practice of Pope Gregory VII (d. 1085), reaching its zenith in the pontificate of Innocent III (d. 1226). In this theory, while spiritual power is to be distinguished from temporal, the former is superior and holds a primacy over the latter. The body that is Christendom has one head: the pope. The emperor, and all kings and queens, hold only a delegated power. "As the sun and moon are distinct, such is the difference to be acknowledged between the Pontiff and the Kings," Innocent IV will write, using a familiar image. The comparison is a frequent one of the age, as are other, similar ones, and always tend to underscore the superiority of religious authority: soul and body, gold and lead, and the famous one of the two swords, the spiritual and the temporal, upon which Bernard of Clairvaux insisted.

These authors' position on pontifical power (omitting nuances that would require too lengthy a presentation) is an important premise, some of whose consequences are of direct interest for our subject. One of them concerns the authority of the pope over the heathen. Here there are differences, but areas of agreement as well, among the canonists we have mentioned. Innocent IV holds that heathen, as rational beings, have a right to political authority of their own and the possession of goods. The pope may not deprive them of these by reason of the sole fact that they are heathen, although he may punish them — even by war — if they violate the natural law (as would be the case with idolatry, for example), since the pontiff has by right the powers of Christ on earth. There is also another just cause for war on the infidels: any opposition they may offer to the gospel being preached to them — saving the principle that they may not be *compelled* actually to embrace the faith. That is, they may only be *prevented from resisting* Christian preaching; but to this end, main force may be applied if necessary. These two arguments can justify the pope's authorization of the secular arm to undertake a war effort against heathen peoples.

The Ostian is more severe. For him, since the coming of Christ the infidels have lost all authority and jurisdiction. Such authority and jurisdiction belong to the faithful alone, since they are based on faith, and not reason, as Innocent IV had thought. In other words, the heathen are not the rightful rulers of their lands. They hold no legitimate authority there.[18] This alone will justify a war on the infidels; not even an infraction of the natural law is required. The second motive for war on the infidels (opposition to the preaching of the gospel) advanced by Innocent IV is adopted "as is" by this second author. The Ostian even calls these wars against the heathen — as do others of his time — "Roman" wars, because they are undertaken in the name of the Christian faith, and Rome is the head of the faith.[19]

Palacios Rubios (d. 1524), a royal councilor, one of the most distinguished jurists of the Burgos Commission, who will have a key role in the matter of the Notification, is an ardent defender of pontifical authority in temporal matters. He appeals to the authors mentioned, as well as to others who express the same convictions, and concludes that, by right, Christ held all power, spiritual as well as temporal; but both have been entrusted to Peter and his successors; therefore the power in question is a power over faithful and infidel alike. Spiritual power ought to be exercised by the church, and temporal power by temporal rulers "by grant or permission of the church."[20]

A champion of the theocratic theory, Palacios Rubios is no less a partisan of the power of temporal rulers. He holds theocratism and royalism together — however contradictory that may seem — because on this occasion these positions (so frequently antagonistic in history) converge, to justify a Spanish dominion over the Indies. A talent for combining them, in this case, is one of the fortes of our jurist. Indeed, the king's jurisdiction over these lands, for Palacios, is duly founded on the pontifical authority as expressed in the Alexandrine bulls. Thanks to these documents, the supremacy of the church over the heathen Indians now belongs to the rulers of Spain.[21] What we have, as Silvio Zavala says, is a "royalist seal of approval on the power of the pope"[22] on the part of the illustrious lawyer and servant of King Ferdinand.

The consequences of this way of understanding not only pontifical authority, but also the authority of secular monarchs, over the situation of the heathen — concretely, of the Indians — are not long in coming. However, Palacios posits a curious distinction that places him on this point between Innocent and the Ostian. According to him, unbelief alone does not provide sufficient cause for denying the Indians the right to own the lands and goods necessary for their sustenance; but it is indeed enough to refuse to acknowledge their legitimate political *authority*.[23] In a word: Palacios's position combines the various considerations advanced in justification of making war on and ruling the Indian nations (and places him on the side of the Ostian as to practical consequences): violation of the natural law, the absence of any political right to govern their subjects, and, of course, opposition to those who proclaim the gospel to them. He thinks, however, that the foundation of all of these motives must be presented to the Indians before war is waged on them. Thus, on condition of antecedent exhortation, all is in good order: acts of war are justified.[24]

Small wonder that, despite a personal esteem for that "most learned doctor" and "good Christian," if rather timid royal councilor, Don Juan López de Palacios Rubios, Las Casas censures his positions: "He has ultimately espoused the error of the Ostian, founding upon him the title that the Sovereigns of Castile have to the Indies." Then he adds, with severity and in a tone of admonishment: "And surely, were that erroneous, indeed heretical, opinion the sole basis for the right of our Sovereigns to be in the Indies, precious little of what there is there [in the Indies] would belong to them juridically" (*H.I.*, bk. 3, ch. 7, *O.E.* 2:184a). Las Casas rejects, then, the theory of pontifical power as Palacios Rubios presents it from his medieval sources.

Dominican Matías de Paz (d. 1519) is more of a theologian than a jurist.[25] But on the point at issue, despite his frequent protestations to the contrary,[26] his position is not very different from that of Palacios Rubios.[27] For Paz, unbelief is a sufficient motive for the church to dispossess rulers of the authority they hold over their peoples (*dominio regnativo*). But like Palacios Rubios, he admits that heathen have a right to proprietorship over lower goods (*dominio posesorio*). In support of his thesis he appeals to a passage from Thomas Aquinas.[28]

On this basis, Matías de Paz postulates:

> In my view, what St. Thomas declares is true; even more, I maintain, with all deference to a better opinion and not in a spirit of temerity, the following thesis: The Church may justly deprive of their dominion all infidel Princes, by reason of their unbelief alone, although their subjects not be converted to the faith. This viewpoint seems to be that of the Ostian, although not utterly and absolutely. For my part, I maintain it in its integrity.

The power of the church over the heathen is delegated to the king of Spain by the pope: hence Ferdinand's power in the Indies. Thus, Paz himself is careful to specify his position for us as being nearer to the

Ostian's than to that of Innocent.[29] And he is correct, despite the slight margin — one more clearly recognized by him than by Palacios — that separates those two classic authors.[30]

Hence war may be waged on the Indian nations for the same reasons as we have seen above in Palacios Rubios. But Matías de Paz insists, with all emphasis, that "before a war upon them is begun, they must if possible be admonished to embrace and revere with all their strength the most true faith of Christ." And he goes so far as to assert that, were this not to be done, the Indians "would have a legitimate right to defend themselves."[31] Advance warning, or "Notification," would legalize the Europeans' actions.

Furthermore, unlike Palacios, Matías de Paz places less emphasis on the dominion of the king of Spain over the Indies and the justification of the wars waged on those who dwell there than on the matter of the regime to which these latter are subjected. And on this point his position is favorable to the Indians: for example, he does not mention Aristotle's doctrine of natural servitude.[32] We shall examine that teaching later. But its absence from the treatment of our question by Matías de Paz is, without a doubt, the reason for the sympathy Las Casas feels — despite all — for this theologian.[33]

Palacios Rubios and Matías de Paz played an outstanding role at the Burgos Conference, and their opinions profoundly marked the discussions held on these subjects.[34]

2. To Laugh or to Weep?

As we have recalled, the theological discussions motivated by Montesino's denunciation, rendered the more urgent by the fact of a great armada being prepared by Pedrarias, had issued in the disconcerting text that is the *Requerimiento*, whose theological framework we have just examined. There are propositions in that exhortation that Las Casas does not hesitate to call "irrational, deviant things."

One Expression of Ignorance

Various versions state that Palacios Rubios is one of the document's most important redactors.[35] Las Casas says the same, nor does he attempt to conceal his personal sympathy for the illustrious scholar of the law: after all, despite the latter's mistaken theological position, he is a well-intentioned person.[36] "This Notification," writes Friar Bartolomé, "was ordered by the venerable Doctor Palacios Rubios, my good friend, according to what he himself (if my memory serves me correctly) told me, as I have mentioned above a time or two. Apart from this, he pitied and had compassion for much of the anguish and harm the Indians were suffering. This Notification seems to be his, indeed, and kneaded from his dough, since he founds it entirely on the errors of the Ostian, whose partisan he was" (*H.I.*, bk. 3, ch. 57, *O.E.* 2:309b).[37] "Apart from this": Las Casas takes his distance, which does not prevent him from esteeming the distinguished jurist personally or from appreciating his benign disposition toward the Indians. Besides, as we have seen earlier, Matías de Paz also thought that it was in good order to advise the Indians of the rights granted to the Spanish sovereigns before forcing the issue by means of war.

Las Casas presents this position as "one expression of ignorance afflicting the King's Council in this same matter, a defect most grave and pernicious" (ibid., *O.E.* 2:308a).[38] The *Requerimiento* must be read to the Indians: this will make European domination, and if need be, war, legal and just. On behalf of the Spanish sovereigns (called, significantly, "tamers of the barbarous tribes"), the text notifies the Indians that henceforward they must obey these rulers.

In its opening passage, the *Requerimiento* records that God has created the world and that all human beings ("we and you") are descended from one and the same couple. The sketch is a rapid one, but it crisply emphasizes the common trunk and stock of all humanity, and here, of Europeans and Indians. "The multitude of generations that has issued from them," from Adam and Eve, has had the effect that their descendants are scattered throughout the earth, into "many kingdoms and provinces." Then, in an enormous chronological — and theological — leap, the *Requerimiento* propounds that in some manner this dispersion led to God's giving "charge to one called St. Peter that he be lord and master of all human beings of the world, whom all should obey, and be head of the entire human lineage." This person is called the "Pope, meaning admirable, great father and governor of all human beings." Such are also regarded "all others who, after him, have been elected to the pontificate." This sovereignty embraces, of course, all domains, religious as well as political.

In their curious communication concerning Christian truths, the sovereigns quickly enter upon the matter that interests them. One of these pontiffs, availing himself of the authority ascribed to him by all, "has made donation of these islands and continent of the Ocean Sea to the said King and Queen and to their successors in these kingdoms." With all amiability, the Indians are told that this is all "contained in certain writings that... you may see if you wish." One imagines the scene: the Indians asking to see the writings (in Latin, of course) upon which their translation to the condition of vassals of the newcomers is founded!

For their encouragement, the presumed audiences of this reading are told that others before them have likewise been notified, and "have accepted their Highnesses and received them, and have always served them as subjects." The latter have also welcomed "religious persons whom Their Highnesses have sent to them to preach to them and teach them our holy faith, and all of them, of their free will and good pleasure, without any pressure or condition, have become Christians.... You are bound and obliged to do the same." This is an important point. With the jurisdiction of the sovereigns linked to the dispatch of missionaries, rejection of the royal dominion would mean refusal to receive the gospel — an adequate reason, according to many theologians, to make war on the Indians.

The Indians are then asked to take account of what is being transmitted to them. "In order to understand and deliberate upon it," they may have all "the time that would be just." In practice, the "just time" will grow shorter and shorter, as in the case of Atahualpa, for example. If they accept what is required of them, the natives will be received "with all love and charity" and may retain the free disposition of their goods. They will not be obliged to become Christians, "unless, upon being informed of the truth, you should wish to convert to our holy Catholic faith, as nearly all of your neighbors on the other islands have done." It would have been more accurate to speak of the "survivors" among these neighbors.

Now the tone becomes more harsh. The invitation is accompanied by threats. The audience is solemnly warned:

> Unless you comply, or if you postpone your compliance in bad faith, I certify to you that, with God's help, we shall mightily invade you, and make *war* on you, wherever, and in every manner, we can; shall subject you to the yoke and obedience of the Church and Their Highnesses; shall take your persons and those of your women and children, make them *slaves* and, as such, sell them and dispose of them as Their Highnesses may order; shall take from you *your goods*; and shall do you all the *harm and evil* we can. (emphasis ours)

Take it or leave it. With God's help and in the service of the gospel, of course. Through wars and servitude, which Las Casas will call the twin entries to the Indies.

Furthermore, responsibility for all of this will fall upon the Indians themselves: "And we protest that the death and harm that may accrue are your fault, and not that of Their Highnesses, nor ours, nor that of these knights who accompany us." Finally — a little dark humor — all of the above is to be witnessed by "the notary here present," who is asked "to deliver to us a notarized copy." Dominators always seek to legalize their oppression. But one may doubt the exculpatory force of this notarial act in the judgment of God.

The initial version of the Notification was expanded and modified in the course of the years, but remained substantially the same. This is without a doubt the document that was read by Valverde to Atahualpa in Cajamarca.[39] In fact, it was used well into the sixteenth century, although new norms were imposed on it as well.[40]

Hew to the Line...

As we have remarked, the text is a disconcerting one. But our discomfiture flows less from its content than from the use made of it. Indeed, as for content, the *Requerimiento* reflects — and draws very concrete conclusions from — only one theological current of the time, the one defending the pontifical theocracy, sketched above. But, we must at once add, the position was an extreme one, represented by the cardinal of Ostia, and somewhat (with certain differences) by Pope Innocent IV and other medieval canonists. We say one current, because there were other serious, well-founded theological positions as well at the time. But they were less useful to the interests of the Crown. They had their fundamental inspiration in principles enunciated by Thomas Aquinas and included, for example, the positions of John of Paris (d. 1306), and Juan de Torquemada (d. 1468).[41] Thus, the Notification does not rest on any overwhelming theological consensus. Other options remain. Las Casas will take a different position, as will, later, Francisco de Vitoria in his brilliant retractations dealing with the temporal power of the pope.

Here, J. Muldoon has presented an interpretation of the theology of the Notification that differs from the one commonly accepted.[42] Muldoon attempts to prove two assertions: (1) that the document is based on the ideas of Innocent IV (and not on those of the Ostian); and (2) that its principal intent is to protect the Spanish Crown from the accusation of being based on the proposition of John Wycliffe — which was condemned at the Council of Constance (1414–18) — that seemed to deny the right of power and ownership to anyone not in the state of grace.[43] The Ostian's position would thus come very close to Wycliffe's, as it denies these rights to anyone living in a state of unbelief (which is a sin). This, according to Muldoon, is why the Notification insists that the Indians have genuine dominion, a right that the Ostian denied unbelievers, while Innocent granted it. Consequently, the purpose of the text would not be, as has always been believed, from Bartolomé de Las Casas to Lewis Hanke, to "inform the Indians." It would be rather a matter of "an effort to prove to the papacy that the conquest of America was being accomplished in accordance with lines of thought that the papacy would approve." Hence, Muldoon holds, the famous document has always been understood incorrectly.

The reasoning is more ingenious than convincing. The author's analysis leaves many questions unanswered. The truth is that the difference, within the common trunk of the theocratic theory, between Innocent and the Ostian was well-known in the age in which the document was redacted. Palacios Rubios and Matías de Paz were aware of it and on some points incline toward the Ostian. In Palacios Rubios, the redactor, there is not the least shadow of a suspicion that there might be a connection between the teachings of the Ostian and Wycliffe. Meanwhile, nothing could be clearer in the Notification than that the dominion of the lands of the Indies has been bestowed by the one who holds all power, the pope, on the rulers of Spain. There is no acknowledgment, then, of any dominion on the part of the Indians. Only subsequently is anything said about the obligation to receive the preachers of the gospel. The Indian side is offered no real opportunity to make a decision. The Indians can only accept what is proposed to them; otherwise they will be destroyed. Finally, it would be curious to be speaking to the Indians so that Rome may hear. There are more direct ways.

The theology of the Notification, then, is but one — and surely not the most solid — of a number of theologies prevailing at the time. But it was in this theology that the royal councilors, and all those whose interests would be served by Pedrarias's expedition, found a convenient justification for the fact of the presence of the Iberians in the Indies and a doctrinal buttress for the rights of the Crown.

One of these persons with a special interest was Bachelor Martín Fernández de Enciso, a member of Pedrarias's expedition[44] and a champion of the theology in question in the controversies that preceded the composition of the Notification.[45] He was a staunch, open partisan of the theocratic theory and consequently of the right to undertake a war on any Indians who might refuse to respect papal authority over their domains, a power delegated to the king of Spain. About this person Pérez de Tudela writes:

> The fact is, despite all the blaring of the pretentious Bachelor, that the ultimate basis of the Notification had been implicit in the "natural law" position, from Matías de Paz to Francisco de Vitoria. But in this case, as in so many others, what happened was that the institutional model constituted a grotesque caricature of the principles on which it was based.[46]

But as we have recalled, it is not natural law theory that is at the basis of this text. It is the theory of pontifical theocracy. Vitoria, who rejects the underlying theology of the Notification, speaks of the duty of advising the Indians of the Christian right of evangelization, but not because they need to be informed that their lands belong to the pope, lord of all the earth, and that the pope has granted them to the king of Spain. The "caricature" that has been drawn is not in a mistaken application of the principles of natural law, but in the pretensions of the theocratic theology itself, and in a disregard of the rights of the Indians on the strength of so-called Christian justifications. True, as we shall see, this same mistake was present in currents incompatible with theocratism.

The "intelligence of the faith" is not an atemporal activity. It sinks its roots deep in the history of the Christian community (and not only in one or another conjuncture). It responds to questions asked by the believer living in a "here and now." That believer reaches out for the reflections being practiced in the Christian community, adopts viewpoints in determinate social conditions, and selects criteria according to the urgencies of the moment. Theology is stamped with the thought and culture of its time and, through it all, seeks to be faithful to the datum of faith, although it does not always succeed.

Thanks to his knowledge of the actual situation in the Indies and a theological perception based on a robust common sense, Las Casas helps us keep our bearings in the confusion of a (legitimate or illegitimate) variety of interpretations of this unusual text.[47]

The first thing Las Casas criticizes is that the instruction given to Pedrarias fails to take into account how things happen in the Indies. Before giving norms like that of the reading of the Notification, "those who counseled the King ought to have considered," he writes, "what have been *the deeds* of the Spaniards throughout these islands, and ask how Cristóbal Guerra, Hojeda, Nicuesa, and finally, Vasco Núñez and his followers have conducted themselves with the Indians of Darién, or with the others of those provinces who had been dwelling peacefully on their lands and in their homes." One must begin with the facts. And Bartolomé adds, firmly and fearlessly: "And of these deeds, the King, or at least the Council, were not ignorant." Texts are not valid solely by virtue of their internal logic or the solidity of their arguments. Their consequences, foreseen as probable or at least possible, if not necessary, also weigh in the balance — especially if they refer to deeds already being done.

In any case, before they were read the warnings of the Notification, the Indians had already been attacked, and therefore they had "just cause and right to defend themselves and to persecute the Christians." The affair is poisoned in its very root. The thing to do was to stop the mistreatment and murder of the inhabitants of these lands. But the Christians failed to do so: "because they did not hew very close to the line." They were careless with the logic of their own theology. Rather than "hewing to the line" and letting the chips fall where they might, the members of the king's Council issued an instruction that the Indians simply be told how well it would be "for them to place themselves under the obedience of the King." To which, Bartolomé replies, the addressees of the communication could just as simply "respond with silence, pointing their fingers at this island of Hispaniola and its many neighboring isles" (*H.I.*, bk. 3, ch. 55, *O.E.* 2:304–305).

Indeed the destruction and depopulation of these places were the most telling evidence when it came to giving the lie to the claim that good would accrue to the natives through the submission demanded in the document.[48] Thus, Bartolomé accuses the document of lying, and of attempting — uselessly, for that matter — to deceive the Indians. "There was also," he states accusingly, "a great deal of blameworthy falsehood: [the document] asserted that [the inhabitants of] certain islands, almost all of [the islands], to whom the above-stated had been notified, had received Their Highnesses in obedience and service, as they continued to do, as subjects of their own free will and without any resistance" — which is "not true," he concludes bluntly.

Some things, at any rate, are clear. The Notification was never used to avoid war. The wars were already being waged and had been for some time now. The purpose of the Notification was to justify the wars. It is on this terrain — that of the actual situation in the Indies, which he knows from experience — that Bartolomé's reflection on the text in question is situated. Before reproducing that text, he asserts that its basis is false, which disqualifies it part and parcel: "Since that which transgresses order and justice, founded on a wicked principle, must be in error, not in one part or one article, but in a thousand parts." Ever attentive to concrete consequences, Bartolomé says that, due to this document, there will be "a thousand vexations," and that it will undermine, morally and even politically, everything done in the Indies, "to the point of corrupting, enervating, and establishing in the frankest and most consummate state of evil, the moral or political edifice" (*H.I.*, bk. 3, ch. 57, *O.E.* 2:308a). The principal goal of the presence of Christians in the Indies has been altogether vitiated. The evil is in the system, and not only in persons taken individually.

After indicating that the theology of the Notification is based on "the errors of the Ostian," Las Casas makes some remarks on "the substance and efficacy or effect and justice of the mentioned requirement" (ibid., *O.E.* 2:309–310). Practical consequences (the "effect") and principles (the "substance") must always be taken into account at the moment of pronouncing a judgment, and not divorced from each other. This is no superficial, contingent observation on the part of Bartolomé de Las Casas, something one might say in passing. It represents his ongoing, deep-rooted attitude. To analyze a text without taking its concrete implications into account is to fall victim to intellectualism, which the Sevillian rejects precisely because he is a person of both thought and action.

From the outset, Bartolomé shows the error of the route of approach being taken to the matter. It is a question of method. The Notification bases the dominion of the sovereigns of Spain on "God our Lord, the one and eternal," and on the power delegated by that God to the pope.[49] But for what reason ought the Indians to believe — asks our friar, intrepidly formulating an opposition between two views of God — that "the God of the Spaniards was more a God than their own gods, or that He, rather than the ones they held for gods, would have created the world and human beings?" The question becomes all the more acute in view of the fact that "the God of the Spaniards" is manifested to them by those who abuse them and who present themselves arbitrarily as their lords and the masters of their lands and domains. "And so, what spirit would they have, and what love and reverence would be engendered in their hearts, especially in their rulers and chiefs, for the God of the Spaniards, hearing that, by His mandate, St. Peter, or the Pope his successor, was giving their lands to the King of the Spaniards,...whom they have never seen, known, or heard of?" (*H.I.*, bk. 3, ch. 58, *O.E.* 2:310a). These are incisive questions. They express, as always, a great respect for the religion and cultural world of the Indians, and an attempt — whose persistence in Las Casas we have already observed — to see things from that other angle. The dwellers of the Indies have as much right to believe in their God (or gods) as do the Spaniards in theirs, even apart from the fact that the Spaniards, in their behavior, were unbelievers.

In a polemical vein and in the same perspective he adds: "Were the Moors or Turks to come and announce to them the same Notification and requirement, declaring to them that Mahoma was lord and creator of the world and of human beings, would they be obligated to believe it?" (ibid.). We need only recall the hostility of the Spaniards of the time toward Moors and Turks to appreciate the force of the counterattack.[50] Las Casas throws it in the Iberians' faces: their works are no better than those of their detested enemies. Nor do they give witness to the true God.[51]

Christ's Gift and Human Freedom

As for papal authority, Bartolomé offers a reflection of considerable theological scope. He acknowledges the function and authority of the pope. Faith accepts this, and faith is a free gift of God. Such acknowledgment, consequently, is not determined on natural or political grounds. Its foundation is in the whole of what we accept by faith, which is before all else faith in the God of Jesus Christ. Only thus is it possible to understand the role the pope fulfills. The Council seems ignorant of this in ordering the Notification. Still, this is where one should have to start. "Why," Las Casas wonders, "do we believe that there is a Church, revering, submitting to, and obeying its visible head, the pope, *except* because we believe and have true faith in the Most Holy Trinity, Father, Son, and Holy Ghost?" The foundation of faith in the church, and consequently a condition of the possibility of an acknowledgment of its demands and its leaders, is faith in the Holy Trinity. "How," then, "or whereby, or by what human, natural, or divine right" will the Indian, "who has never heard of Christ, the Son of the True God, or voluntarily received him as such, be obliged to believe that there is a Church or that there are popes?" And if the Indian — altogether inculpably — has no reason to believe "that there is a Church or a pope,... then how will that [Indian] be obligated to believe that the Pope has power to make bestowal of the lands and domains possessed by people who have never known otherwise?" (*H.I.*, bk. 3, ch. 58, *O.E.* 2:311a).

It has been observed, and correctly, that the Notification required not conversion to the Christian faith, but acceptance of the authority of the pope and consequently that of the Spanish sovereigns.[52] Forced conversion would have been diametrically contrary to a long church tradition. (In the following chapter, we shall be concerned with the matter of the freedom of faith.) The learned authors of this text could not have failed to know that. But what Friar Bartolomé is attempting to show is that a true ecclesiology underlies the document to be read to the Indians. Indeed, as with any theology, the ultimate premise is a free acceptance of the faith; but this premise is not verified in the case of the Indians. What is happening here, perhaps, is that, this long ago, there were those who constructed and imposed on others "theologies" divorced from faith and evangelical practice. The important thing is that Las Casas aims his criticism straight at the proper target: missing from the theology of the Notification are *Christ and human freedom*. The former is unmentioned, and the latter is not genuinely extended to the Indians. It is a matter of a bad theology, at least as to its theoretical formulation, since on the level of inevitable practical consequences we should actually have to say that what is missing is any theology whatsoever. Absent here is any reflection on faith in a God of love that issues in love of neighbor.

Lest there be any misunderstanding, let us observe that, besides all that we have said, Bartolomé de Las Casas recognizes only the spiritual power of the pope — with temporal repercussions, yes, but in no way does he recognize the pope as "lord of the world," as the Notification calls him. Las Casas asks a commonsense question: To the Indians, "must not all of this have seemed to be delirium and raving, nonsense and insanity, especially when they were told they were under obligation to submit to the Church?" (*H.I.,* bk. 3, ch. 58, *O.E.* 2:311a).

Here Las Casas mentions an actual event recounted by Bachelor Enciso (to whom we have referred). A few pages later, he cites Enciso's account verbatim. The Notification had just been read to the Caciques of Cebú. And Enciso continues, in his *Suma de Geografía:*

> They answered me that, as for my saying that there was but one God, and that this God ruled heaven and earth and was Lord of all, this seemed well and good, and this is how things must be. But when it came to the Pope being lord of the universe, in the place of God, and that he had granted the favor of bestowing that land on the King of Castile, they said that the Pope must have been drunk when he did that, since he was "bestowing" something that was not his, and that the King who requested and accepted the favor must have been somewhat mad, since he was requesting something belonging to someone else,...and they said that they were lords of their land and that there was no need of another lord. (*H.I.,* bk. 3, ch. 53, *O.E.* 2:322a)

The Indians' refusal could not have been more blunt.[53] And so — still according to Enciso — the peninsulars regarded the war as justified, waged it, won it, and became the Indians' overlords.[54]

Las Casas rejects this so-called way of proclaiming the God of Jesus Christ, and rebukes Enciso — who parades as a witness to the justice of his wars — on the basis of Bartolomé's own view of the evangelical route to this proclamation: deeds of solidarity and persuasion. "I ask you," he writes, "whether they were obliged forthwith to believe you that the God you were making known to them was Three and One, and thus as well with the other particularities of your Notification." And he adds, with a sardonic humor sprung from his horror of the methods being used: "Were you, by chance, with your armed men — you coming to rob [them of] their gold, their lands, their women and children, and their freedom — an adequate witness?" (*H.I.,* bk. 3, ch. 63, *O.E.* 2:322b–323a). The proclamation of the gospel presupposes respect for the lives of the Indians: it requires a spirit of siblingship translated into acts, and a free act requires time to be elicited. Here indeed is the key to evangelization for this missionary. Only by loving the Indians as Christ has loved us can we proclaim him to them. This in turn requires a respect for human freedom, which is a necessary condition for accepting the free gift of faith as for forging a just political order. In the case of the latter, Bartolomé suggests a notion that will come to constitute an important step in his thinking, and we shall return to it in the fifth part of this work: unless the Indian nations — rulers and subjects alike — freely acknowledge the king's authority, the king has no dominion over them. Las Casas, then, maintains a profound democratic conviction. Perhaps it was influenced by the experience of the Spanish communes that we have mentioned, born in the Middle Ages, but still thriving and belligerent in the time of Friar Bartolomé.

In these conditions, how can the wars against the Indians be justified, theologically and politically? The Dominican's response is not long in coming: "Multiply their 'Notifications' as they might, . . . [these wars] have been, shall be, and are now unjust, wicked, and tyrannical wherever they have been or might be waged for such cause and with such title, on such unbelievers as the inhabitants and dwellers of these Indies." From this violation of the natural law, a perilous consequence emerges: "Most just will be the war waged by these [Indians], and by such unbelievers, on any Spaniard and any Christian who should promote such a war" (*H.I.,* bk. 3, ch. 57, *O.E.* 2:311b). We have a delicate point here, which we shall analyze later.

The affair turns grotesque when the reading of the Notification is done "to people who do not understand the language in which it is enunciated" (ibid., *O.E.* 2:312b). Consequently, such utterance has been pure formality ("for ceremony's sake," *H.I.,* bk. 3, ch. 166, *O.E.* 2:582b), at times amid a hail of Indian stones and arrows.[55] In the *Apología,* we find another treatment of the same point: "What language will be spoken by these messengers to make themselves understood by the Indians?" Latin, Greek, or perhaps Spanish or Arabic? The Indians know none of these tongues. "Unless," he says sardonically, "we might think the soldiers to be so holy that Christ will grant them the gift of tongues!" (149–149v).

The question also arises as to the time span to be allowed for making a decision. According to the Notification itself, the Indians must be permitted "the time that would be just." Las Casas shows how ridiculous such a concept is. "What time span will be given the Indians," he asks, in order that they may repent and make an end of their crimes? . . . Within the term to be given them, which must be lengthy, the Indians will not be obliged by said admonition, nor [therefore] incur imputation of contumacy, since the admonition obliges only after expiration of the term." He then inquires incisively: "What will the soldiers be doing during the term granted to the Indians for their repentance? Will they, by chance, like the forty monks dispatched by St. Gregory I, the Great, to convert the English, pass their time in fasting and prayer, that the Lord may deign to open the Indians' eyes to accept the truth and abstain from such crimes?" And he answers his own question with another: "Or rather will they not hope with all their heart and soul that the Indians may blind themselves in such fashion that they neither see nor hear, thus presenting the soldiers with the occasion they so much desire to rob them and reduce them to captivity?" (*Apología*, 149v–150).

On the last page of his *History of the Indies*, Las Casas returns to the question of term or interval and recounts a painful incident. "Concerning those Notifications, made for ceremony's sake by those who went there and ordered by the governors and," he says with irony, "by those known as learned jurists (and it was by virtue of this office that they earned their bread and lorded it over others, and not on account of their pretty eyes, so that it was not legitimate for them to be ignorant of so inhumane, so gross, an injustice), I wish to recount here what blinded *me* when I dealt with it with the greatest of them, who presided over them all." The importance of the personage makes the fact he will report all the more cruel: a number of lines later we are informed that the person in question was the president of an Audiencia. He writes: "I was speaking to him, and giving him reasons and authorities to persuade him that those armed forces were unjust, and utterly worthy of all detestation and eternal fire." Las Casas argues theologically:

> ... And that the Notifications that were ordered to be made, and were being made, were making of truth and justice a laughing-stock and were to the great vituperation of our Christian religion and of the mercy and charity of Jesus Christ, who had suffered so much for the salvation of those people; and that — since no limit might [legitimately] be placed on the time span to be allowed within which they might be converted to Christ, as [Christ] did not limit it for anyone at all, but [gave] everyone all of the time there was and is, from the commencement of their existence to Judgment Day, nor [did limit it] for any particular person, but granted to each all the space of that one's life within which to be converted, using the liberty of free choice — ... human beings were cutting short that divine privilege, in such wise that some were saying that it sufficed to require of [the Indians], and to wait for this span of time, three days, others extending themselves to saying that it was well to wait two weeks.

Faced with this line of reasoning, which takes up the themes of Christ and of human freedom (both of them absent from the *Requerimiento*, or Notification), along with setting in relief the absurdity of the procedure, the personage in question replies, with sarcasm and contempt: "No, two weeks is too little. It will be well to give them two months to make up their minds." Las Casas comments with sorrow:

"I felt like screaming, the moment I heard and saw an insensitivity so profound and massive in the one who ruled such a great part of those regions" (*H.I.*, bk. 3, ch. 166, *O.E.* 2:582a–583a).

In view of the historical "effect" and the "justice" of the famous text, Las Casas is alarmed at the repercussions on the proclamation of the gospel, due to the "defamation of the faith and Christian religion and of Jesus Christ himself, which from that Notification must necessarily emerge and has emerged" (*H.I.*, bk. 3, ch. 58, *O.E.* 2:312a). It is a harsh reproach. The consequences were foreseeable by those who had decided to act in this manner ("they had to go, and they went"). The repugnance we feel for this text today, together with the way in which it was used, is not anachronistic. It is not a matter of something that was justifiable in its day for reasons that would be inadmissible today. Las Casas lived in that time, and so his repudiation could not be more harsh. And he makes it not because he is ahead of his time (an encomium the modern spirit loves to pronounce upon him), but because he accepts the old (and ever new) demands of the gospel, without shortcuts or compromise.

The primary responsibility falls on the shoulders of those who have the mission of governing. "Evident, then, becomes the ignorance of the King's Council (and please God it may have been possible for them to be forgiven it), and how unjust, impious, scandalous, irrational, and absurd has been that Notification of theirs" (ibid., *O.E.* 2:312a). That this is something that will lie very heavy on Las Casas's heart clearly appears in the last lines of his *History of the Indies,* where he reiterates his assignment of responsibility and expresses a desperate hope:

> But this ignorance and blindness on the part of the King's Council, which was the cause of its providing for the making of those Notifications, arose in the past; and, please God, today, which is the current year seventy-one, may the Council be free of it. And with this supplication and glory to the honor of God, we bring this Book Three to a close. *Deo gratias.* (*H.I.*, bk. 3, ch. 166, *O.E.* 2:583b)

The Notification, like any religious justification today of the plunder and exploitation of the poor, "is something" — as the extraordinary Bishop Las Casas put it — "to make one either laugh or weep" (*H.I.*, bk. 3, ch. 58, *O.E.* 2:312a).

Chapter 5 _____

Perspective of Power

The destruction of persons, peoples, and cultures, along with their natural environment, which is what was occurring in the Indies, called forth in Las Casas a profound sensitivity to life and liberty as special gifts of God. As for war, especially war touted as a means of evangelization, the missionary friar will defend the right of the inhabitants of these lands to decide their religious life for themselves.

The power the church found in its hands in medieval Christendom is the historical locus of the practice and the theology of those who, in one way or another, deem that faith may legitimately be imposed. And so they reason upon the advantages of the use of force for the proclamation of the gospel, although some of them are concerned that it be employed only under certain conditions and limitations. What they do not discuss, and surely it would have been difficult for them to do so, is the perspective from which the question is put. The theorists in question tended to authenticate their positions with an appeal to canon law — or in the best of cases, to the teachings of the theology of law — rather than to the gospel. To recall the theological framework of the series of problems implied in this attitude is the object of this chapter.

Las Casas will not confine his production or reflections to the placing of limits on the use of force. He will reject the use of force across the board. Thus, he not only defends the *freedom of the act of faith* (which the teaching of the time clearly maintained), but actually broaches a defense of *religious freedom* — the right of each individual to live in accordance with his or her own religious convictions. In doing so, our friar rediscovers some of the intuitions prevailing in the first Christian centuries and rehabilitated by Vatican Council II in a context of our own times.

For a better understanding of the Lascasian viewpoint, it will be in order to recall two subtle changes that took place in the first centuries of the church on the subject concerning us. The evolution to which we refer constitutes the doctrinal context of the thought of Thomas

Aquinas, an author of the first importance for Las Casas. As Las Casas says so simply in a meaningful text of the last years of his life: For him, "in the matters of the Indies," there is "no proposition of this material, however rigorous, that is not established by principles gathered from [St. Thomas's] doctrine" (*Carta a los dominicos de Chiapa y Guatemala*, 1563, *O.E.* 5:471a, b).

It will be helpful for our understanding of the subject proposed in this chapter to refer to the theologian whose position dominated the sixteenth century in this area, Francisco de Vitoria, as well as to Ginés de Sepúlveda, whose shrewd refinements of similar theoretical premises take no account of the limits originally associated with them.

1. *The Gospel and Violence*

José de Acosta politely expresses his surprise — which continues to be our own — that in his time such disparate things as the "gospel of peace" and the "sword of war" should be joined together.[1] That is well put. Paradoxically, this is how things are presented. In the foregoing chapter we saw the use made of extreme theocratic positions (alloyed with royalism, in the case of Palacios Rubios) in an attempt to justify waging war on the Indians when they refused to acknowledge the invaders' dominion over their lands. But this position is not the only one that affords carte blanche for the use of arms. Even some of the thinkers who reject the theses of a direct temporal authority of the pope (the theses defended by theocratism) consider the waging of war an appropriate means of propagating the faith. For both groups, the church has a right to evangelize, and in the implementation of that task the right, and the duty, to appeal to political power. The assistance of those who wield that power may in certain cases extend to the undertaking of belligerent actions against those to whom the Christian message is addressed — under certain conditions, of course.

The spectrum of positions has been sketched out a number of times, and we refer the reader to the studies that do so for more details.[2] We need not review it here. We are interested, however, in examining what underlies, historically and doctrinally, the various positions taken. We think that the brilliant Ginés de Sepúlveda saw through to the crux of the problem: the perspective of power. This endowed his writings with a consistency that we find less in others who wrote on these matters. In this nucleus, precisely, we find the point of breach that will cause Las Casas to take his distance from the dominant position of his time.

Removing the Obstacles

When Francisco de Vitoria (d. 1546) made up his mind in 1537 to treat of topics pertaining to the Indies, he encountered the problem of the use of force in the task of evangelization.[3] As we have recalled, war had been a fact of life in the Indies for forty-five years now. The conquest of Peru, whose cruelty horrified Vitoria,[4] had begun not long before the year in which he determined to address Indian issues.

The question was an old one. Dating from ancient times, it had become thornier in the high Middle Ages with Christian contact with the Nordic peoples and especially with the Arab world. As for the latter, one might say that Christendom found itself in a state of ongoing war with the infidel nations. In this context, the Indies represented a colossal broadening of the non-Christian world.[5]

The Salamancan theologian had inherited from Christian tradition a basic postulate: "To believe is an act of the will, and fear greatly diminishes the voluntariety of an act" (Vitoria, *Obras*, 696; CHP, 65).[6] Consequently, no one can be obliged to believe.[7] This principle, incisively formulated by Augustine, was turned to even greater account by Thomas Aquinas.[8] It is in Thomas's version that Vitoria receives it, and this enabled him to reject the refusal to hold faith in Christ as an illegitimate title for the Hispanic presence in the Indies.

Following Thomas Aquinas, Vitoria denies that unbelief is necessarily sinful, or that anyone is necessarily obliged to believe upon a first proclamation of the faith.[9] Then Vitoria adds another consideration, expressing his attention to news of the "scandals, cruel crimes, and many impieties" that had come from the Indies. "I am not very convinced," Vitoria writes, "that the Christian faith has yet been proposed and proclaimed to the barbarians in such a way that they would be obliged to believe it under pain of a further sin" (*Obras*, 695; CHP, 65). The expression is a timid one, but it has the merit of pointing to the facts and keeping them in account in the course of a theoretical reflection.

But the scenario changes when it is a question of legitimate titles. Apropos of the second of these ("the propagation of the Christian faith"), Vitoria maintains that "if the barbarians, either the chieftains or the people themselves, prevent the Spaniards from freely proclaiming the gospel, . . . then the Spaniards may preach to them even against their will, . . . and, if necessary, for this cause approve or make a declaration of war, until such time as secure opportunities be available for preaching the gospel." The reason is that to present an obstacle to this proclamation becomes an assault on the right of Christians to proclaim their message (*Obras*, 717; CHP, 89). A few years earlier, he had already asserted:

In case they should impede the teaching of Christ in such a fashion as not to permit us to preach it, it would be licit for us to oppress them under the right of war, in order that the gospel be propagated. Indeed, were there to be imminent danger to our safety, it would be licit for us to take possession of some of their goods, since this is part of the Law of Nations.[10]

In other words, infidels may not be forced to conversion, but force may indeed be employed to *remove the impediments* to evangelization. Both cases have this in common, that they fall on the side of those who *can* employ force. Vitoria's tone is very different from the one Sepúlveda will later employ, but the danger of failing to see a clear line of demarcation between these two actions is present here as well.

And the Salamancan master falls victim precisely to this danger. In his commentary on St. Thomas's *Summa Theologiae,* II–II, q. 10, a. 8 (an article of which we shall treat further on), apropos of compelling infidels to accept the faith, Vitoria introduces a distinction not to be found in Thomas Aquinas. He distinguishes between infidels who are subjects of Christian princes and those who are not subjects, and acknowledges the validity of Thomas's position only in the case of the latter. With infidels living under the rule of Christian princes, however, Vitoria admits the right of compulsion. The Salamancan's position is clearly contrary to Thomas's, but he defends it on the premise that the scope of political authority — by natural law — includes the religious area. Thus, in this situation there would be no violation of the principle of the freedom of the act of faith.[11]

The text is a headache for Vitoria's interpreters. Carro observes that we have it by way of his students' notes and not directly from the hand of the master. True enough; but given Carro's own acknowledgment of "such a Vitorian stamp" on the passage, we cannot escape the fact that we are dealing with a "deviation on Vitoria's part."[12] Obviously this is a step to the rear vis-à-vis both Thomas Aquinas's position and other assertions of Vitoria himself.[13] What we are seeing is that, once one adopts the perspective of power, it is possible to fall into this kind of distinction — and temptation.

Sepúlveda's partisans take solace from these points of agreement with their master.[14] They are undeniable. Nevertheless, if we are to respect the truth, we must recognize that Vitoria employs nuances of tone that we do not find in the Cordovan. Following St. Paul, Vitoria asserts that not everything permissible is appropriate. As for the use of force in evangelization, from his professorial chair he has restricted himself to indicating what is "licit of itself" (*quod per se haec licent*). But it can be inappropriate to put it into practice. Others will not hold this theoretical reservation. On the one hand, Vitoria has no doubt (*ego non dubio*) that "there has been need to have recourse to force of arms for the Spaniards to be able to remain there." This is clear to him. On the other hand, he fears — as he says, with commendable concern — that practice itself "has gone much further than what right and morality permitted" (*Obras*, 718; CHP, 90–91).

There are certain other assertions indicating the Salamancan master's reservations and manifesting his human sensitivity. However, his thesis remains: *per se loquendo* — that is, in principle — if the Indians prevent the preaching of the faith, war may be made upon them. To tell the truth, this doctrine is not original with him. It corresponds to a process of ideas that came before him, and it reflects the manner in which the problem was posed in his age. What is special in Vitoria is his measured analysis of the pros and cons of the application of the right to proclaim the faith to the case of the Indies, and to the wars being waged there. Mark a point for the school of Salamanca.

Many other members of that school will take up the same question. One of them is Domingo de Soto (d. 1560), whom on a number of occasions we find maintaining positions akin to those of Las Casas. His stance is more clear-cut than Vitoria's.[15] His theoretical framework is the Thomist one, of course. Soto defends the right of Christians to preach the gospel (*jus praedicandi*), but denies that one may be compelled to believe. He supports his position with an extensive appeal to arguments from reason and sacred Scripture. Nor is it to be recommended that heathen be obliged to listen to this proclamation, although he acknowledges that this point is "disputed among theologians." Soto explicitly denies — against Vitoria — that Christian princes may impose the faith on their infidel subjects by force. But it is clear to him that if the infidels prevent the proclamation of the Christian message, this impediment may legitimately be overcome by force in the name of self-defense (*jus defendendi nos*).

It is precisely this last position — also maintained by Vitoria — that is the reason for Soto's disagreement with Las Casas on the sole occasion on which Soto, in his résumé of the Valladolid debate, expresses his own opinion. For Bartolomé, the use of force in evangelization is justified under no circumstances, not even when infidels impede the preaching of the gospel. Soto takes his distance from this stance, writing: "It seems to me that, unless I am mistaken, my Lord Bishop is in error here. After all, it is one thing for it to be licit to exercise force in order to be allowed to preach, which is the opinion of many doctors; and another thing again for it to be permitted to compel persons to come to our sermons, which seems less probable" (O.E. 5:305b).[16] Soto indeed grasps Las Casas's position, and thinks instead that it is acceptable and obligatory to exercise force in order to be allowed to preach, whenever no greater evils would be entailed.[17]

Soto is clearly in favor of a peaceful evangelization, but with the reservation indicated. Las Casas, from his experience in the Indies, believes that this thesis opens the door to dangerous abuses — despite its moderation as compared with that of the liceity of a preemptive war or a war for the purpose of compelling the hearing of the gospel message.

Vitoria and Soto thus establish the parameters of the school of Salamanca. Variations among its representatives are nuances of a core position shared by the theologians and many missionaries to the Indies. Some will be more rigid, and will even defend the use of force with an appeal to secondary reasons.[18] Others will limit or condition such use. But none will reject it outright. The Salamancan theoretical framework will not permit them to.

It will be worth our while here to introduce the position of an author who wrote later than Las Casas, but who had close ties to the Salamancan school, as well as extensive experience in the Indies. We refer to José de Acosta. His position, like that of the others, is complex and nuanced. He distinguishes three methods of preaching the faith: without military apparatus; among peoples already subjugated by Christian princes; and with troops and the protection of soldiers. The first, that of the apostles, is the best. Unfortunately, it is not applicable in the Indies. Anyone who would defend it "in the case of the majority of the peoples of this Western world would be condemned for extreme stupidity alone, and rightly so."[19] This harsh attitude, Acosta goes on to explain, is justified by a number of considerations. Today no miracles accompany evangelization, as they did in the time of the apostles, enabling them to practice the first method. Furthermore, in these lands, unlike those of the Asian, Oriental world — where Acosta had always wanted to go — the condition of the barbarians means that, unless "they were to be compelled like beasts, there would never be any hope [of their conversion], nor would they ever manage to become humanized and attain to the liberty of the children of God."[20] With the civilized people of the East, one could behave differently.

Consequently, the correct method for the Indies is the third: a mission under military protection. Were the infidels to refuse to be preached to and attack the Christians, the Christians should wage war on them. Besides, this would keep the missioners from being killed, as they had been in Florida. In sum, Acosta inclines toward peaceful means in theory, but his realism prevents him from rejecting the use of force. Indeed, he regards it as inevitable — under certain conditions, of course.

Begin with Subjugation

In 1535, in Rome, Juan Ginés de Sepúlveda (d. 1573) had published his *Democrates Primus,* a dialogue on the kinship between the military life and the Christian religion. The occasion of the work was the author's concern at seeing Spanish youths question whether it was correct for Christians to make war. Thus, the Cordovan Latinist sets forth the Christian value of military service and the noble motives that might lead to military action.[21] A number of years later (ca. 1544–45), he wrote another dialogue, which he called *Democrates the Second: The Just Reasons for War against the Indians.* Here he applies to the case of the Indies the material he has presented in his earlier work in favor of the legitimacy, indeed the suitability, of war.[22] This work did not receive permission from the Council of the Indies to be printed, despite the support it had received from important members both of the Royal Council of Castile and the Council of the Indies itself.[23] One of the personages who had supported it was the archbishop of Seville, the president of the Council of the Indies.[24] Sepúlveda bases his theses on four arguments, of which the last bears on the matter with which we are concerned here.

When, at the close of the sixteenth century, Báñez asks, in a commentary on the *Summa Theologiae,* II–II, q. 10, a. 10, whether Christian princes may oblige infidels to hear or receive the Christian faith, he cites John Major and Ginés de Sepúlveda as the principal authors maintaining this position. Báñez is right: indeed these two are forthright representatives of the partisans of waging war before evangelizing. Major had asserted it before Las Casas entered the fray. Sepúlveda, on the other hand — whom Báñez regards as inspired by Major — comes later, and will bitterly lock horns with Bartolomé on this point.[25]

Sepúlveda presents his theses articulately in his *Demócrates Segundo* as well as in his summary of that work called the *Apología* (hereafter *Apología* [GS]) and of course in the other texts of the Valladolid disputation.[26] The last named, as Domingo de Soto rightly points out in his summary, was convoked in order to "inquire into and constitute the manner and the laws whereby our holy Catholic faith may be preached and promulgated in the new world that God has revealed to us," as well as to "seek a suitable manner of subjecting those people to the Emperor's Majesty." Actually, however, the "proposing lords" discussed only "whether it is permitted to His Majesty to wage war on the Indians before the faith is preached to them, in order to subject them to his empire, [so] that after their subjection they may be more easily and conveniently instructed in, and enlightened by, the evangelical doctrine of the knowledge of their errors and of Christian truth"

(*O.E.* 5:295a–b). Indeed this was the crux of the debate. One of the reasons Sepúlveda indicates for answering the question in the affirmative is the need of war for a real and actual proclamation of the evangelical message. Let us see how the Cordovan reasons.

Every Christian has a duty to correct anyone who takes a mistaken path. But in this matter, what is at stake is eternal perdition or salvation. Therefore this duty is more urgent. There can be no doubt but that those outside the Christian religion will be damned. Consequently, "it is right that the barbarians, for their salvation, be compelled to justice" (*Apología* [GS], 65). As we see, the key to the argument is the certitude that the Indians are damned if they continue in their customs and religion. But since God "wishes that all be saved and come to a knowledge of the truth" (*Democrates*, 64), it becomes an obligation of natural and divine law to show the Indians the way of salvation.

Now, the Indians can be shown the way to eternal salvation in either of two manners: either by exhortation and instruction alone, or with a certain force and fear accompanying the same. Sepúlveda clearly sees and acknowledges that the first manner was that of Christ and his apostles. But that was a special situation, in which the Lord cooperated by way of miracles. (Acosta will say something of the kind later, as we have seen.) The second way is that of "the Church, once it has seen that it is protected by the apparatus and power of Christian kings and princes" (*Apología* [GS], 65)[27] — that is, when temporal power has been placed at the service of the task of evangelization.

The Cordovan, altogether justifiably, is very attentive to changes in historical context. Thomas Aquinas's assertion that infidel rites were once tolerated by the church "when the multitude of unbelievers was great" (*ST* II–II, q. 10, a. 11, c.) refers, says Sepúlveda, "to an age in which there were as yet no Christian princes who had the power to compel" (*Apología* [GS], 67). Now we have such princes. For Sepúlveda, therefore, the practice of the primitive church cannot be appealed to as a norm. "Is it thought," his interlocutor Leopoldo asks, "that what was not done in the primitive Church cannot be rightly done in any time, not even on occasions on which [the Church] is reinforced with the strength and power of kings and princes?" The thesis is clear. As Christianity advances in the world, "so the power of the Church increases, not only to invite but to oblige to good" (*Democrates*, 69–70). These new circumstances counsel a change in methods of evangelization. When the church had no power, peaceful means were in order. (Besides, God supported these means with miracles.) But the moment Christianity takes its place among the powers of the world, miracles become "signs for which there is no reason to ask God, when it is possible for us to follow his precept to oblige barbarians to accept the call of the gospel" (*Apología* [GS], 72). War and death, rather than the signs of life that were Jesus' deeds and miracles, are now in order.

The rescue of the Indians from eternal damnation and especially the awareness of confronting a different historical situation are the twin considerations warranting the use of force in evangelization. To this Sepúlveda adds the conviction that, without the previous subjugation of its auditors, the gospel would not be heard. Fear and doctrine, he asserts frighteningly, must march in tandem. "I say," he writes, "that the barbarians must be dominated not only that they may listen to the preachers, but also in order that to doctrine and counsels threats may be joined as well, and fear instilled." Indeed, the majority of the Indians (the barbarians to whom Sepúlveda refers), "thanks to terror joined to doctrine, have received the Christian religion, the very ones who had rejected it when it was only preached" (*Democrates*, 73). The fear inspired in them by their own priests and princes must now be outweighed by the fear produced in them by Christians and their weapons. Sepúlveda even goes so far as to say that this "does not remove their freedom, lest they cease to be able to believe" (*Proposiciones temerarias*, 564).

It is important to observe that from the outset Sepúlveda's argumentation depends on the Indians' not "being obliged to believe," but having "the obstacles suppressed that could hinder the preaching and propagation of the faith." Here he cites the classic text of the Fourth Council of Toledo, which we have already mentioned, in which it is said that "no one can be obliged to believe." This is what Sepúlveda thinks as well. He declares: "I confess that no one may be obliged to embrace the faith, to believe and to be baptized against [his or her] will, or compelled to become a Christian." This, he says, pulling the rug out from under his adversaries' feet, "in sum, is the whole doctrine and testimonial of those who oppose me" (*Apología* [GS], 73). He is in agreement with it. His position enjoys great support from the magisterium and from private theologians, and in the following section of this chapter we shall analyze the process involved in the formation of the teaching of that magisterium and those theologians. It was impossible, consequently, to break out of this mindset: everyone, at least formally, espoused it in theory. It could not have been otherwise.

But as we know, there is more to be said. In this same common doctrine is the notion that the use of force is justified in order to remove impediments to the reception of the faith. Sepúlveda frankly takes this route. Against Soto (and Vitoria as well), he considers that persons may legitimately be compelled to listen to preaching. He is scandalized that Las Casas could deny such a thing: "As for his saying that unbelievers may not be justly forced to hear preaching, this is a new and false doctrine, and one that runs counter to [the opinion of] all of those who otherwise hold his opinion. After all, the Pope has the power, indeed the mandate, to preach the gospel, by himself and through others, throughout the world, and this cannot be done unless preachers are heard: therefore by commission of Christ he has the power to constrain [persons] to hear them" (*Aquí se contiene*, 1552, O.E. 5:314b). It is a "new" teaching, which under pens like Sepúlveda's means "non-Christian."

However, with these statements Sepúlveda is contradicting the Salamancan theologians we have mentioned. At the same time, while the line between *obliging* someone to accept the faith and *removing* the obstacles to preaching was never very clear in practice, with Sepúlveda it seems simply to evaporate. "For when to useful fear," writes the Cordovan humanist, "is joined salutary doctrine, in order not only that the light of truth may scatter the darkness of error, but also that the force of fear may burst the bonds of evil custom — then, as I have said, we rejoice in the salvation of many" (*Democrates*, 73). This use of violence ends in the subjection of the enemy, and that creates the best conditions for conversion to Christianity. The Indians are a case in point. "Once subjected to the power of Christians and withdrawn from their impious religious rites, no sooner do they hear the preaching of the gospel than they run *en masse* to ask for baptism." Thus, subjection through war leads to this fervor and attraction for the Christian faith. Serenely, Sepúlveda gives us the reason: "It is the property of human custom and nature that the vanquished readily adopt the customs of the victors and dominators, imitating them in their works and words" (*Apología* [GS], 69).[28]

Then why *convince*, when *victory* is the more effective means? "Thus, for this reason," the text continues, "in a few days more persons are converted to the faith of Christ, and more securely so, than perhaps might be converted in three hundred years by preaching alone" (ibid.).[29] There is no time to lose then. The human cost of the wars leaves his theses unshaken. On the contrary, on the basis of this "dogma," as he calls it, and in support of which he appeals to, among others, the teachings of St. Augustine, Duns Scotus, and "John Major, who expressly approves this kind of expedition against the barbarians,"[30] the "entire controversy here can be settled" (ibid.).

The narrow line between forced conversion and the removal of obstacles to evangelization has become an invisible one. The distinction becomes one of lip service.[31] The assertion that one cannot be obliged to believe loses its substance. The barbarians must be withdrawn "from the precipice, even against their will," says our author, and conquest by force of arms is legitimated. Indeed, the deed of evangelization "is performed most easily, as we see, after subjecting the people themselves to our dominion, and we know of no other way to proceed in these times" (*Democrates*, 65). And we have what really seems to matter: the legitimacy of the wars of the Indies, for which Sepúlveda thinks he also finds support in the bulls of Alexander VI (and nothing to the contrary in Paul III's *Sublimis Deus*) addressed to the rulers of Spain and charging them with the evangelization of the Indies, preceded by the subjugation of their inhabitants.

Sepúlveda adduces a supplementary argument. Peaceful evangelization constitutes an unnecessary risk to preachers' lives. He recalls that preachers have already been slain in the Indies (see *Democrates*, 72–73). Finally, he wonders whether it is suitable that, before the application of force, use should be made of "previous admonition." In theory, yes, he replies. But then he gives various arguments to demonstrate — not incorrectly, although with different motives from those of Las Casas — that since this would be useless, it is therefore unnecessary. To admonish "such barbarous nations," or even to speak to the Indians, who have no "common language with us, to expect not only their replies, but their compliance as well, would become a thing so difficult, so costly and lengthy, that it would readily discourage all Christian princes from the enterprise."

In fact, the use of the *Requerimiento* — which is what is in question here — hinders "altogether any devout, salutary expedition to the barbarians, and accordingly their conversion, which is the purpose of this war" (*Apología* [GS], 71). It is not the *Requerimiento* itself or its theology that scandalizes him. He rejects it because it delays the start of a military expedition, and so could discourage Christian princes from undertaking one. Sepúlveda concludes his *Apología* with another citation of the two methods of evangelization that he had recalled in the beginning. The reasons he sets forth make his conclusion all the more clear: "Having two routes, then, by which the barbarians can be converted" (this is the point, and indeed Sepúlveda enunciates them as follows, depreciating the former), "the one difficult, long, and beset with many dangers and toils (consisting as it does in admonition, doctrine, and preaching alone), and the other easy, short, expeditious, and very advantageous for the barbarians (consisting as it does in their subjugation), no prudent person will doubt which of these routes ought to be followed" (*Apología* [GS], 72). Nothing could be more obvious.[32] Why waste time?

Major and Sepúlveda are forthright theological champions of armed action before the proclamation of the gospel.[33] Las Casas will meet them on their own ground, that of reflection. But at the same time he is impelled by events in the Indies. There are missionaries there who actually approve the wars. This is the case with the dedicated, and confused, Toribio de Benavente, better known by the Indian name he adopted: Motolinía. In his well-known letter of accusation against Las Casas, which he addressed to King Charles V in 1556, he defends the justice of the wars in the Indies against Bartolomé's onslaughts, writing: "Since it falls to Your Majesty's office to make haste that the holy gospel be preached throughout these lands, and since they who do not wish to hear the holy gospel of Jesus Christ of their own free will *should be forced*, here the proverb applies, 'Better forced to be good than free to be bad.' "[34]

Vasco de Quiroga's (d. 1565) *De Debellandis Indis* is lost.[35] But on the basis of our indirect knowledge of it,[36] as well as by way of his *Información en derecho* (1535),[37] we can state that, despite his preference for peaceful means, he approved and counseled the use of force for the benefit of the Indians themselves, "not for their destruction, as we understand it, but for their edification, as his Majesty and the Supreme Pontiff understand it."[38]

Both examples (Motolinía and Quiroga) demonstrate that it is not easy to swim against the tide of the dominant ideas of an era.[39] Despite the theological interest of all these considerations, however, we cannot escape the sensation that, in the framework of the war being waged, it is a little late to be defending positions for and against its liceity or examining the conditions under which this liceity would obtain. Indeed, a theory that fails to take account of the facts and the scope it will have in a particular situation is fraught with a great weakness even as a theory. This is what is occurring with the theologians of Salamanca, despite their incontestable theological ability, good will, and desire (stronger in some than in others) to know what is going on in the Indies. They are the product of a lengthy process of ideas, as are we all. Let us go back in time, then, and examine this process. This will help us gain a better understanding of their positions, as well as a better perception of Las Casas's contribution.

2. *Two Significant Focal Shifts*

In the question of the legitimacy of the use of force in the proclamation of the gospel, we have constantly met with the distinction between *compelling* an acceptance of the faith, and *removing* obstacles to the preaching of the Christian message. The first is rejected by all theologians of Bartolomé's time (theoretically even by Sepúlveda), in the name of a clear and fundamental proposition: the freedom of the act of faith. This has led many authors to speak of respect for religious freedom and to maintain that the dominant tendency of the era was peaceful evangelization. Such was not the case. It will be worthwhile to examine the subject from a historical viewpoint, for a better comprehension of what is at stake.

This analysis becomes all the more necessary inasmuch as the theologians themselves so readily admitted the second part of the distinction we have mentioned: the right to suppress obstacles to the proclamation of the gospel. But this formula can cover actions approximating a violent imposition of the faith, which of course is rejected in principle. Therefore we have not only risky consequences, but a theoretical inconsistency that it will be important to focus upon and to understand.

All of these theologians that we have seen, understandably enough, work within the theological framework that they have been bequeathed by preceding centuries. The process that has led to the distinction in question explains the ambiguities that we have indicated. As we shall see, over the course of bitter debates, Las Casas intuitively points to positions adopted in the early centuries of the church, and thus prevailing in a different historical context from the one that occasioned the positions on religious freedom maintained in the age of the defender of the Indians.

Indeed, in this matter in the course of history two major shifts, or changes of perspective, occur in the attitude and reflection of the church, and they are fraught with consequences. They will take place so gradually as to escape notice. Their subtlety will even suggest to many thinkers a doctrinal continuity with regard to their basic propositions that was not actually present. It will be in order here to conduct an excursion into this historical process. Chronologically, then, we are working backwards: having seen the later stages, we are now undertaking an examination of the earlier ones. But it has been worthwhile to analyze the way the problems were posed in the sixteenth century first, that we may be more alert to the key points in this evolution.[40]

A certain historical fact, constituted for the most part of a lengthy, complex process, is decisive for an understanding of the two focal shifts in question. We refer to the changes occurring within the Roman empire in the fourth century. Let us first see the overall meaning of these events for the Christian church.

Mediation of the Christian State

The profound religious significance of the sudden, unforeseeable historical events of fourth-century Europe is that of the encounter of the church with a self-contained world. Here was a society that had been formed before the birth of the church (and consequently apart from its inspiration), and that for manifold reasons, after having repressed Christianity, now comes forward in readiness to assist it in its task.

This will occasion the rise of an element of secular mediation — absent in the first centuries — in the salvific dialogue between God and the human being: political power.

Up until this moment, the church has known no human mediation, at least at this level of strength and organization, at the service of religious truth. The values and power of the world appear before it for the first time as presenting an enormous opportunity to carry the word of God to all human beings. The church's acceptance of this mediation will have very profound repercussions on its life — repercussions felt down to our very day.

The encounter with the temporal order occurred in the fourth century, transpiring especially in terms of the political element or, more concretely, of political power. In these new circumstances, what will become of religious freedom, and what will be the faculty of political authority to intervene in such matters?

The Edict of Milan (313) is partly a response to demands for a greater tolerance of Christianity, and it inaugurates freedom of worship in the empire. It is a document of the first importance for the history of the church, of course; but it is equally important for the question of religious freedom.[41] Freedom to practice the religion of one's choice is "regularized," "accorded," "not denied" by the emperors. The notion that religion is a *state affair,* then, is clearly entailed, and in a certain sense, we must say, dominates the text. Freedom of worship appears as a concession on the part of political power.

Thus we find ourselves dealing with a text that grants freedom to practice the religion of one's choice in order to preserve the peace of the empire, resting on the acknowledgment of a supreme divinity that can be worshiped by Christians *as well as* by pagans.[42] The actual acknowledgment of a religious truth is absent. At the same time, the document regards religion as entering into the purview of the state. Therefore, with Christianity extending throughout the empire, the emperors decide, as the culmination of a series of concessions that had been gradually wrested from them, to "tolerate" the Christian religion.

As we know, except for the hiatus of Julian the Apostate, official support for the church will constantly intensify,[43] until in 381 the Edict of Thessalonica establishes Christianity as the state religion. In this text, to be sure, we do find an outright assertion of religious truth. We are far, here, from the ambiguous natural theology that suffuses the Milan text. But this defense of the *true* religion is asserted to the detriment of religious *freedom:* anyone rejecting Christianity will be punished by the civil power. Religious unity is reestablished in the empire, and by force.[44] Emerging from a condition of mere tolerance (accorded by the Edict of Milan), Christianity quickly comes to be a "state religion" (with the Decree of Thessalonica). Thus the ideal of a Christian state is born, and it will have enormous influence in the history of the church all the way to today.[45]

The situation presented to the church is new. The context of the principles and concrete experience of religious freedom and the place of civil power in this area — so ardently defended in the first centuries, as we shall see — has changed. Demands have taken on a gentler tone. It is not the same thing to make demands on an authority hostile to religion, and on a state claiming to place itself at its service. Nevertheless, an echo will remain of the postulates defended in the previous stage. The historical facts just recalled explain how and why the two shifts in accent to which we have referred were produced. Now let us look at these changes themselves.

From Respect to Nonimposition

In the first centuries of the church, Christian thinkers energetically defended personal freedom in *matters of religion*. After the fourth century this continues, but with nuances that are important to underscore and that do not appear always to have had their effect. The change of expression is meaningful: now we have a defense of the freedom of the *act of faith*. This is not the same thing.

Freedom in Matters of Religion. The obstacles and repression imposed by Roman political power on the infant church lead to a quest for arguments in defense of the free exercise of religious life. This occasions a frequent recourse to a general consideration based on the principles of Roman law: the right of each citizen — and Christians are citizens too — to practice his or her own religion.[46] We have two extraordinary witnesses of this "conscientization" or raised consciousness: Tertullian and Lactantius. Separated by more than a century, both have left us texts reflecting the Christian community's experience in the area of religious freedom as well as in that of the right attitude to adopt in the face of the absolutism of political power.

For Tertullian, the terms of the question are clear. Christ has come to lead human beings to a knowledge of *truth*.[47] But the way to this knowledge has its starting point in *freedom* in religious matters. Tertullian then builds his apologia for Christianity, in his *Apologeticum* addressed to the Roman magistrates, on a defense of this freedom.

"It is a crime of impiety," he writes, "to deprive persons of freedom of religion and to prohibit them from choosing their deity, that is, not to permit me to honor whom I wish to honor. No one wishes forced homage, not even human beings."[48] Step by step, thanks to this acknowledgment of a free option in religious matters, Tertullian will prove that the human being is capable of reaching monotheism, and ultimately the Christian faith. His defense of freedom in matters of religion is not, then, something he takes casually. On the contrary, it is the cornerstone of his argumentation in his apologia for Christianity. In order to arrive at the *truth* of the Christian faith, one must begin with the *freedom* of the religious act, and this calls for a legal recognition of such freedom on the part of political authorities. It is not a matter, therefore, of freedom for Christians alone. Tertullian goes into the question in breadth and depth. We are dealing with a "human and natural right." God can be authentically worshiped only by persons who enjoy freedom from coercion.[49]

A century later, we find these ideas expressed in the same perspective, and with the same energy, by Lactantius. While less original a writer than Tertullian, Lactantius nevertheless managed to coin incisive formulas in the area of religious freedom.

Lactantius writes only a few years before the Edict of Milan. His concern, like that of all Christians of the era, is the hostility, to the point of persecution, manifested by the imperial political power. Lactantius echoes his predecessors in his assertion that "Christians long for reconciliation with pagans, for religious peace."[50] However, the peace of which he speaks is not to be obtained at the price of what is special and original in Christian faith: for Lactantius, Christianity is the true religion, and can be known only by divine revelation. Just as with Tertullian, the nonintervention of civil power is based on the rights of all persons to practice the religion of their choice.

Lactantius energetically asserts the value of freedom as a condition of religious life: "Religion is the one thing in which freedom has selected its domicile. It depends especially on the will. One cannot be obliged to worship what one will not worship. One can pretend, but one cannot be obliged to will. . . . No compact is possible between *truth* and *violence*."[51] All religion, and not only Christian faith, depends on free will. Truth and violence are incompatible. This confirms what we have already observed: that Lactantius loses sight neither of the existence of a religious truth, nor, on the other hand, of the fact that access to it must be free and not forced.

Tertullian and Lactantius faithfully reflect the Christian awareness of the first centuries, those antedating the *Pax Constantiniana*.[52] But they also express the permanent values of the Christian spirit and therefore will be cited in the Christian approach to this question throughout all succeeding ages.[53] They bear witness to the basic assertion of the church of the first centuries: freedom in matters of religion.

Freedom of the Act of Faith. Beginning with Constantine, as we have recalled, civil power is placed at the service of the mission of the church, and this new situation will gradually entail a subtle shift from the defense of *freedom in matters of religion* to that of the *freedom of the act of faith*. The freedom demanded will henceforth be focused on the act of faith and for all practical purposes — especially in a positive form — will not exist apart from that act. Freedom in matters of religion will henceforward be synonymous with the right not to be coerced by the forced imposition of the Christian faith. There is a shift in meaning here — one supremely revelatory of a basic mentality brought to the surface by circumstances and of capital importance for the question that concerns us.

St. Athanasius's battle with Arianism and with the support it enjoyed among political authorities rendered him attentive to issues that escaped the other Fathers of the Church. There is an Athanasian text that we might well cite as marking a transition: "Truth is not proclaimed by the sword," he writes, "or spears or soldiers. The special thing about religion is that it does not impose, but persuades."[54] The truth of the faith is not imposed, then, but this seems nevertheless to rest on a more general assertion: we are dealing with something proper to *all* religion.

But beginning in these years, it will rather be a matter, always or nearly always, of protests against the imposition *of the faith* by force. Augustine consecrates this idea in a trenchant formula that will traverse the centuries: "No one can believe without willing to."[55] The rejection of this compulsion responds to the most elementary exigencies of the gospel. The assertion is absolutely basic. Nevertheless, it must be observed that the mere fact of stating things in this way clearly indicates that the historical situation of the church has changed. This state of the question supposes the *possibility* that faith could be imposed by force. This alternative actually exists, and exists for the first time, from the moment Christianity becomes the official religion. This had not been the case in the early centuries, and this is why in those centuries — as we have seen — rather than the necessity of a *free acceptance of the Christian faith*, it was the *freedom of the human person* that was spoken of, as a matter of a "human and natural right," in order that each person might worship what he or she had freely chosen to worship.

Thus, circumstances had modified not only the accent of the assertions, but their very outlook. It is important for us to realize this. A defense of the freedom of the act of faith issues less from the awareness of a basic right of the human person than from a respect for the transcendence of God and for the divine action in souls. God bestows the gift of faith. Its imposition by force falsifies the situation, and therefore is to be proscribed. This expresses a profound, correct religious sense. Respect for God's activity was discernible in Tertullian and Lactantius as well, but it was accompanied by an energetic insistence on personal freedom. It is the latter that now loses momentum.

A reflection on human freedom in this area in function of the act of Christian faith rather than as a condition of all religious life will entail three altogether precise consequences.

1. The dominant outlook from now on will be that of the religious truth that is found exclusively in the church. That truth supposes a free acceptance and cannot be imposed by force. The human being therefore has a right not to be coerced, subjected to violence, with a view to this acceptance. But this is the same as a right not to be forced to adopt the Christian faith. Religious freedom is conceived in function of the act of faith. Apart from the latter, it does not exist in practice. Above all, it does not exist as a right to lead a personal and social life in accordance with one's own religious convictions. And as we know, one of Bartolomé de las Casas's most daring claims in the Indians' behalf is that they do indeed have the right to lead such a life. And so the outlook that we here present will gradually lead to the proposition that only those who profess the true faith have full rights in the matter of religion. The others, those in error, can at most be "tolerated"; and as we shall see further on, according to Thomas Aquinas, following Augustine, what is tolerated is an evil.

2. This explains the celebrated distinction — which we shall find strained to the breaking point in medieval theology — between, on the one hand, *pagans* and *Jews,* who have had no access to the faith, and, on the other, *heretics,* who have abandoned the faith after having accepted it. Thomas Aquinas clearly espouses this distinction, but the idea precedes him. With pagans and Jews, the necessity of a free acceptance of the faith will be kept in account, and this will dictate a more tolerant attitude. Heretics, on the contrary, will be regarded as guilty of withdrawing from the truth after having received the gift of faith and committing themselves to it: therefore they will deserve to be dealt with severely. Friar Bartolomé receives and basically accepts this traditional distinction, but he will take advantage of it in his rejection of the war being waged on the Indians, who are unbelievers of the first type.

3. Third, inasmuch as faith is regarded as a priceless gift to the human being and freedom is viewed exclusively in function of that gift, a series of means of force will be legitimated, not for *imposing* the faith, but — it will be said — simply for *fostering* it. This is what we have seen in the sixteenth-century theologians. The repression of evil, for example, thanks to the fear it inspires, will further good behavior.[56]

The wedge is in, then, for the use of force that will be defended as not intended to impose the faith (the principle will always be saved!) but only to remove the obstacles to its being freely embraced.[57] This is one of the arguments most vaunted in the sixteenth century for making war on the Indians. Its proponents can in this case appeal to a great many authorities, and to a certain tradition. And that is why, in the face of this reasoning, Las Casas seems to fight under difficult conditions.

These three consequences, as we have seen, have played a role in the theological discussions that interest us. But it is important to recall their historical roots and, accordingly, to see their limits and scope too, together with the manner in which they influence Las Casas's theological reflections. The step from a defense of religious liberty to an assertion of the freedom of the act of faith leads to a state of the question in terms of tolerance. But this, as we have said, supposes that civil authority is at the service of religious truth. The significance of that function, in the perspective inaugurated by Constantine, is the subject of our next section.

From Neutrality to the Service of the Faith

In these same centuries, for the reasons noted, another shift occurs that is meaningful for the matter at hand. In a first stage, the demand was that pagan civil power perform its task on its own ground: that of the political. In a second moment, owing to the rise of the Christian state, that power will begin to be expected to place itself at the service of the true faith and to acknowledge the autonomy, indeed the spiritual primacy, of the church.

Where Political Authority Has No Place. We have already cited one vector of the attitude of the first Christians in the face of the intolerance and totalitarianism of the pagan state: the proposition of the freedom of the individual religious act. Political power must not interfere on this terrain. The same conclusion will be drawn — but with limitations that will be of interest to us — by Christian writers of the early centuries, from another perspective: that of the defense of the freedom of the church, as a religious community, to practice its worship and to preach the gospel.

The Christian community, in the face of the claim of civil authority that it can oblige its members to offer sacrifice to pagan gods, is led to an intelligence of the faith that permits it not only to assert the free and personal character of religious comportment, but also to mark the limits of civil power. The latter must not tamper with the relationship between the human being and God.[58] The incompetency of political authority in this area is due to the fact that for Christians, in a manner that will gradually become more closely defined, the areas of power and of religion are distinct.[59] The task of the church is to preach the word of God and to lead human beings to salvation. It alone has a mediating role here. In order to accomplish its mission, it has at its disposition only spiritual means and the strength of conviction that comes from possession of the truth. Thus, it refuses to be trammeled by political authority.

This does not mean contempt for or a minimizing of the function of civil power. Christian writers of this time are fond of repeating St. Paul, to the effect that political authority comes from God and is therefore to be respected. But this supposes that the emperor accepts his place and not usurp that of God.[60] That is, he should keep to his own orbit, that of the preservation and promotion of an order of justice and social peace, and not meddle in the intimacy of religious conscience.

This declaration of religious freedom as a human right and the incompetency of political power in this area did not entail a softening of the demands of religious truth on the part of the first Christians. Rather, they look upon this freedom as the ultimate foundation of those requirements. Indeed, because there is a truth, the human being is bound to arrive at it and freely to put it in practice. At the same time, this truth in matters of religion goes beyond the competency of political power. *Freedom* and *truth*, then, are the extreme terms of the subject that concerns us. In their dialectical tension resides the richness of their relation — but also their vulnerability, as later events will prove. Freedom and truth or, in more concrete terms, free persons and the true God (only *false* gods can accept *forced* homage, Tertullian and Lactantius tell us) are what is at stake. When all is said and done, it is with this relationship (between God and the human person) that we are dealing when we speak of freedom in matters of religion.

In the Service of Religious Truth. The incompetency of political power in matters of religion appeared in the first centuries as a condition of the freedom of the person in this area. We have seen that the situation that emerged with the Edict of Milan caused the accent to be placed on the freedom of the act of faith. A parallel slippage occurs with regard to the role falling to civil power: rather than asserting its *incompetency* in matters of religion, Christians will henceforward maintain that political authority *should not intervene* in internal problems, in ecclesiastical questions. In this perspective, it is the *freedom of the church* vis-à-vis civil power that will be defended. This nuance is of the utmost importance for our subject. It helps us to understand the texts of the era with which we are concerned and to avoid the illusion of a simple continuity when actually there is a change in outlook.

Beginning with Constantine, political interference in church matters will be the common rule. Here is the beginning of a constant struggle on the part of the church to defend its proper originality. In a way, the situation favored the propagation of religious truth. But dangers lurked, so that the church also asserted its distinction from civil authority and claimed its freedom of action.

This line of demarcation between the two powers (temporal and spiritual) seems at first blush to stand in continuity with what had been defended in the early centuries. But circumstances had actually changed, and one of the changes that took place was that the defenders of the freedom of the church now took a different view of the function of civil authority when it came to religion. For these thinkers, temporal power ought to offer a service to the cause of God for which the church labored. Ambrose of Milan, for example, will have no hesitation in declaring that political power should operate in the direct service of the true faith.[61] To be sure, Ambrose places a very high value on the independence of the church.[62] But he does so precisely in the sense of a primacy of the spiritual and of a civil power at its service. The distinction between the two powers is valid especially in one direction: from the state to the church, and less in the opposite direction.

But once this duty to the church on the part of civil power is asserted, is it not likewise being asserted that religion falls within the competency of civil authority, although in subordination to the church? Herein lies the ongoing ambiguity of the situation that came into being with Constantine, and it will give rise to a veritable political pendulum: depending on the circumstances and personalities at hand, the accent will fall now on "service to the church," now on "religion as an affair of state." And the seed is sown for what will later be called theocratism and royalism.

In this perspective, it is only to be expected that the attitude taken toward non-Christian religions will be one of civil *tolerance*. One tolerates an evil. In this case, the evil is religious error: in principle, religious error ought to be eliminated, but in certain circumstances it is permissible not to repress it. Church authorities will frequently direct the civil power not to repel it by violence or to moderate state measures taken with regard to those who are in error. But all of these demands only confirm the attribution to political authority of a right to intervene in religious questions.[63] The spirit of the gospel, of course, imposes an obligation of gentleness and moderation.[64]

We are far indeed from the concept of the incompetency of political authority in religious matters proclaimed in the early centuries.

Nevertheless, the freedom of the church vis-à-vis the civil power is maintained with equal energy, on the basis of something that, despite all, has not been lost from view: the distinction of functions between the powers. The survival of these ideas, despite lacunae and eclipses that may have made us think they had been forgotten, is explained by texts like the celebrated one of Gelasius I (d. 496). The pope sharply and firmly defines the correct relationship between church and state. The teaching expressed in the document is surprising, in the context of the age.[65]

In spite of this great text, however, the union of church and civil society will grow ever closer in the centuries to come. The church will accommodate itself to a situation of privilege that seems to facilitate its task of leading men and women to the faith and maintaining them in the same. This had doubtless been the intention of Constantine himself, who, of course, was a political figure. But personages of the church, too, labored most diligently in its behalf.

3. *Thomas Aquinas's Doctrine of Religious Toleration*

The evolution that we have just sketched, which led to the gradually increasing importance of a perspective of power, constitutes the context in which Thomas Aquinas's thought is situated. Thomas's authority will often be invoked for the purpose of justifying the use of a certain violence with respect to the Indians, under the pretext of evangelization. Las Casas will then have to get right into the distinctions of the common master. But as we have said, he will also delve into the most ancient Christian tradition as well in support of his own position and in order to maintain his polemics with his adversaries.

In Thomas Aquinas we find the first clear, orderly presentation of a doctrinal schema where tolerance is concerned. In the essentials, Thomas reflects the mentality of his age. But he also represents, thanks to his own contributions, a moment of maturation in reflection on the question.[66] His influence in the area of religious freedom will be decisive in later centuries. His teaching will even be used, as late as the nineteenth century, by the proponents of the celebrated distinction between the "thesis" (the ideal, a religion of the state) and the "hypothesis" (the adverse reality that makes it advisable to accept equal status with other religions). Without using the same terms, Leo XIII himself will endorse this theory, and it will be unambiguously abandoned by the magisterium of the church only at Vatican II.

Arguing in behalf of the Indians, Bartolomé de Las Casas will constantly appeal to their condition as pagans to demand in their regard a different treatment from that which heretics ought to receive and criticize his antagonists for failing to notice the difference between the two situations. The distinction between these two kinds of unbelief is confirmed by the authority of Thomas Aquinas. We find a synthesis of his thinking in two questions of the *Summa Theologiae:* "On Unbelief," and "On Heresy." For the sake of brevity and precision, we may well take these two successive texts as our guideline for a treatment of the subject.[67]

As he opens his study on unbelief, the Doctor of Aquino identifies, with all precision, the two senses (as we have recalled them) in which unbelief can be understood:

> It can be regarded as a pure negation, as when someone is called an unbeliever on the basis of the simple fact of not having the faith. Or again, unbelief can be understood in the sense of an opposition to the faith, that is, when someone refuses to hear [the proclamation of] the faith or holds it in contempt. (*ST*, II–II, q. 10, a. 1, c.)

In the second case, we must impute a *sin* to the unbeliever, as someone rejecting the true faith. In the first, on the other hand, we are witnessing one of the results of original sin: here unbelief is a trial, a hardship, and not a fault. The distinction dates from the early centuries. But here it is formulated clearly and systematically.

What renders unbelief culpable — sinful, and thus deserving of punishment — is a voluntary rejection of the faith. For Thomas, then, heresy will constitute a graver matter than the unbelief of pagans and Jews.[68] This leads him to propose a different manner of behavior with regard to the two groups. On the basis of a common position of the canonists of his time, he further maintains that the church's jurisdiction — and inalienable right of coercion — extends only to those who have received the faith, the baptized.[69]

Having made these distinctions, the Dominican master asks, apropos of each of the two kinds of unbelief, whether they may be tolerated.[70] For him to tolerate means, following Augustine of Hippo,[71] adopting an attitude that in certain circumstances may be permissible with regard to *evil* — here, religious error and its consequences. But, and this must be emphasized, Thomas is addressing the question of tolerance with regard to unbelievers on the part of "human government." That is, we are dealing with the posture of *political power* with regard to error in religious matters. This state of the question, then, presupposes as already established the principle according to which, in the eyes of that authority — in strict association with spiritual power — to be outside the Christian faith is a social *evil*, so that this will justify direct interference in the religious area on the part of civil authority. This position, a result of the historical process that we have recalled, is fraught with implications.

Under these conditions, may unbelievers and heretics be tolerated?

Civil Toleration for Jews and Gentiles[72]

Thomas Aquinas's position clearly favors toleration with regard to pagan and Jewish religion. His argumentation rests basically on two principles that Friar Bartolomé will frequently appeal to.

The *first* of these principles is motivated by considerations of political prudence. One must act in function of a good to be obtained or an evil to be avoided. Thomas applies it to the case of tolerance from a point of departure in a comparison between divine and human government: the latter has received its authority from the former, and should therefore imitate it in its conduct. But Christian revelation shows us that God is tolerant, in particular circumstances, with persons who are in error. Therefore civil power should also be tolerant, in the case of unbelievers.[73] The competency of political authority in these matters, let us repeat, is acknowledged as a basic principle — a legacy of earlier centuries, and one which in Thomas's time no one disputed. Accepting this principle, then, Thomas tends to provide orientations of political prudence that are inspired by the Christian spirit. After all, we are not dealing solely with the need for a personal attitude of understanding and charity vis-à-vis religious error in religious matters.[74] Rather, what we have is a transposition of this need to the plane of the social order and the common good. That is, we are dealing with a task incumbent upon the civil power.

Let us observe that these considerations preclude any notion that toleration of error is an immoral act in itself. The best evidence is that God proceeds in this fashion. In no way does this mean a renunciation of the rights of religious truth. It simply means that the defense of this truth by political authority must not become something "absolute or unconditional."[75] The reason is that, alongside the rights of truth, other considerations come into play, which make it possible to "obtain a higher good or avoid a greater evil" and make room for a broader attitude, one more adequate to the circumstances.

We are seeing the application of a broader principle, one that plays an important role in the theology of the Angelic Doctor and one that he himself will bring to bear on other matters treated in the *Summa* (see I, q. 19, a. 9). Bartolomé de Las Casas will frequently appeal to it as the basis of his call for a humane and moderate treatment of the Indians.

But what, in the case of unbelievers, are the good to be secured and the evil to be avoided that justify an attitude of tolerance? Here

Thomas distinguishes between Jews and pagans. In the rites of the former, Christian truth is somehow prefigured, and they therefore constitute a testimonial to our faith. Thus there is an actual *good* in tolerating them.[76] Pagan worship, on the other hand, contributes no element of either truth or utility. It can only be tolerated, then, in view of some *evil* to be avoided.

Apropos of this last point, Aquinas maintains the urgency of avoiding the situation that constitutes precisely one of Las Casas's great concerns in the process of the evangelization of the Indian nations: the situation of "scandal or dissent that may arise from this intolerance, or the impediment to the salvation of unbelievers who, little by little, if they are tolerated, will be converted to the faith" (*ST*, II–II, q. 10, a. 11, c.). This "scandal or dissent" is an evil to be avoided, and adequate means must be taken to do so. In the Indies, Friar Bartolomé will say, the harm already done is enormous and is almost irreparable.

All of this reasoning is inspired, within the conceptual framework of the age, by a concern of faith. The good to be gained, and the evil to be avoided, in the attitude adopted by the civil power, are explicitly referred to the exigencies of Christian faith, and to the salvation of unbelievers.

The *second* principle is more important. The actual basis of toleration for Thomas is the free character of the act of faith. We must not lose sight of this. Bartolomé de Las Casas will make freedom one of the hinges on which his argumentation on the subject of the proper manner of evangelizing in the Indies will turn. But between his position and that of the Doctor of Aquino there are differences to be noted. We have already seen the complex historical process underlying the core assertion. Let us now recall how Thomas's teaching differs from that of Las Casas.

In Thomas we find a pellucid defense of freedom when it comes to accepting the Christian faith. When all is said and done, considerations of good to be secured or of greater evil to be avoided are sustained by the crucial importance of being free in order to make an option for faith. The application of this principle of political prudence will depend on concrete circumstances, but will in all cases avoid slipping into coercion. Thomas has indicated the importance of safeguarding the freedom of the act of faith in an earlier article, on which we have just commented. In it, Thomas asks whether unbelievers may be forced to accept the faith (*ST*, II–II, q. 10, a. 8). His response is in the negative, of course, "since to believe is something voluntary," as he puts it, referring to Augustine and with him the ancient Christian tradition that we have seen.[77]

This solicitude to save the freedom of the act of faith appears, paradoxically, even in the Angelic Doctor's justification of the crusade against the infidels. No one can be obliged to believe. All that Christians can do, in this case, is to compel unbelievers *not to prevent others* from being able to make free profession of the Christian faith.

> Therefore Christ's faithful frequently undertake war against the infidels, not, of course, to force them to believe (since even if after having conquered them they were to take them captive, they would leave the infidels at liberty to believe if that were to be their will), but with the purpose of obliging them not to obstruct faith in Christ. (*ST*, II–II, q. 10, a. 8, c.)

The justification is a religious one and will unintentionally open the door to many abuses. Be that as it may, however, our attempt to understand our author in terms of the mentality of his era will require an emphasis on his concern to maintain, even in this thorny, muddled question, his thesis of the freedom of the act of faith.

The same concern, if in more interesting fashion and on the basis of new reasons, appears in the question of the baptism of the children of unbelievers against their parents' will. Aquinas invokes the custom of the church, which is to deny baptism in these circumstances, and justifies this with an appeal to natural law.[78]

With this posture, Thomas Aquinas does not depart from the canonical and theological tradition he receives. However, it becomes particularly interesting that he should found his opposition to this baptism on "natural justice" and the "natural rights" of unbelievers — in the case at hand, on the rights of parents with regard to their children. On this concrete point, there is an echo in Aquinas of the language of the first centuries on the matter of religious freedom. But Thomas does not extend this outlook to other aspects of the question.[79]

Repression of Heresy

Thomas Aquinas's position is considerably different when he comes to the matter of heresy.[80] On this point he will only repeat the theology of his time. Heresy is comparable to other human offenses and is even regarded, in the last instance, as deserving of the death penalty at the hands of civil authority. The conclusion takes us by surprise.[81] The Dominican master softens his opinion slightly when he indicates that, out of considerations of compassion, the church must abandon a heretic to the secular arm only in case of obstinacy and after earnest admonition.[82]

How is one to reconcile this terrible severity with a defense of the freedom of the act of faith as recalled in the foregoing section? Thomas himself has raised this difficulty, citing Augustine, who had said that believing is a matter of freedom, so that "if the will cannot be forced," it would seem that "unbelievers cannot be obliged to receive the faith." His response to this difficulty is based on a distinction between *access* to faith and its *preservation* once it is received: "Accepting the faith is a matter of will; preserving it once accepted is a matter of obligation" (*ST* II–II, q. 10, a. 8, ad 3). According to the mentality of his age, the master does not admit the possibility of an *ignorancia juris* (ignorance of the "law" — here, of Christian doctrine) on the part of dissidents with regard to faith, while he does acknowledge it in Jews and pagans.

The principle of the freedom of the faith does not hold, then, in the case of heresy, as it has held in that of Jews and gentiles. Let us be more precise. We must distinguish two aspects in the heretic's situation. The *first* is that, for Aquinas, the faith cannot be abandoned without culpability, without subjective fault. Once accepted, religious truth binds one's conscience. Anyone rejecting its integrity cannot, consequently, demand respect for his or her religious convictions. Let us note that this aspect of Thomas's rigorous position with regard to heresy will be gradually softened in centuries to come, and this on the basis of another element of his own thought. We refer to his teaching on the erroneous conscience, to which we shall refer at length later in this book. But he himself does not make this connection. Others will establish it, recalling — and invoking Thomas's own statements to the effect — that the immediate norm of moral conduct is in the dictates of one's conscience; and they will show that this is valid even for the dissident in the faith, the heretic.[83]

The *second* aspect that will be important to indicate has more of a political character and reinforces the severity of the position in question. Abandonment of the faith, for the Doctor of Aquino, rends social unity. Heresy is an "infectious vice,"[84] and the salvation of other Christians is at stake (*ST* II–II, q. 11, a. 3, c.). Thomas cites Jerome: "Arius in Alexandria was but a spark, but as it was not quenched forthwith, it became a worldwide conflagration" (ibid.). Heresy, then, is a social evil, and precisely therefore may be castigated with the death penalty. The Dominican master introduces a nuance into his thesis: the application of this punishment by the temporal power is justified only if the offense is sufficiently grave and if such punishment becomes necessary in order to preserve social peace.

In the historical context of Christendom, the social factor is a determining element in the severity practiced toward heretics. Faith, in this context, is a pillar of social unity: religious dissidence, then, constitutes a breach that threatens society itself. Thus, heresy emerges from the confines of the purely religious and impinges on the political world as well. Here we find something like what has occurred with the first aspect, previously indicated, regarding the obligatory character of maintaining the faith. Another element of Thomas's teaching will modify the consequences to be deduced from the concept of the defense of social unity. This time it will be a matter of the defense of the autonomy of the temporal vis-à-vis the spiritual, which Thomas's theology definitely maintains. In the centuries after Aquinas, many will rely on these points of his thought in order to construct a political philosophy that takes its distance from medieval Christendom's symbiosis of the political and the religious. This critique will deprive of its validity the argument from social unity that Thomas himself wields here in favor of the repression of heresy.

Paradoxically, then, in Thomas's own work perspectives are found that permit further progress to positions of greater respect for religious freedom.[85] The Doctor of Aquino, however, does not explicitly incorporate the ideas that he defends at least in seed with regard to the erroneous conscience and the distinction between the respective areas of political and religious power. His own teaching remains at the level of a tolerance for Jews and gentiles and the repression of heretics.

Las Casas does not subject Thomas Aquinas's position on heresy to a rigorous critical examination.[86] This was not his problem in the Indies. If he mentions it at all, it is to show that the case is not verified in the dwellers of these lands. Bartolomé's concern is to deny that the behavior approved by Thomas with regard to heretics is applicable to Indians. The latter must be led to the faith by persuasion, not coercion. Despite all, Thomas constructs the platform of a profitable reflection on how to behave toward the Indians — the manner urged by Friar Bartolomé.[87] But Bartolomé will have to go further.

As we see, sixteenth-century theology is in the debt of a lengthy historical process and of the ideological evolution accompanying that process. Its theses on the freedom of the act of faith and the right of political power to interfere in religious matters do not permit — despite all good intentions — a perfectly clear state of the question in the matter of a peaceful evangelization. For that, one had to go beyond positions that failed to do justice to the first intuitions of the Christian community. The most serious obstacle to accomplishing this lay in the basic factor underlying the itinerary that we have recalled: Christianity's position at the side of power. The change in perspective will presuppose a new historical perspective: the viewpoint of the victims, the dregs of humanity. This is not reached in one fell swoop. It takes time to see things from a starting point in the rights of the scourged Christs of the Indies. It takes time to mount a defense of their life and freedom on this basis. But it will occasion a rich theological reflection.

Chapter 6 —————————————————

The Only Way

Las Casas's initial and fundamental concern for the proclamation of the gospel is his motivation for the composition of his first work in the implementation of that task. We refer to his *De Unico Vocationis Modo*, or *The Only Way*.[1] He never published his treatise. But as J. A. Barreda declares, it is the "doctrinal font" of many other, later works, and Bartolomé will refer to it constantly.[2]

The central thesis of that book is one we know well. There is only one way to evangelize: by peaceful means, that is, by persuasion and dialogue. All use of force is radically to be excluded. Friar Bartolomé argues with erudition and in the grand theological style.[3] All of this has been analyzed altogether competently and profitably, and it would not be to our purpose to enter into the details of what is proposed in that work.[4] The reader who wishes may consult the available scholarly examinations.

Our purpose in citing *The Only Way* is to emphasize its theological aspects. In particular, we shall be interested in the notion of religious freedom and transcendence of faith that forms the basis of Las Casas's enormous respect for Christianity's message of life and for the right of persons to implement that message in all freedom. Precisely because he is aware of the gospel, he is also aware of the viewpoint of the non-Christian peoples destined to hear it and, it may be, accept it. This for Las Casas means taking Christ as one's model for all evangelization.

There is a very special and controversial case. We refer to the matter of human sacrifice and cannibalism. In the minds of practically all of the theologians of the sixteenth century, at least until Las Casas's massive intervention in his *Apología*, human sacrifice or cannibalism on the part of the Indians would plainly justify a declaration of war on the Indians.[5] The position Bartolomé sets forth in his *Apología* is based on an effort to understand the religious customs of the Indians. It shows us how far his notion of religious freedom could go. The analyses we have conducted in the two first chapters of this second part of the present volume will afford us a clear view of the sense of God, and of the gift of life that comes from God, that governs Las Casas's treatment of this most uncomfortable matter.

1. Christ, the Evangelizer's Model

It is sometimes said that in matters relating to the Indies Las Casas and Sepúlveda represent two extreme attitudes and that the correct position would be somewhere on middle ground, somewhere in between the two great adversaries. Besides, it is said, the majority of the theologians of the age will be found to hold such middle positions. But in the field of ideas, the arithmetic of the mean is not necessarily the best criterion for an evaluation of the values attaching to these ideas. On the contrary, it will only afford a facile — and theatrical — ploy, a way of obviating an antecedent critical examination of the reasons brought to bear in defense of an idea, and of the consequences entailed in its practice. A consideration of the latter — the practical consequences — is always the valid approach. But this is especially the case when, as here, what is under consideration are the wars being waged in the Indies under the pretext of evangelization.

Furthermore, these so-called extreme positions have for various reasons exerted an enormous historical influence. And they are obligatory points of reference for all who address these subjects.[6] Briefly, for the reasons noted, let us examine the theological axes of the Lascasian thesis. To this end, while an appeal to the *De Unico* remains of capital importance, we need to see the question in the context of the Lascasian corpus as a whole.

The Real Obstacle to the Faith

We have seen the importance, for those who addressed this topic, of the matter of impediments to the proclamation of the Christian message. This holds for Las Casas too, only his approach is from the other side of the coin. According to Bartolomé, the major obstacle to the evangelization of the natives of the Indies is the countertestimonial of Christians themselves. He says it in a thousand ways and on a wide variety of occasions. Let us examine a text that, additionally, will have other implications of interest to us.

The harassments and injustices of which they are the victims hold the Indians at a distance from the faith. They also explain and justify the sense of aversion experienced by the Indians in the presence of the proclamation of the gospel. Nor are these people alone here. "In my judgment," Bartolomé writes, "there is no other reason why Saracens,

Turks, and other unbelievers refuse to embrace our faith than the fact that we deny them with our conduct what we offer them with our words." What holds for the Indians holds as well for the historical adversaries of the Spanish people, the Saracens and the Turks. These too ought to be called to the gospel through dialogue and persuasion, not war. Military intervention is but "a pretext to rob others of their property and subjugate their provinces." The appropriate thing would be for unbelievers — whoever they are — to "see the Christian life resplendent in our conduct" (*Apología*, 121–121v).[7]

Here, then, is the real obstacle to the faith.[8] Its suppression is in the hands of the Christians themselves. Christian comportment ought to be consistent with Christian words. No weapons are needed to eliminate this obstacle, much less weapons used against unbelievers. Furthermore, unless this hindrance is removed — if Christians continue to behave as they do and theologians continue to advance their erroneous justifications for the use of arms in order to evangelize — the Iberians' sole legitimate title to a presence in the Indies will be vitiated in its very root. We already know why: without freedom, there is no such thing as the preaching of the gospel (see, for example, *Carta al príncipe Felipe*, 1544, *O.E.* 5:215a).

But there is more. Not only are unbelievers not obliged to believe Christians who act in this manner; they actually have the right to use force to repel their invaders, who abuse them and attempt to impose their customs and religion on them. When it comes to the use of force, the justifying reasons are actually on the side of the Indians.[9] The argument will surely come as a surprise to those self-assured persons who act and reason on the basis of their own power, interests, and "truth."

Las Casas does not stop at a denunciation of what is occurring in the Indies. He contributes elements calculated to aid in the discernment of what, in these occurrences, is in conformity with or contrary to the gospel and justice. Engulfed in the hail of fire of those who favored war on the Indians, or permitted it under easy conditions, the Dominican appeals to the canonical and theological distinctions that might contribute to bringing a bit of order into the chaos.

One of these distinctions is the classic one between Jews and pagans, on the one hand, versus heretics on the other, of which we have already treated. Taking careful aim from behind this parapet, Bartolomé rejects any application to the Indians of the rigor of the dominant position of his time with regard to the second member of the distinction: the heretics, dissidents from the faith. Sepúlveda, who acknowledges the distinction only formally, is forced on a number of occasions to pay attention to it. He forgets to apply it, and in his oblivion of something so elementary "the Reverend Doctor injures himself in the face with his own weapons," Las Casas says (*Aquí se contiene,* 1552, *O.E.* 5:321b).

With an attitude that, doubtless, has much of the defensive about it, Las Casas tries to make it plain that in the Indies the only thing under discussion is what to do about unbelievers, or persons corresponding to the first part of the disjunction. The traditional posture with respect to heresy, therefore, remains outside the purview of his critical examination; ordinarily, when he mentions it at all, he only repeats the commonly received doctrine and observes that it does not enter into account in the concrete reality of the Indies. At times, however, he takes his distance from that doctrine and exhorts his addressees to a respect for the person of the heretic. Still in a framework of his polemics with Sepúlveda, for example, Bartolomé applies biblical language figuratively, as was customarily done in those days when one dealt with these matters, and writes:

> To *all heretics,* then, and above all to those who have never received the faith nor offended the Church, the first thing to be offered is peace, with a declaration and proclamation of Christ himself, the Son of God who is truth. And battle done with them must be with the testimonials of Scripture; and their wounding, with the meek knife of the gospel, in a preaching benign and gentle, with meekness and humility. (*O.E.* 5:321a–b; emphasis added)

Peaceful means, paradoxically presented in the terminology of war and weaponry, are the sole appropriate means when it comes to winning to the faith even dissidents. In all cases, the gospel must be offered with kindness and humility.

But as we have already indicated, it is not over this second category of our disjunction that Las Casas lies awake at night. For Bartolomé, the important thing is the category of unbelievers, into which the Indians fall. The key distinction for him, then, will actually be Cajetan's celebrated distinction among three classes of unbelievers:

1. Those who "*de facto* and *de jure* are the subjects of Christian princes, as are Jews and Moors living in Christian territories." This was a common situation in Europe, with Spain constituting no more than an especially striking case in point.

2. "Others, who are subjects *de jure* but not *de facto,* inasmuch as they occupy Christian territories — for example, Turks, those sworn enemies of Christians — and on such, war may licitly be waged." Here too we are on familiar ground. The complex history of the Mediterranean basin had created many intricate situations between Christians and Turks.

3. "But there are others who are subjects of our princes neither *de*

facto nor *de jure,* such as pagans who inhabit lands where the name of Christ has never sounded." This is the case with the dwellers of the Indies.

The law of the age ascribed to Christian princes an authority over their infidel subjects that was of varying scope and disputed status. It likewise endorsed the right of Christian nations to make war on unbelievers in order to recover lands regarded as usurped by them (for example, Asia Minor and North Africa). Cajetan's third category entailed a relative novelty (relative, because it was actually the case of peoples of Northern Europe during the Middle Ages). In this third case, the use of arms is unjustified. "The faith of Jesus Christ," insists the theologian and cardinal, may not be "propagated in this fashion."[10]

We are not surprised by Las Casas's enthusiasm for this text, which sheds a special light of its own on the matter with which he is so concerned. Cajetan's distinction was as mighty an endorsement of his own position as it was uncomfortable for theologians like Sepúlveda.[11] Bartolomé had learned Cajetan's more generous distinction early enough: the cardinal's work had figured among those he read and studied during his first quiet years as a Dominican on Hispaniola.[12] It is not cited in the *De Unico,* but there is a transparent mention of it in one chapter (the third) that does not currently form part of this work (see *De Unico,* 192v; *The Only Way,* 228–29). He does allude to it explicitly in one other text dating from the same period, the *Carta a un personaje* (1535, *O.E.* 5:64b).

In later works, Bartolomé will refer to Cajetan's text and the three classes of "infidels" frequently and explicitly. He builds his fence around Indian rights with all meticulousness. Indians are unbelievers, not dissidents in faith, and unbelievers of the third category to boot. There must be no making war on them under the pretext of evangelization. The Dominican develops his point with a classification that is an amalgam of the two already recalled. He introduces a "second" or "third species of unbeliever": "heretics and apostates."[13] Cajetan's third category is displaced to fourth, and in it fall the Indians, Las Casas declares unequivocally.[14] He concludes that these nations are to be "loved as ourselves, as we seek, by teaching and good example, to attract and win them to Christ" (*Doce dudas,* 1564, *O.E.* 5:489a).

After all, these are nations indeed. Las Casas never lets us forget this. Whenever he examines these topics, which are matters of life and culture, his reference is always to a people. Belief, whatever the religion in question, is always a community affair. Furthermore, as we have had occasion to observe, what Bartolomé is fighting for is respect for the freedom of individuals and peoples alike.

Dialogue by Deeds

Nothing, then, justifies waging war on the Indians. Freedom is an indispensable condition for a genuine acceptance of the faith. Forcefully to deprive the Indians of the possibility of arriving at this acceptance through a process of maturation is to violate the principle indicated. Hence Bartolomé's concern to respect "the time and space for a conversion" of those to whom the gospel is proclaimed (*Apología*, 171v). War is an impossible shortcut to a destination that requires time because human freedom requires time. The results of war are counterproductive. The evils of war occasion either the rejection of faith in a loving God or a feigned conversion on the part of those who feel their helplessness in the face of Christian destructive might.[15]

In the *De Unico*, Bartolomé rejects any manner of evangelizing that would be contrary to the one he champions. He is dealing, he says, with persons who think "it would be quicker and better done if they subjected pagans willy-nilly to Christian political power. Once the pagans were beaten, they could be preached to without trouble" (*De Unico*, 149; *The Only Way*, 117). Here, had we needed it, is proof positive that long before Sepúlveda ever arrived on the scene there were those who maintained the thesis of antecedent subjugation. The Cordovan presented his position, toward the middle of the sixteenth century, in exceptionally articulate fashion, but it was not an exceptional position. Bartolomé's lofty sense of God and of the demands of human freedom forbid him to endorse such methods of proclaiming the gospel. "When I speak of acts of war," he writes, "I speak of the pinnacle of all evils" (*Apología*, 206v).

Las Casas's doctrine is at the antipodes of the proposition that a war may legitimately be waged in order thereupon to evangelize. From his very first texts, he denounces armed intervention as contravening the Indians' right to life and liberty and as contradicting the principal end in view, which is the proclamation of the gospel. His questionable, failed experiment in Cumaná, the Enriquillo episode, and especially his first work, the *De Unico*, lead him to settle his thesis definitively on this point. That thesis resides in his vehement defense and in-depth justification of peaceful evangelization not as the *best* means of evangelization (as some theologians and missioners will be willing to characterize it, thereupon to maintain its inviability), but as the *only* acceptable method of evangelization. Precisely this differentiates our Dominican from practically all of the theologians of the time who address the matter. Closer to his position were some of the outstanding missioners of the age.

Bartolomé's profound evangelical inspiration functioned as a challenge to his contemporaries. It helped render the positions of many of them more flexible and left an indelible mark on the theologians of the so-called second Salamancan generation. But many thinkers reproached him with what they called his stubbornness and lack of realism. Today, on the contrary, it is difficult for us to comprehend the mentality of persons who in one way or another could have attempted to justify the use of arms in a proclamation of the Christian message. And we see Bartolomé's "extreme" position as the obvious, correct one.

Before the composition of the *De Unico* (if we accept the date proposed by Helen Rand Parish), Las Casas declared that Christ, who had come to reveal God, "the Father of mercies," commanded his successors to "make the gift of his peace, do good to all, and, with the sweetness of their virtues and good works, give freely of what they had freely received, endeavoring to exert an attraction — as our forebears were attracted to good works by peace and love, [as they beheld] those who preached God in their holy petition laying down their lives [for their beliefs]." To give gratis what one has received gratis is the great evangelical norm. Bartolomé can only wonder, then: Why are such ravenous wolves and cruel tyrants sent to the Indies? This is not what Christ did when he sent his disciples to the mission fields. And our manner of announcing the gospel ought to be inspired in his example (*Carta al Consejo*, 1531, O.E. 5:49a).

This will be the high theme of the *De Unico.* Jesus' goodness, his attention to all, especially to the very neediest, will show us the route to take. The conclusion is clear as crystal: "Christ gave his apostles permission and power to preach the gospel to those willing to hear it, and that only! Not power to punish the unwilling by any force, pressure, or harshness. He granted no power to apostle or preacher of the faith to force the unwilling to listen, no power to punish even those who drove the apostles out of town" (*De Unico*, 64; *The Only Way*, 77; based on Matt. 10:14–15). There are no gray areas when it is evangelization that is at issue.

Jesus' testimonial is composed of words and deeds. Here Las Casas cites a capital text of the Gospel of Luke (4:16–20), the "messianic program." He begins by observing that Christ sent his disciples to proclaim his message and dispel idolatry without weapons and violence. Their only arms would be "virtue and holiness and doctrine and requests and promises." And today, "by decree of the Holy Spirit," who continues the work of Christ, the task is to convert "these Indies of ours." Let the behavior of the apostles be the model: "As they did with those, so let us do with these."

The source and model must be Jesus. After all, "he was the first to do and perform himself whatever he taught and commanded his apostles." Now, according to the text of Luke in which Jesus specifies his mission with regard to the "manner of converting unbelievers," he showed his disciples "that they must make notification and declaration to them, and bring them the year of jubilee" and the forgiveness of their sins. That is to say, he was bringing these peoples a life based on justice and reconciliation. This same mission of giving life is also the object of the other verses of the text, which Las Casas goes on to quote in Latin (*The Only Way,* 86): Christ has come to evangelize the poor, to preach liberty to captives, to give sight to the blind.[16]

Las Casas rightly says that these are "his proper works" and that they "are no less law than his words." Consequently, it is against "the divine law of the gospel and against the precept and express intention of God...to seek or to contemplate the punishment by any human power of the offenses of idolatry, or other kind of sin, committed by authentically gentile people." It is impossible to preach by death faith in him who said, "I came that they might have life and have it to the full" (John 10:10). This text from the *Octavo remedio* (O.E. 5:81b–82a) is central, and Bartolomé's citation of the Joannine passage governs his entire thesis: a message of life may not — under any pretext — be proclaimed through destruction.

No one, in Las Casas's time, was more sensitive to this contradiction than he was himself.[17] This was no mere question of pastoral strategy. A peaceful evangelization is dictated by the very content of the message to be preached. If the message is life, then the means may not be death. The image of the "Father of mercies," Jesus' divine Parent, would be obliterated. Coercion in evangelization makes God appear as "a violent, wicked tyrant" (*H.I.,* bk. 1, ch. 24, *O.E.* 1:92b) who approves all of the harassments and injustices perpetrated by self-styled believers.

Thus Las Casas's inspiration in the gospel and experience in the Indies converge and fuse, accentuating the role of deeds in any Christian testimonial to the God who is love. In words, perhaps, this testimonial was already being offered, in certain regions of the Indies. But in each case these words were promptly belied by the behavior of those who pronounced them, or at least by the preachers' companions. Christians' orthopraxis, as we now express it, gives substance to the orthodoxy of their proclamation and wins that proclamation a hearing. Bartolomé's whole life was faithful to this perspective. In one of his last works, he writes:

> The one who would teach others must precede the teaching with works that will be an example of the words. Thus, the indoctrination will be more by works than by words, as it was with the apostles, who first taught by examples of how to live, and

then by words: indeed, now there was no need of words, for the works cried aloud. (*De Thesauris*, 54)[18]

It is an affair of far-reaching implications. Deeds speak for themselves. Paradoxically, words of themselves do not.

The way God is proclaimed is also the way one draws near God: along the pathway of deeds. Las Casas refers to the gospel that best emphasizes this perspective: Matthew's. The deeds of Jesus' followers turn others toward their "heavenly Father" (Matt. 5:16, cited in *De Thesauris*, 54v). Here Bartolomé is citing the concluding verse of the first pericope of the Sermon on the Mount, the passage in which Jesus specifies the attitudes that ought to characterize the disciple by enunciating them in the Beatitudes. They are attitudes that must come to expression in deeds addressed to one's neighbor, and in that neighbor, addressed to God. A solid christology underlies this way of seeing things.

Faith: Beyond Noncoercion

In the light of these postulates, which are rooted in his notion of God and of the Reign of life the gospel proclaims, Bartolomé de Las Casas rejects all manner of violence to be exercised for the purpose of evangelization. Obviously this will preclude anything like a war waged for the purpose of "softening up," somehow, the proposed addressees of one's evangelization. But it will also rule out the other kinds of violence, subtly introduced by missioners and theologians, whose essential elements we have seen above. Let us now examine these case by case.

There was general agreement in the church, in Las Casas's time, that any attempt at *coercion to the faith* was to be renounced. We already know the historical process that had led to that thesis: it was but the residue — even after the church had received the support of political power — of a forthright, unqualified demand for freedom in matters of religion on the part of the Christians of the early centuries.[19] Las Casas has inherited this doctrine and maintains it in countless texts. But the thesis of noncoercion to faith is something that in principle has no opponents. It is not, consequently, a viable criterion for identifying the champions of a peaceful evangelization. Were this to be the factor for that discernment, all, in that age, would be basically in the same position.[20]

Besides — and this is the most important thing — the moment noncoercion to faith presupposes the perspective of power, the door is wide open to subtle uses of force instead. Here we have the celebrated question of impediments to preaching. One of these will be *refusing to hear* the preaching. For some, this is a sufficient cause for war. Soto does not accept this, but he acknowledges that the matter is under dispute (see *O.E.* 5:305b, a text we have already cited). Las Casas rejects the proposition outright. In the *Apología*, on the basis of the passage from Matthew that we have just cited (Matt. 10:14–15 and parallels, mentioned in the text of the *Octavo remedio*), he draws the conclusion: "Christ did not teach that those who refuse to hear the gospel were to be forced to do so or be punished" (119v).[21]

Another obstruction to evangelization (and for Vitoria and Soto, a "justifying cause" for the use of force — indeed, when circumstances require, for waging war) is *refusing to permit the preaching of the gospel.* Neither does Las Casas admit this "justifying cause." Hence the disagreement between Soto and his friend, as we have seen (see *O.E.* 5:305b). For the Sevillian, not even the murder of missionaries constitutes sufficient cause for taking up arms against the Indians: "as long as they do not put the preachers to death precisely *qua* preachers, or Christians precisely *qua* Christians, but as their most cruel public enemies, with a view to escaping oppression and murder at their hands" (*Apología*, 122v).

Actually, Las Casas had already come out against the disquisitions, broaching the possibility of a legitimate use of force before theologians like Vitoria or Soto had intervened in the debate. In his *De Unico* itself, he rejects any justification of the use of force that might claim a basis in the right or duty to overcome obstacles to the faith: "Though many Christians and their backers say it is not their intention to force-convert pagans through war," he says, "but simply to remove obstacles to preaching, . . . that is a willful deception. It does not excuse their blindness, their rotten deviation" (*De Unico*, 177v; *The Only Way*, 147).[22] Las Casas is not taken in. It is not a matter of intentions. In the concrete, these "legitimating considerations" become pretexts for the abuses that he knows only too well from his experience in the Indies.[23]

He rejects an intervention that would oblige anyone to listen to the preaching of the faith, or even protect Christians' right to preach. Underlying Las Casas's rejection of these theses is the fact that, for him, it is altogether insufficient simply to maintain the noncoercibility of faith. That postulate is compatible with violence, in the possible — exceptional, to be sure, if one insist — cases that we have observed. Bartolomé's "nays" take him beyond the limits staked out by respect for the freedom of the act of faith. They suppose a blanket disqualification of any perspective of power in these matters. And it is this blanket disqualification that he enunciates by way of rebuttal to Sepúlveda's argument based on the celebrated "Compelle intrare" ("Force them to come in") of the parable in Luke 14:23, to which Augustine appeals in a context of the question of religious freedom. Bartolomé writes:

> This coercion is to be exercised by way of the action of reason and human persuasion or through spiritual and interior persuasion obtained through the ministry of the angels. Consequently, it is false and impious to declare that Christ has obliged us under precept by the expression cited that, when the Church has great power, we should pave the way for the preaching of the gospel with a war waged on peaceful unbelievers, as the Doctor Egregius Sepúlveda has had the shamelessness to propose with his new dogma. (*Apología*, 210–210v)

The church's perquisite of power must not alter an attitude inspired in the gospel, the wellspring that waters the life of the church in all historical circumstances whatsoever.[24]

Las Casas's route is one of consideration and respect for the customs of the Indian peoples and for their right to choose their religion freely. Along the same lines, he repudiates the destruction of the Indians' idols. These people deserve that account be taken of the time they require to make a change of option in all freedom, if it seems right to them to make such a change. Bartolomé, taking his inspiration in Augustine, calls it "erasing the idols from their hearts" (*H.I.*, bk. 3, ch. 117, *O.E.* 2:456; see also *Apología*, 206v–207). It will be a free decision, one that emerges from within. It will be obtained by persuasion, and not by external pressure. Nothing is more foreign to Las Casas's mindset than the mentality that would "extirpate idolatry."

Indeed, a failure to respect this process can entail a terrible consequence. Bartolomé regards what is happening in the Indies as a terrible blunder: "Crosses are erected, and the Indians are expected to reverence them," without having had the experience of an authentic evangelization. The outcome will be disastrous. The Indians think that "they are being given some idol of the figure the Christians regard as God, and so they will be made to commit idolatry, adoring that stick as God" (ibid., 456b). He minces no words. Here is Christianity itself caught in idolatry. Even the cross can be an idol where there has been no free act of acceptance of the faith. The pastoral guidelines to be drawn from Las Casas's denunciation of this risk are still valid in our own day.

While some — indeed, few — renowned theologians hold positions akin to his,[25] Bartolomé finds that those who actually identify with him are certain remarkable missionaries, such as the great bishop Juan Zumárraga (d. 1548), who has such close ties with our Dominican. We have already referred to a text signed by Zumárraga but probably coming from Las Casas's pen. Under the heading of a "First Truth" (as well as under the "Sixth Truth"), it alludes to the distinction of Cajetan that we have already seen, and on that basis proclaims the wars being waged on the Indians to be "unjust and wicked." The correct way to propagate the faith "is none other than the one used and inculcated by Christ, the true Sovereign of all the world and the wisest of all legislators, and taught and followed by his holy apostles. That is: by giving gratis, in peace, wisdom, doctrine, humility, meekness, kindliness, generosity, in the odor of good repute, in patience and poverty."[26] Another Franciscan, likewise very close to Bartolomé, Jacobo de Tastera (d. 1544), was a champion of certain experiments in peaceful evangelization in the Yucatán.[27]

To be sure, we do not have detailed writings from the pens of these two missionaries that would let us know their position regarding the subtleties introduced by the theologians to whom we have referred above. An analysis of these theologians has made us mistrustful of declarations of a preference for peaceful evangelization. Such pronouncements can be compatible with reservations and conditions that — all good intentions notwithstanding — ultimately justify war. Everything indicates that this was not the case with Zumárraga and Tastera. The testimony of their evangelization is adequate demonstration.[28]

These ideas inspired the efforts undertaken by Las Casas, along with other Dominican and Franciscan friars, in a region heretofore thought of as a land of war but now undergoing a meaningful change of name and coming to be called Verapaz, "True Peace."[29] Here, in this "least corner of the Indies," the inhabitants have had the time they required in order to accept the faith freely, the space they have needed that they might attain to an authentic knowledge of God, without fear and without dissimulation.[30] The religious freedom enjoyed by those who live in this region is accompanied by a political liberty that allows them their free decision as to whether or not they will accept the supreme sovereignty of the sovereigns of Spain (see *De Thesauris,* 101–103). We shall return to this important matter (see below, chapter 13). We have alluded to it here because it underscores the importance of this experiment for Las Casas. But its significance outstrips the judgment of its inspirer. Saint-Lu is on the mark when he concludes his long study on Verapaz with the following verdict:

> A singular case, surely, but something very different, despite its limitations, from a simple local or episodic case. No, the story of Verapaz, that remarkable example of the difficult reconciliation of the spirit of the gospel with the hard realities of colonization, rests at the heart of the history of Spanish America.[31]

The Sevillian strives to understand the native religions from the inside. Swimming against the powerful tide of his European contemporaries, so prideful in their condition as Christians, he holds that "the common and final intention of those who practice idolatry is not to adore rocks, but to adore in them, through certain manifestations of the divine power, the orderer of the world, whoever that might be" (*Apología*, 86v–87). Beyond the idol, the faithful of these religions reach out for the one true God. Las Casas accords these religious customs remarkable respect and appreciation.[32]

This will be his focus in his examination of human sacrifice and cannibalism. The subject has not yet received the study that it deserves; it will be worth our while to examine it in detail, as it is of great relevance for the subject before us.

2. Human Sacrifice

The most solid — or so its partisans maintain — of the motives advanced for a justification of the right, and even the Christian duty, to wage war on the Indian nations was the obligation to defend innocent members of these Indian nations who suffer oppression and injustice. The matter was all the more urgent, it was said, in the case of those who not only were sacrificed to false gods, but were thereupon consumed as food in religious ceremonies. Human sacrifice and cannibalism were the gravest of the accusations lodged against the Indians by those who sought to legitimate the wars of conquest. Sepúlveda uses this argument smugly and aggressively. Vitoria, for his part, repudiates from his chair of theology at Salamanca one way of employing the argument. But when all is said and done he accepts this justification of the wars, and only asks that they be waged with circumspection and moderation.

Las Casas rejected the argumentation lock, stock, and barrel. The facts on which it was based had been recalled on various occasions throughout the duration of the controversy on the Indies, especially by those who sought to legitimate a European presence in these lands. Las Casas had already engaged in discussions of these customs, which were present among certain Indian nations, as well as of the number of persons who might have been sacrificed in them. But the question catches new fire with the entry of Ginés de Sepúlveda into the fray shortly after the promulgation of the New Laws (1542). And it culminates in the famous disputation of Valladolid (1550–51), at which point Las Casas is obliged to take it up once more in its entirety.[33] Without a doubt, the matter of human sacrifice constituted the most aggressive argument, and the one most difficult to refute, of all those brought forward in favor of making war on the inhabitants of the Indies.[34]

With a view to a better understanding of Las Casas's outlook, let us pause for a moment to consider the positions of Vitoria and Sepúlveda. The former gives the subject a subtle treatment, and — with his indisputable authority — sets theoretical parameters of the question. In his *Apología,* Bartolomé takes his distance from the Salamancan master, without, however, making explicit mention of him when addressing this point.[35] Sepúlveda, on the other hand, provokes our friar's explicit and energetic reaction. Here his opposition is out in the open and head-on.

To Defend the Innocent

Francisco de Vitoria confronted the subject in his *De Indis* ("On the Indians"),[36] as well as in a fragment of his earlier *De Temperantia* ("On Temperance"). Let us leave for a later chapter an analysis of the significance of these "retractations" concerning matters of the Indies — these "re-treatments," as they were called, when a scholar addressed once more a matter he had already written about in order to have an opportunity to introduce corrections or make additions. For the moment, then, we shall be dealing only with his "re-treatment" of the question of human sacrifice as a potential motive for armed intervention against the inhabitants of the Indies.

In his *De Indis,* Vitoria touches on the matter in two passages, corresponding to the two major parts of his work (dealing, respectively, with "illegitimate titles" and "legitimate titles" of a Spanish presence in the Indies). The great theologian rejects, first of all, one reason that had been presented to justify war on the Indians: "the barbarians' own sins." Surely there are sins against the natural law here, says Vitoria — for example, "the eating of human flesh, and incest or homosexuality." Vitoria admits that these acts are contrary to nature, but he denies that they legitimate a punitive war. On the contrary, he maintains that "princes may not, even by authority of the Pope, use force to withdraw barbarians from sins against the natural law, or punish them for this cause."

As for the biblical testimonials advanced in behalf of the use of force, the theologian of Salamanca declares: "Never in the Old Testament, in times when business was settled by force of arms, did the people of Israel occupy an infidel land on the basis of their being infidels or idolaters, or by reason of any of their other sins against nature, such as the sacrifice of their sons and daughters to the demons. Rather it was by special privilege of God that they did this; or because they were refused passage; or because they had suffered injury" (the texts cited are in Vitoria, *Obras,* 697–700; CHP, 67–72). Rebutting the theologians who had preceded him in this examination, Vitoria thus rejects out of hand a part of Sepúlveda's argument on the point.

But the Salamancan master does not rest here. Faithful to his method and purposes, he returns to the theme with a new focus in the second part of his work. The first authentic motive for making war on the Indians, he says — a conditional one, as are all of the legitimate titles — is given the following formulation: "The tyranny of the barbarians' own governors or tyrannical laws prejudicial to the innocent, as those that ordain the sacrifice of innocent human beings or the slaying of blameless persons for the purpose of devouring them." The means of force in question against those committing such excesses may be undertaken by Christian rulers "even without authority of the Pontiff," since the territory in which these enormities are being committed, Vitoria explains, is not under the authority of the pope. It is the Law of Nations (*jus gentium*), an expression of the natural law, that is in force there.[37]

This time the fundamental reason presented by Vitoria in support of the prowar thesis is the duty we all have to "care for our neighbor; and they are all our neighbors." This obligation weighs all the more heavily on rulers. The requirement is valid even in the case that the victims would not wish to be defended. "Here alone," concludes the Salamancan theologian, "truth is on the side of Innocent IV and the archbishop of Florence, to the effect that barbarians may be punished for *sins against nature*" (Vitoria, *Obras*, 720–21; CHP, 93–94; emphasis added). Vitoria is plainly aware, then, that he is addressing anew, from another perspective, the illegitimate title that he has previously rejected. The restrictive adverbials with which he opens his sentence ("Here alone . . . ") shows that his intent is to limit the scope of any legitimate application. And yet this does not lead him to any concretely distinct practical conclusion vis-à-vis the one arrived at by the other champions of theocratic positions whom he cites (and we have seen their theses). Here is a rare instance: Vitoria agrees with the authors from whom he is generally at pains to distance himself.[38]

As we shall see, the view of the great Salamancan is different from Sepúlveda's second argument (offense to God).[39] But he is basically in agreement with Sepúlveda as to the third (defense of innocent victims of sacrifice, offense to human beings). On the basis of this undeniable convergence, it has been erroneously maintained that on the essentials Vitoria and Sepúlveda hold the same position on the matter of the Indies and the justice of the European presence there.[40] The truth is more complex than this. Vitoria walks a tightrope between Las Casas and Sepúlveda: hence his partial agreement and partial disagreement with each. The conditional restriction Vitoria introduces into his theses (Sepúlveda, as we know, is less nuanced) requires only a factual verification in order to be cancelled. Many in the Indies will be ready, indeed anxious, to offer such a verification — Toledo and Sarmiento de Gamboa in Peru, among others. We shall speak of this later.

The famous fragment from the *De Temperantia* (a work Vitoria composed shortly before writing his *De Indis*,[41] which we have just examined) pertaining to our question, while it contributes nothing substantial to the subject, nevertheless introduces certain nuances that it will be worth our while to note.[42] The entire passage is devoted to the subject of the liceity of "making war on the Indians for reason of their sacrilegious custom of consuming human flesh or of offering human lives in their sacrifices...." Despite the theoretical nature of Vitoria's considerations, he makes explicit reference to the Indies, and adds, to the words just quoted: "...as occurs with those of the Province of Yucatán" (*Obras,* 1039; CHP, 100). On the page immediately preceding (*Obras,* 1038), where he posits the same thesis, he says: "...as are the recently discovered barbarians of the Province of Yucatán, in New Spain." He makes no such allusion to the concrete reality of the Indies in the *De Indis.*

Vitoria operates on the basis of a clear conclusion drawn by him shortly before in the *De Temperantia* (the fragment under analysis here being only a part of that work): "It is forbidden by natural and divine law to offer human sacrifice to God" (*Obras,* 1032). Some pages further on, Vitoria broaches the moral question of the liceity of making war for this motive (and this is the subject of the fragment), having already determined the "illicit character of cannibalism and human sacrifice" (*Obras,* 1038). Having made certain specifications and having advanced certain rigoristic positions on the freedom of the act of faith, Vitoria draws two conclusions (the fourth and fifth of his line of argumentation) that confirm what we have said on the basis of his *De Indis.*

Vitoria denies, first of all, that war is justified "by reason of sins against nature more than by reason of other sins not against nature." Christian rulers have no authority over unbelievers, and the pope cannot give it to them. But, as in the *De Indis,* what is rejected for one reason is accepted for another. Thus, the following conclusion is formulated with all desirable clarity: "Christian princes may make war on barbarians because they feed on human flesh and sacrifice human beings." We already know the reason why: "...not because eating human flesh or sacrificing human beings is against the natural law, but because it does injury to human beings" (*Obras,* 1050–51; CHP, 109–10). This defense of the innocent must be undertaken "even though one not ask it, and even resist." Human sacrifices violate the natural law, but rulers are not thereby authorized to punish those who offer them; on the other hand, they may do so in order to defend the victims of these sacrifices.[43] Vitoria will maintain the same position in his *De Indis,* as he has already done in one of his lectures on the *Summa* of Thomas Aquinas, apropos of unbelievers in general.[44]

Let us observe, however, that, in this text from the fragment, Vitoria does not employ the prudent, conditional tone that we find in the *De Indis* apropos of the fifth "legitimate title." The allusion to the inhabitants of the Yucatán, an allusion to a concrete, factual situation, in his state of the question has already hinted at a more absolute conclusion. It does not come as a surprise, then, when we find Vitoria maintaining: "Inasmuch as it actually occurs that such barbarians murder innocent human beings, at least in order to sacrifice them, therefore princes may pursue them with war, to the end that they leave off practicing such a ritual" (*Obras*, 1051; CHP, 110). The wars being waged against the Indians for this reason are fully justified. This text, which was published earlier than the *De Indis* (and was withdrawn from circulation, perhaps by Vitoria himself), posits not a hypothesis but a thesis: "facts" are brought to bear.

In one aspect, however, the fragment appears more moderate than the *De Indis*. In this new piece, Vitoria teaches that if war is waged, justifiably, for this sole motive, "once this [motive] ceases, it is not licit to prolong the war or take the occasion to seize their goods or lands" (*Obras*, 1052; CHP, 111). In the *De Indis*, on the other hand, the argument would seem to have a broader application, and actually legitimate the Spanish presence in the Indies in itself as well.[45]

Before taking our leave of Vitoria for a time, let us recall one point that is completely plain to him, whether he regards the reason noted as illegitimate or correct, and whether we are reading the *De Indis* or the fragment from the *De Temperantia*: human sacrifice, and the cannibalism that goes with it, are always *sins against the natural order*.[46] As we shall see, Las Casas will emphatically disagree.

Avenging the Offense to God

Sepúlveda develops this subject extensively. He is aware of the great weight it has with persons of his time. His second and third arguments follow this line. Democrates, as representative of the Spanish humanist, opens his argument with a severe indictment of nations who have sacrificed "human victims, and, opening their breasts and ripping out their hearts, have offered them on their abominable altars, thinking thereby to have performed a ritual sacrifice by which they had placated their gods," and who, furthermore, feed "on the flesh of the victims." Beyond any doubt, this is the "gravest, most obscene, most inhumane crime" that can be conceived.[47] This, according to Democrates, is what is done in the Indies. The question, then, is:

> Shall we hesitate to assert that it has been with consummate right and the greatest benefit to the barbarians themselves that

these people so uncultivated, so barbaric, contaminated with such abominable sacrifices and impious religions, have been conquered by so excellent, pious, and just a King as was Ferdinand then and is Emperor Charles now, and by a nation so excellent in all manner of virtue? (*Democrates*, 38)

Accordingly, after a survey of analogies he thinks to find in the Old Testament, he formulates the following principle:

These testimonials and judgments of God are too stark and devastating to leave room for doubt in the mind of pious persons that these crimes, the worship of idols and human immolations (which we now know have been the custom of those barbarians), are most justly punished with the death of those who have committed them and with the privation of their goods, whether it be in the case of believers, as were the Hebrews then, or in that of pagans, before Christ's coming as after, inasmuch as the law [forbidding such crimes] is founded in natural law, as we have taught, and inasmuch as such sins, which are committed against justice and reason, are sanctioned with just punishment by virtue not of temporal law, but of the eternal law of God, according to the unanimous opinion of theologians. (*Democrates*, 42)

Thus, Sepúlveda reasons in function of two crimes: idolatry and human sacrifice. Both, and not only the second, justify war, for the purpose of punishing (by death and deprivation of goods) those who commit them. The position is a rigorous one, and it did not fail to cause uneasiness in his own partisans.[48] For him, these are sins without excuse. They are violations of the natural law engraved on the heart of every human being, so that they "have the same force everywhere, regardless of circumstances" (*Democrates*, 11). After all, the natural law is but "the sharing of the eternal law in a creature endowed with reason" (ibid.). Accordingly, everyone must necessarily know the natural law.

But at this point Leopoldo, with whom Democrates is speaking in the dialogue, reminds his opponent that according to "theologians of great renown" unbelief (the "absence of Christianity," he calls it) "is not sufficient cause" for making war on non-Christians. Sepúlveda's spokesperson admits the content of the objection as it stands. If there be only unbelief, then, to be sure, that does not afford just cause for a declaration of war. But at once he posits an important exception to be applied in the case of the Indian nations. "This case would obtain," he says, "if there were to be discovered in the New World some cultivated, civilized, humane people to whom idolatry would be foreign and whom nature would have impelled to worship the one true

God" (*Democrates*, 44). The Cordovan humanist is thinking, surely, of noble peoples like the Greeks or perhaps even of the nations that surrounded ancient Israel. But this is not the situation with the primitive people of the Indies. Besides being infidels, they are idolaters. In this case, the war in question is legitimated. Only "the worship of idols and the immolation of human flesh" can, as violations of the natural law, constitute "sufficient cause for Christians, with the authority of the Supreme Pontiff, justly to make war on pagans to punish and correct them" (ibid., 44–45), Sepúlveda admits. But this is precisely the case with the Indians.

A few pages further on, he specifies that in the case of the barbaric peoples of the Indies another exception holds as well. With the Indians, "unbelief alone, in itself, would be sufficient cause" to justify these wars (ibid., 62). True, faith must not be imposed by force, as we have seen. But force is admissible as a means of withdrawing unbelievers from their crimes (see ibid., 59). The theological doctrine — which Sepúlveda accepts — to the effect that unbelief does not legitimate such war is not good, then, for the poor peoples of the Indies. Here the Cordovan breaks with the theological authorities of his time, among whom a consensus to the contrary had been reached.

Rather, the inhabitants of these lands may well be grateful, Democrates expatiates, that the Spanish sovereigns in their magnanimity, while "subjecting these barbarians to their dominion and that of Christians, have in mind not punishment for their sins, but the emendation, salvation, and public welfare of these very people" (ibid., 43). That is, in strict justice they deserve even harsher treatment.

It is not a matter, Sepúlveda cautions, of individual infractions of the natural law. Any personal sin is such an infraction, at least to some extent. It is a matter of publicly approved deeds among these peoples. This is what is serious. We are dealing with the responsibility of entire nations, beginning with their political authorities. Therefore these nations and authorities may legitimately be punished by Christians. The offense is an offense to God directly: hence, "with a sacred war like one waged by the faithful on idolaters, it is not so much offenses to human beings that are avenged, but those offered to God, which by reason of their greater gravity are more deserving of being avenged" (ibid., 60). The reason invoked for the war transforms the military action into a holy war.

There is likewise offense — and this is important — to human beings. But the offense to God is greater. "By this war are avenged human injuries as well, and not only divine; although it is the latter that weigh the more" (ibid.). Thus, to offense of God is added offense of human beings. Sepúlveda presents this as a further argument (his third) for the legitimacy of the wars being waged against the Indians.

Human solidarity ought to entail the defense of innocent victims. Our author cites the case of Mexico, where the custom, he says, is to "immolate to the demons more than twenty thousand innocent human beings" (ibid., 61).[49] The figure is taken from one of his sources on the Indies, G. Fernández de Oviedo's *Historia general de las Indias.* Neither must we forget that Sepúlveda had a great admiration for Hernán Cortés, to whom he was bound by ties of friendship.[50]

In the face of these facts, the conclusion is plain: "*Not only unbelief,* but *also* the incredible sacrifice of human victims and the extreme offenses done to innocent people, the horrible banquets of human bodies, and the impious worship of idols, constitute most just causes for waging war against these barbarians" (*Democrates,* 62; emphasis added).[51]

Among these reasons, of course, Sepúlveda emphasizes the scandal that is surely occasioned by the sacrificial offering of human beings. Thus, he wonders: "Could any devout person deny that a just and religious prince has an obligation to deliver so many innocent human beings from such serious offenses?" Indeed, the obligation in question is incumbent especially on "heads of temporal states" (ibid.).[52] We are not dealing with an appendix to the previous argument (based on idolatry and human sacrifice, which are offenses *to God*). Sepúlveda moves his piece with care, in the knowledge that this will improve his position. To offense of God is now added that *of neighbor:* now human solidarity is involved. Both must be punished by war. Neglect of this obligation is sinful. This last reason in favor of the wars moves Sepúlveda closer to the position taken by Vitoria, which we have recalled above.

Idolatry and human sacrifice are sins against the natural law. Thereby they offer offense to God and deserve punishment at the hands of Christian rulers. And here Sepúlveda adds a powerful consideration: solidarity with and defense of the innocent. He asks: "Who will doubt that for this reason alone it has been and continues to be licit to subject them?" (*Apología* [GS], 65). Sepúlveda's espousal of this position will occasion a lengthy and meticulous treatment of the subject at the hands of Las Casas.[53]

State of the Question

Las Casas confronts the question of the wars being waged on the Indians for the purpose of punishing human sacrifice especially in his writings concerning the disputation of Valladolid. He situates his argumentation on two levels. He deals with questions of *law* (divine and human) in his *Apología*. He addresses questions of *fact* in his *Apologética historia.*[54] The former was read out (at least in a first version) at Valladolid. Its intent is to refute, point by point, the assertions of Sepúlveda. A single idea governs its considerations: respect for the Indians' religious customs.

The bishop of Chiapa propounds his argumentation in the *Apología* with an impressive array of weapons of logic, despite the erudite excursions that at moments seem to distract from the development of his thought. That thought may disconcert at first. But once we enter into the framework of his ratiocination, the presentation arises before us possessed of an internal clarity of its own, the work of this particularly lucid and orderly mind. Still, none of these conceptual disquisitions, any more than Bartolomé's rebuttals and replies lodged throughout the subsequent course of the debate, must make us lose sight of what is concretely at stake and actually transpiring: *the destruction of the Indians "in body and soul."* No argument will be more massive and urgent for the Dominican than the actual cruel reality of the Indies.

With that reality as his point of departure, Las Casas makes it utterly clear in the first chapter of his book that he rejects all manner of argument in defense of the wars being waged on the inhabitants of these lands, including arguments to the effect that "these wars are just provided they are properly conducted." Our friar comments ironically:

> I suppose that they mean, provided they are conducted with moderation, slaying only those whom it is necessary to slay in order to force the rest to submit, as if [the Spaniards] had shut up all the peoples of the New World in cages or dungeons and decided to cut off as many human heads daily as were sold in the meat markets each day for the nourishment and support of the people. (I suggest this by way of comparison.) (*Apología*, 13)

The reference to Sepúlveda is unmistakable. But neither is an allusion to Vitoria to be excluded — at least to the interpretation that some readers might make of the latter's "legitimate titles."

Las Casas is aware that the prowar argument most difficult to refute is the one based on human sacrifice and cannibalism. And so he will give it extensive treatment in his *Apología*. The bishop of Chiapa makes a distinction here that may guide us in our examination of his development of the subject. That distinction is formulated in these terms: "Although they are not excusable before God (*apud Deum*), they are indeed totally so before human beings (*apud homines*)" (*Apología*, 152). Bartolomé repeats the distinction on various occasions, which indicates the importance he attributes to it. In fact, it is repeated in Domingo de Soto's résumé of the Valladolid disputation.[55]

The *Apología* concentrates on the "before human beings" question. This is what is decisive in the war being waged on the Indians. But the bold hypotheses Bartolomé formulates in his treatment seem to entail a position on the "before God" question as well. Sepúlveda notices this, and calls it to his attention. Las Casas will respond in his published replies (accompanied by the texts of Soto and Sepúlveda), in *Aquí se contiene una disputa o controversia* (1552). Let us examine the treatment he accords to the first point. We shall see the second (on the "before God" question) in our next chapter, in a framework of the question of a theology of salvation.

3. Before the Powers of This World

Las Casas posits a number of different arguments on the matter of human sacrifice. It will be of interest to us to stop to consider those that more directly point to the question of freedom in religious matters. Besides, this is the heart of our author's discourse in the *Apología.*

Who Are the Idolaters?

Bartolomé's effort to demonstrate an "excusability before human beings" relies on an argument he now proposes to the effect that human sacrifice does not constitute a just cause for war against the Indians — which Sepúlveda, as well as Vitoria, thought it did. It is here that he brings the entire weight of his reflection to bear.

He begins by discarding the reason (Sepúlveda's second) based on an obligation to punish "the crime of idolatry and human sacrifice by which that people offends God" (*Apología*, 31). Las Casas's argument is the one we have seen used by Vitoria (and here the positions of the two Dominicans converge): the church has no jurisdiction over infidels. Thus, to speak of a war of punishment for the sins of the Indians is out of place.[56] Our friar supports his reasoning with citations and commentary on the bull *Sublimis Deus*, which proclaims the human status of the Indians and their right to freedom and ownership, while reproving the violence committed against them. The argumentation is solid and is well supported by theological tradition.

But as we have seen, Sepúlveda's third argument, constructed on the basis of the solidarity obliging human beings to defend the innocent, is more serious and more troublesome. As we have recalled, Sepúlveda defiantly maintained that this motive alone would justify war on and subjection of the Indians. As for Vitoria, he had actually anticipated Sepúlveda in this position, maintaining the validity of this conclusion "not for reason of sin, but for reason of injury to others," a position in which he was followed by other theologians. Las Casas is facing heavy artillery, then, and he is obliged to address his subject with care and precision.

That the church has no jurisdiction over heathen is a principle accepted by all.[57] On its basis, Las Casas — agreeing with Vitoria, as we have noted — rejects punitive wars. But our author acknowledges certain exceptions to this absence of ecclesiastical jurisdiction. There are situations in which "the church has only contentious jurisdiction *in habitu* over other infidels, in such wise that it may reduce it to jurisdiction *in actu* in certain cases" (*Apología*, 75v). Only in those cases can the church — at a given moment — come to have actual jurisdiction. And he lists six cases.[58] In addressing the sixth and last, Las Casas responds directly to Sepúlveda's third argument.[59]

The form in which he draws up his state of the question is of the highest interest for us. This sixth case occurs when "the church can exercise coercitive jurisdiction *in actu* over unbelievers *if* the case were to arise that the latter should oppress and offend innocent persons, *if* they were killing them in order to immolate them to their gods or to eat the flesh of their corpses, which some people of the world of the Indies are reputed to do."[60] Las Casas observes that this case corresponds to "the third argument, or third cause, introduced by Sepúlveda in order to justify those expeditions of his," and he specifies: "This error of his in this matter will also be eliminated in our following exposition" (*Apología*, 126; emphasis added).

What brings the jurisdiction of the church to pass from "habit" (potency) to "act"? Las Casas prepares the ground for a presentation of his position. This occurs, he replies, not because the immolation of human beings is an act *"contrary to natural law,* which binds all human beings to deliver the oppressed and those unjustly delivered to death, as we read in the Book of Proverbs, chapter 24 [v. 11]: 'Rescue those who are being dragged to death' — an obligation from which the church is not exempt" (ibid.; emphasis added).

The first argument in Bartolomé's rebuttal is aimed explicitly at Sepúlveda. Obliquely, however, he is referring also to Vitoria, who, while not admitting that this act alone could justify war, does regard it as contrary to natural law. In the second stage of his rebuttal, Las Casas sets his sights on both at once. He is responding to Vitoria, who regards it as an obligation in virtue of the *jus gentium*, the Law of Nations, which is an expression of natural law, to go to the aid of these innocent victims. (Vitoria frequently cites the same text of Proverbs, as does Bartolomé in this regard). And certainly, once more, he is responding to Sepúlveda, who has presented this same argument, if with less nicety. Bartolomé's precision in this text shows us how informed and alert he was when it came to the various opinions, regardless of whence they came, maintaining the legitimacy of wars that he regarded as unjust and cruel toward the Indians.

As we might have expected, the bishop of Chiapa adds to his two objections the reason he actually regards as the only one that will ever base the church's acquisition of the jurisdiction in question. That reason corresponds to his great concern as a missionary friar: "Such innocent persons are, *in potentia*, members of the church; wherefore they come under its protection. For this reason it is incumbent upon the church and the Pope, its head, to see to their eternal *salvation*. But innocent persons would not obtain this salvation were they to be sacrificed" (*Apología*, 126; emphasis added).[61] Nothing could be more elementary.

Salvation, then, is a consideration that might justify an intervention. But in the case at hand, that of the Indies, the same concern leads Bartolomé to reject war and domination. It is a matter of the salvation of the victims and consequently of the entire people to which the victims belong — as well as, surely (and let us not forget this), of those who might intervene in the affair or think that they ought to do so. The first perspective, then, is that of the salvation of persons, and not of the natural law, as maintained in the two theses Las Casas rejects. The question of whether or not the natural law is at stake does have importance for Bartolomé in any argumentation concerning human sacrifice, as we shall see below. But the important thing here is his shift of focus in the discussion: he moves it, part and parcel, to a strictly theological level. In this way the matter is fastened to the heart of the Christian message and removed from the place where theology meets canon law, and where Vitoria and Sepúlveda preferred to take their stand.

When the principle just enunciated, based as it is on a concern for salvation, is applied to the case of the Indian nations, it becomes altogether plain that waging a war against them cannot be justified. To conduct such a war would be to apply a greater evil as an antidote for a lesser one (see *Apología*, 146v).[62] Armed intervention would only aggravate the situation, and the deaths it would cause would work counter to the salvation of the dwellers of the Indies. Las Casas has built his bunker. Here he will dig in, to resist the onslaughts of the enemy. It will be impregnable to their mightiest weapon: a call to solidarity with the victims of human sacrifice and cannibalism.

On the basis of his familiarity with the concrete reality of the New World, Las Casas — first of all — rejects the figure of twenty thousand alleged annual victims of the ceremonies held by the Aztec nation, the figure cited by Sepúlveda in reliance on Fernández de Oviedo. Then he counterattacks, insisting that deaths in the wars of conquest surely outnumber the victims of the sacrifices:

> These pagans sacrifice yearly thirty or a hundred or a thousand persons out of invincible ignorance (as I shall set forth hereinafter), while the soldiers in question in waging war for this motive in a single day slay ten thousand innocent persons, with grave injury to their own souls. (*Apología*, 139v)[63]

The cynicism of the argument is transparent. How could anyone doubt that the wars were the greater evil?

Later, replying to Sepúlveda, Bartolomé will consider all of this in the light of another theme, but a theme no less central to his thought: the idolatry being committed by Christians. He writes:

> The Doctor has reckoned ill. In all truth, it would be far more accurate to say that the Spaniards have sacrificed more to their beloved adored goddess Codicia ["greed," "covetousness"] every single year that they have been in the Indies after entering each province than the Indians have sacrificed to their gods throughout the Indies in a hundred years. (*O.E.* 5:333b)

This, he adds, "not even the tyrants who have perpetrated it deny" (ibid.). They know perfectly well how the Indies lie in ruins today.[64] If they want to talk about idolatry, let them begin with the most murderous kind.

Thus Las Casas dispels the specious validity of Sepúlveda's argument, settled as it is on a purely theoretical level. The conquistadors never intervened to rescue the innocent. It is a matter of the facts of the case: what they were doing was offering worship to the god Gold. On which side, then, do we find the more grave, and less excusable, idolatry and the greater number of victims?

Bold Conclusions

But the matter goes beyond any question of relative proportion. The human sacrifices of which they heard and the cannibalism involved obsessed and horrified sixteenth-century Europeans almost beyond description.[65] This lent additional (and emotional) force to the argument.

Now Bartolomé de Las Casas decides to put the adversary in his place. Employing a wide historical lens, he recalls in his *Apologética historia* that the Indies have no monopoly on this enormity. It was the custom of "many ancient peoples" and was always practiced in a religious context (*A.H.*, ch. 161, *O.E.* 4:98a). In fact, the people of Spain themselves did these things, "sacrificing hundreds upon hundreds of human beings" (*A.H.*, ch. 163, *O.E.* 4:104a). Obviously these facts are not being cited in defense of such customs; it is a simple matter of summoning the opponent to greater humility. Accordingly, Bartolomé will say, basing himself on Strabo, and with evident polemical intent: "Our Spaniards, who reproach the pitiable people of the Indies their human sacrifices, immolated captives and horses to Mars" (*Apología*, 154). Thus it is a matter of the practice of many peoples, including those of the Iberian Peninsula. Las Casas recalls the religious context of these deeds and demonstrates the deep roots they have among the peoples who perform them. This is one of the reasons he will use to say that "in offering this kind of immolation for so many centuries, the Indians have certainly fallen into probable error" (ibid.). Below, we shall examine the role of probable error in Bartolomé's assessment of the Indians' conduct on this point.

With his softening-up operations completed, Las Casas plunges into the heart of his argument, proposing four principles for an adequate understanding of human sacrifices. Concretely, these postulates seek to establish that "the Indians cannot see all at once that it is illicit to immolate human beings to their gods, since no evidence could have been presented to them in a few words, or even in many words, that would have shown them that human sacrifice to the true or putative God (if the latter is worshiped as the true God) is forbidden by natural reason." Our author goes further and daringly asserts that "by the same natural reason, they can demonstrate not only that human beings ought to be sacrificed to God, but that it would not be enough to sacrifice the angels themselves, if angels could be sacrificed" (*Apología*, 154v–155).[66] Bartolomé has thrown his opponents' arguments back in their faces. He proceeds by careful steps in the enunciation of his premises, from which he then draws the conclusion that responds to the matter under consideration.

1. "There is no people so barbarous as not to have a certain knowledge, however confused, of God" (ibid.). This general principle expresses a frequent conviction of Bartolomé's time, although it usually referred to the historical period prior to Christianity.

2. "It is to be supposed that by natural instinct human beings feel inclined to worship God, in conformity with their abilities and their particular manner of existence." As a consequence, it is evident that "by natural law human beings are obliged to honor God with the best means at their disposal and to offer him, in sacrifice, the best things they have" (ibid., 155v–156). Belief in God is necessarily expressed by way of external gestures, by cultic acts.

3. "There is no better way to worship God than by means of sacrifice, which is the principal act of adoration and is due to God alone" (ibid., 157).[67] Thus, Bartolomé de Las Casas opens the way for a presentation of his last principle, in which a distinction between the

exigencies of natural law and those of positive law bring him to the threshold of the daring conclusion he will reach.

4. "It is a duty in natural law to offer sacrifice to the true God or to the one regarded as such. Now, it falls to human law and positive legislation to determine which things ought to be offered to God; this latter determination is incumbent upon the entire community, whether upon those who represent it," such as the prince, or, in the absence of such a representative, upon each private individual, who will decide which things are to be used for sacrifice. This fourth premise will be the hinge of our author's argumentation (ibid.).[68]

The development of these four principles, in whose support various arguments and authorities are invoked, issues in the following conclusion: "Within the limits of the natural light [of reason], that is, where human or divine law ceases to be in force — and we may add, where grace and doctrine are lacking — persons are bound by the duty [*deben*] of immolating human victims to the true God or to the putative one regarded as true" (ibid., 160). The offering of human sacrifices constitutes a moral duty ("…*deben inmolar víctimas humanas*"), according to the daring friar. It is a duty proceeding from the natural light of reason, in the absence of positive law to the contrary. We are very far from Vitoria and Sepúlveda, for whom such deeds represent flagrant violations of natural law. But Las Casas will not rest content even with this seemingly paradoxical moral obligation. He goes a step further. He adds a positive argument, adducing a consideration based on something fundamental in his theology: *the value of human life.*

After all, human beings are convinced that there is nothing "better or greater" than God, and that they must sacrifice to God what they consider to be their "most precious and excellent things." Consequently, Las Casas will say, breaking entirely new ground, "*nature itself* dictates and instructs those who lack faith, grace, or doctrine, those who live within the limitations of the natural law, that in default of a positive law to the contrary they must immolate even human victims to the true God, or to a false one regarded as true, so that in offering this God the most precious thing they have they may show themselves especially grateful for so many benefits received" (ibid.; emphasis added).[69]

The requirement is one of human nature itself. "We are obliged" by human nature "to offer [to God] what seems to us the most important and precious good, that is, *human life*" (ibid., 161; emphasis added). The restrictions cited (absence of faith, grace, and doctrine, absence of a positive law, a god held to be the true God) only set in even sharper relief the astonishing conclusion: the Indians *do well* to offer God their very best: *human life.*[70]

Las Casas will employ the argument from the value of human life

in various ways, as we have seen, for example, for the purpose of rejecting both "satanic expeditions or so-called conquests carried out by
our people" and the labors and hardships imposed on the "Indian
oppressed." This time the context is different, as is the objective being sought. Provocative as the point of arrival may appear, however,
one thing remains clear: the profound relationship between *God* and
human life. This is certainly a key element in the theological thought of
Bartolomé de Las Casas. It is the obverse of what made him link, from
the beginning, idolatry of *gold* and the *death* of the Indians.

Unjustifiable Wars

To offer to God the best that they had, their own life, is on the part
of the natives of the Indies to evince a *profound religious sense*. That is,
with this they show that they acknowledge God as the origin of all
things. This acknowledgment is plainly expressed in the biblical account of the sacrifice of Isaac, which Friar Bartolomé regards as solid
support for his whole argumentation concerning human sacrifice.[71] In
that passage from the Book of Genesis, if we look beyond the anecdote, we clearly see that "God is the author of every creature, and all
creatures belong to God. As it is written: 'The Lord's are the earth and
its fullness' (Psalm 23 [Ps. 24:1]); and in the Second Book of Maccabees,
14, we read: 'You are the Lord of all things' [see 2 Macc. 1:24, 14:35].
Thus this must be Lord of life and death" (ibid., 164v–165).[72]

This is what the Indians experience. Thus, human sacrifice does
not seem to them to be clearly contrary to natural reason (which, as
we have seen, many theologians regarded as sufficient cause to justify
waging war on them). On the contrary, their religious sense actually
makes them see these sacrifices as a moral obligation.

In light of all this, how can one think that before any contact with
the preachers of the gospel the Indians would have been in a position
to alter a conviction so deeply rooted in their customs and tradition?
And our friar writes:

> It is plainly impossible, then, in a short space of time and in few
> words to make it evident to unbelievers, especially to ours here,
> that the act of sacrificing human beings to God is contrary to na-
> ture. Accordingly, the fact that the natives sacrifice human beings
> to their gods or even eat human flesh *is not a just cause* for making
> war on them. Furthermore, this inveterate custom cannot be sud-
> denly torn up by the roots. There is no reason, then, why these
> completely innocent Indians should be condemned because they
> fail to repent upon hearing the first words of the preacher of the
> gospel.[73]

Add to this, Las Casas recalls, that they do not understand the preacher's language. Thus, they are "under no obligation to abandon the religion of their forebears forthwith, since they do not understand that it would be better to do so." Here is an interesting assessment of the religious traditions of a people. "On the other hand, the act of immolating human beings, although they be innocent, when it is done for the welfare of the entire republic, is not as *contrary to natural reason* as if what were at stake were something immediately abominable and contrary to the dictates of nature. Thus, this error may have its origin in probable natural reason" (ibid., 166–166v; emphasis added).[74]

Below, we shall touch on the question of involuntary error in these matters. For the moment, suffice it to say that the conclusion to which Las Casas's argumentation leads is clear:

> Inasmuch as in some regions of the New World, whether by law or by custom handed down from time immemorial and confirmed by order of the princes, teachers, and priests, and thus by public authority, it is deemed as something pious and holy to sacrifice human beings to the gods, who are regarded as the true God, it therefore follows that this custom and common error establishes a law among them and consequently will excuse those who perform such sacrifices. (Ibid., 177v)

It is not in order, then, to use violence against them for their violation of natural law. This may be done neither by the church nor by Christian rulers.

To the reasons adduced thus far for declaring the wars against the Indians unjustified, Las Casas adds — in a perspective of salvation — what he calls the "universal argument": that "God and the holy church by means of which God desires that human beings be saved and come to a knowledge of the truth not be frustrated" (ibid., 177v). After all, these wars stand as an obstacle to a correct and persuasive proclamation of the gospel.

The rejection of war on the Indians is one of Las Casas's great themes, but this time he has had to wrestle with the most difficult of all of the reasons advanced to justify such wars: the sacrifice of innocent persons and the consequent obligation of Christians to enter into solidarity with them. This argument carried weight with practically all of the theologians of the time.[75] This is why Bartolomé feels compelled to reason in theological isolation (we might almost say, orphanhood) and daringly face a particularly thorny question addressed by theologians who had had no direct contact with peoples who practiced these customs.

Bartolomé himself was aware of having taken an uncharted path. In a letter to the Dominicans of Chiapa and Guatemala, written in the last years of his life, he will refer to the question of human sacrifice in the controversies of Valladolid:

> I read out the *Apología* I had written against Sepúlveda, which runs for more than a hundred pages in Latin plus some more in [Spanish], in which I drew, and proved, many conclusions that *no person before me had dared to touch* or write about. One of these was that it is not against *natural law or reason, seclusa omni lege positiva humana vel divina* [in the absence of any human or divine positive law] to offer human beings in sacrifice to a god false or true (holding the false as true) — along with other questions involving all of the most difficult, prickly, and vexing questions then arising both here and abroad in this material. (1563, *O.E.* 5:471a; emphasis added)

Indeed the matter vexed all who sought a facile justification of the use of arms against the Indians. And Bartolomé concludes, affirming with a mixture of both candor and pride: "He and all of the other theologians and lawyers were quite satisfied. In fact — and I could swear to this, without fear of succumbing to a vain arrogance — some were struck with admiration" (ibid.). The "he" in this case is Domingo de Soto, eminent theologian and defender of the Indians, whom Las Casas always held in great esteem.[76] The "other theologians and lawyers" were those before whom Bartolomé conducted his public polemic with Sepúlveda (and among the group, Melchior Cano).[77]

Doubtless they all appreciated his argumentation. But there were also some who rent their garments on hearing his bold theses — especially Sepúlveda, for whom the enunciations of the bishop of Chiapa were "so outside Christendom." They must have been "outside" the human race as well, since, according to Sepúlveda, even among the gentiles of Old Testament antiquity there were those to be found who rejected such acts with horror — "so that to say that ignorance is an excuse in so abominable a sin against nature runs contrary to all reason." And Las Casas's adversary draws a sharp conclusion: "As for the ignorance that he says excuses them in sacrificing human beings to their gods, this is a doctrine which cannot be maintained among Christians" (*Aquí se contiene*, 1552, *O.E.* 5:315a–b). For the Cordovan, then, the matter is utterly plain. Later he will once more energetically reject Las Casas's assertion to the effect that human sacrifice is not forbidden by natural law:

> This, then, is the impious error of someone who either knows little of theology, or is puffed up and insolent, or has a very poor sense of the Catholic faith: to say that to sacrifice human beings to false gods is not against the law of nature, when it is idolatry

and homicide. It seems not to have come to his notice that the precepts of the Decalogue are all natural laws, and that anyone who acts against any of them acts against the law of nature, as all theologians agree. (*Proposiciones temerarias,* 549)

Sepúlveda actually goes even further with his objections. But to follow him in these would lead us into the second question that Las Casas distinguishes, that of a consideration of the matter "before God." We shall treat of this question below. It will enable us to see further implications of the point that we have just examined, but we reserve it for later discussion because of its direct relationship with the question of the salvation of unbelievers, with which we shall be concerned in Part Three of this book. Indeed, the question of religious freedom always has repercussions on that of salvation.

Respect for Religious Customs

To conclude this section, let us observe that underlying Las Casas's considerations on the matter of the human sacrifices offered by the Indians is a profound — and astonishing, for the time in which he wrote — respect for the social customs and religious rites of the Indians.[78] This respect actually leads him to say that

> [the Indians] would be acting very light-mindedly and would be deserving of reprehension and castigation, if in a matter so diffi-cult, so important, and so ingrained, as St. John Chrysostom says, they were to give credence to those Spanish soldiers, ignoring *so many mighty testimonials and such great authority,* unless, through convincing arguments, it were to be demonstrated to them that the Christian religion is more worthy of adherence and belief — something that cannot be done in a short space of time. (*Apología,* 154v; emphasis added)

Indeed, "there is no undertaking more important and more diffi-cult than the abandonment of religion once it is embraced" (ibid.). Let us keep in mind that Las Casas is referring to religious expressions re-garded as barbaric and degrading by the Western Christian world of his day. His appraisal is different; therefore he considers it a difficult task for the Indian nations to abandon their religious convictions.

What is at stake is an authentic norm of conduct in the proclama-tion of the gospel: an acknowledgment of the rights of a people to their own way of life and their own religion.[79] These are rights that belong not only to individuals as such, but to an entire nation. Bar-tolomé's attitude is free of all contempt for the customs of others on the basis of cultural or religious considerations.[80] His effort to adopt the viewpoint of the dwellers of the New World ("as if he was an Indian") enables him to discern the religious sense of actions such as the sacrifice to God of human beings' lives — without approving these actions ethically — however much they might provoke revulsion in his contemporaries.[81]

Let us note that our friar makes no attempt to find an easier, softer way. He does not respond to the "defense of the innocent" argument for war by beating around the bush or by limiting himself to a rebuttal of his adversaries' secondary points. He confronts the major difficulty, and he confronts it head on. He addresses that element of the issue at hand that seems to him to be the most difficult to handle because it arouses in his contemporaries the greatest disgust. He sets himself the task of developing this element from a viewpoint that deprives the wars being waged against the Indian nations of all justification. At the same time, then, he blazes new trails for the missionary task and for a theology of salvation in Christ.

What we have just seen with regard to human sacrifice makes it abundantly clear that Las Casas aims his defense of freedom in matters of religion in the direction specified in our chapter 5, which in turn is an expression of his defense of human freedom as such. This explains why he refuses to approve the use of force of whatever kind in evangelization. A certain use of force, as we have seen, might be compatible with that minimal — but precious — demand of non-coercion to the faith that sometimes bewilders certain scholars to the point that they confuse it with respect for religious freedom.

An observation by T. Urdanoz can be helpful in perceiving this point. Scandalized by the Lascasian reflections upon human sacrifice, this modern author declares: "It is paradoxical and contradictory that a Las Casas who could be so enormously zealous, all his life long, for the Indians' conversion to the faith, should here so earnestly defend an absolute respect for religious freedom, religious pluralism, and freedom of worship — even in its most abominable forms — in a way as advanced as that of the postconciliar theologians."[82] Urdanoz is lodging an accusation, not singing a paean. But he is mistaken. He sees paradox and contradiction where there is nothing of the kind. On the contrary: precisely because Las Casas desires that the Indians receive the faith, he respects both their freedom of religion and the transcendence of the gift of faith.

Obviously Urdanoz is not in great sympathy with the religious liberty proclaimed by Vatican II and postconciliar theologians. But, perhaps despite himself, he is correct on two counts: Bartolomé has what he calls an "absolute respect" (Urdanoz's own words) for religious freedom, and this does indeed align him with the theology that we are accustomed to characterize as that of the Council. As we know, the most controversial of the schemas proposed at Vatican II was that of the Declaration on Religious Freedom (which is why this document went through the largest number of preparatory schemas). And for good reason. The modern age had left the doctrine maintained by the church in recent centuries lagging far behind the democratic structures and mindset of contemporary society. The position to which we refer rested ultimately on the doctrine of civil toleration enunciated by Thomas Aquinas. What may have been something of a theoretical disquisition in the Middle Ages became, in the sixteenth century, a theology encouraged by relationships between Catholics and the Protestant dissidents, as well as — although the repercussions in Roman and European spheres were not always very strong — by the situation in the far-off Indies. The challenge grew even more urgent with the proclamation of the "modern liberties" that burst upon the scene with such unique force in the French Revolution. The status quo to which things had settled in Europe, with Catholic and Protestant nations content merely to glower at each other across their respective borders, had met its demise.

Among these modern liberties we find religious freedom. The papal magisterium was doggedly opposed to them. From Pius VI, a contemporary of the French Revolution, to Pius IX (d. 1878), the church's polemics with liberalism were bitter in the extreme. It was during the pontificate of Pius IX that a doctrine arose calculated to pacify spirits within the church (where Catholic liberalism was lobbying for a rapprochement with the modern mentality), but never accepted outside it. We refer to the distinction between *thesis* and *hypothesis* in which, ideally, the Catholic religion would indeed be the religion of the state and enjoy the support of political authority, but in particular circumstances, when this could not be, freedom of worship on modern society's terms could be regarded as legitimate.[83]

Without explicitly adopting it, the magisterium of the church had for all practical purposes taken this stance since Leo XIII. In the framework and terms of the nineteenth century, the magisterium was only reflecting what Thomas Aquinas had propounded six centuries before, although the teaching of Thomas enjoyed a consistency with the conditions of his age of which the nineteenth-century doctrinal schema under consideration here was deprived.[84] But the position of the popes (especially with Pius XI, Pius XII, and John XXIII) gradually veered, over the course of the twentieth century, toward greater sympathy with contemporary demands. The matter was not yet doctrinally clear when Vatican II convened — hence the lively controversy on the preparatory schema for the Declaration on Religious Freedom. The weight of the passionate, painful discussion that was now more than a century old was still too great. Not all were ready to accept the required 180-degree turn.

Finally, the Council abandoned the indefensible theory of toleration (in the sense of tolerating evil) and courageously asserted the right of every person to proceed according to his or her conscience and to practice the religion of his or her choice. This was now seen as a right in whose exercise no political authority had any right to interfere. This position implies no indifferentism in religious matters, as we shall have occasion to observe below (in chapter 9).

At the heart of the Declaration on Religious Freedom is Vatican II's assertion:

> This Vatican Synod declares that the human person has a right to religious freedom. This freedom means that all men are to be immune from coercion on the part of individuals or of social groups and of any human power, in such wise that in matters religious no one is to be forced to act in a manner contrary to his own beliefs. Nor is anyone to be restrained from acting in accordance with his own beliefs, whether privately or publicly, whether alone or in association with others, within due limits.
>
> The Synod further declares that the right to religious freedom has its foundation in the very dignity of the human person, as this dignity is known through the revealed Word of God and by reason itself. The right of the human person to religious freedom is to be recognized in the constitutional law whereby society is governed. Thus it is to become a civil right. (No. 2)

This is indeed what is at stake: a right possessed by every human person, regardless of that person's religious option. It was this — expressed here in a language of our own time — that Las Casas defended in his time with regard to those persons who were Indians. That right ought to be respected — by what the Council document calls individuals, social groups, and human powers and Las Casas specifies as conquistadors, royal councils, and Christian princes. The Council text just cited avoids making any pronouncement at this point concerning truth or error in matters religious. (It will do so elsewhere.) The essence of its declaration here does not require such an enunciation. Whether the content of a given religious belief or object of a religious practice be objectively true or false, in either case freedom of choice is to be respected. Respect for religious freedom rests, in the first instance, with the civil sphere.[85]

No one may be obliged to act against his or her conscience, even if that conscience is in error. The Indians, individually and as nations, have the right to practice their religion openly. The Spanish Crown may not wage war on them on this account, not even in the difficult and extreme case of human sacrifice. The judgment to be rendered upon the practices of these persons in the light of Christian faith, as well as in virtue of other considerations, is important; but it must not be cited as a pretext for the destruction or forced submission of those who believe and live differently from Christians. This is a right that ought to be recognized by everyone living in human society.

We are aware of the differences in historical context and vocabulary between the position of Vatican II and that of the early Christian centuries in this matter. But it is scarcely open to doubt that, in the essentials, the positions coincide.[86] In the first centuries, the church maintained both the truth of the Christian message and the urgency of respecting free access to that message without interference on the part of civil authority. Las Casas, in his era, and in terms of the problems of the Indies, intuitively adopts these early ideas — as, in its own language, Vatican II will do.

Noncoercion to the faith is a part, a consequence, of this religious freedom. Taken in isolation, such noncoercion is compatible with intransigent attitudes toward the practice of non-Christian religions. We have seen this to satiety. But in a framework of freedom in matters religious, the freedom of the act of faith wins its authentic meaning and acquires its full scope. Without blurring legitimate distinctions or making facile identifications, this is how the Council document sees it. "In consequence," we read, "the principle of religious freedom makes no small contribution to the creation of an environment in which persons can without hindrance be invited to Christian faith, and embrace it of their own free will, and profess it effectively in their whole manner of life" (Vatican Council II, Declaration on Religious Freedom, no. 10).

In his own fashion, it was this that Las Casas thought too. By attending to the customs, lifestyles, and religious freedom of the Indians, one created the necessary conditions for a dialogue to be conducted in respect for the equality of both parties. In this manner of dialogue, reason, and not undue pressure, makes possible an integral presentation of the gospel message: now that message is offered — without prejudice to the values of the one proclaiming it — for the free acceptance of each hearer.[87]

The matter is fraught with consequences and retains all its relevance today. Inevitably, the terms in which we have presented the debate over these questions as well as the categories used bear the stamp of the age. But the core is fully valid today. If evangelization is a dialogue, it will not exist without an effort to understand the positions of one's interlocutor from within, in such a way that one may sense the vital thrust of these positions and grasp their internal logic.

Neither will evangelization be possible unless one is ready to give as well as to receive.[88]

Despite these efforts of Las Casas and so many others, much was destroyed in the sixteenth century; but the truth is that the process of annihilation has continued throughout all centuries since, and not only during the colonial period. Today the native peoples, like the extensive black population of this continent, continue to see their lifestyles, their values, their customs, their right to life and liberty, trodden under foot. We must undertake once more, in our age, the colossal endeavor of Bartolomé de Las Casas if we would forge a liberating evangelization of Latin America. Or rather, we must seek to develop what has been under way for some decades now on our continent, from the moment the Catholic Church began to chart a new course with the Bishops' Conference of Medellín (1968). But let us examine certain other aspects of our author's thought as well. His witness and his reflection still have much to teach us.

Conclusion to Part Two

If Las Casas was moved with compassion by the sight of the Indians' untimely, unjust death, the waging of war under the pretext of evangelization utterly scandalized him. We have just examined his reasons. These led him to break with a theology postulating a duty on the part of political power to be at the service of the church's mission.

One of the arguments advanced in an attempt to justify use of force in the evangelization of the Indies was the absence of miracles — that privileged means, it was said, of the church's first evangelization — for the winning of unbelievers to the truth. Our friar, who always looked at things from the other side, will say: Actually you have what you want. A great miracle is taking place in the Indies. After all, the atrocities of which the Indian nations are the victims "have made the name of Jesus Christ detestable, in such a way that what God is doing in the Indies is the greatest of miracles: that this people should believe in the things of faith while they behold the deeds of those who bear the name of Christians" (*Doce dudas*, Providence version, folio 179; the text is not found in this form in the BAE edition).[1] An evangelization that is miraculous indeed, if for unexpected reasons.

Written in the last years of Bartolomé's life, the *Doce dudas* has the character of an evaluation. The Christian faith was received by the tribes and nations of this continent in spite of the behavior of many of those who were there to transmit it. The meeting with Christianity was a nonmeeting with Christians. Against this inconsistency Las Casas struggled all his life. Consistent with the guidelines of the document *Christ the Evangelizer*, he championed a peaceful proclamation based on persuasion and dialogue. This meant a testimony running counter to that of those self-styled Christians. What is required are gestures of love and welcome. For this there is no need to be "great scholars in theology, nor eloquent and accomplished preachers." The gospel can be proclaimed by plebeian idiots and the ignorant, if they have "strong faith, and some little instruction on the articles of faith." Indeed, by giving a "good example of Christian living, these can attain the lot and place of holy apostles" (*H.I.,* bk. 1, ch. 76, *O.E.* 1:231b). This simple persons can do. Intellectual refinements are unnecessary. The important thing is that they bear witness to what they believe. This is how the love of God, which is the content of the gospel, is expressed.

This attitude implies a deep respect for the Indian nations, with an understanding of their culture and its religious elements. Bartolomé's important analysis of human sacrifice — so chilling to certain of his contemporaries — is a mighty effort to understand from within the behavior and values of the native people of this continent. The whole of the *Apologética historia,* in a certain sense, was written from this viewpoint. With the encounter between evangelization and an acknowledgment of the right to be different in matters of religion, the question of freedom in these matters arises. This impelled Las Casas to chart a course up river, to the headwaters.

Part Three _____

God's Memory

═══

✠ In the Indies, Europeans encountered entire nations that had no knowledge of the gospel. This was an altogether new experience for them. Furthermore, these unbelievers, or infidels, were not enemies, nor were they usurpers of Christian lands. Nothing of the kind had ever been known to medieval Christendom, which, for that matter, was little concerned (apart from the remarkable case of Raymond Lull) with the evangelizing of the Jews or the Muslims.[1] To this it must be added that the historical relationship of Jews or Muslims to Christian nations was very different from that of the dwellers of the Indies.[2]

The novelty was so overwhelming that it gave rise to strange theses about the Indians — such as that they were descendents of the lost tribes of Israel[3] or of peoples who had once received a proclamation of the gospel by the apostle Thomas.[4] Bartolomé de Las Casas's concerns were different. He never entertained such bizarre notions. One of the reasons he held aloof from theories like these — and the point is worthy of mention — was that certain individuals appealed to them to justify the wars being waged on the Indians. After all, in the supposition of a first Christianization, or evangelization, the natives of the Indies would have to be regarded as apostates from the faith, which they had once received, or at least as recalcitrant hearers of a gospel that had been proclaimed to them once upon a time. On this supposition, in the thinking of the age, acts of violence against the Indians — in defense of the true faith, which they had abandoned — became legitimate. There is no innocent theology!

The proclamation of the gospel, as we have seen, was the major concern of the great missionary Bartolomé de Las Casas. But precisely here, on this central point of the Christian message — the proclamation of the gospel — Bartolomé's experience of the New World stirs

him to a rereading that will lead him to interesting theological intuition, and distance him from the Western, and ultimately comfortable,
theology of salvation dominant in his time. The concrete problem with
which Bartolomé de Las Casas begins, without knowing where it will
lead, is how to proclaim salvation in the Indies, that is, under the conditions (and with the implications) dictated by the concrete reality. We
speak of "intuitions," and of a "distancing" from a certain theology
of salvation, because in fact we are dealing with something rich and
promising but still incipient. It could scarcely have been otherwise.

God's salvific activity is the content of evangelization and "is the
end, or final cause, for which these [Indies] have been granted by the
Church to the Sovereigns of Castile and León, who until now have had
no stake in them" (*Treinta proposiciones*, 1552, O.E. 5:255a–b). This "final
cause" is the criterion which allows one to sift events of the Indies and
by which the legitimacy or illegitimacy of the Spanish presence in the
Indies must be judged. On this foundation, then, a norm of behavior
arises. The required behavior will be "obligatory under pain of the
eternal damnation" for those who have responsibility in these matters
(*Carta al Consejo*, 1531, O.E. 5:44a). The idea is plain and exacting: the
eternal salvation of believers is rightly linked to that of unbelievers.

Teresa Silva Tena makes a perceptive observation apropos of two
of Bartolomé de Las Casas's most important works:

> If we compare the *Apologética* with the *Historia*, both works ex-
> plain their author's entire vocation. While the first is the story
> of *faithful infidels* (faithful to their own religions), the second, to
> a great extent, is that of *faithless faithful* — Christians who fail to
> put their beliefs into practice, and thus are not only inconsistent
> with themselves, but unfaithful as well to the providential mis-
> sion entrusted to them by God of Christianizing the inhabitants
> of the New World.[5]

Each of these books, the *Apologética* and the *Historia*, enriches the focus
of the other.

Salvation of unbelievers and believers, proclamation of the gospel
to both,[6] and defense of the Indians' life and liberty: here are Las
Casas's great concerns. They all have their foundation in his experience — and his notion — of God, whose solicitude for the abandoned
of history Bartolomé expresses in a beautiful phrase of profoundly
biblical inspiration: "God has a very fresh and living memory of the
smallest and most forgotten" (ibid., O.E. 5:44b).

In the three chapters of Part Three, we shall see how Las Casas
confronts the questions presented to him by the deadly reality of the
Indies with respect to the salvation of unbelievers. The thorny matter of human sacrifices, which we have begun to examine, endows the

problem with all the more urgency once freedom in religious matters is presumed to be required. How is this concrete reality to be appraised from a theological viewpoint? As he begins to address the subject, Bartolomé is forced into uncharted territory. The only map he has consists of the distinctions he finds in scholastic theology, which he makes use of but goes beyond as well, and on more than one occasion.

Bartolomé begins with the theology that has been bequeathed to him, but he endeavors to extract from it the greatest possible advantage for his combat in defense of the life and rights of the Indians. His notion of God and his concern for the eternal destiny of those who call themselves Christians will assist him in broadening his perspectives. Las Casas will not divorce salvation from justice. The observance of the latter is a condition for gaining the former.

The theology of the age was very rigid concerning the salvation of non-Christians. But Las Casas, like certain others of his time, gradually comes to perceive that the new facts do not fit into the abstract mold of the dominant doctrine. This leads him to glimpse pathways little trodden in his day. Paradoxically, along these "new" routes he rediscovers positions maintained in the first centuries of the church (and thus more traditional than the soteriology of his time), which theology and the magisterium of the church have recovered only in our own day. Once more his sense of the mystery of God and of the certainty of God's love for the last and least of history enables him to chart routes.

Chapter 7 _____

Conscience in God's Sight

The concrete reality of the Indies posed new challenges to sixteenth-century missioners and theologians. But very few of them had had any practical experience of this reality with which to combine their theoretical acumen. Bartolomé's case was different. Thus, we see the most original elements of Las Casas's reflection when he faces these challenges, which he does within the framework of a polemical confrontation that stirs his creative faculty. This is what occurs in the matter of the salvation of the dwellers of these lands. His defense of the Indians thus becomes his great theological catalyst.

A case in point is the complex matter of human sacrifice. The problem is a key one in the dispute that raged over the legitimacy of the wars against the Indians. Furthermore, it posed once again, and with renewed urgency, the questions of freedom in matters of religion and of the salvation of the natives of the Indies. Las Casas will be facing these questions in a struggle that he will have to wage alone, against all the other thinkers who address the matter. Nor will he be intimidated. On the contrary, the confrontation will occasion his discovery of unprecedented and surprising ramifications of one of his great theological intuitions: *The God of Jesus Christ is the God who gives life.* Here he will underline his point of continuity — as well as of daring breach — with received theological tradition. New, if rough and rocky, paths now open before him in the question of salvation.

Nothing authorizes Christians to wage war on the Indians — not even the customs that so scandalized and obsessed Las Casas's contemporaries. The question "before human beings," after a laborious but well-founded process of reasoning, has been resolved. Our author's main objective has been attained. What he has sought to do is refute the most powerful argument for armed intervention against the Indian nations: solidarity with the victims of human sacrifice. Vitoria had given in to it. Las Casas rejects it on the basis of his own concerns for a peaceful evangelization and the salvation of the Indians. His daring theses were gradually making inroads. Among his contemporaries, only his constant ally, Domingo de Soto, sympathized with them for the moment. But later on, the great masters of Salamanca will do so and will cite Las Casas as their authority in the matter.[1]

1. Duties and Rights of Conscience

But the issue has another vector, and Bartolomé had painstakingly distinguished it from the question of responsibility "before human beings." Namely, what is the subjective moral situation — the responsibility in conscience, the sin if there is one — of those who perform these immolations? This is a question that will have to be resolved in terms of their *relationship with God*. While distinct from the other, this problem is nevertheless inseparable from it. Las Casas barely touches on it in the *Apología*. He does not have it directly in his sights. But neither can he escape the implications for this second question of the treatment he has accorded the question "before human beings."

Sepúlveda will note the connection in words of scandal and indictment, and Las Casas takes account of his adversary's objection in his reply (see *Aquí se contiene*). In the *Apología*, Bartolomé appeals to the Thomistic teaching on the *erroneous conscience* and applies it to the unprecedented case of the Indies. Thomas's teaching will also permit him to respond to his adversary's harshest criticism. Let us recall Thomas's doctrine, before analyzing Las Casas's use of it.

The Erroneous Conscience

The very expression "erroneous conscience," which we meet in medieval scholastic philosophy and theology, reflects a concern for the subjective aspects of moral comportment, which traditional theology had once neglected. The terms composing it express elements in tension. "Erroneous" denotes a materially false content and thereby posits the existence of an objective religious and moral truth. "Conscience" denotes the subjective aspect, the personal appropriation of that truth.

It was the celebrated and controversial Peter Abelard who, by underscoring the importance of the subjective intention, gave the first impulse to what would come to be a more complex assault on the series of problems involved. In reaction to Abelard, the Franciscan school, taking its inspiration in St. Augustine, steps forward as the advocate for the objective order: in case of a contradiction between the verdict of conscience and the objective imperative, an erroneous conscience may not be followed. We shall attempt to make our way through the morass of controversy that this reaction now produced among the various theological schools by focusing on Thomas Aquinas.[2] And this for two reasons. First, Thomas offers us, in this matter as in so many others, a clear, creative synthesis among the various positions of his time. Second, Thomas is Las Casas's principal theological source.[3] Let us note, however, that the Angelic Doctor finds himself addressing a supremely difficult question. Thus, as we shall see, his attempt at a synthesis will be only that — an attempt. There will be certain elements that he will not succeed in integrating.

Thomas touches on the subject throughout his writings, and we note an evolution in his position with respect to it. We shall concentrate on his *Summa Theologiae*, which represents his final position. Here he lays down the basic principle in all its pellucidity: morally correct behavior will always entail following one's conscience. In other words, conscience always places its subject under obligation. After all, the will moves according to the good as presented by reason. But reason can err. Now, conscience depends on reason's apprehension of good or evil. "The goodness of the will depends on reason as on its object" (I–II, q. 19, a. 3, c.). Here let us recall that for Thomas Aquinas conscience is not the *ultimate norm* of morality: it obliges only insofar as it is the interpreter of the most basic norm of all, which is in God.

If conscience always obliges, the question inevitably arises whether one has a duty to follow an erroneous conscience too, and not only a correct one, that is, whether there is a duty to follow an imperative of conscience based on a faculty of reason that presents an error as if it were truth. The Angelic Doctor poses two questions here, and we must distinguish them as carefully as he does himself.

The first question may be enunciated as follows. When the will fails to follow an erroneous conscience, is that will thereby *evil*? This is tantamount to asking: Does an erroneous conscience bind always, in every situation?[4] Now, some authors, Thomas begins, think that an erroneous conscience binds subjectively only in the case of objectively indifferent acts, never, therefore, when enjoining an action or an abstention that would be against the objective good. Thomas rejects this opinion altogether.[5] And he gives an example that will be of particular interest to us because it refers to the question of heathenism. "To believe in Christ is in itself good and necessary for salvation, but the will is directed to it only under the appearance in which it is presented by reason; so that if the reason proposes this act as evil, the will, in tending to it, does evil — not, of course, because it is evil in itself [to believe in Christ], but because of the incidental apprehension on the part of the will" (I–II, q. 19, a. 5, c.). The conclusion follows immediately: "It is to be asserted absolutely and without qualification that any will that is in nonconformity with reason, whether that reason be right or false, is evil" (ibid.).[6] This thesis, which the Franciscan school of his time did not accept, for Thomas admits of no exception whatever.

In the next article, article 6 of question 19, Thomas poses a further, more difficult problem: "Whether the will that conforms to an erroneous reason is *good.*" Actually, the phrasing of this title promises more than the article delivers. The article limits itself to an examination of whether an erroneous conscience excuses the person who follows it, to which question Thomas responds in the affirmative. But there is actually no clear pronouncement on the moral goodness (or evil) of the act in question. Let us note that this absence of a definitive judgment is itself an important step in Thomas: it expresses a significant evolution in his thought. And it is important for our own purposes, since it will leave its mark on Las Casas's discourse on the topic. The decisive point in Thomas's maturation on this point is to be found in the *type* of ignorance meant. Let us explain.

In his earliest works, Thomas has maintained a rigoristic position on the morality of an act performed in conformity with an erroneous conscience: a sin is committed not only in acting against an erroneous conscience, but in acting in conformity with it as well.[7] Lottin explains the rigorism of this posture: up until now, our doctor has not introduced the question of the different *kinds* of ignorance, which would have helped him to a more precise understanding of the erroneous conscience. Thomas will supply for this omission in the *Summa.*[8] But for the moment, he merely recalls that an act is good or evil only if it is voluntary, and this depends on one's *de facto* responsibility for a knowledge or ignorance of what is concretely at stake. Two situations can present themselves:

1. "If reason or conscience are erroneous through voluntary error, direct or indirect — in the form of an error concerning what it ought to know — then that error does not exonerate of evil the will that has conformed to that erroneous reason or conscience" (*Summa Theologiae,* I–II, q. 19, a. 6, c.). We are dealing with *culpable* (because it is vincible) ignorance, which renders morally evil any voluntary action that is in conformity with the erroneous conscience in question.

2. But "if the error renders the act involuntary by reason of ignorance of some circumstance without any negligence, then that error will excuse from all culpability the will that obeys such an erroneous reason or conscience" (ibid.) Here we have an *inculpable* (since it is invincible) ignorance, which has the effect that the ensuing act is not a *moral* evil.

Now in this second case, not only is there no culpability, but indeed (as we have already observed) to depart from the dictate of conscience — even of this erroneous conscience — would be morally evil.[9] At this point, however, we feel a profound uneasiness with

Thomas's teaching on the question, a malaise that leaves its stamp on the difficulties Bartolomé de las Casas himself will have elucidating the matter. After all, the situation is as follows. Not to follow an erroneous conscience is a sin. To act in conformity with it, on the basis of a culpable ignorance, is likewise a sin. At the same time — and this is the contribution of the distinction that we have recalled — while one does not commit evil when acting in conformity with an inculpably ignorant conscience, *neither* does one perform a morally *good* act. In other words, *even though an erroneous conscience obliges one to perform an act, it does not render that act morally good.* Why not? Because an erroneous conscience, as such, is not in conformity with the ultimate objective norm of morality: the divine law. Such a conscience, therefore, cannot render the act morally good. Moral goodness presupposes the presence of all of the elements required for the same: if one is missing, integrity is missing, and thus goodness as well.[10]

Good or Evil?

And so Thomas is on the horns of a dilemma. After all, he holds that human acts are always concretely either good or evil. No middle ground is possible in the concrete. Then what is the status of the behavior of a person who follows an erroneous conscience based on invincible ignorance? How will moral theology pronounce? Will this concrete conduct be good? Or will it be evil? It must be one or the other. Aquinas does not seem to have resolved the difficulty.[11] For all the daring of the principles with which he begins, then, with their acknowledgment of the place of subjective actors in moral behavior,[12] still Thomas ends up restricting the logical scope of their applications. Why? Perhaps, among other reasons, in order to avoid falling into the position of Abelard, who had not hesitated to acknowledge the concrete act in this case to be morally good.[13]

One of the consequences of Thomas's principles is of special interest to us in terms of our subject. If it is a *duty* to follow an erroneous conscience, how far does the corresponding *right* go? Thomas Aquinas does not address the question specifically.[14]

Here let us recall that according to Thomas's doctrine three conditions are required for a subjective right, which is defined as the competency to possess, do, or demand that which is one's due. First, only a person can be the subject of a right. Second, this right is exercised with regard to a good, an object. Third, a subjective right involves a relationship among persons: a moral power over a good is a right against another person (see *Summa Theologiae*, II–II, q. 57). In our case, the subject of the right would be a person with an erroneous conscience; the good would be an action, in the context of an obligation to follow one's conscience; the "person against" whom the right is asserted will be constituted by all other persons, society, and those who wield societal authority.

However, neither in Thomas Aquinas nor in the other medieval theologians do we find any assertion of the rights of persons in error.[15] The social context of the time, like the vagueness that prevailed in the matter of the moral quality of the behavior prescribed by an erroneous conscience, scarcely facilitated the task. Still, as we have seen, the foundation has been laid for this development. Theologians will build on it later. Las Casas will be among the first.

Before resuming our examination of the Dominican missionary's ideas, we must first say something more about the teaching of Thomas Aquinas. There is another distinction to be made concerning ignorance, and it plays an important role in the question of human sacrifice. There is such a thing as ignorance regarding facts (*ignorantia facti*) and such a thing as ignorance regarding law (*ignorantia juris*). The former can be invincible and, as we know, excuses from guilt. Taking adultery as his example, Thomas asserts that, "if the error is due to ignorance of person, and the husband mistakes another woman for his wife in the fulfillment of her conjugal duty, his will excuses him from sin, since the error proceeds from a circumstance that renders the act involuntary" (*Summa Theologiae*, I–II, q. 19, a. 6, c.). This would be ignorance of a fact.

On the other hand, it is impossible to be ignorant of *law*. In this case, then, there is no excuse whatever. On the basis of the example already cited, it will have to be said, then, that "when an erroneous reason enjoins adultery upon a human being, the will that follows it cannot be excused, as it is error due to ignorance of the divine law, which one is obliged to know" (ibid.). Indeed, Aquinas admits ignorance of divine law or ecclesiastical law[16] as an excusing cause only in the case of insanity or feeble-mindedness.[17] The foundation of this rigid position lies in the conviction that everyone can and ought to know the natural law, as well as in the presumption that the gospel has by now been proclaimed to the whole of humanity, so that every person of good will is in a position to know its principal exigencies.[18]

It is not hard to see the implications of this position for the case of the dwellers of the Indies. Bartolomé de las Casas will have to come to grips, then, with these scholastic theses.

2. The Right to Be Different

The concrete situation Bartolomé de Las Casas must face is different from the one confronting Master Thomas. New facts offer new challenges and lead to different positions. Las Casas discerns this and even blazes new trails — always moving within a scholastic framework, however, since to take too great a distance from it would actually weaken his defense of the Indians, and he is perspicacious enough to realize this. Theologically speaking, the human sacrifices offered by the dwellers of the Indies seem to him to correspond to an erroneous conscience on the part of the Indians, as he repeatedly states in the *Apología*. Thus, it has been important for us to recall the basic elements of the problem of the morality of human comportment as they appear in the commonly received theology of the sixteenth century. In that context we have a better understanding of Fray Bartolomé's limitations and contributions.

Moral Responsibility

How do the human sacrifices fare "before God"? What responsibility in the sight of God lies with the subjective conscience of those who offer them? In other words, is there moral culpability in these deeds? Clear as he has been as to the inadequacy of this consideration to justify the wars ("before human beings") Fray Bartolomé wavers on the second question ("before God"). He is less clear-cut and at times contradictory. He knows he has hot coals in his hands.

Let us cite just one among the several passages in Las Casas on the role of an erroneous conscience in idolatry and human sacrifice:

> Both the voluntary victims of such sacrifices and the members of the common people in general, such as the ministers who sacrifice them to the gods by mandate of their princes and priests, act under the effects of an *excusable and invincible ignorance*, and their error ought to be forgiven, even under the supposition that there would be some judge at hand with the authority to punish these sins. (*Apología*, 166v; emphasis added)

Nor, indeed, does our author admit this supposition, however great the authority of these hypothetical judges. That is, no one — no Christian prince, not the church itself — may arrogate to itself the right to castigate these misdeeds. And even if they might, they may not exercise it in this case, since these acts spring from an erroneous conscience: the conscience of those who believe themselves to be performing a good deed.[19] Once more, the objective is to disqualify the use of force against the Indians; but the argument also points to the question of the ethical responsibility of those who perform the human sacrifices.

Bartolomé sees further still. Taking his point of departure in Thomas Aquinas, for whom an erroneous conscience always obliges so that to fail to follow it would be sinful, Bartolomé draws bold conclusions:

> Inasmuch as they are pleased to maintain the sacrilegious opin-ion that in worshiping their idols they worship the true God, or that such idols are God, and despite the supposition that they have an erroneous conscience until the true God is preached to them with better and more credible and convincing arguments and especially with examples of a Christian behavior they are surely *obliged to defend the worship of their gods and their religion and to sally forth with their armed forces* against anyone who would attempt to deprive them of such worship or religion, or occa-sion them any injury, or prevent their sacrifices. They are obliged to struggle against the latter, slay them, take them captive, and exercise all rights that qualify as corollary of a just war, in con-formity with the Law of Nations. (Ibid., 168–168v; emphasis added)

Let us pause a moment at this unusual text. Once more, Las Casas records his personal revulsion for human sacrifice. It is an act that con-forms to what he calls a "sacrilegious opinion." But he observes that, due to the fact that they are in a situation of erroneous conscience, the Indians in their idols "worship *the true God*." The point is important for him. And so, just above the text we have just cited, he has specified an important exception: "If it is to idols *as such* that the heathen offer sacrifice, it surely does not seem that they can be excused on grounds of invincible ignorance, according to the common opinion of the doc-tors" (ibid., 166v; emphasis added). In that case, there is no invincible ignorance; consequently, neither is there any excuse from culpability for the deeds performed on the basis of an erroneous conscience. But exculpation *is* at hand if *in* the idols the true God is the goal. It will be superfluous to state that, for our friar, the latter is precisely the case with the Indians.[20]

Furthermore, Las Casas draws conclusions that must have made his contemporaries' hair stand on end. The Indians "are obliged" to defend their own traditions and religion by force of arms against those who would seek to suppress them by force. So we have a just war in-deed. But contrary to the position maintained by the theologians who sought to justify the acts of the conquistadors, it is the Indians who are waging the just war, against the Christians, as they battle for their false religion that they regard as true. No wonder the Dominican's contemporaries were scandalized. But neither is it surprising that they found Las Casas so hard to refute. He is simply drawing conclusions consistent with a rigorous scholastic logic.

Entirely apart from the rent garments that strew Bartolomé's path, however, it is the theological meaning of his position that interests us. From the *duty* to follow an erroneous conscience, our author deduces (as Thomas Aquinas did not) the corresponding *rights*. In this case, he concludes to the right (in the face of the interference of foreign peoples and new political authorities) of the Indians to see to it that their own religious convictions and customs are respected (and let us not forget that among these is human sacrifice) and even to fight for these in a war that will be altogether justified: a war on the Christians.

Bartolomé's defense of the Indian has taken him very far indeed. Concretely, it has led him to go one step beyond what medieval philosophy explicitly states and acknowledge the *social and political rights of a person in error*. In the case at hand, it is worth noting, this will be the *right of an entire people,* since it is a matter of an interest "common to them all, who, in the presence of a cause that they regard as just, will reap the advantage that they will be even more encouraged to struggle valiantly and will prefer to die rather than to leave unavenged the offenses offered to their gods and to fail to expel such aggressors from their country" (*Apología,* 168v). The assertion of this right is added to the response given to what, as we have seen, Las Casas (and Domingo de Soto) regarded as the question "before human beings."

Personal rights are exercised in society. Bartolomé calls on Christians to acknowledge and respect the rights of the Indians in matters of religion. Differences in religion ought not necessarily lead to acts of war. Indeed, Bartolomé's reflections on the justice of a defensive war against those who violate religious customs are only that same call applied to an extreme theoretical case. And yet this extreme case is concretely verified in the situation of the natives of the Indies, by reason of unjust wars of conquest waged on them and the upheaval these wars occasioned throughout their world of values. With this position on the rights of persons who act in accordance with an erroneous conscience, Las Casas becomes an innovator in the theology of his time.

It is interesting to observe that in Europe from the end of the sixteenth century onward — beginning with the second generation of Christians after the Protestant Reformation — in a move beyond medieval theology the way will gradually be paved for an acknowledgment of the rights of a person who is in error,[21] although the point will actually remain unclarified up till recent times. The bishop of Chiapa, then, enters the scene as one of the first theologians to affirm these rights.

Bartolomé's defense acquires even greater interest if we keep in account that in sixteenth-century Europe this acknowledgment is made in a perspective of the relationship between, on the one side, persons taken individually and, on the other, civil power: political authority ought to guarantee the liberty of individuals in matters of religion. Las Casas's concrete situation leads him to broach the same question, but from a more comprehensive, collective viewpoint. For him, it is a matter of the rights of individuals, indeed, but also — let us repeat — of the *Indian nations* vis-à-vis the Western Christian countries that had undertaken the conquest and occupation of the Indian continent. What is in question are not only individual rights, but, especially those of a whole people: here, their right to require that their religion, however mistaken it be, be respected.

"The Doctor Would Compel Me..."

All of this is too much for Bartolomé's most dogged adversary, who thinks that the bishop has finally lost his mind.

After the first session of the controversy of Valladolid, Sepúlveda presents twelve objections to Las Casas's reading of his *Apología*.[22] The eleventh objection deals with our subject and indignantly rejects the Lascasian thesis that has concerned us in the preceding section: the right of the Indians to defend their religion. The matter annoys him, as the Dominican was to say. Sepúlveda asserts: "If these barbarians justly defend their religion and idolatry, as the main thrust of his book would have us believe and as my Lord Bishop has plainly stated in his *Confesionario*, it would follow that they justly approve and consequently justly and sinlessly honor idols, since it is a more serious sin to approve crime than not to commit it. But this is inadmissible among Catholics, since idolatry, in the opinion of all theologians, is the most serious of all sins *and against natural reason:* after all, ignorance of the natural law excuses no one, as theologians and canonists agree" (1552, *O.E.* 5:316a; emphasis in original).

There can be no invincible ignorance among the Indians: idolatry (and human sacrifice; see ibid., 5:315b) is contrary to the natural law. What we have, rather, is inexcusable ignorance on the part of Las Casas himself.[23] The text is trenchant and perceptive. Sepúlveda's argument takes as its premise Las Casas's own most daring notion: the rights of persons in error. In his eleventh reply (corresponding to Sepúlveda's eleventh objection), the bishop of Chiapa specifies with agility and clarity the meaning of his reasoning on the matter of responsibility "before human beings" and defends himself — not altogether unhesitatingly — against the accusations being made with respect to the culpability of the Indians (that is, the question of responsibility "before God"). But this time his adversary obliges him to link the two questions even more closely.

Under Sepúlveda's onslaught (on the alleged nonculpability of the Indians), Las Casas replies, "The Doctor would compel me to accept his logic" (*O.E.* 5:334a). What he had proposed to do — he repeats — was "to prove, based on evident premises, that [the Indians] suffer an ignorance and plausible [or invincible] error such as would prevent them from believing, the first time or even after many times, what the Christians tell them to the effect that it is against natural law, or a sin, to sacrifice human beings. Consequently, they cannot justly be punished for this by human beings or by a human verdict" (ibid.).[24] Because there is no culpable violation of the natural law here — among other reasons, but this one responds to Sepúlveda's most powerful argument — Christians may not rightly proceed to punish the Indian peoples.

This is precisely the key to the Lascasian interpretation when it comes to the supposed punitive right of the Iberians. But now he incorporates it into the question of responsibility before God, and now there will be no turning back. Nor is this lost on Sepúlveda, who therefore insists — echoing a traditional teaching — that such sacrifices are contrary to natural reason. Consequently, they constitute a sin. "After all, ignorance of natural law excuses no one." Bartolomé does not dispute that principle. His position is a more subtle one. He has already broached the question of the "nature of the error" afflicting the dwellers of the Indies, and that has led him to audacious conclusions that set him apart within the Thomistic school. His point of departure is in the question of invincible ignorance. Again and again he will say that the Indians cannot possibly overcome their error, as error it surely is for Bartolomé. However, the bishop of Chiapa knows perfectly well that, in Thomas's teaching, there is no such thing as invincible error in the area of natural law (or even church law).

An appeal to the exception posited by the Doctor of Aquino for the feeble-minded and the insane would contradict Bartolomé's lofty concept of the Indians' human qualities, values that he defended all his life. With this facile solution, so antipathetic to his deepest convictions, out of reach, what is he to do? As we have seen, Las Casas comes forward with a bold assertion: he denies that the offering of human sacrifice is contrary to the natural law. And he arrives at his position, as we have also seen, through a shrewd analysis of the religious meaning of such sacrifice. We have cited texts from the *Apología* and the *Apologética historia* in which he declares that *natural law* simply enjoins the offering of sacrifice to God. It is left to *positive law* to determine the material of that sacrifice. Human sacrifice, consequently, is not a violation of the natural law.

He appeals to this same analysis in his reply to Sepúlveda's objections. He writes:

It is not easy to prove to them that it is against natural law to offer human victims in sacrifice to the true God (or to a false one, if the latter is held and deemed to be true). In fact, there are good, probable, and all but irrefutable reasons that might be adduced to the contrary, and we have set forth these at length in our *Apología* and read them out in the presence of many theologians and scholars. (*Aquí se contiene*, 1552, O.E. 5:334b)[25]

The withdrawal of the question of human sacrifice from the terrain of natural law is precisely what aroused the towering wrath of Ginés de Sepúlveda, who maintained the opposite position. Nor, we must admit, was he alone in this. Here, truth to tell, Las Casas was at odds with the common opinion of theologians of his time — as Sepúlveda reminded him, altogether correctly, in the text that we have cited above. For the most notable of these theologians, Francisco de Vitoria, there was not the shadow of a doubt about this matter: "It is forbidden," he writes in a text that we have already cited, "by natural and divine law to offer to God human sacrifices" (*Obras*, 1032). The matter is of capital importance. When it comes to natural law, according to theologians, ignorance is never invincible. Thus, the offering of human sacrifices will inevitably be sin. This is what Bartolomé denies, transferring the question of the content of these sacrifices to the level of positive law, the area of human determinations. Actually in the area of positive law, ignorance can be invincible.[26] Thus does Las Casas take his distance from Vitoria.

3. *Situation before God*

But in acting in this way, do the Indians commit a sin in the eyes of Christian faith or not? Or instead, do they perform a morally good act? This is the next question. The answer will not determine the justification of the wars being waged on the Indians: no sin the Indians could commit would make acts of war against them legitimate. Nevertheless, Las Casas cannot avoid undertaking an explicit treatment of the subject, such as he has offered in his *Apología*. His adversary will not permit it. And this is the second point of his reply.

Between Thomas and the Indians

Las Casas is conscious of having gone terribly far with the theses he has propounded. (See his letter to the Dominicans of Chiapa and Guatemala, cited above.) He is sailing in treacherous, uncharted waters. In the *Apología*, he had said that the Indians are under an obligation to defend their religious traditions by force of arms. This means, as we have observed, ascribing social and political rights to an erroneous conscience, an ascription absent from medieval theology. In his reply to criticism, he maintains his stance. His position is clear. But under the salvos of his opponent, he enters upon an examination of the correlative question — that of the moral responsibility implied in all of this.

Sepúlveda concludes that, having asserted that the Indians "justly defend their religion and idolatry" against other peoples, Las Casas must likewise hold that they "justly and sinlessly honor idols" and offer human sacrifices. Actually, Fray Bartolomé has been careful not to assert this explicitly. Thus, his reply will be unprejudiced. He had postulated two things:

1. The Indians are obliged to follow their conscience, which presents them with something evil as if it were something good — the offering to God of human life itself. But, following Thomas Aquinas, he does not say that, in acting accordingly, they are doing something good.

2. The Indians have a duty to defend their religious customs. This second point, enunciated in the *Apología,* is developed in the eleventh reply. Las Casas writes:

> Given the error or erroneous conscience that the idolaters have, to the effect that those gods are true God, or whom they hold for true God that they honor and worship, they have not only just — or probable, if you will — cause to defend their religion; but they are actually obliged to that [defense] *by natural law,* in such a way that, if they omit it, even at the cost of their lives were that to be necessary, for the defense . . . of their idols or gods, *they sin mortally.* (O.E. 5:336a; emphasis added)

In the *Apología* he had spoken of the obligation to undertake such a defense, without entering upon a moral qualification of the act. Now he specifies: to omit it would be sinful. And so, if Sepúlveda would hear of the Indians' moral transgressions, the first one that Bartolomé lists for him will come as a surprise: the sin they would commit if they failed to require that their religious customs be respected. Natural law, indeed, requires it, Las Casas maintains, with unintentional irony. Indeed, that defense is a demonstration of the love and service of God (see ibid).

This is what the Christian martyrs did, continues Las Casas imperturbably, when they laid down their lives in defense of their faith. Furthermore, in conformity with his methodological principle of reasoning "as if we were Indians," he declares that the Indians are under obligation to defend their God and their religion, "just as we Christians are to defend our true God and the Christian religion, so that unless they did so they would sin mortally, just as we should sin should we fail to do so when necessity arose" (*O.E.* 5:336b). What is valid for Christians is valid for Indians. It is the same right. Why? Because "an erroneous conscience binds and obliges just as does a right conscience" (ibid.), says the Dominican, in the footsteps of his theologian, Thomas.

Thus Las Casas can impute to Sepúlveda an invalid illation. After all, it is one thing to say that the Indians have the duty — and the right — to defend their religion, and another thing altogether to say (as Sepúlveda tries to make him say) that this relieves those who offer human sacrifice of moral responsibility *before God*. (It does excuse them before human beings, as we have observed.) Bartolomé writes: "And thus what the Doctor infers does not follow, namely, that they can 'justly and sinlessly honor' and serve idols and commit idolatry simply on the basis of the justice and probable [or plausible] cause in defending them or being under obligation to defend them" (*O.E.* 5:337a). Sepúlveda's inference is precisely what Las Casas rejects. His adversary's fallacy lies in his having "failed to observe the nature of the error suffered by the idolaters and the material of the erroneous conscience," and he concludes crisply: "…hence the paralogism of his argument" (ibid.). Here we are, on this last point, with Thomas Aquinas's position on the duty to follow an erroneous conscience that mistakes an evil for a good. Las Casas recalls it, and profits by the occasion to tweak Sepúlveda's ear for not knowing it.[27]

A few lines earlier, Bartolomé had buttressed this reasoning with Thomas's principle, "An erroneous conscience binds and obliges as does a right conscience, although in a different way." Las Casas then appeals to a text for which he cites, first, the *Summa Theologiae*, I–II, q. 19, aa. 5, 6 (the articles that we have studied above), and second, the *Commentary on the Sentences*, II, d. 39, a. 3, q. 3. The passage he cites is not actually part of the *Summa*, however. It seems to have been picked out from the *Sentences*. In the *Sentences*, in the postulate that we have recalled, it is stated — and we have briefly alluded to this — that whether one follows an erroneous conscience or not one sins.[28] As we know, Thomas held this rigoristic position before addressing in the *Summa* the matter of the various kinds of ignorance. The distinction he makes in the *Summa* divides in two the question of the morality of any behavior that would flow from an erroneous conscience.

After all, as we have recalled, if the ignorance is voluntary, to follow an erroneous conscience is wrong: the ignorance on which it is based is vincible, and consequently to maintain that ignorance is to violate the moral law. On the other hand, if the ignorance is involuntary, and therefore invincible, it exculpates the person following his or her conscience. In the *Sentences*, however, likewise cited by Las Casas, no account is taken of the two cases resulting respectively from these two kinds of ignorance. This situates the assertion in a more rigoristic line: the subject of an erroneous conscience, whether he or she follows that conscience or not, always commits a moral wrong, whether of action or of omission.

Despite having come so far toward ascribing an invincible ignorance to the Indians, nevertheless, when it comes to a moral qualification, Las Casas allows himself to be carried off by the text he cites from the *Sentences*, without appealing to its later correction in the *Summa*. Accordingly, after maintaining that idolatrous Indians as well as Christian Spaniards are obliged under pain of mortal sin to defend their respective worship of God, he adds: "The similarity fails in this, that we, in doing so, perform a meritorious act, and they, in doing so, incur eternal damnation. After all, whether they do so or not, they act against the divine precept" (*O.E.* 5:336b). Here is Thomas's "Si fiat, peccatum non evitatur; si autem non fiat, peccatum incurritur." ("If it is done, sin is not avoided; but if it is not done, sin is committed.")

Doubtless the fact that in the change he makes in the *Summa* Thomas does not explicitly pronounce on the moral goodness of a conduct flowing from an erroneous conscience is part of the reason for Las Casas's failure to take cognizance of the change. (And we know that neither for Bartolomé nor for Thomas is there such a thing as a morally neutral act.) It had not been noticed in Bartolomé's time that Aquinas had changed his teaching on this matter. Had this change been noticed and had it been noticed that the change took place precisely between his early works and the *Summa*, it would have been possible for Las Casas to introduce some nuance, at least, into his own opinion. Bartolomé must pay a high price for the poor state of his sources.

In the *Apología*, in spite of his frequent reference to the case of the erroneous conscience and the obligation to follow it, Las Casas does not allude to the texts of the *Summa* and the *Sentences* to which he alludes here and which, mistakenly, he seems to regard as equivalent. We do not believe, however, that there is any radical change in his position in the eleventh reply — under Sepulvedian pressure — by comparison with the *Apología*. In fact, even in the latter, at the very moment he distinguishes the two great questions that have served as our guidelines in these pages, Las Casas expresses the *possibility* that the human sacrifices may involve moral fault: "Although *they are not excusable* before God, they are indeed *totally* so before human beings" (*Apología*, 152; emphasis added). The hesitating tone of his statement is maintained in the reply to Sepúlveda despite the straitjacket it is forced into, as we have just seen, by Thomas's most rigid texts.

This attitude is manifested from the beginning of his reply to

Sepúlveda's objection; the best answer that comes to his mind to Sepúlveda's imputation of moral fault on the part of the Indians is: "I am
not excusing them *before God*. I know not that judgment of God; it is inscrutable" (*O.E.* 5:334a; emphasis added). In the *Apología*, speaking of
the Indians' "excusable and invincible ignorance," he had maintained
a similar attitude: "If with such immolations they offend God, *God
alone* will punish this sin of sacrificing human beings" (166v; emphasis
added). God, not human beings. There are things that surpass human
understanding. Only God can judge the presence or absence of sin.
What is important to Las Casas, and this he does consider himself in
a position to establish, is to specify the illegitimacy of any punishment for those acts that other nations and persons might presume to
mete out. Upon this point — which sufficed for his thesis — Las Casas
brings all the effort of his intelligence and argumentation to bear.

On the other question, his last word is to abstain from an opinion
as to whether the offering of human sacrifices, under the conditions
in which it occurs in certain places in the Indies, is a sin or not. He
prefers to leave this question to the inscrutable judgment of God. "We
are ignorant of more about God than we know" about God, he can say,
with the same humility as his master, Thomas.

But none of Bartolomé's distinctions and specifications will satisfy
his adversary. Indeed, this closing appeal to the mysterious designs of
God scandalizes him. Sepúlveda writes:

> He says near the beginning of the eleventh reply that *he knows not
> what God judges* of the idolaters who sacrifice innocent human be-
> ings. But to doubt of the judgment of God is a thing manifestly
> contrary to Catholic faith and the precepts of the Decalogue. It is
> evidence either of not being a Christian, or of a lack of the knowl-
> edge and common sense of prudent and perspicacious persons.
> After all, anyone who knows that in evangelical and natural law
> alike God condemns homicidal idolaters, such as are those who
> sacrifice innocent persons to false gods, and nonetheless says
> that he does not know what God judges of them is consequently
> saying that he doubts the evangelical and indeed the natural
> law — since "knowing," here, is done with the certitude of faith,
> according to the common understanding of the doctors,... and
> not in virtue of any *a posteriori* demonstration. Does he hope to
> escape by way of this puerile quibble? (*Proposiciones temerarias,*
> 553–54; emphasis added)[29]

The Cordovan humanist pursues Bartolomé relentlessly, on grounds
of both natural reason and faith.

For Sepúlveda, the sin of the Indians is all too plain. Furthermore,
it is committed in the area of faith, so that to deny it will be hereti-

cal.[30] Or at best, such a denial will constitute a "puerile quibble" on the Lord Bishop's part, the hallmark of persons of little "prudence and perspicacity." Indeed, Sepúlveda invokes the sin the Indians commit to justify Christians' punitive wars against them. This is his final word in the debate. Las Casas — in conformity with his concern for evangelization — stands by his statements in concluding his reply on this point:

> As for the rest of this objection, I say that, from now till Judgment Day, never will any unbelievers be obligated, neither *as to God* nor *as to human beings,* to believe the faith of Jesus Christ, were the heralds of that faith to be men of war, killers, robbers, tyrants such as Doctor Sepúlveda would have and is dying to introduce. (*O.E.* 5:338a; emphasis added)

To his rejection of the reasons alleged for waging war on the Indians, Bartolomé adds the considerations that we have seen on the question of whether or not the human sacrifices are sinful. As we peruse these considerations, we cannot escape the impression that for Las Casas, in the concrete circumstances of the Indies, no moral fault is committed in the offering of these sacrifices. Nor does this escape the notice of Sepúlveda (or one of his followers) in a curious text. Apropos of Bartolomé's eleventh reply, the author in question states: "The Bishop himself says that he does not seek to excuse the infidels from sin in this matter. But this is untrue, since he is clearly laboring to excuse them when he says, first, that he does not know what the judgment of God is in their regard in this case — which to doubt is un-Christian" (*Proposiciones temerarias,* 567).[31] Indeed, for Las Casas, when all is said and done, God alone knows whether immorality has been committed, and God alone has the right to punish it if it has. Yes, this is indeed the position of the bishop of Chiapa on this thorny question.

Toward the True God

The question of responsibility "before God" for Bartolomé reinforces the argumentation he has brought to bear in his treatment of the question of their responsibility "before human beings." It is not the same question, however. The wars waged on the Indians for reason of their human sacrifices are not justified *in any case.* It is beyond the competency of Christian nations or the church to castigate such acts. This is the point he wishes to make plain. In fact, these acts — always keeping in account the concrete situation of the Indian nations — express a high degree of religious sensitivity; and mistaken though they may be, it does not seem to those who perform them that they are acting in contravention of the natural law. Las Casas is trying to understand the Indian world from within. This leads him to ascribe a value to behaviors that, in a Eurocentric perspective, provoked scandal.

Indeed, as we have seen, Bartolomé asserts that in offering these immolations the Indians evince a lofty sense of God, since they present God with the best thing they have: human life. That is to say, the very dynamics of his reasoning have led him — although his expressions are very cautious here — to a view that the Indians perform morally good acts (or at least, restricting our terminology to that of Thomas Aquinas, we may not say that they commit evil) in offering these sacrifices. Accordingly, these sacrifices do not represent an obstacle to their salvation. The dynamics of his discourse sometimes fail to find the most proper and precise language — or else they are caught in a trap of contradictory texts of Thomas — but they are certainly undisguised. Nor is this lost on his adversary.

Understandably, it was no easy task for Las Casas to make these assertions with all the clarity that might have been desired. Traditional doctrine in these areas left him a very narrow margin with which to work, and he stretched that margin to a point that his opponents regarded as dangerous and even heretical. Clear and bold as he has been in the *Apología* read out at Valladolid, he is led by Sepúlveda's attacks (the twelve objections provide us with supplementary testimony, as they refer to things that the bishop added verbally at the disputation), and perhaps by the discomfiture of friendly theologians, to explain again his positions. He reiterates them in the question of the Indians' responsibility *before human beings,* but he sees himself obliged to pare down his earlier conclusions regarding the moral responsibility of the Indians to defend their religious traditions by force of arms (even though this is not really the point; his main concern here is the question of their responsibility *before God*).[32] But he does not deny what he has said at Valladolid. His tone may be different, but the fundamental elements of his declarations abide. His central theses are the same. We can see this from Sepúlveda's last composition with regard to these same points (see *Proposiciones temerarias*).

Ten years before the Valladolid disputation, in condemning the *encomiendas* Las Casas had entertained reflections that touch on the matter concerning us here. The *encomenderos* argue that if they are deprived of their Indians, all the Spaniards will leave — which would jeopardize not only the sovereignty of the king, but the Catholic faith as well in the Indies, since their inhabitants would then return to their idolatry. Here, Las Casas lodges a daring rebuttal: "In order to be good Christians all ought to maintain, that even were it possible that Your Majesty lose all of his said royal sovereignty and that the Indians *never be Christians,* if the contrary could not be *except by their death* and their total destruction, as has been the case until now," then it would not be "inappropriate that Your Majesty cease to be sovereign over them and that they *were never Christians*" (*Octavo remedio*, 1542, *O.E.* 5:118a; emphasis added). The Dominican administers the *coup de grâce*. The proposition is fraught with consequences.

There is more than implacable logic here; there is a deep sense of God and the gifts of God. Texts like these enable us to grasp why Las Casas got a hearing, surely. But they also show us why he was — as he himself recognizes — "held in odious repute throughout those lands" by the conquistadors, *encomenderos*, and civil officials. Here Bartolomé is referring to the colonists of Hispaniola. But the antipathy he has aroused will promptly spread to the rest of the Indies. The reason is obvious: his opponents knew "that he meant to set the Indians free and deliver them from their murderers — which included each and every Spaniard there" (*H.I.*, bk. 3, ch. 54, *O.E.* 2:554a).

According to the passage that we have quoted from the *Octavo remedio*, it would be better for the Indians to follow their religion if the price of making them Christians is their death. In other words, a live pagan Indian is worth more than a dead Christian Indian, as J. Friede sums it up.[33] Here Las Casas shows himself a true disciple of the first Dominican community of Hispaniola, which, as we have seen, asserted something similar. These persons value the life of the body, too, as a gift of God, so that it is to be carefully respected.

One thing is certain. Through vacillation and perplexity, Las Casas enunciates audacious propositions when it comes to the respect due the religious convictions and customs of the Indian nations (the *rights* of an erroneous conscience), as well as with regard to the difficult question of the salvation of the heathen.[34] To the passages already cited, we may join these forthright lines: "After all, the idolaters believe what they are taught: that those idols are the true God, or that in them the true God is served and worshiped, or ought to be served and worshiped. And indeed, their universal concept is directed toward, and can only terminate with, *the true God alone*." Las Casas appeals to John Damascene, Gregory Nazianzus, Augustine, Boethius, St. Thomas, and "all the saints who treat of this matter" (*O.E.* 5:336b; emphasis added).

His adversaries perceived something new in the Dominican's assertions and sought to confute him. Bartolomé defended himself with courage and diligently strove to strike connections with tradition. In the effort, he risked entrapment in the limitations of scholasticism. But his opponents were not deceived in their perception that, at times, he tried to break out of his scholasticism. Today, from our broader perspective, we are in a position to form a better appreciation of both the continuity and the novelty of the theological paths he trod from his starting point in his defense of the Indians and his profound vision of the mystery of God's love.

It remains for us to investigate one further stage of Las Casas's journey. His theses on human sacrifices and on the religious customs of the Indians in general trenchantly pose the question of freedom of religion (and not merely that of the freedom of the act of faith, which we saw in Part Two). And this, in turn, will call for certain specifications on Las Casas's position with regard to the salvation of non-Christians. Very concretely, this will have a bearing on the possibility that the dwellers of these lands may attain to that salvation. This is the matter that will concern us in the following chapter.

Chapter 8

Salvific Will and Human History

Death or life. For Las Casas it is an either-or proposition. But this places him inevitably on the horns of a second dilemma: that of the salvation or perdition of the inhabitants of these lands. The soteriology, or salvation doctrine, prevailing in the church in Bartolomé's time seemed an invincible stumbling block to any understanding of the situation in the Indies. In this soteriology, Europeans, being Christians, were at an advantage over the Indians when it comes to being saved by God. But it is our friar's deep conviction not only that God has created all human beings equal, but that God wills them actually to be treated as such, in all regions of the earth. This, indeed, is the reason for God's special concern for the "insignificant of history" — persons who are treated by others as if they were somehow inferior. God "remembers" the injustice to which these persons are subjected. But how is this memory of God's to be expressed in the area of soteriology? Bartolomé will make his way laboriously, but doggedly, in this knotty theological question.

Arguing against the wars being waged on the Indians, Las Casas appeals to two classic postulates in the doctrine of salvation. After presenting a number of considerations against the use of force, he adds "this universal reason: that God and His Holy Church, by means of which He desires that human beings be saved and come to a knowledge of the truth, not be frustrated therein" (Apología, 177v). On the one hand, a universal salvific will and, on the other, the need for the church: in Las Casas's time, it was the latter principle on which the accent fell, to the detriment of the former.[1] Our author will adopt them both, but will read them in terms of his concerns for the Indies. Neither God nor the church of God must see their salvific will frustrated in the Indies.

1. *Faith and Defense of the Indians*

In continuity with ancient, authentic theological tradition, anchored in Scripture (see 1 Tim. 2:4), again and again Bartolomé de las Casas recalls the universality of God's salvific design. Frequently he does so within the narrow corridor conceded by the salvation doctrine of the Middle Ages for the difficult passage of the unbaptized. To be sure, this theology constituted an important component of his missionary motivation (as it did with that other great missionary, his contemporary Francis Xavier).[2] Nevertheless, the novelty of the situation he experiences in the Indies will enable him to discern a broader scope for the traditional teaching in these matters. His theological framework imposes certain limits on him; but his sensitivity and tenacity move him to seek responses to the questions that his experience and his evangelizing concern pose for him. They are very similar to the questions that disturbed the Christians of the early centuries.

Aptitude for the Faith

Las Casas must have begun his first work, *The Only Way*, of which only certain chapters have come down to us, with a reassertion of the universality of the salvific will of God. Indeed, at the beginning of chapter 5 (the first that we have), Bartolomé sums up what he has said in his "foregoing chapter," chapter 4, as follows:

> It was due to the will and work of Christ, the head of the Church, that God's chosen should be called, should be culled from every race, every tribe, every language, every corner of the world. Thus, no race, no nation on this entire globe would be left totally untouched by the free gift of divine grace. Some among them, be they few or many, are to be taken into eternal life. We must hold this to be true also of our Indian nations. (*De Unico*, 1v; *The Only Way*, 63)[3]

The declaration is simple and clear. The point is also made, as we have said, in many other passages in his works.

It is worthy of note, however, that for Las Casas an insistence on the universal salvific will of God gains a special importance due to the concrete, dynamic potential that he finds in this postulate. One of its consequences is of particular importance to him: if every human being is called to salvation, then *all are capable of receiving it*. This correlation had a very important meaning for him. The universal aptitude for accepting the gift of salvation is a basic theological argument in favor of the equality of all human beings and consequently of the human dignity of the Indian. The entire *Apologética historia* is written with this objective in mind, and Bartolomé concludes his demonstration with a justly celebrated text:

> There is no generation of human beings, however rude and politically unorganized, or wallowing in the gravest and most detestable sins, that they are without a capacity for the teaching of Christ and incapable of being healed by it: for [God] has made them all teachable and curable. And thus he is seen to have ordered his apostles and disciples and their successors: that without any discrimination or exception they should preach and proclaim his gospel to all nations, to the exclusion of no single one of them. (*A.H.*, ch. 253, *O.E.* 4:431b)

All are called to the gospel, and all are in a condition to make it their own.

These seemingly general statements on the capacity of every human being to receive the word of God have a particular motivation: a predilection for the very weakest, for the Indian. This is what is really at stake for Fray Bartolomé when he proclaims the equality of all human beings. Thus, he will maintain — to the discomfiture, no doubt, of those who would have preferred a formally egalitarian assertion unencumbered with his "sides-taking" and coming down to cases — that the Indians are "most apt to receive our holy Catholic faith, to be endowed with virtuous customs, and to behave in a godly fashion" (*La Brevísima,* 1552, *O.E.* 5:136a–b). Here is one of this missioner's most stubborn themes. And here is another text in the same vein, but more polemical in tone: "There is not in the entire world any people as ready to learn, or possessed of more fortitude and perseverance, or more ready and willing to receive the yoke of Christ, than these. And this is the very certain truth, the contrary being patent error and falsehood" (*Carta al Consejo,* 1531, *O.E.* 5:49a). The Dominican is indeed beset with numerous *encomenderos,* civil functionaries, and even missionaries who repeat this utterly baseless falsehood *ad nauseam.*

From the radical similarity of all human beings, so authentically attested by their capacity for the faith, Las Casas deduces the legitimacy and urgency of attempting to bring that faith to the Indians, especially by way of a proclamation of the gospel. Abominating the comportment — with its alleged Christian motivations — of the Portuguese toward African blacks, Las Casas holds instead:

> Wherever we find that we may offer a first sample of ourselves, by words and works, let it be peace. And let it be no different with the Indians, gentiles, Greeks, or barbarians: for there is one Lord of all, who died for all without distinction. (*H.I.,* bk. 1, ch. 17, *O.E.* 1:65–66)

Blacks and Indians, Greeks and barbarians — there is no difference. All are equal in God's sight, as Jesus' death attests.[4] Thus, "the
heavens and the earth and all that descends from the skies, as the influences and the elements on the earth, are common benefits granted
by God to all human beings without distinction, and God has made
them natural sovereigns over it all no more or less than the others"
(ibid., 1:66a). The equality of persons has its source in the love of God.

In a similar vein, in response to the presumption of those who arro-
gated to themselves the right to punish the Indians for their supposed
sin of unbelief and idolatry, Las Casas consigns the matter to the judgment and goodness of God, who wishes all creatures well. In an early
letter to the Council of the Indies, he maintains:

> Although God decree by secret judgments of His own that these
> people be castigated, woe to the instruments by whom He cas-
> tigates them! For it is His will that all be saved and come to a
> knowledge of Him; and that all might believe, after He came and
> took our flesh, that His name is called Father of mercies, there-
> fore with mercy, sweetness and mildness, peace and piety did
> He desire that the world be converted to His faith. (1531, *O.E.*
> 5:48–49)

The universal salvific will of God protects the Indians from over-
zealous Christians with their selfish interests, who would do better
to emulate the behavior of the God in whom they claim to believe.

It was important — and urgent — to emphasize this capacity and
these rights of the Indian. These rights were being denied in order to
justify the subjection of the Indian to the European. Thus, the proposition that this aptitude has its ultimate foundation in God, in the
universal salvific will of God, cannot be maintained without taking
account of the viewpoint underlying it. It is not a matter of the simple philosophical assertion of the equality of all human beings, so
complacently emphasized by the many scholars of Bartolomé de Las
Casas who would see him as a precursor of the liberal doctrine of
human rights. This interpretation is a good deal more sensitive to the
mentality and ideology of modernity than to the specific reasons that
have induced our Dominican to take up the defense of the "Indian
oppressed": *an evangelical preference for the last and least of history.*

The Eleventh Hour

We are actually dealing with a privilege based on the free, gratuitous
love of God, on the divine memory of the "least and most forgotten."
We find a good example in something with which Las Casas was very
familiar and which he recounts to us a number of years later. In a

letter to a personage of the royal Court, he relates the sad affair of a young Indian woman burned alive by a Spaniard whose advances she had rejected. Her life was regarded as of such little value that the murderer had only been sentenced by a judge to pay the ridiculous sum of five *castellanos*. Bartolomé concludes his account: "I could tell of this and other, worse things that have occurred, here and elsewhere on this continent and on these islands. I know that God will not forget this girl: I know that 'pupillum et magnum diligit Deus, et ipsi cura est de omnibus' ['God loves the small and the great and cares for all'], as Scripture says" (1535, *O.E.* 5:61a). No one is out of reach of God's solicitude, least of all the abandoned and insignificant, like this young Indian of Nicaragua — whom Las Casas remembered, too. God's concern is for all.

Bartolomé proposed to make God's memory the guideline of his life and reflection. His outlook has deep biblical roots. The "memory of God" is an expression of the divine fidelity and accordingly places a demand on every Christian as well. In the Bible, God exhorts at least those who believe: "Remember..." (Exod. 13:3; Deut. 15:15, etc.). Apropos of the abuse to which the Lucay Indians are subjected, when they were brought as slaves to the island of Hispaniola, Bartolomé writes of those who perpetrate such abuse:

> Who with a heart of flesh and human entrails could abide such inhuman cruelty? What memory must there be of that precept of charity, "You shall love your neighbor as yourself," among persons so oblivious of being Christians, or even human, that they have dealt thus with humanity in these human beings? (*H.I.*, bk. 2, ch. 43, *O.E.* 2:108b)

Some Christians forget their own human and Christian condition.

Bartolomé's labor is an attempt to recall to the minds of his contemporaries the recollection that God has of all persons, especially of those persons who constitute the refuse of history. To neglect to love a person in need is to forget that one is a Christian. This is the strength and inspiration of Las Casas's *intelligentia fidei*. It is also what differentiates it from the other theologies of his time.

God's memory is founded in the gratuity of the divine love. Here is the point of departure of another aspect of the salvation theology of the time, and Bartolomé stresses that aspect: in numerous texts, he maintains that in order to be saved one must have received the faith and the sacraments in the church. This is the second principle to which we have referred: the necessity of membership in the church in order to be saved. Indeed, on various occasions — always, it is true, in a context of the universality of God's salvific will — he adopts the consecrated formula, accepted by all Christians of his time, "Outside the church there is no salvation" (see, for example, *Apología*, 121, 177v). This implies the reception of baptism, as well as the knowledge of certain truths.

But as we have seen, the interesting thing is the application Bartolomé makes of this traditional position. It always appears in a context of the profound evangelical exigency that leads him to denouncing the conquistadors and *encomenderos* for their inability to teach the faith — after all, "they know it not even for themselves" (*Octavo remedio*, 1542, *O.E.* 5:77a) — and especially for their creation of a situation that denies the dwellers of the Indies the necessary conditions for salvation. It is these plunderers, indeed, who are responsible for "casting the Indians into hell" (*Carta al Consejo*, 1531, *O.E.* 5:49b). They put them to death "before their time," depriving them of "time and space for penance and conversion," and thereby sending them to burn "in the flames of hell" (*Confesionario*, 1552, *O.E.* 5:237).[5]

Let us examine a meaningful text in which Las Casas denounces persons showing no interest in the evangelization of the Indians working for them. One of them was Nicolás de Ovando, who, as Commander Major of Santo Domingo, is regarded by Bartolomé as being under an especially strict moral obligation to set an example. It is great blindness, our friar declares, to "forget the divine precept, addressed to us all, of teaching and instructing those who have not known divine things, without the knowledge of which it is impossible for human beings to be saved" (*H.I.*, bk. 3, ch. 50, *O.E.* 2:124a). On the theological level, the assertion is straightforward and traditional. In context, however, the main emphasis of this passage, whose point of departure is an acknowledged obligation, falls on a condemnation of Ovando's behavior toward the Indians. And so Bartolomé introduces into the text an aggravating element on the culpability of those guilty of this oblivion: "The more they made use of these people, in their sorrow and anguish and the loss of their freedom and their very lives," the more these people "seemed to be purchasing the teaching of Christ" (ibid.).[6]

By their afflictions, the Indians have "earned" the right to receive the gospel. Thus, a fresh obligation is superimposed on the one that all Christians already have of communicating their faith. These persons' sufferings give them an unanticipated right to receive that message. God, the "father of families," has saved these people for the "eleventh hour of the world, that they be summoned and invited, not by the yoke of hellish servitude, as they have suffered and do suffer it, but by the promise of the daily wage of life eternal, to the vineyard of the Church, with sweetness and enticements." The faith, after all, must be transmitted to others without payment, as the gospel tells. But this has not happened in the Indies. On the contrary, "it has been sold dear indeed, and terribly dear," Las Casas's denunciation runs, "and not given to them, while by Christ's mandate we must freely give what we have freely received" (*Octavo remedio*, 1542, *O.E.* 5:77a).

The gratuity of the intended gift is underscored by the allusion to the parable of the laborers of the eleventh hour. This gospel tells us of the proprietor of a vineyard who, flouting the conventions of any strict conception of justice, pays those who have toiled in his vineyard the whole day with the same wages as the laborer of but a single hour. Just so, the fact that the Indians should have come to know the gospel centuries after the Europeans will not be to their disadvantage. They will receive the same "wages" as those who have become Christians before them, and if the latter complain, the Lord will answer in the words of the landowner in the parable: "I intend to give this man who was hired last the same pay as you. I am free to do as I please with my money, am I not? Or are you envious because I am generous?" (Matt. 20:14–15). At the eleventh hour, what is at stake is God's free and gratuitous love. No person or thing can impose terms and conditions on God.

Elsewhere we find a reference to the same passage from Matthew, to which Bartolomé makes a powerful appeal in support of his proposition of God's salvific will for the Indians. The Indian nations, Las Casas explains, have been "called by Christ, now at the eleventh hour, for their eternal salvation" (*Carta al Consejo*, 1531, *O.E.* 5:43b; see also 1:236a). The gratuity of God's love is the ultimate foundation of the equality of all human beings and of their basic rights.[7] One of the arguments sometimes invoked to establish the inferiority of the Indians was precisely that God had "forgotten" these peoples who dwelt in such far-off lands. In the gratuity of the divine love, Las Casas finds a basis for maintaining the contrary: God's memory of them is living still.

2. Salvation of the Faithful

Bartolomé de las Casas never stopped reflecting on the question of salvation. It sometimes carried him to unexpected conclusions. One was his concern for the evangelization not only of the pagan Indians, but of the Christians as well — the Spaniards themselves. In fact, in his mind the two matters are intimately connected. Thus, his missionary zeal was at once comprehensive and radical. He managed to strike to the very heart of what we understand by salvation.

We have seen how sharp and how painful Bartolomé's concern is for the salvation of the heathen of the Indies. With all his debt to traditional theology, he strives to keep account of the complexity of the matter. And simultaneously — since he begins with concrete facts and the reality of the Indies such as he has it before his eyes — his uneasiness also regards those who boast of their membership in the church. Let us begin with the latter aspect of the problem. It will help us in a later examination of our author's indications concerning the soteriological status of the Indians. The quality of what is involved in the salvation of the *faithful* will enrich his focus on *unbelievers.*

The Faithless Faithful

For Las Casas, Christian behavior is a condition for the proclamation of the gospel in the Indies. In this perception, to be sure, his personal history plays a decisive role. We must be on the lookout for the broad and inclusive missionary and pastoral zeal that underlies our friar's invective against his compatriots. The harshness of his expressions is explained by his lofty concept of the demands of Christian faith in those who have received it and have been nourished by it so that they consider themselves disciples of Jesus Christ.

This is how Bartolomé comes to maintain that in the Indies what is at stake is not only the salvation of the Indians, but that of those who claim to be Christians as well. Thus the question arises of the *salvation of the faithful,* and this question is at least as difficult as, or more difficult than, that of the salvation of the heathen. We are dealing with one of those dazzling changes of outlook that take place in this exceptional bishop who leaves the beaten path and thus always catches his contemporaries by surprise — as well as ourselves. Scholars of his thought have everlastingly sought to encapsulate that thought. Fray Bartolomé Vega, Las Casas's fellow Dominican, interprets his thinking aright when, in a letter to the Council of the Indies with an introduction to the Lascasian *Apología* and a request that it be published, he writes: "It is almost impossible to express in words, illustrious Judges of the Royal Council, how deserving with regard to the Sovereigns of the Spains is the author of this work, as he has been the first to uncover the truth in the matters of the Indies — matters at once so difficult and crucial for the salvation *first and foremost* of the people of Spain, not to mention of all the Indies" (in Las Casas, *Apología;* emphasis added). Yes, first and foremost. But not all of the "people of Spain" will thank Las Casas for his solicitude.

The salvation of the peninsulars was surely one of Bartolomé's great concerns. Speaking of the introduction of the system of *encomiendas* in Hispaniola, he says that those on whom these holdings were bestowed "were as much in need of doctrine, or very nearly, and would be more difficult to convert, at least from their corrupt customs, than in their purely negative unbelief were the Indians, who had no memory on the island of Hispaniola of idols or of any other vice that might prevent them [from such doctrine or conversion], as they were all most simple" (*Carta a Carranza*, 1555, *O.E.* 5:444a). It is more difficult for Christians to be converted (and indeed they need conversion) than the Indians, who have never heard of the Christian message. And Las Casas appeals to a profoundly evangelical notion of conversion: trust in God and fidelity to the divine commandments (see Mark 1:15). That would imply a conduct that Las Casas fails to observe in these self-styled Christians. The expression "negative unbelief" is a scholastic term. It denotes simple, blameless unbelief. Positive unbelief, on the other hand, is that of those who culpably reject the Christian faith. By virtue of their condition, then, the Indians will have less of a problem in accepting faith in the God of Jesus than will the Spaniards who have moved to their lands.

In a letter to the Council of the Indies apropos of what is occurring there, Las Casas speaks of the "perdition of such an infinite number of souls, more and more each day, both of *our Christians,* and of these other people called by Christ at the eleventh hour of the evening to be saved eternally" (1531, *O.E.* 5:43b; emphasis added).[8] It is the danger of the damnation of Christians that is mentioned first. That of the heathen occurs because, as Bartolomé declares so often (for example, in one of the texts that we have cited), peoples called to salvation — and Las Casas reiterates that the Indians are summoned — are unjustly deprived of "time and space for penance and conversion." The perilous state of the Christian soul in these lands, cited in this penetrating observation, is owing precisely to the oppression wrought by Christians upon the natives here. The question of salvation concerns all who are in any way connected with the Indies, as well as (nor is this to be passed over lightly) those who, while living in Spain, nevertheless have responsibility for things that transpire across the ocean.

The king himself has a special responsibility for the salvation of his subjects. He will do them a great favor if he declares to them the state of their souls before God. In a memorandum to Charles V, Bartolomé writes: "And in this Your Majesty will bestow upon Christians themselves a signal boon, for You will be withdrawing them from most grave and pernicious errors that have taken root in their hearts, as they believe that it is permissible to rob and kill and destroy those people only because they are heathen, and that they will not be adding great sins to great sins, or stand in any need of performing the penance and making the satisfaction without which they can in no way be saved" (*Memorial*, 1543, *O.E.* 5:191a). The behavior of the Europeans toward the Indians closes to them the gates of heaven, unless they should repent. And as is known, for Las Casas — as for the best tradition of the church — this is a matter not of words alone, but of deeds.[9]

That is the point. The spiritual harm done the Indians, by denying them the opportunity to become Christians, has a strict relationship with the social and economic oppression of which they are the victims. Let us cite one of the many texts we find in this vein, one in which the rhetorical questions include declarations and hard indictments of the conquistadors and *encomenderos:*

> Tell me, what satisfaction will such damnable men make for the multitudes of souls who burn now in fiery torment forever, put there by the godless cruelty of their conquerors? How will they make up for the overthrow of peoples, the emptying of places by the thousands, all the adulteries, all the kidnappings, all the rapes, all the violations of wives and daughters of the elders, pagans though they be, all the splittings-off of parents from sons and daughters, all the abasements of the natural rulers from status and dignity, all the enslavements, deprivations of freedom for so many free people, all the injuries, all the insults, infinite in number, by which they ruined those poor wretches? (*De Unico,* 215; *The Only Way,* 180–81)

Eternal salvation cannot be divorced from temporal life. Through their conduct, these Christians are unfaithful to their profession of faith, and it is they who first reject God's saving love.

The lamentable state of affairs in the Indies reflects a want of concern for the faith on the part of those whose life — despite what they say — is an ongoing refutation of their condition as Christians. Fray Bartolomé writes, in apocalyptic tones:

> The screams of so much spilled human blood has now reached heaven. The earth can no longer bear such steeping in human blood. The angels of peace and even God, I think, must be weeping. Hell alone rejoices, although this many damned souls will surely stop up its entryway. (*Carta al Consejo,* 1531, *O.E.* 5:48b; see also *Carta a un personaje,* 1535, *O.E.* 5:61–62)

The possibility of the eternal perdition of the Indians is always found in Las Casas's writings in close causal connection — an aggravating connection — with the responsibilities the plunderers have in that perdition. Indeed, from the condemnation of the Indians, due to the absence of any real proclamation of the gospel, derives that of the Spaniards as the ones responsible for that absence. In fact, this will be one of Las Casas's sharpest weapons in his assault on the quality of the Christian presence in the Indies. Let us cite a typical text expressing this attitude and this argumentation. It is framed in the salvation doctrine of the age, and once again in provocative, challenging language, Bartolomé de Las Casas unleashes all his fury:

Was it not enough that these pitiful people trickle into hell one by one with their unbelief? Or must their self-styled saviors, our Christians, come and in the space of a few days, out of sheer greed, with their exquisite new cruelties and tyranny, pluck them from the world and head off with them to the place of endless dark and wailing? (*Carta al Consejo*, 1531, *O.E.* 5:48b)

"Head off *with them*" to hell — this is what is happening to the Christians who mistreat "these pitiful people." Here is where the main accent in his denunciation falls.

Further, they too risk their salvation who refuse to see and denounce the gravity of the atrocities being perpetrated against the Indians. That includes those who neglect their pastoral responsibility. "If they die in the state in which they live," he writes, "holding the Indians and extracting tribute from them, neither doing penance nor making restitution," the *encomenderos* "will go to hell, along with the *confessors* who have absolved them, and *the bishops* who appointed them" (*Respuesta al obispo de Charcas*, 1553, *O.E.* 5:428a; emphasis added). The extent of responsibility is proportionate to the gravity of the fault. Those in the church (priests and bishops included) who justify — or tolerate — these atrocities will receive the same punishment as those who commit them. While in some way for Las Casas (in conformity with the ancient axiom) "*outside* the church there is no salvation," just as surely for him it is insufficient for salvation to be, or to believe that one is, *within* it.

Responsibility of the Mighty

The traditional theological view that unbelievers cannot be saved unless they receive the faith and the sacraments renders Las Casas's denunciation of the wickedness of the wars of conquest all the more energetic. Those who undertake them are responsible for the fact that salvation has not been proclaimed.[10] In fact, we can even say that it is really in order to condemn the behavior of those whose only legitimate reason — as he holds — for being in the Indies is to announce the gospel that Bartolomé so frequently alludes to the eternal perdition of the heathen.

For example, we have passages like this one:

What pardon will they have? . . . You will suffer torment as the damned, not just for damning yourselves, but also for damning others. You cut off with a quick death the time they needed for conversion and repentance. You sent them straight to the torments of hell. You damned also those who grew to hate our faith because of the awful example you have given, grew to ridicule the universal Church, grew to blaspheme God. (*De Unico*, 181; *The Only Way*, 150–51; see also *De Unico*, 163v [*The Only Way*, 133]; 165v [134]; 173 [141]; 200v–202v [165])

These passages are particularly significant in a work that some Lascasian scholars regard as more academic in tenor, a work in which the author would seem to be referring to the concrete reality of the Indies only indirectly.[11]

The greater responsibility, however, lies with those who have authority in the Indies, the higher-ups, not just the rank and file. Las Casas asserts this from the outset of his struggle for justice:

> The main culprits have been those who have commanded and governed in these lands, who for the satisfaction of their own unbridled appetite to become great have maintained all this horrible tyranny, and continue to maintain it, and will continue to. They deserve no other remedy for their sins than that God should cut them short with death and eternal damnation, as we have seen to have occurred in so many of the most wondrous of the divine judgments. (*Carta al Consejo*, 1531, *O.E.* 5:51a).

Bartolomé de las Casas refuses to sidestep difficulties by setting up a distinction — as so many do today when it comes to modern ways of violating human rights in Latin America — between high-ranking civil or military officials and their subordinates. According to this distinction, the former, the titled nobility, for example, or other "respectable" persons, are not held responsible for the transgressions of the latter (their "excesses," as these are called in official parlance), who, of course, are of an inferior social condition.

Our friar refuses to play these subtle, cowardly games. When he raises the accusing finger, he points it where it ought to be pointed. Elsewhere he writes sharply: "So it is clear that the instigators are primary causes of the great wickedness and devastation worked on pagan peoples in the wars of conversion waged against them. The instigators sin worse than the rest" (*De Unico*, 205; *The Only Way*, 170). Their fault is proportionate to their responsibility. It is easy to understand why Bartolomé's bitterest enemies were always the "great" of the Indies, along with those who placed themselves at the service of the great, either in the Indies or in Spain.

Bartolomé de las Casas goes even further. Immediately following the text that we have just cited, he says:

> Whoever counsels crime causes crime, as much as the one who gives the command. So everyone who counsels a war to convert commits grave mortal sin, akin to those who commanded it, if

the counsel proves efficacious in causing the war or something likewise wicked. (Ibid.)

No one escapes responsibility for deeds of the magnitude of those occurring in the Indies. The very members of the Council of the Indies, yes, these high dignitaries themselves, are not blameless in what is happening in these lands. And so Las Casas warns them: "Look, look to your souls, Your Lordships and Mercies! For I *greatly fear and greatly doubt of your salvation.* And avoid like the plague, if you would be saved and would apply remedy to all of this misery, placing any credence in the counsel, letters, or spoken words of the ravening wolves here" (*Carta al Consejo,* 1531, *O.E.* 5:51a; emphasis added). The "Lordships and Mercies" themselves, then, are guilty of having dispatched to the Indies persons who give a Christian countertestimony and of listening to the wolves, ravenous for gold, that roar about the Indies.[12]

It is more than a matter of incompetence or neglect. Venality, greed, and an eagerness to toady to the Spanish sovereigns play a decisive role in the affair. Las Casas writes:

> The cause of these abominations has always been, in greater or lesser degree depending on the moment, blindness and insensitivity. Nor do I know whether it will be charged to the members of the Royal Council as a signal and wicked evil in God's awful judgment that they have not held as their aim and target — as the main end to which all of their works and ordinations, laws and commands and determinations ought to have been ordained and addressed — the conversion and spiritual and temporal utility of those people rather than the acquisition of a fortune for the King, or for themselves, or for their relatives and friends. (*H.I.,* bk. 3, ch. 102, *O.E.* 2:418a)

We find Las Casas's verdict on the responsibility of the Council in works written in the last years of his life as well.[13]

Remedies, Not Bandages

Nor were the Spanish sovereigns spared the accusing finger. While often receiving poor advice from the Council, they too were directly responsible. As a person of his age and time, Las Casas appealed again and again to the justice of the sovereigns over that of other authorities. But he never erected that justice into a myth. He was simply appealing to the justice that corresponded to their obligation as rulers. Their justice was obligatory, but it was not automatic. For Bartolomé, rulers are just *if* they act with justice. The reader will pardon the redundancy:

its purpose is to show that for our friar rulers too are persons capable of proceeding unjustly (as indeed practice demonstrated). If they did so proceed, their salvation was at risk as was anyone else's, and this had to be said forthrightly.

In his *History of the Indies,* for example, Las Casas recounts how King Ferdinand as early as 1507 — the year he regained the throne — under pressure from his allies permitted the enslavement of the Indians:

> In order to be rid of [certain persons] and spare himself their importunities, not realizing what he was about or that he was granting them Indians, he issued them certificates to be shown to the governor, ordaining that he should grant them two hundred Indians, as he had been doing in the case of neighbors of theirs on this island. (*H.I.,* bk. 2, ch. 61, *O.E.* 2:101b)

The affair ended in the death of the inhabitants. The only possible mitigating circumstance, then, in Las Casas's eyes might have been some ignorance, however doubtful, on the part of the king. Bartolomé also records the ominous words Cardinal Cajetan had addressed to Pedro de Córdoba on the subject of Ferdinand: "Et tu dubitas regem tuum esse in inferno?" ("And do you doubt that your king is in hell?"), and comments:

> What Cajetan said, to the effect that there could be no doubt but that the King was in hell for having consented to or permitted such inhuman injustices, ought to be understood in the sense of the King standing for his Council. For if without the advice of the Council, the King had voluntarily mandated entry into these Indies so that the Spaniards entered there and perpetrated upon these people the evils, cruelties, and injuries that they did perpetrate upon them, then there could be no doubt that according to the law of God he was in hell, unless he had been spared by a deathbed repentance. (*H.I.,* bk. 3, ch. 38, *O.E.* 2:264b)

But ultimately the responsibility lies with the Council.

Still more assertively, in bitter dialogue and in response to an accusation lodged against him by Bishop Fonseca (councilor of King Ferdinand for affairs of the Indies), Bartolomé seizes the opportunity to recall the sense of this first initiative of his with the Court: "A more welcome visitor, My Lord, is Casas, who has come from the Indies, two thousand leagues distant, with such risks and perils, in order to warn the King and his Council *not to go to hell* for the tyranny, or destruction of people and realms, being committed in the Indies" (ibid., ch. 139; *O.E.* 2:514b; emphasis added). "Casas" had come all the way to Barcelona to issue this warning. Being king does not exempt one from guilt. On the contrary, it aggravates it. In the case of the king, the road to hell may be even shorter, owing to his lofty responsibilities. Las Casas warns him on various occasions. This is why he has visited and will continue to visit the royal Court: to rescue the king and his collaborators from eternal damnation.

He urges the Council members (letter of 1531), while indicating the king as well, to bring every effort to bear on the establishment of justice in the Indies and to assure an adequate, peaceful evangelization. After all,

> entirely apart from the enhancement of the glory of God and the abundant multitude of souls that would be saved, which is the King's principal end as it is that of Your Lordships (with whom the Royal Conscience acquits itself ever and in all affairs), if you desire to be saved, you must strive [for justice in the Indies] with extreme and signal diligence. (*O.E.* 5:44a)[14]

Those in Spain who bear the responsibility for the Indies will be eternally lost unless they duly procure the salvation of the Indians. In a text dating from two or three years earlier, Las Casas reminds the sovereign of his obligations, expressing — as he stands before the desolate panorama of the isles of the Antilles — his concern for the salvation of the Indians and of the king himself: "From all of the above, the gravest evils and losses follow; and the greatest is that of the souls of those who have been in charge, as well as that of your Majesty unless You ordain a remedy."[15]

In the *History of the Indies,* Bartolomé indignantly refers to the agreement entered into by King Ferdinand and the first bishops of Hispaniola and Puerto Rico, in conformity with the recommendations of the Council. According to this pact, the bishops were supposed not only to commit themselves — scandalously — not to withdraw the Indians from the toil of mining gold but even to encourage them to do the very best that they could, explaining, with unintentional dark humor, that the gold would be used for "making war on the heathen." Las Casas cites this pact as evidence that

> the King knew little about the perdition of these miserable people, and that the bishops were ignorant and the Council blind when it advised the King to force himself on the bishops by way of a contract — almost violent — by which they would commit themselves not to oppose, either *directly* or *indirectly,* the Indians' being made to mine gold and, what is more, [would promise to] encourage and advise them to do so.

This hard labor was the principal cause of the extinction of the population of Hispaniola.[16] The members of the Council had manifested precious little concern to "know how the Indians fared when they mined gold."[17] And our friar exclaims: "The Royal Council ought absolutely to have taken account what this profiteering really was, and not oblige the bishops to it when it was incumbent upon the latter, in virtue of the natural and divine law, to do just the opposite: to oppose and resist and extirpate it as a devastating plague upon their entire flock." In other words, reasons higher than those of a contract with the king place a particularly demanding duty on the bishops. Here again, consequently, any excuse offered by the shepherds on the basis of a signed document was disqualified.[18] The passage goes on to criticize the Council for being "more on the alert, obviously, when it came to getting gold for the King than to lighten his conscience, unconcerned as they have been with the salvation of these people for whom they have a greater responsibility than the King has for themselves" (*H.I.*, bk. 3, ch. 2, *O.E.* 2:173a, b). The members of the Council were more concerned with obtaining gold for the royal treasuries than with the evangelization of the Indians, or with what that evangelization implies in respect for the natives' lives.

In a letter (the so-called Long Letter) to Bartolomé Carranza, then confessor to Charles V, Las Casas goes still further. Complaining about the matter of the perpetuity of the *encomiendas*, he writes: "For threescore years and one these innocent people have been plundered, tyrannized, and destroyed, and for forty the emperor has reigned in Castile *without ever having applied remedies — only bandages*" (emphasis added). The reproach aims directly at Charles V, for whom, nevertheless, he has more liking, understandably, than he will later have for Philip II. Then, unmistakably referring to current events (the king was once more away from Spain) and touching a sore point, he declares that "kings of Castile" can scarcely pass judgment on the Indies "from a corner of England or Flanders." The criticism continues implacably as Las Casas now turns to the poverty of the Indians and the legitimacy of their protest to God for the humiliations they suffer at the hands of the Iberians — with the endorsement of the Spanish sovereigns. The text is a lengthy one, but it is of capital importance, and it will be worth our while to reproduce it in its entirety. "What obligation have they, Father — these unfortunate, oppressed victims of tyranny and annihilation, submerged in a poverty of goods the like of which has never been seen or heard, nor has ever existed, in all the world, these neighbors of ours in the Indies — to supply, amid their own weeping and tears, the necessities of the Sovereigns and rescue the Crown of Castile?" Las Casas is alluding to Charles V's new plans for the Indians motivated by his need for money from the *encomenderos*. And Bartolomé goes on:

Are they not tired of groaning and weeping and begging God for justice and revenge against the sovereigns of Castile themselves, by whose authority, although not by their will (but *this does not excuse them*), from the discovery of the Indies up until our own day they have been made into mincemeat through wars most unjust — invasions perpetrated in contravention of all reason and justice and surpassing in cruelty all of the wars of the infidels and barbarians, indeed of the beasts themselves, in cruelty, in ugliness, in injustice, in wickedness, in horror and terror? And after these wars, the unheard-of, pitiable, lamentable servitude to which they have been subjected — this hellish slavery that is the parceling-out of human beings as if they were beasts, which the tyrants beautify with the name of *encomienda* — has caused more than twenty to twenty-five million souls to perish without faith or the sacraments.

The fact that these extortions (the wars and distributions) have perhaps not been explicitly enjoined by the sovereigns does not excuse the latter, for in some way they have authorized or tolerated them. Thus, the Indians have the right to call down vengeance from God upon these wicked rulers. The Dominican does not beat around the bush.

And now a sore financial need constrains the king to accept new conditions imposed by the *encomenderos:* the perpetuity of their privileges. This will redound to an even harsher spoliation of the Indians. The bishop of Chiapa indignantly exclaims: "And that now the sovereigns should again be trying to place them in perpetual servitude, so that no memory or vestige of them remain!" Indeed, the emperor himself is responsible. And Las Casas asks the king's confessor:

Will there be no priest to disabuse these Catholic princes of ours and give them to understand that they can in good conscience receive not a single *real* from the Indies if they so much as consent — not expressly permit, but merely consent, *consensu expreso non interpretativo* ["by express, not merely interpretable, consent"] — to the subjection of such multitudes of tribes and Indian peoples to the bitter despairing lives they must lead in this, the ultimate captivity, even apart from the murders and perditions of the past? (1555, *O.E.* 5:431a–b; emphasis added)

As we see, the writer cares nothing for the eventual consequences of pointing out the culpability of the sovereigns themselves.[19] Let us not forget that he is writing in 1555, some years after the disputation of Valladolid and of course after the promulgation of the New Laws (abrogated by Charles V, precisely in the matter of the *encomiendas,* in

1545). The situation in the Indies is not improving. Patchwork and pal-
liative — as always — are of no avail. The assignment of responsibility
becomes plain, once certain illusions are dispelled.[20]

In the most authentic prophetic tradition, Fray Bartolomé demonstrates that no human dignity is exempt from God's judgment. On the
contrary, God is more severe with those who have greater responsibilities. It is an old position of Las Casas, and carefully thought through.
In this respect, the *History of the Indies* provides a revealing report. Bartolomé tells of a meeting of those who wished to "destroy the Indies"
that was held in the palace of the bishop of Burgos. Meanwhile, those
who sought to "secure a remedy for these Indies" met in the Monas-
tery of St. Catherine — Las Casas himself and eight preachers to the
king. (He lists their names.) The latter gathering came to a number of
conclusions:

> The first thing they determined was that they must observe the
> evangelical form of "fraternal correction," and by these steps
> fulfill it: first, to exhort and correct, in the manner of brothers,
> the Council of the Indies. If that body were not to apply a rem-
> edy with insistence and efficacity, they would exhort the Grand
> Chancellor. And if he exerted no efforts, they would "correct"
> Lord de Xevres. If no remedy were to be forthcoming from that
> source either, then they would appeal to the King. And if the
> King, having been advised and exhorted to do so, did not at once
> and with all diligence order a remedy applied, they would pub-
> licly preach against all of them, assigning the King his share of
> the blame. With this decision made, all swore by the Cross and
> the Holy Gospels to perform it and carry it out and to expose
> themselves to any risk in so doing. Then they signed their names.
> I saw this. I know it because I was there. (*H.I.*, bk. 3, ch. 133, *O.E.*
> 2:497b–498a)

The text is powerful. The decision is firm. The step-by-step approach is
based on Matthew 18:1–5, the great text on "fraternal correction." Occasion warranting, the king will have to be confronted with "his share
of the blame." Las Casas never forgot the commitment he assumed
with these preachers "by the Cross and the Holy Gospels," even if
this meant "exposing themselves to any risk."

Bartolomé's profound sense of God and acute awareness of the exigencies of the gospel impel him to confront the great of this world
without hesitation or fear. When all is said and done, it is a matter
of seeing clearly that it is not possible to be *a Christian and an oppressor* simultaneously. It is that simple, and that demanding. Thus, our
friar concludes all of his keen criticisms and accusations with a call
for the conversion of all those whose injustices he has denounced. To

express it biblically, we may say he calls for a breach with the status quo and the choice of a new path. This is no harmless, abstract summons. This is a call for a commitment: Las Casas spent his own life proposing concrete, immediate forms of following a path of justice in the Indies, a path of respect for the Indian nations, of love of neighbor, and of conversion to God. If we can say with Las Casas that "God has a very fresh and living memory of the smallest and most forgotten," Bartolomé himself for that very reason always remembered the great and powerful of his time, reminding them of their duties toward the small and most insignificant of history.

3. *Facing Reality in the Indies*

If the Christians who come to the Indies make themselves unworthy of the grace of salvation, it is because they behave unjustly toward the inhabitants of these lands. The experience of Bartolomé de Las Casas in the Indies allows him to see keenly the relationship between justice and salvation. For Bartolomé, it is clear that practicing the former is a condition for reaching the latter.

Without Justice There Is No Salvation

When an atrocity has been committed, it must be undone. "Without restitution and complete satisfaction it is not possible to be saved" (*De Unico,* 207v), he writes in his first book. And in the last, he will take up the same idea:

> As it is necessary to do and observe justice, without the observance of which it is impossible for someone to be saved, hence it follows that restitution of unjust harm and usurpation is necessary for the salvation of each, and without it it is impossible to be saved. (*Doce dudas,* Providence version, folio 179v)

Justice means respecting the rights of all, building a social order calculated to protect and promote all persons as human beings — indeed, to make them agents of their own destiny. Among these rights, the first and foremost correspond to the life and liberty of persons, and it is precisely these rights that are trampled underfoot in the Indies by the wars of conquest and the system of the *encomienda.*

The salvation of every human being is at stake in his or her behavior toward others and ultimately in behavior toward the God who requires that we love our neighbor. This includes rulers. Bartolomé writes:

No person on earth, not even the King of the Spaniards (and we mean this with all due reverence for his Royal Highness), is permitted without the license and free and gracious will of the Inca King or his descendants — to whom it belongs by right according to their laws or customs to receive his goods in legacy — to seek out, examine, exhume, or remove with intent to possess, the treasures, wealth, or precious objects that these persons have buried with their departed in sepulchers or in what are called *Guacas*. And if they were to act to the contrary, they would be committing a mortal sin of theft or robbery. And unless they make restitution and did penance for their sin, it will be impossible for them to attain salvation. (*De Thesauris*, 12v)

For Las Casas, what is occurring in the Indies is more than mere human history or relationships among persons and nations. At its heart is the decision for or against the God of Jesus Christ, that is, salvation history. The establishment of justice among persons is a requirement of friendship with God.

In no text, however, does he go as far in his demand on the king as in what he calls the codicil to his last will and testament: the *Tratado de las doce dudas*. This time the king is Philip II, and as we know Las Casas's attitude toward him is very different from the one he had had toward Charles V.[21] The situation in Spain and the Indies had changed in an important way. This moves Bartolomé to write his final trilogy, his most forceful and critical works, the *De Regia Potestate*, the *De Thesauris*, and the *Doce dudas*.

The polemical nature of the last named is very clear in the Providence version, to which we have already alluded. Having come to the end of his days and his lengthy battle, Bartolomé finds himself impelled to tell everything he has in his heart. The case of Peru, with which he had been so concerned in recent years, gives him the opportunity to express what he really thinks about the Indies as a whole. In their relationship with them, those who govern Spain are compromising their situation before God.

In the letter to Philip, he reminds him of his obligations as king and makes a special point of what the peoples he rules expect from him. The finest reward the king may have for the performance of his duties will be in this world the veneration and loyalty of his subjects (folios 135–135v). Las Casas goes further, however. "It seems to me," he says, "that I am obliged under pain of my salvation to disclose to Your Majesty a secret and to disabuse You of a very great and most perilous deceit" (f. 136). He is referring to events in the Indies that have been concealed until now. Not only his own, but the king's salvation as well, is in question, as the treatise indicates.

This "deceit" consists in the belief that the gold and silver coming from the Indies are well-gotten. Such is not the case.[22] Las Casas regrets any pain his composition will cause the king, but feels he must "look first to His Majesty's eternal salvation (which is no less involved here), as well as to His temporal felicity" (f. 137), and therefore he is obliged to speak. That is what is at stake: the king's eternal salvation. The Dominican is confident that with God's help the king will understand the obligation he has "to correct those evils, and to take a very different way from the one that has been taken," so that the divine wrath may not be poured forth upon Spain (ibid.).

He asks the king to have a committee of scholars examine what he asserts in the *De Thesauris* and the *Doce dudas,* treatises that he has sent him. If what is said there is false, "I shall make a retraction and shall sign my name to the very opposite and do penance for my error and audacity," the bishop says. But if it were to be true, then the king ought to put a stop to the injuries being committed and thereby "render sure Your Majesty's salvation" (ibid.).

The lines that we have cited are taken from the letter of presentation of his treatise and reflect its content well. The work maintains his proposition firmly and plainly: in the government of the Indies, in the restitution of what belongs to the Indians, in the restoration of their legitimate authorities, the king's very salvation is at stake. Politics cannot be divorced from ethics.[23] Unless the king puts an end to the injustices being committed in the Indies, he will make himself an accomplice in these deeds and will authenticate the opinion of the Indian nations that the "king of Castile" is the "worst king on earth" (f. 205v). The expression is hard and bold. It is impossible to say how much of Las Casas is in this judgment, but he is certainly afraid it may be true.

On the other hand, it is not a matter of Peru alone. The problem has a wider scope. We are hearing a denunciation of and a reflection on a situation prevailing throughout the Indies. Las Casas concludes his composition with the observation that, while his "little treatise appears to address only occurrences in Peru, we say, profess, and assert that the same must be done and that His Majesty is obliged to place it in operation throughout the Indies." And he adds meaningfully: "...under pain of salvation" (f. 226v). The circle is complete. The "little treatise" began with the question of salvation, and it concludes with the same. The king must not follow the advice of those who defend the regime of the *encomiendas.* "And I pray to God our Lord that I may be so certain of my salvation, and that I will see his face," he says, taking his inspiration in Paul, "as I am of the damnation of those who give you such advice." The matter is urgent. There are no alternatives.

The book ends with the expression of a wish: "Today, if His Majesty were to take some respite from his concerns for the present and set Himself to penetrate the dangers, spiritual and temporal, in which he is placed by those who give him such opinions, truly Your Majesty will find himself to be great in the grand manner" (ibid.) A hope and a warning.[24]

Surely we are dealing with one of Las Casas's most penetrating treatises, and we shall return to it. It is a dagger, piercing deep into the flesh of the relationship between the Indies and the king. Its point is of steel: the eternal salvation or damnation of the one who has been anointed to watch over the good of the persons falling under his responsibility. The handle, which forces the blade deep and true, is constituted of the experience of an entire life and by the boldness and valor (the *parrhēsia* spoken of in the Acts of the Apostles) required for the proclamation of the gospel. Without misgivings, the bishop of Chiapa places the king before the great choice of his life.

Requirements of Friendship with God

Salvation and everyday life go hand in hand. The first embraces all of life as a gift of God. Unacceptable, then, is a so-called salvation of souls at the price of the unjust death of bodies. In a treatise addressed to the king the Dominican expresses it in a terrible but electrifying comparison: "It is disorder and a great mortal sin to fling a child into a well in order to baptize it and save its soul, if it must drown in the well" (*Octavo remedio*, 1542, *O.E.* 5:118b). The end does not justify the means.

Bartolomé de Las Casas is implacable, then, with despoilers of the Indians who think to lighten their consciences with this or that free-floating act of piety or so-called charity. With an irony that rips the disguise from such a piece of hypocrisy, he declares:

> They die as calm as anchorites who lived long in the desert practicing severe penance! They blithely confess that God is merciful, compassionate. So they think God will not impute their sins to them, their evil deeds committed against God to the damnation of thousands upon thousands of their neighbors. They append to their last will and testament the command to clothe ten or twenty paupers from their estate, or to endow an altar in some monastery on which three or four masses a week can be said for their soul. (*De Unico*, 180; *The Only Way*, 149–50)[25]

It will not be by niggardly, posthumous charity or religious formalities that the injustices committed in this life will be repaired. Years before writing the work from which we have excerpted this passage,

Las Casas had already broached the matter of restitution for wrong-doing — so insisted upon, for that matter, by the traditional teaching on the Sacrament of Reconciliation. We shall examine this question below. For the moment, let us simply observe that our author's considerations on deathbed generosity — of which certain persons are so fond — are as relevant today as they ever were.

All through Las Casas's declarations we hear the echoes of a text from the Gospel of Matthew. It is a passage charged with the experience of the infant church, and this is why it is so sensitive to the distortions of Christ's message that can occur even in a Christian community: "None of those who cry out, 'Lord, Lord,' will enter the kingdom of God but only the one who does the will of my Father in heaven" (Matt. 7:21). The will of that divine Parent can be done in the Indies only along the path of justice toward these nations wrongfully subjugated and wickedly dispossessed of their right to live and to be free. And we have seen the importance for Las Casas of works in Christian witness. Thus, he believes that "what God is doing in the Indies is the greatest of miracles: that this people should believe in the things of faith while they behold the deeds of those who bear the name of Christians" (*Doce dudas*, Providence version, f. 179). This is not the kind of wonder that some missionaries (Acosta, for example) wished for in order to render evangelization more effective. We are once more before a Lascasian reading from the "other side": we are seeing things "as if we were Indians."

Since there is no justice there, the kingdoms established in the Indies are but "robbers' dens, as St. Augustine puts it" (*Carta al Consejo*, 1531, *O.E.* 5:50b). And one who robs and strips the poor rejects God. The crime is all the more heinous where the acts in question are not isolated and individual, but perpetrated in function of an unjust social order, a seeming "kingdom" that is in actuality no more than a den of thieves, from which, consequently, God is gone. This is what is happening in the Indies.

We shall return to the relationship between justice and salvation when we analyze the role Las Casas assigns to *restitution* in his work. For the moment, let us merely underscore two implications of the point with which we are dealing. If there is no salvation without the practice of justice, then we can understand Fray Bartolomé's concern for the salvation of those who call themselves Christians. We have already indicated this worry of his in the foregoing section. Here then let us recall the theological foundation of this concept: the crucial importance of works of justice if one is to be worthy of the salvific grace received. The Dominican is not underestimating the value of a profession of faith or of reception of the sacraments. He is only warning against the separation of these aspects of Christian life from a practice of sibling love — which finds its first and basic expression in just conduct. Las Casas makes this urgent requirement of biblical inspiration and authentic Christian tradition his own. Tirelessly he repeats: Without that practice, faith is vain, and the reception of the sacraments a profanation.

The other side of the coin of the importance of just conduct in order to correspond to the gift of the Reign of God regards the salvific status of those who do not profess the Christian faith, but who, in their own way, live a life of sibling love and the works of justice. Concretely, what is the status of heathen who remain faithful to their traditions and their religion? We have already made one observation in this respect in our study of Las Casas's efforts to draw all possible profit from traditional theology, within the framework of the relationship between the Christian faith and pagan religions. But we have not exhausted the question. An insistence on the practice of justice as an indispensable condition for the salvation of those who claim to be believers leaves the door open for a rethinking of the situation of the unbeliever who behaves with respect and love for others. Bartolomé de las Casas repeatedly praises the goodness and sense of justice of the natives of the Indies. In the logic of his assertions, we might say that God "appropriates" the actions of a love of siblingship on the part of those whom the wars of conquest deprive of "time and space for penance and conversion." Understandably, Bartolomé de Las Casas favors us with no systematic, detailed treatment of the matter. But the question is posed — actually, more than posed.

Indeed, the wealth of Bartolomé's experience in the Indies brings him face to face with other aspects of the problem as well, enabling him to discover new pathways along which he will call into question the commonly received theological opinion of his time. We are in a better position to examine these new routes after having addressed in earlier chapters the difficult question of human sacrifice.

Chapter 9 _____

A Heaven for Indians

On numerous occasions, as we have observed, our friar declares in criticism of the conquistadors and *encomenderos:* unless the Indians receive the faith and the sacraments, they cannot escape eternal damnation. Bartolomé shares this rigoristic attitude with many of his contemporaries who have not yet recovered from their surprise at having encountered these new populations in the Indies.

At the same time, we have seen the breadth of vision and depth of penetration with which our author, under the impact of his experience in the Indies, has nuanced his acceptance of this traditional teaching. Furthermore, his defense of the life, liberty, and religious customs of the Indian nations enables him to discern other opportunities as well, and to take courageous steps and blaze new trails. To be more precise, we must say that Bartolomé's experience of the Indies — his intimate knowledge of the natives of these lands and his commitment to them — enables him to plumb the depths of his faith in God and thereby to find new foundations for his reflection on the mystery of the salvific will of God. This changes his way of understanding the salvation of the Indians.

1. Las Casas and the Theologians of His Time

We shall better appreciate Bartolomé's efforts to make his way in this intricate matter (this "most celebrated question," as Domingo de Soto calls it) if we briefly recall how the subject was presented in his time.

Outside the Church There Is No Salvation

Cyprian's expression is a familiar one. "Extra Ecclesiam nulla salus": outside the church there is no salvation. A great deal of ink has been spilled on this topic. Let us limit ourselves to saying that there is a consensus that Cyprian was indicating the oneness of the church as a route to salvation.[1] Later, the Augustinian school gives the expression a more rigoristic turn, applying it to the matter of the salvation of non-Christians.[2]

But there came a moment at which the formula in question seemed to acquire an obvious meaning. Historical and geographical conditions caused the church to identify itself with the known world of the time (except for areas of no great moment in the European mentality). Here was "Christendom." Now to say, "outside the church," was tantamout to saying: outside the social universe of the time. And objections to Cyprian's formula fall mute. No one is interested any longer in its original sense.

In this context, the conviction grew in the Christian world — a conviction we encounter in the fourth and fifth centuries — that the gospel had now in some manner been preached throughout the entire world. Thus was fulfilled, it was often asserted, the scriptural cry, "Through all the earth their voice resounds, and to the ends of the world, their message" (Ps. 19:5). To be sure, there is a great deal of naiveté in this thesis. But we must not forget that all thought is in some way dependent on a historical and cultural framework. The consequences of the notion under consideration are important. For example, it is maintained that once the gospel has been proclaimed to everyone, not to be a Christian implies a conscious rejection of the salvific message.

It is within this framework that Thomas Aquinas develops his reflection on the subject. It is not strange, then, that he asserts the necessity in order to be saved of believing explicitly — from the moment the grace of their revelation has been received — in the three great truths of Christianity: the Incarnation, the Redemption, and the Trinity (*ST* II–II, q. 2, aa. 7, 8). For one who thinks that some echo of the gospel has reached all the corners of the earth, this teaching will somehow be understandable.[3] The other side of the coin of Thomas's doctrine is that, *before* the coming of Christ — and therefore before the promulgation of the gospel — pagans could be saved through a certain implicit faith in the triple truth just cited. The Fathers of the Church, just as the scholastics after them, were always especially concerned about the salvific status of the great pagan philosophers and thinkers. The text of Hebrews 11:6 ("Anyone who comes to God must believe that he exists, and that he rewards those who seek him") played a central role in these considerations. Anyone who believes in a provident God (see Heb. 11) implicitly asserts the mediating role of Christ, Thomas says, and in this he is following an old tradition (*ST* II–II, q. 1, a. 7).

But with the age before Christ over and done, Thomas deems, we are under the law of grace. To be sure, there will always be exceptional cases, and then the salvific means will be just as exceptional. Thomas then poses the celebrated hypothesis of the wild or savage child, one reared among barbarians, who after attaining to the use of reason follows that natural reason in the quest for the good: we must regard it as certain that God will intervene in some extraordinary manner to give that child to know the truths of faith, whether by an antecedent illumination or by sending some missionary.[4] It will not be to our purpose to develop this point here or to enter into the tangle of interpretations of Thomas's uncomfortable supposition in the circle of his commentators.[5] We indicate it only because it opens a breach in his principle that the gospel was generally known everywhere and that therefore it would be unusual to encounter a situation in which it was not, the situation that becomes precisely so usual and regular from the sixteenth century onward, the age with which we are concerned.

Of course, Thomas's position constitutes the theological context in which the matter is approached in the sixteenth century. But the historical and geographical conditions will be completely different from those in which the Angelic Doctor lived. Contact with the New World — and other continents — created a different, unprecedented situation. Las Casas always had an acute awareness of this novelty in the Indies and writes:

> Without great labors, without any impossible expenditure of wealth, but rather with an unlimited gain of the same, and with unimagined rejoicing, [divine revelation], as he saw, was more loftily and more widely propagated and God through that revelation better known, worshiped, and magnified by unbelieving people, than has occurred at any time since the age of the Apostles. (*Carta al Consejo*, 1531, O.E. 5:43b–44a)

It was inevitable that a phenomenon of this historical magnitude would collide with a theology of salvation that was developed in other parameters.

As the sixteenth century opens, speaking before a committee of experts summoned by Maximilian, emperor of Germany, the priest Trithemius asks: "What should a good Catholic think with regard to the dwellers of these recently discovered islands in the Ocean, islands unmentioned by the old geographers?" The emperor had asked whether these newly discovered populations could be saved without the Christian faith. No, Trithemius replies, "Apart from the Christian faith no salvation is possible. Thus, there will be no Indians in heaven." However, Trithemius makes a kind concession. True, the Indians will be damned, there is no escaping that. But their lot will be less hard than that of Jews and Muslims who refuse to accept the faith proposed to them.[6]

At the other end of the spectrum were the humanists of the time. Their sensitivity to the pagan world of antiquity inspires a broader perspective. This is the case with the great Spanish humanist Luis Vives. Around 1522, Vives writes: "Those among the gentiles who have taken nature as their guide, who are not stained or corrupted by mistaken judgments and opinions, may have been as acceptable to God as those who have observed the Mosaic law." Up to this point, Vives is maintaining a classic position, which we have already seen in Thomas Aquinas. He has simply invoked a distinction, accepted in his time, between natural law (which prevailed from Adam to Moses), the written, Mosaic law (from Moses to Christ), and lastly, the law of grace (from Christ onward). It is this last step that poses a problem when it comes to the so-called New World. The Spanish humanist approaches the point altogether directly, simply applying to these new phenomena all that theology had so readily accepted in the past. "The same will hold," he says, "in our own time, in the case of someone born in the remotest lands of the Ocean, who has not heard of Jesus Christ, but who has kept the two greatest commandments, in which Truth Itself has asserted that the Law and the Prophets consist: love of God and neighbor." Love is the path to salvation. Those who practice it already have the essential. That is why "it is so great and so important for them to have sought to be good, regardless of whether they had had anyone to teach them virtue." Finally, an allusion to baptism: "To this kind of persons, what is lacking? Water alone," Vives declares.[7] Let us observe the excellent indication of the central role of love of God and love of neighbor.[8] This opinion, however, was not to the liking of the Inquisition. It was not easy, in those times, to maintain this kind of thesis.[9]

The School of Salamanca

Academic theology proceeds more cautiously in the new situation. The most renowned theologians of the age strive to confront it in terms of the legacy received from earlier centuries. Francisco de Vitoria, with his ever alert mind, addresses the problems arising from the collapse of the old conviction that the gospel had been promulgated throughout the earth. Treating of the Indies, he says that it does not seem to him that the faith "has up until now been proposed and proclaimed to the barbarians in such a way that they are obliged to believe it under pain of new sin" (*Obras*, 695; CHP, 65). Accordingly, there is the possibility that they are in invincible ignorance with regard to the Christian message. Furthermore, they have been positively alienated from the faith by the spectacle Christians have given them of "many scandals, cruel offenses, and many impieties" (ibid.). Vitoria, then, is aware that the historical context of the question has undergone a profound change.

The life of the Indians plays a role in his considerations on the necessity of explicit faith in Christ in order to be saved. Vitoria's position on the question is a complex one. The Salamancan theologian introduces a curious distinction between *justification* (or "first salvation") and *glory* ("second salvation"). The former (by means of which one can live in this world in the state of grace) can be obtained with implicit faith alone, for which a natural knowledge of God will suffice.[10] However, Vitoria maintains, not altogether without hesitation, it will not be enough for glory, or eternal life. For that, explicit faith in Christ is required. The question, which has at times been awash in a sea of confusion, has been thoroughly studied.[11] Let us merely observe that, despite the concession he makes in terms of "justification," when all is said and done Vitoria introduces no substantial change into the salvific situation of the dwellers of the Indies.[12] To be saved, one must have an explicit faith in the Christian mysteries.[13] True, in a special retreatment of the subject, Vitoria treats of the question of the obligation to be converted to God upon attaining the use of reason. Here he invokes Thomas's famous theory of the child reared among barbarians, to which we have alluded.[14] But as we have noted, Vitoria does not complete his retractation, nor does he enter into the most decisive and significant point at issue.[15]

Domingo de Soto does not like the distinction between "first" and "second" salvation. Instead, he is inclined to admit that a natural knowledge of God — with the supernatural aid required for an authentic conversion — can issue in salvation. In other words, he accepts as conducive to a single salvation what Vitoria rejects except for "first salvation," or justification. The familiar text of Hebrews 11:6 supplies him with a good argument for showing that the basic element of the Christian message is comprised in belief in a provident God. His argumentation comes to daring, but logical conclusions in terms of the hypothesis of the child reared among savages. Here Soto introduces a distinction (to be found neither in Thomas nor in Vitoria) that is destined for great fortune in this matter: the distinction between the "necessity of precept" (the necessity attaching to the normal, divinely prescribed route to salvation, the route required in principle) and the "necessity of means" (the absolutely necessary minimum, which Soto calls the necessity of "end").[16] In Soto's opinion, explicit faith in Christ is required only by "necessity of precept." And so implicit faith in Christ is actually sufficient for salvation.[17] This Salamancan theologian, a great friend of Las Casas, believes his distinction to be entirely applicable to the case of the dwellers of the Indies, who have lived in invincible ignorance of Christian truths. He appeals to Thomas's hypothesis of the child who has not been brought up among Christians. Toward the end of his life (he died in 1560), under heavy fire from Melchior Cano, Soto retreats and places certain restrictions on his thesis of a broad faith — without, however, retracting it completely: he continues to maintain his forthright opposition to Vitoria's two-tiered salvation, which Cano accepts.[18]

Franciscan theologian Andrés Vega (d. 1560), a frequent associate of Soto and like him a theologian at Trent, deserves special attention. Like Soto, Vega defends implicit faith in Christ as sufficient for salvation and makes many very precise references to the Indies. Vega is the author of a commentary on the Decree on Justification of the Council of Trent. Explicit faith is the common way to salvation, he holds, but there are exceptional situations. This is the position of the majority of theologians with respect to the era preceding the proclamation of the gospel. As we know, the debate arises with regard to the time after Christ. Thomas Aquinas had maintained the inculpability of "negative unbelievers" — those who do not profess the faith, but do not reject it either. If they are damned, it is for other sins, and not for that of unbelief. Vega appeals to this thesis (as Vitoria had done for "justification" and Soto for the whole of salvation) in order to understand the new situation. If explicit faith in Christ was not necessary before the preaching of the apostles, then "why would it not be the same thereafter? It is the same faith, the same gospel, the same law, before as after." The promulgation of the gospel "cannot exclude from the grace of God or from beatitude those who have continued to be ignorant of it with the same good faith as before." This, Vega declares, is the case in the Indies.

"Take, for example," he says, "the peoples of the West Indies, discovered in our times by the activity of our Spaniards. No sufficient traces of a preaching of the gospel are found in those regions. Furthermore, whether preachers have been there or not at some other time should not alter our opinion of these peoples." Vega's allusion is to the thesis of a first evangelization of the Indies by the Apostle Thomas, who had supposedly gone to India. When he says that, if this was the case (which he is not very inclined to believe), it ought not to change our way of looking at things, this is an important remark. Some thinkers of the time appealed to the theory of the "Thomas Christians" to support their claim that the Indians were apostates. They had once been Christians, but they had abandoned the faith — with all of the consequences that might ensue. And he goes on:

> When they were discovered, they were all as ignorant of Christ as if he had never been preached in their country. Will this not be a case of unavoidable, invincible ignorance? . . . This want of faith

in Christ is not culpable in them, although it may have been that for reason of their grave sins God had abstained from showering upon them the bounteous rain of the evangelical doctrine.

For heathen, it is enough to have the implicit faith that Vitoria requires for first salvation and that Vega, like Soto, accepts for all salvation, rejecting Vitoria's strange distinction. The heathen of today "are saved by the merits of Christ. Those who are saved without explicit faith in Christ are not justified without Christ, although they are justified without that explicit faith."[19]

Melchior Cano returns to the matter of the savage child, but follows Capreolus — and not Cajetan, as Soto does — in his interpretation. Thus, he emphasizes the crucial importance of supernatural aid in the case of conversion to God through conversion to the *bonum et honestum.* As for explicit faith in Christ, Cano maintains that the debate centers on whether it is necessary *necessitate medii,* since it is obviously necessary *necessitate praecepti.* Thereupon he adopts Vitoria's questionable distinction between justification and glorification. For the latter — which is what really matters — Cano requires knowledge of Jesus Christ. "I would not dare," he writes, "to decide at what time the general preaching of the gospel came to an end. But I can unhesitatingly state that, apart from explicit faith in Christ, no one today can attain to salvation."[20] Then, on the basis of these guidelines, he criticizes Soto and Vega.[21]

Humanist Vives, then, and more strictly in the area of theology Soto and Vega, constitute something of an exception. (It is difficult to pinpoint Vitoria's position.) The majority of the great Spanish theologians of the sixteenth century, contemporary with or immediately subsequent to Las Casas, insist on the necessity of an explicit faith in Christ (although at times, like Báñez, for example, who comes somewhat later, they do so in terms of the difficulty of accepting Vitoria's distinction). However, even in the case of the first three — Vives, Soto, and Vega — certain questions arise. Their theses hold for heathen who have not had an opportunity to hear the preaching of the gospel. This will be the case with the Indians *before* the arrival of the Spaniards, and then we shall simply have a new application of the classic thesis on paganism before Christ. And of course we must lay aside the supposition that the voice of the gospel had already echoed to the ends of the earth. But what is the situation *once evangelization has begun* in the Indies, in these same concrete conditions? This point is less clear in Domingo de Soto and the few theologians who share his position.

And yet, this is the question that concerns Las Casas. We have seen him confront it in a number of different manners. He was always searching. Let us also see how, along varied, arduous paths, he comes to the daring assertions that we shall see him maintain in the next section of this chapter. His outlook is a concrete one. We do not find him employing the fine, complex distinctions of the scholasticism of his time — and in some cases involuted to the point of deviousness — with regard to implicit or explicit faith. What we do find is an understanding, based on biblical revelation, of the opportunities available to history's rejected ones for a definitive encounter with their divine Parent.

The Challenge of the Indies

The concrete reality of the Indies has already figured in the discussions we have just sketched. But the problem became even more urgent for those who were involved in any special way in the affairs of the Indies.

We have cited Ginés de Sepúlveda as an example of a theologian who maintained a progressive thesis with regard to the salvation of the heathen.[22] We know his position from a letter in which the Spanish humanist posits the possibility of salvation for pagan philosophers like Aristotle, for whom he professed a great admiration and some of whose works he had translated into Latin. The letter in question is addressed to Pedro Serrano, who had maintained (in a book about Aristotle) that "none of the philosophers and sages of paganism have obtained salvation."

Sepúlveda manifests his disagreement. He bases his argument, and justly, on Thomas Aquinas, who had asserted that "heathen, before the coming of Christ, obliged as they were solely to the observance of the natural law, were able to obtain salvation merely by its observance, although they would have been able to attain to it more easily with the help of the Mosaic Law." Sepúlveda cites other writers as well and declares: "Appealing to the authority of these authors and to the lines of reasoning that I have now set forth, I have defended the cause of the pagan philosophers who have led a life in complete conformity with the Natural Law." The conclusion is plain, then: "Accordingly, we can assert that everyone who has fulfilled the conditions just propounded has attained salvation, and that therefore there is not the slightest doubt that Aristotle can be reckoned among the first, if we attend as well to his reputation as to his writings." The letter goes on with a warm defense of Aristotle's moral qualities.[23]

There is nothing theologically new, however, in Sepúlveda's position. He is only rehearsing medieval theology. In that theology, as we have seen in Thomas Aquinas, a clear distinction was maintained between the possibility of salvation for the pagan world *before* the proclamation of the gospel (and therefore for the pagan philosophers) and the situation *after* its promulgation. This distinction is important for an understanding of what Sepúlveda is writing to his friend. The theology of the age had no difficulty in admitting the possibility of salvation for the pagans of antiquity, especially for the great philosophers. The question of the salvation of unbelievers *after* the coming of Christ is not examined in Sepúlveda's letter to Serrano.

Sepúlveda had also treated the matter in the *Democrates,* a work still unpublished at the time of his letter to Serrano,[24] in a section that is missing from some of the manuscripts we have of that work today.[25] That section had been a long elaboration coming, significantly, among the pages devoted to human sacrifice. And indeed there is a relationship between human sacrifice and salvation, as Las Casas has shown. The considerations we find in these pages of Sepúlveda will be of interest. Leopoldo, Democrates' adversary in the dialogue, begins by inquiring about the salvation of the great figures of paganism before Christ. Democrates' answer is clipped and clear. Thomas Aquinas has already explained the point, he says. Before Christ, the natural law was enough. Yes, faith in Christ is necessary. But in these pagans, it need not be explicit.

Then Democrates takes a further step. Since there are still persons today who "have never heard the name of Christ," he asks, will this same doctrine be applicable to them, "to pagans who live today, or have lived, in right conformity with the law of nature"? The question is a simple one. Theologians give various answers, Democrates says, but his own opinion is that "no one who pursues justice and who does all that in him lies has ever found the divine assistance lacking, either before the coming of Christ or after." Under these conditions, pagans can be saved — "although," he notes, "with more difficulty than if they had been enlightened by the light of the Mosaic Law" (*Democrates,* 52–56). The road is there, but it is a narrow one.

The imperial chronicler, following many authors of the early Christian centuries here but stirred as well by the esteem in which Greek philosophy was held by the humanism of his time, is obviously speaking of the case of the so-called *noble* pagans — those whose human qualities and intellectual aristocracy distinguished them. What about the Indians? The fact that they live after the coming of Christ is no absolute obstacle to their salvation in Sepúlveda's mind, as we know, although it will be difficult. However, the dwellers of the Indies are a special case for Ginés. They are "savages and inferior creatures" and stubborn violators of the natural law. As they do not fulfill the requirement of living "in conformity with the law of nature," then, they are concretely excluded from the opportunity of salvation offered to all pagans in theory. Thus, the principle expounded in this section of the *Democrates* will not likely be all that our author has to say on the subject at hand.

And surely enough, a few pages further on in the same work, Sepúlveda calls on Christians to wage war to convert the heathen to Christianity, convinced that otherwise they will be damned. After all, he says, "all who wander about without the Christian Religion are on the wrong road and are headed for certain downfall, unless, even against their will, we rescue them, take what it may" (*Democrates*, 64–65). The "certain downfall," of course, is eternal damnation. The same notion, but in more explicit terms, appears once more in Sepúlveda's *Apología*, a book intended to summarize the theses of the *Democrates* and published before the latter. The context is the same, that of the right to wage war in order to bring the Indians to the faith. Sepúlveda writes:

> To correct human beings caught in a most dangerous error, who are headed straight for damnation, whether knowingly or out of ignorance, and to bring them to salvation is an obligation of natural and divine law and a duty that all persons of good will would wish to perform even toward those who might not wish them to. He is no Christian, then, who doubts that they will die an everlasting death who wander about at a distance from the Christian religion. It is right, then, to force the barbarians, for their salvation, into the way of justice. (*Apología* [GS], 65)

The text minces no words. Anyone who disagrees with the author is not a Christian. The same rigorism prevails in a later composition attributed to Sepúlveda (and which at all events is the work of someone who holds his positions) and stating, against Las Casas's doctrine regarding the Indians: "It is express heresy to say that one does not know what God's judgment is concerning the heathen, since it is of Catholic faith that God has already judged and damned heathen who do not believe."[26]

Finally, it will be worth our while to refer to José de Acosta. While he flourishes later than Las Casas, the situation in the Indies enters into his reflection. Hence his interest for us. The illustrious Jesuit dwells on our topic at length. Despite his tendency to stand on middle ground, in this case his teaching is trenchant and rather rigoristic, as he too limits non-Christians' opportunity for salvation. Furthermore, we are struck by the harshness of the language he uses in referring to theologians whose position is different from his own.

Acosta is well abreast of the discussions that had been held in the school of Salamanca. He had known them as a student at that university. "I cannot overcome my astonishment," he says, "at what has occurred with certain masters of scholasticism in our days." He is referring to their thesis of the possibility of salvation without explicit faith in Christ. This opinion, he claims, has arisen "since the discovery of this immense New World." It is an "absurd opinion," Acosta says, and "unworthy of a theologian." Indeed, it is "openly heretical" and lacking any foundation in tradition.[27] He regards it as beside the point to appeal to Thomas Aquinas's wild child. He confesses that he would like to adopt "the defense mounted by these authors in favor of the salvation of the Indians,"[28] but insists he cannot do so.[29] "I am prevented," he writes, "by the datum that no one comes to the Father but through Christ, and there is no other route to follow or door through which to enter into life."

Furthermore, in Acosta's judgment acceptance of the thesis of salvation without explicit faith in Christ would render the preaching of the gospel superfluous. That preaching, that gospel, "is necessary, not for the salvation of more persons more easily, but strictly, that human beings may attain salvation" at all. The position is rigid, but the writer's conviction is deep. He adduces texts of Paul that posit the necessity of hearing the gospel in order to believe, and for Acosta these texts are obvious. All of this deprives the thesis he opposes of its entire foundation, he declares, and he goes on mordantly: "Not for one second longer shall I engage in disputation with anyone who does not hold it for absurd." One factor leading him to his black-and-white position is his sure conviction that the promulgation of the gospel has created a radically new situation: "Should anyone yet undertake to verify at what concrete moment explicit faith in Christ has become necessary for justification, I shall respond altogether plainly: from the precise instant that the gospel was promulgated to the world for the first time." Then he adds, without batting an eyelash: "I shall be told: But until recently the gospel had not been promulgated to the Indians. So I, too, believe. But this *has nothing to do with the question.* We are not dealing with a type of promulgation that would simply wipe out all ignorance, but with a solemn promulgation in conformity with the will of the legislator that abrogates all laws to the contrary and dissolves all contracts." Some Salamancan theologians thought that, quite the contrary, the events of the sixteenth century transformed the historical situation, and thereby presented new challenges.

For centuries — ever since the coming of Christ — the Indians have lived in a time that falls under the law of grace, and this poses new requirements.[30] Consequently, Acosta says, what some authors maintain "is in no way to our liking: that if these heathen do what they can, they can attain salvation without explicit faith in Christ."[31]

Acosta actually holds the most accepted thesis of his time. Soto and Vega, as we have said, are something of exceptions to the rule. As for the magisterium of the church, we shall have to await the nineteenth century to see the gates of heaven swing ajar for heathen. In his allocution *Singulari Quaedam* (1854), Pius IX reiterates the thesis that outside the church there is no salvation — but also denies that anyone can "set limits to the divine mercy, which is infinite," and reminds us that the "hidden counsels and judgments of God . . . are impenetrable to human thought."[32] Pius IX goes no further. The mentality of the age would have forbidden it. But his intervention supported theological positions that were making their way with difficulty. Finally, contemporary theology, Paul VI's *Ecclesiam Suam*,[33] and Vatican Council II[34] have delved deep into the matter and have indicated new routes, taking into account the whole of tradition as well as the novel historical and cultural conditions of our times.

Having recalled this context, we are in a better position to grasp Las Casas's thinking on this thorny subject.

2. *They Will Outnumber Us*

To what extent was Las Casas familiar with the debate on the necessity of explicit faith in Christ? It is difficult to know. His theological training on the matter of salvation corresponds to the dominant doctrine of his time, as we have seen. But Bartolomé refuses to resign himself to the concept of an exclusively Christian European heaven. His appreciation of the human quality of the Indians and their aptitude for the faith prevents him from entertaining such a notion.

God's Inscrutable Designs

In his important introduction to the *History of the Indies,* there is a lengthy section in which Las Casas explains his notion of predestination, thereby furnishing us with certain specifications of his position on the question of the salvation of the Indians.

He points to a number of causes of the sad situation of the Indies: neglect of the main purpose of the colonization, ignorance of the dignity of the Indians, and so on. One of these causes, he says, is ignorance of a "necessary, Catholic principle." And Bartolomé goes on to indicate that principle:

> One must know that there neither is, nor has ever been, any generation or lineage or people or tongue, among all the nations that have ever been, . . . from which, especially since the Incarnation and Passion of the Redeemer, there is not to be gathered and composed that multitude past reckoning seen by St. John (as recorded in the seventh chapter of the Apocalypse), which is

the number of the predestined, and which St. Paul calls by another name: the mystical body of Jesus Christ, and the Church,
or perfect man. (*H.I.,* Prólogo, *O.E.* 1:10b–11a)

"Predestination," then, has the same meaning in Las Casas as in
Revelation and Paul. It is synonymous with salvation — the outcome
of the free action of God, who saves in Christ, and of human liberty.

"Predestination" (a frequently used term in Bartolomé's time)
means simply the providence of a God who — being omniscient —
knows in advance who will be saved, in conformity with the free behavior of each one's life and the presence within him or her of salvific
grace.[35]

Las Casas applies this perspective to the reality of the Indies:

Consequently,... divine Providence must have disposed these
nations too — in what is natural, endowing them with a capacity for doctrine and grace, and in what is gratuitous, furnishing
them with the time of their calling and conversion — as [this
same God] has done, and we believe shall do, in the case of all of
the other nations who dwell afar from [God's] holy Church, as
long as the course of [the era of] the First Coming shall endure.

To none is God's salvific assistance denied: not even to those outside the church. The grace of God is offered to all, although God
alone knows who will freely accept it. And these latter Las Casas calls
predestined.[36]

Therefore at the level of concrete human history we cannot make
distinctions that outstrip our knowledge:

For as we must believe that God has predestined some persons
in each and every nation and stored up for them the time of their
calling, salvation, and glorification, and as we cannot know who
are the elect, we must so appraise and regard, opine, judge, address, and assist *all human beings* (as we desire that [all] be saved),
and this so far as in us lies, as if we were certain that *all are
predestined.*

All are called. God alone knows who will respond adequately. We
cannot close gates that the Lord wants permanently open. No theology
can exclude anyone from salvation (especially with the certitude and
arrogance with which, as we shall see, Oviedo so excludes them). Las
Casas maintains the possibility of the salvation of the Indians despite
their condition as heathen. He hopes that they will accept this calling
and act in such a way that it may so be.

It is in our hands: "Let us with our own works secure a share in
the effect of their predestination." Let us make ourselves sharers in

the process leading to the hearing and free acceptance of the salvific call. Charity obliges us — he continues, citing St. Augustine — to proceed as if we wished *all* to attain salvation (1:11a–b; emphasis added). Predestination is not fate. It is not something imposed by God, but is an expression of the divine knowledge. It is not something for us to know.[37] Rather, in Las Casas it expresses the demands made on our commitment by God's salvific will.

In the first chapter of the same work, the *History of the Indies*, Fray Bartolomé sketches an outline of the history of humanity since the creation. This is certainly a text written toward the end of his life. Its outlook is a balanced one, and it is written in a somewhat solemn style. In terms of the providentialistic interpretation of history proper to his time, which he obviously espouses, our author treats of the moment when, in conformity with the designs of God, the Christianization of the Indies occurs. With regard to when "the notice of this way" of salvation occurs, Las Casas shows the irrelevance of wondering "Why now?" or "Why so late?" or "Why later?" Why are these such idle questions?

> Because the counsel of the One that sends it is impenetrable to human capacities; and because, with a view to a more fulfilled and plain manifestation of the most benign and sweet divine grace, in the disposition of the salvation of the nations [God] has chosen the times of their conversion.

Thus has it occurred "with these nations, who, being without God, wallow so much the more in ignorance and in the defects that come upon them."[38]

But then comes a beautiful, profound passage in which Bartolomé states that the saving grace of God has never been wanting among these nations, not even before the historical moment of their conversion. "However, to them, as to all others, never has that general means of the supreme and divine assistance been denied that has always been granted to all human beings for their succor." Although that divine assistance may have adopted a discreet, indeed concealed, character, nevertheless it has been sufficient for the forgiveness of the faults of those who have had no direct, explicit knowledge of the truths of faith. That assistance, he goes on, "while more inward and more hidden, nevertheless (as it has pleased [God] to ordain) has sufficed — for some in remedy and for all in testimonial — that it be altogether evident and observable that those who have had no share in grace would be plainly guilty for their fault." The ways of the Lord are impenetrable; but our faith in the God who is love enables us to glimpse the divine presence.

All is grace. God's universal salvific will rests ultimately on the free, gratuitous love of God, and we can only bow our heads and contemplate that love. The text concludes: "This light gleams that we may glory not in our merits, but only and precisely in the benignity of a Lord so benign" (*H.I.*, bk. 1, ch. 1, *O.E.* 1:19a–20a). God's love knows no boundaries. In the face of the inscrutable divine designs, all theologies of salvation fall mute. The gratuity of God's love belongs to the core of the Lascasian reflection.

The case of the Indies in this passage is set in the broad theological framework of a comprehensive providential view of history. Furthermore, in terms of what Las Casas sets forth in his account of what has occurred in the Indies, the life and death of the Indians pose urgent questions and call for answers that take this concrete reality into account. Among these questions comes that of the situation, or, more concretely, the historical confrontation, of Christians and heathens before the judgment seat of God.

Another text, too, cites the profound, inscrutable designs of God, as well as reaffirming the presence of God's salvific grace in every human person. We refer to the important passage in the *Tratado comprobatorio* on the Indians' membership in the body of Christ, which we have already mentioned in our second chapter. On the basis of this concept, Las Casas also presents certain considerations on the subject of salvation. First, he repeats that "the saving of human beings is Christ's activity in his capacity as head of *all* human beings." Then, in a departure from Thomistic teaching, Bartolomé maintains that unbelievers (such as the Indians, from whose membership in Christ he will draw conclusions bearing on the responsibility to evangelize) belong, in some manner, *in actu* to Christ. In them, the grace of Christ is "often invisibly" present, withdrawing them from evil and inspiring in them good desires, thereby disposing them "to receive the teachings of the faith once they have heard them." Thus the "minds and wills" of those persons are enlightened.

> And although in his divine providence Christ currently takes constant care to inspire good thoughts in unbelievers and ultimately to stir them to good and withdraw them from evil — in some more, in others less, according to His profound, inscrutable judgments — nevertheless, for their part, they are Christ's subjects [only] *in habitu* or *in potentia*, for want of his true knowledge, which is by faith, and his love and obedience, which is by charity, and therefore are not his subjects or dependents *in actu*.

As head, then, Christ has care of all who form part of his body, whether *in actu* (Christians) or *in potentia* (unbelievers, of whom at least in part Christ is head *in actu* as well). This is true in a special way for the predestined, that is, those who love God in the manner

Las Casas specifies when he refers to the Letter of Paul to the Romans (Rom. 8:28: the "called" for Paul are those who have responded to the summons to faith). This does not prevent him from repeating that God's solicitude is for all, as the Book of Wisdom declares: "For neither is there any god besides you who have the care of all" (Wis. 12:13; our extended citation is from the *Tratado comprobatorio*, 1552, *O.E.* 5:353a–b; emphasis added). The universal salvific will of God is reaffirmed, but this time the active membership of the Indians in the body of Christ is considered, and formulated in certain daring ways.

At God's Right Hand on Judgment Day

In book 3 of his *History of the Indies*, throughout a number of chapters, Bartolomé responds to the opinion of Fernández de Oviedo, one of the first and fiercest of his adversaries where the Indians are concerned. Oviedo regards the Indians as vicious, indolent, and practically without memory, hence incapable of any interest in the gospel or of any understanding of what they were being taught. Otherwise, with the time elapsed and the preachers they have had, "these tribes ought already to have understood something as important for them as the salvation of their souls."[39] He thereupon adduces "reasons" to explain this incapacity on the part of the Indians, which must lead to a negative position in regard to their salvation.

Las Casas does not overlook the relationship Oviedo establishes between human inferiority and eternal damnation. "It will yet be well," he writes, "to respond to each of Oviedo's allegations to the effect that the Indians are somehow defective, as he lodges many. Thereby he practically excludes them all from any remedy that might bear upon their conversion and salvation — as if he were very certain of his own" (*H.I.*, bk. 3, ch. 144, *O.E.* 2:523b). The assurance with which Oviedo speaks of the damnation of the Indians is without foundation. Pricked by the specious arguments advanced by this detractor of the Indians, Las Casas is driven to undertake pioneering reflections on the subject of their salvation.

The Dominican responds, first, that the accuser is "highly uninformed" when it comes to a knowledge of concrete reality, since he had spent his short time in the Indies exploiting the Indians without attempting to know anything about them. Second, to accuse them of sins against nature is only a pretext for waging wars of conquest. As for the Indians' supposed poor memory, Bartolomé rejects Oviedo's claim and recalls that the Indians recount the history of their peoples orally, and with astounding retention.[40] But Oviedo would not likely know anything about that.

The historian also reproaches the Indians with mendaciousness. In response to this accusation (which is still lodged against the Indian today), Bartolomé gives the reason for the Indians' lies. The Indians are merely defending themselves against the abuse and harassment they suffer at the hands of their oppressors.[41] Besides, adds our friar scorchingly, by lying they are only imitating Christians, who deceive them constantly.[42]

Finally, Oviedo accuses the Indians of committing suicide for group entertainment. Fray Bartolomé denounces the cynicism of the assertion. Yes, suicide is frequent, he acknowledges, but it is a new phenomenon among the Indians and is to be explained by "the hellish toils with which they are overwhelmed" (*H.I.*, bk. 3, ch. 145, *O.E.* 2:527a). It is a painful way of escaping an even more painful situation, indeed an unbearable one.[43]

These so-called reasons lead Oviedo to draw a conclusion with theological repercussions that our Dominican rejects with all his might, but that give him an opportunity to fine-tune his thinking concerning the eternal lot of the Indians. Oviedo writes:

> Not without cause does God permit their destruction, and I doubt not that, in view of the multitude of their transgressions, God intends to make a very speedy end of them. They are people without any promise of correction, nor does punishment profit them at all, nor cajolery, nor kindly admonishment. They are an impious people by nature, nor do they feel shame at anything. They are people of abominable desires and deeds and of no good inclination. God can surely correct them, but they have no concern to be corrected or saved. It may very well be that those among them who die in childhood go to glory, if they have been baptized; but once they come to adolescence, very few desire to be Christians, even if they have been baptized, because [Christianity] seems to them a laborious charge.... And so God is requiting them in conformity with their deserts.[44]

Las Casas questions these supposed "permissions from God" for the destruction of the Indians.[45] But above all, he denies that Christians, who ought to be the bearers of the gospel to the Indies, are permitted to be "instruments for the destruction of others," in punishment for the sins of the dwellers of these lands. If there are grave failings among the Indians, that is God's affair. "But no license is granted to us to contemn them on this account, or rob them, or kill them. Woe to us were ever we to be among their plunderers and murderers!" — worse still, if ever "we were to corrupt them by bad example, when we ought to have drawn them to Christ by good example, and been an impediment to their salvation!" (ibid., *O.E.* 2:528a).

That they are an obstacle to the salvation of the Indians has been one of the strongest of Fray Bartolomé's accusations against his fellow Iberians. But this time, appealing to the eternal designs of the divine goodness, he shows that despite the Christian counterwitness the salvific will of God abides and reaches non-Christian peoples:

> However much the divine justice afflicts and straitens them, punishing them in this life, and seems to leave them helpless by delivering them over to our greed, none of those among them that the divine goodness has predestined — nor may anyone who is a Christian doubt of this — will slip from the hand of [God] without [God's] bearing that one to the enjoyment of [God] unto everlasting life. (Ibid.)

Despite their punishment — falling into the hands of greedy Christians, Las Casas says ironically — God has not forgotten them and wishes to bring them precisely to God.

The cruelties and injustices committed against the Indians, then, will not prevent the accomplishment of the will of God, but they will entail the sanction merited by those responsible for them. Oviedo's theses cause the Dominican to exclaim:

> And perhaps,... having through our cruel hands done away with these people, the wrath of God will be poured forth upon us for reason of our violence and tyranny and incite other nations to do with us what we have done with these, and at the last destroy us as we are destroying them. (Ibid., *O.E.* 2:528a)

This mournful prediction will be repeated many times in the last writings of his life (for example, in his "testament": see *O.E.* 5:540). Bartolomé's declaration will be harshly censured by his compatriots in centuries to come. His critics will fail to perceive that with this exhortation the great Spaniard expresses, along with the anguish of a Christian conscience that knows no national boundaries, an afflicted love for the land of his birth.[46]

The text ends with an important, solemn declaration of the salvific status of the Indians, which presents a synthesis of the results of Las Casas's inquiry into the matter. In terms of the situation of conflict to which he has pointed, Bartolomé shows what is actually at stake, over and above any formal considerations, in the judgment of God: "It may be that there will be more of these that *we have held in such contempt* at the right hand [of God] on the Day of Judgment than of ourselves." The number of heathen saved may be greater than that of the "faithful." The last shall be first. We are far indeed from the hasty consignment of non-Christians to eternal perdition that we have seen above. The section concludes with a warning: "This consideration ought to inspire us with great fear night and day" (ibid.; emphasis added). The allusion to Matthew 25:31–46 is evident. Here is a gospel text that, as we have had occasion to observe, is key in the Lascasian theology. Works are decisive for entry into the Reign of God.

Works, Not Words

In the next chapter of the *History of the Indies,* concluding for the moment his polemic with Oviedo, Las Casas recalls that God's judgment will be made upon works, not prattle. He says:

> Oviedo also calls [the Indians] "impious people." Let God be the judge of that, as God will judge and has already judged — as can any human being with a modicum of judgment, who can easily render judgment at the sight of the deeds we have perpetrated upon them with such impiety and cruelty.

Then he repeats, in another form, his prophecy that the Indians will outnumber the Spaniards at the right hand of the Father on Judgment Day. "Whom will God more rigorously convict of impiety on the Last Day? Will it be we, the Christians, or the Indian heathen — when we have such mighty testimonials to the effect that immense populations such as have never been seen or heard, from so many realms and regions and provinces, shall stand before him?" (*H.I.,* bk. 3, ch. 146, *O.E.* 2:530a). The question is a rhetorical one, since — for reasons we know — Christians' impiety obviously takes the prize. Posing himself the question of the salvation of believers has enabled him to make out the route to the grace of salvation. It is the route of works, and the Indians too must traverse it, of course.

In the "Long Letter" to Carranza, Bartolomé reiterates these reflections, proof that the subject is important to him. He argues in favor of the concern the Spanish sovereigns ought to have for "the spiritual and temporal good of the Indians," citing the universal salvific will of God in concrete terms of Jesus' sacrifice: " ... inasmuch as Jesus Christ, the Son of God, shed his blood for the Indians just as for the Spaniards." This leads him to venture an opinion on the possibility of the salvation of the Indians. Making a comparison similar to the one we have just seen, he continues:

> And [inasmuch as] we believe that it is from among all nations that the divine goodness and mercy is determined to gather and draw the number of its predestined, ... in consideration and comparison as well of the excess of the infinite number of those souls with the tiny [number] of the natives of this corner of Spain, it would appear that we may piously believe that [the

former number] incomparably surpasses the number of those whom it has ordained to be borne to the heaven of Spain. (*Carta a Carranza*, 1555, *O.E.* 5:440a, 441a)

There is no need here to examine in detail the figures Bartolomé assumes to be correct when it comes to the Indian population or the use he makes of his assumption in his bid for a greater interest in the Indies on the part of the Crown. What is important is that, as he says, it seems that more are called to the "heaven of the Indies" than God has "ordained to be carried to the heaven of Spain." The heaven of the Indies thus presents a huge challenge to those entrusted with the responsibility of proclaiming the gospel and establishing justice. And it calls for an authentic witness on the part of all who glory in the name of Christian.[47]

The *De Thesauris* (one of Las Casas's last works) also contains a meaningful passage. Las Casas denies that the Iberians have any right to be in the Indies: after all, the inhabitants have never consented to their presence.[48] Consequently, he declares that "all acts implemented in their regard and against them [are to] be held for null and void." Of course, he continues dejectedly, this will not be of much use to the Indians who have already died or to those who are currently undergoing torment. Nor does his thinking end there. He adds an interesting and provocative notion:

A single consolation and remedy, I think, they may have: a vision of the Day of Judgment, when all persons will be summoned and heard and the merits of their cause disputed as that of all others. Then shall every deceit and machination of tyrants and the nullity of their works be laid bare, and the perpetrators consigned to eternal torments by sentence of the just Judge. In turn, the innocence of those who here have suffered such wickedness at their hands (unless other sins, on their own part, should outweigh these sufferings) shall be manifested and vindicated and shall abide secure. (*De Thesauris*, 123, 123v)

On the day of the Last Judgment, to which other Lascasian texts have also referred, things will appear in a light that we lack today. At the left hand of the King of Heaven, the guilt of those who have mistreated the Indians and have been unable to see the presence of Christ in them will be plain for all to see. In like brilliance, at his right will be seen the innocence of the victims of that oppression. Indeed, their innocence will be "vindicated and secure." Beyond any doubt, Jesus Christ will say to them, "Come, ye blessed of my Father." The Indians may be punished for "other sins," our friar concedes, if they have committed them; but not for inculpable unbelief. In this concrete point, Bartolomé is simply following his master, Thomas Aquinas. Furthermore, the turn of his phrase suggests that such faults may not exist and that accordingly the Indians — despite their condition as heathens, which includes absence of the sacraments — will attain salvation. The "vision of the Day of Judgment" shows us what is at stake *now.* All his life Las Casas made an effort to see through the superficial appearances of history and behold it in all its truth and depth. That is, he strove to see it in the light of his faith.

All of these texts summarize, briefly and succinctly, various concepts to which we have pointed in earlier chapters. Let us emphasize three points.

Heathen — those who make no explicit profession of faith in Christ (partly through the fault of Christians) — will perhaps, according to Fray Bartolomé, enter the Reign of God in greater numbers than will the faithful. They will be called to that Reign by the Son of Man, and only because — within their religious world and in their cultural categories — they will have given "to eat and to drink" to their sibling in need, and in him or her to Christ himself. Works in behalf of one's neighbor are an exigency of salvific grace. The gift of the Reign is bestowed on those who practice a love of siblingship, the love that the Lord regards as addressed to himself, to put it in Las Casas's terms, which we have cited above. By contrast, many Christians will hear: "Depart from me, ye cursed." Baptism is no warranty of eternal life. Unless the profession of faith be accompanied by the practice of justice and a love for one's sisters and brothers, that profession will be in vain. In fact, the "Christian" who fails in this practice will be professing precisely a denial of faith in the God of love. Oppression of the Indians, the profound injustice of the system of the *encomienda,* based on slavery and dispossession, sows death in the footsteps of the quest for gold. It makes a laughingstock of the name of Christian and transforms the profession of faith into a lie and a sacrilege. Those responsible for these things will be most strictly judged by God.

In other words, once more we see that Bartolomé de Las Casas refuses to divide the question of the salvation of *unbelievers* from that of the salvation of *believers.* But on this occasion he places the behavior of the latter in the Indies of his time before the judgment seat of God. The eschatological judgment confronts history, illuminates it, and stipulates criteria for exercising discernment within it, here and now. This discernment fires and explains our friar's opinion of his contemporaries. Bartolomé's prophetic strength and courage have their root in the will to life of the God of the Reign.

The second point to which we wish to call attention can be stated with greater brevity, but it is no less important. We refer to the *viewpoint* Las Casas adopts in these considerations. He not only declares that the Indians may be "more numerous than we at the right hand of God on the Day of Judgment" and that their innocence will be made manifest; but he observes that he means those "whom we have held in such contempt." The outcast of history, those who are esteemed as nothing, the "uninvited" to the banquet, are the privileged citizens of the Reign of God (see Matt. 22:1–4).[49] The ones whose heads (whose "skulls") Oviedo says are so hard that they break the swords of those who seek to kill them, the ones who barely deserve to be called human beings and whose destruction, he states, is just punishment for their crimes — these last shall be first. Death and the disdain for the Indian that some manifest impel Fray Bartolomé to swim against an entire theological current, and drink at the evangelical sources themselves. And there he finds that the poor, the hungry, children, publicans, and prostitutes enter the Reign of God before those who publicly proclaim God with their lips without doing the divine will of love and justice, however enthusiastically they claim to be more "religious" than the others.

Finally, Las Casas's assertions shed a new light on an attitude of his, based on his lively sense of human freedom, that we have already encountered: a profound — and perilous, in the eyes of many of his contemporaries — respect for the religious customs of the Indians. Cortés had decided to destroy the idols of the population of Cazumel and replace them with crosses. Bartolomé comments:

> This is one of the errors held and blunders committed by so many in these regions. It is a great and calamitous mistake to deprive the Indians or any nation of idolaters of their idols without having first instructed them at length. They never surrender them willingly. The assault is perpetrated [not upon the idols], but upon the idolaters, who cannot freely and willingly abandon that which they have held for so many years to be God, drinking this in at their mother's breast and receiving it from their elders, without first hearing that that which is given them [instead], or into which they transform their god, is the true God. (*H.I.,* bk. 3, ch. 117, *O.E.* 2:456a, b)

Religious convictions, in Bartolomé's opinion, are not abandoned overnight, as we have seen in the foregoing chapter. The friar from Seville stands poles apart from any extirpator of idolatry (see *Apología,* 39–43).

May we speak of a systematic teaching of Bartolomé de Las Casas on the question of salvation — a Lascasian soteriology? This would be a great deal to ask. He is blazing new trails. We should like to indicate, however, that it would be a great oversimplification and an error to assert that on this point Las Casas basically limited himself to rehearsing the common opinion. Actually the context in which his thesis is situated, the thread he pulls out of old themes, the implications he perceives in terms of his concern for justice and his respect for Indian cultures, as well as the new roads he opens, render his theology on the subject of salvation complex and stimulating. Here is the main theme of his practice and reflection. He has arrived at this complexity and novelty from a point of departure in his defense of the Indian and his deep sense of God. This is where he has sunk the foundations of his denunciation of a Christian justification of oppression that has been foisted upon the sovereigns of Spain, and this is how, to our very day, those are stripped of their peace of conscience who have stripped the Indians of all they had and plunged them into a premature death.

Las Casas was a person of his age, with all of the strengths and limitations of cultural formation that this implies. How could it have been otherwise? But at the same time, he was immersed in a practice that required him to formulate a theory that would go beyond the narrow notions available to him in the theological arsenal he had been bequeathed.

This sent him scrambling over hard ground and cutting his way along altogether new paths in order to try to understand the Indians' equal rights to heaven. What do we have here? From a starting point in the poor, from the underside of a history in which the powerful dominate and repress and then falsify the account, it is possible to discover certain aspects of the demands of the God who delivers. We also discover that, in order to proclaim the gospel and practice theology, we are sometimes obliged to abandon the terrain to which we are accustomed, break with the familiar, the comfortable, and the secure, and walk — like Abraham — toward an unknown land, along a desert trail where the only solid footing is faith in God and hope in the Reign of life.

3. Freedom and Salvation

As we have seen, Las Casas's audacious positions on religious freedom led him to pose the question of the salvation of the Indians in pressing terms. That is, it led him to a neuralgic point of Christian revelation, before which the theology of his time had a definite and rigoristic position, rooted in the exprience of medieval Christendom. With this doctrine, many other aspects of the Christian message got tangled together around this subject; hence its delicacy and the risk entailed in a theologian's approaching it. That is the reason for the care taken by Las Casas in treating the point.

The truth is that the bond between human freedom and salvific truth is a constant in the history of the church. It was posited in the first centuries and was present as well in the impassioned discussion on religious freedom at Vatican II. Let us specify that the question arises sharply when looked at from the angle of respect for the religious options of persons, but not so much if we restrict ourselves to asserting their right not to be coerced to accept the faith. The latter is perfectly compatible with a strict interpretation of the axiom, "Outside the church there is no salvation." In a different historical context, the theme has repercussions in our own age on our understanding of a liberating evangelization.

A Classical Question

Not out of a sheer fondness for history, but because we think it will help us to situate Las Casas within this question as well as to perceive its importance today, let us undertake a schematic presentation of how matters appeared at moments of heated debate. Lest we be over-lengthy, let us restrict ourselves to the early Christian centuries and our contemporary age.

We have seen in Tertullian not only the remarkable witness of a forthright and lofty defense of religious freedom, but someone as well who has a deep perception of the meaning of revealed truth.[50] Therefore he ties his defense of religious freedom to the manner in which he conceives God's salvific work.

Confronted with a pagan world, the first Christian thinkers are especially attentive to the religious values to be found outside Christianity. This was likewise the case with Las Casas. But there is a noteworthy difference. For Christians of the early centuries, generally simple persons ostracized by society, the pagan world was at once a world of a lofty culture and the owner of political power. In Las Casas's age, on the other hand, paganism was linked to what was regarded in Christian countries as a socially and culturally inferior world. Accordingly, the religious values of these nations had to be perceived under more difficult and less clear conditions. It is to our friar's credit to have overcome these obstacles. But it is also the reason for the difficulties he will encounter in so many of his contemporaries.

In the broad-minded context of early Christianity, Justin represents one of the most affirmative positions. For him, there are pieces of truth in pagan philosophies and religions. His theology of the Word provides him with a basis for this opinion. "Christ," he writes, "is the firstborn, the Word in which all human beings share....Those who have lived according to the Word are Christians, even when they have been regarded as atheists, as were Socrates, Heraclitus, and others."[51] Tertullian himself, while he emphasized the difference between Christianity and the pagan philosophies more than did Justin, declares very plainly that through creation, and especially on a basis of the evidence of his or her own spirit, the human person is capable of reaching God. Left to itself and "in its normal state of health," the soul "names God with this name alone, because it is the proper name of the true God." In a celebrated and oft cited passage, Tertullian refers to "the testimony of the naturally Christian soul" — of the *anima naturaliter Christiana*.[52] In fact, in his defense of Christianity, Tertullian declares that pagan thought, where it is at its best and most respectable, has taken its inspiration from Sacred Scripture. This is what gives that thought a kinship with ourselves.[53] These considerations enable him to lay the foundations for the possibility of salvation for those who have not reached the Christian faith and, consequently, to establish a fruitful dialogue with the pagan world — before which, let us repeat, he nevertheless emphasizes the originality of the gospel.[54]

Like Tertullian, Lactantius holds a very broad view of the salvific status of persons outside of Christianity. For him, pagan philosophers and religious figures have discovered, partially and by the grace of God, many Christian truths. This does not dissuade him from strongly maintaining that the church is "alone in maintaining integrally the worship of the true God and is the wellspring of truth, the domicile of faith, God's temple."[55]

The swift advance of Christianity and the rise of a confessional state (see above, our chapter 5) bring in their wake a change in the way in which the situation of humanity is understood with regard to salvation. Now it began to be thought that there are only two classes of persons: those who have accepted the faith of Christ and those who have culpably rejected it.

The Fathers of the Church continue to teach the doctrine of God's universal salvific will: all human beings are saved, in principle, in Christ, although this salvation is actualized only with free acceptance on the part of the individual. But they also say that in the circumstances there is no excuse for ignorance of the Savior: as we have recalled, thanks to the ministry of the church, the voice of the gospel was deemed to have come in one fashion or another to all human beings.[56] Jews and gentiles have no real excuse then.[57] A change of attitude in the area of religious freedom will be a necessary consequence in this evolution of views on access to salvific truth on the part of those outside the church.

The case of St. Augustine is typical. Despite what some of his apologists might say, there is a great distance between what he asserts in the area of religious freedom and salvation at the beginning of his career and what he says at the end. Augustine begins with a respect for the personal process within every individual in the search for truth. This comes from his own experience. But his position gradually becomes more rigid. This evolution, which Augustine himself acknowledges,[58] parallels the development in him of the other question of concern to us. From an appreciation for pagan virtues and a broad solution to the problem of those outside the church, as we have in the *De Libero Arbitrio* or in the *Ad Simplicianum*,[59] we pass to the well-known declarations about the *massa damnata* found in the *De Dono Perseverantiae* or the *De Predestinatione*. True, as in the case of religious freedom, his polemics — this time with the Pelagians — serve to harden St. Augustine's position. But it is no less certain that the parallelism in these two doctrinal developments is particularly instructive. Religious freedom and access to salvific truth are interconnected questions, each bearing upon the other.

These ideas, presented in hesitating, at times even anguished, fashion in the fourth and fifth centuries, will gradually be affirmed. The Middle Ages, with its church coextensive with the then-known world and powerfully compenetrated with it, has a vital, and finally secure and peaceful, experience of the axiom that we find a number of times: "Outside the church there is no salvation." To be for or against Christ is fully identified with being for or against the church. It is not surprising, then, that there is no more talk of parcels of truth to be found beyond the boundaries of the church. There is no consistent world outside the church. The church is the sole depository of religious truth. In such conditions, freedom in matters of religion seems to place the salvation of persons at risk.

The conviction is affirmed throughout the Middle Ages. In this context, the theological reflections on the matter of tolerance that we have examined are produced. The concrete, historical situation of the church changes, beginning with the sixteenth century, in virtue of Christendom's internal breach and the discovery of new peoples. But the logic of thought on the question before us will be the same, by and large, as the one that we have recalled in the preceding subsection.[60]

Modern Freedoms and Salvation

Only in the nineteenth century do the elements of a doctrinal evolution begin to make their first appearance. The set of ideas stirred up during the French Revolution gradually overflowed and were assimilated, with certain distinctions and refinements — and hesitation and polemics — in their essentials by Christian reflection. But once more the topics of religious freedom and access to salvific truth are seen in their intimate interconnection. We have two particularly significant examples.

We know the eminent role performed by Félicité de Lamennais (d. 1854) on this question, especially in the first stage of his reflection. His daring, vigorous defense of religious freedom — not exempt, however, from a certain romanticism — the perceptiveness of his analyses concerning the church's situation, and the depth of his reflection make his thinking on this subject the most personal, original, and influential of the nineteenth century.

It would not be to our purpose to indicate the nuances presented by Lamennais's position on this matter. Our only interest is to underscore the fact that his fervor for freedom and his confidence in the use that could be made of it by persons are not isolated pieces in his thought. They have, it seems to us, their foundation and explanation in his ideas on the situation of the human being when it comes to truth. Wrapped in an envelope that is very much the reflection of its times and not always couched in very felicitous terms, we find in Lamennais a reflection on the human being's relationship with religious truth that gives us a better understanding of his political positions, and endows his thought with a certain affinity for the theological questions of today.

We are referring to Lamennais's philosophical concepts, or, if one prefer, his work as an apologist for Christianity. In his *Essay on Indifference in the Matter of Religion,* he states that human beings have always believed in the great religious truths: the oneness of God, the immortality of the soul, the need for expiation.[61] All of these truths have been preserved by tradition.[62] Nations untouched by Christian preaching, "having no other lights, neither will have other duties, and if they faithfully carry out [the duties they have], they are actually Christian."[63]

In his polemic with Jean Jacques Rousseau, who declared in *Emile* that according to Christianity human beings who had not heard the preaching of the gospel were damned, Lamennais replies:

> A good person,...who seeks the truth, will not be damned....
> That person will be saved in Christianity, because one who has not heard the evangelical preaching and believes the dogmas proclaimed by universal tradition...believes *implicitly* all that we believe and lacks not the faith, but a developed teaching....
> That person is a Christian.[64]

That it was possible to be saved outside of the church was not a new idea in the nineteenth century. What is important for us to notice is that for Lamennais human beings have access to salvific truth through universal tradition.[65] There are, then, religious truths sprinkled throughout humanity. This makes him contemplate the movement of history with great optimism and finally trust in freedom as a means of discovering the truth. Thus, contact with a non-Christian world, just as in the early centuries, arouses sensitivity to God's activity in that world, leads to the reassertion of certain human values, and enables one to see different modalities of access to religious truth.

That Lamennais expressed himself on these points with some ambiguity and that his thought was not free of a certain doctrinal imprecision is beyond a doubt, and his later evolution will confirm this. But it is not our purpose here to pass judgment in this area. It will be enough for us to indicate the essential relationship of Lamennais's notions on the presence of religious truths in humanity and the activity of God in history with his defense of religious liberty and his optimism in the face of the new age being inaugurated on the basis of individual freedoms.

At the other extreme and as a counterpoise to what we have maintained apropos of Lamennais, it will be in order to consider the ecclesiastical magisterium of the era. A perusal of the papal documents issued in response to nineteenth-century liberalism shows us that, ultimately, the reason for the intransigence of the church in condemning what were then called "modern freedoms" was a concern for human beings' eternal destiny. Only in accepting truth through an act of faith do we reach salvation. To tolerate the propagation of error is to place that salvation at risk.

The declaration of Leo XII (d. 1829) is typical. According to the pope, religious freedom certifies that "each individual, without risk of salvation, may choose and adopt the sect and opinion that is to each one's liking, in his or her private judgment."[66] Over against this the pope sets the truth of which the church is the depository and recalls that only that truth saves. To proclaim the civil equality of truth and error is to go counter to the salvation of persons.[67] In order to attain salvation, it is not enough to observe "customs conformable to justice and uprightness."[68] Only a society that acknowledges the Christian faith will favor human beings' adherence to the truth and assure the obtaining of the redemption that Christ merited for all.

Without seeking to make light of the factors of historical inertia, defense of acquired positions, and difficulty in understanding the values of the modern world, it seems to us that, in the last instance, the intransigence of the popes in the area of religious freedom reflects a religious and pastoral concern. This concern in turn presupposes a particular theology of salvation and consequently a particular conception of the mission of the church as exclusive depository of religious truth.

Vatican II and Las Casas

The Declaration on Religious Freedom went through more preparatory schemas than any other document of Vatican Council II. Opposition to this document was stubborn and occasioned its repeated rewriting. Its adversaries made the most of the breach it represented with what they considered the traditional position of the church in the matter. There is something to be said for this, despite the efforts of some interpreters to minimize it. The problem is to come to an agreement as to what is regarded as tradition in this case. It is clear, for example, that the dominant posture of the church in the nineteenth century does not correspond to the position maintained in the first Christian centuries.

One point interests us especially. The opponents of the schemas drawn up for the declaration wield an argument based precisely on the matter we are considering, that of salvation. According to them, to assert religious freedom is to ignore the religious truth present in the church.[69] It is, once more, an echo of "Outside the church there is no salvation." The opposition mounted by the adversaries of the declaration generated an impasse that was only overcome at the intervention of Paul VI. The matter ended with an important insertion in the exordium of the declaration, preceding the central text on freedom in matters of religion that we cite above. The text to which we refer now is of the nature of a profession of faith in revealed salvific truth:

> First, this sacred Synod professes its belief that God himself has made known to mankind the way in which men are to serve Him, and thus be saved in Christ and come to blessedness. We believe that this one true religion subsists in the catholic and apostolic Church, to which the Lord Jesus committed the duty of spreading it abroad among all men. (Vatican Council II, *Dignitatis Humanae*, no. 1)

After citing Matthew 28:19–20, the Council lays the question to rest with: "On their part, all men are bound to seek the truth, especially in what concerns God and His Church, and to embrace the truth they come to know, and to hold fast to it" (ibid.).[70]

The possession of that truth constitutes genuine freedom. A very apposite text links salvation and freedom, stating: "In the end, when He completed on the cross the work of redemption whereby He achieved salvation and true freedom for men," Christ "also brought His revelation to completion" (ibid., no. 11).[71] As we have already recalled, the aim of two of the great redactors of the document upon which we are commenting, John Courtney Murray and P. Pavan, was to place the matter on a juridical plane and withdraw it from the theological field. Indeed, they rightly asserted, respect for the right of religious freedom is a matter involving political authority. It falls to the latter to create the conditions in which citizens may believe and practice the religion of their choice. But it was not possible to escape the theological dimension, as is proved by what happened at Vatican II.[72]

The fact is that the interpolation at the head of the document calmed spirits, and the text was approved. What we are interested in bringing out is that the document's strong defense of religious freedom refers its audience to the question of salvation. At the beginning of this subsection, we said that that relationship was a constant in church history. We sketched this in broad strokes there. Now we confirm it in a contemporary ecclesial event of the magnitude of the Council.

A similar process — the same logic, let us say — led Las Casas from the question of evangelization and ultimately from respect for the religious convictions of non-Christians to the question of the possibility of salvation beyond the visible frontiers of the church. Las Casas not only opposes the antievangelical use of arms — in any circumstances whatever — to proclaim and testify to the Reign of life and peace. He does not limit himself to protesting injustices, or proposing a pastoral style or strategy, or even defending the Indians. "Thrusting to the foundations," the Sevillian takes on himself all of the theological problems implied in the battle in which he is engaged. The starting point of his reflection is not that he must give a course on the matter, which, let it be said in passing, would have been a serious, stimulating motive. Only, it happens, it is not Bartolomé's motive. His "intelligence of the faith" takes its point of departure in what is happening, sorrowfully and daily, to the dwellers of the Indies far from the great centers of theological elaboration. He allows the light of the gospel to fall on these happenings in order to understand what it is that he must do as a Christian.

There are two different doorways to doing theology. The second has its own rigorous requirements no less than the first, with the advantage of the breath of life that comes from its proximity to reality. Hence Las Casas's weight among the theologians of his time, to whom we have already referred.

At Vatican II, the new historical context leads to a profound revision of the dominant position of the last centuries. The Council took a most important step, which enabled it to adopt once more — in other terms and with another purview, to be sure — the demands of the first centuries of the church. The thinkers who debated the point were aware of the influence of historical frameworks on the ideas they defended. The availability of enormous means and the support of political authority influence the way in which the gospel is transmitted. And of course there is the mentality of the age. But Vatican II does not represent a simple retreat to the past. It does mean an effort to go back to the sources.

It is to those sources that Bartolomé de Las Casas's intelligence of the faith recurred, under pressure of the concrete reality of the Indies. Therefore it abandoned the perspective of power, which had begun to be asserted from the fourth century onward, to consider the more evangelical, and more effective, way to "draw all peoples to the true religion" — more precisely, the only way.

Las Casas would have read with great joy a passage like the following (to take a very recent one) of Pope John Paul II:

> Once again I wish to recall: Rigorous respect for religious free-dom and for its corresponding right is the principle and foun-dation of peaceful coexistence.... Finally, I exhort the heads of nations and leaders of the international community always to demonstrate the *greatest respect for the religious conscience of every human being,* and for the valuable contribution of religion to the progress of civilization and the development of peoples. Let them not succumb to the temptation to use religions as tools, as a means of power, especially in the course of a military action undertaken against some adversary.[73]

John Paul's vision embraces humanity's current situation and alludes to points of conflict issuing from various places on our planet. Las Casas asks respect for the religious customs of the dwellers of the In-dies and rejects the imposition of the gospel by means of power, not only military power, but other forms that power may take as well, ignoring the transcendence of faith and the dignity of the person. To defend the dignity of even one person, as such, is to point to a universal perspective.

Respect for religious freedom is linked to respect for other basic human rights — among them, the most important of all, the right to life. And of course it is connected with everything that flows from human freedom. Here is the core of what we call today a liberat-ing evangelization. Its urgency on our continent today has not waned since the times of Bartolomé de Las Casas.

Conclusion to Part Three

Part Three has placed on the table the difficult problem of the salvation both of Christians and of those who have not accepted the faith. Las Casas could not sidestep this challenge once he had taken his stand on the side of freedom in religious matters. The question of how these two groups could respond to the salvific will of God led Las Casas to glimpse avenues that the theology of the age was not eager to traverse. His considerations are important and bold, and fraught with consequences.

We know the universal salvific memory of God thanks to "Our Lord Jesus Christ, who died for those people" (*H.I.,* bk. 3, ch. 109, *O.E.* 2:536a). In behalf of these disdained, forgotten peoples, *Christ Our Savior* demands respect for their condition as human beings and as children of God in whom what the Fathers of the Church call "seeds of the Word" are present. The final destiny of Christians who fail to practice justice and love toward them will not be full communion with God. This attitude will be expressed by respecting them as equal in human dignity and by acknowledging them as culturally and religiously different.

The Reign of God is the content of the evangelical proclamation. However, this Reign is not a reality of the next world alone. It must become present in today's history. The vocation of the native nations to salvation ought to make them forthwith into a Christian community, a church. In one of those chapters of the *History of the Indies* in which the friar from Seville interrupts his narrative and reflects on the concrete reality he has just presented, we find interesting indications along these lines. Bartolomé asserts that "the souls of the predestined" (and we have already defined the meaning of "predestination" for him), in accord with his summons, have been "gathered" by the Lord "until now, and are ever gathered, and will be gathered as grains of heavenly wheat for storing in his divine barns." The allusion to the gospel parable of the wheat and the weeds is obvious. ("Let them grow together until harvest" — Matt. 13:30.) It implies something that Las Casas always demands for the Indians: time and space for their conversion, for their free choice — time and space of which the wars of the Conquista violently deprive these nations.

But if this passage has an eschatological tone, the next reference is to current reality. The text continues: "...or as living stones [*piedras vivas*] far more than precious for the building of that royal and divine house and city" of God (*H.I.*, bk. 1, ch. 76, *O.E.* 1:231a). This time the images are classic ones for the church, even in its presence in concrete history. The Indians are invited to be part of it. Las Casas unfailingly believed in the vigor and potential of "that new church" being born in the Indies (*Memorial al rey*, 1543, *O.E.* 5:203a), in the "living stones" of these lands. But the condition for this is that it be left "to the free will of each one to believe or not to believe, as each one may wish" (*Tratado comprobatorio*, 1552, *O.E.* 5:357b). Salvation is a grace, and gifts are not imposed, but accepted.

Part Four

A Republic of Dirt-Diggers

✚ We have considered the themes of evangelization, religious freedom, and salvation in light of the challenges presented by what
Las Casas calls the first kind of tyranny: the entry, the hostile conquest. Now we need to look closely at the second entry, "tyrannical
government" (*Memorial al Consejo de Indias*, 1565, O.E. 5:537a).

Las Casas rejects the justice of the use of force against the Indian
nations, but he likewise combats the socioeconomic system that is immediately established. Not only are lives lost in the wars but freedom
(and, in the extreme, life as well) is lost under the subjugation implied
in forced labor, such as we find in the *encomiendas*. The *encomiendas*
are radically unjust because "freedom is an inborn human right of necessity and 'per se'... it is a natural right" (*De Regia Potestate* I, 1), he
would say on numerous occasions.

At the royal Court, in Barcelona in mid-1519, negotiating the terms
for his experiment at Cumaná, Bartolomé requests that the preachers
to the king support him in his denunciation of the *encomienda* system before the Council of the Indies. The result was a written opinion
signed by eight learned persons, which he transcribed in full in his
History of the Indies. It says that in a well-constituted society (a republic, they say with precision) the citizens fulfill various duties. But this
is not what is happening in the Indies. "There everything is confused,"
they maintain, "and is reduced to the lowest and basest task of the republic, which is to dig dirt." They ask, therefore, in protest: "Who ever
saw such a huge republic made up completely of dirt-diggers?" They
respond: This republic "is reduced to the most vile and lowest exercise
that can be imagined, which is to dig and turn over the dirt." Moreover the excessive work brings on the death of those who are obliged
to do it (*H.I.*, bk. 3, ch. 135, O.E. 2:502).[1]

This is what was happening in the Indies. It was not a question of
the occasional mistreatment of the Indians; a stable order was being

forged, a true republic, based on these outrages. Bartolomé and the aforementioned opinion challenge this situation; they perceive that one of the reasons for it is that the *encomenderos* — and the cohort of people that surround them — have little or no regard for the indigenous people. With the intention of reversing that state of affairs the Sevillian friar writes his *Apologética historia;* his position is based not only on personal observation, but also on reasons of a philosophical and theological nature.

He says it clearly at the beginning: "The final cause of writing this was to make known the infinite number of nations from this [perhaps meaning "of this," i.e., *deste* instead of *desde*] exceedingly wide world, nations that have been calumniated by those ... who have published that they were not capable of governing themselves, that they lacked human *policía* [= social and political organization] and well-ordered republics." To regard the indigenous people in this way wounds their dignity and offends God; indeed, they speak "as if Divine Providence had been careless in the creation of such countless numbers of rational souls" (*A.H.*, Argumento, *O.E.* 3:3a). To assert that the Indians are inferior beings and incapable of grasping the faith is in the last analysis to accuse God of negligence. The God who loves all equally is the ultimate basis for equality among all persons. In Las Casas theological reflection continuously accompanies historical observation; in this case both lead him to reject the *encomiendas.*[2]

"All the nations of the world are human beings" (*H.I.*, bk. 2, ch. 58, *O.E.* 2:144a), Las Casas proclaims repeatedly. He seeks a social order that has this postulate as its point of departure. In these cases he always speaks of the Indian peoples (see *Memorial al rey,* 1543, *O.E.* 5:181b; *Respuesta al obispo de Charcas,* 1553, *O.E.* 5:428b), not of isolated individuals. He is conscious of what we today call the structural causes of the poverty of those nations in the new situation. His struggle for just legislation is an effort to "aid and defend them," to which all are "obligated, which is clearer than the sun" (*Representación a la Audiencia de los confines,* 1545, 158). But such an end will not be achieved if we do not have a full understanding of who the inhabitant of the Indies is.

These clarifications lead us to examine one of the most important efforts — and achievements — of Las Casas. Together with his fellow missionaries, also Dominican friars, he obtains from Pope Paul III an early and clear intervention on behalf of the Indians. It is a solemn pronouncement on the human dignity of the Indians that, notwithstanding its historical limitations, still has relevance and vigor. Thanks to their initiatives we have a document of great significance in the history of Christianity. Bartolomé goes further; he not only affirms the human condition of those to whom he dedicated his life, but he also sees them as the poor in the gospel sense. Not without difficulty, he extends this notion to the black slaves brought from Africa and even to the whites who worked their misery on the Indian peoples. This perception is a key to understanding his life and reflection.

Finally it will be worthwhile to compare these viewpoints with those of Francisco de Vitoria, the great master of Salamanca. This comparison has caused much ink to spill and has provoked impassioned debates that continue to this day. There are without doubt major convergences, but what makes many uncomfortable are the discrepancies, which, nevertheless, are undeniable. To recognize them is not to enter into a game of simplistic evaluations and condemnations; it supposes situating ourselves on the terrain of intellectual truth and honesty. Since the two came from such different worlds, it would have been surprising to find a total harmony of their views.

Chapter 10 _____

The Trouble Is in the System

In his defense of the Indian peoples, Las Casas points an accusing finger at those responsible for their humiliation. But he is convinced that the actual cause will not be found in isolated deeds. The problem would not be solved by calling attention to a particular individual or by meting out some exemplary punishment. Las Casas has a special gift for perceiving the objective character of the injustices being perpetrated on the Indians and for seeing how they move from individual attitudes to a social and institutional context. And he sees too how that framework conditions other personal behaviors, turning them into law, lifestyle, and routine habits that ultimately spring from a contempt for and exploitation of other persons.

Bartolomé frequently calls for a change on the part of individuals. But he especially demands a change in the social order, if there is to be any hope of creating different living conditions for the natives. Hence his experimental projects in peaceful colonization and evangelization, his interest in laws that would really take account of what is happening in the Indies, and accordingly his constant concern and struggle that the Crown be kept honestly informed.[1] His more comprehensive projects for the Indian continent spring from the same source.

When the priest from Seville joins the battle of the Dominican friars, he collides with a first systematization of the laws of the Indies — the "Burgos Laws." Las Casas denounces them, later contributes to the elaboration of the "New Laws," and radicalizes his positions when a considerable part of the latter is revoked. We shall not enter into detail here about these changes. What is of interest to us is Las Casas's remarkable perception of the existence of a social order that marginalizes and oppresses the Indian nations in their own land and, more basically, his intuition of the Indian as a poor person in the gospel sense. He never stopped deepening this insight.

1. Colonial Society

Very early, the distribution, or *encomienda* (commission, entrustment), of Indians became the axis of the economic and social order being established in the Indies. Christopher Columbus takes the first steps in this direction. And as we saw in chapter 1, the system is implanted, anointed, and sacramentalized by royal decrees, beginning under the military command of Nicolás de Ovando in 1503, shortly after the arrival of young Bartolomé on the island of Hispaniola.

In a sense, we can say that Las Casas's long life was an ongoing struggle with the *encomienda*. The *encomienda* was more than a scandalous bestowal, a "giving away," of persons and their lands to other persons on the pretext of evangelization. It was the structural root of the injustices of colonial society. Its rejection was a central aspect of Las Casas's battle for justice.

The Burgos Conference

Montesino's protest and the ensuing activity of the Hispaniola friars led to the convocation of meetings of scholars for the purpose of studying the situation in the Indies. One of the outcomes of these conferences was the handing down of the Burgos Laws. Later, additional legislation was obtained through the Dominicans' tenacity. The story of the development of these norms and of the debates occasioning it has been told many times and with solid documentation.[2] Let us limit our considerations to certain points that will provide the framework for Las Casas's position on the matter.

In the conference held by the councilors assembling at Burgos, different positions confronted one another. The extremes were represented by two preachers to the king: on one side the priest and licentiate Gregorio and the Dominican Bernardo de Mesa; on the other Matías de Paz, also a Dominican. A middle position was maintained by Palacios Rubios. The questions discussed were, in embryonic form, those that we will meet throughout the sixteenth century and beyond. They can be summarized in two issues of dispute. The first is rooted in the *fact* of the wars against the Indians and sparks a debate on the legitimacy of Spanish power over the Indian nations as well as on the manner in which the gospel ought to be preached. The second likewise emerged from a *fact:* the distribution of Indians (the first form of the *encomiendas*). And this led to a discussion on the freedom and servitude of the Indians. These two broad topics include the questions that concern the two "entries" that we have previously recalled. Here we shall take up the second.

With an appeal to Aristotle and to a text regarded as being of

Thomas Aquinas that we know today to be spurious,[3] Licentiate Gregorio distinguishes two styles of rulership: the "royal," which "is the government of free subjects for their own good and utility," and "the despotic," which is that of a "sovereign over a servant" or slave. It is the latter that is rightly exercised in the Indies, continues the royal preacher, always following the Stagirite's teaching, because "the governance of sovereignty, that is, the tyrannic, is just when it is of natural slaves and barbarians, those who are lacking in judgment and understanding." This is the case with the Indians, "who, as all say, are as animals endowed with speech." These, then, will "profit by serving the sovereign without any recompense or reward." Gregorio also cites Duns Scotus in favor of this servitude. His conclusion is plain and had already been proclaimed: those are in error (the Hispaniola Dominicans) who maintain that "Your Highness may not make use of them by sending them to serve the Christians of Spain, by excavating and extracting gold, for the alleged reason that they are free persons."[4] It is already a matter of gold, obviously.[5]

Neither, to be sure, is the religious motive for servitude missing here: "Chiefly, this is a more suitable means by which the faith may be received and persevered in — this communication and sharing with Christians — than that [the Indians] should be left to themselves, so that we should have to see them return to their old idolatry and vices" (the texts cited are from *H.I.*, bk. 3, ch. 12, *O.E.* 2:198–99). With the Indians, social servitude and the Christian faith are more than compatible: They are mutually implicating. Gregorio's doctrine does not rest solely on a particular notion of the inhabitants of the Indies. It is also due — and with equal urgency — to a particular way of understanding the faith and the life inspired by it. In Gregorio's theology, the ritual and formal aspects of the Christian faith are of prime, perhaps even exclusive, importance.

The position of the other royal preacher, Dominican Bernardo de Mesa, is a bit more moderate, though with regard to the basics and their consequences Mesa's view coincides with Gregorio's. The Indians, according to the friar (and future bishop of Cuba, although he never arrived there), are the king's "vassal subjects," not his "servants." Accordingly, they may be "asked such services as might be within the bounds of the feudal regime." But he immediately specifies that the Indians are servants neither *de jure* — by right of law — nor by reason of their unbelief (which in them is not culpable), nor by purchase, nor "by birth." "And he said," Las Casas writes, "that he saw no other reason for their [legitimate] servitude but their nature, which was without understanding or rational capacity and lacking in the fortitude necessary for perseverance in the faith and good habits. Here was a natural servitude, according to the Philosopher." In effect the Indians have always been formally declared free and thus cannot be called slaves; nevertheless, for their own good they ought to be "ruled in a quasi-servile manner, which need not be so great as to justify calling them slaves, but in which there is not so much freedom as to harm them."

Mesa's conclusion is that, since "idleness is the worst evil they can suffer" and the source of all vices, especially among those who live in idolatry, the Indians ought to be distributed "among the faithful of good conscience and good habits, who, besides keeping them occupied, will teach them the things of faith and the other virtues" (*H.I.,* bk. 3, ch. 9, *O.E.* 2:189–91a).[6] We already know what Las Casas, who did know the Indies, thought of the conscience and habits of these "faithful."

The opposite position from the one we have just sketched is represented by Matías de Paz, also a Dominican friar, who had hastily composed a treatise to read aloud at the Burgos Conference. We have already mentioned this composition. Here we have someone who moves with ease in the theological field and who seems to have better information on the reality of the Indies, since he constantly refers concretely to the situation of servitude prevailing in those lands. Paz takes Spanish rule for granted and recognizes the distinction between the royal and despotic rulerships. But unlike Licentiate Gregorio, he holds that the former alone is applicable in the Indians. "By authority of the Supreme Pontiff, and not otherwise, it will be permitted to our Catholic and most invincible Monarch to govern the said Indians with a royal, but not despotic, authority, and thus maintain them perpetually under his dominion."[7] And he goes even further: in a corollary to this conclusion, anticipating a theme that in the course of the years will become one of Bartolomé de Las Casas's most formidable weapons: "Whence it follows that anyone who has heretofore oppressed them with a despotic servitude after their conversion to the faith is necessarily obliged to *restitution,* at least of the harm inflicted and the profit obtained."[8] Later we shall see the role Las Casas assigns this traditional aspect of the sacrament of penance in his defense of the Indians.

Thus, the assertion of the Indians' freedom is maintained not only as a matter of principle by this Dominican master, but with an energy and consistency not to be found in the authors that we have seen until now. Matters become a bit more complex, however, when he makes potentially dangerous concessions. "Taking into account the expenditures and labors spent in getting to them" and in order to hold on to "a land so distant from us," Paz accepts the legitimacy of "requiring of the Indians certain services that will be *perhaps greater* than those required of Christians residing in those regions." But then he adds a caution: "...provided such services be in conformity with the faith and the dictates of reason."[9]

Palacios Rubios, for his part, addresses briefly the question of the Indians' freedom and servitude. The weight of his argumentation impinges rather on the other subject we mentioned, namely, the legitimacy of the Spanish dominion, which we took up in connection with the *Requerimiento*. For Palacios, the Indians are free creatures and have a right to possess their goods. But if — after being warned — they resist accepting the gospel and acknowledging the authority of the king, based on the power of the pope, Christians may justly declare war on them. The subjection of the Indians, who shall have to serve the Spaniards "as subjects their lords," will be the consequence of that war. Palacios Rubios is speaking of legal servitude, then, not natural servitude.

Given the enormous pressure exerted by the mighty of the Indies, by the power of their allies at Court (Bishop Fonseca and Secretary Conchillos, among others), and by the theological and juridical theses placed on the table, the final outcome of the Burgos Conference is scarcely surprising. First of all, seven general principles were enunciated, on the basis of which, after a formal declaration of the freedom of the Indians (a polite salute that will be constantly repeated in the official texts, as well as in those of some theologians), the distribution of the Indians among the colonists was accepted, although a humane treatment and the payment of a suitable wage were likewise enjoined. "These propositions," writes Las Casas, "show how well-intentioned the scholars were." But he immediately points out the danger of the fact "that the Indians were to be distributed and to come under the power of the Spaniards" (*H.I.*, bk. 3, ch. 8, *O.E.* 2:187b–188a). Great evils would ensue for the Indians. Las Casas thinks that this is due to ignorance of the concrete reality of the Indies. Thus the door was wide open for a reinforcement of the Indians' de facto slavery, at the same time that lyrical declarations about their freedom were being made.[10]

Legalized Injustice

But these were general norms. It remained to translate them into laws, "because they were like principles, implying many particular rules" (*H.I.*, bk. 3, ch. 9, *O.E.* 2:188b). This was done, and the Burgos Laws were promulgated in December 1512.[11] Las Casas criticized them bitterly, as they only consolidated and legalized the exploitation of the Indians. "Of these laws," he writes, "which were some thirty in number — to describe their qualities in brief — some, by far the majority, were wicked and cruel, tyrannical, and contrary to natural law, which no reason, specious argumentation, or fiction might in any way excuse. Others were impossible to observe, and others irrational and worse than barbaric" (*H.I.,* bk. 3, ch. 13, *O.E.* 2:201b).[12] Bartolomé's verdict is sharp, in no way toned down. But what interests us are the reasons he adduces for his condemnation. Let us consider four.

The most important one is that these laws perpetuate and definitively establish the system of distribution, or *encomienda,* that is, the servitude of the Indians and the exploitation of their labor. The royal councilors had laid down "as a foundation that it was appropriate to parcel out the Indians, that they might be converted and be well treated" (*H.I.,* bk. 3, ch. 13, *O.E.* 2:201a).[13] Here is the root of all evils, the "fault for everything" (*H.I.,* bk. 3, ch. 14, *O.E.* 2:206a). It is not, then, a matter of moderating or softening an ignominious, oppressive system. The system itself must be suppressed. "No law," Las Casas writes, with the insight and outspokenness that won him so many enemies, "no moderation, no remedy, was enough, or could be implemented, to prevent [the Indians] from dying, or keep the island as it collapsed from becoming a desert" (*H.I.,* bk. 3, ch. 13, *O.E.* 2:201a). The gravity of the situation, in which the life and death of the Indians are at stake, leaves no room for subtle nuances or compromise solutions. The reality of the Indies disqualifies such postures and places them unerringly on the side of oppression. Las Casas's so-called intransigence is the product not of any doctrinal or principled dogmatism, but of the raw realism dictated by his concrete experience.

A second motive for his rejection of the Burgos Laws is that in their opening paragraphs they echo the calumnies the colonists had spread about the Indians. "From the prologue onward," he indicates ironically, "one effortlessly guesses with what reputation and appraisal those *good Christians* have reported the Indians to the king" (ibid., *O.E.* 2:201b; emphasis added). Indeed the document in question imputes to the Indians sloth, vices, and lack of abilities, as well as scant inclination to virtue. That situation of human inferiority seemed to provide an argument in favor of the distributions, and we know that Las Casas energetically rejected this judgment.[14]

Bartolomé adduces a third reason for his rejection of the Burgos Laws: the importance of a Christian indoctrination of the Indians. He indicates the absolute incompatibility of the regime of the *encomienda* with the presentation of the Christian faith. The latter calls for the testimony of believers' lives, while the cruel, legalized servitude of the Indians at the hands of those who called themselves Christians was more than sufficient motive for the Indians to reject the faith.[15] The distributions were achieving precisely the opposite of their avowed purpose. In other words, the laws presupposed, or alleged, something that unfortunately was wholly and utterly false: a will to Christianization on the part of the colonists (see *H.I.*, bk. 3, ch. 14, *O.E.* 2:203b).[16]

The fourth consideration brought forward by Las Casas against the Burgos Laws is a particularly courageous one, given the political conceptions of the age. In addition to everything Las Casas has said so far, the laws in question were unjust because they had been framed without any consultation with the party most affected by them: the Indians themselves. The legislators had of course never so much as dreamed of such a thing. But it is more than polemics that stirs Las Casas to this criticism. We shall see later how important it was to him to consult a people before making political decisions in their regard. Bartolomé is altogether clear on the matter and appeals to the opinion of the scholars in his audience. It is worth reproducing the text in its entirety.

> Let the jurists say whether that entire legal decision and any of those laws or ordinances had any juridical entity or validity. And concerning this effect, bond, and substance, let it be hereby known that all of the determinations, laws, and ordinances made by the Sovereigns with regard to all of these Indies and their peoples have been made to the irreparable detriment and perdition of the same, *without summoning them, without hearing them,* and without any attempt to persuade them, the very ones who would have been more principal contributors than any others, since it was they and they alone, and their entire status and estate, that was affected by what was ordained and determined. (Emphasis added)

As we see, Bartolomé's verdict is far-reaching. It goes well beyond the Burgos Laws. It questions the whole juridical order given by the Crown for the Indies. And it concludes with a disqualification of the legality and justice of all that had been enacted: "Thus, all that has been done and ordained has been done and ordained in the absence of the concerned party, in contravention of all natural, divine, and human law" (ibid., *O.E.* 2:205a–b). It will be superfluous to observe that the force of our friar's argument resides in the fact that for him the Indian is a free human being, endowed with a capacity for social organization and in full possession of all human rights.

In a word, these are laws inspired by the mighty "on behalf of their own greed and tyranny" with the endorsement of the members of the Council, who "cannot ignore" their own responsibility in the matter, and who have condemned the Indians "to perpetual servitude, and to the death that has ensued, necessarily, therefrom" (*O.E.* 2:204a).[17] Injustice and pillage are erected into an economic and social system, and they forge a legal apparatus for their justification. It is the inauguration of what the bishops at Medellín will call, centuries later, "institutionalized violence" (Medellín Document on Peace, no. 16), and at Puebla, "institutionalized injustice" (Puebla Final Document, nos. 46, 509).[18]

2. *Expropriation of Life and Liberty*

All of the foregoing refers to events at the beginning of the second decade of the sixteenth century. Las Casas's account of them is from 1559 (see *H.I.*, bk. 3, ch. 8, *O.E.* 2:186b). However, Bartolomé's opposition to the *encomienda* is already presented in his first writings. The Indians' forced labor and the other abuses underlying their unjust, premature death are scored right from the start. We read of them in his *Representación a Cisneros* (1516, *O.E.* 5:5b), for example. "The reason the Indians have died, and are dying daily," he says in another text from the same period, "is first and foremost [*principalísimamente*] their bestowal on and distribution to particular individuals [the *encomenderos*]" (*Memorial de remedios*, 1516, *O.E.* 5:6a). This is precisely the starting point for his celebrated communitarian plan, with which we have dealt. Here was his first alternative to the *encomiendas*. Tirelessly, he will propose others.

Encomienda *and Tyranny*

In the letter to the Council of 1531, the Dominican maintains that the only possible remedy for the island of Hispaniola is "to liberate the Indians," removing them from the power of the Christians (*O.E.* 5:54b). The *encomienda* is simple tyranny and the cause of the depopulation of the island, for which Las Casas so frequently indicts the *encomienda* system. The liberation Bartolomé demands — and this demonstrates the concreteness with which he treats human freedom — must entail the Indians' right to live in any village they please (an allusion to the forced displacements), where they may rest "without paying any tribute whatever."[19]

Some years later, in his full maturity, Las Casas will write his most devastating tractate of all against the regime of the *encomienda*.[20] From the outset he will insist that "the principal and most substantial" remedy to be applied in the Indies is the suppression of the *encomienda*. Without this, "all others will be worthless, as all are ordered to and arranged around this one" (*Octavo remedio*, 1542, *O.E.* 5:69b). Las Casas adduces sixteen reasons to substantiate that thesis. The first four are central and definitive. They are calculated to fracture the alleged relationship between the *encomienda* and evangelization, adduced in favor of those concessions.[21] If the only motive justifying the presence of the Spanish Crown in these lands is the proclamation of the gospel, then the very existence of the *encomienda* renders that presence illegitimate.

Indeed, this cornerstone of the colonial order, besides being an ongoing cause of death for the autochthonous population, is the greatest impediment to the credibility of the gospel and the reception of the faith. The counterwitness of exploitation and mistreatment by the *encomienda*, we read at the end of the fourth consideration of the *Octavo remedio*, makes the Indians "think and weep for it night and day, that their gods were better than our God, since they suffer such evils with ours, and with theirs things had gone so well.... And so they will withdraw from the faith and hold it in abhorrence." The conclusion Las Casas reaches is ineluctable: "Your Majesty is under obligation... to remove them from the power of the Spaniards, and not to give them away *en encomienda*" (*O.E.* 5:78b).

In this treatise, Las Casas insists on the insufficiency of enacting laws calculated merely to soften the exploitation of the Indians. It is necessary to go to the causes of this state of affairs.

> Now there are some good laws, and there have always been prohibitions and penalties and ordinances and levies in tribute imposed [on the Spaniards] and services they must render, but none of this stops them from extorting, stealing, or killing just as they always did.

What must be done is to suppress the *encomienda* completely. Half measures will avail nothing. His personal experience has shown him that. It is the *encomiendas* that have destroyed, and continue to destroy, the Indies. They have been "the true and effective cause — not just one among many nor a simulated cause — of the annihilation and decimation of all of these peoples, almost since their discovery." Since the greedy will stop at nothing, to maintain the distributions — regardless of the form they may take — is to set the Indians "on the horns of raging bulls, and throw them to wolves, lions, and tigers starved for days on end" (*O.E.* 5:91b, 89a–b).[22]

For Las Casas the *encomienda* is the "root of tyranny" (*H.I.,* bk. 3, ch. 134, *O.E.* 2:499b) that brings death to the Indians and deprives the Christians of any reason for coming to the Indies. It is the core around which the colonial system crystallizes.[23] It constitutes the real purpose of the wars of the Conquista, euphemistically called "pacifications." Around it revolves the established order, with its functionaries at the service of the *encomenderos*, with its special interests and corruption among the high and mighty of the Council of the Indies and other authorities in Spain, with its merchants who do business with the new lords, and with its forced Indian labor. It is a whole social fabric, and

Las Casas will take it into account, for example, in his *Confesionario,* where the various agents of colonial society are identified in terms of their respective and interconnected culpabilities.

What is important to emphasize is that in Las Casas's judgment the social system now being established in the Indies is responsible for the current condition of the Indians, with the expropriation of their right to life, liberty, and the gospel as well. According to Bartolomé, the Indians in his time were what a colonial order centered on the *encomienda* had made of them. Their poverty — to which we shall return in this chapter — is the result of their dispossession.

Bartolomé's conviction prevents him from simply protesting against particular injustices and leads him to add to that protest what in contemporary terms we would call a social analysis. Without a knowledge of the concrete reality in question and the interplay of interests and forces, the defense of the Indian nations remains on the level of empty rhetoric or, at best, of good will. What endows Las Casas's work with its remarkable penetration — and wins him irreconcilable enemies, to our own day — is his sense of the concrete conditions required for a historical transformation. Those who limit themselves to a defense of the poor without denouncing the causes of poverty and oppression fail to question the "social mechanisms" that produce them.[24] Despite their good intentions, the lack of lucidity or courage leaves the "root of the tyranny" untouched. Not so with the friar from Seville.

The *Octavo remedio* and the *Brevísima relación,* both written in 1542, are the two-edged sword wielded by Las Casas in convocations destined to culminate in the promulgation of the New Laws.[25] Years before, in cooperation with other missionaries and bishops, he had played a preponderant role in obtaining from Paul III the bull *Sublimis Deus,* which proclaimed the human dignity of the native American.[26]

A Failed Attempt?

The New Laws (1542–43) introduce radical change into the regime of the *encomienda* through a series of dispositions that favors the freedom of the Indians.[27] They do not fully respond to our author's desires, but they constitute an important step in that direction, especially the article declaring the *encomienda* incapable of being handed on as an inheritance. Thus, it would eventually disappear. Without a doubt, a partial — and very fragile, as we shall see — convergence had occurred between the demands of the defenders of the Indians and the interests of the Crown, which, like any central power, was anxious to exercise greater control over events in the Indies. A number of writers have indicated this, and they are correct. But this convergence of interests does not mean that the new orders could not alleviate the excruciating plight of the native peoples. Hence Las Casas's efforts to obtain them.[28]

It was an important moment in Bartolomé's life. His influence at the Court was considerable now. Not only did his opinion carry great weight at this time in the selection of bishops who would be "protectors of the Indians,"[29] but he himself was offered the episcopal see of Chiapa.[30] The reaction of the *encomenderos* to the new legal norms, however, was violent, and turned the tables. Hostility to Las Casas grew more bitter, and he was threatened with actual physical harm. And what was still more grave, the *encomenderos* managed to get Charles V to revoke the heart and soul of the New Laws (what "stung" the most, Las Casas would have said), especially the order cancelling the hereditary character of the *encomiendas*.[31]

Some, not incorrectly, speak of a kind of political defeat suffered by Las Casas at this time on the heels of an apparently significant victory.[32] But to go on to say that from this moment the bishop of Chiapa takes his distance from the actual reality of the Indies and gradually slips into an unreal utopianism or disenchantment and the bitterness of frustration is to reach a conclusion unwarranted by the facts. Doubtless his defeat came as a blow. But just as at other moments of his life (in the failed experiment in Cumaná, for example), adversity sharpens his understanding of concrete history and strengthens his will.

On the other hand, it had not been difficult to foresee the *encomenderos'* reaction. Las Casas himself had anticipated it in a *Representación* to Charles V, in which he had said that if the king intended to strike at the interests of the mighty of the Indies, "probably a great scandal would arise throughout the Indies." As events were to demonstrate, he was surely correct. Meanwhile, our friar does not confine himself to sending out danger signals, but in accordance with his inveterate custom proposes solutions. His analysis leads him to predict that there are two places where the issue could really become a burning one: Mexico and Peru. For both cases he suggests the king withdraw the "most dangerous and rowdy" *encomenderos* from the two regions — some twenty from New Spain and a like number from Peru.[33]

All scholars agree that these years are decisive in his life and that an important change now occurs in his focus on questions of the Indies.[34] What basically changes is his attitude toward the Spanish Crown. His hopes gradually wane for a solution to the problems of the Indies by royal intervention that, in his view, would have to be freely accepted by the Indians.[35]

The Battle against Perpetuity

Bartolomé's disillusionment and concern are heightened when the idea of a perpetual *encomienda* is proposed. Beset with serious fiscal difficulties, the Crown lends a favorable ear to the proposal. Various meetings are held, with important people linked to the Indies in attendance.[36] The story has been told in minute detail and with competency on a number of occasions.[37] Opinions were voiced both pro and contra, and the matter was on the point of being settled between Philip II (who was favorable to the concession) and the *encomenderos* of the Indies. But in the end the accord was not signed.[38]

Las Casas intervened with all his energy. One of the most important items in his plea is the famous letter to Carranza, in which he insists that the *encomienda* is the cause of the depopulation of the Indies (1555, *O.E.* 5:435b) and is incompatible with evangelization (*O.E.* 5:436–437b). We have already seen the far-reaching scope Las Casas gives this last subject.[39] The *Memorial* that he and Domingo de Santo Tomás send to the king (1560, *O.E.* 5:465a–468b) is part of the same effort. The pair had been authorized by Peruvian caciques to make a monetary counteroffer more advantageous to the Crown than that of the *encomenderos,* in order to avoid the concession of the perpetuity.[40]

Our only purpose is to underscore the fact that Bartolomé's struggle with the *encomienda* in the various phases that we have cited (the Burgos Laws, the New Laws, and the perpetuity) has the aim of eliminating the root of the system that manufactures poor and oppressed people. Las Casas insists that the Indians who toil to exhaustion and death on the *encomiendas* are no longer the same persons as existed before the coming of the Europeans. Exploitation has transformed them into very different people. Indeed,

> those distributions have taken from them, destroyed, their administration, government, and political order. As [the distributions] have stripped and robbed the kings and lords of their status and jurisdiction and reduced them to the condition of the most oppressed and unfortunate — indeed, even more sorely humiliated, belittled, afflicted, and tormented than any of the others — all these multitudes of their subjects and vassals are left without leaders, or anyone to obey, fear, or respect, without rule or law, abandoned. (*Carta a Carranza,* 1555, *O.E.* 5:437a)

It is not only wars and hard labor or death and the deprivation of liberty. The very world of the dwellers of the Indies has been destroyed — "deconstructed," as today's anthropologists like to say. And yet much remains. To appreciate it, one must go beyond appearances to the underlying human and religious values that survive all the harassment and abuse. With Las Casas we find a titanic effort to know these peoples from within, as well as from behind (in time). At the same time, he is convinced that if the machinery that murders them, expropriates their freedom, and destroys their world is not stopped, there can never be any real solidarity with them, nor will they be loved as neighbors. And then the gospel cannot reach them.

In the final analysis this is what is at stake in his projects and his failures, his offers and his counteroffers, all these laws and rescissions of laws, his letters to sovereigns and his pressure on authorities. The driving spirit of the constant Lascasian efforts is an evangelical sensitivity to the poor and an urgent sense of God.

3. The Right to Dominate

The regime established around the *encomienda* was transformed into institutional practice almost from the moment of the Europeans' arrival. The situation was basically confirmed by the Burgos Laws. Later certain norms contradicted these laws in part, but others reinforced them. Only the New Laws signified, at this level, an effort moving toward an important change. Its effect was diminished by the rescission of a capital point of these orders. But, despite their evident limitations, they constituted an impressive attempt to create a juridical order in conformity with justice.

It is not, however, a mere matter of a society that functions by stripping the Indians of their elemental rights. This society is the expression of a mentality, indeed a theology, that accepts as self-evident the human superiority of the European. Hence Las Casas's battle on the theoretical front, as well.

Two Classes of Human Beings

John Major, a theologian we have already met in connection with the legitimation of the wars of conquest, appeals from 1508 onward to the text from Aristotle that Licentiate Gregorio would cite a few years later.[41]

Besides the right to evangelize, to which we have already alluded, another reason is adduced to justify European dominion in the Indies: the human inferiority of their inhabitants. These persons, in the Aristotelian text in question, are relegated to the category of *slaves by nature*.[42] For their own good, consequently, they should be subjected to the Europeans born to be lords.[43]

In his *Apología*, Las Casas devotes a little monograph to a rebuttal of Major's thesis. The text is well known. In it Las Casas reiterates some of his key ideas on the point that we shall have occasion to see below. Here we need only recall that his rejection of Major's theses hinges on his assertion that Major is unaware of "el hecho y el derecho" — the *de facto* as well as the *de jure* state of things. Major's ignorance of the reality of the Indies makes his theoretical lucubrations particularly dangerous (see *Apología*, 229–237v).

Sepúlveda takes up the same ideas as Major but sets them forth with a greater and a disturbing assurance. In the course of the some forty years that separate Major from Sepúlveda, a great number of authors, theologians, and even missionaries express themselves in like fashion, if with less precision. We may not, then, regard Major and Sepúlveda as extreme or exceptional figures. They are only the more articulate exponents — especially in the case of the second — of a very widely held position.[44] Their stance did nothing more than provide reasons for the way soldiers, conquistadors, *encomenderos,* and numerous functionaries spontaneously thought — and acted.[45]

But as we have said, Sepúlveda is the champion of this way of seeing things. To be sure, it is not out of a desire to defame the Indians but rather with the aim of propping up the rights of the Crown and the privileges of the *encomenderos.*[46] We have seen the first three "justifying reasons" the Cordovan advances in treating the duty to proclaim the gospel and to come to the rescue of victims of human sacrifice. One reason remains to be considered, which is, moreover, the first one he presents. We mean the barbaric nature of the Indian peoples (*Apología* [GS], 61). In his *Apología*, he devotes a scant page to the subject and later a brief response to Las Casas's argumentation at Valladolid. In his *Democrates*, on the other hand, he offers an extensive development of the subject.

Sepúlveda takes his starting point in Aristotle.[47] A war is justified when the natural condition of some is such that they ought to obey others who are superior to them (see *Democrates*, 19). The former are "slaves by nature," and "it is not only just, but useful [to themselves] as well that they should serve those who are lords by nature" (ibid., 22).[48] The authority of superior persons "over their inferiors" (ibid., 23) is beneficial to both. Consequently, if those born to be slaves refuse to accept this dominion, the lords may impose it by force. This is what the Romans did.

Through many pages, Sepúlveda presents these principles. Then in support of them he calls on Augustine and Thomas Aquinas. The concrete reality of the Indies is his backdrop and more: He does take it up explicitly as well. His sources are the reports of Hernán Cortés to Charles V and Fernández de Oviedo's *Historia* (see *Democrates*, 29, 33, 36).[49] The judgment he renders upon the inhabitants of the Indies could not have been more harsh. The rights of Europeans over these peoples are clear since "in prudence, invention, and every manner of virtue and human sentiment, they are as inferior to Spaniards as children to adults, women to men, the cruel and inhumane to the gentle, those intemperate beyond all bounds to the continent and moderate." All but one of the extant manuscripts of the *Democrates* add one more clause: "…finally, I might almost say, as monkeys to human beings" (ibid., 33).[50]

There is no point in trying to soften the harshness of Sepúlveda's expressions with subtle distinctions, or in quarreling over the meaning of certain words.[51] The Cordovan is to be credited with the clarity of his opinions and his forthrightness in proposing them.[52] This is precisely what lends trenchancy to his position. And at times Las Casas is at sixes and sevens when it comes to formulating a reply. But this also forces him to fine-tune his replies, as well as to venture into such difficult areas as that of human sacrifice.

Sepúlveda's clarity and courage in expounding his ideas have made him a favorite target of those who have taken up the defense of the Indians. But they have likewise caused some to try to isolate him, and at the same time Las Casas, by presenting them as representatives of unacceptable and extreme positions. This facile view of the issue at stake artificially opens the door to so-called middle and moderate positions. It should not be forgotten that in his ideas the Cordovan humanist enjoyed the company of eminent theologians like his friend Alfonso de Castro and many others who express themselves very much as he did — or even more harshly than he. He was also supported in the fundamentals by a goodly part of the legislation of the time and especially by what was practiced in the Indies. Sepúlveda is not, then, an unusual or isolated case.

The native world seemed so remote and so different from the European world that a sense of human and cultural superiority arose almost spontaneously in a Europe that had for centuries lived closed in on itself. Its extracontinental contacts were sporadic. The peoples composing it had drawn closer together racially, culturally, and religiously.[53] This includes Spain, a land always somewhat distant and different from other European nations, a land that recognized on its soil the presence of various and important cultures.

To appreciate the Indian universe for itself, not to see it as a no-man's-land culturally and religiously, was to navigate against the tide. Few, very few, did so. It was not easy. Witness two remarkable missioners of solid intellectual formation: one, a great achiever, the other, one of the most outstanding intellects of the second half of the sixteenth century. We refer to Vasco de Quiroga and José de Acosta. We present them here as significant examples because they are two men who without a doubt sought to draw near the natives of these lands.

"Tata Vasco" — Papa Vasco — whose memory abides in the minds and hearts of the Indians of Michoacán, Mexico, by reason of his social works in their behalf, nevertheless had little respect for their *policía* ("policy" — i.e., social order, political organization), as it was called in those days. He writes that these natives live "in notorious offense to God their Creator, in the worship of many and varied gods, against natural law, and in ignorance of everything including decent political life. They live *sin ley y sin rey* ('lawless and kingless'). Above and beyond being infidels, they are cruel, barbaric, and fierce toward one another. Their very nations are barbaric."[54]

Even so, Quiroga regards the enslavement of the Indians as unmerited and unjust and staunchly opposes it. He vehemently denounces the harassments of which they are the victims.[55]

In the Introduction to his *De Procuranda Indorum Salute,* Acosta distinguishes three classes of barbarians. These are not different meanings of the word, but distinct levels of human beings within the definition he gives for barbarian: "those who withdraw from right reason and the customary practice of human beings." The first class consists of those who "do not withdraw very much from right reason." To this class belong the great peoples of Asia, who can thus be called to salvation almost like the Greeks and Romans in other times. This level does not exist in the Indies. The second class is further from right reason, but they have important attributes. The best examples are "our Mexicans and Peruvians." In their "customs, rites, and laws there are so many monstrous deviations" that force and authority are required for such people to receive the light of the gospel. The third class is constituted by beings "like unto beasts." "There are droves [of them] in the new world."[56] If these can be attracted, so much the better. Otherwise, "they shall have to be obliged by force" so they will not place obstacles in the way of the gospel. The view is severe, but Acosta proclaims that "the salvation of them all, under the guidance of Christ, must be secured."[57] He approves the use of a moderate force, but denies that a war may be waged on them that would entail their death and servitude.[58]

We have cited these two examples in order to show how difficult it was for persons of that time to appreciate the human and cultural level of the Indians. As we have said, the positions of Quiroga and Acosta are very different from that of Sepúlveda. There is nothing in these zealous evangelizers about the theory of "slaves by nature."[59] But there is a conviction about the aboriginal population's clear inferiority that civilized persons could help them overcome through education. The sentiment of the age exerted a decisive influence on them,[60] despite their genuine concern for the aboriginal population.

Racial discrimination in Latin America, of which Indians and blacks are objects, doubtless owes a great deal to currents of thought affirmed in Europe in the nineteenth century. But in Latin America these currents found lands prepared since the sixteenth century. Indeed, the concealment of racism among us today and our determination to deny its existence (one of our social lies) must not block us from recognizing its deep rootedness on our continent.

This context affords us a better understanding of the scope of the ideas Las Casas defended. Against the background of the mentality of the age, his position in defense of the Indians and their human capacity stands out sharply.

Barbarians of the First Class

Taking their inspiration from a Greek custom adopted in the Middle Ages, sixteenth-century writers and theologians frequently refer to the peoples of the new world as barbarians. The term is an ambiguous one. Some writers use it to indicate a cultural distance, often with a connotation of contempt for those nations. Sepúlveda invokes the concept in support of his thesis of the natural slave (see *A.H.,* ch. 264, *O.E.* 4:434a). In order to refute these notions, Las Casas undertakes to specify what is understood by "barbarian." He sets forth his viewpoint at the beginning of his *Apología* and as an epilogue to his *Apologética historia.*

Basing himself on Aristotle, as everyone did in those days, he distinguishes three categories of persons to whom the Philosopher applies the label "barbarian." To these three he adds, reluctantly, a fourth type — the only one applicable, if must be, to the dwellers of the Indies.

In the first class, the word "barbarian" is taken in a "broad, improper sense" and refers to "any cruel, inhumane, savage, pitiless human being who has withdrawn from human reason." Such a person, blind with passion, plunges headlong into the commission of "deeds so inhuman that wild and savage beasts of the mountains would commit no worse." In this sense, the Greeks themselves, like the Latins, can be called barbarians — Spaniards, too, if they perform cruel deeds unworthy of a human being (*Apología,* 14–14v; *A.H.,* ch. 264, *O.E.* 4:434–435a). Las Casas readies his guns.

To the second class belong those who know no Scripture or, more generally, who speak a different language, or "do not pronounce another's language well." Here, rather than being improper, the term becomes narrow. It is possible, as was said, that wise and valiant nations might be called barbarian by people not belonging to those cultures. Thus, he comments, the Greeks regarded the Romans as barbarians and vice versa (see *Apología*, 14v–16; *A.H.*, ch. 264, *O.E.* 4:435–36).

Only to those of the third class is the term "barbarian" properly applied. Here are those who, either by reason of their character or owing to the aridity of the region they inhabit, "are cruel, savage, obtuse, and uncultured." They do not have a government based on laws, respect no friendship, have no cities, "do not live socially," and inhabit "mountains and woods." It was these that Aristotle denominated slaves by nature. They need to be "governed by Greeks; they need to learn from those who are wiser." The barbarians of this category "are rare in any part of the world, and few in number." They are as rare ("extremely rare," *rarísimos*, Las Casas calls them) as persons of heroic virtue. Bartolomé goes on minimizing the possibilities for using this category. These persons are "nature's mistakes or monsters in a rational nature." We are talking, then, about something exceptional that can occur in any part of the world. This approach alone will suffice to invalidate the theses and generalizations of Major and Sepúlveda. Las Casas need not even say explicitly that this category does not apply to the Indian peoples. He insists that these cases are too infrequent for the "limitless numbers of natives" to be included among them (*Apología*, 16–19; *A.H.*, ch. 165, *O.E.* 4:436–439a).

This difficult, extreme human case leads Las Casas to express a courageous evangelical judgment. Even those few barbarians who fall in this class, despite their limitations, "have been created in the image of God and are never so utterly abandoned by divine providence as to be incapable of entering the Kingdom of Christ — as they are our siblings," he specifies, "and redeemed by the most precious blood of Christ." Let us not forget that we are speaking of persons who were just labeled abnormalities of nature. Christ died for them too; therefore "we owe these savage, ignorant persons, in their extreme barbarity, that to which they have a right, that is, to be treated fraternally and with Christian charity." This, he continues, "we owe all human beings without exception" (*Apología*, 20–21).

We are reading a beautiful humanistic and evangelical page about a matter apparently outside the polemic. It is not about the Indians; that is clear. It is not they who are the "siblings" in this text. We are confronting the situation of people who, owing to various considerations, are even called monstrosities, strange human beings who often provoke horror and fear. Even with them Las Casas does not lose his bearings; they are siblings in Christ, just as are those persons more familiar to us, or those who — like the inhabitants of the Indies — belong to other cultures. Here is an energetic reassertion of the universality of Christian love. If no one is outside God's love, then no one can be outside our own. All are called to enter the Reign of God.

As we see, in Las Casas's defense of the human condition there is no "obsession with Indians" that some like to talk about. The matter goes far beyond that.

The friar from Seville uses the occasion to remind Sepúlveda the Aristotelian that in theology philosophical sources must not take priority over Christian revelation. The Greek philosopher had said that barbarians (understood as serfs by nature) might be hunted like wild beasts. Sepúlveda had relied on this assertion to make his case for the war against the Indians (*Democrates*, 22). Las Casas rejects such a thesis. Aristotle, he says, was ignorant of "Christian truth and charity." No one may subject "barbarians" to "wicked, cruel, exacting toils as if they were beasts of burden, so that they might be hunted down and taken captive by more intelligent persons." And he cries, "Too bad for Aristotle!" ("Valeat Aristoteles!").[61] As Christians our norm is Christ, "who is eternal truth." And his commandment is love. Las Casas is issuing a warning, this time indeed alluding to what Sepúlveda's doctrine would mean for the inhabitants of the Indies. "Whoever desires that a great part of humanity be such that [following Aristotle] one might behave toward them like cruel butchers, oppress them with slavery, and thus grow rich, is a tyrant, not a Christian." This time it is a question of exceptional, battered human beings, the last and the least, in whom we as Christians ought also to be able to perceive the hand of God. The image of God, in which they have been created, is present in all of them. This is the root of their most elementary human rights (*Apología*, 21–21v).

Obviously the Indians do not belong to this third category. They are peoples of a high level of civilization and a prudent political government. This provides Las Casas with the opportunity to make certain distinctions and use them against Sepúlveda. In the first place, he tells him, he has falsified Aristotle's teaching in attempting to include the natives of the Indies in the strictest notion of barbarian, the third. The reproach must not have pleased the Cordovan scholar, who had translated Aristotle. For Las Casas, there are no inferior races and according to him not for Aristotle either. Not only are all persons equal before God, but we should regard them as such as we live together as human beings.

Bartolomé's second observation consists in an argument *ad hominem*. In the past Spaniards too were adjudged barbarians by the Romans, and Las Casas asks, "Was it perhaps just to wage a war on them to deliver them from their barbarism? Did they perhaps have the right to distribute the men and women among themselves?" And he asks his opponent directly: "Would you, Sepúlveda, have tolerated St. James's evangelizing your Cordovans in this fashion?"

With great concreteness Bartolomé makes a third observation. The inhabitants of the Indies are admirable artisans, an area in which they surpass "all of the peoples of the Western world." But Sepúlveda cannot see the enormous human *and rational* value of these "mechanical labors." Las Casas is accusing him of being a prisoner to a narrow way of understanding rational activity as that of a disincarnate intellectual. Manual labor, for Sepúlveda, is inferior work. Through these spectacles, he is incapable of seeing what the Indians can do. Many today would like to say that with this argument Bartolomé reveals a modern perspective ahead of its time.[62] Perhaps they are correct, but the important thing is to underscore that for him this comes from a humanism without borders nourished by the waters of Christian springs.

Finally, even were we to admit that these people are "bereft of any sharpness of ingenuity" (which Las Casas denies), they are not on that account "to be subjected to those more intelligent and," he adds significantly, "made to adopt their manner of life" so that if they refuse, war may be waged on them.[63] No people should renounce its own customs and lifestyle. We have already met with this respect for the personhood of the native peoples (*Apología*, 23–25v).

On the other hand, while the Indian nations plainly do not fall in the third class of barbarian, some of their members could be labeled as such in terms of the first category. Indeed, this category is applicable to individuals of any group, however civilized it may be. But in the Indies, the ones whom the term "barbarian" (in the first sense) best fits are certain Spaniards, "by reason of the awful deeds they have perpetrated upon those peoples." This is typical of Las Casas, who loves to turn back on the Europeans the accusations they make against the Indians (*Apología*, 14).

He will do the same — on the basis of elementary common sense — with the second sense of the word "barbarian." If the Spaniards regard the people of the Indies as such because they are ignorant of European languages, then the Indians must have "regarded us as barbarians, that is, as foreign, since they did not understand us" (*A.H.,* ch. 264, *O.E.* 4:435b). Obvious as this reciprocity may appear, it never occurs to the minds of those who feel secure in their superiority. When two peoples meet, both are barbarians, each for the other. This did not occur to the minds of those who had come to these lands.

Both cases that we have just cited — like the goad with which he pricks his opponent — are expressive of what we have called the Lascasian methodological perspective: "If we were Indians..." To this the Dominican adds that if the Indians must be understood as barbarians ("Let us grant for the sake of argument that they be called, or be, barbarians," *Apología*, 22v), a fourth category will have to be established. In this fourth category, "barbarians" would be those who do not know Christ — not because of any urge to call such persons barbarians (which Bartolomé obviously does not like to do), but because, by putting them in the category of unbelievers, he obtains two results. First, he is able to apply to them the term "barbarians," so frequently used of them, but gives it a completely new and different meaning, radically excluding its common pejorative usage. Second, the identification of barbarians as unbelievers permits him to invoke all of the reasons — already presented — for rejecting war on the Indians and the subsequent domination that unbelief can in no way justify.

A Disorder Provoked

To conclude this chapter, we should like to make a few observations about something we frequently hear concerning Las Casas's opinion of the autochthonous population of the Indies. Some criticize him and others give him faint praise for his "idealization" of the Indian. They regard him as a precursor of Rousseau and the "noble savage."[64] Let us admit that certain passages in Las Casas's writings may invite such a comparison. But the differences between the two seem to us to outweigh the coincidences.

The myth of the noble savage, created after Montaigne by Jean-Jacques Rousseau in the *Discourse on the Origin of Inequality among Men* (1754), is an attack on modern civilization.[65] Here is an enlightened person who at the same time is a critic of the Enlightenment. According to Rousseau, human beings are born good; then civilization — as it had been constructed up to his day, and so proud of itself — corrupts them.

But this is not Las Casas's accent. True, he is enchanted with the natural world of the Indies. But he was in love with a universe that had captivated him since he was eighteen years old. Granted also, he praises the human qualities of its inhabitants, but now we know why. Because the Indians were held in contempt by the Europeans and were seen as borderline animals, Bartolomé's praise of their humanity and virtues is intended to show that they are subjects of rights and that war may not be made on them with impunity. Nor may they be subjected to servitude. Las Casas's aim is not to criticize what Rousseau calls the "civil state" versus the "natural state."[66] This is not the function of his encomium of the Indians.

For Bartolomé, the inhabitants of the Indies are not in a "natural state" except in certain regions. In the *Apologética historia* he is trying rather to demonstrate that they are capable of forging lofty civilizations, living in great cities, creating prudent political governments, and making wise laws. He shows that they are proficient in the arts and in music.

Las Casas does not oppose the noble savage to the civilized person. We may even say that, rather, he contrasts the "well-civilized" with the "ill-civilized" persons who abuse their power and refuse to acknowledge the rights of others, and such persons do this not because they are civilized or because society has corrupted them, but because of their neglect in practice of the values they trumpet in theory. Thus, he tells us, members of peoples of an elevated cultural level (Greeks, Romans, Spaniards) will sometimes fall in the category of barbarians of the first class. And this is all the more grave when, at the same time, they proclaim themselves Christians.

The myth of the noble savage is a by-product of modern society and its intellectual awakening in the Enlightenment. Las Casas is not a child of the century of light. He is, however, someone seeking to shed the light of Christ on the concrete reality of the Indies.

For this reason, one of Bartolomé's approaches to these matters seems to us to be supremely incisive and charged with consequences. To the considerations he entertains in behalf of the human quality of the natives, Spaniards in the Indies can simply reply that they see no such thing in them. The Dominican rises to his rebuttal. That opinion, he observes, is based on "a great error [found] in many of us — laity, ecclesiastics, and religious — with regard to these Indian nations." It so happens that "those who, from our nation, have come to these lands [arrived] after these peoples had lost their republics and the order that they had had for living and governing."

Not only does he invoke his own long experience in the Indies, and thereby deprive of all foundation a judgment based on a newly deformed reality, but he indicates the causes of the deformation. It is the result of "our having thrown [the Indians' polity and order] into such disorder and having humiliated them to the point of utter annihilation." This state of affairs has been created by the invaders, who, having destroyed the indigenous world, think that "the confusion and abasement in which [the Indians] now live has always been there and has proceeded from their barbaric nature and disorderly administration." Such, however, is not the case. Of that you may be sure, says the old expert on the Indies. This state of affairs has been provoked by the very ones who now accuse the Indians of being barbarians (*A.H.*, ch. 264, *O.E.* 4:435a–436b)![67]

This situation originated with the initial shock. But it has been stabilized by the *encomienda* and everything around it. That is, the socioeconomic order that has been installed here continues to turn these peoples, who at one time lived according to their customs and were ruled by their laws, into displaced persons who have no direction or guiding star and who today seem humanly inferior.[68] We have already seen Las Casas lay the blame at the doorstep, not of individuals alone, but of the entire colonial system. With this observation, Bartolomé places under interdict the very criteria employed by the Europeans to qualify other peoples as barbarians. Here are persons who for their own profit organize a society that shatters the Indian nations and thereupon, confronted with the human and civilizing impotence that they themselves have produced, now declare themselves these nations' protectors. Las Casas's observation is penetrating. It is correct, then, to say that he laid the foundations of an anticolonialist position.[69]

Chapter 11

Persons and Poor

The protest of the Hispaniola Dominicans, to whose cause the Franciscans and Bartolomé de Las Casas presently soon rallied, was not long in coming to the ears of the Spanish Crown. But the results were not what the missioners had sought, nor, still worse, did they afford any alleviation for the sufferings of the dwellers of the Indies. The friars' struggle, twenty years old now, in defense of the humanity of the Indians and their capacity to receive the gospel, had failed to change things. Furthermore, there had arisen — even, as we have seen, among missionaries in the Indies — the notion of the inferiority and irrationality of the Indians.

The friars now decided to appeal to the highest instance of all. The newborn church of the Indies made a daring representation to Pope Paul III. Las Casas played a role in the project, whose precise dimensions have only recently begun to be appreciated. The result was a series of extremely important papal texts calling for respect for the dignity of the Indian nations. Las Casas studies the matter in depth and sees in the members of those peoples not only subjects of human rights, but persons who must be understood as poor in the gospel sense of the word — that is, according to the love God. A consideration of all this allows us to take an important step in our understanding of the Lascasian thinking.

1. Las Casas and Paul III

The bull of Pope Paul III, *Sublimis Deus* (June 2, 1537), is regarded as the most important papal pronouncement on the human condition of the Indians. Two other pontifical documents, promulgated mere days before, must be taken into consideration as well: the brief *Pastorale Officium* (May 29), and the bull *Altitudo Divini Consilii* (June 1).[1] Las Casas always cited these (especially the first two) with satisfaction. Their concurrence with his ideas is indeed remarkable. It will be worth our while to recall the context in which they were issued as well as their actual scope.

A Complex History

The history of these texts was for a long time a muddled one. What was known was that these decrees had been obtained due to steps taken in Rome itself by a curious personage, Dominican friar Bernardino de Minaya. Minaya himself relates the matter in a memorial to Philip II.[2] From Mexico he sails to Spain with the intent of going on to Rome to present the truth about the Indians' predicament. In the judgment of Friar Bernardino, the Indians had been calumniated by another Dominican, Domingo de Betanzos, the author of a report that endorsed the low opinion of the Indians held by Cardinal García de Loaysa, president of the Royal Council of the Indies and former master general of the Dominican order. Minaya carries with him a letter to the pope from Bishop Julián Garcés (likewise a Dominican)[3] and in Spain obtains a recommendation from the empress for the pope.[4] This is the version of the story given by Friar Bernardino and followed by historians of the matter up to now.

Today, thanks to Helen Rand Parish, we have a better knowledge of what actually occurred. In her recent *Las Casas en México,* the illustrious historian has shed light on little-known aspects of the life and work of Las Casas on the basis of unpublished documents. With regard to the point that concerns us here, she has identified more precisely the role Bartolomé played in the issuing of the pontifical documents in question.[5] She has accomplished this through the meticulous reconstruction of an important meeting of bishops and religious superiors that took place in Mexico in 1536, in which Las Casas — having recently arrived from Nicaragua — participated. Three great themes were addressed: the controversial matter of the baptism of adult Indians, the slavery of the inhabitants of the Indies, and the question of their evangelization. The meeting concluded with three *Acta,* corresponding respectively to the three points addressed, which together with three other treatises and Garcés's well-known letter,[6] were thereupon carried by Minaya to Paul III.[7] The three pontifical decrees correspond to these acts and treatises.[8]

One of the treatises would be Las Casas's *De Unico Modo,* which concerns the method of evangelization. The second treatise was by the Augustinian Juan de Oseguera, on the baptism of the Indians (this one is no longer extant), and the third was by Vasco de Quiroga, on their slavery. Parish holds that Las Casas began to write his *De Unico* after the famous episode involving the cacique Enriquillo. Thus, Bartolomé's first book would have been a theological reflection on his own experience of peaceful evangelization. Las Casas now abandons a position that had led him in earlier years to encourage the establishment of military garrisons that would provide missionaries with any necessary protection. The case of Enriquillo definitively reinforces his thesis that the gospel must be proclaimed by persuasion only. His new view had received further impulse from Betanzos's report on the Indians and by the abrogation of the antislavery law of 1530. For that reason Parish dates the work around 1533–34.[9] We no longer have the _De Unico_ in its complete form, but it is possible to reconstruct it on the basis of various references. Using these, Parish maintains that "section for section, the original work was exactly parallel to the future encyclical, _Sublimis Deus_."[10] And indeed their thematic similarity is striking.

The Sublime God

Sublimis Deus is addressed to "all the faithful in Christ."[11] On the basis of the love of the "sublime God" for the human race, Pope Paul III recalls a universal principle:

> And inasmuch, furthermore, as the human being has been created for a share in eternal life and happiness and can attain to this everlasting life and happiness only by way of faith in the Lord Jesus Christ, as Sacred Scripture attests, it necessarily follows that the human being is of such condition and nature as to be capable of receiving the faith of Christ, and that anyone endowed with human nature is capable of receiving that faith.

Every human being without exception is called to eternal happiness. Faith responds to this universal salvific will; everyone is fit for receiving this grace.

The pope demonstrates the presence of this capacity through a scholastic type of reasoning that we frequently find in Las Casas. "Nor, surely, can anyone be supposed to be so foolish as to believe that he himself can attain the end or in any way reach the supremely necessary means" to that end. Christ's words and witness establish the universality of the message and the possibility of accepting it: "Accordingly, Truth Itself [Christ], who can neither deceive nor be deceived in assigning preachers of the faith to the task of preaching, said: 'Go and teach _all_ nations.' All, said he, without any exception, since _all_ have the capacity to receive the doctrine of the faith" (emphasis added). Here we have a straightforward declaration, along Lascasian lines, of two universalities: the gift of faith and the fundamental equality of all human beings in terms of the gospel.

The matter is seen in all its implications when we take into account the circumstances of the age. Ever since John Major had defended his theses in Paris, many other persons had maintained the human inferiority of the Indians.[12] Even more serious than these ideas, however, was the practice of the colonizers,[13] who appealed to (or ignored, as it suited them) the ambiguous, contradictory laws enacted by the Spanish Crown.

For example, in an effort to palliate the Indians' plight, Charles V in 1530 forbade their enslavement.[14] In the Indies, scant attention was paid to this royal decree.[15] Furthermore, let us recall that it was soon abrogated, in February 1534.[16] Las Casas must be referring to this abrogation when he speaks of the "sad license granted by the Royal Council to enslave" (*Carta a un personaje*, 1535, *O.E.* 5:64a). This "license" was due above all to pressure exerted by the powerful Cardinal García de Loaysa.[17] It gave slavery back its green light. The everlasting inconstancy of measures taken by the royal authority in this area doubtless played a relevant role in the immediate context of the bull we are studying.

This is why the papal text takes on a polemical tone, pointing directly to what is occurring in the Indies. It censures those who "often dare to assert that the West Indians (and others who have come to Our notice in these times) ought to be placed in our service like brute beasts, under the pretext that they are excluded from the Catholic faith." Then the bull decries the oppression to which the Indians are subjected, condemning "those who reduce them to slavery, oppressing them with such afflictions as they scarcely oppress the brute beasts they use." In the face of this the pope reminds us that the Indians are "genuine human beings" and "not only have the capacity to receive the Christian faith, but (as we have learned) approach that faith with great alacrity." And indeed this was what numerous missioners maintained, with Las Casas among them.

The practical consequences are obvious:

> The aforementioned Indians and all other people who in the future come to the knowledge of Christians, although they be outside the faith of Christ, neither are nor ought to be deprived of their freedom or dominion over their goods. Indeed, they may freely and licitly use, possess, and enjoy freedom and such dominion and must not be reduced to slavery.[18]

The universal summons to salvation is the rock-solid basis that supports the affirmation of the equality of all human beings. The inhabitants of these lands are free and owners of what is found in them. The Indies are not a no-man's-land, as those who sought to conquer them thought. All, including the Indians, are capable of receiving the gospel and "must be attracted to that faith in Christ by the preaching of the word of God and the example of a good life." The main concern of the bull is evangelization.

Bartolomé de Las Casas wrote his *De Unico* precisely to demonstrate that the way to proclaim the gospel is persuasion, since it is addressed to free beings. These are persons endowed — in equal measure — with natural reason. So true is this that, in presenting Paul III's text, Bartolomé asserts of the Indians: "Many of those persons could rule us in the monastic, economic, and also political life, as well as guide us to good customs." In terms of a received classification of his time, he opposes head-on (in language that cannot have pleased the *encomenderos*) those who dared so say that the inhabitants of the Indies "were beasts or quasi-beasts, openly detracting them; and that consequently it was right and legitimate to subjugate them by means of war, or to hunt them like animals, and then to reduce them to slavery and so make use of them at whim" (*De Unico*, 137). As we see, Las Casas's text runs very closely parallel to the pope's.

The ideas Garcés presents in the letter we have mentioned, written in elegant Latin, are similar. The bishop of Tlaxcala bitterly criticizes the Indians' detractors and defends the natives' human status. He also asserts their enormous readiness to receive the faith. Those who speak ill of the Indians seem to forget that the church excludes no one from its proclamation of the gospel. He therefore asks the pope to facilitate the evangelization of the Indians and to send them missionaries. Thus the church will grow in "Asia," and thus perhaps compensate for its losses in these years in Europe.[19] This text, too, surely carried weight in the decision for and content of the pontifical document.

Against Slavery

The brief *Pastorale Officium* is addressed to the archbishop of Toledo, Juan de Tavera, who had played an important role in the enactment of the royal decree against slavery in 1530 — which had been rescinded, as we have said, through the influence of García de Loaysa, president of the Council of the Indies. Paul III's step is significant because it was Loaysa, and not Tavera, whose duty it was to see to the affairs of the Indies. Loaysa would have been the expected addressee of this letter.[20] The text reasserts the teaching of *Sublimis Deus*, but adds very precise sanctions against those who mistreat the Indians. Like the bull, the brief as well includes the Lascasian ideas. In particular, the pope threatens the enslavers of the Indians with excommunication, a measure urged by Bartolomé in various writings antedating the pontifical texts.

The pope recalls that, although the Indians are "outside the bosom of the church, nevertheless they neither are nor ought to be deprived of their freedom or of dominion over their goods. For as they are human beings and accordingly endowed with a capacity for faith and salvation, they must not be destroyed by slavery." Declared under excommunication, then, with absolution reserved to the Roman pontiff alone and "regardless of their dignity, state, condition, rank, and preeminence," are all those who might "dare in any fashion to reduce the said Indians to slavery or despoil them of their goods."

Seemingly unaware of the revocation of the royal decree prohibiting the Indians' enslavement, the pope begins his brief to Tavera with a reference to the same:

> It has come to Our notice that Our most beloved son in Christ Charles, Ever-August Emperor of the Romans, who is also King of Castile and León — in order to restrain those who, burning with greed, show an inhumane spirit against the human race — has by public edict forbidden all of his subjects from daring to subject the West or South Indians to slavery, or to deprive them of their goods.

The intent of this allusion is to place the pontifical document in continuity with the decree of Charles V, and thus avoid any conflict with the emperor. Of course, the effect was just the opposite. Having abrogated the antislavery law, the king could scarcely have taken kindly to this encomium of himself for something no longer in force. Thus, instead of "rendering the hearer benevolent," the brief's exordium became a piece of unintentional irony.

It is not difficult to understand Las Casas's enthusiasm for these documents. He reproduces them in his *De Unico* (137v–140) in support of his thesis that the gospel must be proclaimed by persuasion and not by force. He does the same in his *Apología*, where he provides a more detailed commentary (see 64–66v). Both papal documents, especially the bull, use terms very similar to his (and now, thanks to Helen Rand Parish, we have a better understanding of why this is so), and are for him an important confirmation of his positions.[21]

The other bull, *Altitudo Divini Consilii*, is addressed to the bishops of the Indies (and we should note this) and deals with sacramental questions, especially those involved in baptism and matrimony. It governed the life of the church in the Indies for a long time (and was still cited in the 1917 Code of Canon Law). In language calculated to be as inoffensive as possible, it bears on a point under heated debate in the Indies: the requisite conditions for the reception of baptism. Franciscans (who favored an accelerated preparation for the sacrament) and Dominicans (who maintained the need for a solid antecedent evangelization) had engaged in a bitter debate over the question. The papal document supports the Dominicans' position, which had found in Las Casas one of its most determined advocates, without in any way reproaching the Franciscans.

Those who have baptized the Indians "without observing the ceremonies and solemnities kept by the Church" have not sinned, the document says, in view of "the circumstances of that time." Henceforth, however, they must comply with "that which is observed by the Church." Norms are also prescribed for marriages and for abstinence. Finally and with good judgment, the document notes the distance separating the Indies from Rome and grants its episcopal addressees "full and free faculty" for the resolution of "any cases reserved to the Apostolic See" — an early and useful instance of decentralization.[22]

2. An Emperor's Wrath

As we know, however, none of these texts — not even the papal ones — that challenge very concrete privileges put an end to the discussion, let alone the practices in question.

What Was Revoked?

Emperor Charles V will oppose both the bull *Sublimis Deus* and the brief that ratified its doctrine and indicated corresponding guidelines of behavior. At the same time, the *encomenderos* and their allies, despite their claim to be Christians, will ignore the papal directives. Such is the immemorial custom of the great ones of this world when their interests are threatened.[23]

Charles V now solicited and obtained from Paul III the brief of revocation, *Non Indecens Videtur* (June 19, 1538), whose effect is so much disputed.[24] Some think that the pope annulled all three documents — or at least the first two — that we have considered in the foregoing pages. Others hold that only the letter to the cardinal of Toledo was affected. The text of the new brief opens with these words:

> It does not seem inappropriate for the Roman Pontiff, who must watch over a number of matters, to revoke, correct, and change [dispositions made] to someone's detriment when these have been wrung from him by deceit [*per circumventionem*], and enact others, as may seem useful and proper in the Lord.

The opening sentences enunciate a matter of principle: If the pope has been misinformed, intentionally deceived, he may emend what he decreed. Justice requires it. In this case, a powerful person has brought the error to light. In effect, the pope openly acknowledges that he is writing in response to an initiative on the part of the king of Spain. The passage is a key one for an interpretation of the document: "Our most dear Son in Christ, Charles, Ever-August Emperor of the Romans and Catholic King of the Spains, has recently caused Us to be informed that a certain letter in the form of a brief had been extorted [*in forma Brevis extortas fuisse*] from Us." His Majesty felt that the earlier letter had harmed his interests in the Indies, the text continues, and so asks the pope to give further attention to the matter.

Paul III proceeds accordingly to the request, acknowledges his error, and declares that it was not his intention to be prejudicial to Charles V or to place obstacles in the way of the king's efforts in the Indies. He grants the emperor's request and solemnly declares: "By apostolic authority, through these presents, We revoke, invalidate, and annul the aforementioned letter [*litteras praedictas*] and anything contained therein." Thus, any conclusion drawn from it will be, says the pope emphatically, "null and void and of no validity or effect."

Exactly what did Paul III revoke? De la Hera has correctly observed that the pope speaks of a "certain letter in the form of a *brief*" in the singular, and not in the plural, as the Latin expression "litteras in forma brevis" has sometimes been translated (Lewis Hanke and López de Lara, for example). Furthermore, he refers to a brief and not a bull. Strictly speaking, therefore, only the letter to the archbishop of Toledo (*Pastorale Officium*) would have been revoked while no mention of the bulls (*Altitudo* and *Sublimis*), which are of greater doctrinal authority, is made. This is also the position of Parish, who, furthermore, thinks that a reading of the brief of revocation as a whole shows that only *Pastorale Officium* is being referred to.[25]

This indeed seems to have been the case. De la Hera goes further, suggesting that the king asked only for the revocation of this brief.[26] But this is not how Charles V himself interpreted the controversial brief of revocation, *Non Indecens*. In fact, on September 6, 1538, the king issued an order to the effect that, henceforward, papal "bulls and briefs" dealing with affairs in the Indies be presented to the Council of the Indies before being forwarded to those lands. Otherwise they were to be withdrawn from circulation. If such documents were judged inappropriate by the Council — says the king — "our Most Holy Father" would then be asked, "upon receiving better information, to rescind them. Meanwhile, let the Council see that they not be executed or applied."[27] Thus the king of Spain is invoking the rights of the Patronage, granted by Pope Julius II.[28] Furthermore, the royal order only confirms the countermeasures (confiscation of the documents, arrest of Bernardino de Minaya) taken by the sovereign against Paul III's decrees months before. Jealous of his authority, he is anxious to prevent interference in his policy in the Indies.

Still more plainly, only days afterward (September 10), Charles writes to the viceroy of New Spain (Mexico) about the texts of Paul III, saying that he had been "informed that one Friar Bernardino de Minaya, of the Order of St. Dominic, moved by good intentions, had obtained from Our Holy Father certain *bulls* and *briefs* concerning the natives of this land, and their instruction, freedom, and manner of life, in derogation of Our Royal prerogatives and of that which We have so ordained with such care and watchfulness." He informs the viceroy that he has seen to the withdrawal of "said original bulls and briefs and has informed His Holiness of this, that he might order the revocation of *any and all bulls and briefs* for which the said Friar Bernardino had pleaded." And, confident that he speaks the truth, he adds significantly: "His Holiness has seen to this, as you will learn by the copy of the brief that I am having sent to you."[29]

This time the language is in the plural and obviously means for the king *bulls and briefs.* According to the king of Spain, then, *Sublimis Deus* — and not only the letter to Tavera — has been annulled by the brief *Non Indecens*, which he dispatches to the viceroy. Everything indicates that this is what he requested and — mistakenly — thought he obtained.[30]

There is every indication, then, that only the brief *Pastorale Officium* has been abrogated. But even in this case we must say that we are faced with a surrender by the pope to the emperor. We have already pointed out, following Hanke, some of the reasons for this retreat. But the delicate nature of Charles's request has led Paul III to take certain precautions. Parish, who has made such an important contribution to a clarification of these matters, furnishes us with a revealing memorandum — hitherto unpublished — dictated by Cardinal Ghinucci, who played an important role in the issuing of Paul III's decrees on these matters, and preserved on the verso of the original first draft of the brief *Non Indecens* (now kept in the Vatican Secret Archive). Here is the text:

> The Pope said that, if it were said that the letter [*litteras*] was obtained by subterfuge [*per subreptionem*], he would therefore readily grant its revocation [*earum revocationem*], as punishment for deceit, etc. But if it is said to be simply extorted, and is revoked, and also the processes and condemnations and censures and all their consequences, it seems to him that this could be imputed to rashness (*levitati imputari*).[31]

Therefore the former option was taken. But in any case it was a questionable move — despite the shrewdness of the "footnote," which reveals Paul III's awareness of the step that he was about to take.[32]

Subsequent Fate of the Documents

For his own part, Las Casas always appealed to the papal texts of 1537, without alluding to any revocation. This is what he did in the *Apología* and probably with the theologians and lawyers at Valladolid as well, in 1550. Nor was he alone in this. Ginés de Sepúlveda too, not in the *Democrates*, but in his objections to Las Casas's positions, did the same. Sepúlveda cites Paul III's bull in support of his interpretation of the texts of Alexander VI. Further, he asserts that Paul's criticisms are directed against excesses committed in the Indies. According to Sepúlveda, this bull "was issued only against soldiers who without authority of their prince were enslaving these barbarians, as well as committing many other atrocities, and treating them as beasts. This is why he said that they must treat them as human beings and neighbors, since they were rational animals" (1552, *O.E.* 5:316b).

Juan de la Peña, too, cites *Sublimis Deus* and uses it to come to a correct interpretation of Alexander VI's *Inter Caetera*. De la Peña writes:

> The first thing that Paul III defined in it was that those unbelievers, the Indians, were human beings with a capacity for eternal life and eternal death. The second thing that he defined was that those unbelievers have not been deprived *de facto,* nor should they be, of the ancient sovereignty that they have over their possessions. On the contrary, he commanded that they be allowed to make free use of them as their own. And as these decrees seem contrary, they must be interpreted in accordance with common law.[33]

As we see, in the second half of the sixteenth century there is not the shadow of a doubt of the validity of *Sublimis Deus*.

It is particularly significant here that the popes who followed Paul III cite these documents (including especially *Pastorale Officium*, of whose revocation by Paul III there can be no doubt) as validly issued and in force. Indeed, a hundred years after, Pope Urban VIII addresses the bull *Commissum Nobis* (1639) to the collector of Portugal on the enslavement of the Indians. Urban cites Paul's brief to Tavera and writes: "With the present letter, we wish once more to confirm the content of that Brief." Then he declares that there exist in his own time the same "reasons that moved Our predecessor Paul to write that Brief." The pope is energetic in his position, demanding that "no one dare or presume to reduce the Indians to slavery, sell them, purchase them, exchange them or give them away, separate them from their wives and children, despoil them of their belongings and goods, move them to other places and displace them, or deprive them of their freedom in any manner whatsoever." Finally, he reaffirms the penalty of ex-communication for those who ignore this reminder. There is not the slightest suggestion of a possible repeal of the brief in question.

Still another century later, Benedict XIV, in the bull *Immensa Pastorum* (1741), which was addressed to the bishops and king of Portugal in the face of the persistence of slavery, repeats his predecessors' proscription of the same. He explicitly states that he is following the brief to Tavera and the bull of Urban VIII. Gregory XVI returns to the topic in his apostolic letter *In Supremo* (1839) against slavery in Africa and the Indies. Paul III's brief is cited as the first link in a chain of condemnations of Indian slavery, with an explicit addition bearing on what was occurring in Africa.

Finally, in his encyclical *In Plurimis* (1888), written to the bishops of Brazil on the occasion of the abolition of slavery, Leo XIII quotes for the first time (without mentioning it by name) the bull *Sublimis Deus,* which he calls a "solemn decree." He adds that this document had been confirmed "by a letter to the Archbishop of Toledo, determining that those who act contrary to this decree would fall under interdict and that the power to absolve them would be reserved to the Roman Pontiff alone."[34]

It would be difficult to imagine a greater endorsement of the brief *Pastorale Officium.* Actually, *Sublimis Deus* is less well known in papal teaching; it would seem that the first reference to it dates from the close of the nineteenth century. For all these reasons, and despite the later changes we have mentioned, which at times make for a tangled mess, we must forthrightly accept the fact that the documents of Paul III — in a special way *Sublimis Deus*; *Altitudo Divini Consilii,* of course; and even *Pastorale Officium* — are part of the magisterium of the church. Paul III's revocatory brief *Non Indecens* did not leave a mark on the church's official teaching.

3. The Intention of Jesus Christ

In the foregoing chapter, we recalled Las Casas's awareness of his confrontation with a social system that strips the Indians of their humanity. In response, he upholds the dignity and rights of those persons and thus boldly battles to remove from their shoulders the stigma of the name of barbarians, which was invoked to justify acts of war against the natives and their unspeakable harassment — or at least to specify what could possibly be meant by this expression in their case. Now then is the moment for him to reiterate the crucial importance of enfleshing the gospel, so that it be a criterion of concrete discernment in history. All human beings — however limited, deformed, crude, or strange they may be or appear — ought to be regarded as our brothers and sisters.

But we have not yet entered upon the most important step along these lines. We already know that Las Casas listed the dwellers of the Indies in a category of unbelievers that made war against them illegitimate. Call them barbarians if you will, but only in the sense of nations who have not yet accepted faith in Christ and not as being inferior to other peoples. The Indians are of equal dignity with Europeans and altogether capable of receiving the Christian faith. Their rights must therefore be respected and defended. It was this that, with the help of his friends, Bartolomé succeeded in having solemnly proclaimed by Paul III.

There is more, however. For Las Casas, the inhabitants of the Indies are not only persons and thereby the subjects of rights; before all else, the Indian is a *poor one in the gospel sense.* And this entails enormous consequences. We have already touched on the point in Part One (see chapter 2). This was also the perspective of Guamán Poma (see the Introduction). It will be worth our while to return to it in connection with what we are seeing in the present chapter. At the same time, Las Casas's vision grows wider and deeper. Not only is the Indian a poor person in accordance with the gospel: so is the black, who has been violently hauled to the Indies. In fact, even whites can be poor. It is not a matter of race. In all of them, in terms of Bartolomé's first intuition, Christ is present.

With Their Poverty on Their Backs

The major cause of the poverty and oppression in which the Indians live is greed for gold. This is what leads to the wars of the Conquista and to the exploitation of Indian labor in the distributions. Having experienced all of this, having had some share in this criminal order, Bartolomé now reads the text of Ecclesiasticus with new eyes. Now, thanks to this passage from Scripture — a prophetic one — he understands that here too, in his own life, to despoil the poor of what is rightfully theirs is to kill them. It has also helped him to regard differently his experience in the Indies and his personal responsibility in the oppression of the Indians.

All of this leads Bartolomé de Las Casas to see in the Indian the *poor* of whom the Bible speaks. Indeed, Las Casas repeatedly refers to the Indians as the "poor." He speaks of them in heavily biblical accents with descriptions reminiscent of the book of Job (see Job 24, which is the harshest and at the same time the most beautiful description of poverty in the Bible), or those which the prophets present us. Thus, he will tell us of Indians whose "belly cleaves to their backbone from pure hunger" (*H.I.*, bk. 3, ch. 14, *O.E.* 2:205a), or who — he complains, with a realism of which false spiritualities are innocent — after working all day are still expected to pray and to absorb religious instruction.

Along the same lines, Las Casas will mention those Indians of Cuba who, believing that the Spaniards would do them no more harm, came to see him with their "poverty on their backs" (*H.I.*, bk. 3, ch. 30, *O.E.* 2:247b). Constantly he will call them "the poorest of people" (*Brevísima*, 1552, *O.E.* 5:138a) and claim that "people so poor in chattels and land have never been seen in the universe nor heard nor been." Fray Bartolomé denounces the attitude that regards Indians as "beneath insects."[35] In one of his last texts, addressed to Pope Pius V, Las Casas will once more insist on the "incredible poverty" of the dwellers of the Indies (*O.E.* 5:542b).

Countless passages could be cited in the same vein. But it is important to emphasize that Las Casas does more than describe a situation. He actually sees the Indians not only as poor, but as oppressed people as well, persons stripped of their rights and of a just wage, as the text from Ecclesiasticus puts it. The "Indian oppressed" is the expression that will come from his pen so many times (e.g., *H.I.*, bk. 3, ch. 82, *O.E.* 2:364a), along with "captive poor" (e.g., *O.E.* 5:541b). Bartolomé is fully aware that the current poverty of the Indian is the result of unspeakable exploitation. The natives of the Indies, "oppressed with the most difficult labor and tyrannies beyond belief, take upon their gaunt shoulders, against all divine and natural law, a most heavy yoke and unbearable burden" (*O.E.* 5:541b). Therefore, he concludes severely, in the last memorial that he sent to the Council of the Indies, "every bit of gold and silver, pearls, and other wealth that has arrived in Spain is stolen property" (1566, *O.E.* 5:538b).

We have dealt with this point in treating of the *encomienda*. Let us now address the obvious conclusion Bartolomé draws precisely at the moment that his reading of the passage from Ecclesiasticus enlightens his conscience. It will be his lifelong task: the Indians' liberation. This alone will be the "adequate remedy for these unfortunate people," cleric Bartolomé writes to his friend Rentería, in communicating to him his decisions (*H.I.*, bk. 3, ch. 81, *O.E.* 2:360a). To secure this remedy will be the undertaking of his entire existence. From now on, that liberation seems to him a condition of justice and a demand from the Lord: the oppression of the Indian "is *contrary to the intention of Jesus Christ* and the way of love with which he charged us in the gospel. It completely contradicts, if you look carefully, the whole of Sacred Scripture" (ibid; emphasis added). From this point on the intention of Jesus Christ becomes the norm of his life. At times this is obvious; at other times it must be discerned in concrete events.

His contemporaries promptly perceived the danger that lurked in these propositions. Las Casas relates how the bishop of Darién, Don Juan Cabedo, echoes at the royal Court the complaint of the conquistadors that Bartolomé "was toiling for the liberation of the Indians and trying to take them away from the Spaniards; they considered him a destroyer of so many grandees that used the Indians and the enemy of their nation" (*H.I.*, bk. 3, ch. 147, *O.E.* 2:530b). Early on, as we see, our cleric is being accused of a lack of patriotism in advocating the liberation of the Indians. This will be a frequent and no less unjust accusation down to our own day. What is happening is that this Spaniard — which is what Bartolomé truly and profoundly was — believed the gospel and the defense of the poor came before false and disguised nationalism.[36]

Las Casas's denunciation of the murder of the Indians and the destruction of their lands led him to a sharp confrontation with the conquistadors and *encomenderos* and their allies at Court.[37] But he lucidly points out that, entirely apart from the question of personal intentions, this was occurring because of the internal logic of the socioeconomic system being implanted. Perceptively he writes:

> I am not saying that they directly wish to kill them, out of some hatred for them. I am saying that they desire to be wealthy and to abound in gold, which is their goal, by means of the toil and sweat of the afflicted, distressed Indians, using them as lifeless means and instruments, and that upon this follows, necessarily, the death of them all. (*Octavo remedio*, 1542, *O.E.* 5:89a–b)

The death of the Indians became inevitable, then, as a consequence of the alienated work upon which the new colonial order, orientated to the satisfaction of the interests and greed of the dominators, was being constructed. The latter, Las Casas maintains, "sought, not to put them to death directly, but to use them as animals, preferring to the bodily and spiritual health of the Indians their own interests, covetousness, and gains, upon which death follows, not doubtfully but inevitably" (*H.I.*, bk. 3, ch. 30, *O.E.* 2:248a). The murderer of the poor (one who "takes their bread from them") is not, then, an isolated individual moved by wicked instincts, but an oppressive political system based on the interests and gain of those who enjoy its benefits and on the accumulation of wealth in the hands of a few. It is a system that uses the poor as "dead instruments" without respecting their character as living creatures. Thus is created a situation of profound injustice, which is therefore contrary to the will of God. On the basis of the Christian faith Las Casas denounces the social order centered on the inordinate quest for wealth that was beginning to take root.

That regime is shattering the Indian nations (in some regions more, in some less, to be sure), isolating their members as they watch the old factors of social cohesion go up in smoke. This, Las Casas remarks, affects the reception of the Christian faith, and he offers a perceptive biblical commentary on the matter. In defense of the autonomy of the Indian nations, he observes that, as the Jews were not yet a people in the time of Abraham, God had not yet bestowed on them their "Old Law" — nor, for the same reason, "when the Hebrews were in captivity in Egypt" either. No, "it was given them when they were a people, and had fled Egypt, and might enjoy their freedom." Being a people and living in freedom are requisite conditions for faith. "Never has there been any religion in the world," he says, "nor has any people been given a law as thoroughly dependent on those receiving it being a people and enjoying freedom as the Christian religion and the law of the gospel."

The text continues most interestingly. If the dwellers of the Indies had been found "scattered like cattle across the fields, in order to instruct them in the faith and give them the law of Christ we should have had to join them together and make peoples of them." And "if they had all been slaves, we should have had to set them free." Being a people and being free are requirements of the Christian faith. But the newcomers in these lands did exactly the opposite. They found peoples "living in good order" and "scattered them, turning them into flocks as if they were cattle" (*H.I.,* bk. 3, ch. 11, *O.E.* 2:197a–b). They had been living in freedom, and now they were subjected to servitude — exactly the contrary of what the gospel message demands.

This is a text of the first importance. It expresses Las Casas's theology of grace, which it does not restrict to the level commonly considered religious. Grace invades everything, including social life. The gospel con-vokes; it calls a people into being. When we destroy nations, we deprive those nations of the concrete conditions for being the people of God. Here we have a rich ecclesiological perspective.

First in the Church

It would not suffice to describe this horrible situation, or even to indicate its causes. A way out must be found. Las Casas proposed — all his life — solutions of varying value. Two of his most important efforts (already noted) were the experiment in peaceful evangelization in Verapaz, geographically limited but intended as a model, and the New Laws, which were more comprehensive, but on another level. Bartolomé entertained few illusions concerning the application of the New Laws. Besides, no sooner had they been promulgated than the news arrived of the resistance they were provoking.

The fear that they would not be put in practice, and would even be rescinded, moves Bartolomé to look for other solutions. Nine days after Charles V annulled a substantial part of these decrees, Las Casas, accompanied by two other bishops, Valdivieso (d. 1550) and Marroquín (d. 1563), presented an extraordinary document to the Audiencia de los Confines.[38]

In this text, Las Casas (who is certainly its author)[39] appeals to a traditional datum: the church has responsibility for the poor, in this case called the "wretched." The origin of this received doctrine is in a law first laid down in the time of the Emperor Constantine, says P. Castañeda.[40] From that time onward, the juridical category of the "wretched" began to take shape — those whose condition of weakness requires that they be specially protected. A catalogue of privileges developed within the juridical norms to reestablish some manner of justice. It was surely the biblical notion of the poor as God's favorites that inspired these efforts.

Las Casas takes up the question once again, but he does so in the new context of the Indies. He does more than merely apply what has already been said; he changes the perspective. He goes back to the biblical sources, and therefore does not limit himself to denouncing the condition of the poor: he also points out the injustice of which they are the object. The traditional position simply spoke of the poor and wretched as weak — and even humanly inferior — persons needing protection. Las Casas departs somewhat from the line of thinking to which he appeals: for him the natives of these lands are "the most wretched and most oppressed and burdened, afflicted, helpless persons, who suffer the greatest injustices."[41] They are people so miserable that those who are not moved to compassion at the sight of them "are bestial, cruel men."

Let us note the point of the matter: the bestial are those insensitive to this situation and its suffering, not those who suffer it, the Indians. Never have nations been seen who were more afraid of "Spanish Christians because of the violence, coercion, oppression, tyranny, robbery, cruelty, unjust captivity, and wicked wars" of which they have been victims. The Indians are poor — wretched, in terms of the tradition to which Las Casas appeals here — *because they have been made such.* Their situation has been created by injustice and cruelty. This viewpoint is absent from the canonical tradition in question, but it is clearly present in the prophetic line of the Bible, and Bartolomé recovers it in this statement to the Audiencia.

Neither is this outlook — which takes causes into account — present in the laws handed down by the Spanish Crown on behalf of the Indians: for example, in the establishment of the Protectorate,[42] eventually identified with the episcopate. The principle of "legislation for the Indies, and the key to its understanding, is a view of the natives as minors, incompetent to be their own administrators."[43] That is, it is the opposite of what Las Casas thought. This enables us to see what his particular petition is based on. For him, Indian persons and nations stand on an equal footing with Europeans. They should enjoy freedom and the right to appoint their legitimate political authorities. Las Casas's point of departure is a deep respect for the Indians' dignity as human beings and for the nations that they have constituted. As we have already pointed out, Las Casas always considers the Indians as members of peoples and cultures.

All of the foregoing constitutes the first part of the text under examination here. The second part is the principal one: here the bishops ask that the Indians be placed under ecclesiastical jurisdiction in accordance with the traditional juridical policy upon which they base their argument. The bishops offer four reasons: (1) because there is no one to secure justice for the Indians or to defend "their lives and freedom"; (2) because of the "tyrannies and injustices" the Spaniards commit against them; (3) because of the "cause and favor of our faith," which fails to reach the natives by reason of the oppression to which they are subjected; and finally, (4) because these people, so ready to receive the faith, "can already be said to belong to Holy Church."[44]

The proposal is extremely bold. It would place the immense population of the Indies directly under the "protection and shelter" of the church. If the laws of civil society have been unable to ensure justice, then the church must step into the breach: "It belongs immediately to ecclesiastical judgment to know and determine the causes of this, and to fulfill all justice in its regard." And the petition adds, in a spirit unmistakably Lascasian: " . . . to defend their lives and liberty from any and all persons, . . . as [one] defends the most wretched, most poor, most helpless . . . and destitute of persons." It is the church's duty. Arguments based on the Fathers of the Church and canon law so certify.

The third part of the text seeks to ensure that the demand not be rejected. It recalls that the bishops are protectors of the Indians, but obviously what the text presents goes far beyond what was anticipated for that institution.[45] The three bishops ask the Audiencia to declare that, by right, they may "learn and determine the causes having to do with the Indian natives," since it is a matter of persons "privileged by divine law and by the holy and universal church" in the face of the "oppression to which they are subjected." If the Audiencia fails to accept this, its members will fall, they solemnly declare, under "papal excommunication *ipso facto*" for hindering them from discharging an obligation that, they say, they are prepared to defend "with their blood, if need be."

The Audiencia rejected the petition out of hand. But for Las Casas, the matter was anything but laid to rest. In various texts from the same period he insists on the same notion: *Representación al Emperador Carlos V* (1542, O.E. 5:124b), *Memorial al Rey* (1543, O.E. 5:184a–185a), *Carta al Consejo de Indias* (1544, O.E. 5:208b). He is seeking to render effective his commitment to the Indians as gospel poor.[46]

Despite everything Las Casas did not slacken in his efforts. With the abrogation of important points of the New Laws, the bishop of Chiapa faced a difficult moment in which he saw many of the things that he had so laboriously constructed fall apart. However, he does not miss a beat. One year after his confrontation with the Audiencia (in 1546), he writes an interesting treatise, unpublished until recently and therefore very little studied,[47] called at the time the *Quaestio Theologalis,* from the opening words of the manuscript. Parish proposes as a title *De Exemptione sive Damnatione* (On exemption or damnation).[48]

Here we wish to highlight only that the work's central thesis is to prove that ecclesiastics are exempt from the coercive authority of secular judges and authorities, including kings and princes. Were such authorities to pronounce any judicial sentence upon an ecclesiastic, they would risk excommunication.[49] Thus, Las Casas strengthens the role of the episcopal ministry, whose divine origin the text likewise maintains.[50] All of this gives more force to his thesis about the role the church should play in regard to the poor of the Indies.[51] The Dominican has come to the conclusion that only in the church can the Indian nations find support and defense. This leads him to emphasize the function of missionaries and bishops in the Indies.[52]

Taking seriously the intention of Jesus Christ carries Las Casas very far. As we have repeatedly observed, Bartolomé's deepest spiritual and theological intuition was to see in the Indians those who are called poor in the gospel and in them to see Christ himself. Las Casas always looked for a way to enflesh his vision in historical realizations. We have just seen an example. But little by little, Las Casas perceives that this approach is not limited to only the original inhabitant of the Indies. The black, violently brought from Africa, has the same rights as the Indian. The black, too, is one of those called "poor" in the gospel. We shall treat the point in detail.

4. A Repentant Man

The colonial order being installed in the Indies will shortly have a cruel — and unforeseen — consequence for the population of another continent: Africa. We refer, of course, to the ignominious slave traffic that began to develop on a large scale around the middle of the sixteenth century and reached staggering proportions in the following century, as various European countries became involved.

At first, like all his contemporaries, Las Casas accepted the fact of slavery as such. Like others, he even supported certain petitions that black slaves be transported from Spain to replace the work force that had been recruited among the native peoples of the Antilles, who were on their way to extinction. As we know, he has been harshly reproached for this. It is also well known that years later he wrote painful, contrite pages about his "blindness" in this matter. Las Casas's final, definitive position is clear today to every serious historian and anyone else willing to consult the facts and the texts.

Nevertheless, the persistence of this accusation against Bartolomé — motivated, in large part, by his polemical position on questions of the Indies — is such that a few pages must be devoted to the matter.[53] It is well to make clear, however, that this is not the only reason for doing so. Bartolomé's defense of the Guanches (inhabitants of the Canary Islands) and Africans will also help us to see that his evangelical perspective on the poor is not limited to the world of the Indies.

Between Legality and Justice

Slavery is an ancient fact of the human race. In Europe (as well as in other parts of the world, especially in the East), it was widely practiced, paradoxically, in the shining age of Greek democracy just as in Rome, even at the time of the Republic itself. In the course of the Middle Ages, for reasons that would be beside the point here, its social and economic importance diminished. But it continued to exist and was legally recognized. The state of war prevailing for centuries between Christian countries and the Muslim nations around the Mediterranean basin kept slavery alive on both sides and in some ways caused its increase during the fifteenth and sixteenth centuries.[54]

Thinkers like Plato and Aristotle and legislation such as Roman law endorsed the legality of slavery. Once converted to Christianity, the European peoples accepted it as a fact, only insisting that slaves be treated well and that their right to life, marriage, and even, in some cases, priestly ordination, be recognized.[55] But the regime as such was always legal.

A number of reasons are given for this. The first is war. In the mentality of the time, the victors — in a just war, to be sure — had the right to slay the vanquished. To make them slaves for life instead was regarded as a concession, almost a humanitarian gesture. Here, then, was the most important cause of slavery, because once someone was enslaved, that person could be bought and sold. Other alleged justifications for the enslavement of persons, besides war, were their conviction of a serious crime, their sale of themselves or their children in order to pay debts that they had contracted, and finally — although this was something of a matter of dispute — having been born a slave.

The Fathers of the Church and the great scholastics — among them, Thomas Aquinas — regard slavery primarily as a punishment. Slavery is a consequence of sin.[56] But they accept as valid the reasons we have already presented in terms of the origin of slavery, and thus they regard it as legal. Thus, slavery is part and parcel of the social and economic order of the age, although, as we have said, it was no longer as extensively practiced as it had been in the ancient world, or as it will later be with the exploitation of the Indies. This is the juridical and theological position that thinkers of the sixteenth century inherited.

In the middle of the fifteenth century there slowly began a phenomenon that would become one of the most wicked and shameful deeds of the human race: the traffic in African slaves. The Portuguese made raids along the western coast of that continent, captured the inhabitants, and took them back to Europe as slaves. They justified their behavior on the grounds that these Africans had been converted to the Islamic faith, which made them, in the mentality of the time, traditional enemies of Christianity and even usurpers of Christian lands.[57] A war on these peoples, then, seemed only an extension of the one being waged against the Muslims. This war, then, is justified, and the enslavement of the vanquished was regarded as legitimate. Another reason was also adduced: slavery existed among Africans, and the Portuguese purchased slaves from black merchants involved in the business. The traffic grew and worsened throughout the fifteenth century. The result was a large number of black slaves in Europe, especially in Mediterranean countries, from the end of that century onward. In Seville, Las Casas's native city, slaves constituted an important segment of the population. Black slaves were part of Sevillians' everyday experience.[58]

In view of all of this, it should not surprise us that theologians and jurists accepted slavery as legal.[59] The situation of the Indians, best known in Spain, posed certain problems and produced controversy. Some defended the legitimacy of servitude for the inhabitants of the Indies. Indeed, various royal decrees authorized their reduction to slavery. Others opposed it and likewise influenced the decisions and counterdecisions of the Crown. The bone of contention was the question of whether the wars being waged against the natives were just or not. As we have seen, war was regarded as the most important and justifiable cause of slavery.[60]

Things looked very different, however, when it came to Africans.

On the legitimacy of the reduction of blacks to slavery there was a consensus among thinkers of the time. For example, Francisco de Vitoria was consulted on one occasion regarding the slave trade established by the Portuguese. With regard to persons who had been captured through deception, the Salamancan claims in a letter to a friend that if this has occurred, then it must have been something of an exception. If the king of Portugal, he thinks, has authorized this traffic, he must have reasonable motives for doing so, as it is not likely that he would "permit such inhumanity, nor that no one would point it out to him." As for those who had been "made slaves in war," he sees no need to be so scrupulous in the matter. The Portuguese, according to Vitoria, have no reason to inquire into the justice of "wars among the barbarians" — that is, among Africans. They are presumed to be just.[61] It is enough that a person be "a slave, *de facto* or *de jure*, and I will buy him without qualms," Vitoria says.[62]

Domingo de Soto and the other great scholars of the Salamancan school adopt the prevailing thesis, although Soto himself asks at one point whether the legitimating reasons for slavery can actually be found in the traffic being conducted by the Portuguese.[63] We have to await the end of the sixteenth century, however, to find real questions being raised.[64] We find them in the Dominicans Tomás Mercado (d. 1575) and Bartolomé de Albornoz and in the Jesuits Luis de Molina (d. 1600) and Fernando Rebelo (d. 1608). Mercado (who had some experience of the Indies, having lived in Mexico), Molina, and Rebelo denounce the injustice and mistreatment of which the blacks are victims,[65] but do not reject the slavery to which they are subjected. Molina, who had lived and taught in Portugal, even makes laudable efforts to gain a first-hand knowledge of what was happening in Africa with the Portuguese raids.[66]

It is Albornoz (who taught for a while at the University of Mexico) who goes furthest with his criticism. In his *Arte de los contratos*, published in 1573,[67] he questions the alleged justifications for slavery (war, conviction of a crime, purchase) that we have recalled (and criticizes Mercado for accepting them). Against those who were saying that enslaved blacks actually profited in the balance, since they received the Christian faith, he replies that according to the law of Jesus Christ the soul's freedom may not be purchased with the body's enslavement.[68]

Alonso de Sandoval (d. 1652) constitutes a case apart. He entered the Society of Jesus in Lima, Peru, where he lived several years. Having generously devoted himself to the service of the black slaves in Cartagena, he wrote an important work based on his ministry: *De instauranda aethiopum salute* (a title apparently inspired by Acosta's work *De Procuranda Indorum Salute*). His concern is for the evangelization of the African slaves and the sufferings they undergo. At a certain point the question of the justification of slavery arises, and Sandoval refers to Molina and other theologians. He does not speak out clearly against the injustice of the phenomenon; he is influenced by persons of great authority who regard it as legitimate.[69] His disciple Peter Claver (d. 1654), who devoted himself so admirably to the enslaved blacks, consumed his life alleviating their sufferings and making them Christians. But he did not ask the larger question about the justice of slavery. He accepted it as a fact of the times, or at least he did not go further than Sandoval on the subject.[70]

Only at the close of the seventeenth century do we encounter a radical rejection of slavery. It is contained in a text, practically unknown until recently, that comes to us from the Indies and is from the pen of a Capuchin named Francisco José Jaca de Aragón. Jaca worked in Cartagena, the great port of entry and an important market for slaves brought from Africa. There Jaca must have had contact with Jesuits who had known Sandoval and Claver. In 1681 in Havana he wrote a lengthy memorial bearing the title *Resolución sobre la libertad de los negros y sus originarios en el estado pagano y después ya cristianos* (Resolution on the freedom of the blacks and their forebears, in the state of paganism, and then as Christians). It is an extremely interesting document, which questions all the reasons given in favor of legal slavery. With great feeling Jaca protests against the subjugation of the blacks to slavery and also against the yoke placed on the Indians. This text can be regarded as the most extensive and spirited abolitionist call of the time.[71]

At the level of church magisterium in these centuries, generally speaking the documents only protest abuses, call for decent treatment, forbid the enslavement of Christian converts, and recall the exigencies of being brothers and sisters in Christ.[72] But beginning with Gregory XVI (d. 1848), the popes harshly censure the slave trade, which they regard as an "inhumane commerce," and at the same time denounce any participation in it by Christians.[73] Leo XIII (d. 1903) speaks in the same vein in a number of texts of his own.[74]

Meanwhile, great jurists and political thinkers of the seventeenth century,[75] although maintaining courageous theses regarding human rights and political liberties, not only do not question, but actually seek to justify black slavery as integral to social harmony and the logic of power. This is the case with Hugo Grotius (d. 1645), one of the founders of international law (with Vitoria, who preceded him), philosopher Thomas Hobbes (d. 1679), and one of the great inspirers of liberal thought, John Locke (d. 1704). None of these questioned the leading roles of their countries, Holland and England, in the African slave trade, which had reached enormous proportions by the time they wrote.[76]

Unfortunately, the situation will endure, by and large, until the nineteenth century. Now, finally, for various reasons — not always very altruistic ones, such as new economic conditions — slavery will be abolished. This is the context of Las Casas's intervention. Let us examine it.

Black Slavery in the Indies

Las Casas was a person of both action and reflection. He was in the thick of various events of his age, never refusing to take sides even in difficult and controversial matters. He was not of the tribe rebuked by Péguy when he said that they kept their hands clean because they had no hands. As a result, Bartolomé always left his mark, although he sometimes regretted the stands he had taken and forthrightly admitted it. This is what happened in the case of black slavery.

Black slaves came to the Indies very early. Some seem to have come with Columbus. A large group landed with Nicolás de Ovando in 1502, on the basis of instructions the latter had received from the Catholic sovereigns a short time before.[77] In the ensuing years, several hundred black slaves arrived in the Antilles.[78] As early as the first decade of the sixteenth century, a motive frequently invoked for their importation was the Africans' greater physical capacity for hard labor. The largest contingent arrived in 1510: two hundred African slaves.

Only in 1516 did Las Casas become involved. In his celebrated *Memorial de remedios*, in the "Eleventh Remedy," he asks the king "to maintain in the mines" of the communities that he, Bartolomé, is proposing "some twenty blacks or other slaves" (*O.E.* 5:9b). These would replace the Indians who, in addition to the other labors they had to perform, also toiled in the mines. What he means by "other slaves" is specified a few pages further on, when he asks the king to grant the colonists permission to "have *black and white* slaves that they may bring from Castile" (*O.E.* 5:17a).[79] Indeed, in the system of slavery accepted at the time, there were not only black slaves in Spain, but white ones as well. Acknowledging the legitimacy of the phenomenon, Las Casas asks that those in that condition replace the Indians, whose legal regime is that of freedom.

Petitions for black slaves to be sent to replace the natives were frequent in those years. One came from Cristóbal de Tapia, procurator and alderman of the city of Santo Domingo;[80] another from the comptroller of Hispaniola, Gil González Dávila;[81] another from the Hieronymites;[82] and there were more.[83] There were two views of the matter. One was that of the Franciscans of Hispaniola as we have it in a letter signed by Friar Pedro Mexía, requesting that *encomenderos* deprived of their Indians "be indemnified" at the rate of one slave for every five Indians.[84] Another appears in a letter we have frequently cited in our first chapter — signed by the Dominicans, among them Pedro de Córdoba — and here the friars ask that the Indians be taken away from the Spaniards and "as a temporary compensation to the Christians and to their farms...His Highness grant them license to import slaves."[85] As we see, Bartolomé was not alone in his request.

Nor was his intervention limited to this petition. A short while later he will once more call for slaves to be shipped, again in very limited number and from Castile (see *Memorial de remedios para las Indias,* and *Memorial de remedios,* both from 1518, *O.E.* 5:34b, 39b).[86] In these years King Charles grants important permits for the transport of black slaves to the Indies. Las Casas makes such a request once more in 1531 (*Carta al Consejo, O.E.* 5:54b, 55a) and again in 1543. On the latter occasion — the last time he will take up the matter in this way — he asks permission to take two dozen of them to Chiapa, where he had just been appointed bishop.[87]

Afterward, for reasons which we shall set forth, Las Casas's attitude toward black slavery changes radically. Our examination of the earlier period shows us that Bartolomé was far from being the founder of black slavery in the Indies. It would be pointless to repeat this, were it not for the fact that we often hear declarations to the contrary, despite the evident absence of foundation. When Las Casas touches the point, he does so from within a prevailing system (this does not remove its profound injustice) that was accepted socially and justified philosophically and theologically at the time. He petitions for the transport to the Indies of persons who were *already* slaves in Spain, and he asks for them in small numbers (except in his letter of 1531, in which he speaks of several hundred).[88] Never did he take part in, or give his opinion on, the slave trade on the grand scale that was beginning at the end of the period we have been examining.[89]

At no time, in the documents we have cited, does Bartolomé consider the legitimacy of slavery; nor does he argue in favor of it. The truth is that he simply does not pose the problem. He merely adopts the mentality of his age in its regard. After his last involvement in the matter (1543), things begin to change. There cannot be the least doubt of a reversal in his thinking. We have forthright, painful documents expressing his repentance for the blindness in which he had lived up to the middle of the sixteenth century.

Around 1547, Las Casas learned what was actually going on in Africa. On the way back from the Indies, the bishop of Chiapa stopped in Lisbon. This is probably where he received certain information about the manner in which the Africans were subjected to slavery.[90] Here he could have had the opportunity to become acquainted with certain works by Portuguese historians concerning their compatriots' expeditions on the African continent.[91] These chronicles made up for his lack of any direct experience of the events in question; and as we know, nothing stimulated Bartolomé's thinking more effectively than what came from experience. For a long time he had lacked such experience in the case of black slavery. His readings now removed his blindfold (which may already have become a bit loose in recent years). Now he plainly saw the deep injustice of black slavery and consigned to writing the transformation that took place in him.

The Same Right as the Indians

Las Casas now appends eleven chapters to the already completed first book of his *Historia de las Indias*.[92] In these he denounces in a language homogeneous with the rest of that work the enslavement, death, and other outrages of which both Canarians and black Africans are the victims. We have cited various passages from these chapters in earlier chapters of our own. The facts reflect a profound injustice, but the way the historian Gomes Eanes reports them reveals an insensitivity as great as that of the Portuguese prince who was their perpetrator. (See also chaps. 136, 150 of book 1 of *Historia de las Indias*.)

We should like to underscore two points from these pages. We have already referred to the first: the crucial matter of the passage from Ecclesiasticus that helped Bartolomé shake off his blindness to the oppression of the Indians.[93] Now those lines once more make their appearance, this time to draw the veil from the deeds of the Portuguese in Africa. In their raids, under the pretext of evangelization they are offering in sacrifice something "robbed and ill-gotten" (*H.I.*, bk. 1, ch. 24, *O.E.* 1:92b–93a). With this second allusion to the passage from Ecclesiasticus, we think that Las Casas has left us a sign of the second change that takes place in him. Just as, once before, he had seen and denounced the injustices being committed against the inhabitants of the Indies, now he sees and denounces those committed against the Canarians and Africans.

The second point to which we wish to call attention is Las Casas's special and careful concern to demonstrate that the wars being waged by the Portuguese are bereft of all justification. (The matter is treated in detail in *H.I.*, bk. 1, ch. 25, *O.E.* 1:95b–97a.) As these wars are not just (although defensive wars waged by Canarians or Africans against Europeans would be), the slavery to which these populations are being reduced is illegal and immoral. What he had once accepted as a fact now loses its foundation and is transformed for him into a horrifying injustice. Emerging from his ignorance, Bartolomé will now resolutely defend the rights of persons whose situation had not stricken his conscience until now.[94]

This is the function of the eleven extra chapters. But Las Casas goes further in the later passages of the same work and leaves clear proof of his new view of things. He does so in two steps.[95] In the first, he once again sketches the circumstances of his initial intervention in the matter. In the face of the Dominicans' refusal, with a view to liberating the Indians, to grant sacramental absolution to Spaniards who had Indians in their service, the Spaniards had besought the king's permission "to bring a dozen black slaves from Castile." Las Casas recounts that he had supported that petition, asking "in his memoranda that the Spaniards' request be granted to bring from Castile some dozen black slaves."[96] But in composing the present pages, Bartolomé regrets what he had written years before, "oblivious," he says, "of the injustice with which the Portuguese take them and make them slaves." He began to suspect this, and his worst fears were confirmed by Portuguese historians themselves, who presented the deeds in question as if they had been glorious exploits. The Dominican fails to be impressed by these paeans, reads between the lines, and perceives the injustice involved.

Accordingly, he adds, speaking of himself: " . . . But after he found out, he would not have proposed it for all the world, because blacks were enslaved unjustly, tyrannically, right from the start, *exactly as the Indians had been*" (H.I., bk. 3, ch. 102, O.E. 2:417a; emphasis added). He laments having given the "advice" that he gave. His sorrow is clear. And his change of outlook could not be more obvious. Not for anything in the world would he repeat what he had said thirty years before. What is happening is "unjust and tyrannical." Besides, the blacks have the same rights as the Indians. We must understand that statement literally. We know why Bartolomé thinks that right is on the side of the oppressed Indians; the same goes for the blacks. In his pages on Africa, he protests the plundering of the "inhabitants of those lands, who are innocent in their regard, be they Moors or Indians, or blacks or Arabs" (H.I., bk. 1, ch. 24, O.E. 1:91b). The same principles hold for all. Let us observe that he includes the Moors, despite the hostile attitude Christians had toward them in his time. (Another text in this vein will be found in H.I., bk. 1, ch. 17, O.E. 1:65b–66a.) On this point too there is an important evolution in Las Casas.[97]

Several chapters further on he returns to the subject with important specifications.[98] Once more he recalls (with more feeling, perhaps) the permission sought by his neighbors on Hispaniola to import black slaves. They had promised the cleric Las Casas that when they had received them they would free the Indians they had. This had brought Bartolomé into the affair in support of their petition that they might be permitted to "bring some black slaves from Castile" — that is, as we have remarked, from among those who were _already_ slaves in Spain. But, the reporter observes, the matter quickly became complicated and evolved into a commercial franchise with the monopoly given to the Genoans. Thus, the complexion of the affair changed: now it had become a business in the hands of merchants, which "was of no small hindrance to the good and the liberation of the Indians."

In other words, Las Casas did not even achieve the purpose for which he had committed his error. Frankly and sadly he expresses his contrition: "The cleric soon regretted the advice he gave on this matter, judging himself culpable through inadvertence." He had been living in ignorance of the facts, accepting the mentality of the age. But gradually he had sought to emerge from this blindness — "in view of what he later saw and ascertained, as will become clear." The data had not come to him of their own accord. He had had to "ascertain" them. He sought them out, perhaps moved by a suspicion gradually forming in his mind. He even promises to develop the point later in the same work ("as will become clear") — a promise he was unable to keep because he could not complete his plan until 1552.[99]

What he "saw and ascertained" was that "the captivity of the blacks [was] as unjust as that of the Indians." The injustices are identical, and both must be done away with. That being committed against the Indians is older for him and had been the first to challenge him; the other had grown (and would grow larger after Las Casas's death), and it had taken him longer to see it. Thus, he is convinced that "the remedy that he had counseled, that blacks be brought so that the Indians might be freed, was wrong." Bartolomé is retracting an error he committed. The reasoning that had led him to this mistake had seemed correct to him: "He supposed that they were rightly captives." These are the reasons adduced in his time to legitimize slavery, and which he thought applied in the case of the Africans. Sorrowfully he confesses that this will not excuse him before the judgment seat of God: "He was not sure that the ignorance and good will he had had in this matter would excuse him before the divine justice."

As we have seen, he always thought that that divine judgment should be a matter of experience even now, right here at the heart of history. He had not seen it in the matter of black slavery, because he had been unable to discern the demands of the gospel. This is the level on which his change occurs before God. A historical and social analysis is altogether necessary. But when all is said and done, he finds himself before the judgment seat of the God who identifies with the hungry, with the unjustly imprisoned, with murder victims. The black is in the same situation as the Indian, but Bartolomé could not see it in the first decades of his defense of the latter. Jesus Christ is present both in the Indian and in the black. Both find themselves in the condition of being "scourged Christs" of the Indies.

The Dominican promptly condemns the traffic in slaves. He declares that the Portuguese "have for many years been in charge of plundering Guinea and making slaves of the blacks, most unjustly." The Spaniards as well have a grave responsibility in the slave trade. After all, he says, once the Portuguese saw that "we demonstrated such need of them and that we indeed purchased them, they hastened to abduct them and make them prisoners, as they continue to do by as many evil and wicked ways as they are able." Spanish interests motivate the slavers. To boot, greed is infectious, with the result that the Africans themselves began to wage "unjust wars" and take other "illicit ways" to make slaves and sell them to the Portuguese. And Bartolomé adds perceptively: " . . . in such a way that we ourselves are the cause of all of the sins committed by both, even apart from the sins we commit in buying them" (*H.I.*, bk. 3, ch. 129, *O.E.* 2:487a–b, 488a).

This last remark is typical of Las Casas, who always seeks to dig beneath the surface. Only a knowledge of the causes of things makes it possible to transform a situation. One must know what is happening in Africa and take account of the various factors in the slave business. This is how Bartolomé proceeded in the case of the inhabitants of the Indies, and now — striking his forehead in repentance for not having perceived it earlier — he does the same with the situation of the Africans.

What Las Casas perceives around the middle of the sixteenth century is that the injustice committed against the Africans is of the same nature as that suffered by the Indians. There is no justification for enslaving these peoples. In both cases, greed, the lust for money, is the cause of an inhumane state of affairs. Bartolomé therefore denounces not only slavery, but the scandalous slave business as well, which in these years began to attain enormous proportions.

Furthermore, if we bear in mind what we said several pages above, we realize that Las Casas is the first of his time to do so.[100] Albornoz's intervention comes only in 1573 (with Molina's, which is much less clear-cut, appearing only shortly before that). The forthright and valiant defense mounted by Capuchins Jaca and Borgoña, so much more comprehensive than those that have come earlier, date from over a hundred years later. In view of the accusations, based on incomplete information, leveled against Las Casas with regard to the beginnings of black slavery in the New World, it is surely paradoxical to find him the first to denounce that injustice.[101] But the chronology is clear.[102]

Las Casas's definitive position leaves no room for doubt.[103] His remorse for his unfortunate "advice" of 1516 (and his "blindness" in the following years) is painful and plain. Besides, it is based on an analysis of historical events that he had gradually come to know better. This attitude, like that of other, later theologians whom we have mentioned, is exceptional in the era in question. Nor did these few manage to change the mentality of the time. In the end the Christian conscience demonstrated little sensitivity, and a slow reaction, to the slavers' wicked business. This has been acknowledged, in truth and humility, by John Paul II on a recent visit to the island of Gorea, the scene of such horror and suffering for so many Africans captured to be sold as slaves.

The pope asks forgiveness for Christians' participation in these events:

> From this African sanctuary of black pain, _we ask forgiveness_ of heaven. We pray that, henceforward, Christ's disciples may be seen to be entirely faithful to the observance of the commandment of brotherly and sisterly love left them by their Teacher. We pray that they may never again be the oppressors of their own brothers and sisters, but may seek instead to imitate the compassion of the Good Samaritan of the gospel in their welcome of the needy. We pray that the scourge of slavery and its consequences may disappear forever.[104]

This penitential attitude ought to be a guideline for behavior in analogous historical situations, such as in Latin America today.

Chapter 12

A Fact Looking for Justification

After some hesitation, Master Francisco de Vitoria, *Catedrático de Prima* of the University of Salamanca — holder of the most important theological chair — decides to plunge into the controversy of the Indies.

In his commentaries on the *Summa Theologiae* of Thomas Aquinas, as well as in his *relecciónes,* or "rereadings" on various problems, Vitoria had made occasional allusions to questions arising in connection with the Indies. He appreciates the difficulty of addressing such questions. It will mean collision with the vested interests of the Spanish Crown, the conquistadors, and the *encomenderos.* Given his position and authority, however, and the climate of the times, he cannot simply ignore the topic. It is his own religious order, the Dominicans, that is most committed (not in all of its members, of course) to the defense of the Indians. Many of his disciples in Salamanca have sailed to the Indies to spend their lives as missionaries there.[1] A former master general of his order is the current president of the Royal Council of the Indies (García de Loaysa). News often comes from the Indies to Valladolid and Salamanca. Things are getting uncomfortable for Vitoria, who feels compelled to make a pronouncement.

The contribution of the individual regarded as the greatest Spanish theologian of the age is taken by many scholars even today as the definitive elucidation of this thorny question, at least in its theoretical aspect. Numerous books and articles have been devoted to his positions on matters of the Indies and furnish us with an abundant systematic, analytical (and also at times dithyrambic) presentation of his important work.[2]

In the following pages we shall engage in a critical reflection on Vitoria's thought in this area, underscoring the points that bear on what we have seen up until now. The Salamancan sets forth his ideas with great clarity, for the most part, in easily available texts on which we have some very valuable commentaries. It would not be of direct interest to us to examine Vitoria's entire contribution to international law, which is doubtless the most significant and enduring part of his work.

This focus will lead us to a comparison of Vitoria's theses with those of Bartolomé de Las Casas, whom many scholars regard — erroneously — as the missionary who put the Master's theology into practice.[3] As we shall see in our examination of the *Yucay Opinion,* the contrast between the positions of the two thinkers is striking, and although the *Opinion* brings this out on the basis of a historical fable (the alleged intention of Charles V to withdraw from the Indies), it makes an important point.

M. Bataillon is correct in maintaining, for reasons different from our own, the need for a "review of the Las Casas–Vitoria problem from the ground up." We call his reasons different from ours because the illustrious French Hispanicist actually opposes a separation of the two. The teachings of Vitoria and of Las Casas are "like twin sisters," he assures us, and "we should need irrefutable proofs, in the face of the massive evidence of the texts, if we are to believe in a serious discrepancy between the two great Spanish Dominicans on the rights and duties of the King of Spain in the Indies."[4] We cannot agree. The observation is intended to be complimentary to Las Casas, who would thus appear to have been illuminated by the light of the Master.[5] It is not difficult, however, to find the proofs Bataillon requires. Recent studies have provided it. There are areas of agreement between the two, surely; but there are differences as well. Indeed the matter ought to be investigated "from the ground up."

1. *Rights of a Progressive Humanity*

We shall keep in mind especially Vitoria's celebrated *relección* known as the *De Indis* (1538–39), along with certain other related texts dealing with the claims — illegitimate and legitimate — of the Spanish Crown in the Indies. We have already seen some of these attempted justifications; now it is time to draw up a balance sheet. In the *De Indis,* a disquisition conducted with brilliance and panache, Vitoria comes forward as the standard-bearer of progressive humanity at a moment of great historical changes.[6]

Legitimate Masters

In the *De Indis* Vitoria poses the problem with great theological style. He cites the evangelical mandate contained in the closing verses of St. Matthew ("Make disciples of all the nations. Baptize them in the name of the Father, and of the Son, and of the Holy Spirit"; Matt.

28:19) and asks how that commission ought to be read in terms of a question that has arisen in actual missionary practice: whether it is permissible to baptize the children of unbelievers against the will of their parents. The problem is a classic one and was dealt with by Thomas Aquinas. But certain facts endow it with a new urgency. "The entire controversy and reconsideration," he says with precision, "have arisen because of those barbarians of the New World, commonly called Indians, who, previously unknown in our world, have some forty years ago come under the power of the Spaniards" (*Obras*, 642; CHP, 2).[7] The question of claims or "titles" to the legal and ethical legitimacy of this power already in hand — we are dealing with a *fait accompli* — is what Vitoria will address in his study. Let us make clear that the word "barbarian" is used in its general sense, without any pejorative tone, at least not directly. But the context of the Indies is explicit.

The steps in the study Vitoria proposes to undertake are motivated, consequently, by the relationship that has been established between the Europeans and the inhabitants of the Indies:

> In their regard, the present dissertation will contain three parts. In the *first*, we shall investigate by what right the barbarians have come under the jurisdiction of the Spaniards; in the *second*, what power the rulers of Spain have over them in the temporal and civil area; in the *third*, what power the rulers ["the bishops," in the CHP version] or the Church have over them in spiritual areas and matters of religion. (Ibid.)[8]

The theological approach is impeccable. Pastoral practice interrogates Scripture, in quest of an "understanding of the faith" situated in a particular historical context. But this context is not a simple stage or empty frame into which one might put just any picture. Any given historical situation sharpens, rearranges, and launches theological questions, but it also opens new paths for responding to them. Thus, we see Vitoria start with a subject that some today would like to call "purely religious" — the baptism of children of unbelievers — only to end up with a new, "political" issue: the reasons for the European sovereignty over the Indies. That this issue is a theological one, Vitoria has no doubt; indeed, he will say that it is more a theological one than a juridical one.[9]

He grants, however, that this has not been the customary approach to the matter. He surprises us by adding: "I am not certain that worthy theologians have been summoned to undertake an examination and determination of this matter who might enjoy sufficient authority to be heard on something of such great account" (*Obras*, 649; CHP, 11). This is surprising because we know of theological meetings that were held in the years before this, and that illustrious Dominicans participated in them.[10] In fact at the end of his critique of the legitimate titles he says: "Let me remark that I have seen nothing written on this question or attended any disputation or consultation concerning this material" (*Obras*, 703; CHP, 75).[11]

It is not easy to understand Vitoria's concern to present his contribution as something new, something independent of previous opinions. To tell the truth, it is little short of impossible that he should have had no contact, theoretical at least, with a matter that had been so hotly contested in the Dominican order in Spain for some quarter of a century now. It may be that the delicacy and controversial nature of the topic is the reason for his reluctance to see himself involved in such discussions. Indeed, in the Introduction of his *De Indis*, Vitoria explains at great length and very cautiously why he intends to treat of a problem that seemingly had already been solved. He acknowledges that the question has been studied (and thus appears to know what has been said up to that moment). Still, things are not clear; some doubts persist. It will be worthwhile, then, to examine the point.[12] But it will be better in that case to avoid reference to polemics that, while not yet as heated as they will become some years later, were already impassioned. What we have, then, it would seem, is a manifestation of the Master's well-known prudence.

Before examining the famous subject of the "titles,"[13] the Salamancan professor firmly lays down a clear and bold principle: "Before the coming of the Spaniards, it was [the Indians] who were the authentic masters [of the Indies], publicly and privately" (*Obras*, 666; CHP, 31). The proof of this proposition is offered in a precise and detailed manner. Furthermore, he responds to various objections to his thesis. He endorses native sovereignty over the Indies with all desired clarity. Let us emphasize that Vitoria posits this sovereignty before undertaking any analysis of potential titles to sovereignty on the part of other "lords."[14] On this solid foundation — already found in his earlier *relecciónes*[15] — arguments ("titles") will now be entertained both for and against Spanish sovereignty.[16] At times the reasoning is masterful. At other times it seems hasty and superficial. At some moments, we shall see it switch sides: the logic will become somewhat confused and uneven, and we shall be perplexed as to what Vitoria's position really is. One result will be a broad spectrum — too broad — of interpretations of the Master's thinking.

It is well known that Vitoria makes a critical examination of seven titles that "are neither appropriate nor legitimate" in favor of an Iberian presence in the Indies. He warns us in advance, however, that side by side with them he will place "other, legitimate titles by which the Spaniards may subjugate the barbarians...seven or eight legitimate, just titles" (*Obras*, 667; CHP, 33). Before coming to the heart of the problem, then, we know two things very well: that the Indians are authentic sovereigns, but that Spanish sovereignty as well is — or can be — just.[17] Let us see why. First, however, we must briefly recall why it might not be just.

The Titles: Obverse and Reverse

The *illegitimate* titles are: that the emperor is sovereign of the whole world; that the pope as well is temporal sovereign of the world; that the right to sovereignty came with the discovery; that the Indians refused to receive faith in Christ; that the barbarians sin against nature; that the Indians have made a free choice; and that God has made a special concession to the Spaniards. One by one, these attempted justifications, alleged by other thinkers, are examined and discarded. Masterfully, Vitoria performs his task of intellectual hygiene. His conclusion is crisp and clear: none of the titles listed is capable of legitimating the European presence in the Indies.

First he responds to the argument based on the notion that the emperor is *de jure* the sovereign of the whole earth. This position, says Vitoria, first of all cannot be based on natural law, in which no one has sovereignty over the world. But neither is it written that by divine law anyone at all has ever been sovereign over the world, either before or after Christ, who left no vicar for temporal affairs. Last, no such sovereignty can be deduced from positive law: no law grants such authority. The conclusion is transparent: "Never has the emperor been lord of all the earth" (*Obras*, 669–75; CHP, 33–42). Thus, Vitoria demolishes the idea of a West united under the aegis of a universal sovereignty.

Great emphasis has been placed, and rightly, on the importance of Vitoria's rejection of the second title, the authority of the pope — so "vehemently" invoked, as Vitoria puts it, by the partisans of a Spanish presence in the Indies. Indeed, as we have seen, this was the most important of all the arguments brought forward in theological discussions held in connection with the Burgos Conference. Vitoria had already undertaken a painstaking labor of clarification of this point in his *relección, De Potestate Ecclesiae Prior,* with a view to clearing the ground for the establishment of the legitimacy of papal authority. That authority is exercised not in the temporal domain, but in the spiritual, he first asserts. But then the illustrious theologian wavers and ultimately ascribes a certain temporal power to the pope.[18] He even goes so far as to maintain that, "with a view to [*in ordine ad*] a spiritual end, the pope has the broadest temporal authority over all princes, kings, and emperors" (*Obras*, 305).[19]

The condition is plain: only with a view to what pertains to him directly and in circumstances that so require is it licit for the pope to interfere in the area of the temporal. The observation is not a casual one, nor could it be. It is a thesis in its own right and is based on the propositions that accompany it. A discussion of the matter fills several pages. In support of his thesis, Vitoria cites texts and authors (like St. Bernard with his theory of the two swords) who maintained the theocratic view. The Salamancan's position is clear.

In the *De Indis,* he presents this same thinking once more. On the basis of principles established by Thomas Aquinas, Vitoria demolishes the arguments advanced in favor of a pontifical theocratism. His approach is akin to the one he has just used against an imagined universal sovereignty of the emperor. Thus, he takes his distance from the Ostian and appeals to Torquemada. He observes, moreover, that the majority of theologians are aligned with him in this discussion.[20] He is not unaware that, on the other hand, most canonists maintain the theocratic doctrine. This is understandable, Vitoria maintains; but he does not think that "much ought to be made of the authority of our adversaries among the canonists, since (as we have said above) these matters ought to be dealt with in terms of divine law" (*Obras,* 684; CHP, 53). Canon law is ancillary to theology.

To be sure, we are witnessing one of the peak moments in all Vitorian thought.[21] But we must not exaggerate. True, the Salamancan rejects a pontifical theocracy. However, he ascribes to the pope a power that, within a short time, few will defend. In fact, theologians like John of Paris had already frankly distanced themselves from such theses.[22] In the *De Indis,* Vitoria's language is more restrained than in the *De Potestate Ecclesiae Prior,* but the fundamental thesis abides. Vitoria declares, for example: "The Pope has temporal power with a view to spiritual ends — that is, insofar as it is necessary for the administration of spiritual things" (*Obras,* 680; CHP, 49). This has been dubbed the "indirect power of the pope in temporal matters" (by contrast with the "direct" power attributed to him in the theocratic position). The expression comes from Bellarmine and Suárez, but the notion itself is already present in Vitoria and his sources.[23]

And so the titles just mentioned, like others that we had already studied,[24] are seen as inadequate to justify Spanish sovereignty or war against the Indians. But we have already been apprised that adequate titles do exist. They are: society and natural communication, the propagation of the Christian religion, the defense of Indians converted to Christianity, the power of the pope to bestow a Christian prince on a nation having a considerable number of converts, the defense of the innocent, a genuine and willing acceptance of the sovereignty of the king of Spain, friendship and alliance, and — perhaps — the ineptitude of the Indians to govern themselves.

The most relevant of these titles, and in some sense the one that supports all the others, is that of *sociability*. It is also the one most highly regarded by academic theology and the one that founds Vitoria's deserved reputation as an innovator in the area of the Law of Nations, specifically, as the founder of public international law. Vitoria calls this title that "of society and natural communication." It is based on the notion — for which it has received great praise — of an international order, which Victoria designates as that "of the whole world," *totius orbis,* that is the product of what human beings have in common as such. With elegance and finesse, he distinguishes from the notion of Christendom, which united peoples on the basis of the Christian faith, what he regards as another authentic polity. Thus, he seeks to base the concrete reality of the human community not only on religious principles, but on principles of the Law of Nations. This title establishes that "the Spaniards have the right to traverse those [Indian] provinces and to remain there, without the barbarians having the right to prohibit them from doing so, provided the latter suffer no detriment thereby" (*Obras,* 705; CHP, 77–78).

It is a question of the foundation, in the Law of Nations and ultimately of natural law,[25] of relations among the nations of the world. One of these relations is that of commerce. The freedom to conduct it had become an acute requirement of the mercantile capitalism that had made its appearance in the more progressive European milieus.[26] Barbarians might not impede this communication, Vitoria granted, and if they attempted to do so, Spaniards, after reasoning with them, might answer with force in the case that the unbelievers should have recourse to violence. "Furthermore," Vitoria writes, "if otherwise they are unsafe, [Spaniards may] build fortifications and defenses; and if they suffer injury, they may with the authority of their prince avenge it with war and carry forward the other rights of war." And if in order to win security they need to occupy Indian cities and subjugate their inhabitants, "they may licitly do so." But, of course, if the barbarians permit Spaniards "to conduct business with them peacefully," he concludes, no just cause will be present for the seizure of their goods (*Obras,* 713–15; CHP, 83–85).

Among the legitimate titles that follow, with the principle of "sociability" as his guideline, Vitoria takes up again, from another perspective, some of the reasons that he has previously rejected, mitigating in part his condemnation of them. Thus, apropos of the *second* reason (which we have already examined; see our chapter 5, above), he asserts the obligation of the church to proclaim the gospel. In fact, the pope may entrust the preaching of the gospel in the Indies to Spaniards "and forbid it to others."[27] Thus, if the barbarians attempt to prevent the proclamation of the gospel, "the Spaniards may legitimately occupy their lands" (*Obras*, 717; CHP, 89–90).

The *third* title derives from the second. Spaniards may even wage war and depose the Indians' sovereigns, if these should seek by force to return their Christian subjects to the practice of idolatry.

The *fourth* is a specification of the third and returns to the matter of pontifical power: if in the presence of an infidel lord, it is feared that his subjects who might have embraced the Christian faith might apostatize, the pope enjoys the faculty of deposing him and replacing him with a Christian prince. (It is significant that Vitoria cites Innocent IV in his behalf here.) Surprisingly, he adds that this holds even though the conversions to faith in Christ may have been made "whether willingly or by violence, that is, by threats, terror, or in another unjust way, provided they actually" — he asserts perplexingly — result in the Indians' becoming "true Christians" (*Obras*, 719; CHP, 92). What astonishes us are the means cited, which do not seem the best indicated for winning "true Christians."[28]

Next, he appeals to a classic motivation of his time (his *fifth* "just title"): the tyranny of the barbarians and the defense of the innocent, especially of intended victims of human sacrifice (a case that we have already had occasion to present and discuss in our chapter 6).

By way of concluding this extended passage, Vitoria offers us a *sixth* title. Spanish sovereignty is justified "if the barbarians, understanding the Spaniards' sense of humanity and their wise administration, should freely wish, both the lords and the rest, to receive as their prince the king of Spain" (*Obras*, 721; CHP, 94). Here is an interesting note on the consent of the governed as a condition of the legitimacy of the governors. The focus here is rich, fertile, humane, and democratic. It will be worthwhile to observe that according to Vitoria this title justifies only the Spaniards' presence in the Indies and not the wars they wage there (which other motives justify), because, precisely, it is based on a free, uncoerced choice on the part of the Indians. It is not to be wondered at then that this is the only title that Las Casas has been able to accept from Vitoria. (And as we shall see, Bartolomé places more severe restrictions on it than does his confrere, while declaring on the basis of his experience that it has been verified but once in the Indies — in the lands of Verapaz, which have been evangelized peacefully by Dominican friars.)

In the latter five titles, the Dominican master has returned in one way or another, as we have noted, to several of the motives he had previously rejected as inadequate. Now he merely imposes requirements of moderation and humane treatment in terms of his first great title, "sociability,"[29] and declares these five motivations to be adequate to justify war upon and domination of the Indian nations. Faced with these lucubrations, we cannot escape the thought that it would perhaps have been more correct to declare these titles from the outset "conditionally adequate."[30] Then we should have been spared the confusion, the subtle distinctions, and the impression of waffling that we gather in a doctrine that, when all is said and done, lends itself to varying, indeed contradictory, interpretations.

The *seventh* title is a case apart. It emerges from considerations of "alliance and friendship" and is based on the supposition that "the barbarians themselves sometimes war among themselves legitimately." Accordingly, inasmuch as "the injured party has a right to declare war, [that party] may call on the Spaniards for help and share with them the fruits of victory." War is justified because friendship and alliance (supported once more by "sociability") supply the faculty of intervening in the Indians' intestine struggles (of course, our theologian hastens to add, the war must be just)[31] and even of sharing the "fruits of victory" (*Obras*, 722; CHP, 95–96).

2. The Weight of the Facts

Let us return to the conditional nature of the titles advanced by Vitoria. But let us observe from the outset that, although these titles are presented in hypothetical form, we are not dealing with a simple, neutral weighing of the pros and cons therein. The needle of the scale swings in one direction only, due to an adsciticious, concretizing factor: the weight of the reality — or of an interpretation of that reality, at least — forged in the decades of the Iberian presence in the Indies.

Severely Retarded?

Vitoria brings forward one last title of legitimation, his *eighth*. He does so with hesitancy: "I dare neither approve it nor condemn it out of hand." But the mere fact of his mentioning it is significant. He enunciates it as follows: "Although, as has been said above, these barbarians are not entirely lacking in judgment [*amentes*], nevertheless they are not very different from the severely mentally retarded [*amentibus*]. Wherefore it would appear that they are unfit to establish or administer a polity that would be legitimate in human and civil terms." The barbarians "are little, if at all, more capable of governing themselves than simple idiots. Nor indeed are they easily distinguishable from the beasts of forest and field, inasmuch as they consume their food practically unprepared and thus do not seem superior to brute animals." Given, then, "the feeble-mindedness and rudeness attributed to them by those who have visited there, of which they say that it is far greater than in the children and incompetents [*amentibus*] of other nations,"[32] the Indians ought to be governed by outsiders. Vitoria concludes: "For these barbarians' utility, the Spanish Sovereigns may take their administration in charge, appoint prefects and governors for their cities, and even bestow on them new [native] princes should it be seen that this would be to their advantage." Thus would Spanish sovereignty be founded as well on the human inferiority of the inhabitants of the Indies.

This attitude, says the theologian of Salamanca, is based on an exigency of the gospel, "on the precept of charity, since these are our neighbors, and we are under obligation to secure their good."[33] And not only that, but they are our neighbors in need. Vitoria remarks that the specified intervention must be not "solely for the profit of the Spaniards," of course, but especially for that of the Indians.

Ending his consideration of the eighth title, the Salamancan master observes that Spanish sovereignty in the Indies "may also be justified on grounds of something to which we have already referred, namely, the fact that some persons are natural slaves. And this is what these barbarians seem to be. Therefore they might in some measure be governed as slaves" (*Obras*, 723–25; CHP, 97–98).

He is referring to his lengthy Introduction. There he had written that the Indians "are not precisely feeble-minded [*amentes*]: After all, in their own fashion, they exercise the use of reason." The proof that they do is that they have their cities, a certain orderliness in their affairs, and even "a kind of religion." Vitoria then specifies: "I think that the fact that they seem to us so senseless and retarded is mostly due to their evil, barbarous upbringing." They are not born that way then. And he reminds his fellow Spaniards: "Neither are there missing from among ourselves certain country folk who differ but little from animals."

Thus he seems to reject the position, which others in his time held, that the barbarians are out-and-out natural slaves. In fact, he doubts that this is what Aristotle meant in the first place. Rather, he believes, the Philosopher was referring to "civil, legitimate servitude, which makes no one a slave by nature," so that that one might be legitimately enslaved and reduced to the status of chattel. What Aristotle really means, thinks Vitoria, is that in those whom "nature has made defective and lacking in mental capacity," there is a "natural need to be ruled and governed by others" who are "their natural lords, that is, who abound in intellectual capacity" and have received "faculties from nature for commanding and governing." The Salamancan reasserts that although the Indians ("these barbarians") were to be "as inept and dull as it is said" of them, they cannot on that account be denied "to hold authentic dominion, nor be accounted among the number of those [legitimately consigned to] civil servitude." He concludes, disconcertingly taking back what he has given: "The truth, however, is that from this reason and title a certain right to subject them can arise, and we shall see this later" (*Obras*, 664–66; CHP, 29–31). In his Introduction he is referring precisely to this eighth title.[34]

Vitoria's tone is vacillating. The Master walks cautiously, but his assertions of the human inferiority of the Indians are there (along with those of European superiority).[35] Vitoria has heard it and believed it. He probably also knew a different judgment of the Indians, but it will have left a less deep impression on him. It is not a matter of an eleventh hour hesitation. He has expressed himself to similar effect earlier, before composing the *De Indis*. In his *Lecciones sobre la Suma Teológica* (dictated between 1521 and 1536), he denies that unbelievers may licitly be obliged to accept the faith and says that this holds for the Indians: "These islanders, while rather bestial and incapable of learning, are under obligation to accept only what they can grasp by natural reason."[36] And since the faith is beyond the reach of reason alone, unbelievers may not be compelled to accept it. The text defends the classic point of the freedom of faith, but it reveals in passing an exceedingly poor opinion of the human condition of the Indians, even while acknowledging in them a certain presence of natural reason.

Granted, we find in Vitoria no depreciatory terms, nor Sepúlveda's sweeping, smug argumentation based on the Indians' alleged human inferiority.[37] Rather, the Salamancan master is forthright when it comes to every human being's natural freedom and a certain right vested with the Indians, even if their human inferiority be admitted, to have both the possessions they need and legitimate political authorities of their own. Important as well are his allusions to the role that should be performed by education. Nevertheless, he seems to have given exaggerated attention to the statements of those who held a pejorative concept of the dwellers of the Indies.[38] Hence his proposal of his eighth title and the arguments on which it is based.[39]

Let us observe that this eighth "reason" does not have its illegitimate counterpart, as do some of the titles Vitoria endorses. Truth to tell, it is strange that in his first series of titles Vitoria does not discard the inferiority of the Indians as a motive, since from the outset (with Major and the Burgos Conference) this had been one of the most frequently invoked and seemingly most evident considerations. No, the Dominican master reserves a place for it — a doubtful place, it is true — among his "legitimate titles."[40]

The Intolerability of Abandoning the Indies

The title "society and natural communication" is doubtless the corner-stone of the whole edifice. This concept provides all of the inspiration for the seventh title, as well as modifying and legitimating, under certain conditions, the considerations previously presented as in-adequate. The final conclusion is clear: Spanish sovereignty in the Indies is legitimate, and the wars being waged against the Indians are justified. Confirmation of this is at hand in the presupposition of the second *relección* "On the Indies" (also called "On the Right of War"), pronounced in June 1539.[41] It begins in these terms:

> Inasmuch as a defense of the possession and occupation of the provinces of these barbarians, commonly called Indians, ulti-mately appears legitimate, especially by right of war: therefore, after having discussed in the first relection the titles the Span-iards may adduce with regard to these provinces, we have deemed it fitting to append a brief consideration upon this right of war in order to complete the former account. (*Obras,* 814; CHP, 97)

The exordium of the second *relección* thus stands as a summary of the previous *De Indis.* The occupation of the Indies is defensible on the basis of the right of war. The titles enunciated above prove this. It will be in order then to study the justifications and conditions of a just war. And that is what Vitoria does, without any further men-tion of the matter of the Indies, but focusing the theme in terms of a more general perspective. A like conclusion had been reached in the first *De Indis:* Closing his treatment of the second legitimate motive, Vitoria emphatically declares — departing for the moment from the conditional language he generally employs: "I have no doubt that it has been necessary to have recourse to force of arms for the Span-iards to be able to remain there." And he adds, expressing a frequent concern of his: "But I fear the affair may have gone beyond what law and decency have permitted" (*Obras,* 718; CHP, 90–91). Indeed it had. Thus, Vitoria postulates the ethical principles of a just war.

In other words, summarizing everything that he has previously stated on this point, but operating now from a very new viewpoint, that of the social and economic order of modernity, the Salamancan master now accepts what he had rejected in a theocratic and imperial perspective (the universal power of the pope and the emperor).[42] A juridical framework was needed that would be adequate to the chal-lenge posed by questions arising in the moment of expansion now transpiring in the life of the countries of Europe. Vitoria supplied that framework.[43] With lucidity and daring, he steps onto the difficult ground of war, laying the foundations for an ethical behavior in that limit case. This is one of his great contributions.[44] But the nuances and distinctions he introduces, subtle theologian that he is, and the calls he issues for moderation in the use of force, moral, Christian human being that he is, will unfortunately not count for much in practice. A great number of those who claim him as their inspiration will retain only what they regard as "substantial" — that is, as legitimizing their interests: the rights of the West vis-à-vis the "barbarians" and the permissibility of war for the vindication of those rights.

What is the reason for Vitoria's seemingly so callous, inhumane position? Have we an "ivory-tower theologian" here, someone totally, or almost totally, out of contact with reality? The Salamancan's scholastic ratiocination might suggest this. But we think otherwise. And we do so not only because no thought is ever produced apart from a relationship to its historical context (especially in a matter like the one Vitoria has elected to address), but because Vitoria explicitly adopts the situation in the Indies as the background of his whole discussion. This is plain both from the exordium of his reconsideration of the Indian problem and from the passage he later withdrew from his *De Temperantia*. His intention was to intervene in the debate. Consequently, he was not unaware that his reflections would have practical repercussions. His abstract approach is only a mannerism, a kind of pedagogical ploy.

Furthermore, our *Catedrático de Prima* holds an a priori position, which his analysis of the "titles" only reinforces. That position is transparent by the time we come to the end of his exposition of the legitimate titles. Surely to the surprise of those who failed to perceive that all thought, even theological thought, carries a specific social weight, Vitoria declares:

> From what has been said in the course of this discussion, it appears to follow that, were all of these titles to cease [from their validity] — the barbarians would give no occasion for war, would not wish to have Spanish rulers, and so on — expeditions and commerce as well would thereby cease, *to the great prejudice of the Spaniards* and great detriment to the *interests of the rulers,* which would be *intolerable.* (*Obras,* 725; CHP, 98)

"...which would be intolerable" ("non esset ferendum"), he concludes. All the quibbling, then, has taken place within well-defined, inescapable parameters. The importance of legitimate titles or theological reflection is dwarfed by the massive, irreversible reality of the Iberian presence — decades old now — in the Indies. If truth be told, what we have here is a *factum quaerens jus,* an accomplished fact looking for some legitimating right. Should justifications fail, the basic reality would still remain: the need for commerce and all that ensues therefrom.

Three supplementary considerations buttress his position here, Vitoria says. First, the cessation of transatlantic commerce would entail the loss of benefits to both sides (Spaniards and Indians). Second, the assault on the interests of the king in that commerce would scarcely be inconsiderable, as "the prince is responsible for the discovery of these sea routes, and the merchants are defended by his authority," so that as a consequence the king may impose tribute "upon the gold and silver imported from the barbarians." The third consideration returns us to the religious area, but this time in terms of a lapse of more than forty years since the barbarians have fallen into Spanish hands. "With so many barbarian converts there," argues the theologian, "it would be neither appropriate nor licit for the prince utterly to abandon the administration of the provinces in question" (*Obras*, 725–26; CHP, 99). By reason of the *commerce* now established and the *faith* now received, the Indies are not to be abandoned, not even in the hypothetical case that the original legitimate titles had lost their validity. And so the second *relección* "On the Indies" comes to a close.[45]

Let us acknowledge the complexity of the problem. A theology that seeks to be responsive to historical realities, especially, as is the case here, when these realities are not known by direct experience, will inevitably execute zigzags. Even so, we cannot help a feeling of malaise at the way the celebrated relection on the Indians concludes.[46] The "reasons" the work advances are regarded as important, but the deeds being done are regarded as even more important. Those who armed themselves with Vitoria's ideas in order to defend their interests in the Indies could therefore make use of certain ambiguities, vacillations, and perplexities in the Master's writings.

We shall not rest, however, with our malaise. As far as possible, we shall want to sharpen our analysis and inquire into the reasons for this disconcerting phenomenon in the great Salamancan. That will also help us specify with greater exactitude the relationship, to which we have alluded a number of times on earlier occasions, between Las Casas's work and Vitoria's.

From Temperance to Prudence

We have recalled Vitoria's position on the basis of his most important and most influential text on our subject. But for some years now we have known that his first sustained intervention took place within his relection *De Temperantia*, which he pronounced toward the end of 1537[47] and hence which antedates the second *De Indis*.[48] Originally part of the *De Temperantia* but subsequently withdrawn by the author himself was the famous fragment whose pages substantially, if only germinally, maintain the same theses as the later relection. We have already had occasion to see, for example, that there are no appreciable differences between these two writings of Vitoria when it comes to human sacrifice. True, in the fragment Vitoria employs a rather more free and straightforward language.

Some authors, however, insist on differentiating the two compositions, and even contrasting them. Let us consider, for example, the view of someone to whom Lascasian studies owe a great deal, Manuel Martínez. For Martínez, the *De Indis* is "vulnerable generally, and in several basic aspects frankly flawed," while the fragment is not.[49] Martínez is surely correct in many of his critical observations on the *De Indis.* However, it seems to us that he goes too far in the course of his appraisal of the pages withdrawn from the *De Temperantia* when he speaks of contradictions in Vitoria. The language of this text, as we have said, is a bit bolder and less cautious regarding the king than the well-meditated introduction to the *De Indis.* This we concede. But in a simple sketch of the latter — in terms of its substance — one finds no essential difference with regard to any central theses. In both retreatments the author calls for moderation and respect for the rights acquired in the execution of a war that he nevertheless justifies. Contrary to the thinking of the author just mentioned, we do not think we find Vitoria maintaining in the *De Temperantia* that although the wars of the Indies have been just "Spain will have won no right of dominion" over the Indies by waging them.[50] Conceptually speaking, there is no opposition between the *De Indis* and the fragment from the *De Temperantia.* At most there is a difference in language and accent, which in a certain sense would make it risky for the Salamancan were that fragment to become known.[51]

The fact is that Vitoria withdraws this text from his *relección* because he regards it as inopportune to publish it. He thinks it would be more appropriate to take up the point at some later date, at greater length with prudence.[52] This is what he will do in his relection, held early in 1539, on the Indies. It is interesting to focus on the precautions he takes before he approaches the problem this time. In the face of the uneasiness that his treatment could provoke, he acknowledges that one could rightly object that "neither the Rulers of Spain nor their counselors are under any obligation to examine and address once more all of the rights and titles upon which deliberation has already been held and sentence pronounced, especially by way of turning their attention to those things that in peaceful possession and good faith our rulers already occupy."[53]

Nevertheless, he justifies his intent with a precisely formulated appeal to the right of theology to have its say: "Nor is the affair of the barbarians so evidently unjust that we might be unable to dissent from its injustice, but rather it appears that, depending on one's approach, either side enjoys a basis for argument." Indeed, he goes on, although the subject is being managed by "learned and good persons," at the same time "such extensive human massacres, the dispossession of so many persons who have committed no offense, so many lords deposed" are spoken of that it will be worth the trouble to examine the question. This can only be an allusion to reports arriving in Spain of outrages of a kind to which the Master has always been very sensitive. He further recalls that "not all theological discussions are always deliberative in kind, but frequently belong to the demonstrative sort, that is, are undertaken in order not to investigate, but to instruct." Thus, the material can be treated without necessarily being called in question. And to other possible objections he responds: "Our discussion has lost none of its urgency; neither do I wish to stir new conflict" (*Obras,* 648–49; CHP, 10–11). Here we have a manifestation of Vitoria's famous prudence.

3. *Between Theory and Practice*

It was long said that Bartolomé de Las Casas did not cite Vitoria. Today we know that this is incorrect. It is true, however, that, except in the *Apología,* he does so only in passing.[54] Some have even wished to see a theoretical shortcoming in Friar Bartolomé here. But now, after the publication of the last work mentioned, these questions are no longer a matter of speculation. Whatever deference he may feel for Vitoria, Las Casas forthrightly expresses his disagreement with him. Sepúlveda, in appealing to Vitoria in defense of his own well-known theses concerning war on the Indians, leaves Bartolomé no other alternative — something he has perhaps avoided up to the moment out of respect for the Salamancan master.[55]

Bartolomé is not afraid to take the bull by the horns:

> Anyone reading both parts of this most learned man's first relection will readily discern that in the first part he proposes, and in a Catholic spirit refutes, the seven claims [there considered] in terms of which a war against the Indians could appear to be just. However, in the second part he introduces eight titles in virtue of which or some of which the Indians might be submitted to the jurisdiction of the Spaniards. In these titles he *supposes* certain *things utterly false,* for the most part, that would be required in order that this war be regarded as potentially just — things re-

ported to him by those *brigands* who, with complete indifference, are sowing destruction across all that world.

Ignorance of the facts. But also, owing to the credence lent to the oppressors of the Indians, a distorted view of reality. Thus, the eminent doctor's reasoning and suppositions lack any foundation in that reality.

Las Casas goes further. Seeking a better understanding of Vitoria in his concrete circumstances, he says that the latter "manifested a certain carelessness [*remissius se habuit*] with respect to some of those titles in an effort to soften what had seemed to the partisans of the emperor [*Caesarianis*] to have been expressed by him in a somewhat too severe manner." The emperor and those around him were on the watch, and this made the theologian's language more moderate. Clearly, however, Bartolomé specifies, "for lovers of the truth, there is nothing of the overly severe in what he sets forth in the first part of his work. On the contrary, it is not only true as to the past, but is Catholic and most true currently" as well. "Lovers of the truth" here means: those who know the reality of the Indies, where destruction continues to reign. What Vitoria has indicated in the first part of his work does not pertain to deeds over and done. They are still being perpetrated at the moment of Las Casas's debate with Sepúlveda.

The Salamancan doctor, Las Casas insinuates, seems to have had some awareness of his ignorance concerning what was occurring in the Indies. In the second part of the same work, says Bartolomé, Vitoria "gives us to understand this by speaking in the conditional form, for fear of approving or uttering erroneous assertions as if they had been true." Despite his respect for this honest precaution, Las Casas's verdict on Victoria's teaching (on which Sepúlveda claims to rely) is plainly condemnatory: "Now, as the presuppositions of this most learned Father regarding the circumstances are *false,* and in view of the fact that he says certain things *with timidity* [*timide dicat*], in no way ought Sepúlveda to have thrown up to me an opinion of Vitoria's that is based on false information" (*Apología,* 237a–238; emphasis added). The false suppositions, along with the prudent conditionals, lead Las Casas to reject the Sepulvedian doctrine. His disagreement with Vitoria's position, indeed his disqualification of his "titles," could not have been more straightforward. But "truth before friendship," as the saying went. Bartolomé's strength resides precisely in the fact that his defense of justice is rooted in the truth of the facts.

We are dealing with a text that at one and the same time is respectful of the great theologian and clear-sighted when it comes to the shortcomings in his much-lauded relections on the Indies. Bartolomé's examination of the celebrated "titles" had already given us a hint of this. Now let us analyze the reasons brought forward by Las Casas for disqualifying certain elements of Vitoria's teaching: *fear and flattery* in propounding his theses, and *ignorance* of the reality of the Indies, which leads him to make unwarranted suppositions. Thus we shall be in a better position to make a judgment on the doctrinal relationship between Las Casas and Vitoria, as well as to return to the core of Vitoria's position: the principle of "sociability."

Fleeing the Peruleros

But such prudent instances of the Master are not always understood by those who have all power in their hands. The emperor's partisans, the *Caesariani,* are uneasy with these disputes over Charles V's dominion in the Indies. The matter has come under broiling discussion, especially among the Dominicans. Charles now addresses a letter, in November 1539, to the prior of St. Stephen's Convent in Salamanca, in which he says he has been informed that "certain religious masters of [your] house have lectured upon and treated in their sermons and law courses Our holdings in the Indies." Now this is "harmful and scandalous," and these "masters and religious" must be summoned and required to state with whom they have treated of these subjects and whether they have distributed documents in their regard. Accordingly, he demands that all "writings that they have in their possession concerning this" be recovered, "without any copy remaining in their power or that of anyone else." Moreover he commands that in the future "without our express permission they neither treat nor preach nor dispute upon the above-mentioned, or cause any document touching upon it to be printed."[56]

The letter unmistakably alludes to Vitoria (and to Domingo de Soto, who addressed the topic before Vitoria did). Attempts to dissimulate this reaction on the part of the king and to see a smooth-as-silk relationship between these two personages are in vain.[57] It was doubtless an instance of the exercise of the privilege of the royal veto in ecclesiastical matters. Vitoria feared this veto. At any rate, Charles had intervened two years before with other import but to similar effect in a matter involving the authority of Paul III himself. We refer to the interdict imposed by the king on the promulgation of the papal documents that we have examined in detail in the preceding chapter. Such may even be the reason why Vitoria does not refer to these documents in the *De Indis.* The *Sublimis Deus* (like the brief *Pastorale Officium*) had dealt explicitly with the matter treated in Vitoria's relection. Furthermore, it constituted a priceless endorsement of certain of his theses. The towering importance of the papal documents makes Vitoria's silence very difficult to understand. A possible explanation, therefore, lies in the fact of King Charles's displeasure with these Roman texts. How, indeed, had it been possible to mention *Sublimis Deus* without referring as well to *Pastorale Officium* — the document that happened to have most disturbed the king? Vitoria's prudence did not, however, spare him the reproval of Charles V's letter. In any event, after the *De Indis* the Salamancan professor never again addressed the question of the titles to a European presence in the Indies.[58]

Vitoria had feared the imperial reaction. A letter to his friend and confrere Miguel de Arcos, published some decades ago,[59] expresses an uneasy feeling in the face of the facts of the Indies and of the reactions that any opinion of them is bound to provoke.[60] In a familiar tone, he expresses to his correspondent the revulsion he feels at the manner in which the wars in those lands are being waged. He does so with an energy that we miss in his public lectures at Salamanca.

With all the intrepidity he had gained in addressing the many thorny problems he has had to confront in his life, when it comes to matters of the Indies, "my blood runs cold," he says, "at their mention." And he adds, "I still work as much as I can."[61] He feels an obligation in conscience to address these problems. But he frankly acknowledges that when confronted with those who come from there, especially those returning from Peru, the *peruleros,* the first thing he does is to "run away from them." He does not seek to set persons at enmity with one another over the matter; "nor do I say more than I understand, or plainly see to be sure and just." And so he would prefer that questioners "consult others, who have a better understanding" of the case.

Besides the difficulty of understanding the facts, Vitoria is aware of the stumbling block encountered by anyone seeking to render an opinion upon them. There are not lacking those who will accuse anyone daring to pronounce judgment on the situation as being an enemy of the pope and the church ("They call you a schismatic"), as well as of the emperor ("and that you condemn the Conquista"). Therefore he seeks to avoid treating the subject. But if pressed to "answer categorically," he says, "I come right out and say what I think."

What is it that Vitoria does not see? He is convinced that the emperor "may [legitimately] conquer the Indies." He even says that he holds "all of these battles and conquests for good and holy." And yet, in the case of Peru, how can he say that things have proceeded with justice? He says he knows that "never have Tabaliba [Atahualpa] or his people wronged Christians in any way." The emperor is possessed of "just titles" to conquer the Indians, and this can in certain circumstances justify the wars — but only with a view to "subjecting them and compelling them to receive the emperor as their prince," not in order to "rob them and cast them to perdition."

The war against the vassals (and the Indians are just as authentically vassals of the emperor "as if they were natives of Seville") must be waged "for their good, and not for that of the prince." In the case of Peru, nothing justifies the plundering or any of the other outrages being committed there. Vitoria is alluding to the position of those who say that, on the contrary, it is they who have been wronged by the Indians and that the latter behave as animals. With good judgment he comments ironically, "If the Indians are not persons, but monkeys, then they are incapable of doing wrong to anyone." There is no way, then, to maintain "the innocence of these *peruleros*" (and he acknowledges that some of his Dominican confreres have attempted to do so). Nor, in consequence, can "these conquistadors be exonerated of the ultimate impiety and tyranny."[62] He would not do so, he says, though his "tongue and hand were to be cut away."

The tribulations of a theologian! The text is interesting, more for what it reveals to us of Vitoria's lofty personal qualities than for any new perspectives it might afford us on his doctrinal position with regard to the Indies. He expresses his conviction (already voiced in the writings that we have examined earlier), along with the fears that have obliged him (or that now oblige him) to proceed with caution. At the same time, the private nature of his letter enables him to vent his feelings and to manifest to his friend the visceral revulsion provoked in him by the mistreatment perpetrated upon the Indians of Peru. His reflections show well the concrete conditionings of a reflection on the faith in questions so controversial. Here is the sensitive heart of a good person, the frustration felt by an illustrious professor — and fear on the part of a public personage who finds himself in confrontation with power.

Despite our malaise at Vitoria's vacillations, we must confess that he has the great merit of doing theology upon concrete, controversial problems. This is to his great honor and credit. The Salamancan could have spared himself a great deal of anguish if, like so many others of yesterday and today, he had concerned himself only with irrelevant matters that fail to touch, even obliquely, the interests of the mighty of this world. But between his fears, perhaps exaggerated, and his Christian and theological honesty, despite the wealth of the principles he has enunciated, Vitoria has fallen into the trap of the Indies, and it has left a scar on his thought. Las Casas perceived this and lamented it.[63]

Writing in the Conditional Mood

Las Casas's other objection, that Vitoria is *ignorant* of the reality of the Indies, is recognized by all. But it ought to be sketched out with greater precision. True, Vitoria himself seems to reveal his awareness of this lack of knowledge in his constant use in his argumentation of conditional forms and equivocal examples that enable him to treat rather aseptically of things that had now meant the death of millions of human beings. This is what has prevented him from perceiving, in spite of his sensitivity to that reality and his generous calls for moderation, that his entire demonstrative apparatus could issue in practice, for all his good intentions, in an apparent justification of the wars that had been waged as well as those yet to be undertaken.

But it must be said that Vitoria had the opportunity to become informed of the reality of the Indies. He lived in the Convent of St. Stephen, an ideal place to be to receive such information. Las Casas therefore goes so far as to assert that the "most learned man" not only did not know what was transpiring in the Indies, but lent an unduly attentive ear to the versions reported by the marauders [*praedonibus*] who were destroying "all that world." Surely he did so out of his desire for balance and objectivity. Still, what was actually occurring in the Indies — events extensively reported by Friar Bartolomé in his memorials, as well as by so many other missioners even in their official accounts — are a refutation of the conditionality he employs in his discourse upon so-called legitimate titles. Ignorance, then, there surely is, but not necessarily invincible ignorance. At the same time, his letter to Arcos demonstrates that that ignorance deserves a certain consideration. Perhaps what we have — if the letter is from 1545 — is that Vitoria acquired this knowledge in all its evidence only after his public intervention in these matters.[64]

Friar Bartolomé's reproaches of Vitoria's teaching — in a context of great deference to the person — were perhaps spurred by Sepúlveda's appeal to it in defense of his own theses.[65] Worse, Sepúlveda had had good grounds for that appeal. The conjectures of the master of Salamanca had indeed authorized Sepúlveda to lay claim to his support, at least in part. Vitoria's positions are not Sepúlveda's, but neither are they diametrically opposed to them. At all events, the Master leaves a broad margin for interpretation. He opens a spectrum of possible positions.[66] Las Casas was clear-sighted and courageous in his critique of this great theologian of his day.[67]

What is happening, when all is said and done, is that the two Dominicans are operating from different theological perspectives. Vitoria is the theologian of emerging modernity. He treats questions from the viewpoint of the Christian West. Not that he lacks a vision of universal scope or sensitivity to the problems of his time. On the contrary, no one has ever doubted these in him. But his focus is Europe's, and that of the social class maturing and beginning to take economic power in its hands. He is very aware of the dangers inherent in the aggressive nationalism of the sixteenth century and on his guard against them. Accordingly, in terms appropriate to and even in advance of his era, he recalls the exigencies of the international community, on foundations that if not religious are at least ethical. He perceives the new approaches urged by mercantile capitalism, but he tries to ensure that these not bypass the finality of the common good.[68] That is his great merit, and always will be. Vitoria's contribution retains its entire validity in the current concert (or discord?) of nations at the international level.

But his universe, understandably enough, is not that of the poor of the Indies. In behalf of the peoples whom Europe was beginning to colonize, he calls for humane treatment. But his advocacy of the rights of those nations and cultures has its limits. He is discomfited by the injustices being committed in the Indies, but he believes what he hears about the "barbarous customs" of the natives there, and even — now without a certain hesitation — about their alleged inferior humanity. He is concerned, obviously, for the proclamation of the gospel in the Indies. But he is also zealous for social communication and commerce with these peoples. Their spoliation and murder at the hands of his compatriots earn his moral indignation. But in facing that situation it is not enough to propose moderation in wars and conquests that he regards as just if only they meet his theoretical conditions. Vitoria's theology does not fully respond, then, to the complex reality of the Indies. It is high intellectual flight, yes, and it fixes principles of great fecundity. But it is so riddled with incertitudes that despite its author's generous intentions it can be requisitioned, when all is said and done, by those who place their own interests ahead of the exigencies of the gospel — or worse, who seek to justify their privileges by manipulating the Christian faith.[69]

Sociability and Inequality

The experience of the Indies and the reflection this experience stimulates in him lead Las Casas to a different position. In fact, he gains an entirely different theological perspective. Bartolomé's outlook is from within the world of the poor, from among the despised races, from the deep recesses of an exploited humanity — from within a world represented principally, in this case, by the Indian, but also, as we have seen, by the black (and by the impoverished Spaniard). His inevitable (and fertile) limited concurrence with Vitoria's views must not blind us to the difference in his viewpoint and in the practical consequences thereof. An example of this difference of focus is found in a text we cite (see above, our chapter 3) on the rights claimed by the king of France to the silver mines of Guadalcanal, which the king of Spain was unwilling to admit (see *De Thesauris*, 132). The entire refutation here consists in a reversal of viewpoint: Vitoria, and so many others with him, may seem to be adopting a universal language in order to treat of the subject of the Indies; in reality, however, they are adopting, simply and understandably, a particular European point of view.

Being both more familiar with the reality of the Indies and more attentive and sensitive to the practical repercussions of a theoretical reflection, Bartolomé de Las Casas resists a certain application in the Indies of Vitoria's basic postulate of "sociability." That resistance has earned him the resentment of Vitoria's admirers, who interpret his qualified opposition to the application of the principle as a rejection of the principle.[70] But Las Casas had his eyes open when it came to what this principle would entail in the Indies. As J. Friede[71] and I. Pérez[72] have observed, Las Casas does not deny the human value and meaning of "sociability." What he rejects is making it an argument for war and domination in the Indies. Here we have an interesting passage from Las Casas in which it is not difficult, despite the date of the event mentioned, to see an allusion to Vitoria's principle. Treating of the Portuguese expeditions in Brazil (of which he had learned from the book by João de Barros), he presents these soldiers' reasoning as follows: If, when the gospel is proposed to them, the natives "were to be so refractory as not to accept this law of faith and should reject the law of peace that ought to be observed among human beings for the preservation of the human species, resisting that commerce or exchange that is the means by which peace and love among all human beings are acquired, practiced, and preserved (as this commerce is the foundation of all civilized human dealings), then a cruel war, by fire and blood, may legitimately be waged on them" (*H.I.*, bk. 1, ch. 173, *O.E.* 1:460a). The condition enunciated is reminiscent of Vitoria; the text refers to considerations of the faith, but the proclamation includes other forms of "commerce" or interhuman exchange, including the economic. Our friar makes this explicit with the following observation: " ... And even should they not wish to, they must maintain a commerce and trade their possessions for others, unless they were to have need of the former" (ibid., 460b).

The faith may not be imposed and neither may commercial exchange. Still less may nonexistent rights be deduced from them. Faith and commerce revolve in different orbits, but freedom is requisite in both. The more powerful have no right to impose an undesired economic relationship on the weaker. This is what is at stake. Consequently, it cannot "be stated or believed that commerce and exchange must be maintained by any peoples with other, foreign human beings against their will, if not against their entire voluntariety and liberty" (ibid., 461a). Relations, yes, but not in a relationship of inequality, especially if the inequality is camouflaged by a so-called equal-rights doctrine, a pretended right to do business with you even against your will. This is the nub of the Lascasian objection.[73]

Las Casas keeps account of a reality in which — while the theologians wrangled — the life and death of whole populations were at stake. Vitoria, whose reasoning was not intended to "provoke any tragedies," as he declared in his letter to Arcos, seemed oblivious of the fact that the tragedies were under way at full steam and crying to heaven. The exaggerated pathos was not in the denunciations of the atrocities being committed in the Indies, but in the injustices themselves.

The foregoing considerations must not blind us to the value of the principle of sociability Vitoria advances. His proposition blazed completely new trails and laid the foundations for an ethically founded body of laws on totally new terrain. The creative intelligence of the professor from Salamanca was surely able to exercise a problem-plagued but fertile discernment in the turbulent waters of his time.[74] He faced the challenges presented to the European nations and responded to them from a humanistic and Christian perspective. His contribution to international law constitutes the intellectual greatness of this noble, just human being.

What Las Casas rightly called into question was the validity of his principles in the controversial Indian context. In asking his questions, Bartolomé recalled that law must take account of distinct concrete situations — political, economic, cultural — especially when it is a matter of relations among nations of unequal political and military power. Another bridgehead was his insistence on the crucial importance of a thorough knowledge of the *facts*, with a view to forging a *legal system* that not only would take account of reality, but whose norms would express an actual, concrete morality.

In both cases, it is once again the methodological postulate "If we were Indians..." that we must meditate. But here we should like to observe that from that point of departure it is possible to make an important contribution to the theoretical quality of the development of a legal corpus and juridical system based on justice for all in general and for the weakest members of society in particular — witness Las Casas's work. Precisely its theoretical quality? Indeed. A concern for the concrete consequences of a system of thought is intrinsic not only to its formal logic, but to its vital, concrete logic as well.

With his successes and his failures, his revulsion for the atrocities being perpetrated on the Indians and his timidity, the compass of his theoretical disquisitions and his vacillations, Vitoria had the immense merit of treating of these matters from a university chair of towering influence in his time. There at the heart of thinking Spain he opened the door to a fertile reflection and planted the seeds of a school of thought that would place a mighty arsenal of theological arguments at the disposal of the defenders of the Indians.

Conclusion to Part Four

Equality among all human beings was one of the themes dearest to Las Casas's heart. Sounding the depths of this principle, he defends the rights of the despised dwellers of the Indies. With this same intent, he points, ever and again, to the novelty represented (for Europeans) by this continent and those who people it. The same notion enables him to show the newcomers that they cannot simply identify what they find in the Indies with what they already know or mechanically transport interpretations and behaviors sprung up in another context to the context of this new world. Nor is it for any other reason that Bartolomé battles for all he is worth for an understanding among his compatriots that the Indians belong to a different category of unbelievers or barbarians from those of conventional European acquaintance. With clairvoyant eye, he perceives the novelty of the Indies, to which he was always most sensitive, and fights to protect their inhabitants from the theological justifications advanced for making war on them and subjecting them. Dwelling at a great distance from Europe — and this has come as a surprise to Europeans, says the Sevillian — are peoples who have lived "many thousands of years in their villages under their own orderly, peaceful government" (*H.I.*, bk. 3, ch. 18, *O.E.* 2:215a). These are ancient civilizations, however new for the newcomers.

The terrible situation in which the Indians live has its primary cause in the mistreatment and exploitation of which they are the object. It becomes ever more plain to Bartolomé that the objectively most correct and therefore the most appropriate concept calculated to convey that condition is the gospel notion of "poor." This focus overflows on all sides the one who regards the Indians only as non-Christians — as unbelievers, infidels. Seeing in the Indian a "poor one" of the gospel transforms him or her into a favorite person of the God of Jesus Christ, with all of the exigencies that this entails for a believer. *Liberation in Christ* embraces the "deliverance of the oppressed and the succor of those in anguish," as well as the "salvation and redemption of souls"

(*Carta al Consejo*, 1531, *O.E.* 5:46a). The effort to further this liberation is a task incumbent upon all followers of Jesus and indicates a guideline for their action. Thus, with the alleviation of suffering in the Indies, "the whole mystical body of concern to ourselves perhaps be healed" (ibid., *O.E.* 5:43b). As Bartolomé puts it, recounting the outrages suffered from the outset by the Indians of Hispaniola and expressing a beautiful intuition, "God sleeps not when these injustices" occur (*H.I.*, bk. 1, ch. 171, *O.E.* 1:455b). And God's watch must be ours, even in our own day.

Although his initial, principal concern was the defense of the Indians, Las Casas's experiences, readings, and discussions throughout his life open other horizons to him. Asians and Africans (Muslim or not) and even Spaniards begin to appear in his allegations — at times with certain vacillations. These indictments never acquire the weight of those regarding the Indies in Bartolomé's commitment and reflection, which are marked specifically by his experience in these lands, but the mere fact that they are lodged expresses the universality of the outlook he advances.

The novelty of the situation of the Indies calls for a reflection of its own. The "little or no theology" of the Council of the Indies in the early decades, he observes, makes it impossible for that Council to accord the affairs of the Indies an adequate examination. Las Casas was aware that the "intelligence of the faith" is intimately bound up with a knowledge of the reality that that faith seeks to illuminate. Herein lie Bartolomé's differences with Vitoria's positions on the Indies. The Sevillian never left off doing theology in this perspective. His activity was sustained by an ongoing, challenging reflection. Thus, without his ever having taught in Salamanca, his voice in the theological school of that university carried its impact.

Part Five

God or Gold?

✠ Las Casas's involvement with Peru is of long duration and great complexity and is ultimately decisive for his thought and activity. Bartolomé learns very early of what he calls "Peru's apparent wealth" (*Carta al Consejo*, 1534, *O.E.* 5:58a). The gold of these territories has struck the fantasy of all manner of adventurers, and they are greedy for the fabulous treasures of the new land. At the same time, or rather for this very reason, news arrives of the havoc being wrought by "Pizarro and his holy disciples" (*Carta a un personaje*, 1535, *O.E.* 5:61b). Among these abuses is the rapaciousness to which Atahualpa falls victim, as he is dispossessed "of his throne," of "his great treasures," and finally of his life (ibid., 61b). From the very start, then, the picture of Peru that forms before Bartolomé's eyes is not only of a land where the *gold* for which the Europeans have lusted ever since their arrival in the Indies has been found in fabulous abundance, but also of a place where the *God* of Jesus is in the most danger of going unrecognized.[1] This feeling about Peru, devoid of illusions, will accompany him all of his life.

Impelled by this consideration, Bartolomé sets sail, along with other Dominican friars, hoping to undertake a missionary labor in that "unfortunate land of Peru" (ibid., 60b). He reaches Panama, but as he resumes his voyage he meets with shipwreck and lands in Nicaragua. There he will remain for a time, doing what he was unable to accomplish in the country of his original destination. Later, in a crucial hour of his life (and at the moment of his concern with the New Laws), Bartolomé will be offered the episcopal see of Cuzco, which he will refuse.[2] But his interest in this land will never wane, and thanks to reliable correspondents he will always be abreast of events there. With Domingo de Santo Tomás, he will plunge into the thick of the struggle against the perpetuity of the *encomiendas,* thus alienating the

359

peruleros (who will already have felt under attack by the New Laws) once and for all.

But there is more. Peru becomes the very touchstone of Bartolomé's battle for justice in the Indies. He views events there as a profound challenge. The question of whether the Iberians have or do not have the right to make the treasures of Peru's mines and burial sites their own affords him a place to stand for the creation of a comprehensive, synthetic reflection on the European presence in the Indies (see *De Thesauris*). The challenge of Peru assumes a concrete and incisive character with the "twelve doubts" either sent or personally carried to him by Dominican Bartolomé de Vega, perhaps around 1563.[3] Las Casas's responses, all dealing with Peruvian matters, express his definitive position with regard to all that was transpiring in the Indies.[4] With the passage of time, the Indies, generally regarded in Spain as "so remote,"[5] draw ever nearer to Las Casas, even those lands of Peru he has never been able physically to reach.

It is important to denounce the injustices to which the native population of the Indies is subjected, enter into solidarity with their sufferings, and isolate the profound causes of their situation. But he regards it of capital importance, as well, to proclaim openly their right to recover what is theirs and to liberate themselves from the oppression under which they writhe. From the moment of their cry from Hispaniola in 1511, the missioners have pointed to a face of the Indies contorted with plunder and violence and have insisted that the culprits are under obligation to restore what they have taken. As happens so often with other subjects, Las Casas takes up the relays, and goes even further with the same demand: restitution will have to comprise not only material goods, but moral damages as well, including the restoration of the legitimate rulers of the Indies, who have been dispossessed of their authority. To this purpose, he will adduce another point of the church's traditional teaching: since the native peoples have been attacked in an unjust war, their wars of self-defense are just.

Next, Bartolomé executes a foray onto new terrain, where on the basis of the Indies he advances a thesis universal in its scope: a necessary condition of all political legitimacy is the free consent of the governed. Therefore, if this free consent is not verified in the Indies, and in his judgment it is not, the papal donation and the universal sovereignty of the king and queen of Spain cannot become effective. Concretely, he proposes the project of restoring "the Inca," Titu Cusi, to his throne.

The Lascasian theses on Peru arouse great animus there. With energy and determination, Viceroy Toledo organizes a campaign of opposition to them. A principal point of the latter's undertaking concerns the matter of the legitimacy of the native rulers. The viceroy needs to squelch the notions of this restless Dominican friar and his friends in Peru if he is to affirm the authority of the king of Spain and incorporate the mighty *encomenderos* into the colonial order he seeks to establish. The so-called *Anónimo de Yucay* (Yucan opinion) will supply him with the theological ammunition he needs. The truth is that that "opinion rendered" is not an isolated one. The *Yucay Opinion* actually systematizes ideas already sprung from the minds and pens of skillful defenders of the colonial order. The package of notions it presents is by no means strange or unusual for the time, then, and it deserves our detailed study. In an effort to explain the reasons for the existence of the mines of Peru, the author of that text will declare this wealth to have been a gift of divine providence itself: after all, it is thanks to it that the Spaniards, with the encouragement of their sovereigns, have been inspired to come to these lands. And in coming here, they have brought the Christian faith.

Bartolomé always fought this connection between gold and gospel.[6] With biblical lucidity he has analyzed the idolatry of gold being committed by those who called themselves Christian. His reflections show what will be at stake later, in the thesis presented by the Yucay composition. His position is seen as an intolerable paradox by his contemporaries, who are convinced that idolatry was the sin of the inhabitants of the Indies, not their own, and one that must receive appropriate punishment.[7]

Toledo's campaign fails to destroy Las Casas's influence in Peru. Some decades later, a Peruvian Indian who knew the era of the viceroy and felt its impact will take up in a personal and original way certain essential aspects of the Lascasian project for Peru. He will propose to King Philip III solutions of his own in an enormous letter that owing to the huge distance, not only geographical but especially social, separating him from such an illustrious personage, will never reach its addressee. Guamán Poma will be living testimonial that Lascasian ideas have continued to win adherents — and enemies — in the lands of Peru.

Chapter 13

Rights of the Indian Nations

Las Casas energetically denounces the injustices arising in the Indies with the coming of the Europeans. He ferrets out their causes and combats these. He constantly presents projects for altering this state of affairs in its very roots and includes in his effort a theological and juridical reflection enabling him to go beyond contingent, local situations.

Nor are his efforts limited to this. From the outset he maintains the natives' right to life and liberty — and not only as an individual right, but as a collective one. Thus he prefers to speak of "Indian nations." Despite the state of prostration in which they are sunk due to the traumatic events of the invasion and domination, these "free peoples and tribes" (*Carta a Carranza*, 1555, O.E. 5:435b) have rights that must be recognized and fought for. After all, these are "human nations" (*H.I.*, bk. 1, ch. 175, O.E. 1:468a). They must ultimately be the historical subject, the concrete agent, of their own liberation.

The proclamation of those rights leads the author back to a consideration of the current state of oppression obtaining in Peru. The harassments they suffer today, says Bartolomé, are inflicted for the purpose of "cruelly steeping the hearts of the inhabitants in fear, . . . that never may they meditate their wretched, unhappy state and aspire one day to their liberation [*sua liberatione*]" (*De Thesauris*, 108). Las Casas's constant comparison of the oppressive situation of the native population with that suffered by the people of Israel in Egypt — a traditional theme in the history of Christianity — is in the same line.

This subjugation must simply be done away with. If the Indian nations become aware of their situation and analyze its reasons, they will be in a better position to secure their own liberation, an objective that the Sevillian has had in mind from the first moments of his defense of the aboriginal population. The remedy — he will say countless times, and beginning very early — "is very plain and has been most carefully considered here." That remedy is: "that the Indians be set free"

(*Carta al Consejo,* 1531, *O.E.* 5:54b). And Bartolomé is still talking about liberation in his last will and testament (see *O.E.* 5:539b).

Of course, as in his other great reflections, we find a maturation of his ideas here, especially with regard to the routes to be taken to this liberation. Bartolomé sounds the depths of two classic points of the theology of his age: the duty of restitution and the right of self-defense. On the basis of these concepts (especially the first), he glimpses new routes to the restoration of Indian rights. The evolution of Indian affairs and his reflection on evangelization as the sole justification for the Hispanic presence in the Indies lead Las Casas finally, and daringly, to make everything depend on the free consent of those nations. His interest in the problems posed in Peru will make his effort here an unusually telling one.

1. Parasitism Is Unethical

Ever since the about-face effected in his life in the year 1514, Las Casas had become more and more aware of the correlation between thievery and death. To deny the poor their bread (as a symbol of the whole of their life), and worse, to deprive them of it when they already have it, is to become a murderer.[1] In his *Confesionario,* or manual for the conferral of the Sacrament of Reconciliation, which centers on the duty of restitution incumbent upon all who have had a part in the dispossession of the native peoples,[2] Las Casas says: "It is illicit to live on the possessions of another." And it is worse if it is done "with pomp, in high estate, and by the sweat of human neighbors by whom one is owed nothing" (*O.E.* 5:138b). Those who see themselves dispossessed in this fashion have a valid right to defend themselves — by force, if need be.

A Question of Justice

Anyone who by violence or by deceit has come into possession of something belonging to another is under an obligation of restoring it to its rightful owner. This is a classic point of Christian moral theology.[3] The thought spontaneously occurred to the Hispaniola missioners at the sight of the atrocities being committed on that isle. Indeed, these missioners were the first to speak of restitution in the Indies.[4] It was an acute awareness of the duty of restitution that sparked Las Casas's conversion experience, from which his radical change of life emerged. Without his perceiving all of its exigencies as yet, it was by this duty that he was impelled to renounce his *encomienda.* Restitution seeks to reestablish the justice that has been wronged by plunder and extortion.[5]

Bartolomé takes his first theoretical and practical steps in this area by positing the need for a *compositio,* or settlement — the canonical term for the duty, when restitution is impossible, of offering a part of the debt as an alms. This is what the state of things in the Indies requires, "inasmuch as most of the Indians are dead, with neither part nor parcel of them remaining, and they can never again exist" (*Memorial de remedios,* 1516, O.E. 5:14b). Actually the cleric from Seville is only invoking the common doctrine of the time, which was already being applied in the Indies,[6] as it would be — not without further abuses — for long years to come.

The matter matures in Las Casas's mind. Theoretical elements acquired in his years of training as a Dominican will be of great utility to him. We see this in the systematic presentation he makes of the topic in his *De Unico* (ch. 7, paras. 4, 5). There, restitution is tied in precise terms to righteousness and salvation. And here our friar arrives at something he will never surrender: without restitution, there will be no salvation for the Christians in the Indies. He also takes an important step with regard to what is to be returned: what has been stolen, of course — but further, everything of which the Indians have been deprived "by their death and massacre" and "the loss of their liberties" (*De Unico,* 211v). And Las Casas will continue to plumb the matter.

With the *Confesionario,* Bartolomé passes an important milepost in his reflection and in the scope of the subject.[7] His advice to confessors centers on restitution. It is one of his most controversial books and one of those that caused him the most trouble in his life. It is also one of the writings that had the greatest influence on the pastoral activity of the church of the Indies. On a grand scale — the subject had been broached before — Bartolomé urges Christians to realize that the harm they do the Indians is cause for eternal damnation.[8] Unless they repent and make restitution to the Indians of whatever they have taken from them, they are lost forever. The rules of the *Confesionario* indicate what is to be required of penitents in various cases. If the penitent refuses, confessors may not grant absolution.[9] The Dominican's theses are radical. They are rigid, said those who ever ask for moderation from this person driven by the deaths and injustices he sees around him.[10] Still, they enjoyed great acceptance with bishops and missionaries.[11] Consequently, many old conquistadors, *encomenderos,* civil functionaries, and others, on their deathbeds, endeavored to make restitution.[12] Applied in practice, the *Confesionario* doubtless threatened to destroy the huge fortunes of the *encomenderos* of the Indies.

In the *De Thesauris,* Friar Bartolomé poses the question of restitution in terms of the problem of the burial sites, the *huacas,* to which we have alluded. He draws the following conclusion:

> To no one on this earth, not even to the King of the Spaniards (with all due reverence to His Royal Highness), is it permitted, without the license and free and gracious will of the Inca King or his descendants, to succeed to the [natives'] goods, search out, unearth, sort through, and carry off precious objects that they have buried with their departed in the sepulchers and so-called *Guacas.* And if they do, they will commit a mortal sin of theft or robbery. And if they fail to restore it and to do penance for their sin, it will be impossible for them to attain salvation.

Nor does the matter rest here. The injury done the Indians has other implications. With elegance, then, and realism (honor and glory belong to the virtue of justice, according to Thomas Aquinas), our Friar adds:

> Nor must they repent only of the sin of theft or *robbery,* but of the *insult,* as well, that in a special manner they cause the aforesaid living successors or descendants of those whose sepulchers they violate, in that they occasion a diminution of the honor and praise of both living and dead and effect the disappearance of a memory of the latter. Wherefore they are also obliged to give them satisfaction [for insult as well as for theft or robbery]. (*De Thesauris,* 12v; emphasis added)[13]

Although with the *Confesionario* Las Casas had managed to smite consciences and win certain changes in individuals, the matter continued to mature and grow in his mind. It became a mighty weapon in his battle for the overall transformation of the Indies. The *De Thesauris* and especially the *Doce dudas* (Twelve doubts) are an expression of that proposal. For Bartolomé, the Spanish sovereigns themselves are obliged to restitution, since they have ultimate responsibility for events in the Indies. In response to Sepúlveda he even declares that "the illustrious doctor or anyone else seeking to justify or excuse [those unwilling to make restitution] sin most mortally and are obliged to the same restitution" (*Aquí se contiene,* 1552, *O.E.* 5:343b). The injury to be repaired has been in goods both material and moral. Restitution, therefore, must include the restoration of the destroyed monarchical societies of these lands, in which the Indians had led a civilized life in conformity with their customs. This will require the rehabilitation of their legitimate political authorities. Bartolomé then presents his project concerning the Peruvian Inca, with which we shall concern ourselves below. First, we must recall certain further elements in order to see all of the dimensions here.[14]

Natural Right of Self-Defense

Las Casas has inherited another classic theme of moral theology, and he applies it relevantly in his writings on these points. While less central to those works than the doctrine on restitution, the just-war theory enjoys the clear consensus of the theologians of the time. A people violently attacked have the full right to use violence as well, in order to repel that of which they are the object. Our friar disallows the cynical use of this argument to legitimate acts of war on the part of Europeans against the Indians. It is obvious, says Bartolomé, that the Indians have not traveled to Europe to disturb its inhabitants. They had been living peacefully in their own lands. It was they who were invaded and attacked.

In consequence, it is the native nations who have the right to defend their lives, culture, customs, and religion against those attacking these things from without. Such a reaction on their part would be fully justified. In view of the mistreatment and offenses they have received, which "surpass anything of the kind ever received by any of the other nations of the world," these peoples "have the right to wage war in all justice" (*H.I.,* bk. 1, ch. 104, *O.E.* 1:290b).[15] Countering the opinion of some, Bartolomé specifies that it is not a matter of a rebellion or uprising, for the simple reason that these terms are applicable only to subjects, and the Indians for Las Casas are not subjects of the Spanish Crown. After all, as we shall see a few pages further on, they have never voluntarily accepted Spanish sovereignty. Criticizing the punishment administered by Columbus to Indians for their "rebellion," he asks: "How can nonsubjects be rebels?" To make himself understood, he poses another question: If the king of France were to ride roughshod over the rights of the natives of Castile, and the Castilians were to react, "Could the king of France rightly call the Spaniards rebels? I doubt that Castile would confess to this rebellion" (ibid.). This would not be rebellion in the actual meaning of the term. It would be the fully justified defense of a strict right.[16]

An analysis of the case of Enriquillo will serve as an illustration. Enriquillo was an Indian chief of Hispaniola, whom the missioners had known since his childhood — hence the diminutive suffix in his Spanish name. Having had quite enough of the harassment of which he and his people were the object, he determined "to defend himself on his own land." The Spaniards called this an "uprising" and sought to put it down by force. Enrique resisted, and many Indians joined him in his fight. For Las Casas, this was a "just war of natural defense" of the Indians' lives and rights, a judgment in support of which he appeals to Scripture (the episode of the Maccabees) and the history of Spain (King Pelayo). The Indian chief had proceeded with the same titles as had the Maccabees or Pelayo. (Our quotations are from *H.I.*, bk. 3, ch. 125, *O.E.* 2:478a–b.)[17] If this had not occurred more frequently, it was because the Indian peoples had not had the needed strength. But this does not make the injustices they suffer just. "Never is tyranny purged," he says, "by the quiet of the oppressed. This will be for lack of strength," he specifies, "and it is obvious in the case of the Indians" (*Respuesta al obispo de los Charcas,* 1553, *O.E.* 5:428a–b; see the same verdict in *H.I.*, bk. 3, ch. 127, *O.E.* 2:482a).

For this last reason, he boldly proposes that the king of Spain himself would have the duty to wage war on those in the Indies who refuse to reestablish justice there. In that case, the latter would indeed be in rebellion against the will of the king that they proceed with restitution. Thus, "the king of Spain himself is obliged to make war on them, and to die in [that war] if need be, in order to deliver the peoples they hold in oppression." He will establish this conclusion by way of a number of different arguments. To inform the king of this duty "is to do him a very great service," as it means "having a concern for his soul, that it always be happy and live in blessedness" (*Doce dudas,* 1564, *O.E.* 5:532b–534a).

Las Casas asserts this right of the Indians all his life long, and at the close of that life he reasserts it energetically: "The native people of each and all of these regions where we have come into the Indies have the vested right to make war on us most justly and evict us forthwith from the land, and this right will abide with them till Judgment Day" (*Memorial al Consejo,* 1565, *O.E.* 5:536b).

It is plain to Bartolomé that war must be a last resort. War, even a defensive one, is never something good. At best it can be a lesser evil. Actually, in view of the historical context, Las Casas's probable intent is more to emphasize the profound injustice being committed in the Indies than to indicate any realistic possibility that his sovereign might ever wage war on his own soldiers there. The thesis incisively declares what side justice is on. Here, then, Bartolomé is content to repeat the doctrine of the just war, applying it to the situation of the Indies — with sincere conviction, surely, but without deepening it or offering any novel contributions to it.[18]

2. Right to Receive the Gospel

Evangelization is a dialogue. Every Christian has a duty to bear witness, in deeds and words, to Jesus' message. And all peoples have the right to hear this proclamation, thereupon to receive and accept it should they so wish. Gradually, Las Casas comes to a clear perception of the fact that the presence of Christians in the Indies is justified not only by the duty of Christians to evangelize, but also by the right of the Indians to have the Reign of God proclaimed to them. Duty and right are conjoint and mutually conditioning. Together they indicate the criteria according to which the task of evangelization ought to be carried out, the criteria of a discernment between what is correct and what is incorrect in the situation now created in these lands. Let us see how our friar moves forward, arguing his thesis along a path that leads him to one of his most surprising and incisive positions.

Casually Concocted Titles

In one of the rules in his *Confesionario,* Bartolomé trenchantly maintains that everything that has been done in the Indies "has been against all natural law and the Law of Nations, as well as against all divine law, . . . and consequently, null, void, and without any validity or legal effect" (*O.E.* 5:239b). In a most controversial and much attacked work, this is doubtless the most nettling point of all. It was severely reprehended and earned Bartolomé not only a charge of lèse-majesté, but a denunciation to the Holy Inquisition. Around this same time, capital points in the New Laws were abolished (1545), stipulations that, while they had not fully corresponded to his proposals, nevertheless had constituted an important gain. Truly Las Casas was passing through the most difficult moment of his life.

Suddenly Bartolomé was obliged to be more specific with respect to this rule from his *Confesionario,* which was seen as attacking the validity of any claim to sovereignty over the Indies on the part of the sovereigns of Spain. He says as much at the beginning of the book he writes to explain his position: the *Treinta proposiciones* (written in 1548 and/or 1549, published in 1552). The theses of this composition are presented jejunely. Two of them (the most important, in his judgment) are developed in the *Tratado comprobatorio* (dating perhaps from 1550–51). In this last work, the point that interests us is examined with care.

The two propositions just mentioned are the seventeenth, which declares the Spanish sovereigns to be authentic sovereigns of the Indies, a title based on the grant by the Apostolic See,[19] and the eighteenth, which denies that this superior sovereignty annuls the authority of the legitimate native rulers of the Indian nations.[20] We are dealing with a limit case, then, a text whose circumstances — the attacks of which he has been the object — move Las Casas to yield as far as he possibly can to the opinion current in his age. Hence the crucial importance of these circumstances for an elucidation of his position. The same thing is true for the *Tratado comprobatorio.* Before going into the matter in greater detail, let us observe that the second of the two propositions in question (along with other specifications to be made later) limits the first. It will be impossible to analyze them separately. And so, *prima facie,* we have something very different here from the classic theses of theocracy or the direct power of the pope in temporal matters.[21] Let us see this in more detail.

The *Tratado comprobatorio* advances the reasons that specify and shade or nuance the theses of the *Treinta proposiciones.* The author begins by rejecting the titles he sees as having been dreamed up by certain persons wishing to curry favor with the sovereigns and justify the oppression to which the Indians are being subjected. There is no point, as Las Casas will say at the close of the treatise, in "casually concocting various titles" (*O.E.* 5:409b). He then explicitly refutes four such attempted legitimations: Spain's relative proximity to the Indies, the greater prudence of the Spaniards, the illegitimacy of Indian proprietorship (ever since the coming of Christ),[22] and the barbarous, idolatrous ways of the Indian nations (see *O.E.* 5:409b–410a).

The two conclusions that he will prove, naturally, correspond to the two propositions previously recalled. However, the terms in which the demonstrations are couched supply certain clarifications. For Bartolomé the only valid title of the Spanish presence in the Indies is "the grant and donation, not simple and mere, but modal *id est, ob interpositam causam* [by reason of an intervening consideration], made and interposed to them by the Holy See" (*O.E.* 5:352a). Now, a *modal* grant creates an "onerous" right, a right entailing a duty equal to or exceeding the benefit. The granting of such a right is not "simple and mere." Bartolomé's expressions are carefully calculated. A number of pages further on he takes up the point once more after some important specifications. Although we believe that his position is better explained from another angle (as we hope to show in the following paragraphs), we shall first try to understand it within the framework of the European theology of the era.

What authority does the pope have to impose such a charge? He has power over persons and temporal goods "only insofar as it may appear to him, in conformity with right reason, that it is necessary and appropriate in order to guide and direct faithful or heathen (although differently in each of the two cases) onto the road to eternal life" (*O.E.* 5:352b). The responsibility of the pope, as head of the church, is to proclaim the gospel. His temporal power, Las Casas specifies, may be exercised only *in ordine ad finem spiritualem* — solely as a means to a spiritual end (ibid.). He holds it over unbelievers, as well, since they too are potential (and in some respects actual) members of the body of Christ.[23] But his power over them is different from that he has over Christians.[24]

The temporal power of the pope is not a direct authority. This is clear to Las Casas. But the prosecution of the religious end can have repercussions in the political domain. Thus the temporal authority of the pope is indirect, or "directive."[25] This is Bartolomé's perspective. He grants the pope the right to intervene in temporal affairs "insofar as it may be suitable for the purpose of directing persons to their spiritual, eternal end, which is the beatitude for which they have been created" (*O.E.* 5:358b).

He takes his distance from John of Paris, whom he does not seem to know very well,[26] and harshly criticizes William of Ockham for seeming to wish to limit the authority of the pope in order to amplify that of kings and princes (see *O.E.* 5:358b). At the same time he cites authorities in behalf of his thesis, as was the custom. Occasionally he includes theologians or jurists whose position is not precisely his own (for example, Bernard of Clairvaux or Innocent III; see *O.E.* 5:360b, 364a), but who — against authors like Ockham — support the right of the church to intervene in temporal questions. His basic posture, however, is firm and is expressed altogether clearly in a text like this one: "In the promise of the Sovereign Pontificate, our Redeemer unmistakably said to St. Peter: 'Tibi dabo claves regni coelorum' [I shall give you the keys of the Reign of Heaven]; he did not say, 'Regni terrenorum' [Of the terrestrial Reign]" (*O.E.* 5:364a).[27]

However, the theory of the indirect power of the pope in temporal matters always entailed the risk of a slippery slope. Its champions could easily slide into assertions verging on the direct power they explicitly sought to reject. Even in the presence of a denial that this power may be exercised save when the spiritual end (the only one for which the pope has competency) would otherwise be at risk, the door is open, almost inevitably, to conclusions that outstrip their premises.

How Far?

Las Casas did not escape the danger. While his principles are crystal clear in these works, one of his theoretical conclusions is less so: that proclaiming the possibility for the pope to interfere in the government of temporal polities if it is appropriate to do so for the sake of the propagation of the faith. Bartolomé likewise cites, again only theoretically, the case of a prince who out of malice and hatred of the faith would oppose the proclamation of the gospel with consequent harm, including oppression, to his subjects. In that extreme situation, the pope could charge some Christian prince with intervening, even by force of arms, "in behalf of and for the liberation of the oppressed," presupposing that this would not cause still greater harm to the persons of the polity in question (see *O.E.* 5:366–71). We are faced with an exceptional case, then, and a rather isolated text.[28] But Bartolomé has surely gone very far with his deductions.

Two remarks seem to us to be in place here. First, this is a difficult moment in Las Casas's battle. He is under siege at the hands of his most relentless adversary: Ginés de Sepúlveda, who is accusing him of treason to king and country. And so he must do his best to explain how the pope could have given this commission to the Spanish rulers. He does so on the basis of an initial intuition that only the proclamation of the gospel could justify the European presence in the Indies. Then he appeals to a number of authorities, among them the school of Salamanca, with Vitoria at its head. And indeed that school held positions like those just recalled.[29]

True, in his *De Indis* Vitoria cites as an illegitimate title of peninsular sovereignty in the Indies the papal grant supposed to have been made by Alexander VI in his capacity as "monarch of the entire world, even in temporal affairs" (*Obras*, 676; CHP, 43). After all, for Vitoria the most important consideration is the principle of "sociability" (and/or "commerce"), which is a principle of the Law of Nations. On the present occasion, however, Las Casas cites the relection that the Salamancan professor specifically devotes to the question of papal authority, or "power," the *De Potestate Ecclesiae Prior* (to which the *De Indis* refers).[30] There, after a correct representation of the position of one of the leading theoreticians of the indirect power of the pope, Vitoria specifies his own position *per longum et latum*. He denies that the pope wields any direct political power. His mission is spiritual. But Vitoria also would have it that in order to achieve a spiritual end the pope has wide indirect power in temporal affairs. The condition is clear: solely in function of what is proper to him and in circumstances that so require the pope is permitted to interfere in the area of the political.[31]

Vitoria's assertion is altogether plain. Domingo de Soto is somewhat more nuanced. Soto is mistrustful of papal interventions in temporal matters. But when all is said and done, his conclusions resemble Vitoria's.[32] At the same time, we must be careful to keep in view in all of this the integral position of both of these great theologians. Their central thesis, like that of Las Casas, is that the pope is not the monarch of the world. His proper domain is that of the spiritual. In saying this, they have performed an important role in the theology of the sixteenth century.[33] But we have already noticed the slippery slope on which the theory of indirect power places us. In fact, the very notion of *power* causes one to fall into these consequences, however earnestly they may be presented as exceptional cases.

This seems to be what happens to Las Casas when he conducts his discussion on this level. He has been criticized for citing Vitoria and Soto in favor of his bold and risky theses on the legitimacy of papal interference in temporal affairs. As we see, however, he is not off the mark in appealing to these two thinkers (see *O.E.* 5:367b).[34] Their authority, with the further endorsement of a close friendship in the case of the second, weighs so heavily with Las Casas that he makes the doubtful asseverations that we have now examined.

This leads us to a second observation. Bartolomé presents his propositions concerning papal power in the course of a development of hypothetical and theoretical cases having no reference to the reality of the Indies or to Spanish dominion in those lands. The extraordinary circumstances of his imaginary cases are explicitly stated by Las Casas, such as those of a rejection in bad faith of the proclamation of the Christian faith or the unjust affliction of a ruler's subjects. But as we know, Bartolomé never allows these kinds of propositions to waft about in thin air waiting to be used by anyone who might be inclined to do so. With a scholar's rigor, he indicates that in the Indies these situations do not obtain. In those lands there is no such repudiation of the faith. Thus, his theoretical propositions are not applicable there. And he insists on this point in several ways. In practice, therefore, his hypothetical casuistry will have no repercussions in the places that provoke the Dominican's alert concern. Perhaps this is why he does not develop his own perception of the doctrinal aspects of the matter, but limits himself to declarations of principle supported by the professors of Salamanca. This observation may permit us a better comprehension of the specifically Lascasian perspective, of which we shall treat in the next section.

First, we must recall that Las Casas originally proposed to prove a second conclusion, to which the *Tratado comprobatorio* does not devote many pages. After all, it was the first point that had come under attack and that therefore called for a more extensive treatment. But the second does come in for abundant examination in other works. Its core is the indisputable legitimacy of the Indian nations' own political authority. The imperial dominion granted to the Spanish sovereigns that they might honor their charge to secure the proclamation of the gospel in no way entails the unseating of the native princes and rulers of the Indies. Indeed, these peoples have the right to accept or reject the authority of the European sovereigns. On this point, which is likewise dealt with in some of his earlier works, Las Casas in these same years will radicalize his position.

We shall return to the matter in this same chapter. For now, let us merely indicate that these rights of the native peoples enormously reduce the scope of any political implications in the papal mandate.[35] The fact that those rights are not explicitly acknowledged in the Alexandrine bull only strengthens Bartolomé's case. The pope had been under no obligation to state them, he is at pains to explain: they are obvious, inalienable, and founded in the best of Christian tradition. Consequently: "Of necessity, such grant, donation, letter, and bulls, by virtue of the tenor in which the pope makes and grants them, must be understood, interpreted, and declared in this sense, inasmuch as in the said documents it is neither expressed nor declared" (*O.E.* 5:420a).

The absence of this point from the papal text need afford no obstacle to the Spanish rulers' respect for the native rulers of the Indian nations. That text imposes an inescapable restriction on the dominion granted to the Spanish, a battlement that Las Casas will see to building ever higher and stronger.

A Position of His Own

In view of all of this, after the controversial assertions that we have reported, Las Casas continues to insist, in the same work, that the responsibility of the Roman pontiff is before all else a religious responsibility. In telling terms, he summarizes his position:

> Accordingly, the donation of those realms of these same unbelievers, which the Apostolic See has made and makes or might make to Christian princes, rests and is based solely upon the promulgation of the gospel and the spread of the faith and conversion and salvation of the unbelievers themselves and [is] for their temporal and spiritual good. And this is the cause and ultimate and final reason of the same. (*O.E.* 5:379b)

And not any temporal power of the pope.

Further on, employing the technical terms appropriate to the case, he defines the power he attributes to the pope as follows:

> The power held by the Supreme Vicar of Christ over temporal and secular goods and states (as has been proved above) is indirect and *per quamdam consequentiam* [by virtue of a particular implicit connection]: that is, with a view to and in regard of spiritual matters and to the extent that it is necessary for their attainment. (*O.E.* 5:403b–404a)

It is an indirect power in that it is a consequence of what his authentic area is (*ex consequenti*, as Juan de Torquemada had put it).

These texts must all be situated in their era. The terms have a ring of times gone by. Today we express ourselves very differently. Obviously, for example, the use of ambiguous terms in the various theories — direct, indirect, or directive power — is occasioned to a large extent by an appeal to the concept of "power" to designate the responsibility of the church on the dividing line between politics and ethics. (*Ratione peccati*, "by reason of sin," was another expression used to justify this "power.") Yves M.-J. Congar, in an article to which we have already referred, regards the formula "directive power" with a certain sympathy; but he astutely observes that the adjective would seem to cancel the substantive, so that what we ought to do is to get rid of the word "power." And Congar continues with an interesting suggestion: instead of speaking of a "directive power" perhaps we should speak of an activity, and not a power, in the temporal area.[36] The church works through consciences, not by way of coercive means.

When we view matters in this way, we perceive that the heart of the problem is still with us. Today it presents itself in the form of the following question. May the church have an opinion on social matters? The question has been posed ever since the social teaching of the church began to be voiced. In his latest social encyclical (*Centesimus Annus*), Pope John Paul II has once again insisted on the right of the church to intervene (from an ethical perspective) in secular affairs, something privileged groups have always looked upon with a jaundiced eye.[37] This right is inherent in the church's mission of evangelization. Not that the church has political programs or technical proposals to present. But the political and the social affect human beings. And the defense of the worth and dignity of human beings is an intrinsic part of the church's mission.

Let us return to Las Casas. We have yet to sketch out a more adequate outline of his thought. To this end, we shall find it useful to appeal to other Lascasian texts from more or less the same period, surely key years for the shaping of his position. In the *Apología*, read out in Valladolid in 1550 and subsequently revised, he reiterates his central thesis:

> The Sovereign Pontiff is not lord of the world, but the chief steward of the Supreme Prince and Universal Lord of all the world, inasmuch as in his area, that is, throughout the world and among all nations, by way of the cultivation of his apostolic teaching and in accordance with the prophecy of Jeremiah, he must establish virtue and make it prosper, and eradicate vice. (*Apología*, 180)

The text of Jeremiah refers to the Prophet's calling to proclaim the word (Jeremiah 1). But the word in question is one that renders a judgment on historical events. The pope must do this as chargé d'affaires, as "chief steward" (*mayordomo*) of Christ, not as a monarch in his own right. His function has been specified a number of lines earlier: the Lord has ordained that the sovereign pontiff "ensure the preaching of the gospel throughout the world" (ibid., 180). This is his proper and sole sphere of authority.

In a brief writing attributed to him (*Sobre el título del dominio del rey de España sobre las personas y tierras de indios*),[38] dating from 1554, Las Casas repeats a strong thesis from the *Apología:* War may not be waged on the Indians for reason of their idolatry. And he goes on:

> Nor can the Pope give such title or license to the sovereigns of Spain: *quia nemo dat quod non habet* [since no one gives what one does not have]. The Pope may send preachers throughout the world, and he has a faculty from Christ for this, but *not for depriving any king of his kingdom.*

The reason he advances is especially interesting: "because Christ lived poor and disavowed temporal realms, as he professed before Pilate: *Regnum meum non est de hoc mundo* ['My kingdom is not of this world']." Christ's poverty is incompatible with temporal power. It ought to be the same with those who continue his mission. The consequences, including the exceptions, are plain:

> To his successor St. Peter he left no faculty over the realms of the earth in the area of the temporal; although *per accidens* he might licitly interfere in the same. And since Christ gave him no such power, he does not have it by legacy, nor can he give anyone license to deprive their neighbors of their homes. Not even over the temporal goods of his subjects, who include only Christians, has he any sovereignty or power, except in certain rare and restricted cases.

And at once he adds: "...all the less where unbelievers are concerned." The pope may interfere in temporal affairs only *per accidens,* only incidentally: that is, only in special cases, which are even more rare in cases involving the unbaptized.

All of this frames and conditions something we already know: that the Spanish Crown has universal sovereignty in the Indies. But here Las Casas emphasizes a concept that, although it is substantially present earlier, he will continue to develop and from which he will conclude to bold propositions. "The title that His Majesty holds," he asserts, still in the text we are quoting, "is this one alone: that all, or the greater number, of the Indians should *of their own will* seek to be his vassals and regard it as an honor to themselves. Thus, His Majesty is the natural king of them as also of the Spaniards." The ultimate determinant in the matter is the free will of the Indians. We shall take up this point again below.

We find a third text in the "Long Letter" to Carranza, the *Carta grande a Carranza* (1555). To implement the papal mandate in the face of the crying outrages being committed in the Indies will now mean "to relegate the temporal welfare of the Sovereigns and the temporal, bodily, and spiritual welfare of the Spaniards, to second place, in order to rescue the temporal, bodily, and spiritual welfare of those realms and nations" (*O.E.* 5:440a).

Two objections arise at once, and Las Casas attempts to answer them. First, is it not too much to require of the Spanish rulers that they give more than they receive?[39] Second, would secular rulers not thereby be setting foot on spiritual ground, ground not their own? Las Casas is quite well aware, contrary to what we sometimes hear, that the spiritual realm is not his sovereigns' proper charge. But he regards the Indies as a case apart. Here the rulers have a papal mandate to assume a spiritual task. He writes: "It is mainly and directly incumbent upon the sovereigns to have care not of the souls of their subjects, but of what regards their peace and good moral customs, nor indeed all of these," he specifies, "but only civil [customs] which dispose a person to lead a good political life." This is the normal, proper order of things. Any exception will be in function of that normal, proper order:

> The care, charge, and offer given and committed to the sovereigns of Castile by the Church, and taken on by them of their own free will and by solemn public agreement, is mainly and directly for the purpose of laboring with supreme diligence, relegating to second place all things besides, for the conversion and salvation of those millions of souls, who have all of the necessary prerequisites to be converted and won to Jesus Christ. (1555, *O.E.* 5:440–41)[40]

In requesting the papal bull, the king and queen have freely accepted its terms and are under an obligation to comply with its demands.[41] At the same time, it is plain that we are dealing with a situation *sui generis*. Let us take careful note of the consequences of this Lascasian conviction.

A "Modal" Grant

As we peruse and ponder Bartolomé's texts on these subjects, we become convinced that an approach to them in terms of the centuries-old European debate will not be the only approach, or even the best one. True, Las Casas himself invites us to use it, with its world of citations from the jurists and theologians who debated the temporal power of the pope. But it is equally true that for our friar all of this is merely instrumental (in a nonpejorative sense). He had to make himself understood. And so he had to speak in the customary, received terms of the theology of the day. But he was always very sensitive to the *novelty* of the Indies and to the need to find responses, theoretical and practical, fitted to that reality.

In this quest he labels the papal grant made to the Spanish Crown "modal." He uses the term in the exordium of his *Tratado comprobatorio* in a passage that we have cited. And he returns to the expression at the end of his proofs for his "first conclusion," which, as we have said, takes up the bulk of this work. He does so in a lengthy section written mostly in Latin ("for scholars of the law," he specifies, *O.E.* 5:424b). The bishop of Chiapa avails himself of a technical legal expression.[42] The grant in question, he says, was neither "simple, nor absolute, nor mere" (*O.E.* 5:413a). It carries a condition, a charge, a proviso — a "mode." Unless this condition is observed, the grant will be invalid.

He is speaking of the Alexandrine bull. There is the grant, but with a charge: that of "introducing the Catholic faith and Christian religion into these lands and securing the conversion of those peoples" (*O.E.* 5:413b). Next he analyzes the papal text and specifies that it was this "mode" that moved the "Vicar of Christ to grant and donate the supreme civil authority, *otherwise* he would not have conceded or granted it, since he would not have been able to do so in conformity with law. This is readily seen," he adds emphatically, "from the frequent use of [the expression, 'in conformity with law'] throughout the treatise" (*O.E.* 5:415b–416a). Further on he repeats that since "the pope has no jurisdiction over temporal things, or concerning the area of the temporal, or over secular and worldly states, except for the sake of the spiritual — that is, *in ordine ad* the spiritual (as has been proved above)" (416a–b) — therefore the establishment of the sovereigns of Spain as supreme rulers of the Indies can only have been "for a very important reason, and one necessarily to be regarded as the final cause: that is, for spiritual good" (*O.E.* 5:416b).

It is his final word on the point. "This donation, consequently, is modal. And thus we have fully established our first conclusion" (ibid.). It is an onerous grant: the charge conditions its own implementation, prescribing particular guidelines for the comportment of the Spanish Crown. Furthermore, as we know, Bartolomé's "second conclusion" abides: the condition of a free acceptance of Spanish sovereignty by the dwellers of the Indies.

Our own interest, however, lies in our discernment of Las Casas's lucidity vis-à-vis the novelty of the Indies. He appeals to the theology and law of his time (what else could he do?), but he also seeks to be attentive to differentiating factors. When all is said and done, from a point of departure in the best elements of these disciplines he was able to confront his own particular, concrete problems in the light of the word of the Lord and the legacy of tradition. He perceives, of course, perhaps somewhat confusedly, that he must not confine himself to the repetition of interpretations developed in another historical context.

Bartolomé must do his thinking in terms of the Indies. His position on the meaning of Alexander VI's bull keeps account of the theology and law that have been bequeathed to him, as well as of the new reality and the intellectual challenge implied therein. Therefore, it seems to us, his position resists enmeshment in the involutions of traditional interpretations of the power of the pope, even of the one that had begun to appear in Europe at that time (that of direct power versus indirect power, as a medieval mentality began to cede to a modern one).[43] For Las Casas, what was at stake in the Indies, more than territory, were persons — children of God, to whom the gospel ought to be preached (his first intuition). Everything else must be subordinated to that task. Furthermore, those persons were to be protected from the oppression and outrages they had suffered for so many decades.

For these reasons, the pontifical donation of a superior sovereignty invested in the Crown becomes a conditional one, and from two sides. First, it has its meaning only as an instrument for evangelization. If there is no evangelization, or indeed if evangelization is not carried out appropriately (that is, peacefully and without harm to the Indians), the grant becomes ineffective and invalid. The sword of Damocles hangs over the right bestowed by the pope. Second, the right to dominion granted by the donation is likewise conditioned (and strictly conditioned) on an acknowledgment of the legitimacy of the authority of the natural, native rulers (Proposition 18 of the *Treinta proposiciones,* and second conclusion of the *Tratado comprobatorio*). Las Casas goes further still. It is not enough that the pope grant the dominion: *The Indians must freely accept it.* This is already sketched out in Proposition 19, but, as we shall see below, Bartolomé will correct it and radicalize it in the same year.

What we need to emphasize here is that under the knife of these two conditions the papal donation, and the dominion it implies, is whittled away. As Las Casas reworks the point, the nuances and distinctions grow. The papal donation evaporates almost to the point of disappearance.[44] Can we continue even to speak of a theocratic mentality? Or of the direct power of the pope? The least that must be said is that there are no precedents for this way of understanding things in the classic exposition of that interpretation of papal authority.

On the other hand, does the Lascasian conception fall purely and simply under the rubric of indirect power? Plainly the Dominican seeks to move in the direction of this second theory when he reasons within the framework of the European world. We think that, being abreast of the debates on the subject, he is able to weigh the various elements of these different theories, but he strives to develop a formulation of his own that will correspond to the reality of the Indies. That is the reason why his position is understood in such different and even contrary manners, as we have recalled.

It seems to us, then, that Las Casas's position resists classification in terms of the categories of the theology of law that were dominant in his age. To try to force them into those categories will only lead into a blind alley and contradictions. Our friar's reference is to reality: to the gospel and to his own experience. These dictate the object of his strivings: on one side, respect for faith and for the God who grants that faith as a grace; and on the other, the abused Indians, who are persons endowed with freedom and in whom Christ is present. His expressions are frequently juridical, but their sustenance is evangelical. His question is: how to satisfy the right of the autochthonous population to receive the gospel. After all, for Las Casas this is a right. That is the concern that governs his argumentation.

The pope has no direct power in the ambit of the temporal. He can only make a commission, impose a charge, of evangelization, and this charge must be implemented in respect for the freedom of its addressees. In other words, the papal donation to the Crown is conditioned by this assignment to evangelize, limited by an acknowledgment of the natural dominion of the autochthonous nations, and subject to the free acceptance of the Indians. These are all pieces of a single whole. They cannot be separated. To attempt to separate them would be to eviscerate our friar's precious synthesis. To pick them apart and examine them one by one would be to fail to understand Las Casas's effort, an effort undertaken in function of a new situation, of whose radical novelty perhaps no one was as acutely aware as he. Were we to try to take the various elements simply one by one and try to stuff them by turns into the pigeonholes of the various prevailing theories, we should indeed find inconsistency and contradictions. In order to perceive the unity of all of the elements of the Lascasian doctrine, we must see things from where Bartolomé has sought to take his stand. From that starting point, he has developed — in depth, gradually, and not without hesitation — an interpretation of the bull *Inter Caetera* and consequently of the Hispanic presence in the Indies, whose norm must be the requirements of the faith and the protection of the Indians. Theology is precisely the "intelligence of faith," and faith, according to St. Paul, works through charity, through love for our sisters and brothers.

For purposes of his interpretation, Las Casas has fused old elements with new ones. That had always been his forte. However, had he contented himself with merely stating that in conformity with the letter of the documents of Alexander VI and Queen Isabella, the Crown ought to seek the salvation and conversion of the Indians, he would not have gone beyond the mentality of his time, as formally asserted in these official texts. We need only think of the pontifical documents bearing on the Portuguese expeditions to Africa. These expeditions had originally been authorized as an undertaking of evangelization. That is the purpose for which they had been mandated by the pope. But once they were launched, the door was open wide for war on the African peoples.[45] By "formally" we do not necessarily mean insincere. But we do mean having little or no concrete impact on the treatment accorded the Indians, over whom dominion was thought to be held either because the pope had a temporal power to grant it, or for other reasons (right of discovery, or principle of sociability, for example).

Bartolomé's approach was entirely different. His first and last goal is not an abstract proposition, but a *criterion* that allows him to make judgment upon what is going on in New and Old World alike. The horror of the wars and oppression, all this Indian suffering, appear in all their raw realism in the light of what *ought* to have been done instead and what ought to be done now — in other words, in light of the reason why the Europeans are in the Indies at all. War and oppression tread elementary human rights underfoot. They also violate the one consideration that might have justified the presence of Christians in these lands. In combination, the two transgressions amount to a great offense to the God in whom these persons say they believe. Las Casas will remind them of this at every turn and on each occasion will draw concrete, exacting conclusions. Had he spoken solely of the missionary purpose (as did so many theologians in his time), his life would not have been filled with difficulties.

Against this background — and Las Casas's enemies must acknowledge it — we gain a better understanding of what Bartolomé has said in his *Confesionario.* To assert that everything that has been done in the Indies is "null, void, and without any validity or legal effect" (*Confesionario,* 1552, *O.E.* 5:239b) is to stand amid the facts. The facts of the case give the lie to any claim to a respect for "the purpose of this whole business" (*Aquí se contiene,* 1552, *O.E.* 5:347b). Unless the "mode," the commission, of the papal grant is observed, the grant itself ceases to have legal effect. It is not Las Casas, then, who denies the Spanish rulers' dominion; it is those who forget the reason why they are in the Indies and mistreat, slay, and oppress the inhabitants there. If there is lèse majesté and unpatriotism here, it is on the part of the Dominican's adversaries. Flawless.

Vitoria agrees with Las Casas that the finality of the papal bull is evangelization. But this is not the basis for his foundation of Spanish dominion in the Indies. The key principle of his own reasoning, as we have seen, is the principle of sociability. If Las Casas ties the universal sovereignty of the Crown as granted by the papal act to the proclamation of the gospel, it is because this gives him a warranty of protection and defense of the weakest of the weak. Sociability fails to do this, since, when all is said and done, it can legitimate acts of war and the domination of the native peoples. That is, Las Casas's foundation seems to him to be a better response to the exigencies of the gospel.

Las Casas does not abandon his interpretation of the Alexandrine bull (as we have seen, he was the first and most stubborn champion of this understanding of it) when he sees his patriotism and his loyalty to the Crown under attack, not even when he steps into the minefield of papal power in temporal affairs. In fact, it is precisely this understanding that keeps him from blowing up on his way through. He may lose a few feathers along the way, get stuck in a trap or two, hesitate at a fork in the road — but he forges ahead, fusing *hecho* with *derecho* — fact with right and law. For Bartolomé it is not a matter of the proclamation of the gospel in the abstract. We are dealing with its communication to the suffering, oppressed inhabitants of the Indies — in whom Christ is present.

The proclamation of the Reign of God is the first and last end of what ought actually to be happening in the Indies. Therefore it is this proclamation that provides the basis for reverence for the human dignity of those who dwell there. It is the right they have to hear of the universal love of God that founds a defense of that human worth.

3. *Consent of the Governed*

The extent and consequences of the right to receive the gospel freely will continue to provide Las Casas with material for reflection. As we said at the beginning of Part Five of this book, the Peruvian situation is an important factor in his view of the Indies. Indeed, his reflection on the Indians' right to receive the gospel persuades him to make a bold proposal for the redirection of that situation. His ideas will have repercussions in these lands for a long time. The case of Guamán Poma, understood within his own perspective, is particularly significant (see below, chapter 15). Before looking at what Bartolomé says about Peru, we should take notice of one of his most daring political intuitions: the voluntary acceptance of political authority, i.e., the consent of the governed, as a prerequisite for the legitimacy of that authority. This thesis is the foundation on which he builds his proposals for Peru.

Liberty of Peoples

We know of the central place in our Dominican's thought, from his first writings onward, held by his insistence on the Indians' freedom in light of their status as human beings. We have also seen his energetic position with regard to religious freedom and his insistence on a peaceful evangelization by persuasion and dialogue.[46] But, as always with his great intuitions, he continues to delve and never stops. As a result, some of the conclusions he draws can be unexpected.

The topic of freedom arises in terms of opposition to the exploitation that pervades the system of the *encomienda*. The connecting link is Las Casas's intuition that the use of force in the proclamation of the gospel is morally wrong. At first the defense of the freedom of every person, and that of the Indian in particular, merely renders certain forms of domination and colonization inadmissible. But gradually the Sevillian perceives implications that had not been clear to him at first. The pristine liberty of the inhabitants of the Indies will come to constitute an absolute condition of any manner of Hispanic presence among them. Unless that presence were to be accepted voluntarily by the Indian nations, it would be altogether bereft of legitimacy. Now it becomes important to specify that this holds even in a case where the Spanish Crown might comply with the requirements of the "modal donation," which we treated in the previous section. Only by way of the Indians' free decision can that grant become effective.

It is a long process through which Las Casas arrives in his final years at one of his deepest convictions and sharpest weapons in his defense of the Indian nations. He sketches the process in his important *Octavo remedio*.[47] He reiterates his thesis that the faith must be freely accepted "because God has left it in the hand and choice of each individual whether or not to be willing to receive it." Nothing may be done against the will of the Indians. All must be done "according to and in conformity with it, and with their approval and consent" (*O.E.* 5:94b–95a). From here he moves to the sovereignty of the king over his vassals, which "is based on the voluntary consent of the subjects" (*O.E.* 5:95b). The question of religious freedom leads him to that of political liberty.

And he will apply this to a concrete case: that of the *encomiendas*. In continuity with his previous assertions, but with new specifications, he maintains that one of the considerations that "render the [legal basis for the] *encomienda* null and void [is] the want of the consent of all those peoples, . . . who are doomed to lose their liberty, their souls, and their lives *in absentia*, without their being cited or appearing" (*O.E.* 5:108b). If this acceptance does not occur, the mandate received from the rulers of Spain is invalidated. After all, "the prince may never do anything prejudicial to the people without the people's consent" (*O.E.* 5:96a).[48]

In other words, the outrages and injustices entailed for the Indians by the *encomienda* are not the only reason why that system should be abolished. After all, that would still leave the door open — and how many persons of good walked through it in those days! — for tolerating a "good" *encomienda,* one on which the treatment of the natives would be more moderate. Bartolomé learns this lesson and carries his thinking further. It is not enough to reject the actual cruelties involved. One must strike at the root and repudiate the entire system. This is what is implied in his declaration that even though the *encomiendas* have been ordained by the Spanish Crown, if the Indian nations do not consent to this kind of labor (and they surely could not), then the *encomiendas* are not just. The proposition rests on a general principle: the prerequisite of the voluntary consent of the governed in order for any political regime to have legitimacy. The step the Sevillian has just taken is pregnant with consequences.

The following year he returns to the point with energy and clarity. Early in 1543, he sends a memorandum (co-signed by his great friend, Friar Rodrigo de Ladrada) to King Charles. It is a thick document, packed with perceptive observations. It recalls that the proclamation of the gospel is the sole purpose of a Hispanic presence in the Indies. This objective does not militate against the sovereignty of the "great peoples, polities, and communities such as are those of the Indies." Their "altogether just jurisdiction," Bartolomé asserts, taking an important theoretical step, is guaranteed by "natural law and the Law of Nations." Only when these peoples acknowledge "Your Majesty as universal sovereign," he says, "will this dominion be a dominion *in actu* ['in act,' actually], whereas it is now such *in potentia* [merely 'in potency,' merely potentially] insofar as notification to them is concerned." Then he specifies that, with their acceptance, "they will not lose their particular and general sovereignties, since our faith does not dispossess them of these. Rather, such will be confirmed: thus, the supreme sovereignty and universal jurisdiction of Your Majesty as king of Castile can be compatible with their particular or general sovereignties and jurisdictions" (*O.E.* 5:192a).

In the same memorandum, he has just said that the "sovereigns and *caciques* and peoples" must be invited "to consent of their own free will (since it concerns them all, and they cannot be deprived of what belongs to them by natural law, which is freedom) and their own consent, because they would be subject to Your Majesty" as "free peoples and vassals" (*O.E.* 5:183b).

Let us note that from these first formulations onward the notions of the supreme and universal sovereignty of the king of Spain and that of the voluntary consent of the people go hand in hand. Las Casas will maintain this bond and analyze it further. The second intuition, then, is not simply tacked on to the first for the sake of nuances and limitations. Actually we have but a single thesis: There is no sovereignty without popular consent.

In the last text cited, Bartolomé is appealing to an ancient juridical axiom going back to Roman law: "Quod omnes tangit, ab omnibus tractari et approbari debet." ("What affects all, must be known and approved by all.") In the Middle Ages, the maxim continued to be applied in its original context, that of private law. But it had begun to be applied to what today would be called public law as well. In the latter domain, the consent of all interested parties as a requirement for the validity of a particular norm appeared especially in the secular area. But there were those who sought to make it count in ecclesiastical affairs as well. Las Casas gives this principle unusual weight and extension. On its basis he posits a democratic coexistence of peoples as the only legitimate form of government. Moreover, this norm becomes of capital importance for an assessment of the justice of the Spanish presence in the Indies.[49]

Two Stages of Acceptance

In the texts that we have cited, Las Casas's enunciations are declarations of principle. There is no beating around the bush: The consent of the governed is required for the legitimacy of royal jurisdiction. Thus far he has not distinguished between two potential stages in the acknowledgment of the dominion of the king of Spain over the Indies — before and after his potential subjects' possible conversion to Christianity. He will do so, much later, in Proposition 19 of his *Treinta proposiciones*. There he will declare the natives to be "under an obligation" to recognize the sovereigns of Castile only after having received the faith, and not before.[50] Here the bishop of Chiapa establishes a principle in virtue of which any first contact with the dwellers of these lands must be moderate and peaceful (like all evangelization, for him). Thereby he takes a position at the opposite pole from those, like Sepúlveda, who postulated that the Indians must *"first* be subjected to the sovereigns of Castile, and *then* have the gospel preached to them" (*Aquí se contiene*, 1552, O.E. 5:316b; emphasis added).[51]

Las Casas's argumentation is roughly based on the concept that once the Indians have accepted the faith freely, through dialogue and persuasion, they will come under the jurisdiction of the church. Such dominion is thus added to the church's responsibility to protect them. But this in turn will entail on the part of a Christian ruler obligations with regard to the neophytes. (We must not forget that this is one of Vitoria's "legitimate titles" for the continued presence of the Crown in the Indies.) And these obligations will necessarily correspond to some right over the natives. Bartolomé seems to see himself restricted to this position by the bull *Inter Caetera*.[52] But he will soon perceive the risks for the cause he defends that lurk in the distinction he has introduced. Sepúlveda himself will undertake to show him these. In his *Apología* Las Casas offers a detailed commentary on the papal bull. The text speaks of "subjection," which ought to be interpreted, our friar says, as a "civil and Christian" one (*Apología*, 250v). It denotes a human relationship that respects the "human rights" of all (*Tratado sobre los indios,* 1552, *O.E.* 5:268b).[53] The submission in question "will spring from the gentle, meek preaching of the divine word" (*Apología*, 252).[54] That is, it will keep pace with the process of evangelization.[55]

Sepúlveda is shocked: "To say, as he [Las Casas] says that they are to be subjected not at the beginning, but only after being made Christians, is altogether mistaken" (*Aquí se contiene,* 1552, *O.E.* 5:315b). In Sepúlveda's view, subjugation should come first, then evangelization. Bartolomé's considerations are self-contradictory, he holds: if the king may use armed force to require obedience of the Indians who have become Christians (and therefore have accepted his authority), why may he not wage war on them from the outset, and for weightier reasons?[56] It is nonsense, then, to make a "distinction between these two stages" (ibid.). This was surely not the purport of the Lascasian propositions. At first Bartolomé replies that his opponent confuses the two stages that he had distinguished (see *Aquí se contiene, O.E.* 5:341b).[57] Our friar recalls the traditional teaching on this point: Christians are more restricted in their behavior in the first case, since they are dealing with persons who have never accepted the faith.[58] Thus the contradiction his adversary seems to see is chimerical.

But the foregoing response must have seemed inadequate to Bartolomé. In the published texts of the debate with Sepúlveda, he adds quite an extended section in the very framework of his Twelfth Reply.[59] The objection — along with, perhaps, his own brief initial response — has shown him that he must offer a more profound and precise response. He introduces a new distinction. It is one thing, he now says, to reject the supreme and universal authority of a monarch (even though it may have been proposed by the pope), and quite another to abandon the faith. If the former occurs, "it does not therefore follow," he now observes, "that war may be waged on them (as Doctor Sepúlveda says) while they abide in the faith and the observance of justice" (ibid., *O.E.* 5:342b). In other words, being a Christian and being a subject of the king of Spain are not equivalent. The Indians need not be vassals of the Spanish sovereigns in order to be followers of Jesus. The important thing is that they keep the faith and practice justice. This is all that counts.

For that matter, the supreme sovereignty postulated by Sepúlveda is but a means (in conformity with the historical conditions of the age) at the service of the presence of the gospel in the Indies. If it becomes "harm, catastrophe [*ruina*], and destruction," or if it is more calculated to serve the "interests and advantage of the sovereign than the common good and utility of the subjects, then it becomes by natural reason and by all human and divine laws...utterly detested and detestable" (ibid.). The possibility cannot be excluded.

This line of reasoning concludes with the most important assertion of Bartolomé's entire book: "And in this sense *I understand, declare, and limit Proposition Nineteen,*...in which I say that the rulers, sovereigns, and communities of that order of the Indies are under an obligation to recognize as sovereign rulers and imperial governors the King and Queen of Spain" (ibid.; emphasis added).[60] Here is a categorical correction of Bartolomé's earlier formulation.[61] It is due to his adversary's having seen the need for it. It flows from the distinction between Christian and subject: A free acceptance of the faith does not oblige one to acquire the condition of subject of the king of Spain. The Indians retain their liberty to accept or reject that authority.

The rectification seemed so important to Las Casas that he solemnly repeated it in his *De Thesauris*. "We desire that what we have said in our *Tratado comprobatorio del derecho real* be *understood and corrected.*" He proposes that there be added to the "proof of the first conclusion" of that tractate: "...after they have given their free consent, as is prescribed." He likewise writes an annotation to Proposition 19: "In this paragraph," he says significantly, "it *seems* to be presupposed that after having received baptism, if they fail to make such acknowledgment, they might be compelled to make it and punished" if they resist. Bartolomé says, "seems," as he wishes to make it understood that this was not even his original intent; but, Sepúlveda's interpretation has shown him the ambiguity of his own text. And so he wishes that "this text be understood as follows: that neither *after* baptism, any more than *before*, if they are unwilling to accept our sovereigns," may anyone oblige them to do so, since "they have the right to consent to or dissent from the above-cited papal disposition in both states in which they find themselves, those antecedent and subsequent to their conversion" (pp. 96v-97; emphasis added).

Being and Not Being in the Indies

The correction written by Bartolomé for his Proposition 19 has caused us momentarily to swerve off course, from an examination of Bartolomé's replies to Sepúlveda of 1552 to a consideration of our friar's next-to-last book of 1563. Between those two dates, Bartolomé ruminated on the question of popular consent, and it matured in his mind. In the *Tratado comprobatorio* he reiterates the importance of the consent of the governed for the legitimacy of any political authority. No one can wrest this right from a people, he says.[62] We find the same point expressed more forcefully in another treatise, also published in 1552: the *Principia Quaedam.*[63] In it Bartolomé only lays down a series of principles, without making any express allusion to the reality of the Indies. The key concept of the book is that of human freedom, both individual freedom and the liberty of a people as such. In this work he tersely founds his democratic theory of power: Only "through choice on the part of the people has any just dominion or jurisdiction of rulers over persons, throughout the world and among all nations, ever arisen" (*Tratados,* 1245).

Three years later in his letter to Carranza he returns to the point, but this time to include the specification he has enunciated in the Twelfth Reply. The king of Spain must be acknowledged by the Indians "as emperor over their many kings, *after* being converted to the faith and becoming Christians" — the Indian rulers as well as their subjects — and the acknowledgment must be made "of their own free will and not coerced through violence or force" (*O.E.* 5:444b–445a; emphasis added).[64] Throughout, that for which Bartolomé strives is respect for the rights of the Indian nations to their lawful possessions[65] and their own political leaders. This will also contribute to their being offered the gospel peacefully.[66] Bartolomé perceives that these different elements are intertwined in such a way that they reinforce each other. There can be no evangelization by dialogue and persuasion without respect for the persons, customs, and traditions of nations.[67]

What is occurring in the Indies places him, however, in a situation that the Sevillian can express only as "this contradiction in terms of the Spaniards being, and not being, in the Indies" (ibid., *O.E.* 5:447a). And he explains. The Spaniards *are* present in the Indies in terms of the supreme sovereignty of the Spanish sovereigns and *are not* present there in the sense of a negative presence, by which they "hinder and corrupt the faith and religion of Christ with their exceedingly corrupt deeds and lethal example" (ibid.). He ends with the proposal that "they all be ejected, except for a few carefully chosen individuals, that the Indians may receive the faith." This, he repeats, he proposes "before Jesus Christ if need be and is the best imaginable thing that could be provided." In fact, if the conditions previously maintained are allowed to prevail, the "sovereign jurisdiction of the rulers of Spain" will be "superfluous" to the Indians (*O.E.* 5:439b).

Let us briefly recapitulate and fine-tune what we have so far presented in this section before addressing a case of the application of the principles laid down. From a point of departure in his first intuitions concerning human liberty, and consequently that of the Indians, Las Casas rejects the servitude of the *encomienda* and the forced imposition of the Christian faith. A voluntary acceptance of the faith, supported by a thousand arguments (see his *De Unico*), is the fertile soil in which he roots his notion that the voluntary consent of a people is the necessary condition (or "efficient cause," as he will often call it, using Aristotelian language) for the legitimacy of any political authority or of the decisions made by that authority.[68]

The tree grows higher and stronger and supports (and conditions) the thesis of the supreme sovereignty of the king of Spain, which has been taking shape against the background of another intuition: evangelization alone justifies the Hispanic presence in the Indies. Both vectors converge to yield a bold stand: as long as there is no consent on the part of the Indian nations, the dominion of the Spanish monarch (and this, for Las Casas, is the meaning of the *Inter Caetera*) is one "in potency" only, and not "in act."[69]

Severely questioned by his adversaries, Bartolomé seeks to explain the difficult — and new — theses he maintains. For this he transports a notion from canon law to the area of the political. *Before* baptism, unbelievers are not under the jurisdiction of the church. They are, however, *after* having accepted the faith, since at this moment they become part of the ecclesial body. Our friar then advanced the notion that in the former stage they are outside not only the jurisdiction of the church, but *also the royal dominion;* but in virtue of the papal mandate to the king they fall under it in the second stage. The Valladolid disputation will show him the danger inherent in this assertion. He corrects it immediately, and with all the clarity that one could wish. Was the initial assertion the result of some inadvertence, or was it a tactical ploy under heavy fire? Conjecturing as to someone's intentions can be like finding a needle in a haystack. There are so many possibilities. One thing is certain: the rectification comes hard on the heels of the discussion and, even more strikingly, was published along with the expression to be modified. Both declarations, then, became publicly known *simultaneously.*[70] It therefore seems to us that what we are seeing here is a maturation of thought. We are not denying that there is a new departure, a radicalization, in Las Casas's ideas here. But the elements of continuity are equally clear.

The stumble at Valladolid gave greater scope to his democratic thesis on the origin of power. He is now in a position to make an important leap. He will do so in three important works that it will be useful to examine together. There is a relationship among them that does not always appear at first blush. The challenge of Peru will draw his bow and sharpen his aim.

4. Restoration of the Inca

Apart from the texts from the treatise *Principia Quaedam*, those that we have cited thus far concerning the democratic theory of political power bespeak an unmistakable relationship with the reality of the Indies. Something similar occurs with the trilogy of works that we are about to examine. The first, chronologically speaking, is the *De Regia Potestate* ("On Royal Power").[71] It is a very unusual document, in that it deals with its subject from a purely doctrinal and theoretical viewpoint, without explicit allusion to the Indies. This case is different with the other two: the *De Thesauris* and the *Doce dudas,* which are devoted explicitly to Peruvian questions. However, there is a connecting thread, and despite appearances it runs through all three. Furthermore, truth to tell, neither the *Principia Quaedam* nor the *De Regia Potestate* are really foreign to "that most broad universe and extensive orb of those Indian oceans" (*Tratado comprobatorio,* 1552, *O.E.* 5:409b). Las Casas's concern for the Indies is always translated into concrete projects. One of the last was that of the restoration of the Inca in Peru.

Peru, Unhappy Land

The treatise *De Regia Potestate* opens with the establishment of the solid principle of the primordial liberty of all persons, which includes freedom as to lands and other possessions (see bk. 1, ch. 1). All political authority must take this into account (see bk. 3, ch. 1). Upon this foundation rests the second principle: "Never has subjection or servitude or charge been laid on any people but that that people voluntarily consented to it" (bk. 4, ch. 1), writes Bartolomé. And he specifies: "All authority, power, and jurisdiction of kings, princes, or of any high magistrates who impose taxes and tributes proceed from the free people" (bk. 4, ch. 2).

Human freedom and its political consequences with regard to consent, then, are the underpinnings of Las Casas's position on political authority. The crucial importance of the consent of the governed is the core of this treatise. All depends on the free acceptance of the (potential) subjects. "The people," he says, "naturally and historically, are antecedent to kings" (bk. 4, ch. 4). Accordingly, the agreement of the people will be necessary for the legitimacy of public measures taken within any polity (see bk. 4, ch. 6). The power of kings and queens has as its finality the "securing of the common good of peoples," without prejudice to their liberty (bk. 5, ch. 1).

Slowly but surely, Bartolomé is moving closer to the matter that interests him. He asks: "If a king has a number of kingdoms, are these obliged to come to one another's assistance in case of war?" And he answers: Only if it may be without detriment to the kingdom affording the assistance, and with the voluntary endorsement of its people (bk. 6, ch. 1). What Las Casas has in mind is doubtless the matter of the perpetuity of the *encomienda,* whereby King Philip hoped he could alleviate the economic difficulties of his European possessions. The controversy over the *encomiendas,* which raged so hotly in Peru, constitutes the background of the *De Regia.*[72] For that reason, a considerable part of the work is devoted to proving that the king may not alienate his subjects' property to their detriment without their approval; least of all may he alienate those subjects themselves (see bks. 8, 12). This is a "natural and divine right" on the part of those subjects (bk. 13, ch. 1).

The *De Regia* is surely one of the high points in the development of Las Casas's democratic thesis, whose ancient roots we have recalled.[73] Despite the solemn trappings of its academic style and its plethora of scholarly references, the tractate is scarcely an innocuous one in a context of the overheated polemics of the problems of the Indies. It is the longest and most biting approach to this question in the Lascasian corpus (together with the *Doce dudas,* on the latter score). The greater part of the treatise is devoted to it. The theme of popular consent runs all through its pages. This affords its author the opportunity to sum up the central theses of his thought. It stands, then, as his last will and testament.

Without the consent of the governed, the papal mandate making the sovereigns of Spain universal sovereigns of the Indies can have no effect. Entering upon an examination of this point, Las Casas here distinguishes three stages in the condition of unbelievers: *before* becoming Christians, *after* being baptized, and a third stage, with which we shall not concern ourselves here: *after having* "suffered at the hands of the Spaniards invasions, wars, catastrophes," and other oppression (*De Thesauris,* 83). His thesis with regard to the first stage is plain: "As long as those people were unbelievers, it was illicit for our Sovereigns to oblige them to give the consent in question" (ibid.).

The second stage is more important, and Bartolomé dwells on it at length. He enunciates the conclusion that he will prove, which will be along the lines of the correction he has first introduced in his Twelfth Reply. "It is illicit for anyone to punish or molest those people, after their conversion, with temporal or ecclesiastical penalties, for having refused to give the consent in question or to accept the papal establishment of our Sovereigns" (ibid., 85v). Among the arguments he adduces in support of this assertion, we shall find it interesting to emphasize one that sheds a great deal of light on Bartolomé's viewpoint.

To this thesis, he says, "serious objection" could be raised. It can be formulated as follows: "Inasmuch as the Christian faith implies an acknowledgment of the authority of the Pope in the church, and as this authority has been exercised in the commission entrusted to the sovereigns of Spain to proclaim the gospel in the Indies, it would seem that it ought to be obeyed in this case as well." Thus, the new Christians must offer it "their free consent, just as to the other articles of faith." They fall into heresy, then, unless they believe, and into contumacy unless they obey (ibid., pp. 92–92v).

The objection is without foundation, responds the Sevillian. The domain of the pope is that of faith and morals. Here "the Church cannot err, nor consequently can its head, as head" (ibid., 92v). But in other questions ("positions and determinations referring to particular facts, as to property, crimes, etc.") "the Pope can err, since he is following reason, which can err, as St. Thomas says. Accordingly, there are cases in which the judgment of the Church can be erroneous and inculcate error." Now, the case before us "does not pertain to faith or good morals." Whence it follows that the papal grant to "the sovereigns of Spain...*is neither included in nor founded on faith* or divine law or natural reason." It functions on another level: "It is a particular determination of human law, which can be made," Las Casas specifies, "in different manners and depends on *human will*, that is, on the human will of the Pope" (ibid., 93v; emphasis added). It is not a matter of faith. Thus, the papal decision may be accepted or not by one who has received baptism.

Now everything is in its proper place. Not every determination of the pope obliges the faithful under pain of sin. Neither in the articles of faith, nor in Scripture, "nor in the teaching of the Church," Bartolomé writes, "do we find a basis for any universal sovereignty of the rulers of Spain over that world [of the Indies] for the purpose of seeing to the preaching of the faith there, nor [do we find there] that the Pope can grant this" universal sovereignty. Consequently, "those nations are not obliged to believe that the Pope can appoint our sovereigns universal sovereigns of their own world" (ibid., pp. 94–94v). Such a duty prevails only in matters of faith.

These important considerations on the substance and the various levels of the papal magisterium support, in the *De Thesauris*, Bartolomé's correction of the celebrated Proposition 19 (as well as what is stated in the *Tratado comprobatorio*). We have had occasion to see the apposite texts in the *De Thesauris* (see pp. 96v–97). The important thing for the moment is this new step taken by Las Casas in his reflection on the papal donation. With it he infuses with new vitality a conclusion he has already advanced, which he now presents on the basis of a juridical distinction: As long as the Indian nations "do not freely consent to the establishment" decreed in the pontifical bull, the Spanish sovereigns have only a "right in the matter" (*jus ad rem*), and not a "right to the thing" in question (*jus in re*) (ibid., 101).[74] The transition from the one to the other is pending, depending on the will of the population of the Indies. Thus, the Dominican specifies a bit further on, in the absence of this consent the sovereigns "lack the more important right" (ibid., 103).[75]

These are not mere declarations of principle. Where it is a matter of the Indies, Las Casas never speaks in the conditional. He knows the facts too well for that. The consent in question has never at any moment occurred in these lands. "The obedience that until today and up to now has been offered is and has always been owing to violence and involuntary, and all see themselves coerced to offer it" (ibid., 106; see also 120) — except in Verapaz, the friar adds. The conclusion is simple and sharp: None of the concrete conditions for the validity of the papal grant are at hand, so that it has never been in force.[76] We might as well be back in 1493, since the "most important right" has been prevented from its exercise. There has been no free acceptance of Spanish sovereignty on the part of the Indian nations.[77] The papal grant continues to be "in suspension and pending" (ibid., 127).[78] And so in one of his last texts Bartolomé will say that up to the moment the king of Spain is universal sovereign of the Indies "in name only," since, he vigorously concludes, the Spaniards who are there "have usurped" those Indies (*Memorial al Consejo*, 1565, *O.E.* 5:537b).

Titu Cusi, the Inca

The most trenchant document of this great trilogy is the *Doce dudas*, the "codicil" of Bartolomé's last will.[79] In it he discusses the solutions he sees for the situation of the Indies: restitution, defensive war, consent of the governed. He deals with all three, but he spends more time on the first and third. It is these that lead him to his concrete proposals here. Las Casas carries his demands of restitution further in this writing than anywhere else in the corpus of his works. Restitution becomes the key to the "remedy" he postulates for the Indies. In the course of his battle, he has been broadening the field of application of this requirement. His last effort along these lines will be in this text. The Indians have been despoiled not only of their goods, their human rights, and the respect due their human dignity; they have also been stripped of their legitimate political leaders. For Bartolomé, the duty of restitution involves something comprehensive and radical: the restoration of the empire of the Incas.

Here is where the vector that we have just examined, that of the consent of the native population, converges with the one presently under consideration.[80] Bartolomé's sixth principle addresses this point, with annotations that will be to our profit to observe.[81] We shall follow the "Providence" version here, which develops this postulate more extensively.[82] Las Casas opens with an enunciation of the thesis to be defended:

> In order that our Sovereigns may attain to a just possession of the supreme rulership over the Indies with legitimacy, that is, in consideration of rights and due circumstances, it is a necessary requisite that a consent of the rulers and peoples of that world intervene — that these give their consent to the institution or donation bestowed upon our Sovereigns by the Apostolic See. (*Doce dudas*, folio 155)

We are already familiar with the arguments Las Casas will now adduce in support of this proposition. But amid the repetitions, he sometimes adds the unexpected. For example, now he proposes that the free consent of these nations "be asked and obtained *judicially*" (f. 156; emphasis added).[83] Thus, a legal obligation would supervene.

Furthermore, Bartolomé makes an urgent appeal to Scripture. He finds "two juridical processes" in the designation of the kings of Israel: one on the part of God, who selects someone, and the other "on the part of the people," who "voluntarily receive the one selected by God, and it is the people who freely ratify this" (f. 156v). In other words, divine providence does not force a king on the people. It respects the will of the members of a nation. As illustrations he cites the cases of Saul and David. In both, the people intervene to confirm the divine election. The same should be the case in the Indies with the donation made to the rulers of Spain.[84]

Comprehensive restitution and the need for a voluntary consent are the twin pillars of a daring and very concrete proposal: the restoration of the legitimate heir of the Incas, Titu Cusi, to the throne of his ancestors. Las Casas offers this suggestion in bringing his treatise to a conclusion, and does so in detail. He even indicates the person who ought to go in search of the Inca in the place where he has taken refuge: "that cleric who was vicar general [of the See] of Cuzco" (f. 119v).[85]

"Our Lord the King is obliged under pain of salvation, then," he says peremptorily, "to restore those realms to King Titu, the successor or heir of Guayna Cápac and the other Inca lords, and to repose in him all his power and authority" (f. 218).[86] In view of this, the envoy should declare to Titu that "it is in his hand to consent or not to consent" to the "institution that the Apostolic See has made to the sovereigns of Castile and León of that universal empire" (f. 220). Titu is free to do so or not, but if he does so, it must be under appropriate conditions. He must therefore desist from "all terrorism and all deceit" (ibid.). If he persists in terrorism, "we shall do nothing, for everything will be utterly and absolutely null" (ibid.). There would be no free act.

In order to reach an accord, the king of Spain must promise *"good government* in every way," of these peoples: respect for their "laws, statutes, and customs that were not against the Christian faith and religion, their status and freedom," together with the restitution of "all of those peoples that His Majesty now holds, and those possessed by the *encomenderos*" (ff. 220–220v; emphasis added). For his own part, King Titu must acknowledge the aforesaid sovereignty and in the manner of the age send the rulers of Spain "certain jewels in gold and silver" (f. 220)[87] — a symbolic tribute, the expression of an accord that must put an end to the injustices being experienced in Peru. One of those injustices is precisely the demand on the people of a tribute to the Spanish rulers over and above that offered by them to their own legitimate political authorities (see f. 224v).

What Las Casas proposes for Peru he understands as valid in one way or another for all the Indies (see f. 226). We are reading of a comprehensive project of restitution to the Indian nations and, consequently, of their liberation.

Chapter 14

Two Deceptions

The writing we know as the *Yucay Opinion* (*Parecer de Yucay*, 1571) is an important source of information for the discussions in the theology of law occasioned in Peru by the Spanish presence in the Indies. The original text is to be found in the Madrid National Library and has been published in *Colección de documentos para la historia de España* under the following heading: "Copy of a letter that, according to a note, was to be found in the general Indies archive, which we have corrected against another that we have under our hand, treating of the true and legitimate dominion of the Rulers of Spain over Peru, and impugning the opinion of Father Friar Bartolomé de Las Casas."[1] The heading is accurate. What we have here is indeed a criticism intended to demolish the positions maintained by Las Casas. The author does not affix his name to his "opinion," but he testifies that he writes from Yucay, a place near Cuzco, in the very heart of the Tawantinsuyu. Today the author is thought to be García de Toledo, a Dominican and a cousin of the viceroy of Peru.[2]

1. Inca Sovereignty and Idolatry

The document acknowledges and decries the influence the writings of Bartolomé de Las Casas have had on discussion of the policy of the Spanish Crown in the Indies. It therefore enters upon a polemic against these writings in terms of the series of problems being experienced in Peru at the time. Those called at that time the *peruleros* — the conquistadors, *encomenderos*, and functionaries of these lands of Peru — had little love for Bartolomé. Actually, the New Laws (1542), of Lascasian inspiration,[3] provoked the energetic protest of the *encomenderos* throughout the Indies. But nowhere did that reaction reach the pitch of turbulence that it did in Peru with Gonzalo Pizarro's rebellion and its aftermath.

Bartolomé de Las Casas, who always had a special concern for

396

what was occurring in Peru, was therefore a particularly controversial figure in these realms. The *Yucay Opinion* stands as a testimonial to this fact. The composition is both an attempt to refute the key theses of the bishop of Chiapa and a judgment upon his intentions. Its historical context is the Peruvian situation in those years. The Yucay document enters the scene as the antithesis of the Lascasian *Doce dudas*.

All Due to One Person

The *Yucay Opinion* is one of the tracts commissioned by Viceroy Francisco de Toledo in his effort to demonstrate the legitimacy of Spanish dominion in the Indies. At stake is "all the good or evil" that is occurring in these lands. Its author opens his memorandum with the following words:

> Your Excellency commands me to give him my opinion concerning a thing that I have observed and considered with great diligence: the [question of the] dominion of the Incas, and that of His Majesty in these realms, in which consists the foundation of all of the good or evil of the Indies, as shall be shown below. I obey Your Excellency, first, because to do so will be a thing of service to God and His Majesty, whom Your Excellency so reverences in matters great and small, as well as because thus I have been commanded by Your Excellency, whom, after those two, I most desire to serve on earth. (*Yucay,* 105)[4]

In the final third of the century, native resistance plus Las Casas's disturbing proposals have made of the turbulent Peruvian situation the place and moment of a decisive option for all the Indies. There the whole affair is at stake. With this in mind, the author, good "servant" that he is, proposes to develop three points: the alleged legitimacy of the Incas' sovereignty, the harm that that sovereignty has caused, and the reasons warranting Spanish dominion in the Indies.

A study of this document, if we compare it with the other works commissioned by the viceroy in these same years, will present us with the interpretation of the Christian message to which it appeals in support of the Toledo regime established in Peru in the last third of the sixteenth century.[5] That theology collides with the one Las Casas, who had long ago joined the group of Dominicans on Hispaniola, maintained all his life. The theology of the *Yucay Opinion* is akin to the position of Ginés de Sepúlveda, the great adversary of the bishop of Chiapa, and dovetails at certain moments with some of the stances taken by Francisco de Vitoria.[6]

The first point the author of the *Parecer* proposes to treat is the question of "by what door a deception so great has entered almost all the world as that which would attribute to these Incas an authentic, legitimate sovereignty in these realms" (*Yucay*, 105). In his judgment, a second "deception" accrues to the first. It lurks in the "idolatry" in which the Indians have lived prior to the coming of the Europeans:

> And I believe that it is the most subtle deed of the devil suddenly to have persuaded the world of this deception. After the first in which he held this wretched, idolatrous people, no one has been under nor seems to discover in the Indies a greater one than this, which he has perpetrated on the world by a man who is a religious. (*Yucay*, 106)

To the falsehood of idolatry, then, which comes from the Indians, is now added a new lie, fomented by Las Casas: the legitimacy of Inca sovereignty.[7]

García de Toledo will attempt to show throughout his memorandum that the second deceit occasions the Indians' relapse into the first. After all, he explains, if the king of Spain were to withdraw from these lands, their inhabitants would return to idolatry. Intend it or no, Las Casas collaborates with this return. The author of the *Opinion* proposes to avoid it at all cost. The discussion centers on the question of idolatry.

If this situation is to have a remedy, it will be necessary to point the accusing finger, ruthlessly, at the person who is the source of all the ill:

> The cause of this enormous deception of the Emperor's Majesty and his Council and his viceroys and governors and Audiencias and of theologians and holders of great university chairs and preachers and, finally, of all of Christendom, indeed all of the faithful, has been one person who was wrong. That was a friar of St. Dominic called Friar Bartolomé de Las Casas. (*Yucay*, pp. 105–6)[8]

Against him and his work this memorandum is being penned.[9]

He is only one person. But how many he has been able to deceive! "He had good qualities. He was a very good religious. But when it came to the Indies, he was much overcome with passion and, in the most substantial of those affairs, much deceived" (*Yucay*, 106), says the viceroy's cousin. And that passion led him to falsify reality, to which enterprise he bent stubborn, cunning efforts, thereby winning approval of his viewpoint from respectable persons of lofty authority in Indian affairs.

> The abominable conclusions, corollaries, and inferences drawn by that Father from his false documents were mixed in with others that were well drawn and rigorous, thereby terrifying the

Emperor, the Council, the *encomenderos*, the friars, the bishops, the confessors, and for that matter all of the theologians in Spain, the students and teachers and professors, the chapters of the religious houses, the universities — with all of them approving his false doctrine, opinions, and conclusions on the strength of the false information he had given them all to the effect that a legitimate sovereignty lay with these Incas and native chiefs. (*Yucay*, 111)[10]

The consensus the intrigant has managed to gain is impressive, and García de Toledo acknowledges his argumentative logic and ability to persuade. Unfortunately, all of this is placed in the service of a wicked cause.

A Disillusioned Lascasian

To concentrate his fire, the author focuses on Bartolomé's propositions concerning political legitimacy in Peru. On this point, he says, Las Casas thought matters stood "as he was literally reporting them, as if he had seen them, or," the viceroy's cousin admits, "as perhaps they might be elsewhere, where he had actually been" (*Yucay*, 111). Curiously, the last clause seems to leave open the possibility of an authentic native sovereignty in other places of the Indies, of which Las Casas may have had direct knowledge. Thus, as raw possibility, it is suggested that Friar Bartolomé's argumentation might perhaps be applicable to other cases and other Indian rulers. But not here in these lands. The *Yucay Opinion* insists on Las Casas's ignorance of Peru, "where he has never come in his life, although they say he twice intended to, setting sail without being able to reach his destination" (*Yucay*, 106).[11] Accordingly, what was happening here "he knew only by hearsay" (*Yucay*, iii). Consequently Las Casas is not entitled to an opinion on the realm of Peru.

The author's own case, he goes on, may serve as an illustration of Friar Bartolomé's powerful influence over others. We are actually reading the words of an old Lascasian, he says, but one who had grown disillusioned on closer acquaintance with the reality of the Indies. "I was one of those who most believed him," he says, "and to whom it seemed worst to deprive these individuals of their dominion, until in Peru I saw the contrary, along with other instances of the blindness" afflicting those who had credited Bartolomé (*Yucay*, 113). Contact with the Peruvian situation — of which he says Las Casas is ignorant — has changed the way of thinking of the Dominican religious who arrived in Peru as a member of Viceroy Toledo's family, we read. Little is known of his life, and so we do not know in what his so-called Lascasianism may have consisted while he was still in Spain.

Ignorance of the facts was now joined by poor scholarship. "This friar, before becoming a religious, was a secular cleric with a licentiate in law. He had not studied theology" (*Yucay*, 106).[12] And this makes Las Casas's great influence all the more surprising: "...since, as he had such authority with the Council, he needed only to approve or disapprove a thing, whether it were in an ecclesiastical or in a secular matter, and that is what would be done on the strength of the credit he enjoyed with His Majesty" (*Yucay*, 113). A number of times the author remarks this weakness on the part of the Council of the Indies — and on the king's, as well — when it came to Las Casas (see *Yucay*, 108, 112, 113). Had it not been for that, despite Bartolomé's being a "friar, and a good one" (*Yucay*, 107), and despite his "good life and his authority as a bishop" (*Yucay*, 112, 113), things would not have come to the pass that "almost nothing was decided by the Council; everything was up to him" (*Yucay*, 107). The greater Las Casas's influence, the greater the danger.

As an example of the authority enjoyed by Las Casas, the author cites the promulgation of the New Laws, so detested by Peru's *encomenderos*. Bartolomé's efforts to obtain them had to be viewed in the context of the restless friar's longstanding battle with the new owners of the Indies. And the author talks about Bartolomé's harsh disputes with the *encomenderos* and royal functionaries in defense of the Indians. He concedes that these can be partly explained by certain abuses and problems in the first years of the Spanish presence in the Indies. But he thinks that all that is a thing of the past now and that one ought to be able to rise above all the squabbling. "At first there was so much abuse of these natives, and, with well-placed zeal, he defended them." However, "he seems to have been so excitable with these laity, in this defense, and they with him, that neither side deserved to be believed" (*Yucay*, 106). There were abuses at first. Then things changed.

Thus, neither the *encomenderos* nor Bartolomé are to be trusted, especially the latter:

> After all, nothing so hobbles the attempt to persuade persons to undertake such a grand and unusual business as does this excitability and passion. It used to shoot out of this religious's eyes and mouth. He would downright sputter when he spoke of these lay people. So devoid of modesty was his manner that his passion would spread to the other side. They might as well have been declared enemies. (*Yucay*, 106–7)

As we see, the author's objectivity and impartiality have their limits — and their sputtering!

Las Casas's intrigues bore on the notion of granting "titles to the Incas as legitimate kings of this land and to the chiefs as legitimate natural lords" (*Yucay*, 107). But this, García de Toledo maintains, is "the greatest falsehood that has been uttered concerning the Indies" (ibid.).

One must call a spade a spade, then, and realize that the Inca was "one of the greatest and newest tyrants of the world and had no more legitimate dominion over this land than over Spain. Nor were the chiefs or masters any more lords for having been put there by a tyrant a few years before the Spaniards came" (ibid.). Tyrants and upstarts, the Incas were. What legitimacy could they have as rulers? This was one of Viceroy Toledo's pet theses, and he set his collaborators to work on it. The king of Spain, then, need have no scruples when it came to exercising his own authority, especially in Peru, since "of no realm," says the memorandum's author, "I believe, is His Majesty more the legitimate and absolute lord than of these" (*Yucay*, 109). With all his lies, Las Casas was endeavoring to "deprive His Majesty of eight parts in ten of the sovereignty that God and his Vicar had given him."[13] And so he was closing in the Indies "the gates to the greatest benefits, and opening them to greater evils" (*Yucay*, 108–9).

Bogey of a Withdrawal from the Indies

By way of illustration of the gravity of this second deception, the *Yucay Opinion* advances a claim whose historical authenticity has been the object of heated scholarly discussion. The question is of interest to us because, on one particular point, it places Francisco de Vitoria at odds with Las Casas.

Leaving certain details aside, the matter is as follows. While on the subject of the justifications for a Spanish presence in the Indies, of which we have spoken above, our Yucay author maintains that Las Casas had persuaded Emperor Charles V to abandon the Indies. Such a catastrophe, he says, was avoided only by the sensible, last-minute intervention of Francisco Vitoria, a theologian to whom Viceroy Toledo and his followers will refer with high praise on a number of occasions. The author does not neglect the opportunity to lash out once more against Las Casas and his devilish machinations. The "Prince of Darkness," he says, is making use of this friar in order to deceive and to snuff out "the light of the gospel."

Thus, then, did he contrive, in such a way that the Emperor conceived scruples, which this Father had instilled in him, and all the theologians with him, owing to the [aforementioned] false information, so that he intended to yield to these tyrant kings of the Incas, until Friar Francisco de Vitoria told him that he must not, that Christendom would be lost. So [the Emperor] determined to [do so] when [the Indians] should be capable of maintaining themselves in the Catholic faith. (*Yucay*, 112)

The success of the Lascasian campaign — which had managed to bedazzle "all the theologians" and enlist them in its cause — is said to have caused a return to the first deception: idolatry. Our scandalized author comments: "Behold the refined trickery, that the darkness of unbelief, idolatry, human sacrifice, cannibalism, and bestial living might once more come upon" these poor, benighted natives of Peru (ibid.). Thus, human sacrifice, cannibalism, and a subhuman way of life are said to have characterized the natives of Peru before the arrival of the Christians. (García de Toledo says this in passing. Sarmiento de Gamboa will emphasize it directly.) The horrors of idolatry render even more worthy of repudiation and condemnation the cooperation Las Casas, with his ideas, lends to the reestablishment of these abominations.

The authenticity of this proposed withdrawal from the Indies has its partisans as well as its determined opponents. The latter seem to advance more convincing considerations. M. Bataillon has devoted an incisive article to the point and lists the authors who credit this assertion of the Yucay memorandum.[14] With minute attention to detail and the erudition that is his trademark, Bataillon dismantles one by one the arguments advanced (indicating certain inconsistencies, as well) and concludes that, "from whichever direction one approaches it, the story of a Charles V prepared to withdraw from the Indies, under Las Casas's influence, and snatched from temptation by Vitoria is scarcely convincing."[15]

Indeed, no document of those same years echoes the report of the Yucay paper.[16] The texts in which we find any allusion to it, which have been presented by Manzano,[17] all date from 1567–73. And as Bataillon observes, they are more easily explained in terms of the time of Philip II than of Charles V.[18]

The renowned French Hispanicist closes his study with a firm rejection of all of the arguments so far presented. Ever the good, cautious historian, however, he leaves open the possibility that new evidence may come to light: "Until we find an authentic document dating from the reign of Charles V and testifying to an imperial offer of restitution of sovereignty, or at least to an official debate on the matter, the prudent view would be that what we have here is a late myth that caused great passions in Peru."[19] Bataillon considers furthermore that the history of Peru on the eve of the execution of Túpac Amaru I has been insufficiently examined. "A study of the historical context would doubtless shed more light on the actual route of what I propose to call the *bogey of a withdrawal from the Indies,* and of its localization in Peru."[20]

The argumentation against the existence of a plan to withdraw from the Indies, which Vitoria is supposed to have thwarted, is solidly based. We should like to add only two remarks. The first will merely be an addition to the considerations already recalled here. As we read the authors who support the claim of the Yucay memorandum, it is easy to perceive in the majority of cases that this "bogey of a withdrawal" is particularly welcome as an enhancement of the complex figure of the emperor.[21] These writers wish to combat what has been called (for anything but self-evident reasons) the "black legend" and have it thought that Las Casas's *ideas* were almost heeded, but that the *facts* (reported by the *Informaciones Toledanas*) ultimately gave those ideas the lie.

This is indeed the context of the question, says Porras Barrenechea, over the course of that "great epoch of Hispanicity" that was the Toledan period.[22] The "bogey" fits in well with a whole interpretation of the historical reality of those years based on the notion of a sensitivity and nobility of conscience to be ascribed to the rulers of Spain. That conscience is said to have been burdened by Las Casas's denunciations, then lightened upon the acquisition of a better knowledge of the tyranny and illegitimacy of the native rulers of the Indies. Hence the persistence of the thesis of a Spanish withdrawal from the Indies and the facility with which its partisans launch into their categorical assertions on such flimsy grounds. No argumentation, however well-founded objectively and presented by scholars of the stature of Bataillon, Basadre, Lucena, and others, will ever have any effect on this mentality and its special interests.

Our second observation concerns a point of direct interest to us. Although we do not regard the notion presented in the *Yucay Opinion* concerning a withdrawal from the Indies as tenable, one thing does become quite plain (nor does García de Toledo's intuition fail him here). And that is that Vitoria's position on the Indies is not the same as Las Casas's. We think that on this point Bataillon is mistaken in arguing, against that memorandum, that no important distance separates these two great Dominicans in the matter of the "duties of the king of Spain in the Indies."[23] As we have seen, the difference between the two, despite certain points of agreement, is great.

2. *Root of All Evils*

Viceroy Francisco de Toledo is a key figure in the establishment of Spanish dominion in Peru. His viceregency (1569–81) will be marked by an unbridled anti-Lascasianism that is but the other side of the coin of his fervent defense both of the presence of the Spanish sovereigns in the Indies and consequently, de facto, of the essentials of the social regime imposed by the *encomenderos* in the lands of the old Tawantinsuyu. The Yucay paper faithfully expresses this attitude on the part of Peru's grim governor. To Toledo, the ideas of Bartolomé de Las Casas and his followers (and here he was correct) seem to be subversive of the recently established order and consequently to represent a danger for the permanent Spanish domination that Toledo proposes to establish.[24]

In the viceroy's effort, the question of the legitimacy of Inca rule wins his particular attention. Friar Bartolomé has been concerned with it a number of times. Besides, the subject is intimately bound up with a particular manner of conceptualizing the human status and concrete historical lot of the Indian nations. The Yucay memorandum is clearsighted here. But the viceroy is not satisfied. As we have said, he now commissions other works, as well, calculated to eradicate the thesis of a legitimate Inca dominion and with it everything that might present the Indians on a footing of equality or as endowed with rights vis-à-vis the Iberians.[25]

The Junta of 1568

Toledo had known what he would face in Peru. In 1568, shortly before setting sail for the New World, he had attended a general meeting of the Royal Councils (which some historians like to call the Junta Magna, the Great Conference), presided over by Cardinal Diego de Espinosa, bishop of Sigüense and president of the Council of Castile, and held in his palace. The meeting had been convoked for the purpose of examining Indian affairs and turned out to be decisive for the policy that would be followed in the Indies.

In the decade of the 1560s, a series of events occurred in the Indies (manifestations of social unrest, an uprising of *encomenderos,* the overthrow of the viceroy of Peru, Huguenot colonies founded in Brazil and Florida) that shaped, says B. Escandell, an "American crisis" coinciding with the crisis undergone in Europe in these same years.[26] To this we must add Rome's new interest in the evangelization of the Indians, as manifested in the bull *In Coena Domini* (1568) of Pius V.[27]

Philip II and his collaborators sought a magical escape from this sorry state of affairs in the convocation of the general conference of which we have spoken.[28] There, directives were issued to the viceroys who had recently been appointed for Mexico and Peru.[29] Francisco de Toledo participated in the deliberations and took his cue, all during his Peruvian tenure, from the decisions that emerged.[30] The acts of this meeting have not been found,[31] but we have the text of certain instructions that Toledo received.

In the matter of interest to us, Philip II's indications are clear:

> According to information received concerning the religious who have resided and do reside in those lands, under the pretext of seeking to protect, favor, and defend the Indians, they have attempted to interfere in matters judicial, governmental, and of state, in an effort to impugn Our legal sovereignty over the Indies; and [interfering in] other matters as well, occasioning a great deal of scandal, especially when they address these points in their pulpits or in other gatherings and speeches. You will take care to warn their provincials and [other] superiors of this, lest in any way they give occasion for it, and you, for your part, will likewise see to the observance of the decrees, provisions, and chapters of instructions that concern this matter.[32]

Difficulties with friars were old hat.[33] They had been denounced to the Spanish authorities by Licentiate Jerónimo de Valderrama, who had been dispatched to Mexico in 1563 to implement a series of fiscal reforms intended to better the condition of the royal treasury. The friars there had energetically opposed his project of increasing the tribute imposed on Indians, maintaining that the great poverty in which they lived rendered the proposed measure unacceptable. Scandalized, Valderrama reported that these Fathers had actually made bold to question the rights of Spain in the Indies, declaring that "his Majesty has nothing else here than the Pope has given him, and the Pope can have given him this land only for the spiritual good of the Indians. The day they have a government and have been instructed in the things of faith the King is under obligation to leave these realms to their natives."[34]

And so the members of the conference, like the king himself, were anything but well disposed toward these Las Casas–inspired agitators.[35] This is Toledo's understanding, as is plain from what he says in a letter to Espinosa:

> The first and deepest root, Most Illustrious Lord, of all of the damage being done to the governance of this land I understand to be an inadequate appreciation of the tyranny prevailing there at the moment [this land] was acquired, and the consequent failure to ascribe to His Majesty all of the juridical liberties residing

in a sovereignty over this land. From the moment the Most Illustrious Conference began to hear of these challenges and of
the harm wrought by the indiscretions and inexperience of the
bishop of Chiapa on the strength of the influence he enjoys in
these realms, as well as through the impression here and abroad
caused by his book, I had the intention of verifying there by personal experience the truth of the facts that he so distorts, never
having been present in or having had any experience of that
country.[36]

The text is pellucid. The root of all of the ills of the Indies is ignorance of the rights of the Spanish Crown over the Indies. It would
seem that this, along with Las Casas's role in the matter, was seen
as the problem even at the Conference of 1568. Toledo had come to
Peru, then, knowing full well that he would have to maintain a firm
hand with those who disputed the king's rights in the lands under his
charge and put order into the world of the *encomenderos*. The viceroy
even considered making use of the Tribunal of the Inquisition, whose
installation in the Indies had also been decreed at the Conference of
1568,[37] in order to impose silence "on the contrariety of opinions that
has ever prevailed among preachers and confessors in those provinces
concerning jurisdiction and security of conscience."[38]

"The Heart of Most Friars of This Realm"

The full reestablishment of the king's authority and the silencing of
all who questioned his rights would require an "antecedent measure:
the recall of all of the Dominican's books, which have been the principal cause of the spread of that dangerous opinion."[39] For Toledo,
the enemy is Las Casas. The problems are due to him and his fairy
tales and not to what was actually occurring in the Indies. In a letter to Spain, the viceroy tersely expresses his way of seeing things,
maintaining, according to Lewis Hanke, that "the books of the fanatic, virulent bishop of Chiapa have served to spearhead the attack
on Spanish dominion in America."[40] The argumentation is a familiar
one: the difficulties are due to those who denounce the outrages, not
to the outrages themselves or their perpetrators.

Shortly after Toledo's arrival in Peru, Las Casas's works began to
be recalled there (especially the treatises published without authorization in Seville in 1552). That this action had royal authorization
is plain. In December 1571, Philip II wrote to his viceroy: "As for recalling the books written by the bishop of Chiapa and found in [Peru],
you have done well. Complete the task. Gather them up, along with
any others that may treat of matters of the Indies that have been pub-

lished without our license, to be conferred by members of our Council, wherever any such works are to be found."[41] But Toledo encounters obstacles. The owners of the books have been won over to Las Casas's ideas. According to Toledo, the "heart of most friars of this Realm" has been lost to the royal cause, and he petitions his sovereign for "some censure or precept of obedience," under which he may be able to oblige the resisters.

The task of collecting all of these books is under way, Toledo announces. "The books of the bishop of Chiapa, as well as any others printed without license of the Royal Council," he writes, "will be gathered up *as Your Majesty commands.*" But the evil caused by the Dominican friar has been great:

> Chiapa's doctrine has taken root in the heart of most friars of this Realm, and enormous damage has been done. Indeed, even had they not been printed without Your Majesty's authorization, as they have been, and had they not been from the pen of a "witness" who has never seen or visited these parts, they are replete with such falsification of the facts and so much ignorance as to matters of government, that it would have nonetheless been of the utmost urgency to recall them and have them proscribed by Your Majesty's Royal Council. The intervening delay, since the holding of the Conference, has occasioned no small amount of harm.

Viceroy Toledo means the 1568 conference that, as we have seen, inspires all his work. And so he laments the slow pace of the application of its directives.

Toledo likewise petitions for a direct warning from the king to the church on the eve of the ecclesiastical council to be held in Lima. The church and the council must tend to the matter of the writings of the bishop of Chiapa. Toledo writes: "Nor let Your Majesty neglect to have the council about to convene here informed that You are pleased to have the matter of Chiapa's books addressed and settled." But the viceroy perceives the insufficiency of this step, since the friars (as "exempt religious") are not under the direct authority of the bishops and will be little affected by the decisions of the council. In order for a battle with the subversive ideas of the bishop of Chiapa to be won, a personal intervention on the part of the king will be needed:

> And even if in order to get them to appear as summoned I resort to the censures of the ordinaries, the friars are not obliged by such — indeed, it is the ordinaries who are under the control of the friars — so that some censure or precept of obedience will be required on the part of those actually enjoying authority over them in order to get all of the books.

Zealous Don Francisco would dearly love to be able to get into the religious houses and poke through their libraries.[42]

Despite all of these measures, the turbulent affair seems to go on and on. A short while later, Toledo will still be denouncing the influence Bartolomé de Las Casas wields over religious who, according to him, unduly meddle in political matters and "foment Chiapa's doctrine, which is founded on false allegations, as Your Majesty will already have understood in part from the evidence heretofore dispatched...." The viceroy avails himself of the opportunity to laud the work commissioned by himself and being executed by Sarmiento de Gamboa: "...and will come to understand entirely by reading the history presently being composed with such care and diligence in verifying the truth of its assertions. This, too, will profit Your Majesty's rights, the good governance of this land, the conscience of the Spaniards, and the good of the Indians themselves, those subjects of the false allegations everywhere trumpeted by Chiapa in his books and preached and taught by his disciples today." Exasperated, Toledo concludes that this evil is one that must be made to disappear without a trace. "Until this Chiapa business is torn up by the roots," he maintains, "it will always be able to sprinkle its seeds somewhere or other, and there will always be someone found to poison the soil therewith."[43] And this seed, for all the efforts of the stubborn viceroy and his obsequious retinue, still yields its harvest today.

Toledo's assignment was to implement the directives of the 1568 conference and fully reestablish the rights of the royal Patronage.[44] For him, then, the missionaries' independent attitude was unacceptable. In their defense of the Indians Toledo saw undue interference in political affairs. They were meddling in matters that did not pertain to them.[45] An evangelical denunciation of the injustices being committed against the Indians was seen as interference in matters of "government and state,"[46] especially when these denunciations sought to go to the root of the injustice. Paradoxically, some of the most ardent defenders of the "purely religious" nature of the task of evangelization are often persons who hold political power in the service of the mighty.

3. Power and History

Nor was Toledo off the mark here. An assertion of the Indians' liberty, like that of their equality with the Europeans, was diametrically opposed to the social system beginning to be implanted in the Indies. The viceroy rises up as a champion of that order. Hence his harassment of Las Casas's ideas or of any other missionaries who defended the Indians. However, this did not prevent the seed of the gospel, then

being sown by Las Casas and many others, from sprouting and bur-
geoning into a concrete history. The difficulties were great; the process
would be a slow one. But it would have all its consequences.

Illegitimacy of Inca Sovereignty

For the one who represented the king in Peru, the withdrawal from
circulation of the works of Las Casas was but one part of the task
to be performed. In the dispute over what just titles Spain might
have to dominion over the Indies, the proposition that the Incas'
government had been — and, de jure, continued to be — legitimate
constituted a powerful argument and was able to disturb some consciences. The interests of the Crown and the *encomenderos* — which
had been contrary, some decades before — now coincided, and Bartolomé's thesis was to be rejected.[47] Toledo perceived this and with
the support of those powerful allies proposed to show that the Incas
had simply been tyrants, enjoying no authentic right over their peoples, whom they had forcefully subjugated. Friar Bartolomé, like other
Spanish missioners and jurists of the age, maintained the legitimacy
of the natural Indian rulers' authority and accordingly the injustice of
the conquistadors' attitude in ignoring it. Las Casas's preaching had
succeeded in winning over influential individuals in the Indies government, although not everyone drew the same logical conclusions as
he.[48]

A demonstration that there actually had been no such natural
rulers in Peru and, what is more, that the Incas had been despots
and tyrant newcomers, would stifle these shrill friars once and for all.
Furthermore, now one would be able to justify the waging of war on
the Indian peoples and their subjugation — for example, through an
appeal to Vitoria's ambivalent titles, which left the possibility open.
Indeed, Levillier holds that Vitoria's teaching meant a great deal to
Toledo.[49]

The *Informaciones,* while denying the *factual* legitimacy of Indian
sovereignty, leaves untouched Vitoria's disquisitions on the consequences flowing from the *right* of these unbelievers to govern themselves. Meanwhile, with its appeal to the natives' alleged idolatry,
human sacrifice, and sins against nature, the work attempts to place
the doctrine of the master of Salamanca at the service of the Toledan
theses.[50]

In a fine piece of strategy, Toledo joins the battle on different
fronts. Beginning late in 1570, he issues his *Informaciones,* intended as
a demonstration of the illegitimacy of Inca sovereignty.[51] What a puz-
zled Manzano calls these "strange Toledan research projects"[52] have
this perfectly clear intent. The thesis to be proved stands at the head

of the communication: "Following is information and proof, gathered by mandate of His Excellency, of the origin and descendency of the tyranny of the Incas of this realm and of the certainty that neither are there now nor have there ever been any natural rulers in this land."[53] The work has been executed on the basis of the testimony of Indian leaders summoned by the viceroy.

Standing as a preface to the *Informaciones* is a letter from Toledo to Philip II summarizing the content of the document. In closing his letter, the viceroy presents the conclusions to be drawn from the data that have been collected. The third of these points very precisely to one of Las Casas's propositions bearing on the perpetuity of the *encomiendas,* a particularly delicate matter in Peru, as we have observed. "Presupposing," says Toledo, "the authentic dominion held by Your Majesty in these realms, inasmuch as it will serve good governance, let Your Majesty give and distribute to the Spaniards in this land, temporarily or permanently, without the scruples heretofore occasioned by the casual assertion that these Incas had been legitimate rulers and the chieftains natural lords, because all of that is false, as witness the following demonstration."[54]

The king and the Peruvian *encomenderos* — who had invested so much time and money in the defense of the perpetuity of the *encomiendas* in opposition to Las Casas and his loudmouthed friars — could be satisfied. Philip II certainly was, and once again approves the efforts of the enterprising viceroy. "This is good," he writes. He lauds "the diligence you have exercised and continue to exercise in gathering all of these papers bearing on the truth and title and sovereignty with which we possess those Realms, and the information you gather from the principal descendants of the Incas and the various other factions."[55] With these *Informaciones* Toledo hoped to put an end to the influence the bishop of Chiapa had even in the Council of the Indies, from which that hierarch had obtained provisions for the governance of this land "that," according to the viceroy, "so destroyed [that governance] in the spiritual and temporal that today it can raise its head no longer."[56] The royal official hopes to put an end to this state of prostration, at least in Peru.

For Love of Neighbor

With the same intent, the viceroy commissions a book by one of his own councilors, Sarmiento de Gamboa: the *Historia Indica.*[57] Insistently he recommends its publication.[58] Here is another effort — in the genre of history this time — to demonstrate the illegitimacy of Inca dominion. But Sarmiento goes further. He reveals in his book that he is abreast of the juridical and theological discussions of recent years, and this provides the focus of his historical report. For him, not only the colonization (the "second entry," as Las Casas called it), but the war on the Indians (the "first entry") is justified.

In the introduction to his work, Sarmiento indicates his starting point very precisely. The devil, at the height of cunning, "has contrived to enlist in his armies the very soldiers who had been fighting against him — the preachers themselves, who now began to raise difficulties over the right and title of the sovereigns of Castile to these lands." Due to a "want of attention on the part of the governors of those times" and to the information provided by Las Casas, Charles V had been given to believe that there already were legitimate rulers in the Indies, so that the emperor "was on the point of abandoning" those lands. The author therefore proposes to certify "the fact of the truth of the abominable and worse than inhuman tyranny of these Incas and of their autonomous chieftains, who are not nor ever have been independent rulers, but were appointed by Topa Inga Yupanqui, the greatest, cruelest, and most pernicious tyrant of them all. And the chieftains have been and are now enormous tyrants appointed by other great and violent tyrants, as history so plainly and surely shows." It is a thesis with which we are familiar, and it coincides — almost verbatim — with the *Informaciones* and with the *Yucay Opinion*.[59]

The author adds that the situation prevailing in the Inca empire fully justifies a war to be waged on it, by reason not only of its illegitimacy, as explained, but of its inhumane practice as well.

> Furthermore, their tyrannical laws and customs explain Your Majesty's genuine, sacred title especially to this realm and realms of Peru, inasmuch as Your Majesty and His most holy predecessors on the throne have forbidden the sacrifice of innocent human beings, the eating of human flesh — that accursed, execrable sin — casual sexual commerce with sisters and mothers, the abominable use of beasts, and all of their [other] nefarious, accursed practices.[60]

And so, thanks to their holy enterprises, the sovereigns of Spain have become the defenders of the victims of barbarous Inca practices and the reestablishers of natural law in these lands.

Sarmiento advances a powerful consideration in favor of the conquest of these peoples, and one that he hopes will be regarded as adequate. Love of neighbor has made this conquest a duty, he says, in a curious excursion into the theological area, "since each of us, especially princes, including Your Majesty, is commanded by God to love our neighbor." Love of neighbor, which is the duty of every Christian, but which is incumbent upon rulers in a preeminent way, justifies the presence of the Spaniards in the Indies. As we see, the adventurous spirit of the famous navigator is not restricted to the field of geography.

Sure of his argument, the author of the *Historia Indica* makes bold to posit the hypothetical case of a legitimate Inca sovereignty and states that even in that situation the actually prevailing practices in violation of natural law would justify an armed action against the perpetrators. "For this reason alone," he writes, "war may be declared, waged, and prosecuted in all justice against the tyrants, even were they the natural and authentic rulers of the land.... After all, for these sins against nature they may be castigated and punished." Even if the natives of these lands are to opposed to these practices (as the *Informaciones* acknowledges they are) or if the victims were unwilling to be avenged by the Spaniards, the fact would remain that those who commit such crimes "may be compelled to observe the law of nature, as the archbishop of Florence and Innocent teach, and Friar Francisco de Vitoria confirms in the report that he has made concerning the titles to the Indies."[61]

Vitoria's opinions seem to have been known to Sarmiento from the start (as they were to the author of the *Yucay Opinion*), since they were known to Toledo.[62] No more effective appeal could have been made than to the authority of the prestigious master of Salamanca. His doctrine, after the bitter dispute between Las Casas and Sepúlveda at Valladolid (1551–52), had appeared on the scene as a satisfactory, less controversial, middle road and furthermore was open to an interpretation favorable to the theses of the able Toledo.[63]

Sarmiento's contribution to the polemics concludes with a concise paragraph in which he reiterates a point he has already made a number of times: that the Indians' sins against nature are easily sufficient to give the sovereigns of Spain full rights over the lands not only of Peru, but of all the Indies.

> By this title alone, then — even without all of the many others — Your Majesty has the most sufficient and legitimate title to all the Indies of all the princes of this world to any sovereignty whatever: inasmuch as in greater or lesser degree and whether it be relatively public or more concealed and dissimulated, there prevails in Your Majesty's lands of North and South this general violation of the law of nature.[64]

The reestablishment of morality in these matters justifies the European presence, the exploitation of these lands, war, and domination of the native populations. Enormous political consequences (and they are matters of life and death for whole populations) therefore flow from Sarmiento's ethical considerations. Our illustrious author defends them without a moment's thought for the violations of natural law involved in the slaughter of the Indians, their forced labor, and the abuse of Indian women by those who had come to establish "moral" order. Responsibility for one's neighbor, especially the responsibility incumbent on rulers, is the theological principle that in the mind of Sarmiento justifies everything he knows is happening in the Indies.

4. Falsifying the Memory of a People

A power held in the present tends to make provision for the future, as well, by dominating the past of the vanquished. A people afflicted with amnesia are an unstable people, subservient to the idols of the status quo, vulnerable to the self-serving, mendacious word. Conquerors always try to erase or block the memory of those whose necks they have bent. The Aztecs and Incas had sought to do it with the nations they had subjected, and the Europeans strove to do it more thoroughly and more radically when they came to these lands. After all, in the judgment of most of the Europeans, that past contained no human values worth preserving.

A Divine Election

The viceroy receives the backing of the mighty *encomenderos* of Cuzco, who see that in this instance Toledo's effort to provide a basis for the rights of the Crown is a bolster for their own pretensions. A memorandum they send to Toledo is revealing. It energetically impugns the notion of the legitimacy of Inca sovereignty as failing to correspond to "the truth of the matter." Those who are ignorant of the actual situation, they say, are letting their imaginations run away with them. The signatories allege that practices and opinions have been introduced among the Indians "with which are contaminated, by necessary consequence, not only our evangelical law, but natural law itself, which is left with practically nothing whose contrary is not inculcated by whatever most recent enterprise might be under way." As a result, "in the customs of these barbarians we find the most extraordinary manner of teaching ever employed by the demon with any kind of new peoples of all of those that have been discovered in the world." The deviant practices promoted by the enemy of God are to be combated. With theologians and moralists behind them, the *encomenderos* assert with heartfelt conviction: "We truly believe ours to have been the most justifiable cause of all those of which we read to have been championed by the citizens of any realm." After all, here the enemy is the devil who gives bad advice to the dwellers of the Indies.

A legitimate title for the Spanish presence, then, emerges from violations of natural law on the part of the Indians. To this another is added: "the merciful grace bestowed by our Lord and his Vicar General of our Church on the sovereigns of Castile" — a "grace," say the *encomenderos,* that is now precisely the one "held by ourselves." They are in Peru in the name of the king and the service of God. There is a theological basis for their presence: "God our Lord has chosen us as a means for the accomplishment of his divine predestination, seeing that such a great number of people have plainly been saved through the discovery of these realms that are under the dominion and protection of Your Majesty and are being saved and shall daily be saved till the end of the world." To the *encomenderos,* now transformed into missionaries, the Indians owe their eternal salvation. Well might they at least attempt a partial repayment of the enormous debt they have contracted with their saviors, by means of their labors and their lives.

This divine election is further endorsed, say the *encomenderos,* enriching even further their own, most original, theology of salvation, by the obvious divine protection they have received since their arrival in these lands, "in arming and defending us from the beginning from such great numbers of people with favors almost miraculous and beyond nature." This is what happened, for example, at Cajamarca, "where Atabaliba, arriving with two hundred thousand armed men, was captured and saw his army put to flight by well under one hundred seventy men, without any of the latter being killed." Perhaps the Indians who died on that occasion were the first beneficiaries of the salvific deed that had brought there the future *encomenderos* of Peru. All of this leads to the conclusion, with regard to the dominion that they exercise in Peru jointly with the Crown, that "we know of no sovereignty possessed anywhere in the world with such just and reasonable titles and of such utility and profit for the service of God."[65]

The Cuzco municipal council closes its with letter an expression of gratitude to Viceroy Toledo for all that he has done to demonstrate the illegitimacy of the political authority of the Incas and for defending the rights of the king, which are warranty for their own rights.[66] Their quarrels with the Crown are a thing of the past. This is to the credit of the viceroy, who, with such political perspicacity has so effectively strengthened their alliance against the common enemy: a handful of bishops and missionaries who are mounting a defense of the Indians and their rights on the basis of the gospel.

The zealous Toledo goes still further. He conducts a veritable campaign among the Indians themselves, attempting to demonstrate to them the illegitimacy and tyranny of the authority exercised over them by the Incas.[67] Early in 1572, he calls a meeting of the "descendants of the twelve *ayllus,* to view the genealogical tree that had been painted and to have the *Historia Indica* read to them"[68] and then in obedient submission to signify their endorsement of that work. To falsify the memory of an oppressed people is to mutilate their ability to rebel. Thereby an effective weapon is acquired for their continued subjugation. The manipulation of history has always been a prime resource in the hands of dominant groups for the maintenance of their power.[69] We have always suffered on our continent, despite recent praiseworthy efforts to correct it,[70] a version of history according to the ruling class. The consequences of this for a discourse on Christian faith are greater than is commonly recognized.

In the arsenal of arguments amassed by Toledo with such patience and devotion, the *Yucay Opinion* has a place all its own. Here is a weapon having the important function of indicating the author of the evils this writer wishes to combat: Bartolomé de Las Casas. The viceroy and his hangers-on seem to think that it is the Dominican's writings, and not historical events, that are at the root of all of these protests against the injustices being perpetrated upon the Indians. The confusion is a curious one, but it constantly recurs. A power is attributed to books and ideas that they actually do not have, and this enables us to close our eyes to an inhumane reality — the true prime mover in the opening of minds and the commitment of hearts. Writings can help in this process, but they have no power without the support of the cry arising from a situation unacceptable to human and Christian conscience.

Rather than the recall of Las Casas's books and the imposition of silence upon the missionaries, what was needed was an acceptance of the demands of justice, radical as these might be.[71] But that would have required a different perception of what was occurring at that time. It would have required a special attention to the victims of the social order that was being established. Furthermore, a rare courage would have been needed to enunciate in words what, it is true, the eyes could scarcely overlook.

Las Casas acquired this perception and mustered this courage. Nor was his attitude that of an isolated individual. No, he was accompanied by many along his way. Let us read, for example, what Pedro Cieza de León says ("the prince of chroniclers," Jiménez de la Espada called him, and Porras Barrenechea liked to repeat the expression) about occurrences in Peru in those years:

> Surely it is no small occasion for grief to contemplate that it was the pagan, idolatrous Incas who had had a fine, orderly government and could maintain such broad lands, while we Christians had destroyed such great realms. Yes, wherever Christians had

passed, conquering and discovering, nothing now remains but a universal conflagration.[72]

Here is one of the numerous documents of the time that some like to regard as having been composed in a "Lascasian" style. We think the formula a poor one, calculated to minimize the importance of these testimonials. All of these denunciations indeed have a common origin. But that origin is antecedent to any possible Lascasian inspiration. It lies in concrete historical reality. The real question is not whether the author is an ally of Las Casas, but whether he is honestly observing what is happening in the Indies. And, of course, whether he has the courage to declare it.[73]

Las Casas's consistency, however — his tenacity in drawing the ultimate conclusion, not only in words but in his life — may well have made him the most annoying gadfly of all.

Manzano, for his part, eulogizes Toledo's efforts and thinks they snuffed out the spark Las Casas and his followers had kindled. "The tyranny of the Incas," he declares, "became clear as day." And he adds significantly: "The Catholic sovereigns of greater Spain could put their fears at rest as to the legitimacy of their dominion over the Indies. No 'natural sovereign' had been stripped of any rights."[74] According to this, then, Toledo had achieved his objective. The waters riled by the turbulent friars were settling again.[75] Sovereigns and *encomenderos* alike could breathe easy now, while the Indians died. As we know, one of Las Casas's war horses was his concern for the truth of information sent to the Crown.

What ultimately motivated the efforts of the viceroy, who was related to the noble house of Alba, is plain to see. Consequently, so is the motivation of his collaborators. The reason for their assault on the ideas and friars he calls "Lascasian," then, is evident. In all honesty, we ourselves have no wish to idealize these Tawantinsuyu that Toledo seeks to disparage. Today there is a consensus as to their relatively late arrival, as well as with respect to the game of bloody wars and political alliances they played to win their dominion.[76] What is unacceptable — and Las Casas indicates this with all lucidity — is the use of these deeds, their negative side, their unjust aspects, as an argument in favor of the legitimacy of European power in the Indies, and as a pretext to declare those Indies arbitrarily and unilaterally a *res nullius* — something dropped in the street, a "lost and found" item belonging to no one, under no legitimate authority, and with their inhabitants lacking any rights over their own wealth. The crime becomes all the more grave when the plunder and destruction of these territories is carried out on the pretext of "liberating" the Indians — and proclaiming them the gospel.[77]

José de Acosta, an important figure in the church in Peru at the close of the sixteenth century, who was close to Toledo for a time, renders a succinct judgment on this kind of argumentation:

> I am at a loss to appreciate, let alone approve, other titles that some strive to maintain in their eagerness unnecessarily to broaden the royal authority, indeed perhaps to toady to it. Concretely I refer to those who appeal to the alleged tyranny of the Incas, who have usurped the empire of Peru by force.... Upon these bases they pretend to settle the right of Christian princes to reign there. But obviously one may not despoil robbers of the plunder they have taken from others and appropriate it oneself. And so I ask: With what right or justice can that sovereignty over the Indies be wrested from the tyrants of the Indians (supposing that this is what they are) and kept for oneself?... Are others' crimes to give us the right to commit new crimes ourselves?

Then he adds, with good judgment: "Although these empires have been violently usurped, they now have the confirmation of at least six hundred years. And if it be said that that period of time is insufficient for the prescription claimed in any of so many other empires, we shall inevitably end in a universal chaos where human relations are concerned."[78] Let us note that Acosta regards the presence of the Crown in the Indies as legitimate. But he renders an independent judgment, and in so doing rejects the allegations so minutely developed by Toledo and his servants.

In his treatise *Doce dudas* Las Casas had written years before: "To hear our Spaniards, it would be licit to steal from a robber and keep what one has stolen, since they offer no exculpation from their sin but to say that Guainacapac had tyrannized over that realm." However, he concludes, "we do not excuse our tyranny by alleging his" (*O.E.* 5:530a). Plain common sense.[79]

Inferiority of the Indian

To be sure, the matter was not limited to the question of the legitimacy of Inca sovereignty. The viceroy and his collaborators bent their efforts to the establishment of another point as well. It was a profound conviction of theirs: the human inferiority of the Indians. Indians were incapable of leading a decent life in society or of approaching the gospel without the ongoing assistance — material and spiritual — of Spaniards. In the letter to the king in which he presents and summarizes his *Informaciones,* Toledo argues:

> Let the record show that these natives are a people in need of a caretaker. Grave affairs arise, touching their souls and their

treasures alike. Were there none to guide and govern them, they would be lost in all these matters. And were there no Spaniards in the land to teach them faith in Jesus Christ, they would not understand that either. They would be deceived in everything.[80]

The text is plain. Without help from the Europeans, the Indians (who do not even have a word for "love"; *Yucay*, 136) would be in no condition to live in a human and Christian manner. We have already met the problem in this deception. Now it reappears: The Indians, ignorant of what is best for them in religion as in economics, are at the mercy of every lie and illusion. This renders still more pernicious the theses of those who raise obstacles to or question the king's titles over these lands.[81]

From the outset the inferiority of the Indians has been one of the favorite arguments of the defenders of the Conquista and the *encomienda.* Las Casas has energetically confronted these persons. Toledo takes the same tack, an approach explicitly maintained, as we have seen, by Ginés de Sepúlveda and others. In a memorandum he composes at the close of his tenure of office in Peru, the viceroy deals with the matter of the human condition of the Indians and publishes his considered judgment: "As I have already told His Majesty, in order to learn to be Christians, they must first know how to be human beings and be introduced to governance and a political and rational lifestyle."[82]

Those unable so much as to know that they are human beings ought to be given norms of a social conduct, which of course must be European. Any other form of living in society is inferior, indeed subhuman.[83] Friar Bartolomé will battle this Eurocentrism his whole life. A great part of his literary production (especially the *Apologética historia*) is devoted to a demonstration of the human character of Indian society and culture, as well as the full equality of the Indians with their unexpected and aggressive visitors. For Toledo and his allies the inferiority of the Indians is a proven fact.[84] From it they deduce a great many political and religious conclusions.

Toledo's celebrated ordinances regulating the Indians' life are marked by that conception. His measures come in for harsh judgment on the part of an important anthropologist and expert on Peru of our own times, John Murra:

> His administration was a disaster. We need only think of the massive deportation of millions to the reductions of which other viceroys spoke, but which he actually completed. . . . One cannot read the registers amassed even by a favorable source like Levillier without realizing that the intent was the destruction of the Andean societies.[85]

Execution of Túpac Amaru I

Shortly after the appearance of the *Yucay Opinion,* the *Informaciones,* and the *Historia Indica,* Toledo ordered the execution of Túpac Amaru I,[86] the living symbol of the resistance of a people who refused to be subjugated. The campaign against Inca sovereignty and for a social order based on a balance between the rights of the Crown and the privileges of the *encomenderos* had come to a climax.[87] Thus ended the stage of the *Reconquista* initiated by the Indians after the death of Atahualpa, whose high points were the siege of Cuzco and other cities by Manco Inca and in the dogged defense of Túpac Amaru I himself undertaken by the city of Vilcabamba.[88] Guamán Poma regards that execution as an act of pridefulness on the part of the viceroy. He passes the same judgment on Pizarro's execution of Atahualpa, whose death he presents with an aura of martyrdom.[89] The two executions, presented by Guamán Poma in identical terms down to the last details, wrought a profound effect on the Indians and left a deep trace on their memory.[90]

The execution of the Inca was no isolated phenomenon. Toledo was prepared to impose Spanish sovereignty by every means at his disposal.[91] In 1574, after having been duped by the Chiriguan Indians and having failed in an expedition against them,[92] the viceroy called a meeting at Chuquisaca on the topic of the just war. Toledo was in no mood for opposition. When it was suggested that Charles V in 1530 had issued an order proscribing the enslavement of captives, the viceroy retorted that he had never seen such a law.[93] He pressured the assembly into sanctioning the justice of the wars in question and the enslavement of all captives. Shortly thereafter, in 1580, Toledo urged the king to publish a general declaration of the justice of a war waged against rebels and apostates.[94] The question of the just war continued to be a matter of dispute with the conquest of Chile and the Philippines.[95]

With an astute political eye, the viceroy had waged his battle through the use of several weapons. His theological arm is the *Yucay Opinion.*[96] In the so-called research reported in the *Informaciones,* as well as in the view of the past expressed in the *Historia Indica,* there are signs of an attempt to justify the Spanish presence in the Indies in terms of the Christian message. But in any case the document attributed to García de Toledo directly indicates the development of an actual theology, that is, an interpretation of the faith in the context of the era that was inaugurated for humanity with the encounter of the old and new worlds.[97] The time was "so new and so unlike any other," as Las Casas had put it. In our next and final chapter, we shall examine this theology that sought to justify the order being installed on our continent.

Chapter 15 _____

Christ Did Not Die for Gold

The immediate context of the *Yucay Opinion* is the power game and confrontation of interests that we have just recalled. Thus, its author undertakes a theological reflection calculated to defend both the rights of the Crown over the Indies and those of the conquistadors and *encomenderos* to exploit the wealth of these lands. The memorandum is explicit as to its objectives. García de Toledo is not unaware that many other writings have already been produced along these same lines, but he is convinced that he has something of his own to say, something that no one has noticed before.

He indicates that original point at the beginning of his composition. The author proposes to examine "how good and necessary it is to shatter these mountains of gold and silver and carve out mines, with all the good means Your Excellency has provided — a thing that until now had been pursued more owing to the wiles of the devil than to reason and truth" (*Yucay*, 105).[1] It is the "reason and truth" of the existence and exploitation of the gold and silver mines that will govern the author's efforts. The framework in which he places his contribution is the providentialistic view of history typical of the age but now to be reinterpreted by himself. That view will enable him to discourse upon the role that, to his understanding, the treasures of Peru play in God's plan for this realm.

1. God's Two Daughters Fair and Hideous: The White and the Indian

The author of the *Yucay Opinion*, like others who took up their pens in these times, regarded the Indies to have been bestowed on the sovereigns of Spain by God in exchange for the lands of the Iberian Peninsula, which they had reconquered for the faith by wresting them from the hands of the Moors.

And in token of this, that we might clearly understand, they were given them the very year that they completed the restoration to his Divine Majesty of the Kingdoms of Spain. And that we might still more plainly understand, unless we were to be blind, they were given them by God through the [holder of the] loftiest title of all Christian sovereigns, granting them not by arms but by the hand of his vicar on earth. (*Yucay*, 109)[2]

García de Toledo next specifies that God has granted them the Indies without there having previously been in them "any manner of universal or particular lord, since they had given Him [the kingdoms of] Spain just so, without a single Moor being left there having any dominion: all that had ended with Granada" (*Yucay*, 109). A kind of historical reciprocity, then, prevails between God and the sovereigns of Spain. Ferdinand and Isabella and God exchange lands unencumbered by let or lien, and there are no particular domains to impose conditions on the swap.

A Bargain with God

We are familiar with the thesis of the illegitimacy of Indian political authority. Now we see the Indies bestowed on the Spanish Crown in terms of a kind of bargain with God, and suddenly there exists a title to the possession of these realms that has never existed before. It also appears as providential to the author's mind that shortly before the arrival of the Spaniards in this no-man's land of the Indies certain tyrants called Incas had subjugated various peoples there. Now these groups were under a single sway, and Christians "would find them all subjected, however tyrannically, and would have nothing left to do but baptize them." Thus had the Inca tyranny by divine design been enlisted in the service of Christianization. The domain of the Indies, then, represents a perfect accord between church and state, without any preeminence of the former over the latter, cautions Viceroy Toledo's loyal servant, so that "by one hand, and simultaneously, without the Church having any precedence over the rulers of Spain, both [the Church and the Spanish rulers] become sovereigns of this world" (*Yucay*, 110). Any superior jurisdiction on the part of the church — appealed to by the friars who defended the Indians — would have been to the detriment of the royal dominion and is excluded here.

God had been gradually preparing the way for the arrival of the Spaniards in the Indies and making straight their path. "A wondrous thing," says the author of the *Opinion*, "is the ignorance of these [overlords], who in the nearly one thousand years since the commencement of their tyranny have never succeeded in becoming legitimate rulers"

(*Yucay*, 137). He does not mean the Incas alone, then, whose dominion according to the memorandum is of recent vintage. ("It began
a mere eighty years before the Spaniards came in"; *Yucay*, 136.) He
means the chiefs, too, and any other (so-called) Indian authority of
the past. We too are surprised that over the course of so much time
there had never been any legitimate authority in these lands. The author is simply overcome with astonishment, and we must confess to
the same. "How wonderful too," he writes, "is the wisdom of God in
maintaining these Realms all these years without legitimate titles so
that the rulers of Spain might find for them the loftiest and most secure [title to authority] of any in all the world" (*Yucay*, 137). Another
providential measure.

The use of hyperbole in alleging the justice of the rights of the
Crown over Peru, which we have encountered in Sarmiento de Gamboa as well, belongs to the style of the period. Of greater interest is
what follows. By a disposition of divine providence, says the author,
the Indies were seized by the Spanish sovereigns "without the need
for so much as a venial sin on their part" (ibid.). After all, explains
García de Toledo, "the many mortal ones that were committed have
been against their orders, being perpetrated through the disorder of
their ministers, who would well be punished for it" (*Yucay*, 137). The
Indies had been so well prepared by God that the Spanish rulers might
take possession of them without a guilty conscience. According to the
memorandum, the scruples aroused in them by Las Casas were without the least foundation and manifested a total ignorance of the plans
of divine providence. The sins committed in the Indies are the work
of subordinates and involve not so much as a venial sin for the sovereigns. The "excesses and murders and cruel acts committed by the
Spaniards *in the beginning*," the statement will repeatedly say, were not
"the deeds of many soldiers, but of a few inhumane derelicts, who often performed them against the will of their superiors" (*Yucay*, 119;
emphasis added). The more serious the guilt, the lower the social or
military rank of the guilty and the lower the number of guilty persons.
In our own day as well we are familiar with the argument: atrocities
are laid to the account of subordinates when it is a question of the
abuse of the poor and marginalized. Obviously, from all that we have
seen, "these cruel deeds wrought by a few" (*Yucay*, 119) do not change
the essential: the crystal-clear right of the Crown over these lands.

The *Yucay Opinion* emphasizes the coinciding dates of the Spanish
Reconquista and the discovery of the Indies. The observation was a frequent one at the time under the pen of anyone seeking to support the
role of divine providence on behalf of the king and queen of Spain
in these two towering achievements. But other consequences as well,
the author of the memorandum thinks, ought to be drawn, and these

have been overlooked. Up until now, he asserts, forty years after the winning of these Peruvian realms, no one has been able to justify the Spanish exploitation of Peruvian mines and treasure-troves.

> A justification for working the gold, silver, and quicksilver mines has not as yet been formulated. This is difficult to believe, after all the time that has elapsed. These mines have never been exploited until our own times. Now this exploitation is occurring under the guidance of our king, who is acting under the influence of the divine Spirit and a particular movement of God, and with the encouragement of our Most Holy Father, who is so filled with the Holy Spirit as his own works declare, as voiced to this Holy League that we have formed against the enemies of our Catholic faith.

The author will show us the required justification. It will be found in the age-old struggle being waged in defense of European Christendom, which had entered a crisis in these same years. Writing mere months before the Battle of Lepanto, the author shows that he knows of the Holy League formed by the Pope, Philip II, and Venice for the purpose of combating the Turks. The need for resources for the defense of the Catholic faith (and European society) against its enemies, as well as for "the great riches of God's glory and the souls that with these riches are sure to be led to the Kingdom of Christ Our Lord" justify, our author says — a posteriori but altogether evidently — the exploitation of the mines of Peru: "I believe and hold it for a certainty," he says, "that it has justified the labor of these mines and treasures" (*Yucay*, 140).[3] The gold of Peru, then, plays a providential role in the defense and propagation of the Christian faith.

The same conclusion was reached by "the flower of the Realm among the jurists and theologians" of Spain, summoned by the king, who decided in favor of "the work of the mines." And our author, who as we know has a proclivity to amazement, enthusiastically declares this "marvelous thing": that "the wealth uncovered is so great. It is a matter of awe and amazement." From these, "His Majesty draws so much gold and silver, in his so Catholic and generous determination, that he has more than enough not only to subdue the Turk, but to shower with benefactions as well those Realms from whence he draws them" (*Yucay*, 140–41). Something may be left over from the mines of Peru then, the author concedes, for the benefit of those who actually dwell there. He means the spiritual boon of the faith.

These arguments represent a fresh attack on Bartolomé de Las Casas. Las Casas regarded the exploitation of these mines as an act of plunder. In fact, he had advised the Indians to hide the mines from the greed of the Spaniards, who, he would tell them, were only there for gold and silver.[4] We have already seen that García de Toledo complained about the advice being given the Indians by the friars in the face of the extortions of the colonial administration. The blindness of "this Father Bishop of Chiapa" is surprising, maintains the viceroy's cousin. After all, he asks, sure of the response: "What does it mean for God to have placed these Indians, so miserable in their souls, so Godforsaken, so incapable and bestial, in Kingdoms so great, in valleys and lands so delightful to the eyes and so filled with the wealth of mines of gold, silver, and many other metals?" (*Yucay*, 141).[5] Ah, the heart of the matter.

Sacred Odor of the Mines

Such appetizing natural goods cannot be there for vulgar, animal-like people. The contrast is evident to the author, and he poses a question that can only be resolved on the theological level. García de Toledo undertakes that task by proposing a kind of parable, which reveals his mentality.[6] God behaved "with *these* miserable pagans and with *us* as a father with two daughters." And the parable continues.

> One was very pale and fair, and modest, graceful, and charming, while the other was altogether hideous — bleary-eyed, stupid, and crude. When it came time to marry them off, there was no need of so much as giving the first girl a dowry. She only needed to be seated in a palace, where all the lords vied with one another over who would marry her. With the ugly, lazy, foolish, clumsy one, there was nothing to do but give her a great dowry — many jewels, rich, sumptuous, and expensive clothing — and leave her to heaven.

Without a plenteous dowry there would have been no marriage for the ugly daughter, nor therefore any security for this unfortunate ("y con todo esto dios y ayuda": leave her to heaven — pray for a miracle).

Then the parable is applied to the history of Christianity. "God has done the same *with these and with us*. We were all infidels, in Europe, in Asia. But in our natural aspect, we had great beauty, much knowledge, and discretion." The infidels of the Indies lack all of these human qualities. Accordingly, "little else was needed in order for the Apostles and apostolic men to dispose our souls, with the help of Jesus Christ, for the faith of baptism. Of course, these other nations were God's creatures as well, and destined to beatitude and an espousal to Jesus Christ. But they were ugly, rustic, stupid, inept, and bleary-eyed, and so, a great dowry was required" (*Yucay*, 141–42; emphasis added).

Once upon a time, the Europeans and the inhabitants of Asia Minor were infidels. But they were handsome, worthy, and intelligent.

That was all that was needed to attract apostles and evangelizers. Now these Indians are infidels to be converted too, but ugly ones, unworthy, and dull. Here, then, is the reason for the existence of their mines. This is their dowry, to compensate for the lack of natural endowments in these clumsy, subhuman Indians: "And so he gave them veritable mountains of gold and silver, fertile lands and fair, since, in this sweet odor there would be people who, *for God*, would be willing to go preach the gospel to them and baptize them, and these souls would become spouses of Jesus Christ" (*Yucay*, 142; emphasis added). For God! A curious link is forged between the physiological and the spiritual: the odor of gold stimulates love "for God" on the part of these singular evangelizers and inspires them to come to these lands.

One might look in vain for a more openly racist and Eurocentric affirmation. We declare the superiority of the white race and Western culture ("we"), and our contempt for the native (these "others"). Thanks only to the fragrance wafting from their mines and other riches, these wretched people, so helpless, so lacking in natural qualities, have awakened an interest in some so-called evangelizers. The text goes on to develop the idea, with a cynicism verging on the incredible:

> But I state and dare to affirm without fear of contradiction that in the order of predestination, not only the goods of grace, such as grace, charity, and the virtues, are means of predestination and salvation, but temporal goods as well. Some are means of predestination and salvation, and their default, means of damnation. There are persons who are saved because of their wealth, and others who are damned for lack of it. (*Yucay*, 142)

Salvation or perdition can depend on gold.

Here is an entire Christian theology, that is, a manner of understanding the Christian faith. Our utter rejection of it must not prevent us from seeing the level at which the author seeks to place himself. Not only are grace and charity gifts of the Lord and means of predestination and salvation; temporal goods — in which the author of the *Opinion* has a manifest interest — are as well. The absence of wealth can entail damnation, says the author, emending the gospel of Jesus Christ without batting an eye. Salvation may depend on whether or not one has the material means to attract those who are to come and proclaim God to them. ("Proclaim what God?" we may wonder.) Without wealth, one does not receive the gospel: this is what would have happened, we read, in the case of the wretched inhabitants of these lands if they had no mines. Indeed. Just as we suspected.

The text continues:

> Thus I say of these Indians that one of the means of their predestination and salvation has been these mines, treasure-troves, and wealth, since we clearly see that wherever these are the *gospel spreads by leaps and bounds,* and where they are not, this is a *means of reprobation,* since the gospel never arrives there, as we see by so much experience: The land where this dowry of gold and silver does not exist, there neither soldier nor captain wishes to go, nor any minister of the gospel either. (Ibid.; emphasis added)

As we see, the author has a sorry opinion of those charged with proclaiming the gospel. Their motivations for coming to the Indies go no further than that of soldier or captain.

But his idea of the gospel is even worse. Shamelessness knows no limits. Wealth attracts the gospel (which "spreads by leaps and bounds"). Poverty resists it and is a sign of reprobation. After all, who would want to preach the gospel to the poor? Here we have a genuine rereading of Scripture from the viewpoint of the historical and religious meaning of gold and power. The result is a crying inversion of the teaching of Jesus Christ.

The terms García de Toledo employs shock us. But he is not alone in his position with regard to the function of the mines in the proclamation of the gospel. With a bit more subtlety and complexity and perhaps somewhat resignedly, this position is also found in the celebrated and balanced José de Acosta (celebrated, precisely, for his balance). Acosta, as we have already observed, is among the defenders of the legitimacy of the Spanish presence in the Indies, although not for the reasons adduced by Toledo and his followers. Nevertheless, it is strange that this great expert on the Peru of his time should echo the painful, grotesque text on which we are commenting.

The famous Jesuit admires the wisdom of God in placing in far-off lands, in the Indies and particularly in Peru, "the greatest abundance of mines that has ever been known, in order to attract persons to seek those lands, hold them, and, in passing, communicate their religion and the worship of the true God to those who had not known him." The evangelizers will evangelize in passing, on their way to gold and wealth. After all, the Christian message is spread "not only by those who preach it sincerely and with charity, but also by those who proclaim it with temporal and human ends and means." This is what has happened among us, since "we see that the lands of the Indies most abundant in mines and wealth have been the most advanced in the Christian Religion in our times. Thus does the Lord make use of our efforts for loftier purposes." It is a painful discovery: where the richest mines are, there too is the greater commitment to the "advancement of religion." And then, perhaps indicating the source of these peculiar opinions, in an implicit reference to the author of the Yucay memorandum, he praises him: "In this matter, a *wise man* observed that what a father does with an ugly daughter in order to marry her off is to give her a large dowry. This is what God had done with this so unpleasant land — give her a great wealth of mines so that by that means someone might be found to desire her."[7]

The surprising allusion to a "wise man" on the part of this sensible, remarkable scholar — who, while he did not question the prevailing system, nevertheless denounced in no uncertain terms the more gross abuses of the Indians — unfortunately proves that the mentality reflected in the *Yucay Opinion* was not an exception in the Peru of the time.[8]

A short while before, in his well-known missiological work *De Procuranda Indorum Salute*, José de Acosta had energetically denounced the shameful labor of the mines. To force "free persons who have done no evil" to perform hard labor "seems out and out savage and cruel." This is what is happening in the case of the mines. "Such labor involves the commission of an injustice against the liberty of the Indians, inasmuch as they are obliged to serve the profit of another at the cost of such great personal disadvantage of their own, as they must abandon their land and their children."[9]

But then he at once confounds us:

> On the other hand, if the exploitation of metal mines is abandoned, . . . if the rocky river banks are left unmined, and the various metals are neglected, then will all advancement and public organization of the Indians be abandoned. This is the objective sought by the Spaniards with their great sea voyages. This is the reason why merchants barter, judges sit, and even, often enough, priests preach the gospel.

Acosta comes right out with it. He agrees with the Yucay memorandum, then, on how matters would stand were there no gold in the Indies. "The day gold and silver run out or disappear from circulation, all human cooperation, all ambition for voyaging, all efforts in the civil or ecclesiastical field, would immediately vanish."[10] As we see, Las Casas is not the only one to regard greed for gold as an important factor in the Spanish presence in the Indies.[11] Let us also note that when it comes to the motives of the missionaries, Acosta's terms are at least as hard as Bartolomé's.

The Jesuit confesses himself confused in the matter. "On one hand, I ought to complain of the calamity of our times and such a great cooling of charity." Indeed, he wonders, is it not true that "greed for gold and silver is of so much more account among us that, were these to fail, the salvation of souls would no longer count for anything at all?"

And yet, on the other hand, he profoundly admires "the goodness and providence of God, which accommodates itself to the condition of human beings, and in order to draw to the gospel peoples so remote and barbarous has provided these lands so copiously with metals of gold and silver, as if thereby to arouse the covetousness of our own people." He then asks himself: "If charity for souls does not spur us on, will greed for gold in that case lure us sufficiently?" The flagging Christian zeal of the age discourages him, and he hesitates between disgust and admiration.

Acosta's perplexity does not afflict him long, however. He seizes upon the theological significance of the second alternative. "Who, then, will not gaze in fear and awe upon the secrets of the wisdom of the Lord, who could make silver and gold, that plague of mortals, the salvation of the Indians?" He thinks that we may say, then, that just as from the unbelief of the Jews has come salvation for the gentiles, so too from the covetousness of Europeans issues the salvation of the Indians. Thanks to gold, God's saving love reaches the inhabitants of this faraway land. Having accepted this mediation, Acosta can only ask decent treatment of the Indians working the mines, in conformity with existing laws: "First of all, those who toil in the mines must not be deprived of ministers for their upbringing and spiritual care."

And he brings to a close his study of the function of the mines in the salvation history of the Indies with the following resigned reflection: "If our people rightly observe the conditions of the laws, as these have been conceived by scholars, then it seems to us that tolerance ought to be exercised in their regard, lest, abandoning commerce, they abandon as well the work of the preaching of the gospel." Such a turn of events would be perilous for the Indians: the Spaniards might depart and leave off their evangelization. In all realism, it becomes necessary to accept behavior motivated by the thirst for riches. But the condition will be that the guidelines proposed by learned persons be respected: "If they fail to fulfill these premises and deal cruelly with the Indians, as if they were slaves, let them see the account that they shall have to render to God, who is Father of the poor and Judge of orphans."[12]

A nick in the armor of evil. Mere tolerance is being asked. (Only something evil can be "tolerated.") Acosta's Christian heart may be overgentle in the eyes of some of his compatriots, but this does not mean he rejoices at this reason for the Iberian presence in the Indies.

2. *No Gold, No God*

The author of the Yucay text at least deserves credit for not concealing his reasons and coming right out and preaching what so many still practice today, if in more sophisticated forms (for motives of power and social prestige instead of money, for example), forms more "presentable" in society. Let us not forget, however, that the viewpoint of the poor, a preferential option for the dispossessed (as demanded with renewed vigor in our days by Medellín, Puebla, and John Paul II), was the soul of the practice of many missionaries and bishops as early as the sixteenth century. Then as now, this meant an upheaval, a radical change in practice and perspective, and therefore a change exposed to all manner of attacks at the hands of the established order and the political theologies that justified that order. The Yucay document's criticism of Las Casas and other missioners is a clear example of this intent.

Primacy of the Temporal

The conclusion of all of the foregoing reasoning is ineluctable: "It is good, then, that these barbarians have their mines: God has given them to them to lead them to faith and Christendom and to preserve them in the latter and to save them" (*Yucay*, 142). What Jesus called "devil's dung" has become something sacred. The dilemma between the worship of God and Mammon has been resolved (see Matt. 6:24). In that perspective, Las Casas plainly appears once again as a tool of the demon:

> And now I seem to see from what mold this Father Bishop of Chiapa has extracted the projectile of his opinion that it is a pity that these mines exist: from the same from which that of the demon emerges today. Speaking with the Indians today, one of the things that [Chiapa] most urges upon them is that they conceal the mines and treasure-stores, telling them that were it not for the mines the Spaniards and Christians would leave, and they could return to their idolatries and past life.

"This Father" is a bishop, the text recalls. It is even more scandalous, then, that he would take a position in favor of the Indians' return to idolatry.

The text goes on:

> And this is what the Indians do. They had rather be slain than reveal the location of the mines, since the devil knows full well that these are an effective means of the gospel being in these regions, and that by means of these riches the [Indians] are saved,

and have deprived him of his realm and cast him out. And he has taken as his tool this religious man to conceal these mines and treasures and cast human beings to hell.

In having persuaded the Indians to hide the mines, Bartolomé de Las Casas is actually sending them to hell. This missionary is deceived, then, as he deceives others, by the forces of evil. After all, were there no gold, there would be no gospel, nor any salvation, for the Indians ("by means of these riches the [Indians] are saved"). In that logic, the conclusion is scarcely surprising. "Whence I conclude that this Father has had much of the human spirit and little of the divine in this case, and has been infected by the Evil One — which often occurs even in the holiest of men" (*Yucay*, 142, 143). Admit the premises, and the conclusions follow inexorably.

The devil sees very plainly that gold is an "effective means of the gospel being in these regions" and seeks allies to conjure away this danger. Diabolical knowledge indeed: it is the very devil, then, the "father of lies" (John 8:44), who, it seems to our author, conceals the mines and treasure-stores through certain sadly misled missionaries, friars, and bishops. The most surprising thing is that the devil does this to prevent a greed for gold (which is idolatry; see Col. 3:5, where in the Greek the term used is *pleonexia*) from bringing to the idolatrous inhabitants of the Indies the message of love of the God of truth. What a topsy-turvy world!

In a word, without gold there is no God in the Indies. And the reason for this is that between the desire for gold and the presence of God in these lands comes the intervention of the king, whose task is precisely to see that God be proclaimed. The author is explicit about this: "I say that it is so necessary, morally speaking, that there be mines in these Realms, that were there not, neither would there be a king or a God." That there would be no king without gold "is clear" for our author, so clear that, paradoxically, it shakes (evacuates?) the thesis that the main purpose of the Crown for its presence in the Indies is evangelization. Indeed, in the maelstrom of his argumentation, García de Toledo plunges into an intrinsic contradiction. The king is present, he explains, only because of the gospel:

> Had His Majesty not the charity of the Apostles, he would not have taken upon his shoulders the two precepts he observes: one of having the gospel preached in this new world, and the other of preserving it once it has been received. Furthermore, he would have no more interest or utility here: No longer would he have his double-tithe or his export and import duties, as these would lapse once no more gold and silver were to be had. Trade would

come to a halt, and no king would wish to be king here. (*Yucay*, 143)

The royal "charity," for all its resemblance to that of the apostles, has its motivations and its limits according to the author: it is driven and maintained by gold.

But that without mines there would be no God "is even more clear inasmuch as, in these realms more than in others, the spiritual depends on the temporal" (ibid.). As we see, the *Yucay Opinion* does not make its assertions casually. An entire political theology lies behind its asseverations. The temporal and, more concretely, wealth decide the concrete presence of the spiritual and hold it enthralled: *Where there are mines, there is the gospel.* Here in the New World, things are just the opposite of what the title of a famous book by Jacques Maritain suggests: what we have here is a "primacy of the temporal." That primacy obtains particularly "in these realms, more than in others" — by reason of the beastliness of their inhabitants, of course, which renders them incapable of attracting the heralds of the gospel on the basis of their own qualities and human level. After all, they are hideous, inferior human beings. God's intervention in the Indians' history depends on gold. That intervention is implemented by way of the Spanish Crown and the *encomenderos* of the Indies.

Indeed, the presence of God in the Indies requires that of the king:

> The preaching and preservation of the gospel, which is what I mean by "God," would be unattainable were it not for the Catholic King. How could justice be maintained, without all these ministers, garrisons, and armed forces of the Realm, without all of the clerics and friars, without the security of these Realms on land and sea, without the corsairs we see and without which we should be helpless, without the best of everything and every daily advantage? (Ibid.)

The mines, providential gift of God to the homely, bleary-eyed Indians, will keep the king from going home (and with him the soldiers, civil officials, and *encomenderos*). These excavations are to their advantage. And as we know, this presence ensures that of the evangelizers, also drawn, it would seem, by the sweet odor of wealth.

The conclusion of this bold reasoning is obvious: "The mines, then, are as morally necessary as having a king. Without them, just as without His Majesty, the gospel would not survive. *Holy and good*, then, are they, and for anyone to deny it would be great blindness, and the wickedness of the devil and his works" (*Yucay*, 144; emphasis added). Were the king to withdraw from the Indies, the gospel would take its leave as well, and "there would be no God" in these lands. This is

how things would be were there no gold and silver mines in the Indies. They are "morally necessary." The chain is forged of strong links:
God is present because there is a king, and the king is here because
there are mines. The strongest link in the chain is gold, then — thanks
to which the king remains, incidentally triggering an evangelization.

Now we see in clearer outline the problem the *Yucay Opinion* had
posed from the outset, as it undertook to report the remarkable history
of Las Casas's unfortunate advice and Vitoria's judicious intervention.
By placing gold and silver mines in the Indies, God has provided the
finest reason for the king and queen not to abandon these lands. These
holy and good mines constitute the basis of a theological argument —
one even more incisive than that wielded, presumably, by the master
of Salamanca — that will surely preclude this *spiritual* catastrophe.

Gold thus becomes the authentic *mediator* of the presence of God in
the Indies. The proposition of the Yucay text is a kind of reverse christology. Ultimately, gold holds the place of Christ as intermediary of
the Father's love: Thanks to gold, the Indians can receive the faith and
be saved; without it, they will be damned. This is the heart of the *Yucay Opinion.* This is what gives meaning and vitality to its arguments
in defense of the rights of the Crown and the *encomenderos.*

To this twisted "christology," Bartolomé de Las Casas will oppose — in an evangelical perspective — that of Christ present in the
poor, in the scourged Christs of the Indies. Here we are at the heart of
the matter. Here is a theological difference. In fact, here is a difference
in the manner in which one receives the faith and puts the gospel into
practice. Here is a person who, along with others, rejects the majority
opinion of the world of his days and takes a different one. Actually we
are dealing with two christologies. But before examining Las Casas's
analysis of greed as idolatry, we have one more important point to
consider from the Yucay memorandum.

A Wasteland

In the same vein, García de Toledo adds a number of considerations,
which he acknowledges he has not "proposed at the beginning" (*Yucay,* 144), on the matter of the mines and the *huacas.* In his *Tesoros del
Perú,* Las Casas had written that the gold and silver buried there are
not *res nullius,* something nobody owns, but that they belong to the
Indians.[13]

The problem is posed in the first lines of Bartolomé's *De Thesauris:*

> In the realms commonly referred to as those of Peru, in our
> world of the Indies, there have been found, and continue to be
> found, in the ancient sepulchers called *guacas,* grand and won-

drous treasures of various precious objects — vases and chalices in various shapes, of purest gold and silver, precious stones, decorations or furniture wrought of rich materials, wondrously fashioned, as well as gold and silver in such quantity and of such quality that their existence seems impossible in the world of things and are ascribed rather to the artisanship of the departed. The question before us is whether all of this will belong indifferently to anyone who, whether by private authority or by authorization of our Sovereigns of the Spains, or by that of the governors who rule these regions in the name of the King, seeks it out, attempts to dig it, finds it, and takes it with intent to retain it, and thereby acquires dominion over such things and objects and may possess them in good conscience. (*De Thesauris*, 1)

Las Casas's answer is clear. To appropriate the wealth of the *huacas* "without the authorization and free and gracious will of the Inca King or his descendants" is to commit a "mortal sin of theft or robbery" (ibid., 12v).[14]

The author of the *Yucay Opinion* alludes to this position when he attacks the bishop of Chiapa.[15] The matter, he says, "has become clouded over by the passions that prevail in these realms between religious and laity." The situation has been provoked by Las Casas: the whole difficulty "is owing to the originator and master of this sect and opinion, who was the bishop of Chiapa" (*Yucay*, 144). The "sect" in question, as we know, was composed of numerous missionaries and bishops of the Indies. Once again the author claims to base his position on the facts. The king and his counselors must have a knowledge of the facts, he says, before laws are passed with regard to these territories, or else they will constantly be publishing and abrogating laws: "It will be of great security for the royal conscience and of great [benefit to the royal] authority that he not undo tomorrow what he has done today" (*Yucay*, 145). We hear the echo of the Toledan criticism of persons in Spain, the Council of the Indies itself at times, who paid too much attention to Las Casas and then had to retrace their steps.

In the style of an academic lecture, the Yucay author observes that "these Indians have two kinds of goods: one consecrated to their idols, such as gold and silver;...[and] other goods that have been dedicated to and bestowed on the dead" (ibid.). In both cases, the king, and any Spaniards who found this wealth, have a right to it. After all, gold and silver "must not float about without an owner"; nor can its owner be the devil or an idol, or indeed the "Indian who has had them buried with him, as he is now in the next life, or better, next death," the author specifies sarcastically, in terms of his particular theology, "which is hell, and has voluntarily given them to his gods" (*Yucay*, 146).

García de Toledo likewise staunchly refuses to assign ownership of these goods to the church on the basis that they have been presented through the idols to the true God. No such intention was present, he maintains: in fact, those who offered them "erred, and thus were idolaters, who sinned mortally and were damned" (_Yucay_, 146). God cannot have accepted their intention, and "still less did he receive their offerings of gold or silver or animals" (_Yucay_, 146). Thus, the goods in question were like a stray dog. The conquistadors may, then, without perturbation and in good conscience dispose of these properties — except, of course, the fifth part belonging to the king.

The case is even clearer with regard to other goods. The author slips in a curious argument here, simply applying Western categories to the cultural reality of the Indies. The Indians, he says, have no positive law regulating inheritance. But the only obligation in natural law is that of supporting one's children until they are old enough to support themselves.[16] Consequently, the wealth that the caciques and other important persons bury with themselves in the _huacas_ do not belong to their offspring, who have doubtless emerged from their minority of age. "That part which he has given to no one," writes the author in utter confidence, "but has left for himself, belongs not to his children or his creditors, but to His Majesty, as _res nullius_" (_Yucay_, 149). In fact, for García de Toledo all the Indies are _res nullius_, something no one owns, a no-man's land, given in grace and providence by God to the gold-hunters (and bearers of the gospel, according to this writer) coming from Europe.

Furthermore, the seizure of these goods entails certain secondary benefits of a religious import. It would prevent the Indians from going to the _huacas_ and continuing to practice their idolatrous customs. On this basis, the _Yucay Opinion_ is able to conclude that this wealth is "_res nullius_, the property of his Majesty for expenditure in such lofty works as engage him outside these realms against the infidels, and in these works destroying the errors that are daily professed with these treasures and burials" (_Yucay_, 151–52).

The complacent author brings his composition to its conclusion.[17] He has expounded ideas not to be found in the other texts commissioned by Viceroy Toledo at the same time:

> This, Most Excellent Lord, is my opinion, and Your Excellency commands me to render it. My mind is very satisfied that Your Excellency has thus employed me in my profession, which is to shed light and to have in some measure imitated our Lord Jesus Christ,[18] who tells us that he has come into the world to give testimony to the truth, as I to this new world to give testimony

to that truth so rich of spiritual and temporal goods as this same
world was once full of darkness. (*Yucay*, 144)

His satisfaction comes from having fulfilled his role as a theologian,
shedding the light of the Christian message on things controversial.

His conviction of having reflected on the faith is a firm one. Doubts
arise in us, not in him. Just as Christ came to give testimony to the
truth, that is, to proclaim that God is love, so also the author of the
Yucay Opinion has come to the Indies to enlighten this new world with
"reason and truth," as he has declared to us in the opening lines of his
composition (*Yucay*, 105). He attains this through his reflection, which
counteracts the darkness stirred up by his confrere, Bartolomé de Las
Casas. To shed light on these problems is, for García de Toledo, a way
of imitating Jesus Christ.

The author bids the reader farewell with the wish that from these
shades of night "God may deliver us, that we may presently see light
everlasting. In the meantime may our Lord watch over Your Excellency's most excellent person for many years, that you may complete
such services to these realms as will be of equal grandeur with those
you have begun" (*Yucay*, 152). To this end he has written his little
tract.

An Anxious Heart

It is not easy to resist the temptation to irony in commenting on this
astonishing text. Even allowing for the mentality of the age, its cynicism is shocking, indeed, at times, grotesquely, shatteringly comical.
To attempt to explain it in terms of "the way people thought in those
days" would be a complete mistake. In that same century, we have
the evangelical witness and practice of great missionaries and bishops like Pedro de Córdoba, Montesino, Juan de Zumárraga, Antonio
Valdivieso, Julián Garcés, Vasco de Quiroga, Juan del Valle, and so
many others. Dating from this era, as well, is the great Spanish theology of Vitoria, Soto, Cano, Veracruz, Peña, and many another; and
whatever our observations, even reservations, with regard to one or
another thesis of these theologians when it comes to the Indies, a wide
chasm yawns between their reflections and the theology of García de
Toledo's composition.

Very concretely, this text must be regarded as a testimonial to a
specific mentality, a particular attitude (tied to political and economic
power) toward the Indians and toward poverty in general. The same
will have to be said of its exasperated reaction to the battle being
waged by Bartolomé de Las Casas. Thus, paradoxically, or seemingly
so, the argumentation of the *Yucay Opinion* only corroborates what

Friar Bartolomé already thinks of this kind of defense of the wars of conquest and the regime of the *encomienda*.

In the debate with Las Casas at Valladolid, Ginés de Sepúlveda has alleged that unless there were some profit for the conquistadors, no one would be willing to travel to the Indies. If the king were to lend an ear to Las Casas in this matter, "even were he to be willing to make the expenditure and send men, no one would be found willing to travel so far, not for thirty ducats a month, whereas now they place themselves at such great risk and go to all this trouble for the sake of the profit they expect from the gold and silver mines and from the help of the Indians once these have been subjugated." Like the author of the *Yucay Opinion* (and, to some extent, Acosta), the Cordovan acknowledges the role these mines play in the Iberian mind with regard to the passage to the Indies. Were this enticement to be withdrawn, the consequences for the task of evangelization would be devastating. "Preachers would not go, or if they did go, they would be dealt with as were those who this past year in Florida had been sent without an armed guard, on the same recommendation and urging of this same Lord Bishop." Las Casas's counsels respecting a peaceful evangelization are regarded as having already occasioned the murder of missioners unaccompanied by soldiers (including, in the case alluded to, Friar Luis Cáncer, friend of the bishop of Chiapa).

Furthermore, ever faithful to his thesis of the need for war before the proclamation of the gospel, Sepúlveda continues: "And even if they are not killed, not in a hundred years will their preaching have the effect it has in two weeks *once [the Indians] are subjugated,* as in the latter case [the missionaries] are free to preach publicly and convert anyone so willing, without fear of priest or cacique. The contrary is the case with those who have not been subjugated" (Sepúlveda's Twelfth Objection, 1552, *O.E.* 5:317b; emphasis added). Having decimated the Indians and "disordered their order," as Las Casas puts it, the Spaniards assist the Indians who remain in more readily becoming Christians, according to the royal chronicler.

According to Sepúlveda, then, in whose thinking the Yucay document takes its inspiration, were there no gold, no one would come to the Indies. Bartolomé de Las Casas has said exactly the same thing. The difference is in the ethical and Christian judgment deserved by all those who have come. Las Casas's reply is prompt, then, and he ironically expresses his agreement with Sepúlveda: "He says that it is the hope of gold and silver mines and of the help of the Indians that brings them there. So I too, indeed, believe, as this is what they have always demonstrated by their deeds." And he adds pithily:

After all, they are guided neither by the honor of God, nor the heaven of their faith, nor the intent of succoring and saving their neighbors, nor of serving their king either, of which they ever so falsely boast, but only by their greed and ambition, that they may exercise their tyrannical lordship over the Indians, whom they desire to have distributed to them as if they were beasts, in a perpetual, tyrannical, and hellish distribution.

This, he concludes, making an effort to stay with the objective consequences and not pronounce a moral judgment on the person of his bitter adversary, is "what the Very Reverend Dr. Sepúlveda urges with all his might, although I do not really believe he has any idea of the evil he is doing" (1552, *O.E.* 5:347–48).

The Indians well perceived the lust for gold that consumed the newcomers. "To this very day," writes Guamán Poma some decades later, "that desire for gold and silver abides, and the Spaniards kill one another and ravage the poor among the Indians, who for gold and silver are annihilated — part of this realm, the peoples of the Indian poor. For gold and silver!"[19]

In the old drama, *Tragedia del fin de Atahualpa*,[20] Felipillo, an interpreter, appears, translating the following words addressed by Almagro to Atahualpa:

> This mighty Lord tells thee:
> We, we have come
> in quest of gold and silver!

In the same piece, the princesses (Ñust' acuna), confronted with the demands of the invaders, supplicate Atahualpa:

> Sole Lord, Atahualpa,
>   my Inca,...
>
> The bearded enemy,
>   my Inca,
>
> Has a heart anxious for gold and silver,
>   my Inca.
>
> If gold and silver he will have,
>   my Inca,
>
> Let us bestow it on him, even now,
>   my Inca.[21]

Thus we find many of the great topics of the theological and political controversies of the sixteenth century (the relationship between gold and the gospel, the salvation of unbelievers, the right to war, Indian sovereignty, the just titles of the Spanish Crown, the *encomienda,*

and so on), discussed in the *Yucay Opinion*. This political document —
which it obviously is — written in order to justify Spanish power
and concretely at the service of Viceroy Toledo's political policy, argues theologically. It will be one of the first, but not the last, to do
that on this continent. And so, despite all, Bataillon is not off the
mark in his judgment: "Few documents are more interesting for the
'moral history' of the Indies than the so-called anonymous memorial
of Yucay."[22]

3. "Covetousness, Which Is Idolatry"

At this point it will be helpful for purposes of comparison to bring in a
key text of the Lascasian theology. Writing several decades before the
Yucay document, Bartolomé seems to anticipate the perspectives that
it poses. We refer to a small but beautiful treatise on what St. Paul calls
"covetousness, which is idolatry" (Col. 3:5, according to the Greek). It
is called the *Octavo remedio* (Eighth remedy). It will be worth our while
to examine it in some detail.

In the Service of Greed

The *Octavo remedio* amasses reasons (twenty of them) for not dis-
tributing the Indians as an *encomienda*. This, as we know,[23] is the
principal remedy proposed by Bartolomé for the inhuman situation
afflicting the inhabitants of the Indies. The seventh consideration adduced to demonstrate the harm entailed in the *encomienda* consists
in a reflection on the inordinate thirst for gold, to which we have
referred.[24]

Las Casas begins with the observation that greed is insatiable.
"The void or vacuum of a wealthy person's appetite to be wealthy can
never be filled in this life, since the proposition of acquiring wealth
is always endless." He appeals to Scripture: "The covetous man is
never satisfied with money" (Eccl. 5:9). Consequently, Las Casas maintains (and this is the point of his argumentation), such persons are not
to be entrusted with command or dominion over others: it is imper-
missible to allow "the greedy and covetous person, holding authority
and power over others, to flay them alive and plunder them of their
substance and very blood."

Our author undertakes to detail this basic proposition under three
points. The insatiable quality to which Las Casas has referred, with
an appeal to Boethius, is owing to the fact that the appetite to be rich
"resembles the appetite for total beatitude: just as beatitude promises
one a blessedness sufficient unto itself and all unfailing, so wealth too

promises self-sufficiency." Indeed, "through money human beings acquire all of the temporal things of which they feel the need and desire, such as honor, nobility, status, family ties, pomp, fine garments, alimentary delicacies, the delight of their vices, revenge on their enemies, and great esteem of their persons." Therefore, quoting the First Letter to Timothy, Bartolomé will say: "The love of money is the root of all evil" (1 Tim. 6:10). The covetous plunge into the attainment of their end without respite or rest. Whence it follows that "the appetite of the greedy one is infinite and vehement," so that it is never satisfied.[25]

Hence the fact that the attraction for money is "humanly incurable," as Las Casas says in a second observation. It is worse than the concupiscence of the flesh, "since money is more universal" and, when possessed, "has the faculty of slaking concupiscence," and not the other way around. Besides, "the appetite and greed for money and wealth is hardier and more enduring, because it is constant, than is the lascivious [appetite]." And according to Thomas Aquinas it is more dangerous, the friar from Seville reminds us.

This leads him, thirdly, to treat of a matter especially fraught with consequences. The greedy will stop at nothing in order to satisfy their ambition. That ambition has deprived them of their freedom. Gold has become their lord: "And in the end," Las Casas perceptively observes, "they become captives and slaves of money and must do what their lord commands, walking ever with care and diligence and on the alert to please it and keep it satisfied, since it is from it that they await all their consolation, their good and the purpose of their desires, and all their beatitude." Their lord (at whose service they are — to use Matthew's expression) is money. That makes their judgment of things to be *enajenado,* alienated, under the control of another, and they are no longer in a position to "do the deeds of one who is free." By their works you shall know whom they serve.

Las Casas delves into the motivations of those who travel to the Indies. They are persons who "have once for all surrendered as slaves and captives to avarice, as appears in the works they have done here." Not what they say they believe, but their works prove that those who will stop at nothing to gain gold have made riches their lord. Las Casas takes a further step and goes to the root of the meaning of greed: in the Indies "God is less esteemed, revered, and worshiped than is gold." Gold is the real god of those who abuse the Indians. Greed is idolatry, as St. Paul says. In a similar vein, Guamán Poma, addressing "Spanish Christians" on the basis of a text of Luis de Granada, speaks of a Spaniard who had fashioned an idol of silver and throws that in their faces: "And you have idols in your possessions and your silver!"[26]

Indeed we are speaking about idolatry in the Indies. Las Casas says this explicitly in his first book, speaking of those who provoke "death and butchery by which they inundate all with human blood" and thereby contravene the precept not to spill innocent blood, to seek justice, to succor the oppressed, to render judgment in behalf of the orphan, to defend the widow, to give bread to the hungry. Those who behave in this way do not believe in the true God.

> Rather they spill forth libations to Baal, that is, in other words, they worship the particular idol of those who do these things, which is the idol that dominates them, holds them enthralled, and is in possession of them. That idol is ambition for power and an immense desire to become rich, which has neither escape nor end. "Greed is idolatry, too," as St. Paul says. After all, according to St. Jerome, *baal* means "my idol, that which *possesses* me." All of these things suit very well any ambitious, covetous, or greedy person, especially preachers of this ilk — or better, these wretched, unhappy tyrants. (*De Unico*, 165v–166)[27]

Las Casas is particularly scandalized that what is actually idolatry is disguised as a service to the true God. Apropos of the origins of the *encomienda*, he says:

> With a view to gilding over their most cruel and bitter tyranny, which consumes so many peoples and persons only for the satisfaction of human greed and to get gold, those pretend to teach the faith who do not even know it for themselves, and this is their excuse for the destruction of the innocent in order that from their blood they may extract the *wealth they hold for their god*. (*O.E.* 5:77a; emphasis added)

A *pretended* proclamation of the true God serves to disguise an idolatrous behavior on the part of those who know nothing of the faith. Bartolomé adopts a forthright prophetic perspective here. The idolatry of self-styled believers in the God of biblical revelation must be stripped of its mask. Let us remember that.

In Scripture, the rejection of God is presented as idolatry rather than as atheism. And idolatry is an ongoing risk for the believer. Idolatry consists in placing one's trust in something or someone that is not God, or playing on the ambiguity of asserting God with one's lips while actually seeking other securities and motivations. This, when all is said and done, is the core of the teaching of the prophets and of their denunciation of this perversion of the worship of Yahweh. A text from the First Book of Kings says it with all clarity: "Elijah appealed to all the people and said, 'How long will you straddle the issue? If the Lord is God, follow him; if Baal, follow him'" (1 Kings 18:21). The disjunction is obvious. Yahweh's rejection of idolatry is zealous and energetic. The prophets prove that. To place one's trust in an idol leads to a comportment foreign to the will of Yahweh as expressed in the Covenant between God and the people. Hence God's energetic rejection of idolatry.

Let us take a further step. The Bible specifically denounces the idolatry of gold. The topic comes up in the Old Testament, but it is not expressed there with the force that we find in Jesus and, in his footsteps, in Paul. The familiar text from Matthew reads: "No man can serve two masters. He will either hate one and love the other or be attentive to one and despise the other. You cannot give yourself to God and money" (Matt. 6:24). It is the same exacting disjunction that we find in the First Book of Kings. Only this time the idol is not the god of a neighboring people, but wealth. This god can exercise a subtle attraction on the heart of any believer and thus place him or her at its service. Thus does Mammon (see Luke 16:9–15) confront God in a struggle for the loyalty of persons.[28] The believer must choose. The option for God shuts out all others. "Love" and "hate" here underscore this rejection and call for a decision.

This stark contraposition between God and wealth is part and parcel of the message of Jesus. The option is made not with lips, but with deeds, with a *service* that cannot be offered to God and money at the same time.[29] To serve wealth is to transform it into an alternative to the Lord. In that case God is shut out of our lives. "The lure of wealth choke[s] [the message] off. Such a [person] produces no yield" (Matt. 13:22). And so Paul does not hesitate to call the covetous one an idolater (see Eph. 5:5, Col. 3:5).[30]

A Prophetic Standpoint

Las Casas has adopted this prophetic standpoint with the new and radical precision he receives from the teaching of Jesus. The problem in the Indies is the affirmation of the God of biblical revelation and the worship due that God. Bartolomé's profound biblical sense enables him to see what is at stake in the abuse and the demands suffered by those who dwell in these lands. They come from persons who give over their lives to a false god, persons who place their trust in gold and serve that. The root of what is occurring in the Indies is the idolatry of people who call themselves Christians.

This had already been denounced by the missionaries of Hispaniola, to whose position Las Casas had rallied some years before. They had complained that the "mad lust for gold" in the hearts of the conquistadors had them committing murder without giving it a second thought and making a laughingstock of the work of evangelization. Indeed, there were areas where the missionaries had come in first, and then once the Indians had been "instructed and baptized the Christians came to settle there, and the newly baptized were the first to die in the mines digging gold for the newcomers. Hence the opinion among them that the friars had only come to tame them, so that the Christians could take them and kill them." This tragic end even led the Indians to think that "the crosses they had been taught to trace on their foreheads and breast meant nothing but the ropes they would presently have tied around their necks so that they could be led to their death in the mines." The countertestimonial of Christians nullified the toil of the missioners.[31]

The friars indicate that that behavior had persuaded the Indians, not without reason, that gold "was the god of the Christians, which is what the Indians said: This was their God, and that is why they loved it so." The Christians' practice is leading the natives of Hispaniola to think their god must be gold. And so, the Indians think, were they only to rid themselves of their gold, they would be delivered from the presence of its fervent followers. The friars recount an instructive, pitiful story here:

> A certain chief summoned all of his people and ordered them each to bring their gold to one place and make a pile of it. And he told his Indians: "See, friends, this is the Christians' god. Let us dance before it a bit, and then sail out upon that sea and cast it into the waters. Once they know that we do not have their god, they will surely let us be."[32]

This example shows how the religion of the Christians was understood from an outlook that was likewise religious. For the Indians, gold did not have the commercial value that the Europeans saw in it. The conclusion to which the Indians came — and correctly, in many respects — is fraught with implications for the task of evangelization. The authors of the letter cited are fully conscious of that.[33]

The more serious idolatry, accordingly, is to be found on the side of numerous Christians. To trust in an idol instead of in God is the first mark of idolatry in the Bible. Las Casas finds it again in his experience in the Indies. The consequence of this "error with regard to the end," says Friar Bartolomé in his scholastic language, is the root of all the evils. "This error and exchange of ends has destroyed . . . the Indies." Due to it, human beings are regarded as less important than material goods. "Thus," he writes, "the Spaniards use the Indians as no more than means and instruments to acquire the gold and wealth they desire and hold for their end."[34]

By contrast, Scripture makes us see persons as the end or purpose of social life, and not mere tools for the acquisition of riches and power. This inversion of values is due to the fact that the idol at whose service idolaters place themselves is but the product of human hands. The prophets seize upon this second mark of idolatry and ridicule it:

> The carpenter...cuts down cedars, takes a holm or an oak.... Half of it he burns in the fire, and on its embers he roasts his meat; he eats what he has roasted until he is full, and then warms himself and says, "Ah! I am warm. I feel the fire." Of what remains he makes a god, his idol, and prostrate before it in worship, he implores it, "Rescue me, for you are my god." (Isa. 44:13–17)

Isaiah's sarcasm (part of the wood is kindling, for cooking, and the other part for making into a god) reinforces his denunciation. The idol is a product of the hands of a human being, and therefore inferior to that human being. Yet this is what the idolater transforms into a god.

Las Casas tries to fight this inversion of ends and means, supporting his outlook christologically. Apropos of the utilization of the Indians as means for obtaining wealth, he takes careful aim and writes ironically: "Not so acted *Christ, who came into the world not to die for gold,* but to suffer for human beings in order to save human beings." Jesus' death on the cross reveals God's love and emphasizes God's will "that human beings be the purpose of all things, and not inferior things the purpose of human beings." We go against God, says Las Casas, adopting expressions from the gospel in order to designate money, when "rational creatures whom God loves so much are relegated to a status inferior to trash, dung, and the filth of the earth." Jesus' life and death indicate the authentic order of things.

In denouncing idolatry the prophets tie it to the shedding of innocent blood. For example, Ezekiel says:

> [The] nobles within [the land] are like wolves that tear prey, shedding blood and destroying lives to get unjust gain....The people of the land practice extortion and commit robbery; they afflict the poor and the needy, and oppress the resident alien without justice. (Ezek. 22:27, 29)

They are the victims offered in sacrifice and service to the false God.

Las Casas is sensitive to this cruel aspect of the idolatry that he regards as the root of what is occurring in the Indies. Energetically he denounces the fact that the Indians "now as before, even as I write, are being sucked dry of the substance of their body, since they have nothing else left in their homes." The greed of the conquistador has wrested everything from them. Only the blood of their bodies remains. Bartolomé's reading of Ecclesiasticus has helped him to perceive that he himself had been spilling innocent blood in managing an *encomienda*. The Bible often condemns those who gobble up the poor.

Along these same lines Bartolomé denounces those, whoever they be, who offer human victims on the altar of false gods.[35] He will say, for example, of the violence committed by the Portuguese against the blacks of Africa that the former "had no other purpose but their own interest, and to become rich on others' anguish and on human blood" (*H.I.*, bk. 1, ch. 25, *O.E.* 1:97b).[36]

In a letter to Domingo de Soto, he speaks of *encomenderos* who pay friars to keep them in their service and who support themselves and abide "in their tyrannies by ever maintaining themselves on human blood."[37] And it was bloodshed indeed. In rejecting the figure Fernández de Oviedo gives for the number of persons sacrificed by the Aztecs each year, which Sepúlveda adopts in order to argue in favor of the legitimacy of the wars against the Indians, Las Casas replies by showing which side commits the most murderous idolatry:

> I say that the Doctor has counted very poorly. It would be far more true to say that the Spaniards have offered [more victims] in sacrifice to their beloved and adored god Greed in every province of the Indies, each year that they have been there since they first came, than the Indians have sacrificed to their gods throughout all the Indies in a hundred years. (*Aquí se contiene*, 1552, *O.E.* 5:333b)

Idolatrous worship, in this case the worship of gold, sows death. In these lands, "because there were goods and riches there, which we have plundered and usurped with supreme cruelty, injustice, and tyranny, we have destroyed populations and created a wasteland" (ibid., *O.E.* 5:334b). Gold is mediator not of the gospel of life, but of injustice and death.[38]

4. A Project for Peru

The Toledan reaction did not stifle the voices that called for justice toward the indigenous population, nor did it end Las Casas's influence in Peru. But it had an effect on both. Furthermore, at this time the depth of the confrontation between the Andean world and the order being systematically and oppressively installed in that world became more evident. Bearing witness to this situation is Felipe Guamán Poma de Ayala, to whom we have referred elsewhere in this book. He writes from a mental universe that has made him difficult reading, especially for persons of a deeply ingrained Western outlook. But Guamán proposes to respond to the chaos prevailing in the ancient lands of the Tawantinsuyu. In his battle with a world set on its ear, a battle on behalf of good governance, he utilizes ideas and topics he finds in his own reading, which he incorporates into his project. Among the authors whose concepts he cites is Bartolomé de Las Casas, although he never mentions him by name.

A World Turned Topsy-Turvy

All indications are that Guamán Poma's book-length letter to Philip III failed to reach its addressee. His contemporaries seem unaware of its existence. Consequently it has no place in the disputes then raging over questions of the Indies. Strive as he might to make himself heard (boasting in his letter of a real or fictitious royal lineage), the fact remained that Guamán Poma was an Indian.[39] The lot that befell him, then, was the same as that of the rest: he was ignored by the mighty of this world. His manuscript languished in a corner, forgotten for centuries in the northern cold, to be found in Copenhagen and finally published in 1908.[40]

The text is painfully labored, written with great difficulty in the language of the illustrious personage to whom it is addressed.[41] It reveals the intense life, the anguish, and the hopes of its writer. It also reveals someone who has read widely — more widely than he explicitly claims.[42] Whatever the accuracy of the data and information he provides, what leaps out at us from the page is the speaker's outlook: he writes as an Indian and a Christian who is trying to right once more a world that the coming of the Europeans had turned upside down.[43]

An *Indian* racially, he makes himself one reflexively, as well, taking up the viewpoint and defense of his sisters and brothers. There was no lack of natives of these lands who had become oppressors of their fellows (as has also happened since), and Guamán repeatedly denounces them. He is an Indian also in terms of the cultural universe he expresses, both in his language and in his imagery. With Guamán, not only the text counts; the visual is also of great importance. Word and picture intertwine and shed light on each other.[44] The monotony of the sketches describing the outrages the Indians suffer effectively conveys the daily, repetitive nature of the harsh situation in which they find themselves and makes for a better understanding of the scope of his proposals. These have the litanic force of the clause that comes so frequently from his pen: "And there is no remedy."

Guamán's world, the means he uses to express himself, and the peculiar internal logic of his composition have disconcerted some of his readers. Today, however, valuable analyses have plumbed the thought of this author and have shown that despite the historical inconsistencies, the fictionalized reports, the difficulties of expression, and the at times wobbly appropriation of Western categories, we find an Andean view of the events that have taken place in Peru and a well-pondered proposal for a "good governance" that will be able to deal with the current chaos.[45]

Granted, Guamán's testimonial is atypical. His is an original, complex voice and manifests more than "the Inca reaction." His view of history and his proposal for its betterment have deep roots in the strata of the remote generations of the peoples inhabiting the lands of Peru.[46] Our writer is aware that he will be focusing things differently from the chroniclers of his time, whose works he knows well: hence his title, *Primer nueva corónica* ("First New Chronicle").[47] For purposes of his proposal as well as in order to win a hearing, he adopts European cultural categories, while not renouncing his own. Thus, he attempts to create a worldview of unaccustomed breadth and scope. Like any other creator, Guamán Poma has a world of his own, whose various elements fit together with a precision and a fertility that cannot be observed when they are taken in isolation. Hence the enormous fascination he arouses in those who really decide to enter into this mental universe.[48]

In Search of Christ's Poor

Guamán Poma writes as a *Christian*, as well. Faith in Jesus Christ, who loved the poor with a preferential love, is for him a basic criterion in the discernment between justice and injustice in the Peruvian Andes. Hence the sense and meaning he assigns to his long journey through the ancient Tawantinsuyu. He goes in quest of an intimate knowledge of the spoliation and mistreatment the Indians suffer. He goes in search of "the poor of Jesus Christ."

It is a difficult pilgrimage, that of our scrivener ("true witness of what his eyes have seen," as he says), into the world of the poor, where he loses himself among them. Speaking of himself, he declares:

> The author walked in the poor world with the rest of the Indian poor, to see the world and manage to write the present book and chronicle, as a service to God and His Majesty and crowds of Indian poor of this realm. Thirty years he toiled, leaving his people and buildings and farm, and donning the poorest of sackcloth. And thereby was acquired the author's poverty, which he wished to have in order to see and reach what there was in the world.

This act is reminiscent of a fundamental Christian theme: the *kenosis*, or self-emptying, of God in the Incarnation (see Phil. 2:7). And indeed, immediately after the passage just cited Guamán Poma writes: "I truly say that God became human — the true God and poor."[49] The observation is incisive. God not only became a human being, but concretely a human being who was poor. Jesus' followers must do the same. This is what Guamán Poma declares that he has done. He has walked "with all of his poverty on the way."[50] The reason for his journey was love "for God and the Virgin Mary. . . . For their love he walked in all of this poverty and toil, aged as he was — eighty years old."[51]

Plunging into the world of the Indian poor — abandoning his lofty social condition, he likes to recall[52] — Guamán Poma acquires a firsthand knowledge of the outrages suffered by those poor. Unrecognized, he has suffered just as they: "Since they know me not," he reports, "and see me poor, in my presence they take their farms and wives and daughters with little fear of God and justice. I tell the truth, recounting my poverty: Entering into their midst as a poor one among so many animals who devour the poor, I too was devoured, even as they."[53]

This last phrase has a distinct biblical ring. In Scripture the exploitation of the poor is denounced as an act of voracity. The psalmist says, "Will all these evildoers never learn, they who eat up my people just as they eat bread?" (Ps. 14:4). Guamán is severe with those who comport themselves in this way. Addressing "Spanish Christian readers," he attacks them on the basis of their own faith: "You say, when you flay one another (and much more so the poor Indians), you say you shall have to make restitution. I do not see that you make restitution, either in life or in death. It seems to me as a Christian that you all damn yourselves to hell."

Why are these Christians damned to hell? Because the exploitation of the Indian is a personal offense to God. "The poor," he declares, "are despised by the rich and prideful, who think that there is no God or justice where the poor are. But it ought to be obvious from the faith that where the poor are, Jesus Christ himself is. Where God is, justice is."[54] The writer's evangelical inspiration is evident: He is paraphrasing Matthew 25:31–46. He is writing his book-length letter lest the "poor of Jesus Christ" continue to suffer contempt and persecution.[55]

Christian behavior is based on love, especially love for those in need. "To serve our Lord," he writes, "and to favor the poor" are two sides of the same coin.[56] Thus, he presents himself as someone who "has traversed the world to see where justice lies, and to provide the poor with his justice and remedy."[57] And when meeting anyone indigent, "from my own, from what I had out of my poverty, I gave that person to eat."[58]

The situation seems devastating to Guamán Poma, and once more he finds biblical ways to express it. He cites the prophet, "Lord, how long shall I cry and thou not respond to me?" (see Ps. 13:1–4). Later, addressing "Christian readers among good Christian Indians, male and female," he comments: "Together with [the prophets], speak with tearful voices, groaning with your heart and soul and mouth, tongue and eyes." Speak with all your being. Here is the prayer of protest. It recurs frequently in the Old Testament, but is neglected by Christians today. Its refrain: "And there is no remedy."[59] And finally an expression of confidence: "Cease not to weep with the prophets, who will help you. And everyone answers me, 'Amen, Jesus!' "[60]

It is an expression of hope, as well, both eschatological and for the present. In discussing with a Spaniard the ordinances of Viceroy Toledo, Guamán Poma appeals to God's justice: "Sir, I have the hope that Jesus Christ is to come again to judge the wicked and punish them, and that he will give glory to the good. It is a good and holy thing to favor the poor of Jesus Christ."[61] The certainty of the Last Judgment will provide a guideline for one's behavior: One should favor the poor. Ultimately, no one is mightier than "the poor and their God."[62] Meanwhile, the thing to do is to keep walking "toward the remedy, and service in the world to God."[63]

As we see, the phenomenon of the poor, regarded from a christological viewpoint, is a capital element in Guamán's worldview. Guamán will even personally identify with Christ. According to Scripture (Phil. 2), though Son of God, Jesus annihilated himself as such, becoming one of us. His first thirty years are called his hidden life. He was but another artisan of Nazareth. He lived in poverty, he was crucified by the powerful of his time, and before he died he cried out, "My God, my God, why have you forsaken me?" (Mark 15:34).

Guamán sees a parallelism with himself. He too has had his hidden life, to which he assigns the unlikely, but symbolic, duration of thirty years, the length of time he has wandered all up and down the Tawantinsuyu. He has lived among the poor, having abandoned his lofty social estate, has raised his protest to God for the sufferings of which he has been a witness and which he himself has suffered, and has been devoured by those who were abusing the Indian poor, taking him for one of them.[64] And so the search for Christ's poor acquires certain crucial connotations. Jesus declared them privileged addressees of the Reign he had come to proclaim. To be a Christian, that is, another Christ, means proceeding in the same way. Conversely, in the poor we find Christ himself. In other words: we find Jesus Christ at both the point of departure and the point of arrival. This effort to identify with Jesus — and with his deed of redemption and liberation — reinforces Guamán's quest for the "Indian poor" and freights with towering implications his will to put an end to the cosmic and concrete chaos transpiring in the "Indies of Pirú."

Good Governance

The same framework houses Guamán Poma's concrete proposals for Peru. These have been examined many times. Our own interest lies in emphasizing the points of contact with Lascasian notions. This will demonstrate the influence of the Dominican's ideas in the land that robbed him of his sleep in the last years of his life.[65]

As we have observed, Guamán does not mention Las Casas. It would certainly have been risky to do so after the Toledan campaign against the friar, who was regarded by the Peruvian *encomenderos* as an enemy of the interests of the Crown.[66] The Indian chronicler is concerned with the feasibility of his project and seeking to avoid obstacles along the way. But this does not deprive his denunciation of its force. He is convinced of the radical injustice of the way in which the Hispanic presence in these lands has materialized. The religious perspective in Guamán is not an irrational element (in the pejorative sense of the word), as it has at times been said to be. On the contrary, his Christian motivation lends strength and radicality to his critique.

There are revealing convergences between the principles enunciated by Las Casas in his *Doce dudas* and Guamán's position. Both reject the thesis of a just war to be waged by the Spaniards. Our chronicler repeats the idea that the Indian rulers are legitimate political authorities.[67] That coincides with a Lascasian postulate, of course,[68] but it is also true that other theologians, including Francisco de Vitoria, maintained it. Guamán also holds the second Lascasian principle, which requires respect for the usages and customs of a people who have caused no offense (ibid., *O.E.* 5:487–91), and he will repeat it on numerous occasions.[69] The claim implied here is one we meet in both authors: the Indians are of equal worth and dignity with the Europeans.

Particularly important is the matter of restitution.[70] No one insisted more on this than did Las Casas, or endowed it with the comprehensive scope it has in his work. Guamán also makes this point an ongoing demand,[71] which he carries — as did Las Casas — to the extreme of proposing the restoral of the realm of Peru to its legitimate rulers. While for Las Casas the legitimate sovereign is the direct descendant of Guayna Cápac, the Inca Titu Cusi, according to Guamán the Peruvian dominion should be handed over to his own son, in whom, he declares, are combined both the Inca legitimacy (which Guamán claims for his family) and that of the Yarovilcas, who were local rulers before the coming of the Incas.[72] Here we have not only a familiar theme, but doubtless as well the reverse influence of the aggressive Toledan attempt to demonstrate that the Incas were tyrants and usurpers of the legitimate sovereignties that preceded them.

The candidate proposed by Guamán, then, is less vulnerable to this criticism.[73]

But Guamán's proposal and its ties with Lascasian ideas go much further than this. The project of the restoration of the rightful "king of the Indies" is part of another, much larger one. Guamán boldly posits a kind of planetary political organization, where each nation has its place and where the rights of all are respected. In other words, he envisions the contrary of what is occurring in the Peru of his time. The model he has in mind is one that had once prevailed in the Tawantin-suyu. There the Inca "had four kings, of the four parts of this realm."[74] Thus, he recommends to King Philip that he declare himself "monarch of the world, . . . for the governance of the world and the defense of our holy Catholic faith, the service of God," and that he have under his authority the kings of the four parts of the world: the Indies (his own son), Guinea (as he calls Africa), Rome ("the king of the Christians of Rome, or another king of the [Christian] world"), and, surprisingly, Turkey (the "king of the Moors of the Grand Turk"). These four kings will wield equal authority and must acknowledge the supreme dominion of King Philip.[75]

Guamán's treatment of this subject is typical of his use of his sources. He is creating his own original rereading of the Lascasian thesis of the universal sovereignty of the king of Spain, which, upon acceptance by the Indian nations, would permit them to deliver themselves from the domination they suffer at present, to have their autonomy respected (within certain limits), and to reestablish justice. We may even say that Guamán's proposal is more ambitious than Las Casas's: after all, what he recommends is a new world order, in which peoples of different cultures and religions would coexist.[76] The universality of his outlook does not militate against the fact that his major concern is the Peruvian situation. But once again we have what in our own days we see in someone like J. M. Arguedas: in plumbing the depths of the singular, of his own cultural values, of the rights of every person and every people, he acquires a universal voice.[77]

So much for the areas of agreement. There are divergences, as well, if minor by comparison. One of them has already been noted.[78] In his eagerness to deny the justice of the wars against the Indians and their consequent subjugation, Guamán attempts to show that the Indians are descended from Noah and that they were Christianized in the apostolic age. Inca idolaters effaced that faith, but it is plain to Guamán that the Christian message did not come to these lands only with the arrival of the Spaniards. Evangelization, then, would be no justification for a Spanish presence in these lands. But his argument turns against the one who wields it: in that hypothesis, the theology and law of the time would regard the Indians as apostates and consequently deserving of punishment. For these reasons, Las Casas not only does not propound this theory, but explicitly rejects it.

A less relevant difference lies in Guamán's report that the Inca, through an emissary, Don Martín Guamán de Ayala (the chronicler's father), had agreed to hand over the realm of Peru to the king of Spain through Pizarro.[79] In this context, the use of force against the indigenous peoples would have been the violation of an accord, and thereby an additional reason for a denunciation of the injustice of the present situation. There is no such thing in Las Casas, for whom the manner of the Spaniards' entering Peru is in violation of natural and divine law, not of a pact between two nations.

To be sure, Domingo de Santo Tomás plays a decisive role in Guamán's familiarity with the Lascasian ideas.[80] Usually more reticent with respect to his own reading, the Indian chronicler cites Friar Domingo explicitly. Nor could he ignore the interventions on behalf of the Indians of the author of the first Quechuan grammar — some of them executed jointly with Las Casas. But there is one connection with the Lascasian theses that seems to us to have passed unobserved until now. We are thinking of Friar Luis de Granada (d. 1588), likewise mentioned by Guamán.

Friar Luis's influence on our chronicler is well known and has been analyzed by R. Adorno.[81] To her important findings we may add the datum of the bonds of friendship and ideological intimacy that joined Luis de Granada with Bartolomé Carranza[82] and Juan de la Peña, Dominicans like himself, and through them (if not directly, as well) with Las Casas. Luis could not have been ignorant, then, of what was happening in the Indies.

Or consider this passage from a sermon of Luis de Granada for the feast of St. Dominic:

> Against the Indians, who have been discovered in the New World almost in our own days, the soldiers have so raged and treated them with such cruelty that the name of Christian has become hateful and abhorrent in the extreme by reason of these horrible atrocities. And thus when religious come to them to preach the gospel, lest they take fright and flee at hearing the name of Christ, a friend advises them in advance that these are not Christians, but certain Fathers who come for their good, and to instruct them in the faith. What more lamentable thing could be imagined? What could be more unworthy?[83]

This concern on the part of the friar must have been an additional reason for the sympathy Guamán expresses for him, and perhaps another route by which he has become familiar with the Lascasian ideas. What is certain is that, if these ideas have a repercussion on Guamán's work, it is because they were so firmly anchored in the reality of the Indies — in the sufferings and hopes of their inhabitants — and in the gospel of Jesus.[84] More than a project, then, with particular accents in each writer, perhaps it is a common attitude that Las Casas and Guamán share, a manner of regarding the death and life of the Indians, injustice and justice in the Andes, and the encounter with Christ in the poor.

This attitude brings Las Casas's name to the fore again at other moments of the history of this continent and our country.[85] Not always well known and understood, Bartolomé's voice is nevertheless, all admit, the voice of the most forgotten among us. A revived interest in Guamán's work in our day has revitalized Bartolomé's own challenge. The hoary texts we read keep alive, amid the untimely, unjust death of so many in our own day, amid the contempt of their neighbors, amid their marginalization, the proposal of a Good Government.

Conclusion to Part Five

It is impressive to see Las Casas advance in age and wisdom. His view becomes more and more organic and acquires long-term dimensions. His vision and project for Peru take shape gradually, going hand in hand with his growing conviction that the consent of the people is an indispensable condition for the validity of any decision affecting a nation. Not that he did not stumble along his way or that no stones lay in his path; but little by little his step grew firm and his route less encumbered. A little rivulet at first, the democratic theory swells in his mind to a raging torrent, as it incorporates its tributaries — the themes Bartolomé has developed in earlier years (restitution, for example) — and pours into the land of Peru.

There are those who dispute the feasibility of his proposal. But no one doubts the enormous respect that proposal implies for the Indian nations, their rights, and their values. And in this alone there is an important, imperishable message (to which Guamán Poma was sensitive). And we pay attention today for, despite the disappearance of the immediate political framework, the substance remains of the protest of these marginalized peoples, to whom, in one manner or another, many of us who live in Latin America belong.

For its part, the Toledan era sought not so much to declare the Lascasian ideas incapable of realization as to undermine their foundations. To this end, it attempts to prove that the Incas are not legitimate natural sovereigns, but simple usurpers: thus Bartolomé's project for Peru would be meaningless. The friar's works are recalled to prevent their doing still more damage in Peru. The theological extreme of the viceroy's campaign was the fashioning of a kind of theology that would justify the exploitation of the mines and the sack of the *huacas* (the subject of Las Casas's last two works). In the end, contrary to every requirement of the gospel, that theology serves ill-gotten wealth. "The worship of Mammon," Las Casas had once called this behavior and this legitimation, and he identified it as the Christian idolatry that scandalized Indians accused of idolatry. Here the Dominican will remind us of the poor Christ and the poor in Christ, as the authentic motivation and privileged addressees of the proclamation of the Reign.

The situation in Peru causes Bartolomé to hasten his step. True, the lust for gold had prevailed since the times of Columbus; but a few decades later, to say gold was to say Peru. For these reasons, in the important dedication of his *Doce dudas* to Philip II, still unpublished today, Las Casas warns the king to "trust more in the Providence of that supreme King and most almighty *God*" than in "the gold of Collao" or "the silver of Potosí." Besides, "with a little money, well spent, and a tiny army," the king will win more victories and greater glory than "with the millions that come to him ill-gotten — as is everything that is brought to him from the Indies" (*Doce dudas*, Providence version, folio 136; emphasis added).

Those of us who find in Las Casas and in Guamán Poma inspiration to learn about and confront the problems of Latin America and Peru may well make our own the lovely expression of Garcilaso de la Vega — who spoke from a very particular experience of his own and his family — regarding Spain and Peru: "I have things on deposit in both nations."

Conclusion _____

And They Said
They Would See It...

══

Las Casas's reflections lead us down to the most profound levels of the history of the peoples caught up in the whirlwind of sixteenth-century events. They thrust us beyond the conjunctural. They help us not to become enmired in the anecdotal or lost amid the peaks and valleys of the age. They set us inexorably before the high stakes of the Indies: the life and death of their inhabitants. It is that simple and that scandalous. Here, according to Bartolomé, is the ground on which Jesus' resurrection — life's definitive victory over death — is to be proclaimed.

At that time, many considered that the Indians lacked any values of their own. As Columbus himself had said, they were a *tabula rasa*, a clean slate. Consequently, their lot was to toil for the newcomers and ultimately to be assimilated by them. By contrast with those who thought and acted in this manner, Bartolomé de Las Casas, and certain others with him, saw in the Indians the *other* — the one who was different from Western culture. The route to this genuine discovery was longer and more hazardous than the one Columbus had undertaken across uncharted seas. Not without sluggishness, not without limitations, these persons, whose cultural distance from the Indians was so great, gradually divested themselves of their spontaneous sense of superiority and sought to move to the viewpoint of the dispossessed. This effort enabled them to read history in a different way and to understand the meaning of the swift and violent events of those years from the other side of that history.

The attitude was necessary also in order to avoid evangelization becoming just another way of subjugating the Indian nations.[1] This is precisely what happens whenever the gospel is unduly linked to a particular culture, whenever the evangelizer fails to follow the path of what we call today the inculturation of the faith. The word is new, but the reality is old. For believers it rings of incarnation and of a presence

455

of God that is respectful of the human condition. Thus, for Las Casas the "only way" to evangelize is by persuasion and dialogue.[2] Seeing things "as if we were Indians" — that is, from the viewpoint of the race, customs, cultures, and religious practices of the Indians — makes us more sensitive to the injustice of the treatment being inflicted on the autochthonous population, as well as to the rejection of evangelical values that this violation of their rights implies.

Bartolomé had another penetrating intuition. He saw in the Indian, in this "other," this one-different-from-the-Westerner, the poor one of the gospel, and ultimately Christ himself. This is without a doubt the very key to the Lascasian spirituality and theology. It sketches Bartolomé's "intelligence of faith" with original strokes, giving it its own physiognomy among other theological reflections of the age. The right to life and liberty, the right to be different, the perspective of the poor — these are intimately connected notions in the experience our friar has of the God of Jesus Christ, in whom he believes with all his strength, a strength he therefore places at the service of the liberation of the Indian. Despite the obvious distance between historical contexts, Bartolomé's commitment constitutes a challenge for us today. In our times, too, the rights of the poor and oppressed must be defended according to the guidelines of the Medellín Conference.[3] We are called on to defend these persons' values — and in a way, to defend their very existence, inasmuch as they continue to be treated as if they were "nonpersons."

In view of all of this, Las Casas's witness is particularly important for the self-discovery that the peoples of Latin America must make today. The sixteenth century was decisive in our history. Things happened and options were made then that marked the centuries to come. From the Christian viewpoint, Bartolomé sees it as the "time of vocation" and calling of the Indian nations, the time when God "decided to open the treasures of the divine mercies." But greed and arrogance transformed that time into a "time of tribulation, a time of drought, of revenge, of rage, of affliction and dissipation, a cruel, deadly time." That age became an age when not only the bread that feeds the body was denied and withheld from the Indian, but also "the bread that feeds souls, which is the teaching of Jesus Christ." The text we cite, which expresses a lucid historical intelligence and a faith sensitive to persons' daily lives, concludes with a painful, acute question: "And when ever, in another time, was death so sorely, or at any rate so speedily, sovereign?" (_Carta al Consejo, O.E._ 5:47b–48b).

How often we have asked ourselves the same question, in this, the hour of Latin America and Peru! Why indeed does death continue to be so sovereign among us? Ours is a time of drought and tribulation, but also, in terms of the rich Lascasian focus, of calling and mercy. These two times frame, and press, our freedom, our projects, our hopes. When we have transformed the one into the other, we shall have embraced the ultimate meaning of Las Casas's life and work: to be a witness of the God who is "rich in mercy" (Eph. 2:4) in the Indies. This witness cost some missioners their lives in Bartolomé's day, as it has other Christians in our era. In between, how many dear, beloved friends have fallen as well — our companions along our way, with whom we have shared concerns and perplexities, joys and sorrows, projects and leisure, Eucharist and silence! It is certain that their death has left an indelible trace on our lives. This martyrdom is the wealth, a sorrowful wealth, of the church of yesterday and today on this continent.

We have no intention of positing facile equations between eras endowed each with its own coordinates and personality. But neither must we fail to perceive the points of contact between them or the teachings that we can gather from the past. The present acquires density and substance when it is nourished by the memory of a journey, when the courage is found to identify unsolved problems and wounds not yet healed. Here are gaping maws that hunger still and voraciously consume so many energies today. The historical view gains effect and luminosity when maintained from the present. This has its risks, of course, and consequently must be done with great respect for a far-off age so different from our own.

Part of this memory means acknowledging our responsibility in what the poor have always had to suffer. The Christian manner of assuming this responsibility is to beg humble forgiveness from God and the victims of history for our complicity, explicit or tacit, past and present, as individuals and as a church. To ask to be forgiven expresses a will to change in our behavior and reasserts the obligation of being an efficacious sign in the history of the Reign of love and justice.[4] It is not a fixation on the past. It is a step toward the future.

Only historical honesty can deliver us from the prejudices, narrow interpretations, paralyzing ignorance, and the deceptions foisted on us by private interests, which lay our history on us like a permanent mortgage instead of transforming it into a thrust to creativity. The recovery of our memory will inspire us to fling to the trash heap as inadequate, and consequently useless, the so-called white legend and black legend of what occurred in the sixteenth century. A concealment of the complexity of what occurred in those years for fear of the truth, in order to defend current privileges, or — at the other extreme — a frivolous, irresponsible use of offensive expressions, condemns us to historical sterility.

At the same time, our interest in and revulsion for much of what occurred with the various Indian nations and cultures in the sixteenth century must not incline us to ignore the intricate process of later centuries, with the arrival of new races and cultures, or the situation of injustice and dispossession in which the poor of today find themselves on this continent. In view of current problems, it would be a grave error to allow concerns aroused by the fifth centenary to confine us to the sixteenth century. In our day, as well, we have a destruction of persons and cultures, and we continue to hear "the just cries, which everywhere have mounted to heaven," as Túpac Amaru said, in accents identical with those of the Bible. Latin American reality is variegated, and cannot be explained through summary, jejune analyses.

One of the major challenges of Latin America and Peru is our cultural plurality. Here a wealth becomes a stumbling-block when its enormous possibilities go unrecognized and undeveloped. Many different racial, cultural, and spiritual families live in these lands, but they have not yet learned to live together. None of them must arrogate to itself alone the representation of the continent, none must be marginalized and despised. All should participate on an equal basis in the building of a just and democratic society. Racism is an assault on human dignity and Christian conscience.

In the quest for this life of social harmony, the proclamation of the Christian message — in deed and word — has a role to fulfill, inasmuch as that message can be fittingly proclaimed only in profound respect for the cultural values of peoples and the freedom of persons. Rightly have Medellín and John Paul II so insistently called for the undertaking of a "new evangelization," one that will take into account the unprecedented aspects of the current situation, a situation as new as the commandment of love is ever new (John 13:34). The special bearers of this evangelization — as Puebla demanded[5] — must be the poor, the members of the races, cultures, and social classes that our society marginalizes.

The witness of martyrdom, to which we referred a moment ago, demonstrates that those members of the people of God on pilgrimage in Latin America were speaking very seriously in these lands when, more than twenty-five years ago, they provided the church with the impulse for a preferential option for the poor. Thus did they lay the foundations for a new evangelization. And thus did they blaze a trail to a new set of social relations in Latin America.[6]

In this task, the example of Bartolomé, a "witness of the gospel before the eyes of the poor," as M.-D. Chenu described him,[7] has much to teach us. It requires a great deal of effort to find new avenues for the transmission of the gospel message. It requires a dogged attention to a changing situation to find an evangelization for our times. Creativity and tenacity were precisely two characteristics of that prophet of his time that Las Casas was. And both were maintained by a great sensitivity to the human suffering that makes Juan Gonzalo Rose say, with poetic intuition:

> Ah, militant of Christian love!
> In the name of my people I baptize thee:
> friar human being,
> friar friend,
> friar sibling. ("Epístola a Bartolomé de Las Casas")

Here is a human being who defended the equality of all human beings, a friend of God who is in turn the "friend of life" (see Wis. 11:26) and the brother of all those in whom he read the face of Christ, our elder Brother. Las Casas, who could not recount "without tears" (*Apología,* 237) what was occurring in the Indies, who seemed to have been born "to mourn for others' griefs" (*Carta al Rey,* 1559, *O.E.* 5:463a), is one of those who have not appeared before the Lord with dry cheeks and who therefore have received the tender consolation of which the prophet tells: "The Lord God will wipe away the tears from all faces; the reproach of his people he will remove from the whole earth" (Isa. 25:8).

Toward the end of his life, Las Casas dispatched a memorandum to the Council of the Indies in which he summarized the position he had adopted throughout his life in matters of the Indies. His poor state of health prevented him from presenting his petition personally, and his close followers and friends took up the relays. One of them, the great theologian Alonso de Veracruz, has left us a revealing testimonial. "And this is the truth," writes Veracruz, honestly adding an indication that seems sad and ironical to us today: "They [the Council] provided nothing in this respect. Instead they said that they would see to it" (*O.E.* 5:538b). This is the answer the poor continue to hear on this continent. We are still "seeing to" the memorandum they have been formulating for centuries in defense of human beings' most elementary demand: the right to God's gift of life.

A response to the call of the poor requires that we pose ourselves a question in all honesty. How can we make faith in the God who "has a very fresh and living memory of the smallest and most forgotten" the inspiration of our lives? How can we transform this time of dissipation and death into a time of calling and grace? In other words, how can we make our own today the counsel the great apostle Paul received from the "pillars" of the church — to be "mindful of the poor" (Gal. 2:9, 10)?

Neither Las Casas nor Guamán Poma shows us the way. This is our charge and responsibility. They do give us the impassioned witness of their own quest, which they carried forward with determination and hesitancy, in success and failure, right on target and missing the mark, amid light and darkness — but ever with hope and with love, in the footsteps of Christ's poor. Rather than fixate on the past, we are called by them — each of us from his or her own cultural world — to make the present our own and to shape and forge the time to come.

They both challenge us to hurry to write our names, in all haste and urgency, with purpose and determination, on the pages of that history of long duration that is the coming of the Reign of life proclaimed by Jesus.

Appendix 1 ———————————————————

The Demographic Question

A consideration of the question of the population of the Indies will afford us a better understanding of why the debates of the first century of the European presence were so heated and invested with such a sense of urgency. The first missioners used the word "destruction" to express their terrible experience. They are speaking of the decimation of a population. It is very difficult, however, to arrive at a precise calculation of the population of these lands before the coming of Columbus. We are dealing with an area in which it is impossible to move with certitude for want of adequate data, as well as with a question that for many is emotional in the extreme.

The Indies

Calculations vary enormously. The lowest estimates of the total population of the Indies at the moment of the arrival of the Spaniards are those of Kroeber (8.4 million), Rosenblat (13.4 million),[1] and Steward (15.5 million). The highest are those of Dobyns (90–112 million) and the Berkeley school (100 million).[2] Sapper (37–48 million) and Rivet (40–45 million) stand midway. Denevan offers a state of the question in the form of a carefully pondered balance sheet of the studies devoted to the matter: after reviewing the criteria used to calculate the pre-Columbian population of the Indies, he settles on the figure of 57.3 million persons, with a margin of error of 43–72 million.[3]

Reacting to the use of high figures for the pre-Columbian population by other European countries for centuries now to disparage Spain, Spanish historians have always been reluctant to accept relatively high estimates. Spirits are calming, however, as two recent studies demonstrate. A. Gutiérrez recalls some of the data we have noted above and takes the following position: "From all of the information available, certain mean calculations can be arrived at that would place the indigenous population of the territories colonized by the Spaniards at some seventy million natives."[4] M. Lucena, for

461

his part, calculates "the native population of the Ibero-American territory" at 65 million.[5]

But we shall not appreciate the point of these calculations, which is the extent of the *de*-population of the Indies, unless we also refer to calculations of the indigenous population some years after the arrival of the Europeans. Here too estimates vary, but less widely, since the available sources are more reliable. We may speak of a population of some 9 million for so-called Spanish America (by far the more populous area) as a whole by 1570, the date of an important taxation census in these lands.[6]

Rosenblat, who as we know prefers a relatively low count of the original population, estimates 10 million by 1625 (and 8.5 million in 1825, the lowest point, in his calculations, of the native population), signifying a decrease of 25 percent in the initial population as he estimates it. At the other extreme, Dobyns thinks that the population fell to a bare 4.5 million by 1650 — a decrease of some 95 percent. Lucena speaks of the disappearance of 60 million natives by mid-seventeenth century (including Brazil).

Whatever estimate we may select, we are surely faced with a demographic catastrophe. This is the case even if we accept Rosenblat's low estimate. And it is especially the case if we realize that we are speaking of living persons — that is, beings who reproduce and who, consequently, normally (even in the case of a low rate of growth) increase in number with the passing of time. That is, the sole fact that in the course of a century-and-a-half a population would have — in the proportion indicated by the above hypothesis — declined by 25 percent would actually mean that the number of persons who had lost their lives was far greater than 25 percent of the initial population. Furthermore, practically all demographers and historians reject Rosenblat's position and incline, as we have seen, to higher numbers. Thus, the decline in population becomes far more rapid.

Hispaniola

According to historians, there are reliable data to support an estimate of between 20,000 and 30,000 Indians on Hispaniola by 1510.[7] Calculations of the original Taino population vary, to be sure. The first Dominican missionaries spoke of 2 million, Las Casas (on the basis of an estimate by Columbus) of 3 million, figures some regarded as overblown. But the celebrated Berkeley school says 8 million. Years before, Rosenblat had declared that it was no more than 100,000 to 120,000. A recent study attributes to the island an original population in the vicinity of 400,000.[8] The truth is that, whatever the calculation one accepts (even discarding the highest estimates), we are confronted with an impressive demographic collapse, which becomes even more catastrophic when we reflect that by 1540 there were no more than 300 natives living on Hispaniola.[9] It is not difficult to imagine that this decrease in population must have been a terrible experience for those who lived on the island in those years, and this helps us understand the tone and sense of the missionary friars' defense of the Indians.[10]

Peru

Different calculations have also been made for the population of Peru. The most important work in this area has been done by N. D. Cook. This author analyzes in detail the various methods employed to estimate the original native population, cites the results of those studies, and concludes that it must have declined from 9 million (in 1520) to somewhat more than 1 million in 1570 and a bit over 600,000 in 1620. According to this, the population drop was dizzying, especially along the coast.[11]

The Causes

The causes of this huge demographic decline are various. Four basic ones are acknowledged: malnutrition and dietary changes, new illnesses (smallpox, measles, typhus, influenza, and so on), against which the indigenous population had no immunity, the wars of conquest, and hard labor. But clearly these factors do not simply act in parallel: they combine, with the result that the effect of each is exponential. Furthermore, there were other causes, like suicide, the forcible separation of men and women,[12] and the "loss of appetite for life" (Sánchez Albornoz).

In a documented article F. Guerra affirms that illnesses were actually the prime factor in the frightful population decline.[13] Doubtless that was a very important cause, but it should not be overestimated in the case of Hispaniola. Indeed, the first epidemic (smallpox) reported there began in 1518, when the population had already plummeted.[14] It is curious, nevertheless, that Guerra, who seems to admit that a demographic collapse did indeed occur in the sixteenth century,[15] censures Las Casas for not having perceived the role played by diseases, as if the culture of that time must have had an understanding of contagion such as we have with modern medicine.[16]

Conclusion

Obviously all of this is approximation and must remain open to further determinations and corrections. We may indeed say that in light

of all of today's studies and taking into consideration all the imprecision that these inevitably have, the figure of 20–25 million dead for the
whole continent, advanced by Las Casas around 1552, is a rather mid-
dling one,[17] especially in view of the fact that the demographic drop
occurred preponderantly in the first decades, with which Bartolomé
was familiar.[18] Thus, Las Casas's estimate is close to while somewhat
below current conjectures — which is all the more remarkable since
in his time the means that we use today to make these calculations
were not available. But unquestionably this is a subject that will long
continue to be discussed.

A New Document of Las Casas

In chapter 10, note 25, p. 552 above we alluded to the discovery of a text by Las Casas related to the New Laws. We now have access to it thanks to the Biblioteca Nacional of Madrid, which has just published it in a beautiful facsimile edition of the manuscript under the title *Conclusiones Sumarias sobre el remedio de las Indias* (1992). The publication includes two brief but important studies by Helen Rand Parish and Isacio Pérez Fernández, who in various ways have been involved in making the document known and in establishing its authenticity.[1]

The document is of great historiographic value. And it is definitive with regard to Las Casas's central role in the enactment of the New Laws (1542–43). In a way that is characteristically his, Las Casas (with R. Ladrada to be sure) presents six truths (the basis for what follows) and then sixteen "universal remedies" for all the Indies and eighteen "less general remedies" addressed to the "terra firma," that is, the continent, and to the islands that "are already destroyed." The text includes only those remedies regarding the continent.

With regard to content the memorial takes up again the basic themes that we have seen in his better-known works. In this writing he insists, of course, on the pernicious character of the *encomiendas* and on the necessity of guaranteeing the administration of justice and similar points. We note his petition for "a universal procurator of all the Indians, an ecclesiastical personage of great virtue, a lover of justice, and an enemy of greed" (eighth general remedy). He also asks for the selection of "the poorest of bishops, holy men who walk with the downtrodden," because "the great poverty of the Indians cannot withstand extravagant bishops" (tenth general remedy). He presents the same demand of poverty for the friars who go to the Indies. For Las Casas this was always a condition of the proclamation of the gospel, here articulated with the clarity with which we are familiar. Also important is his reiteration that the king cannot give the Indians "without their will and consent . . . to whomever he wishes, since they are free and enjoy the highest degree of freedom that can be imagined" (ninth reason of the eighth less general remedy).

Without doubt the text enriches the Lascasian bibliography. And it reminds us that we need to be open to other such textual discoveries.

Notes

(Full information for abbreviated titles is given in the bibliography)

Introduction: Upstream to the Source

1. For simplicity's sake, we shall cite Las Casas's works in the text rather than in the notes. Our reference apparatus for Las Casas's works is indicated in the bibliography at the end of the book. It also has complete bibliographical data on the studies (both books and articles) that we will be citing in these pages.

2. See the testimonials of natives in J. Llaguno, "500 años de evangelización en México." To the "offenses" (*agravios*), as Enrique Dussel recalls, correspond the "memoranda of acts of vindication" (*memoriales de desagravios*) appearing so frequently in this era.

3. See "Appendix 1: The Demographic Question" (p. 461). *La Iglesia frente al racismo,* from the Pontifical Commission for Justice and Peace, says: "The first great current of European colonization was de facto accompanied by the massive destruction of the pre-Columbian civilizations and the brutal subjection of their inhabitants" (no. 3).

4. As José Carlos Mariátegui says: "The Conquista, evil as it was, was a historical fact. The Republic, as it exists today, is also a historical fact. Against historical facts little or nothing can be done through abstract speculations of the intelligence or pure conceptions of the mind. The history of Peru is but a tiny piece of human history. In four centuries a new reality has taken shape here, created by the alluvion of the Occident. It is a frail reality, but it is, for all that, a reality. It would be excessively romantic to decide today to ignore it" (*Peruanicemos al Perú,* 66).

5. John Paul II said in Santo Domingo that the church "seeks to approach the celebration of this centenary with the humility of truth, without triumphalism or false shame, only looking at the truth; it seeks to give God thanks for what has been correct and to draw from its errors motives for moving in a spirit of renewal toward the future" (Address to the Latin American Bishops' Conference, October 12, 1984). The episcopal conference of Medellín spoke of the "lights and shadows" of the history of Latin America ("Introduction").

6. Las Casas's life is frequently divided into broad periods: from his prophetic call to his entry into the Dominican order (1514–22); from that moment to his departure from the Indies (1522–47); and the period of his final years, in Spain (1547–66). Occasionally these dates are shifted one way or the other depending on how much importance is attributed, for example, to the promulgation (and partial abrogation) of the New Laws (1543–45) or to the disputation at Valladolid (1550–51). Doubtless there are elements in favor of a division of Bartolomé's life into stages; but, as such a classification will tend to do, it sometimes fails to do justice to the complexity of a person's life and evolution of his thought.

7. The works of Helen Rand Parish (who has granted us access to the important studies she is about to publish), I. Pérez Fernández, Francesca Cantù, and R. Marcus, among others, have shown us, in recent years, often on the basis of unpublished material, relevant points of Las Casas's biography. These valuable contributions specify dates and places; more than that, they provide excellent information for a better understanding of the thought of a person who always tied life and reflection together. We may say that these studies (we shall be citing them in the course of this book) have changed, in capital aspects, the historical physiognomy of the Sevillian friar. From them, a hitherto largely unknown Bartolomé emerges, depriving of all foundation so many earlier judgments concerning the course of his life and his intellectual itinerary — opinions, declarations, and incorrect data still to be found in manuals, encyclopedia articles, and even works of loftier academic pretensions. We still have no comprehensive biography of Las Casas available that would include the new contributions mentioned; but the studies just named are bringing us close to one. For the moment, we may refer to H. Wagner and H. Parish, *The Life and Writings of Bartolomé de Las Casas;* Marianne Mahn-Lot, *Bartolomé de Las Casas et le droit des Indiens;* and I. Pérez Fernández's precise *Cronología.* For the first decades of Las Casas's life, see the minutely detailed work of M. Giménez Fernández in his *Bartolomé de Las Casas: Delegado de Cisneros* and *Bartolomé de Las Casas: Capellán.*

8. *Indígena* [a noun, which we shall render in English as "native" — Trans.] means "born there." We shall also use, without fear of objection, the word "Indian," since that is what the inhabitants of these lands (regarded, for well-known historical reasons, as the "West Indies") were called in Las Casas's time; indeed it remains common usage today, even among native persons and organizations of Latin America.

9. We are referring, of course, to the friars of Hispaniola, of whom we shall speak at some length. Let us observe from the outset that these were persons of solid spirituality, the product of the reforms in progress in their religious orders, the Franciscans and Dominicans, in these years. The renewal in question — as happens so frequently in the history of the church — emphasized prayer and a life of poverty.

10. Indeed, many persons of that time denounced the injustices and mistreatment of which the natives were the victims. See, for example, the testimonials of Las Casas's contemporaries collected by J. Comas, "La realidad del trato dado a los indígenas de América entre los siglos XV y XX."

11. J. M. Chacón y Calvo, "La experiencia del indio."

12. This is the case with — among others — V. Carro, for whom whatever is theologically valid in Las Casas comes from Salamanca, and especially from Vitoria (*La teología y los teólogos-juristas;* see, for example, his "Introducción"). These judgments have inclined many scholars to think that the proper, original things about our restless friar were only his deeds, his polemics, and his projects, and not his theoretical elaborations. It is symptomatic that the famous *Dictionnaire de Théologie Catholique* should devote only a few lines to Las Casas, while going on for several columns about Ginés de Sepúlveda. Nor are histories of theology concerned with Bartolomé's ideas; see, for instance, the detailed work by M. Andrés, *La teología española en el siglo XVI*. Vilanova, on the other hand, devotes several pages to him, in a framework of what he dubs, in terms of the periodization proposed by Enrique Dussel ("Sobre la historia de la teología en América Latina"), "prophetic theology in the face of the Conquista and evangelization" (E. Vilanova, *Historia de la teología cristiana,* 2:715–19).

13. This is the focus of one of the rare comprehensive works on our author's thought: R. J. Queraltó Moreno, *El pensamiento filosófico-político de Bartolomé de Las Casas*.

14. To be sure, most of Las Casas's works have been published. But we must remain open to the possibility of discovering new texts. At the same time, the identification and publication of letters, both written and received by him, would shed light on certain episodes of his life. (Marcus is working in this area.)

15. J. Pérez de Tudela speaks of Las Casas as an "encyclopedic wellspring of culture" ("Significado histórico," xxxix). (Earlier, Lewis Hanke, in his celebrated *Lucha por la justicia en la conquista de América,* as well as in other works, called attention to this same quality of our author's writings.) Hence the respect with which Las Casas is cited by the theologians of Salamanca.

16. Writing from the Indies, José de Acosta makes a sagacious observation: "Our theologians of Spain, celebrated and illustrious though they be, nevertheless fall into not a few errors when they pronounce upon matters of the Indies. But those close to [the Indies] see them with their own eyes and touch them with their hands: although they be less celebrated theologians, nevertheless they reason with much more logic and more soundly.... Great, doubtless, is the importance of direct experience, as it provides such occasions for knowledge" (*De Procuranda Indorum Salute,* 1, IV, ch. 11, p. 95). To all evidence, Acosta is not thinking of Las Casas, who wrote before him but whom he never mentions; but his remark, and requirement, are perfectly fulfilled in the Dominican.

17. Las Casas himself saw this clearly, for example vis-à-vis the role played by money or power in the "impartial information" sent to Spain concerning the Indies and in doctrinal justifications of what was occurring in those lands (see Bartolomé's letter to Domingo de Soto, 1549, published by Bataillon, *Estudios sobre Bartolomé de Las Casas,* 262; as well as his *Carta a Carranza,* 1555, O.E. 5:449b–450a). But this does not mean that discussions at the theoretical level have no meaningful content of their own (least of all in Las

Casas's time) or are reducible to ideological disputes having no purchase on reality.

18. J. A. Maravall, "Utopía y primitivismo," 382.

19. L. Hanke, "Una palabra," 263.

20. Mistrustful of his reforming zeal, the confreres of John of the Cross hoped to have him sent out of Spain, and in the Carmelite chapter held in Madrid in 1591 he was assigned to the Mexican mission. But weak in health and conscious of his frailty, the saint ultimately declined the assignment. He writes to the friar in charge of the undertaking that he had "now lost the idea of the Indies, and had come to La Peñuela, to embark for other, better Indies.... The true Indies are those others, so rich in everlasting treasures" (according to Juan de Santa Ana's version, in San Juan de la Cruz, *Obras Completas,* 1096).

21. Guamán Poma entitles his work, *Primer nueva corónica y buen gobierno.* We shall use the edition of J. Murra and Rolena Adorno. Our pagination is that of the facsimile.

22. Ibid., 1109; emphasis added. Countless times, Guamán Poma uses the expression, "Christ's poor," "the poor of Jesus Christ."

23. Ibid., 903.

24. Ibid., 1. Just below, he specifies that he is writing "for the emendation of the said distributors [*comendadores*] of Indians, and magistrates, and priests both religious and secular, and the said miners, and the said caciques and Indian bosses, common Indians, and other Spaniards and persons" (ibid.). No one escapes.

25. We shall return to Guamán Poma elsewhere in this book, especially in chapter 15.

26. *La larga marcha* is the title of his anthology of Lascasian texts, with extensive and valuable introductions.

27. Las Casas uses the expression in speaking of the difficulties suffered by Sebastián Ramírez de Fuenleal (d. 1547), the great friend of the Indians who was bishop of Santo Domingo and president of its Royal Audience.

28. Here is Casaldáliga's poem, "A Bartolomé de Las Casas," translated from the Spanish:

> The poor, for thee, have played
> a greater Church and a surer God:
> against the baptism of a dead Indian,
> thou pourest the first baptism of life.
>
> *Encomendero* of the good news,
> on the Court and Salamanca
> hast thou served notice!
> And this thy impassioned heart
> bears five hundred years of witness.
>
> Five hundred years shall they be, O seer,
> and today, more than ever, the continent roars
> like a volcano of wounds and burning coals.

Teach us once more to evangelize,
along a sea delivered of its caravels,
holy father of America, Las Casas!

Introduction to Part One

1. In a draft of a letter discovered, transcribed, and placed in its context by M. Bataillon, *Estudios sobre Bartolomé de Las Casas*, 245–65 (here, 261).

2. *Fontano,* the lovely and little-used adjective in the term *fontano lugar* [here translated as "wellspring"], is actually not a neologism "forged by himself," as Bataillon thinks ("Las Casas, ¿un profeta?" 290), but an old Spanish term.

3. It is thought, with good reason, that the "personage of the Court" to whom the letter was addressed must be Juan Bernal Díaz de Luco, a person of influence when it came to questions of the Indies and Las Casas's good friend. He will have an important role in the steps leading up to obtaining *Sublimis Deus* (see below, our chapter 11).

4. The text goes on: " . . . Because then they tell us that the Spaniards have come to the Indies to be wealthy, and to be lords of the Indians, and that, in order to escape the poverty of Spain, they have come over here to take their lands from them" (*Doce dudas*, 1564, *O.E.* 5:512b).

Chapter 1: Dying before Their Time

1. Bohío and Babeque were among the native names for other parts of the island.

2. On the mighty Pasamonte and his supporters at the royal Court, see M. Giménez Fernández, *Bartolomé de Las Casas: Delegado de Cisneros*, 29–32.

3. Text reproduced by Las Casas in *H.I.,* bk. 1, ch. 33, *O.E.* 1:122b–23a; also in R. Ruiz de Lira, *Historia de América Latina*, 168–69.

4. Giménez Fernández, *Bartolomé de Las Casas: Delegado de Cisneros,* 24. The point is disputed. R. García Villoslada (who reacts vehemently to Giménez Fernández's thesis on the Alexandrine bulls and their context) regards the missionary perspective as having marked the Columbian enterprise, fostered by the Spanish rulers, from the very beginning. He admits that perhaps "the missionary aim was not the primary aspiration of the royal couple," but explains that it "would have been a piece of Quixotism, scarcely in keeping with human nature, which is not only spirit but body as well, to plunge into such a risky and costly adventure for spiritual ends alone, without the incentive of economic and earthly profit. What I hold, perhaps naively, but not without a basis in the documentation, is that the Spanish sovereigns, especially Doña Isabella, while they sought both gold and souls, valued the souls more than the gold: that, in their judgment, and in their conscience as Christians, the preaching of the gospel had precedence over the exploitation of the mines" (R. García Villoslada, "Sentido de la conquista y evangelización," 385). A. Rumeu de Armas, for his part, holding the same position as Giménez Fernández, thinks that "when Christopher Columbus

agreed, at Santa Fe (1492), to attempt a voyage to India by sailing west, his objective, and that of his patrons, the Catholic Sovereigns, was expansionistic and economic, not missionary" (*Política indigenista de Isabel*, 127; the author thinks that the missionary purpose takes shape only later, with the bull *Inter Caetera*).

5. Apropos of a gift by Columbus to the city of Genoa, P. E. Pérez Mallaína remarks that this was a very significant deed "for someone this attached to money" ("Tierras por descubrir y ganar," 57).

6. Cristóbal Colón, *Textos y documentos completos*, 327. The text is some-what obscure. It is intended as an encomium on gold and the practically unlimited diversity of its power: it can even dispatch souls to heaven, through alms or any other assistance to someone in need.

7. T. Todorov, for example, thinks Columbus's interest in wealth is in terms of "the recognition it implies of his role as a discoverer" (*La conquête de l'Amérique*, 17). For his part, Las Casas, who admired many things in Colum-bus, criticizes his concern for money. For example, after citing the pretexts Columbus has advanced for selling the Indians into slavery, he says: "All these are the Admiral's words: fine ignorance indeed — if ignorance it was, and not greed" (*H.I.*, bk. 2, ch. 37, *O.E.* 2:92b).

8. For example, we have his dreams for the Holy Sepulcher in Jerusalem. A. Milhou has given an excellent description of the complexity and ambigui-ties of Columbus's personality in *Colón y su mentalidad mesiánica en el ambiente franciscano español*.

9. "They never refuse anything they are asked for, whatsoever it be,... happy to exchange it for anything at all of any kind....They have even ac-cepted pieces of broken barrel staves, exchanging their animals for them," Columbus says, and then recounts how he forbade that "such worthless things" be offered them (Letter to Luis Santángel of February 15, 1493; in Colón, *Textos y documentos completos*, 142).

10. Ibid., 33.

11. In a letter from Hispaniola addressed to "Señor de Xevres" (or Chièvres — Guillermo de Croy, grand chamberlain to King Charles I), a group of Franciscan and Dominican friars (including Pedro de Córdoba and Antón Montesino, to whom we shall refer below) present the facts as follows: "And the Spaniards remaining on the island did such things to the Indians that the latter killed all forty of them, and although none of them remains to be ques-tioned as to the reason, it is believed that the Indians killed the Christians for crimes the latter had committed" (letter — hereafter, Franciscans' and Do-minicans' Letter — *DII* 7:399). In the version we cite it is dated June 4, 1516, but Giménez Fernández (*Bartolomé de Las Casas: Capellán*, 1220 n. 4222) thinks the correct date should be December 4, 1519. M. A. Medina (*Comunidad al servicio del indio*, 180 n. 291) holds that, "on internal evidence, as well as by reason of the identity of the signatories and the importance of the addressee," the date of the letter is actually June 4, 1517.

12. In 1496, Columbus writes in a letter: "From here we can send, in the name of the Holy Trinity, as many slaves as can be sold,...of whom, if the information I have is correct, four thousand can be sold, for (conservatively)

twenty million" (*H.I.*, bk. 1, ch. 110, *O.E.* 1:397a). Las Casas comments that it is astounding how a person so "good by nature" could be "so blind in a matter so clear" as that of the injustice of the business enterprise he had chanced upon "in the traffic — or rather the blood — of innocent Indians." He protests the enslavement and death of African and Canary blacks (mentioned by Columbus in the same letter) and thinks that the Admiral must have caught this mentality from the Portuguese (in some of whose expeditions the Admiral had participated) in their "most execrable tyranny in Guinea" (ibid.; 1:397b, 398a). It is worth noting that Indian slavery comes up as one of his projects as early as the letter to Santángel (see Colón, *Textos y documentos completos*, 145). Some historians think that, obsessed with reclaiming the holy places of Jerusalem, Columbus saw the Indies as a means of gaining the funds necessary to finance that undertaking.

13. See the royal order addressed to Bishop Fonseca: "Concerning what you have written to us of the Indians who come in the caravels, it seems to us that they can be sold better here, in Andalusia, than elsewhere; you must have them sold as you think best" (Madrid, April 12, 1495; in R. Konetzke, *Colección de documentos*, vol. 1, no. 2).

14. Four days later they write to Fonseca once more that they desire to be informed by "scholars, theologians, and canonists whether, in good conscience, these may be sold as slaves or not." Therefore they inquire in what circumstances they were taken captive (the celebrated question of the just war). They then order that the sale be suspended (ibid., no. 3). They do not declare the Indians free; they simply suspend the traffic in question pending an examination of the pertinent documents. At issue, doubtless, is whether the Indians had been enslaved in conformity with legal norms.

15. This time the royal order (of June 26, 1500) is addressed to Pedro Torres: "As you know, by Our mandate, you have in your power, in sequestration and deposit, *some* Indians of those who have been fetched from the Indies and sold in this city, its archdiocese, and other parts of this Andalusia, by mandate of Our Admiral of the Indies. These We now command to be set at liberty, and We have ordered the Prefect Friar Francisco de Bobadilla to receive them under his authority and transport them to the said Indies, there to do with them what We have commanded." (The royal document is reproduced in its entirety in V. Rodríguez, "Isabel La Católica," 663; emphasis added.) Let us observe that the text speaks of "some" Indians "on deposit." Actually, Pedro Torres had in his power only twenty-one of the five hundred that had been transported to Spain, of whom two remained there, while the other nineteen returned to the Indies. One supposes, therefore, that other persons received similar texts; see Rumeu de Armas, *Política indigenista de Isabel*, 138. On this subject see ibid., 137–41; Rodríguez, "Isabel La Católica"; and D. Ramos Pérez, "El hecho de la conquista de América," 22–27.

16. There is no documentation of any reproach having been addressed to the Admiral on this account (nor for the famous sentence attributed to Isabella, "Who is Cristóbal Colón to make slaves of my subjects?"). In March 1502, however, before his fourth voyage, Columbus received from his sovereigns the following indication: "And you are not to traffic in slaves. But if

someone were to be willing to come here as an interpreter, with the intention of returning, bring him" (cited in Rodríguez, "Isabel La Católica," 657). This did not end the matter. In 1518 Las Casas was still asking King Charles to send home the Indians who had been brought to Spain, since the Spaniards had "enslaved them unjustly and against God" (*Memorial de remedios*, 1518, *O.E.* 5:36b).

17. Elsewhere, reporting similar opinions of Columbus concerning the Indians, he says that it is "to be noted that these were the principles whence, little by little, sprang the distribution which we now call *encomiendas*, and consequently the utter perdition of all of these infinite nations" (*H.I.*, bk. 1, ch. 155, *O.E.* 1:409b).

18. A curious text from Las Casas's pen may represent the harshest of his judgments regarding Columbus. After censuring his military expeditions against the Indians and his enslavement of them, Bartolomé writes — likewise alluding to the last stage of the Admiral's life — with cruel and sorrowful irony that "Divine Providence" had seen to the withdrawal "from the Admiral's hands . . . of this traffic, lest so much selling quickly depopulate the island in too little time and nothing be left for *so many other* murderers of these people to go to hell for, once their eyes have lighted on such a lamentable enticement" (*H.I.*, bk. 3, ch. 94, *O.E.* 2:398b; emphasis added). Other Indians were left so that they might be crushed and enslaved. Columbus, so admired by Las Casas in other respects, is one of these murderers, then, and as such is liable to eternal damnation. A defense of life, and of the weakest, takes precedence over personal sympathies.

19. In Konetzke, *Colección de documentos*, vol. 1, no. 9; emphasis added. Issued in Zaragoza, the document decrees other dispositions in favor of the Indians, and approves marriage between Indians and Spaniards.

20. Ibid., no. 11; emphasis added. The royal order is "given at Medina del Campo."

21. See for example one of the best studies of the institution: S. Zavala, *La encomienda indiana*, 13–17.

22. The document is a memorandum presented to Charles V in 1542, probably part of a larger work in which Las Casas has proposed "twenty remedies" for the Indies. Of the latter, we have only the pages that treat of the "eighth remedy," devoted to the subject of the *encomienda* and published by Bartolomé himself in 1552 (as one of eight treatises published simultaneously). It has been translated, into various languages, many times. See I. Pérez Fernández, *Inventario*, 296–309.

23. Indeed, "if Her Highness had known that the said instruction that she had decreed was so harmful to the Indians, who could doubt that she would not have abominated and detested it? But a few months after the decree was issued, she died" (ibid.).

24. Secret Instruction for the Governor, Friar Nicolás de Ovando (Cartagena, March 29, 1503) (*DII* 31:175–76). F. Moya — the first, we think, to have called attention to this text — comments: "Thus, the hidden idea in the 'noble' plan [of Zaragoza] to 'reduce' or move the Indians to villages in which they would supposedly be educated, Christianized, and well treated, was to

create reductions in which a sufficient labor force would be available to exploit the mines on behalf, not any longer of the Spaniards on Hispaniola, but of the Crown. The Indians were to be attracted to these villages 'of their own free will,' lest there be any recalcitrants who might undermine the execution of the plan" (F. Moya, *Después de Colón*, 37).

25. A fine testimonial to the desolate situation of Hispaniola before 1520 is to be found in the memorandum by Hernando de Gorjóa, *DII* 1:428–29. Many years later, José de Acosta (in an ideological context to which we shall return in chapter 14) says: "The island of Hispaniola, and that of Cuba, and San Juan de Puerto Rico, were once densely populated, and awash in gold, whereas now they are practically deserted and wild. The Indians have been wiped out, and the precious metals that abound there can no longer be mined" (*De Procuranda Indorum Salute*, bk. 3, ch. 18, p. 533). The state of the Indians is well described. Acosta is mistaken, however, in thinking that there was an abundance of gold on the Antillean island, especially by the time of his writing. See Appendix 1, above.

26. Contrary to what one frequently hears, the friar from Seville was never of the opinion that everything that happened in the Indies before 1492 was beyond reproach. For example, we have the text in which, referring to the pre-Columbian era, he speaks of "the oppressions" perpetrated by "some lords, when they turned out to be prideful or greedy, or failed to exercise their sovereignty with the moderation and justice to which they were obliged by natural reason (for the utility and profit of the realm)," and rejects "the public sins that nature abhors," which these native rulers committed "publicly, believing it to be licit for them [to do so] — mainly, in sacrificing innocents and eating human flesh, where such [victims] were available" (*Tratado comprobatorio*, 1552, *O.E.* 5:400b; he specifies, however, that this last custom is not generalized in the Indies). But it is clear to him that these reprehensible acts committed by the Indians in no wise justify the wars of domination waged against them by the Europeans.

27. Las Casas describes the arrival of this little band of missionaries. They were "received by a good Christian of this city called Pedro de Lumbreras, who gave them a cabin for their lodging, at the head of one of his corrals, since there were no houses there at that time other than of straw and bundled branches. There he fed them bread made from cassava roots — a bread of very little substance if eaten without meat or fish" (*H.I.*, bk. 2, ch. 53, 1:133b).

28. Pedro de Córdoba is a first-rate spiritual personality, who has not yet received much scholarly attention. See, however, E. Rodríguez Demorizi, *Los dominicos y las encomiendas*; R. Boria, *Fray Pedro de Córdoba (1482–1521)*; and especially, Medina, *Comunidad al servicio del indio*.

29. In Giménez Fernández's judgment, Ferdinand V's religious policy had transformed the church and its representatives, "during the tenure of Ovando and Diego Colón, into mere chaplains to the slavers, whose abuses they dissimulated or emulated, as is evinced by the distribution of Indians to bishops, other prelates, clergy, and even the Conventual Franciscans, whom distance had spared the Cisnerian reform" (Giménez Fernández, *Bartolomé de Las Casas: Delegado de Cisneros*, 43). Huerga, who cannot be accused of dis-

476 _____ Notes to Pages 28–30

liking King Ferdinand, acknowledges the latter's policy to have been "a bit Machiavellian" (A. Huerga, "La instalación de la Iglesia en el Nuevo Mundo," 230). Indeed, as we know, Niccolò de Machiavelli cites Ferdinand and his disregard for promises and signed treaties as an illustration of the figure he champions in *The Prince.*

30. Death is the inevitable consequence of oppression. Las Casas censures the members of the Royal Council for not seeking to be duly informed regarding the Indians' situation, and thus condemning the latter "to perpetual servitude, and to the death necessarily ensuing therefrom to this day" (*H.I.,* bk. 3, ch. 14, *O.E.* 2:205a).

31. Actually, Pérez de Tudela observes that the first protest against the enslavement and exploitation of the Indians came from Cristóbal Rodríguez (known as "La Lengua," "The Tongue," having been the first to learn the native language), a seaman on one of Columbus's voyages. Nicolás de Ovando regarded him as an enemy. (See "Significado histórico," in Las Casas's *Obras Escogidas,* xxvii.) On this curious personage, see Las Casas, *H.I.,* bk. 1, ch. 158, *O.E.* 1:415a, and *H.I.,* bk. 1, ch. 177, *O.E.* 1:470b–71a.

32. Las Casas emphasizes that "all of the most scholarly of them" participated in the work (ibid., *O.E.* 2:175b), among whom, besides the vicar (Pedro de Córdoba) and the preacher, may have been Domingo de Mendoza, Tomás de Berlanga, and Bernardo de Santo Domingo. As the text of the sermon was drawn up in advance, it is not out of the question that Bartolomé could later have had a copy in hand.

33. There is a bit of controversy concerning the precise date of this sermon. The great specialist on the life of Fray Bartolomé, M. Giménez Fernández, indicates a date of November 30 ("Fray Bartolomé de Las Casas: A Biographical Sketch," 74). Actually, however, Las Casas's own indication and the scriptural text point rather to the Fourth Sunday of Advent. (See José de Martín Rivera, "El sermón de Fray Antonio de Montesinos," 113–17.) Pérez Fernández ("La fidelidad del Padre Las Casas a su carisma profético," 85–89 n), with his customary attention to detail, has clearly and definitively established that the sermon must be dated the last Sunday of Advent, which in that year fell on December 21.

34. The reasons adduced by Antonio García y García ("El sentido de las primeras denuncias," 70–71) for calling in question the basic accuracy of Las Casas's report are not very convincing. Nor do we understand his argumentation based on the written text of the sermon; a book of sermons to aid preachers is not the same thing as a particular homily for a special occasion such as this one. Instead, see the excellent observations of Noé Zevallos, "Acerca de un discurso liberador: El sermón de Montesinos," on the *artes praedicandi* in the Middle Ages and the sermon, at once traditional and free in style, that concerns us here. We believe, with V. Carro and the vast majority of experts on the question, that "the veracity" of Las Casas's version of the famous sermon "is undeniable as to its basic content and fundamental expressions" (*La teología y los teólogos-juristas,* 1:54).

35. Ibid., 1:55. It is true that they are Dominicans; but Thomas Aquinas

did not have the influence in the formation of these missionaries that he came to have later in Spain, thanks in large part to Vitoria's teachings.

36. J. M. Chacón y Calvo, "La experiencia del indio," 224.

37. Further on, in a comment on the deeds (or rather, misdeeds) of Pedrarias, he observes: "Killing or robbing the Indians has never been held as a crime in these Indies" (*H.I.*, bk. 3, ch. 50, *O.E.* 2:316a).

38. See, on this subject, Medina's detailed study, *Comunidad al servicio del indio*, 121–38, as well as that of J. M. Pérez, *¿Estos no son hombres?* The text of the *Doce dudas*, found in the John Carter Brown Library (Providence, R.I.; hereafter Providence version), was made available to me by J. B. Lassègue and will appear in the *Obras Completas* of Las Casas to be published by the Instituto Bartolomé de Las Casas foundation of the Dominicans of Andalusia. In that version Las Casas himself describes the facts in this way: "From the year ten, in which the friars of St. Dominic went to Hispaniola, persons considered to be saints, prudent and very learned, they saw the oppression and destruction that was happening to the Indians and knew that there had been a great multitude of people and that few were left. So later in the year eleven they very openly and vigorously preached about it and denounced it, condemning all that had been done and was being done as tyrannical and abominable. The news arrived in Spain, as did the religious in pursuit of the truth" (f. 170v).

39. P. Borges's reservations concerning Las Casas's version and the reactions it provoked ("Drama lascasiano") are unclear, apart from certain minor points (for example, a supposed excessive preference for the Dominicans over the Franciscans) which do not affect the substance of the Lascasian report (as the author himself recognizes; see p. 779). Borges seems to present Bartolomé as dissimulating Montesino's objections to the king's power to bestow the *encomiendas* (indeed, to his right to hold the Indies). We fail to see what he seeks to insinuate by this supposition. Las Casas always decried the *encomiendas*, and many have interpreted this as a rejection of any reason for the Spanish presence in the Indies. We do agree with this author that the colonists of Hispaniola interpreted Montesino's sermon correctly: it did not stop with asking for a decent treatment of the Indians; his denunciation went further. Hence the role Bartolomé attributes to it in his defense of the Indians. Borges further suggests that the incongruities he believes he sees in the Lascasian text are due in part to the fact that the Sevillian friar began to compose his *History of the Indies* only in 1552, completing it in 1559 at the age of eighty-five (see Borges, "Drama lascasiano," 779). But as we know, both dates are incorrect.

40. This was done by a royal decree of November 28, 1548. It was the result of an accusation of Sepúlveda before Prince Philip (and before the Inquisition); see on this I. Pérez Fernández, *Cronología*, 747–65.

41. Sepúlveda will likewise characterize as a "new doctrine" Bartolomé's refusal to approve the use of force in propagating the gospel in the Indies (*O.E.* 5:314b).

42. This royal order (as well as the *mensajeras* of the Dominican provincial, which we shall presently cite) are found in Chacón y Calvo, *Cedulario*, 427–31.

43. Carro, *La teología y los teólogos-juristas*, 1:61.

44. Las Casas attributes this in large measure to the power exercised at the royal Court by Fonseca, bishop of Burgos, and by Lope Conchillos (ibid.).

45. "Mensajera del provincial de los dominicos para el Vicario general que está en las Indias, sobre lo de los sermones" (March 16, 1512), in Chacón y Calvo, *Cedulario*, 425–26.

46. "Mensajera del provincial de los dominicos para el Prior que está en las Indias" (March 23, 1512), ibid., 443–44.

47. "Mensajera del provincial de los dominicos para los dominicos que están en las Indias, de reprehensión" (March 1512), ibid., 445–47.

48. Altogether credibly, Las Casas presents the complaints of the grandees of Hispaniola and the reactions provoked in Spain itself as follows: "These letters, arriving in the Court, threw the same into great confusion. The King wrote to, and sent for, the provincial of Castile, who was the prelate of those who were here,…complaining of his friars whom he had sent here, to the effect that they had done him great disservice in preaching things against his state and to the great commotion and scandal of all the land; [and ordering] that he at once apply a remedy, or rather that he order a remedy applied." And he continues: "You see here how easy rulers are to deceive, how unhappy kingdoms become by reason of [mis]information furnished by the wicked, and how oppressed and buried, lest it sound or breathe, is truth" (*H.I.*, bk. 3, *O.E.* 2:178–79). Bartolomé's version is corroborated by the royal order and the *mensajeras* just cited, which are known to us from other sources as well. The ease with which rulers are deceived will be one of the major obstacles to be encountered by Bartolomé over the course of his life.

49. On the scope of Montesino's sermon, Pérez de Tudela asserts, first, that "the preachers' criticism strikes not so much at the basis and justification of the slavery in which the natives had been placed, as at the manner and outcome thereof." But he adds: "On the other hand, it is true that Montesino's invocation pointed to the root of the evil" ("Significado histórico," xxviii). We agree with the latter statement. Obviously, we cannot expect a detailed treatment of the subject in this early sermon. However, the clear demand it makes based on the gospel lends a special incisiveness to its claims. Those who heard it perceived all that it implied — hence the vehemence of their reaction. While Lewis Hanke may exaggerate when he characterizes Montesino's sermon as a "decisive turning point in the history of America" (*La lucha por la justicia*, 31), J. Friede is surely not justified in going to the other extreme and minimizing the importance of an event that he regards as having produced only "a local disturbance" (*Bartolomé de las Casas: Precursor*, 19).

50. See below, chapter 13.

51. A letter, written by Pedro de Córdoba, but signed by all of the Dominicans of Hispaniola, begins: "Your Reverences have ordered me to give you my opinion and that of these Fathers of this House concerning the traffic in Indians; and although we have spoken upon this matter many times before now, and therefore there was no need to render an opinion a second time, *nihilominus* [nevertheless], in order to comply with Your Reverences' demand, I have agreed to set forth here, in very summary form, the opinion of us all" (in *DII* 11:211–12, undated; hereafter, Letter of the Dominicans).

E. Ruiz Maldonado supposes that we are dealing with a missive dispatched by the signatories to their confreres of the Convent of San Esteban, and that it would have been written toward the end of 1516 or in the middle of 1517 (*Libro Anual,* 159 n. 2). Medina, *Comunidad al servicio del indio,* 248, thinks instead that the letter was written in response to the Hieronymite fathers who were Cisneros's commissaries in the Antilles: in this case, its date would be April or May 1517. The text of *DII* reads *nihil hominos.* The transcription of *Libro Anual* (the same version in Medina, *Comunidad al servicio del indio,* 248) seems more correct; it has *nihilominus* (nevertheless). I owe the observation about this word to Pedro de Guchteneere.

52. See below, chapter 10.

53. See *DII* 11:221; hereafter, Letter to the King.

54. The original is in Latin. We use Medina's Spanish translation, *Comunidad al servicio del indio,* 261, which dates the letter May 27, 1517; hereafter, Latin Letter.

55. Letter of September 26, 1517, published by V. Rubio as "Una carta inédita de Fray Pedro de Córdoba, O.P." We use Medina's version, in his *Comunidad al servicio del indio,* 288–91.

56. Letter of the Dominicans, 212.

57. There can be no question that the term is well chosen (see Bataillon, *Estudios,* 55–56). Historians like Fernández de Oviedo or López de Gómara regard the tragedy as a punishment for the sins of the Indians. For the context, use, and purport of the term "destruction," see the keen analysis of Milhou, "De la destruction de l'Espagne à la destruction des Indes"; idem, "El concepto de 'destrucción' en el evangelismo milenario franciscano."

58. Pedro de Córdoba describes the destructive consequences (suicides, abortions, infanticides) of the exploitation of the Indians as follows: "By reason of these afflictions and hard labor, the Indians themselves chose and still choose to kill themselves, demonstrating in their choice that they are free and not slaves, and that no one can make them such." The expression is a bold one: the elimination of their world of reference drives the Indians to this incredible, terrible manifestation of freedom, in de Córdoba's terms. In further describing this reality, the friar goes on: "Women, weary of their toils, have sought to avoid conception and childbirth, lest they be compelled to work during pregnancy or at childbirth. Many indeed, finding themselves pregnant, have taken measures to do away with, and have done away with, their unborn infants. Others, when they have given birth, have killed their own children with their own hands, rather than placing them or allowing them to be placed under such harsh servitude" (Letter to the King, 218–19).

59. Franciscans' and Dominicans' Letter, 412. We find corroboration in another letter: "Where are they, Most Reverend Lords, the countless people that were discovered on [the island], whose number the discoverers compared with the grasses of the field? Of them all, there remain on the island no more than ten or twelve thousand, men and women together, and these, crushed and enfeebled, and, as it were, in their last agony" (Latin Letter, 259). The year is 1517, when Las Casas, sometimes together with these friars, presents his first memoranda to the Court.

60. The text continues: "That these souls were so many, we know from the late Don Bartolomé, brother of the former Admiral, God rest his soul, who tallied them himself at the Admiral's order." Further on, the friars say that there were perhaps "more than two million, as many have declared who came in the beginning" (Franciscans' and Dominicans' Letter, 400–401). Even making allowance for the rhetoric of the age, to claim that these testimonials are one-sided represents an ideological decision to refuse to face the facts and to ignore the best historiographical sources.

61. Ibid., 423.

62. Latin Letter, 258.

63. Letter of the Dominicans, 213.

64. Letter to the King, 218.

65. Ibid., 220.

66. Ibid., 217. Within a few years, the Indian population of Hispaniola was nearing extinction. The colonists then brought in natives who had lived on neighboring islands — so-called useless places, as there was no gold there — as we have seen. Las Casas recounts the facts as follows: "The Spaniards, seeing themselves that the Indians were being consumed in the mines digging for gold and in the other labors, such as farming, that were killing them, and that they were becoming fewer by the day by reason of their death, and having no other consideration than for their own temporal harm and for the profit they were losing, they chanced upon the idea that it would be well to make up for the loss of those who were perishing, the natives of this island, by bringing in from other islands the people that could be brought, so that their business in farming and the mines and other interests would not cease" (*H.I.*, bk. 3, ch. 43, *O.E.* 2:106b; cf. bk. 3, ch. 83, *O.E.* 2:365a). Giménez Fernández reports that the king acceded to the request that the colonists of Hispaniola be allowed to do this, at first with certain restrictions, but then giving them, for all practical purposes, carte blanche for this slave policy (see *Bartolomé de Las Casas: Capellán*, 472–74).

67. Letter to the King, 218. "Neither Pharaoh nor the Egyptian people mistreated the children of Israel so cruelly, nor the persecutors of the martyrs the children of the Church. For these have not even spared the weaker sex, women, as so many nations are accustomed to do" (Latin Letter, 259).

68. Letter of the Dominicans, 212.

69. "For the moment, this is our goal: that they not disappear. They are going to their death in droves, and unless help comes at once, voluntarily, even though it is now almost too late, what will happen is that, when we do wish to help them, it will not be possible to do so" (Latin Letter, 260).

70. Letter of the Dominicans, 212.

71. Letter to the King, 219.

72. Letter of the Dominicans, 214.

73. Letter to the King, 218.

74. Ibid., 217.

75. Ibid., 218. Years later, Las Casas would express himself in the same terms, denouncing the *encomenderos* for oppressing the Indians under the pretext of "teaching them the faith that they themselves did not know" (*Oc-*

tavo remedio, 1542, *O.E.* 5:77a). This is one of a number of similarities, even verbatim, between Las Casas and the letters of the Hispaniola friars.

76. Ibid., 220. The matter of restitution also comes up in the Letter of the Dominicans, 213. And the reason for raising the issue is forcefully expressed by the Latin Letter: "All that any Christian has acquired here has come out of the Indians' entrails, sweat, and blood" (Latin Letter, 261).

77. Letter of the Dominicans, 213–14.

78. This is a profound conviction in the mind of Pedro de Córdoba and his companions. In his letter to the king, the Dominican even maintains that "if among [these nations] preachers alone were to enter, without the force and violence of these miserable Christians, I think that nearly as excellent a Church could be founded among them as the primitive one" (Letter to the King, 217). The Indies offered this possibility, and that aim reinforced the zeal of many missionaries of that time.

79. Franciscans' and Dominicans' Letter, 428.

80. The work has been edited, with a lengthy introduction and notes on its history and doctrinal content, by Medina, ed., *Doctrina Cristiana para instrucción de los indios por Pedro de Córdoba.*

81. Ibid., 210. De Córdoba also posits, on a number of occasions, the equality of men and women (see ibid., 209).

82. Letter of the Dominicans, 213.

83. See below, chapter 11.

84. Pedro de Córdoba's Letter to the King begins with an allusion to the misinformation the king has received and declares that "the false informants ought to be known and held for such" (Letter to the King, 216).

85. Ibid., 220–21.

86. The friars likewise tell Lord de Xevres: "We likewise think that if, while able to provide a remedy, Your Excellency dissimulates [the facts], he will give a special account to God" (Franciscans' and Dominicans' Letter, 430). Shortly before they had said with all desired clarity: "Those who have been the cause of all these deaths of which we have spoken, Your Excellency, were principally two governors who came to this island after the former Admiral. One of them was called Bobadilla, and was here only briefly; the other was the Comendador Major, whom we have mentioned above, and who was called Nicolás de Ovando, during whose tenure nearly all of the havoc occurred to which we have made reference" (Franciscans' and Dominicans' Letter, 411). Las Casas's judgment will be the same.

87. Letter to the King, 221. In a postscript to their letter, the Franciscans and Dominicans give Las Casas an effusive recommendation: "All of the above, Your Excellency, and a great deal more that might have been said and that has been omitted here in order to avoid greater prolixity, is very well known to Bartolomé de las Casas, a cleric here, who is a person of truth and virtue, and a special servant and friend of God, most zealous for His law. We commend him to Your Excellency most affectionately, begging You to accord him much credit, for he is a person who merits it, as he is moved by nothing in the matter of the traffic in Indians but by the desire to perform a service

to Your Majesty" (Franciscans' and Dominicans' Letter, 430). Las Casas refers to these letters of recommendation in *H.I.*, bk. 3, ch. 95, *O.E.* 2:401a–b.

88. Henríquez Ureña, *Las corrientes literarias en la América Hispana*, 21. Along the same lines M. A. Medina rightly states that the problem that these missionaries "surfaced in Hispaniola" was "the liberty of the American man" (*Comunidad al servicio del indio*, 241).

89. Medellín Document on Peace, no. 22.

Chapter 2: Scourged Christs of the Indies

1. We frequently hear of Las Casas's "conversion." It is not difficult to understand, however, why he did not use this term to refer to the turnabout in his life in 1514, and the reason is worth noting. I. Pérez Fernández mentions a passage in which Bartolomé seems to refer to himself as someone who "had been converted" (*H.I.*, bk. 3, ch. 138, *O.E.* 2:366a). But, besides being a "somewhat irregular text" (Pérez Fernández, *Cronología*, 227), the passage in question is not very clear. However, Las Casas will explicitly refer to his decision to become a Dominican after the failure at Cumaná as a conversion (see *H.I.*, bk. 3, ch. 150, *O.E.* 2:566b). M. Bataillon (*Estudios*, 48 n. 9) already made this observation. Consequently, we may refer to the event of 1514 as a prophetic call, which will only become stronger and deeper in the years to come. Time and again in his writings Las Casas refers to this originating moment in his life. Below, we shall examine some texts bearing on this. (See the analyses of Enrique Dussel, "Núcleo simbólico lascasiano como profecía crítica al imperialismo europeo"; Pérez Fernández, "La fidelidad del padre Las Casas a su carisma profético"; F. Cantù, "La dialectique de Las Casas et l'histoire.")

2. The date of Las Casas's ordination has been the subject of dispute. I. Pérez Fernández (*Cronología*, 183–86) thinks it took place at the end of February 1507. Helen Rand Parish has confirmed that Las Casas was ordained a priest in Rome (after receiving the diaconate in Seville) in 1507; and on the basis of a manuscript she found in the Vatican Library, she initially dated it March 3 (see Helen Rand Parish, "Introduction: Las Casas's Spirituality," 15). But on the basis of the same document she now believes the ordination took place in the last days of February (personal communication). We are likewise indebted to Parish, a keen researcher, for our knowledge of the correct year of Las Casas's birth: 1484 (see Parish and Weidman, "The Correct Birthdate of Bartolomé de Las Casas"). Pérez Fernández has called attention to other documents that support this dating (*Cronología*, 91–95).

3. In his *History of the Indies*, Las Casas recounts that Pedro de Córdoba had studied in Salamanca and that he "would have been an extremely fine scholar, had it not been for the fact that his harsh penitential practices gave him severe, constant headaches, which forced him to curtail his study a great deal." But, he continues, this very circumstance led him to greater holiness of life: "We may be sure that he left this life as pure as his mother bore him." Our cleric heard a sermon of Pedro's — profitable for the Indians as well as for the Spaniards — which he was never to forget (see *H.I.*, bk. 3, ch. 54, *O.E.* 2:133a, 134b). Elsewhere, after de Córdoba's death, Las Casas will say

that he "died of *hético*" — meaning, he explains, that he died of the "severe penances that he had performed in his life" (*H.I.*, bk. 3, ch. 148, *O.E.* 2:557b). The manuscript says *etyco* (data provided by M. A. Medina); *ético* or *hético* — it can be used as an adjective or noun — refers to tuberculosis.

4. On the friendship and influence of Pedro de Córdoba (who was only two years older than Las Casas), we have the testimony of a Dominican historian: "He was greatly favored by the religion and doctrine of the saintly Friar Pedro de Córdoba, whom he loved as a father and esteemed as a saint. Upon hearing the sermons of that blessed father, he had given up the Indians of his *repartimiento* and was attempting to persuade others to give them up. These sermons also moved the blessed cleric to a more structured piety" (Augustín Dávila Padilla, *Historia de la fundación y discurso de la provincia de Santiago de México de la Orden de Predicadores*, 1596; cited in *Libro Anual*, 137). From the point of view of Fray Augustín, to become a religious was to comply with that "more structured piety," and to enter the Dominican order would be, of course, all the better.

5. As we have said, Las Casas held lands on Hispaniola and then received a *repartimiento* in Cuba from Diego Velázquez (see *H.I.*, bk. 3, ch. 32, *O.E.* 2:251b).

6. Parish, in her edition of *The Only Way* (see Parish, "Introduction: Las Casas's Spirituality," 15, 17–19), thinks that a good part of Las Casas's work was directly with the Indians. His work was an experience of evangelization — despite the conditions under which it was carried out, and very different, of course, from his later experiments — at least until the terrible massacre of Caonao. Las Casas himself speaks of letters he has addressed to Indian caciques, or chiefs, and of sermons he gave at this time. In fact, he speaks of his experiences in evangelization and of the many baptisms performed at this time, all those becoming Christians whom God "had predestined for His glory" (see *H.I.*, bk. 3, chs. 29–30, *O.E.* 2:243b–244a, 248b, 249b–250a). See Pérez Fernández, *Inventario*, 31–41.

7. The passage goes on: " ... no greater unless death finds that someone not in the state of grace" (*De Unico*, 220v; *The Only Way*, 168).

8. D. Ramos Pérez, " 'Conversión' de Las Casas," maintains, on the basis of a detailed analysis of the texts, that Las Casas's "first conversion" was a process of several months. Thus he contradicts Giménez Fernández's "road to Damascus" thesis (*Bartolomé de Las Casas: Delegado de Cisneros*, 50). We have no problem in accepting Ramos's position on this point. Indeed such processes take a certain time. In a way, the same thing occurs with Saul of Tarsus, who goes to the city of Damascus, spends three days there without eating or drinking, and then goes to meet Ananias and other disciples (Acts 9:9–19). We hesitate, however, at the insinuations of this author with regard to a connection between the crisis of the Colombist party and the call Las Casas experienced to devote his life to the defense of the Indians. Historical contexts are always important for an understanding of personal attitudes, to be sure; but it would be simplistic to see a mechanical cause-effect relationship here. We do not believe that the great historian succeeds in establishing such a relationship between a decline in the fortunes of Diego Colón's allies

and Las Casas's perilous commitment. Thus, we wonder what he means by a number of statements in the following vein: "Actually, the moment of Las Casas's 'conversion' cannot be an independent, autonomous factor, since it occurs precisely at the moment of a conjunctural change, we might almost say a radical one, occurring in the Indies and characterized by a complete power crisis for the second Admiral, Don Diego Colón. The latter phenomenon has genuine importance, since the Las Casases had always been loyal to Colón" (Ramos Pérez, " 'Conversión' de Las Casas," 252). Ramos continues to emphasize these connections without any mention of Las Casas's criticisms — in his defense of the Indians — of the first Admiral as well as the second. Does he mean that Las Casas's radical breach with the *encomienda* was due to the fact that he was going to lose it in any case with the fall of the Colombist party? Ramos does not come right out and say this, but he seems to imply it. For example, he suggests that the passage from Ecclesiasticus did not demand this breach, since it is compatible with an *encomienda* "managed with the demand for decent treatment that had been prescribed by the laws of Burgos of 1512, with the modification of Valladolid of 1513" (Ramos Pérez, " 'Conversión' de Las Casas," 251–52). Among other things, this ignores the severe criticisms leveled at these laws by Las Casas and his Dominican friends.

Ramos is clearly on solid ground when he underscores the processual nature of this enlightenment of Las Casas's conscience. But he is less so when it comes to the cleric's motivations for changing his position when he is confronted with the mistreatment of the Indians. There is nothing in Bartolomé's later life to confirm the thesis of a circumstantial, and hence superficial, option. Ramos acknowledges this himself when, bringing his article to a conclusion, in a sentence carefully calculated to offer Las Casas a rose along with the thorns, he says that Las Casas has simplified the account of his "conversion," moved "perhaps by the desire to feel himself the emulator — as he was and even more in strength, knowledge, and constancy — of the then renowned Father Montesinos" (Ramos Pérez, " 'Conversión' de Las Casas," 257). When is the "then" of which this author speaks? At the time when Las Casas (who never had a rivalry with Montesino) wrote his *History of the Indies,* he was much better known than the friar who had been his precursor.

9. Here the Latin version of the Bible known as the Vulgate makes an interpolation, as it does elsewhere in Ecclesiasticus. It adds a line not found in the Greek text, which Las Casas, too, omits, and which modern editions of his *History* enclose in brackets. It would be translated: "The Lord alone is sufficient for those who look to him for the way of truth and justice."

10. This line is also omitted by Las Casas. But it is found in the Greek version (as also in the Vulgate).

11. F. Moreno cites a similar, beautiful passage from Domingo de Soto: "When the poor are deprived of the opportunity to beg alms, they are deprived of life as well. They are left with no other hole to hide in but the grave.... How often God proclaims Himself Advocate and Father of the poor!" (Domingo de Soto, *Deliberación en la causa de los pobres,* cited in Moreno, "Historia, ética e Iglesia en América Latina," 33; see this author's commentary on these and other texts of de Soto).

12. As to this way of seeing things, the rules of his *Confesionario* are revealing when they speak of settlers "who would not have been conquistadors" and of those who sell arms, especially horses, although they had not taken part in the wars or in the *encomiendas*. They are all responsible and required to make restitution (see *Confesionario*, 1552, *O.E.* 5:239b–242a). The notion of sins of omission does not come from an anxious rigorism; on the contrary, his source is the perception of the evangelical dynamism of love that knows no bounds.

13. Las Casas relates that the massacres and other atrocities of which Africans were the victims occurred on the Feast of Corpus Christi and adds, with trenchant irony: "...A good day for good works" (*H.I.*, bk. 1, ch. 24, *O.E.* 1:91b).

14. We shall return to this in chapter 11.

15. The Providence version has some variants of which we note one: the Indians are called "most miserable" instead of "most poor" (folio 203). We shall see the importance of these terms later (see chapter 10, below). We have another allusion, this time implicit, to the passage from Ecclesiasticus. Referring to the villainy of "Vasco Núñez and his companions," Las Casas says that they thought they were "offering God a pleasing sacrifice under the pretext that they were punishing those who had broken the natural law" (*H.I.*, bk. 3, ch. 47, *O.E.* 2:285b).

16. Las Casas always speaks very highly of Rentería, and even recounts that, while he was making the decisions we indicate, his friend in Jamaica was arriving at similar conclusions of his own. Rentería had even thought of the suitability of building "some boarding schools, where children could be reared and taught, and thereby spared such a violent death" (*H.I.*, bk. 3, ch. 80, *O.E.* 2:359).

17. Las Casas adds, ruefully: "One of those who cooperated in these tyrannies was my own father, though he is no longer involved." Pedro Las Casas is known to have accompanied Columbus on his second voyage. Thus, Bartolomé regards the oppression of the Indians as having been committed from the very beginning of the colonization.

18. The point has been extensively studied by Giménez Fernández in his *Bartolomé de Las Casas: Capellán*, 647–1173.

19. This does not mean that during the previous years he remained in "dry dock." H. Parish, for example, thinks that he is the author of a petition in 1528 that is presented as written by two Dominican religious. The historian believes, moreover, that this text played an important role in the enactment of the antislave law of 1530 (see below chapter 11). Moreover, during this time he begins to write his *Historia de las Indias*.

20. This is an unpublished text. It is found in the Providence version of the *Doce dudas*. The texts that we cite are in folios 135v–136.

21. In the prologue to his replies to Sepúlveda, he says: "Therefore I beseech Your illustrious Lordships, Graces, and Paternities to regard this most important and perilous business not as mine, unconcerned as I am to defend it except as a Christian, but as an affair of God, and that of his honor, faith, and universal Church" (*O.E.* 5:318b).

22. In a letter to Domingo de Soto, he writes: "I have become inured to the adversities, rebuffs, and enmity that I have had to suffer and undergo in the thirty-three years that God has had me bear witness to this, His truth" (in Bataillon, *Estudios,* 261). The content of Las Casas's testimony is God's truth, not a personal truth.

23. See Bataillon, *Estudios,* 45–136: "Cleric Las Casas, Heretofore Colonist, Reformer of the Colonization." On Las Casas's first years in the Indies, see R. Marcus's suggestive article, "El primer decenio de Las Casas en el Nuevo Mundo." For the sociohistorical context of Las Casas's first years of activity, the reader may consult the observations of P. Chaunu, "Las Casas et la première crise structurelle de la colonisation espagnole (1515–1523)."

24. See below, chapter 15.

25. In another work, he speaks of "those who glory in bearing the name of Christian" but who in their deeds constitute "an obstacle to the conversion of all those who have not yet passed through the doors of the Church" (*De Unico,* 436).

26. With Fray Bartolomé's first denunciations, two former acquaintances of his, Pánfilo Narváez and Antonio Velázquez, procurators of the island of Cuba, tried to invalidate his testimony, asserting that the "cleric is an imprudent person, with little authority or credibility; he speaks of what he neither knows about nor has seen, so that his facts contradict each other." Therefore "one so lacking in credibility or authority should not be believed; what he speaks about has no title of credibility. He is only engaged upon an imprudent quest for an ecclesiastical office of his own, through the backbiting in which he is involved, believing that this will enable him to achieve the reform of the evils that he describes" ("Informe de los procuradores de la isla de Cuba, Pánfilo Narváez y Antonio Velázquez, en respuesta a una consulta del Consejo de Indias," in *DII* 7:12–13). This was an early attack on Las Casas, which would be repeated many times in similar terms throughout his life.

27. Dominican Friar Bernardino Minaya recounts that, having accompanied Pizarro's expedition to Peru in its early stages and with an encounter with Atahualpa imminent, he proposed to the future marquis "that we explain to the Indians the reason for our coming, which was none other than to bring them the knowledge of God, and in no wise to rob them and expropriate their lands." To which, he continues, "Pizarro answered me that he had come from Mexico to relieve them of their gold and that he would by no means do what I asked him" (Minaya, "Memorial," 491). The greed of those who had recently arrived has marked the memory of the period. The Mercedarian M. de Murúa, a late chronicler strongly criticized by Guamán Poma, says the same thing happened to Pizarro with gold and silver as happens to "hydropic persons whose thirst and desire to drink only increase the more they drink" (*Historia general del Perú: Origen y descendencia de los Incas,* 189). On this controversial friar, see the interesting study of X. Pikasa, "Religión pagana y conversión cristiana en el antiguo Perú."

28. In *DII* 7:401.

29. The word "destruction" figures in the title of Las Casas's best known (at least until recently), but not most important work, *Brevísima relación de la*

destrucción de las Indias. But as Saint-Lu has observed, it is the expression of a key category in Las Casas's thought (see A. Saint-Lu, "Significación de la denuncia lascasiana").

30. And so, in a play on words as he begins his account of certain expeditions undertaken just a few years after Columbus's arrival, he will say: "Tras Viceinte Añez salió otro descubridor, o quizás destruidor" ("After Viceinte Añez, there sallied forth another discoverer, or maybe destroyer") (*H.I.*, bk. 1, ch. 173, *O.E.* 1:459a).

31. Las Casas criticizes the destruction of the Indian world wherever he finds it. Against those who claim that he was obsessed by the excesses committed by Spaniards in particular, let us recall what he writes about the Germans to whom Charles V had granted a *concesión*, for which they paid him well, in Venezuela. In that region, "which the Germans have at their disposal to rob and destroy, the transgressions and corruptions are as wicked as any the devils do. They have horrible, exquisite things in their minds, cruelties that those more than unfortunate Christians, if that is what they are (which is impossible), have committed against those innocent people." The subject of gold comes up once again in this case. "Does it seem to your Grace," Las Casas complains, "that the king was well advised when for 400,000 gold ducats that the Germans offered him, he had to give them (give them or lend them, I know not which) a land so great — hand over to them such meek people, for them to kill, and withdraw them from the world and stuff hell full of souls? . . . Whence, or for what purpose, could our Lord King have made such a contract?" Then he asks, with sorrowful irony: "Are these the 'preachers' the King sends to convert those entrusted to him [by the papal donation]?" (*Carta a un personaje,* 1535, *O.E.* 5:67b–68a). Not even the king is permitted to purchase an economic or political end with the Indians' deaths.

32. Guamán Poma, *Primer nueva corónica y buen gobierno,* 372, 374, 391.

33. It is altogether astonishing that Todorov (in his *La conquête de l'Amérique,* 180–81, 191) should find no essential difference between Las Casas and Cortés. His book presents us with genuinely penetrating analyses, but on this point his subtle arguments remain quite unconvincing. One has the impression that the author allows himself to be carried away by a taste for paradox, something that he himself seems to have perceived (191). As Castillo well says, Todorov "seems to forget the importance of 'otherness' in the mind of the defender of the Indians" (Carlos Castillo, "El problema de los Indios: Bartolomé de Las Casas," 53 n. 10).

34. In a similar vein, Guamán Poma writes: "Jesus Christ, the living God, . . . came to withdraw souls, not silver, from the world, and neither asked nor gave tribute" (*Primer nueva corónica y buen gobierno,* 962a).

35. This contract would be an expression of what Giménez Fernández calls Las Casas's "possibilism," that is, a practical sense that led him to accept, in spite the loftiness of his ideals, what could actually be realized (see Giménez Fernández, *Bartolomé de Las Casas: Capellán,* 647). Thus it is not to be confused with the "probabilism" of moral theology.

36. In an important homily John Paul II applies this gospel text to the contrast between North and South in the world today: "In the light of the

words of Christ, the poor South will judge the wealthy North. And the poor peoples and the poor nations — poor in different ways, not only in lack of food, but also deprived of liberty and other human rights — will judge those who take these goods, accumulating for themselves the imperialist monopoly of economic and political domination at the expense of others" (in Namao, Canada, September 7, 1984, no. 45).

37. See our next chapter.

38. P. André-Vincent has pointed out the importance of this Lascasian text in his "L'intuition fondamentale de Las Casas et la doctrine de Saint Thomas."

39. In the pages that follow, he does not repeat this idea. Without denying it, he limits his characterization of the Indians to their membership *in potentia.* But the thesis remains posited.

40. See Henri de Lubac's classic work *Corpus mysticum.*

41. Jean-Baptiste Lassègue, *La larga marcha,* 157 n. 1.

Chapter 3: If We Were Indians

1. Reproduced in 5:5–27. We do not have the earlier texts listed by H. R. Wagner and Helen Parish, *The Life and Writings of Bartolomé de Las Casas,* 259–60, and especially by I. Pérez Fernández, *Inventario,* 31–52 — except for the abstract, prepared by Lope de Conchillos's secretariate, of a *Memorial de agravios* presented by Las Casas to cardinals Cisneros and Adriano (see 5:3–5).

2. For a reflection on this subject in today's terms, see H. Echegaray, "Derechos del pobre, derechos de Dios."

3. Parish does not think that this document is Las Casas's. She bases her opinion especially on the fact that it concludes with a pronouncement against the alleged rights of Columbus, which does not reflect the Sevillian's mentality (in Pérez Fernández, *Inventario,* 59–60). Pérez, however, does think it is Las Casas's writing (*Inventario,* 60–62).

4. Giménez Fernández is of the opinion that Las Casas may have included the Isabelline text on advice received from Palacios Rubios in the course of the memorandum's redaction (see M. Giménez Fernández, *Bartolomé de Las Casas: Delegado de Cisneros,* 135). He also thinks that the disputed anti-Columbian appendix was added by a non-Lascasian hand (see idem, *Bartolomé de Las Casas: Capellán,* 519 n. 1740).

5. See the examination, by Giménez Fernández, *Bartolomé de Las Casas: Delegado de Cisneros,* 177–202, of the instructions received by the Hieronymites (based on a text prepared by Las Casas and Palacios Rubios) and of the context of the Cisnerian reform. On this and other aspects of the work of the illustrious cardinal, the reader may also consult B. Escandell, *Estudios Cisnerianos.*

6. See *H.I.,* bk. 3, ch. 87, *O.E.* 2:376a. Las Casas makes certain criticisms of the plan being implemented by the Hieronymites. One of them is lodged against the norm prescribing that "one-third of the laborers," by turns, be assigned to "mine gold" (*H.I.,* bk. 3, ch. 89, *O.E.* 2:383b). He refers to a similar guideline — differing in detail — in his *Memorial de remedios,* dating from 1516

(*O.E.* 5:23a). Bartolomé has left us clear testimonials and profound reflections on the actual operation of the project committed to the Hieronymites. These religious complained to Cardinal Cisneros of the cleric's criticisms, thereby disturbing, despite a friendship of long standing, the prelate's relationship with Bartolomé. Matters reached the point that, in July 1517, the cardinal wrote to the Hieronymites ordering them to send Las Casas to Spain — under arrest if necessary (see the text in Giménez Fernández, *Bartolomé de Las Casas: Delegado de Cisneros,* 647–48). Parish appears to be in possession of further material regarding this episode (see her "Introduction: Las Casas's Spirituality," 23–24).

7. Concluding his 1531 letter to the Council, Las Casas says: "I dispatch to your Lordships and Mercies a printed copy of the Pope's bull granting these lands to the rulers of Castile, having personally seen to its printing" (*O.E.* 5:55b). Pérez Fernández thinks it possible that this publication took place in Barcelona in 1519. But obviously we cannot be certain about that (see Pérez Fernández, *Inventario,* 123). As has been observed, Las Casas was one of the first of his time to perceive the importance of the press in the defense of a cause. He will offer a further practical demonstration of this with the publication of his treatises in 1552.

8. Another text contains a rapid but clear reference to the bull and to Isabella's testament: the *Memorial de remedios* read out by Friar Reginaldo Montesino (Antón's brother) at Valladolid in December 1517. Distinguished Lascasists such as Giménez Fernández (see his *Bartolomé de Las Casas: Capellán,* 57) and M. Bataillon (see *Estudios sobre Bartolomé de Las Casas,* 87–88) have attributed the text to Las Casas. Bataillon draws upon it extensively for his explanation of Las Casas's projects for the native communities and even advances the supposition that the Sevillian was influenced by Thomas More's *Utopia*. (In the following section we shall refer to Baptiste's contrary hypothesis. After a meticulous analysis, Baptiste suggests that it was Las Casas who influenced Thomas More.) Pérez Fernández and Parish deny the Lascasian authorship of the text in question (see Pérez Fernández, *Inventario,* 73–75). Regarding the point we are addressing, the text in question says: "The Indians are free,...and this is the conclusion arrived at [by the 1513 conference of theologians and scholars] in view of the Bull of the grant, made to the Sovereigns of Castile and León by Pope Alexander VI, of the said Indies and Mainland, as well as in consideration of a passage in the testament of our Most Serene Queen, of happy memory, in which she commends to the Catholic King, her consort, enjoining the same on his successors, a fair treatment of the said Indians, along with their farms, as these are free persons, so that they may be drawn to our holy Catholic faith" (*DII* 12:107). The passage is surely very interesting and closely akin to the Lascasian thesis that freedom is a condition for the reception of the faith. ("With the Indians in the hard servitude in which the Christians have them, we are unable to preach them the divine law"; *Carta a un personaje,* 1535, *O.E.* 5:66b.)

9. We have a reassertion of the perspective of evangelization in an unpublished text of Juan Zumárraga, which Parish regards as having been written in close collaboration with Las Casas. That document states: "The

final and remote cause, or ultimate end, being striven for by the Sovereign Pontiff in the Apostolic Letter of the grant of these realms to our Most Christian Sovereigns of Spain was not, either de jure or in any circumstantial hypothesis whatsoever, anything other than that the faith of Christ be preached throughout this New World of the Indies and that these people be converted to Christ" ("Parecer ampliado, con seis verdades, sobre esclavos indios y conversión pacífica," 1536, in Parish, *Las Casas en México,* Appendix 1; see our chapter 11, below).

10. Providence version, folio 136.

11. Ibid., f. 136v.

12. The literature here is extremely extensive. See the excellent comprehensive presentation in P. Castañeda Delgado, *La teocracia pontifical,* chs. 11, 12. Castañeda reviews the various interpretations made of these texts, finally rendering his own judgment: that this was "an actual bestowal or donation on the part of the Roman Pontiff in his capacity as temporal sovereign of the earth in view of his spiritual mission." It was "one more link in a long chain of medieval donations" (284, 285). In a more impetuous style, R. García Villoslada also presents a state of the question, in his "Sentido de la conquista y evangelización." And see the presentation by the great historian Zavala (with a survey of the old interpretations of the bulls): S. Zavala, *Las instituciones jurídicas de la conquista de América,* 346–89. Still important is Giménez Fernández's substantial *Nuevas consideraciones sobre la historia, sentido y valor de las bulas alejandrinas de 1493 referentes a las Indias.*

13. Actually Las Casas knew only the second *Inter Caetera,* predated May 4, 1493, the version that entailed more important consequences.

14. To cite one example among many; see T. Urdanoz's important "Las Casas y Francisco de Vitoria."

15. This does not necessarily mean that the Salamancans took their inspiration directly from Las Casas. The question of the contacts among these Dominicans is a very complex one. But some relationship, through other persons, must have existed. Furthermore, the "second generation" Salamanca theologians will uphold the missionary interpretation of the Alexandrine bulls, and one of the authorities they appeal to will be Bartolomé de Las Casas. Abril Castelló even goes so far as to say that, on this point, "the glosses of Sotomayor, Medina, Peña, and Báñez are copied from Las Casas" (V. Abril Castelló, "Bartolomé de Las Casas y la escuela de Salamanca," 511).

16. Controversial, and not always well understood. Pérez Fernández is preparing a critical edition of this book, with its contextualization in the work of Las Casas.

17. Depriving them of both rights were, for example, those who mounted prospecting expeditions along the coasts of Panama and Venezuela (see *H.I.,* bk. 1, ch. 172, *O.E.* 1:459a).

18. He sums them up in two: the "great greed" of those who had come from Spain, and the abuse and starvation to which the Indians were subjected (*O.E.* 5:5b).

19. Las Casas always trusted the qualities and good judgment of the Spanish farm worker, who was very different from the type of person com-

ing to the Indies up to this time. As late as 1559, he still thinks that the remedy for Hispaniola (that "key to all the Indies") ought to be to "people it with simple farm folk, who abound in these realms" (*Carta al rey,* 1559, *O.E.* 5:463b). He had written the same thing ten years before, but with regard to all the Indies (*Representación al Consejo,* 1549, *O.E.* 5:292b). See A. Milhou, "El labrador casado."

20. In the *Historia de las Indias,* recalling these ideas, he says that, through these marriages, "a single republic" will be formed, "one of the best, and perhaps the most peaceful and Christian in the world" (*H.I.,* bk. 3, ch. 102, *O.E.* 2:418b). Urdanoz deems Las Casas the first to propose "the fusion of both peoples by *mestizaje,* or intermarriage" (Urdanoz, "Las Casas y Francisco de Vitoria," 244). However this may be, the phenomenon will be of capital importance for the future of the continent.

21. He says this twice (*O.E.* 5:18b, 21a). The point is an important one. Las Casas is proposing here, in 1516, something that will be refused the Indians for a long time to come: access to the priesthood.

22. In this project, Bartolomé also proposes — showing how much further he has to go — that "slaves, black and white," transported from Castile, be held here (*O.E.* 5:17a). We shall return to this point (see below, our chapter 11). For now, let us emphasize that, in the prevailing context of the universal approval of slavery (appalling as it is in our eyes today), the question was whether, depending on the case, it was legal or not — independently of race, as our quotation shows.

23. For example, Las Casas petitions the dissolution of the agreement struck by the Crown with a certain Francisco Garay on grounds that it cannot be implemented "without slaying many Indians" (*O.E.* 5:10b).

24. This geographical coincidence had already been noted by J.-B. Lassègue, *La larga marcha,* 109.

25. As Baptiste says, "It would be a researcher's dream (or nightmare) to discover, among More's papers (or Erasmus's, or Busleiden's), a copy in Latin of Version A [Bartolomé's text]. Only then would it be possible to make a verifiable comparison between Las Casas's Latin and More's" (V. Baptiste, *Bartolomé de las Casas and Thomas More's Utopia,* 62).

26. That they had failed to keep account of this will be one of his criticisms of the Burgos Laws of 1512. He forthrightly accuses the king's councilors: "This they plotted, and managed to make it the first thing the King would ordain, namely: that they be *removed from their nature* and peoples, where they had been born and reared in all their lineages for perhaps thousands of years, and driven in next to Spanish peoples like a wedge, where the day will come that they will have no single hour's breathing space, and they will perish" (*H.I.,* bk. 3, ch. 13, *O.E.* 2:203a; emphasis added).

27. The importance of the point has already been suggested in Ricardo Levene's old article, "Bartolomé de Las Casas y la doctrina de la libertad"; see also L. Pena, "Presupuestos histórico-doctrinales de la teoría de Las Casas de la libertad"; R. Queraltó Moreno, "Fundamentación filosófica." One may likewise consult J. I. Gutiérrez Nieto, "La idea de libertad en Castilla durante

el Renacimiento"; and of course the comprehensive works on Las Casas's thought.

28. See V. Abril Castelló's pertinent articles, "Bartolomé de Las Casas, el último comunero," and "El comunerismo lascasiano y las libertades políticas del indio americano."

29. Manuel Giménez Fernández, in his eagerness to establish the authenticity of the 1517 text, of which we shall presently speak (and to demonstrate Bartolomé's juridical and theological incompetency at the time — something that Parish, "Introduction: Las Casas's Spirituality," refuses to accept), maintains that this the first occasion on which Las Casas proclaims the liberty of the Indians (see Giménez Fernández, *Bartolomé de Las Casas: Capellán*, 383–403). Maravall had already noticed this error and corrected it (J. A. Maravall, "Utopía y primitivismo," 360); indeed the idea was already present in the *Memorial de remedios* of 1516.

30. *DII* vol. 12. Las Casas reports this meeting, and other details, in *H.I.*, bk. 3, ch. 99, *O.E.* 2:409b–410a.

31. See below, our chapter 10.

32. Here will be found all of the texts whose precise references we shall be omitting in the following pages.

33. The passage continues with a brief reservation as to the Indians' earlier condition under their own authorities: " . . . Rather, if there were any shortcomings in their republics, then Your Majesty's dominion may cleanse and refine them of these, and thus they may enjoy an enhanced freedom."

34. The same idea and expression is found in the *Tratado comprobatorio* (1552, *O.E.* 5:400a) and the *De Regia Potestate* (8:5, p. 83).

35. Three years later, now in episcopal orders, he will tell the king — together with Bishop Valdivieso — that the first thing he asks is that "we set these free, our sheep, the native Indians of these Indies, and set them at all liberty, *in order that* we may preach to them and instruct them, and draw them to a knowledge of their God and Creator" (*Carta al príncipe Felipe*, 1545, *O.E.* 5:222b; emphasis added).

36. See below, chapters 5, 6.

37. Curiously, the sentence quoted is in the first-person singular, whereas, above, it has been the first-person plural that was used, as indeed we might expect in such a case of collective authorship.

38. See below, chapter 13.

39. John Major was a Scottish theologian who taught for long years in Paris (see García Villoslada's interesting *La Universidad de París durante los estudios de Francisco de Vitoria*, especially 106–64). Major was the first theologian in Europe to address the problems posed by the Indies. He does so in the lectures he gave in 1508 and published two years later (his commentary on the Fourth Book of Peter Lombard's *Sentences*, d. 44, q. 4).

40. A. Saint-Lu, "Le cri de tant de sang: Les massacres d'Indiens relatés par Las Casas," in idem, *Las Casas indigéniste*, 45–54. The author takes the cases of the massacres of Cholula and México, which Las Casas describes in the *Brevísima*, 1542, 147b–148b, 148b–149a. The native versions are found in texts published by M. León Portilla in his *Visión de los vencidos* and his *El*

reverso de la conquista. Saint-Lu thinks that, in writing the *Brevísima,* Las Casas was able to make use of old native versions of those episodes (Saint-Lu, "Cri de tant de sang," 53).

41. Saint-Lu, "Cri de tant de sang," 54.

42. León Portilla, *Visión de los vencidos;* idem, *El reverso de la conquista.*

43. See B. Biermann, "Bartolomé de Las Casas und Verapaz."

44. Despite the fact that Las Casas himself mentions and explains — sometimes in detail — words from native languages, we do not know how extensive his knowledge was of the Indian tongues, as we possess no definitive documentation on the point. We do know, however, that Domingo de Santo Tomás, author of the first *Gramática o arte de la lengua general de los Indios de los reinos del Perú,* was an associate of his. See L. J. Cisneros, "La primera gramática de la lengua general," and M. Mahn-Lot, "Transculturation et évangélisation."

45. This is what the natives understood, so that they entrusted him with the defense of their interests (see León Portilla, "Las Casas en la conciencia indígena del siglo XVI"). For example, Peruvian Indian chiefs assigned him, along with Domingo de Santo Tomás, the task of opposing the perpetuity of the *encomienda* (see below, our chapter 10).

46. Parish has rightly called attention to the importance of this fact in Las Casas's life. See her "Introduction: Las Casas's Spirituality," 18.

47. The text continues no less expressively: "When a father, approaching the partition, saw that his son was being taken from him, the husband that his wife was being given to another master, the mother her daughter, and the wife her husband, who will doubt that this was not new torture for them, and double wretchedness and sorrow, as they poured forth their tears, groaning aloud and bewailing their unhappy lot, perhaps even cursing their fate?" (*H.I.,* bk. 3, ch. 156, *O.E.* 2:581a–b). Speaking about the evil deeds of the conquistadors Las Casas will refer a number of times to the Indians as "those sad people" (*H.I.,* bk. 3, ch. 49, *O.E.* 2:315a) or "those miserable people" (*H.I.,* bk. 3, ch. 102, *O.E.* 2:394a), expressions that confirm the feelings that their situation provoked in him.

48. Earlier in the same work, in an allusion to the use of peaceful means to proclaim the gospel to the Indians, he exhorts his readers: "In withdrawing these *siblings* of ours from their error, let us follow the example of the Apostles and apostolic men" (*Apología,* 177; emphasis added).

49. Later, in his reply to Sepúlveda regarding the number of human victims offered in sacrifice, he will say: "If the Very Reverend Doctor Sepúlveda would consider this lovingly, and with charity, he would know that I make a better count than he does. And he would do well to answer how it happens, since he *weeps* for the Indians sacrificed because they died without baptism — somewhere between ten and a hundred (or for that matter had there been a thousand, or ten thousand, which there were not) — his soul does not mourn and his entrails tear and heart tremble for the twenty million souls that have perished in all the rest of this time without faith and without the sacraments?" (*Aquí se contiene,* 1552, *O.E.* 5:334a; emphasis added). Human compassion is one of Friar Bartolomé's motives for action and reflection.

50. See a commentary on this gospel text in Gustavo Gutiérrez, *A Theology of Liberation*, 198–99.

51. Something we find very rarely, according to Pérez Fernández, who thoroughly studies this matter.

52. He even foresees the desirability of joining the North and South Seas (the Atlantic and Pacific Oceans) — through Nicaragua rather than through Panama (see *O.E.* 5:66a).

Introduction to Part Two

1. The Providence version carries the same text but speaks of "December of the year 1563" (f. 157v). This is one of the reasons to consider this manuscript earlier than the one used in the BAE edition.

2. In many texts Las Casas refers to this double entry; see, for example, *O.E.* 5:42b and 48, *O.E.* 5:293b. In the *Doce dudas* (Providence version) this distinction enables him to expound his ideas in long paragraphs (see chs. 12–18, ff. 157v–169).

3. One text among many: "Destroying and killing so many countless meek and gentle peoples and depopulating such large lands, robbing infinite treasures" (*Carta al emperador*, 1542, *O.E.* 5:123a). According to J. Friede (*Bartolomé de Las Casas: Precursor*, 147 n. 7), this letter would be from 1544, after the passing of the New Laws. I. Pérez Fernández maintains that the date is 1532, between May and November (*Inventario*, 314).

4. The Spanish translation, as A. Losada notes (see *De Thesauris*, 296 n. 27), inevitably weakens the expression of Las Casas that here uses an incisive play on words in Latin: "non a verbis sed a verberibus."

Chapter 4: Evangelization at Gunpoint

1. As we know, Bartolomé takes his data concerning these Portuguese forays mainly from historians João de Barros and Gomes Eanes de Zarara. It is these works (which he read surely in the early years of the 1550s) that have taught him of the "destruction of Africa" occurring all through the fifteenth century and have enabled him to perceive the profound injustice of the enslavement of the inhabitants of that continent. I. Pérez Fernández has shown this very plainly in his *Fray Bartolomé de Las Casas, O.P., Brevísima relación de la destrucción de África*. See below, our chapter 11.

2. This is certainly a shortcoming on the part of Bartolomé de Las Casas. But the text we have cited and certain other similar passages show that, had he had more contact with the world of Islam, he would not have stooped to such frequent slurs on Muslims — a commonplace among his contemporaries. Las Casas evolves, in function of his practice and a better knowledge of concrete reality. (This was the case with his radical change with respect to black slavery.) But he lacked that experience and knowledge — especially early in his life — with regard to the present matter. It is possible, nevertheless, to find among his writings various texts along the same lines, and even more precise, than the one just cited.

3. See *History of the Indies*, bk. 1, chs. 17–27. We shall return to this matter below (chapter 11).

4. According to Helen Parish ("Introduction: Las Casas's Spirituality"), this work was written around 1533–34, after the famous Enriquillo episode. Enriquillo, a young chief, had mounted a rebellion on Hispaniola around 1519 and waged a defensive war, preventing the entry of the Spaniards into his territory. In a complex episode, Las Casas, who was very ill-regarded by the Spaniards living on the island at that time, started a dialogue with him, complied with certain previous conditions, and persuaded him to lay down his arms (see ibid., 56–59). On Enriquillo, see Pérez Fernández, "Fray Bartolomé de Las Casas ante el último guerrillero indio del Caribe."

5. Here we differ with P. Castañeda Delgado, who, in his otherwise excellent article "Los métodos misionales en América," speaks of three positions: for, against, and in between. He is led to assert that only Sepúlveda among the theologians and jurists (and almost no missionary) was in favor of the waging of war as a prelude to evangelization. He also expands the list of those who propose a peaceful evangelization by adding those who prefer it as an ideal but accept martial action under various conditions often readily appealed to by conquistadors, *encomenderos*, and certain missionaries.

6. Las Casas frequently presents this situation in terms like these: "The Spaniards penetrated this New World, unknown in previous centuries, with extreme insolence. There, in contravention of the intention of their prince, they perpetrated cruel and unusual crimes. They put numberless thousands of persons to death, burned villages, stole livestock, destroyed cities, and, without cause or pretext of probable cause, and with inhuman cruelty, committed abominable acts against those miserable people." And he ends with the question, "Can those savage, rapacious, seditious persons have any knowledge of the true God, to whose worship the friars had been exhorting the Indians?" (*Apología*, 176).

7. A few lines further on he says: "These were the services offered to God, Their Highnesses, and the conversion of those people to the Catholic faith, in their great zeal, by Diego Velázquez and the rest" (ibid.). Las Casas, we know, has no personal quarrel with Velázquez, who in turn was friendly toward the cleric during the latter's tenure as chaplain and *encomendero* in Cuba. But neither, evidently, was Velázquez's behavior an exception to the general rule among the conquistadors, and it is this that Bartolomé is criticizing.

8. In the *Historia* he recounts the following anecdote of an event that had occurred in the course of the expeditions launched from that island. "Early in the morning the Spaniards saw two canoes coming, with nine persons in them. When they had reached shore, the Spanish captain had them seized and bound, without cause or purpose, but only that his name might stink in the nostrils of all who should ever hear it. He had some of them taken aside and questioned, showing them gold from the island of Cuba and asking them whether that metal was to be had in their land." And Las Casas exclaims: "See the gospel he began to preach to them and the signs he gave them that there was but one true God in heaven!" (*H.I.*, bk. 3, ch. 96, *O.E.* 2:403b).

9. We shall return to the matter of the trade imposed on the Indians when we speak of Francisco de Vitoria, that defender in all good faith of the right of the Europeans to conduct business and therefore to remain in the Indies.

10. Elsewhere he indicates another great "blindness of Portugal": "First, that the infantry ordered those of its number who, being of the stuff of which apostles are made [*idóneos apóstoles*], customarily assaulted and robbed those living in the peace and security of their homes, to work to bring to the faith those *infidels or Moors* who had never heard of it, or if they had had previous notice of it, would readily abandon theirs and receive ours." "Idóneos apóstoles," he calls the assailants ironically — suitable candidates for the office of apostles, these authors of persecutions against Africans and, specifically, Muslims. In passing, Las Casas expresses once again a profound conviction of his: It is no simple matter to change religions. We shall examine this conviction of his below. The text continues with a defense of the transcendence and gratuity of Christian faith: "Second, that they ordered them to bring them to the faith as if they had come to sell them some merchandise or other and that was the end of the matter." Finally, another favorite idea of his: the free will of persons. Christians did not seem to perceive the gravity of their actions: "Third, that, having done the above-named deeds — deeds so wicked, so evil in themselves, so horrible — the infantry [were ordered] to ignore what *will* they might have to receive their preachers, who had given them such fine examples of Christendom" (*H.I.*, bk. 1, ch. 25, *O.E.* 1:95a; emphasis added). This behavior, Las Casas testifies, "first began in Portugal rather than in Castile" (*H.I.*, bk. 1, ch. 173, *O.E.* 1:460b).

11. Quoted by Lewis Hanke, introduction to *Bartolomé de Las Casas: Del único modo,* 28.

12. We are shocked, of course, by this usage of the adjective "mahomético" (Mahometan), which can be explained only by the notion — as persistent in our day as it was in Bartolomé's — that Islam seeks to propagate itself by force. That is Las Casas's understanding: "This, Sir, is not the path of Christ, not the manner in which his gospel is to be preached, not the way and custom by which souls are to be converted. This is the way taken by Mahoma himself, and even worse than Mahoma, who claimed to have come *in vi armorum,* by force of arms. After all, those whom he had subjected by arms and who believed in his sect, he allowed to live. Here, the Indians who so joyfully and willingly submit to and receive their God the Spaniards cut to pieces and bury their souls in hell" (*Carta a un personaje,* 1535, *O.E.* 5:68a). Las Casas denies that this is part of Christianity, despite the comportment — and even worse — of some of its adepts. The question of whether Muhammad and his followers actually preached a "holy war" in that time is a complex one, in which many nuances must be introduced, and it goes beyond the scope of these pages.

13. Beltrán de Heredia, to whom we owe so much for his studies on the Salamancan school, reproaches Las Casas for his "impetuous character," which, says Beltrán, leads him to "anathematize the cruelties perpetrated by the conquistadors on the Indian poor, and in censuring particular acts, to

condemn the Conquista itself and those who had ordered it. Dominican theologians walked more carefully here, restricting their condemnations to invalid reasons [*títulos ficticios*, adduced for the Conquista] but leaving the cause itself intact, as it could be legitimate for other reasons" (V. Beltrán de Heredia, *Domingo de Soto*, 261–62). Las Casas did find these theologians too cautious. For him, justice demanded the forthright, explicit rejection of the Conquista, and not merely of one or another abuse. Indeed, Beltrán de Heredia is criticizing Las Casas for one of his most acute and correct perceptions. The problem, when all is said and done, was "the Conquista itself," and "those who had ordered it."

14. De Córdoba and his friends criticized the Burgos Laws, and twenty years later Francisco de Vitoria will do the same with the Notification.

15. The expedition mounted by this cruel personage — regarded as such not only by Las Casas, who called him a "wolf starved for days on end" (*Octavo remedio*, 1542, *O.E.* 5:107a), but by others as well — was unprecedented. It was the largest and mightiest of all these years (see C. M. Gasteazoro, "El ciclo de Pedrarias").

16. Las Casas lauds the personal quality of this friar, but comments: "Good Franciscan Father Alonso del Espinal, due to his not little ignorance, accepted the ambassadorship because he had failed to notice that he was being sent to keep so many thousands and millions of his innocent neighbors in a captivity and unjust servitude in which they would surely perish — as they had already perished, and in which at last they did meet their end, every last one" (*H.I.*, bk. 3, ch. 5, *O.E.* 2:180a). For a somewhat different version of Espinal's role, see L. Arranz Márquez, "Alonso del Espinar, O.F.M., y las leyes de Burgos de 1512–1513." Arranz does acknowledge, however, that the Franciscan agreed with a number of persons of his time who judged that "by and large, the Taino people were not ready to live in freedom" (ibid., 642). And so the confirmation of the *encomiendas* in the Burgos Laws was justified.

17. A few other authors could be added — always canonists, to be sure (and among them, St. Antoninus, archbishop of Florence, d. 1459). But it is interesting to observe that, in the disputations held at the beginning of the sixteenth century, Thomas Aquinas figures merely as one author among others (despite the extensive use of him by Matías de Paz). It was in these same years that, in Paris (where Francisco de Vitoria studied), Thomas Aquinas's *Summa Theologiae* had just begun to be used in theology.

18. "We believe, however," writes the Ostian, "that it is better to say that the Pope is the Universal Vicar of our Savior Jesus Christ, and that consequently he has authority not only over Christians, but also over all heathen, inasmuch as the faculty received [by Christ] from the Father was plenary.... And it seems to me that, since the coming of Christ, all honor, power, dominion, and jurisdiction have been removed from the heathen and transferred to the faithful, by right and for just cause, by the one who holds supreme authority and is infallible" (cited by Silvio Zavala in his introduction, lxxiv–lxxv, to the Leturia translation of Palacios Rubios, *De las islas del mar océano*, and Matías de Paz, *Del dominio sobre los indios*; Zavala edited the two works and published them together in one volume).

19. Here it is interesting to recall the testimony (1435) of Paulus Vladimiri (Pawel Włodkowicz). This Polish priest and theologian, unknown to sixteenth-century Spanish theologians, including Las Casas, ardently fought against the Teutonic Knights (an order approved by Innocent II in 1199), who, armed with the authority of certain papal bulls, conducted savage wars against the Lithuanian heathen on the pretext of evangelization. Frequently appealing to Thomas Aquinas, Paulos rejects the use of force for the extension of the faith. He regards as heretical the theology adduced in favor of this use of force. The papal donation of the Lithuanian territories was made for the purpose of evangelization, says Paulos, not for sake of the power and wealth of the Teutonic Knights. Present at the Council of Constance (1414–18), Paulos asked for a condemnation of such use of force, but failed to obtain it. Here is a great defender of peaceful means of evangelization and the rights of non-Christians. For further reading on this remarkable theologian, see the excellent study by Stanislaus Belch, *Paulos Vladimir and His Doctrine*. See also B. Przybylski, "Le problème de la guerre juste selon St. Thomas et P. Wlodkowic." I am indebted to my friend Wayne Wytembelski for calling my attention to this interesting figure.

20. J. Palacios Rubios, *De las islas del mar océano*, 87. We have the actual copy of this work that Las Casas used, with interesting marginal annotations in his own hand (which therefore figure among his first "writings"; see I. Pérez Fernández, *Inventario*, 70–71). This work has been published, with an important introduction by Zavala, together with that of Matías de Paz, *Del dominio sobre los indios*. Palacios Rubios asserts that "the coming of Christ has withdrawn from the heathen all jurisdiction and power and has transferred them to the faithful." Las Casas notes in the margin: "Heretical opinion of the Ostian," adding, "You cannot, Lord Doctor, dissolve or respond to those authoritative dicta except under the most absurd premises" (Palacios Rubios, *De las islas del mar océano*, 115). In this fashion, Palacios Rubios continues, Christ, from the very moment of his birth, held "exclusive sovereignty over the world" (ibid.). Once his mission was accomplished, he transferred both jurisdictions, the temporal and the spiritual, to St. Peter and "to the other Apostles" so that "the Pope enjoys the fullness of the power delegated by Christ" (ibid., 84). Secular princes, then, have the exercise of the temporal arm only "by concession or permission of the Church."

21. Palacios Rubios, *De las islas del mar océano*, 132–34.

22. Zavala, introduction to Leturia translation of Palacios Rubios and Matías de Paz, p. lxv. Zavala continues: "In this sense, Palacios Rubios's teaching on pontifical authority would represent not only a prolongation of thirteenth-century theories, which might be expected of a Doctor of Laws and professor of Canon Law, but also an anticipation of the opportunism of the many authors of sixteenth-century tractates who utilized elements of medieval theory to defend their religious and political viewpoints in that turbulent century." And elsewhere Zavala writes: "In Spain, faced with a European political problem (the annexation of Navarre) and another of transoceanic expansion (titles to the Indies), the Councilor of Ferdinand the Catholic, Doctor Palacios Rubios, adopts, as the sixteenth century opens, the

theory favorable to the temporal power of the Pope; but he does so without forgetting the cause of the sovereignty he serves. This confluence of ultramontanism and royalism characterizes the political view of our jurist and permits us to situate it, in unstable equilibrium, between the exaggerated papal theories of the Middle Ages and the rationale of the state as conceived by Machiavelli" (ibid., lxx).

23. "Heathen must not, for sole cause of their unbelief, and in the absence of any other just cause, be deprived of their goods or suffer war in which Christians might seize what they possess" (Palacios Rubios, *De las islas del mar océano*, 42). But he will follow the Ostian in denying the heathen any jurisdiction over their lands except by reason of "a certain tacit, precarious consent on the part of the Church,... inasmuch as the entire world has been granted to the Pope as a bark or diocese so that the Roman Pontiff may reside and render judgment in any part of the world, even among heathen" (ibid., 108). Consequently, the church "may deprive unbelievers of [this jurisdiction], wholly or in part, whenever it may so decide" (ibid., 112). Alongside the latter two passages, Las Casas notes "Absurd" and "False."

24. With obvious reference to the Notification, which Palacios Rubios himself has redacted, after acknowledging the Indians' right to defend themselves (they are not "obliged to surrender the moment the Christians arrive," ibid., 34), he writes that this is all changed once it is explained to them that the "polity of the whole world, and authority over [the world], lie with the Pope, who has made donation and concession to Your Majesty of the province in which they live." In a concatenation that we shall see in the Notification as well he concludes: "And if, after a reasonable interval for making a decision, they have not seen fit to do so, they may be invaded and reduced to submission by war and force of arms, with their goods seized and their persons enslaved, since Christians will now be justified in making war" (ibid., 36).

25. According to V. Carro, the "first qualified theologian to intervene in the *Controversies of the Indies*" (*La teología y los teólogos-juristas*, 1:373; emphasis in the original). In fact John Major is the first, and while he concerns himself with the matter only briefly, his influence is great.

26. See, for example, Beltrán de Heredia, "Un precursor del Maestro Vitoria: El P. Matías de Paz O.P. y su tratado 'De Dominio Regum Hispaniae super Indos.'" Getino says, somewhat ironically: "The title of the article obliges him to relate his imperialist theories to the more humane and generous ones of the Salamancan Master" (L. A. Getino, *El maestro Fray Francisco de Vitoria*, 191 n. 1). Pérez de Tudela expresses similar reservations: "It has been said that Paz essentially anticipates Vitoria's conclusions by twenty-seven years. We regard this as somewhat exaggerated" ("Significado histórico," xxxi). Indeed, despite all of his vacillations with regard to the rights (*títulos*) of the king of Spain and the justice of the motives adduced for making war on the Indians, Vitoria is far from the theocratism of Matías de Paz.

27. Zavala specifies Paz's contributions vis-à-vis those of Palacios Rubios in these terms: "As for a basic comparison between the teachings of Palacios Rubios and Paz, I should dare to think that the latter interprets the authorities with greater knowledge and subtlety. On the delicate points of

the argumentation, where Palacios Rubios conforms to a formal exposition calculated to appeal to the logical taste of jurists, Paz penetrates the difficulty with the depth of a theologian." Then he indicates Paz's distance from Vitoria and his practical agreement with Palacios Rubios (Zavala, introduction to Leturia translation of Palacios Rubios and Matías de Paz, xlvii–xcviii).

28. This is the text: "Although dominion and preference or precedence have been introduced by human law, while the distinction between faithful and infidels is based on divine law, and the latter, as the product of grace, is not abrogated by human law, which is of natural reason, . . . nevertheless, the said dominion or precedence can justly be annulled by determination or ordinance of the Church, which has the authority of God: inasmuch as infidels, by reason of their unbelief, deserve to lose their power over the faithful, who acquire the category of children of God" (*ST* II–II, q. 10, a. 10, c.). Ruiz Maldonado, whose untimely demise is lamented by his friends and scholars of Las Casas alike, has remarked that Las Casas avoids citing this text at certain key moments in his defense of the Indians, since it might have supplied his adversaries with arguments. But he likewise sagaciously observes that neither does Sepúlveda cite this Question of the *Summa,* since it also contains assertions that went against his theses (see E. Ruiz Maldonado, "Tomás de Aquino, Bartolomé de Las Casas y la controversia de Indias," especially 106–107).

29. Matías de Paz, *Del dominio sobre los indios,* 239–40.

30. With reference to questions concerning the dominion the heathen have over their lands, by way of concluding a point in his reasoning he says: "Wherefore it follows that the opinion of the Ostian is more true than that of Innocent, and more in conformity with Sacred Scripture" (ibid., 247).

31. Ibid., 223.

32. Matías de Paz even cites the possibility of restitution to Indians, "once [these are] converted to the faith" (ibid.), when they have suffered injustice. Palacios Rubios, by contrast, maintains some of the islanders to be "so inept and incapable as to be altogether helpless to govern themselves. Thus, they may be called slaves in the broad sense, as having been born to serve and not to command." Here he appeals to Aristotle, the *De Regimine Principum* (at this time attributed in its entirety to Thomas Aquinas), and John Major (Palacios Rubios, *De las islas del mar océano,* 37–38). Las Casas notes in the margin: "False testimonial, the upshot of tyranny" (ibid.). However, if we compare these expressions concerning the Indians with those used later by Tomás Ortiz, Domingo de Betanzos (a controversial figure), García de Loaysa, Ginés de Sepúlveda, and a number of others, Palacios Rubios's judgment seems moderate.

33. Las Casas recalls that Master Matías de Paz "composed a treatise in Latin, in the course of a fortnight, attacking and impugning the despotic manner in which the Indians were made use of and demonstrating that they ought to be governed as persons and free people" (*H.I.* bk. 3, ch. 8, *O.E.* 2:188a). Zavala nuances Las Casas's judgment of Paz's ideas regarding the Indians and believes that Bartolomé read them with a certain benevolence

(see Zavala, introduction to Leturia translation of Palacios Rubios and Matías de Paz, cviii–cix).

34. A. García y García, with a critical bias against Las Casas's opinions in this regard, has turned his attention to these authors in his "El sentido de las primeras denuncias," 75–93.

35. The testimony of Gonzalo Fernández de Oviedo, who had gone on Pedrarias's expedition, runs along the same lines. "Later," he writes, "in the year 1516, I asked Doctor Palacios Rubios (since he had ordered the Notification) whether the conscience of Christians was satisfied by the Notification, and he told me yes, if used as it says it ought to be" (*Historia general*, bk. 29, ch. 7).

36. Cf. *H.I.*, bk. 3, ch. 7, *O.E.* 2:184a. One of Bartolomé's reasons for this appraisal was Palacios Rubios's effort, despite his failing health, to prevent the voyage of the Hieronymites (in 1517). He had been alerted to their project by Las Casas, who, seeing the enthusiasm with which they accepted the task assigned them by Cardinal Cisneros, felt uneasy about it. His feeling was justified by the event (*H.I.*, bk. 3, ch. 87, *O.E.* 2:375b–376a).

37. The text goes on, " . . . As we have stated at length in our first book, whose title is *De Unico Vocationis Modo Omnium Gentium ad Veram Religionem*, written in Latin." This reference to Palacios Rubios's theses is not found in the chapters of the *De Unico* that we have today.

38. We cite the text of the Notification according to the version Las Casas reports to us in his *History of the Indies* (*H.I.*, bk. 3, ch. 57).

39. The text entrusted to Francisco Pizarro in 1533, "that he might be able to proceed with the conquest and population of the provinces of Peru," is practically identical with the one we have followed and may have been read to Atahualpa by Valverde. The document is published in E. Lisson Chávez, *La Iglesia de España en el Perú*, vol. 1, no. 2, doc. 17, and as an appendix in Juan de la Peña, *De Bello contra Insulanos*, 538–41. Let us observe in passing that Dominican Vicente Valverde, a graduate of Salamanca, is a far more complex figure than a summary version of the Cajamarca episode might suggest. See his letter to the king (1539), in which — among other, less clear, assertions — we find a firm defense of the freedom of the Indians (in Lisson Chávez, *La Iglesia de España en el Perú*, vol. 1, no. 2, p. 11). For Valverde and other Dominicans of the period, see Nguyen Thai Hop, "Los dominicos en la defensa del hombre andino."

40. J. Höffner (*La ética colonial*, 275–78), and especially Castañeda Delgado (*La teocracia pontifical*, 319–26), adduce various cases of the application of the *Requerimiento*.

41. See the presentation — accompanied, it is true, by exaggerated praise — of Torquemada's main theses in Carro, *La teología y los teólogos-juristas*, 1:319–29.

42. "John Wyclif and the Rights of the Infidels: The Requerimiento Re-examined." Despite all, the article presents interesting data and suggestive connections; it has the further merit of noting how close the Ostian is to Wycliffe.

43. Wycliffe's position, as Francisco de Vitoria indicates at the beginning

of his *Relectio de Indias,* is not altogether clear. See a brief presentation of Wycliffe's ideas in K. B. McFarlane, *Wycliffe and English Non-Conformity.*

44. Fernández de Enciso is the author of the first book on the Indies to be published in Spain: *Summa de geografía,* Seville, 1519.

45. In a "Memorial" or memorandum reproduced in *DII* 1:441–50. Here, see Hanke, *La lucha por la justicia,* 30–32, and Castañeda Delgado, *La teocracia pontifical,* 320.

46. J. Pérez de Tudela, "Significado histórico," xxxviii.

47. Regarding these interpretations see Hanke, "The 'Requerimiento' and Its Interpreters," and Castañeda Delgado, *La teocracia pontifical,* 326–30. See also J. Manzano, *La incorporación de las Indias,* 41–57.

48. Bartolomé de Las Casas reports something that happened to him on the island of San Juan, when he was a cleric, which he regards as deserving of "attention and even tears" (*H.I.,* bk. 3, ch. 91, *O.E.* 2:391a). A certain Juan Bono had been saying that the Indians had always treated him very well. "Then why, you wretch," Las Casas asked this "famous pirate and waylayer and plunderer of the Indians," "have you perpetrated such ungrateful wickedness and cruelty upon them?" To which Bono responded: "Upon my faith, Father, because I was given them for their destruction and was told to capture them by war or by peace." In receiving his verbal commission from the Judges Advocate of the city, Las Casas explains, the sailor had thought he heard the word "destruction," when the actual term was "instruction"! And so he had been roaming about "assaulting the Indians of isle and mainland," adds our cleric, in profound sorrow. The confusion is as revealing as it is lamentable.

49. It is not beyond the realm of possibility that his rejection of the Notification implies his refusal to accept the thesis that the pope is a temporal sovereign. As we shall see, Las Casas indeed rejects this thesis.

50. What is hypothesized here was what had actually happened in the Turkish siege of Vienna in 1683: "If you become Muslims," the inhabitants were told, "you shall receive protection.... But if you are stubborn, and resist,... no one will be spared.... You shall all suffer armed assault.... Your goods and properties will be given up to pillage, and your children will be deported into slavery" (cited by J. Höffner, *La ética colonial,* 277). It would be interesting to know what the theologians of the Notification thought of this warning to the Christians of Vienna.

51. We must observe, however, that its defenders are not lacking today. Ramos regards the text as expressing "a mighty didactic effort to explain all of the premises of the power of the pope and his function — according to the doctrine of the Ostian, naturally — in terms of which [the pope] might bestow upon the sovereigns of Castile the unknown Indies." It sought "a praiseworthy end: the avoidance of a war of subjection, with its consequent enslavement" of the vanquished (D. Ramos Pérez, "El hecho de la conquista de América," 44). As we see, these observations take the right to occupy the lands of the Indies for granted. But this is precisely what is at issue.

52. See Zavala, *Instituciones jurídicas,* 488.

53. Las Casas perceives the audacity of the Indian response, and the first

time he mentions it (without recounting the occurrence), says: "I should not dare write it down here. Indeed, if it is written anywhere, it cannot be found, although [Enciso] says it in other, shameless words — as we shall report, God willing, below" (*H.I.*, bk. 3, ch. 57, *O.E.* 2:310b). (We already know these "shameless words" about the pope and the king.) Not content with this remark, after citing Enciso verbatim in another chapter, Bartolomé adds: "I happen to know for a certain that much of what Enciso says here was falsification and not history,...and therefore hold it as certain that the Indians said those words neither of the Pope nor of the King" (*H.I.*, bk. 3, ch. 63, *O.E.* 2:323a). Las Casas makes this declaration to exonerate the chiefs, of course; but it may also represent caution on the part of one who knows he has malicious adversaries on the lookout for the slightest pretext for attacking him — even though he can have had no responsibility for the expressions that may have been used.

54. This leads Las Casas to make the following commentary, which indirectly touches Palacios Rubios: "What more powerful or clearer proof could be had than the one confessed by your mouth, of the ignorance and blindness of Bachelor Anciso, and of the one who ordered the said Notification, and of all who believed that it has excused the horrible, impious wars, plunderings, and calamities that the Spaniards have caused those people through [that ignorance and blindness]? What evidence has Anciso given them in his Notification that they were in contempt of legitimate authority so that he might legitimately invade them, occupy their settlements, slay them, and take them captive?" (*H.I.*, bk. 3, ch. 63, *O.E.* 2:322b).

55. Fernández de Oviedo, likewise a member of Pedrarias's expedition, testifies to the foolishness with which the first to have to make use of this document addressed their task. He recounts: "The Governor ordered that I take with me the Requirement *in scriptis* that was to be made of the Indians, and handed it to me personally, as if I knew the Indians' language so that I could read it to them, or we had anyone there to undertake the study of their language should they wish to teach it to him. After all, simply to show them the paper on which it was written would be unavailing. Thus, in the presence of all I said: 'Sir, it seems to us that these Indians are unwilling to hear the theology of this Requerimiento, and that you have no one willing to learn their language.' " And he adds, with a boastful, cynical realism that also belies the purpose claimed for the document: " 'Let Your Mercy keep it until we have some of these Indians in a cage, that they may slowly learn it and the Lord Bishop manage to make them understand it.' And I gave him the Requerimiento, which he accepted with a big laugh, as did all who heard me" (*Historia general*, bk. 29, ch. 7). Oviedo could not have spoken more truly. The Notification presupposes that the Indians had been previously put in cages.

Chapter 5: Perspective of Power

1. *De Procuranda Indorum Salute,* bk. 2, ch. 1, p. 246. We shall cite this work in the Corpus Hispanorum de Pace (CHP) edition. It includes the texts eliminated from the first edition, which was published during Acosta's life-

time, by censorship; hence its interest. But since the noted Jesuit accepted these excisions, our previous version, authorized by him, has a value that we must not ignore. It has been published by BAE. This author's other works will be cited in the versions presented in that same BAE volume.

2. See V. Carro, *La teología y los teólogos-juristas*, 2:233–92; J. Höffner, *La ética colonial*, 45–95; P. Castañeda Delgado, "Los métodos misionales en América."

3. See below, our chapter 12, which will be devoted to Vitoria.

4. He expressed this in a letter to his friend Miguel Arcos (1534 or 1545). See below, our chapter 12.

5. We shall be dealing, of course, with the evangelization of non-Christians alone. As we shall see later in this same chapter, the position of the dominant theology regarding heretics was one of great severity. Heretics, in the canon law of the era — which drew theology along in its wake — were looked upon as persons who had abandoned the integrity of the Christian faith after having once received it, so that they had now violated a pact. This rigidity with regard to heretics is fully shared by all of the authors that we shall be studying. Consequently, any divergences to which we shall allude concern non-Christians alone, who are frequently called infidels, that is, unbelievers.

6. We shall use, in these pages, T. Urdanoz's edition of Francisco de Vitoria's *Obras*. In the case of the *Relección de Indis*, we shall also keep before our eyes the edition of L. Pereña Vicente and J. M. Pérez Prendes. Ordinarily we shall follow these respective translations; in some cases, however, we shall appeal directly to the Latin text. In order to facilitate the reader's consultation of the Spanish, we shall cite both editions at once, indicating the former with the word *Obras*, the latter with the abbreviation CHP. These references, as with our citations of Las Casas, will go in the text itself.

7. See the historical and theological framework of this statement in the pages that we shall devote to the subject in this same chapter.

8. Here, as everyone will do who treats the matter (including Sepúlveda), Vitoria cites the Fourth Council of Toledo (seventh century), which censured the comportment of King Sisebuto in forcing Jews to accept the Christian faith. That assembly also made a distinction between heretics and other unbelievers.

9. The reference is to "negative" unbelief, or simple ignorance of the Christian faith. "Positive" unbelief, in contrast, would be actual rejection of that faith. In this second sense, heretics are at times included under the denomination of unbelievers.

10. Vol. 3, p. 82, of his Commentary on the Secunda Secundae of St. Thomas Aquinas's *Summa Theologiae* (quoted by R. Hernández, "Presupuestos de Francisco de Vitoria," 70).

11. Vitoria says: "I say that it is not evil, but of itself good and licit, that those who govern oblige infidels to receive the Christian faith under sanction and threat of punishment" (Commentary on the Secunda Secundae in the *De Indis* [CHP], 121).

12. Carro, *La teología y los teólogos-juristas*, 2:248–49. Urdanoz (in Vitoria,

Obras, 542 n. 99) sees an evolution in Vitoria on the question of the coercion of infidel subjects of Christians, so that he moved to less rigid positions. See also Castañeda Delgado, "Los métodos misionales en América," 132–33; Hernández, "Presupuestos de Francisco de Vitoria," 70. The last-named author also records that Vitoria approved another, indirect kind of pressure upon persons to accept the faith, for example, "exemption or partial relief from tribute accorded to converts" (69).

13. Scandalized, Carro thinks Vitoria comes dangerously close to Duns Scotus's thinking here, which reproach, given the Dominican fervor of this scholar of sixteenth-century theology, must have been painful to him to make. It is a criticism that he will repeat, furthermore, when he reports Vitoria's considerations on the baptism of children of unbelievers, in which, once more, the Salamancan shifts toward the Franciscan theologian (see Carro, *La teología y los teólogos-juristas,* 2:248, 252). We shall return to this last point in our chapter 12.

14. T. Andrés Marcos and A. Losada, for example, in works that we shall cite below. The latter is of the opinion that this occurs despite a "timorous and ill-defined position" adopted by Vitoria in his "just title" based on evangelization (Losada, "Juan Ginés de Sepúlveda: Su polémica con Fray Bartolomé de Las Casas," 575).

15. Soto intervened in questions of the Indies before Vitoria did. Quite early, he wrote a book devoted to the subject with which we are concerned: *De Ratione Promulgandi Evangelium,* which unfortunately is lost. For Domingo de Soto's position, in addition to the works of Carro, Höffner, and Castañeda already cited, see J. Brufau, *La Escuela de Salamanca;* R. Hernández, "La escuela dominicana de Salamanca"; and for a comprehensive view, V. Beltrán de Heredia, *Domingo de Soto: Estudio biográfico documentado.*

16. A few pages further on, he gives a good summary of Las Casas's position, with which he disagrees, at least partially. His confrere, he says, rejects preventive wars, "and not only that, but, as we have said, neither does he admit the liceity of a war to be waged on those who would place obstacles in the way of our preaching, in the case that the obstacle would be raised by the common consent of the entire polity and all of its elements, so that they might not be forced to hear our preaching" (*O.E.* 5:308a).

17. Abril Castelló has given us a good study of Soto's reservations regarding Las Casas, as well as of the distance separating him from Sepúlveda: V. Abril Castelló, "Bartolomé de Las Casas y la escuela de Salamanca," 496–501. For our own part we think that Soto, although differently from the Cordovan, does not renounce the theology developed in the perspective of power that we shall see later in this chapter — although he does present a more moderate version of it. Las Casas does indeed indicate a breach with it. This is the real reason for Soto's criticism.

18. This is a frequent tendency among the Franciscans, with certain illustrious exceptions, due to the influence of Scotus. The reader may consult F. Aznar Gil's well-documented "La libertad religiosa del indio en autores franciscanos del siglo XVI."

19. Acosta, *De Procuranda Indorum Salute,* bk. 2, ch. 8, pp. 302–6.

20. Ibid., ch. 1, 246. Elsewhere, he reasons as follows. In the first centuries, rude and ignorant persons (Christians) had to preach to people of a high level of culture. In these conditions, miracles were needed. In the Indies, exactly the opposite situation obtains: here, the addressees of evangelization are, vis-à-vis the missioners, "inferior in all: in reason, in culture, and in power" (ibid., 308, 310). Miracles are of no utility here. For Acosta's view of evangelization, see M. Marzal, *Historia de la antropología indigenista: México y Perú*, 94–108; N. Zevallos, "El Padre José de Acosta"; and D. Brading, *The First America*.

21. The *Democrates Primus* was published in Latin for the first time in Rome (1535) and bears a dedication to Fernando de Toledo, duke of Alba. Losada has published it in Spanish in *Tratados políticos de Juan Ginés de Sepúlveda*, 127–304. For this work, one may read the study by H. Mechoulan, *L'Antihumanisme de J. G. Sepúlveda: Etude critique du Democrates Primus*. This author — who is not particularly concerned with the controversy of the Indies as such, any more than is Sepúlveda's book itself — is not one of those who qualify Sepúlveda as modern. On the contrary, he writes, concerning the significance of Sepúlveda's work: "A knowledge and understanding of Sepúlveda's thought affords us a better grasp of the drama of the Spanish decadence of the seventeenth century. We may say that our author, in his battle to *retard* the deepest aspirations of his contemporaries, is no stranger to this destiny" (Mechoulan, *L'Antihumanisme*, 11; emphasis added). Our references to Sepúlveda's works, like those to Las Casas and Vitoria, will go in the text itself.

22. We shall use Losada's edition (henceforth, *Democrates*). Sepúlveda modified and expanded his book on various occasions, hence the difference among the manuscripts discovered by Losada with his diligent work (see his "Introduction" to the *Democrates*). Doubtless a number of these corrections were made after the Valladolid disputation (1550–51). However, we cite the *Democrates* here in the awareness that some of the changes were motivated by Las Casas's arguments presented at that controversy. The same occurs, for that matter, with the final text of the Dominican's *Apología*. We shall note this when appropriate and possible.

23. The Universities of Alcalá and Salamanca opposed the publication of this work around 1548. The Acts of the University of Salamanca in this regard, along with Sepúlveda's own reply, have been published in Juan de la Peña, *De Bello contra Insulanos: Intervención de España en América*, 1:499–503. See Beltrán de Heredia, "El Maestro Domingo de Soto"; Pereña Vicente, "La Intervención de España en América," 45–59; J. González Rodríguez, "La Junta de Valladolid convocada por el Emperador." A role is attributed to Las Casas in the opposition mounted by the great Dominican theologians to earlier publication of this work. However, the exchange of letters between Sepúlveda and Cano shows that the latter illustrious theologian was quite convinced of his own reasons for opposing publication of Sepúlveda's work.

24. Sepúlveda recounts that "certain religious had come from the Indies, sent by the Spanish conquistadors there, to the Emperor and King our Lord, with regard to *certain ordinances* that he had made, as this was said to have

been the occasion of much discussion at Court concerning the justice of the conquest of the Indies. Now, the Most Reverend Cardinal Archbishop of Seville, President of the Council of the Indies, as he had heard tell that Doctor Sepúlveda held the Conquista for just and holy — being waged as it ought, and as just wars are accustomed to be waged, which he would demonstrate with utmost plainness — urged him to write upon the subject, [saying] that he would be doing the King a service thereby. And so he wrote a book in the space of only a few days" (*Proposiciones temerarias escandalosas y heréticas que notó el doctor Sepúlveda en el libro de la conquista de Indias, que fray Bartolomé de Las Casas, obispo que fue de Chiapa, hizo imprimir sin licencia en Sevilla año de 1552, cuyo título comienza: Aquí se contiene un disputa o controversia* [Rash, scandalous, and heretical propositions observed by Doctor Sepúlveda in the book of the conquest of the Indies that Friar Bartolomé de Las Casas, sometime bishop of Chiapa, did have printed without permission in Seville in the year 1552, whose title begins: herein is contained a dispute or controversy]; the reference is to an undated text by Sepúlveda, published in A. M. Fabié, *Vida y escritos de Fray Bartolomé de Las Casas,* 1:543–69; here, 543; emphasis added). The mention of the dispatch of religious to Spain by the *encomenderos* "with regard to certain ordinances" is, without a doubt, an allusion to the New Laws (1542), which provoked such a powerful reaction in the Indies. It is incorrect, therefore, to assert that Sepúlveda wrote his book "simply to prove the justice of the Conquista," without implying any "attack on the New Laws" (Losada, "Introduction" to the *Democrates,* xiv). The testimony of the interested party is transparent here. Besides, the "justice of the Conquista" and the new "ordinances" are connected questions.

25. John Major dissents from the theocratic and royalist theses that we have seen in the foregoing chapter; but he agrees with their representatives with regard to the legitimacy of waging war on infidels for purposes of evangelization. "As those gentiles did not understand the Spanish language," he writes, "nor would admit preachers of the divine word without the support of a strong army, it was necessary to build strongholds here and there, in order that, with time — and mutual understanding — that savage people might grow accustomed to the habits of Christians." Then, curiously, he adds: "And because, in order to accomplish all of this, great expenditures are necessary, which the [Indian] ruler will not defray, it is therefore licit to recover them [by levies of tribute upon the Indians], since the [Indians] ought reasonably to wish this." The peoples to whom the gospel is proclaimed ought to have to pay for any efforts made in this regard by Christian kings. When we think of how matters actually eventuated in the Antilles, this last thesis acquires characteristics of an insulting cynicism. But the author is not aware of that. It happens that we are in the presence of a cold juridical ratiocination that, being innocent of the facts, is therefore theoretically poor as well. The least that can be said is that we are dealing with a doctrine "built on pure theorization." At once we notice "a total ignorance of the actual reality of the enterprises of conquest and evangelization" (A. de la Hera, "La ética de la conquista de América en el pensamiento europeo anterior a Vitoria," 116). What is happening is that these theoretical models also have repercussions on

reality. They help to justify oppressive demands, and injustice. Carro, then, seems to us to have his bearings when he asserts that Major's position "would not be unwelcome to the most unscrupulous *encomenderos*" (Carro, *La teología y los teólogos-juristas*, 1:388).

26. Sepúlveda published his *Apología* in Rome in 1550, under the patronage of exalted personages of the Roman Curia. He thinks that his summary has been written "in the scholastic manner" (*Apología* [GS], 57), and expresses his gratitude to Antonio Agustín, Auditor of the Tribunal of the Rota (August 26, 1549), for undertaking to make his, Sepúlveda's, writings better known (see Losada, *Juan Ginés de Sepúlveda a través de su "Epistolario,"* 165). Sepúlveda is not mistaken. On a number of points, his summary is actually more precise than the dialogue itself, the *Democrates*. Sepúlveda was a great expert on Aristotle, but did not like to be seen only as a philosopher and man of letters. He wanted to be regarded as a theologian. His enemies, he writes to a correspondent, seek to "discredit me as a theologian" (letter to Martín de Oliva, in Losada, *Juan Ginés de Sepúlveda a través de su "Epistolario,"* 162). Juan de la Peña, a Salamancan master, said, for example, that Sepúlveda was "outstanding in canon law, but mediocre in his theological formation" (Juan de la Peña, *De Bello contra Insulanos*, 312). A. Pagden (*The Fall of Natural Man*, 109, 118) recalls the reasons for the scant theological appreciation of the great theologians of the sixteenth century for Sepúlveda's work. Sepúlveda's *Apología*, along with Las Casas's, has been published by Losada. We shall refer to it as: *Apología* (GS). Circulation of this work was forbidden in 1560 by order of the king.

27. He maintains the same thing in an interesting letter (undated but subsequent to the *Democrates,* and without the name of the addressee) published as an appendix in Hanke's thesis and not included in his *La lucha por la justicia.* Here Sepúlveda says that the church used force "wherever it was able to do so, by the hand of Emperor Constantine" (Letter of Sepúlveda in Lewis Hanke, unpublished thesis, 377; hereafter: Letter [Hanke]. The notion of two historical times has its inspiration in a text of Augustine of Hippo. Las Casas also employs the notion (see Las Casas, *Apología*, 212–212v).

28. Commenting on, and supporting, the Sepulvedian theses, Andrés Marcos writes: "Without the conquests of Hernán Cortés, what would Friar Bernardo de Sahagún, Padre Motolinía, and the other heroic Franciscans who sowed the seed of the gospel in New Spain have attained? Before they had converted one single Indian, they would have had their throats slit before the idols, and their skulls would lie nameless in the ossuaries reserved for victims. Force is not truth, or justice; but it is an indispensable element for the spread of civilization — it is necessary in order that the true and the just may be the cement of human society" (T. Andrés Marcos, *Vitoria y Carlos V en la soberanía hispano-americana*, no. 37).

29. In another work he will say: Unless the Indians "submit to the power of the Christians, it will be impossible to bring them the faith of Christ, solely by means of indoctrination and persuasion, even apart from the great dangers, difficulties, and span of time that would be involved" (Sepúlveda, *Historia del Nuevo Mundo*, 59).

30. According to Leturia, Sepúlveda is the first to cite Major apropos of questions of the Indies (see P. Leturia, "Maior y Vitoria ante la conquista de América," 79). In fact, Sepúlveda thinks, there is biblical warrant for "declaring the true religion a just cause for the conquest of those who hold it to be false" (Letter [Hanke], 381). An argument of broad application, as we see.

31. The same occurs with the other important distinction in the common doctrine, the one prescribing a different treatment to be meted out to pagans and Jews, on one side, and to heretics on the other. Sepúlveda applies to the former the severity that the received theology accepted only with regard to the latter. In both cases, he thinks, a declaration of war is legitimate (see Sepúlveda, *Democrates*, 75, and Las Casas, *Aquí se contiene*, 1552, *O.E.* 5:310a).

32. Höffner indicates Sepúlveda's influence in officialdom, regarding it as "probable that the majority of the lawyers of the Court were of the same opinion as Sepúlveda," among them the illustrious Juan de Solórzano Pereira (Höffner, *La ética colonial*, 282–83). His position, then, is not an unusual one. According to a datum furnished by Las Casas (and pointed out by Losada), Sepúlveda attempted to influence Trent with his ideas by sending his *Democrates* there, but without success (see *Apología*, 239).

33. To be added to the list, despite an occasional nuance, surprisingly enough is Alonso de Veracruz, Vitoria's disciple at Salamanca, who became Las Casas's close friend (see his writings edited by E. Burrus, *The Writings of Alonso de Veracruz*). Cerezo de Diego, an expert on this theologian who taught in Mexico, rightly perceives that in this question Veracruz was not immune to the enticements of power (P. Cerezo de Diego, "El pensamiento americano de un discípulo de Vitoria," 264; see idem, *Alonso de Veracruz y el derecho de gentes*, a comprehensive study of this theologian; the pages on this point in the last-cited work are 307–22). On the other hand, Alfonso de Castro and Bernardino de Arévalo defended positions akin to Sepúlveda's. For the latter, one may consult González Rodríguez, "Fray Bernardino de Arévalo en la Junta de Valladolid (1550–51)."

34. See the text of this letter, along with a thorough scholarly study on it and an examination of relations between Las Casas and Motolonía, in I. Pérez Fernández, *Fray Toribio Motolinía, O.F.M., frente a Bartolomé de Las Casas O.P.* On this matter, see also M. Martínez, "El obispo Marroquín y el franciscano Motolinía"; F. Joroshaeva, "Bartolomé de Las Casas y Motolinía." It would be a mistake, however, to judge the work of Motolinía by this unfortunate letter.

35. Biermann thought he had found this treatise (published by R. Acuña, *De Debellandis Indis: Un tratado desconocido*), but Zavala questioned that attribution (S. Zavala, "En torno al tratado 'De Debellandis Indis' de Vasco de Quiroga"). Las Casas was acquainted with it, and was anything but appreciative of its approval of the wars. This in no way invalidates other aspects of Quiroga's work, such as his personal familiarity with, and action in behalf of, the natives of Michoacán, Mexico. On the complex relationship between Las Casas and Quiroga, the reader may consult M. Bataillon, *Estudios sobre Bartolomé de Las Casas*, 267–69.

36. Especially by a text of Miguel de Arcos (a Dominican having ties

to Vitoria) that seems to have been written in response to Quiroga's work: published in Hanke's *Cuerpo de documentos* of the sixteenth century, 3–9.

37. Reproduced in *DII* 10:333–525. Also in R. Aguayo, *Don Vasco de Quiroga*, 86–231. See the text and the study by P. Castañeda Delgado, *Don Vasco de Quiroga y su Información en derecho.*

38. Just above, he says that the purpose of this use of force is "to humble them — from their raw strength and beastliness — and once they are humbled, to convert them, and draw them to the bosom and mysteries of [the Christian faith] and the true knowledge of their Creator and all things created. Against such as these, and to this end and effect, when they are strong, I should hold war, or to put it better, their pacification or compulsion, as just, licit, and holy, *servatis servandis.*" Nevertheless, Quiroga censures the wars being waged in the Indies up to that time. For his position, see Pérez Fernández, "Análisis extrauniversitario de la conquista de América en los años 1534–1549," 125–31; the author reviews the positions of other missionaries in the Indies on the subject. See Zavala, *Ideario de Vasco de Quiroga;* Enrique Dussel, *El episcopado hispanoamericano: Institución misionera de defensa del indio, 1504–1620* (for Quiroga, 311–23); R. Aguayo, *Don Vasco de Quiroga;* and the recent fine study by J. A. Gómez Moreira, *Conquista y conciencia cristiana: El pensamiento jurídico-teológico de don Vasco de Quiroga.*

39. A short while later, another important missionary, this time in Brazil, Manoel da Nóbrega (d. 1570), adopts an approach similar to Motolinía's and Quiroga's. See "Diálogo sobre a conversão do gentio," in S. Leite, *Cartas do Brasil do padre Manoel da Nóbrega* (Coimbra, 1955), cited in E. Hoornaert, "Las Casas o Sepúlveda," *Revista Eclesiástica Brasileira* (December 1970): 860–61. See also O. Beozzo, "O diálogo da conversão do gentio."

40. For what follows, see Gustavo Gutiérrez, "Freedom and Salvation: A Political Problem."

41. The edict is found, for example, in Lo Grasso, *Ecclesia et Status: Fontes Selecti,* nos. 3–7.

42. Licinius (one of the signers of the Edict) was a pagan, and Constantine was a recent convert to the Christian religion. See S. Calderone, "Constantino e il cattolicesimo"; see also the old but penetrating study by P. Batiffol, *La paix constantinienne et le catholicisme,* 188–201.

43. After the Edict of Milan, things change quickly. The choice Christians seem to have to make narrows down to two: either to renounce the world and be uninterested in the temporal city, or to Christianize it by way of domination. Christian worship ceases simply to be accepted alongside other religions: Through a series of measures, Constantine grants the church the exclusive protection of the state. He goes even further, and this interests us particularly, taking measures against heretics and schismatics.

44. "The Edict of Milan is abolished, and oneness of religion is reestablished, but in favor of Christianity" (J. Lecler, *Histoire de la tolérance,* 1:75).

45. See Christopher Dawson, *The Making of Europe,* 43–44. God's cause and the state's gradually come to be seen as one: betrayal of God is betrayal of the empire, says St. Ambrose, a contemporary and friend of Theodosius,

addressing the emperor Gratian (see Ambrose of Milan, *De Fide*, bk. 2, ch. 16, n. 139, *PL* 16:612).

46. "Every province, every city has its God.... We alone are refused the right to have a religion," Tertullian says, in his *Apologeticum*, bk. 24, chs. 7, 9, p. 159.

47. See ibid., bk. 21, ch. 30, p. 137.

48. Ibid., bk. 24, ch. 6, p. 157.

49. "It is a human right and a natural right that each one be permitted to worship the God of that one's choice. One person's religion must neither injure nor serve another's. It is incompatible with the nature of religion that it be forced on a person. It must be adopted spontaneously, not by force. Sacrifice is of no value unless it is offered willingly. Accordingly, when you oblige us to offer sacrifice, you give your gods nothing. They have no need of unwilling sacrifice" (Tertullian, *Ad Scapulam*, ch. 2, *PL* 1:777).

50. Lactantius, *De Institutionibus Divinis*, bk. 5, ch. 12, nos. 3–4, *PL* 6:618.

51. Idem, *Epitome Divinarum Institutionum*, 54, *PL* 6:1061. "True sacrifice," he writes in a work we have already cited, "cannot be offered under pressure from without. Unless it is offered spontaneously and from the heart, it is a sacrilege, as happens when it is obtained by means of violence, prison, torture" (idem, *De Institutionibus Divinis*, ch. 5, no. 21, *PL* 6:619–20).

52. See the texts of Athenagoras, Tatian, Minucius Felix, and Justin collected by J. Rivière, *Saint Justin et les apologistes du second siècle*, ch. 4: "Le christianisme et l'Etat," 71–86.

53. For example Lactantius's texts will be cited in Vatican Council II's Declaration on Religious Freedom.

54. Athanasius of Alexandria, *Historia Arianorum*, ch. 67; *Patrologia Graeca* 25:773.

55. Augustine of Hippo, *In Joannem*, 26, no. 2, *PL* 35:1607. The text is frequently cited, but without taking cognizance of the fact that it dates from 416 C.E., that is, from a period when Augustine's position on religious freedom had become very rigid. Augustine's change of attitude here shows us that, as we shall see throughout our examination of church teaching on the question, a defense of the freedom of the act of faith is *not incompatible* with certain forms of religious intolerance. Augustine's case is instructive, but it is not unique. Las Casas seems to perceive this; hence the discreet distance he takes from this Father of the Church (motivated as well by Sepúlveda's appeal to the ancient thinker). See B. Rech, "Las Casas und die Kirchenväter," 26–43.

56. Augustine, *Contra Litteras Patiliani*, bk. 2, ch. 83, no. 184, *PL* 43:315. Sepúlveda will cite this text with alacrity.

57. Due in large part to the conversions gained through the imperial edict of 405 C.E. suppressing the schismatic church and ordering it to return to unity under pain of grave sanctions, Augustine sees an advantageous facet of these measures and alters his position on religious freedom (see Augustine, *Retractatio 2*, 2, 5, *PL* 32:632). Centuries later, Bernard of Clairvaux, Bruno of Querfurt, and Thomas Aquinas himself will attempt to justify the use of means of force in the same way: it is a matter of combating an obstacle, not of imposing the faith. None of these writers, therefore, will have any problem

being staunch defenders of the freedom of the act of faith (not freedom of religion).

58. Hippolytus writes, 204 C.E.: "The one who believes in God must not be a hypocrite. But neither has that one any reason to fear ordinances of civil power enjoining something that is forbidden in the light of faith in God. After all, if that power imposes on anyone an obligation contrary to that person's conscience, it will be sweet to go down to death resisting the command" (Hippolytus of Rome, *Commentarium in Danielem*, 3, 20–25, 31; and other passages in the same work).

59. Justin Martyr asserts this very early. See his *Apology*, bk. 2, ch. 7.

60. Tertullian will say, sarcastically: "Anyone who says the Emperor is God, assaults the imperial dignity: after all, if he is not a human being, he can scarcely be an emperor" (Tertullian, *Apologeticum*, 28, 34).

61. See a letter of St. Ambrose to the Emperor Gratian (*Epist.* 17, nos. 1, 2, *PL* 16:1002A, 1005A). Ambrose exercised great influence on this emperor. See C. Morino, *Chiesa e stato nella dottrina di S. Ambroggio.*

62. See Ambrose, *Epist.* 21, *PL* 16:1045–49.

63. This was actually accepted by Catholics as well as by heretics and schismatics. See V. Monachino, "L'impiego della forza politica al servizio della religione nel pensiero de S. Agostino."

64. This conception of temporal power at the service of religious truth, and therefore ultimately of the authority of the state in religious questions, will be adopted by the popes. A very familiar text of Leo I, addressed to Emperor Leo I of Byzantium in 457, says (and we reproduce only its most significant passage): "You must keep unwavering account of the fact that royal power has been bestowed upon you not only with regard to temporal things, but especially for the defense of the Church." The "especially" plainly expresses the ministerial function of political power that the Middle Ages will only reassert and seek to establish more in depth (Leo I, *Epist.* 156, ch. 3, *PL* 54:1129; in Lo Grasso, *Ecclesia et Status*, no. 104, 48–49; the same notion occurs in another letter of Leo I, *PL* 44, col. 1122).

65. See the text in Lo Grasso, *Ecclesia et Status*, nos. 108–12. The document does not merely ask freedom for the church, but, in a tone that recalls the writings of the early Fathers, indicates that "temporal things" are the proper domain of the state. See L. Weckmann, *El pensamiento político medieval*, ch. 8.

66. "Before Aquinas, it is impossible to find in the ambit of orthodox thought a univocal, continuous doctrinal orientation in the matter of religious tolerance" (M. Condorelli, *I fondamenti giuridici della tolleranza religiosa nell' elaborazione canonistica dei secoli XII–XIV*, 5).

67. Carrasco observes that, on this point, Thomas's thought in the *Summa* represents clear progress compared with that of his *Commentary on the Sentences* (see S. Carrasco Calvo, "Herejes e Infieles en la obra de Santo Tomás," in *Tommaso D'Aquino nella storia del pensiero*, 2:29).

68. "Denial of the faith once received is more gravely sinful than resistance to the faith not received, just as it is more gravely sinful not to keep a promise than not to do what has never been promised.... Therefore, ab-

solutely speaking, the unbelief of the heretics is worse" (Thomas Aquinas, *Summa Theologiae,* II–II, q. 10, a. 6, c.).

69. Thomas refers to a Pauline text frequently cited in these matters, to which Vitoria and other sixteenth-century theologians will also appeal in order to reject all justification of the use of force against the Indians: "What business is it of mine to judge outsiders? Is it not those inside the community you must judge? God will judge the others" (1 Cor. 5:12–13). The church is judge of the faithful, not of unbelievers.

70. See *ST,* II–II, q. 10, a. 11, "May the rites of unbelievers be tolerated?"; ibid., q. 11, a. 3, "May heretics be tolerated?"

71. "One speaks of tolerance only with reference to an evil" (Augustine, *Enarratio in Psalmos, PL* 36:271).

72. Carrasco thinks Thomas is referring to the gentiles of his time. Thus, the Doctor of Aquino would be addressing a current problem.

73. "Though almighty," he writes, and "sovereignly good, God permits evils to occur in the universe. He permits these evils, which he could prevent, to occur in order not to suppress greater goods, or lest greater evils supervene." Consequently, "thus it ought to be with human government. Rulers are right when they tolerate certain evils for fear of impeding certain goods, or to avoid worse evils." And he concludes: "In this sense, although unbelievers were to sin in their rites, these rites may be tolerated, whether for the good that comes of them, or by reason of the evil that is avoided" by tolerating them (*ST,* II–II, q. 10, a. 11, c.).

74. Vermeersch calls this attitude "private tolerance" (R. P. Vermeersch, *La tolérance,* 43ff.). It presents no special difficulty.

75. The expression, obviously inspired in Thomas, is that of Pius XII, and occurs in a discourse pronounced to Italian lawyers on December 6, 1953. This notion represented an important milestone in the doctrinal evolution of this matter in the years before Vatican II.

76. In these rites, "What we believe continues to be presented to us in prefiguration" (*ST,* II–II, q. 10, a. 11, c). In the same Question, Thomas quotes a passage from St. Gregory defending Jewish worship, which text is included in the celebrated and influential Decretals of Gratian.

77. This negative response does not hold, according to Thomas, for the case of heresy. We have already seen this, but we shall return to the point once more below.

78. "It is of natural law that children, before having the use of reason, be under the care of their parents." It would therefore be "against natural justice" to baptize them before they have the use of reason, since only then, which is when they "commence to have the use of their free choice, do they begin to govern themselves, and become able to decide what is in conformity with divine or natural law." Then at last it is possible for them to be brought "to the faith not by coercion, but by persuasion" (ibid., a. 12, c.). Later, in a discussion of baptism, Thomas returns to the same point: "It would be an offense against natural justice were such children to be baptized against the wish of their parents," which, he adds, would be "as if an adult were baptized unwillingly" (*ST,* III, q. 68, a. 10).

79. Thomas's position on baptism will leave an indelible mark on the Dominican school. We shall return to this matter in our chapter 12 below.

80. It must not be forgotten that, for Thomas, a "heretic" is an active dissident, of the first generation. In his time, heresy as an ongoing condition was unknown. The question of those who have been born in religious dissidence is not posited.

81. "Now it is much more grave," he asserts, "to corrupt the faith, which assures the life of the soul, than to counterfeit money, which enables a person to attend to temporal life. Therefore if counterfeiters or other malefactors are sentenced to death, and justly so, by secular princes, with all the more reason may heretics, once we are convinced of their heresy, be not only excommunicated, but also justly sentenced to death" (*ST*, II–II, q. 11, a. 3, c.).

82. "The church," he writes, "practices a certain mercy for the sake of the conversion of those in error. Therefore it does not condemn them immediately, but only 'after a first and second warning,' as the Apostle says. After this, if heretics remain obstinate, the church, having no hope of their conversion, and for the sake of the salvation of others, removes them from itself with a sentence of excommunication; and thereupon commits them to secular justice to be removed from this world by means of death" (ibid.).

83. See Lecler, *Histoire de la tolérance*, 1:124.

84. Thomas Aquinas, *In IV Sententiarum*, d. 13, q. 9, a. 2, a. 3, c.

85. De Vera adds other reasons for nuancing Thomas Aquinas's position: F. De Vera, "Aportación de Santo Tomás a la doctrina de la libertad religiosa."

86. Bataillon, *Estudios sobre Bartolomé de Las Casas*, 362, dubs this harshness toward heresy "Lascasian" — when, as we have seen, Thomas himself inherits it and systematizes it. Las Casas, concerned as he is with the situation in the Indies, does not address the question *ex professo*. Thus, the doctrine in question antedates him.

87. In the following chapter we deal with this subject at length.

Chapter 6: The Only Way

1. On the date and circumstances of the redaction of this book, see below, our chapter 11.

2. J. A. Barreda, "Aproximación histórica," 1. As Castillo so well says, "For Bartolomé de Las Casas, the problem of the Indians is that of their conversion" (C. Castillo, "El problema de los indios: Bartolomé de Las Casas," 51; Castillo's doctoral thesis, on conversion in Las Casas's *Historia de las Indias*, will soon be published).

3. García del Moral observes that the *De Unico* is an "early model of the concrete utilization of all theological loci" (A. García del Moral, "Estructura y significación teológicas," liii). And this before Melchior Cano's famous work on the subject (*De Locis Theologicis*).

4. See J. A. Barreda's comprehensive *Ideología y pastoral misionera en Bartolomé de Las Casas;* and Helen Parish, "Introduction: Las Casas's Spirituality" (in *Bartolomé de las Casas: The Only Way*). Furthermore, in her valuable appen-

dices, Parish retraces the process of the redaction of this book, and explains the order followed in this excellent translation (by F. Sullivan).

5. The Latin manuscript of this book was discovered in the Paris National Library in 1879 (see A. Fabié, *Vida y escritos de Fray Bartolomé de Las Casas*, 2:578 n. 4). Until then the existence of this text was known through allusions made to it by Las Casas in some of his other works. There is sufficient reason to think that there were two versions of the *Apología*, one in Latin and another in Spanish. Losada, followed by Hanke (see Lewis Hanke, *All Mankind Is One*, 73–74; on p. 108 he also reproduces a clear note of Losada on the matter), thinks that both versions correspond to the same text, whose original language would have been Latin; and that that Latin version, with some parts in Spanish, would have been the one presented at the Valladolid disputation. At the same time, keen-sighted researcher I. Pérez Fernández ("Dos apologías de Las Casas contra Sepúlveda: La 'Apología en romance' y la 'Apología en latín'") offers strong arguments to the effect that the Spanish version is the original; on the other hand, he regards the Latin version as a translation containing such important modifications that it may be called a "recomposition" (Pérez Fernández, "Dos apologías de Las Casas," 151). The latter, reworked, would be the one we have today. All researchers, however, agree that what Bartolomé de Las Casas calls the second part of his *Apología* is what we know today as his *Apologética historia*. The *Apología* was published with a Spanish translation by Losada in 1975, and then, with some improvements in the Spanish version, in the *Obras Completas* of Las Casas, vol. 9. The English translation, by Stafford Poole (*In Defense of the Indians*), also dates from 1975, and is accompanied by valuable notes.

6. See, among many similar references, F. Aznar Gil, "La libertad religiosa del indio en autores franciscanos del siglo XVI," 394. On the other hand, we do not agree with this author when he declares that the divergences between positions represented by Las Casas and Sepúlveda are "less to do with doctrine (both begin with the same theologico-canonical principles) than with whether it is appropriate to apply them" (ibid., 395). It happens that the author does not distinguish between freedom of the act of faith and freedom in religious matters. The differences are indeed plainly theological; but in order to perceive this, it is necessary to specify carefully the particular notion of evangelization that is at work here.

7. Speaking of the Portuguese wars against the Moors of Africa, he writes: "This is the blindness... that has fallen upon worldly Christians: to believe that if persons are unbaptized unbelievers, it thereby becomes legitimate to assault, rob, imprison, and slay them" (*H.I.*, bk. 1, ch. 22, *O.E.* 1:85b).

8. He calls it a "reasonable obstacle" thrown up by the Indians, apropos of the incursions of Hojeda and Nicuesa into the mainland. The inhabitants of these regions "acquired a reasonable obstacle and probable cause not to receive the faith of Jesus Christ for many years, as long as [the Spaniards] believed that they professed it and held them [in subjection]" (*H.I.*, bk. 3, ch. 48, *O.E.* 2:144a–b).

9. Concerning the episode to which we allude in the foregoing note, he

asserts that "from that time forward, till Judgment Day, the Indians have acquired the right to wage war against any Spaniard altogether justly" (ibid., 144a).

10. Cajetan, *Commentarium in II–II,* q. 66, a. 8 (the book is dated 1517–18), in *Operum Sancti Thomae,* Leonine Edition (Rome, 1897), 9:94. Is Cajetan referring explicitly to the Indians? The possibility is difficult to exclude, if we think of the role he played in sending missioners of his order to the Indies and of the communications we know he received from his confreres (see *H.I.,* bk. 2, ch. 44, *O.E.* 2:133b; bk. 3 ch. 38, *O.E.* 2:264a–265b). In 1532, Cajetan responds to six "doubts" sent him by the Dominicans of New Spain, in a little treatise (first published in Latin by V. M. Pollet [*De Caietani scripto*], included by Parish, along with a Spanish translation, in her *Las Casas en México,* Appendix 17). As Parish says, Cajetan was actually "more of an indiophile than had been supposed" (*Las Casas en México,* n. 45). For his role as master general of the Dominican order see R. Moya, "Las autoridades supremas de la orden y la evangelización de América," 855–57.

11. See *Apología* (GS), 78. A theologian very close to the humanist, Franciscan Alfonso de Castro, did not hesitate to list Cajetan as a heretic for questioning the Pauline authorship of the Letter to the Hebrews (see J. González, "Los amigos franciscanos de Sepúlveda," 887).

12. See Parish, "Introduction," which calls Cajetan's work "the new bestseller of the 1520s."

13. In the *Apología* (see folio 185v), the category "apostates and heretics" figures in second place, while in the *Doce dudas* it comes third.

14. Here is how he details it in the *Doce dudas:* "This is the fourth kind, or distinction, of infidels, who neither hold usurped lands that once were ours, nor have wrongfully despoiled us of them; likewise who have never acted wrongfully, harmfully, or prejudicially toward us, nor have the intent to do so, nor act to the detriment or impediment of our holy faith, either because they have never heard of it or because their attitude toward it is one of simple indifference.

"Likewise, those who neither at present, nor in centuries past, have been subjects of the Christian Empire or of any member of the church, neither *de jure* nor *de facto* (i.e., *actu*), nor by reason of origin or domicile, nor on account of any crime they might have committed against us or the church, nor by reason of contract, nor for other of the just causes for subjugation that we have cited above. There are many such nations in the world, who are vulnerable on none of these accounts, especially any pagans or gentiles who have their realms, regions, provinces, and their own lands, at a distance from ours, which nations — namely (before other nations, peoples, and tribes), Greeks, Barbarians, Tartars, Persians, Macedonians, Scythians, Massagetes, Sicacors, cave-dwellers, Dacians, Numidians, Sogdianans, Bactrians, Albanians, Cumeans, Indians or people of India, Ethiopians, Turks, Saracens, who worship idols, honor or believe in Muhammad, or teem with unmentionable superstitions and errors and of abominable vices (provided they do not offend against the Catholic faith or the Christian polity in any of the manners listed above) — along with others, if there be any such, we thus place in the fourth category." (We follow the Providence version here.) The long list of unbelieving peoples (absent from Pérez de Tudela's edition) brings out the peculiarity of the Indian nations. In the previously known version, this text corresponds to the passage found at *O.E.* 5:489a.

15. In the famous letter to his very good friend Carranza, he writes: "How, Father, are those tribes to believe and not blaspheme [the Christian faith], holding it for something horrible, harsh, heavy, lying, and tyrannical? And so we suspect that there may be no true Christians among them and that it is out of sheer fear that they pretend to believe" (1555, *O.E.* 5:437a).

16. See a commentary on this text in Gustavo Gutiérrez, *El Dios de la Vida*, 39–45. In the *De Thesauris*, Bartolomé maintains that in order to evangelize it is important that those sent be "men tested and approved, who first *do* what they teach" (Las Casas, *De Thesauris*, folio 142; emphasis added).

17. He demonstrated this when, as we saw in chapter 2, he gave up his *encomienda*. See also the text from the *De Unico* (folio 158v) that we cited in chapter 2 regarding this surrender.

18. The text continues very interestingly: "And their works so overwhelmingly testified to their most holy life that no one actually censured their life, but only sought to discredit their preaching, according to St. Chrysostom. That is, it was for reason of their preaching that they were accused of being seducers and were so mightily slandered. There was no one, however, who dared to reprehend their lives. No one ever alleged that the Apostles had committed any crime of fornication, impurity, or greed. They were called seducers solely in respect of their dogma. Persons whose life gleamed with such splendor simply must be respected. Truth itself stopped the mouths of their enemies" (Las Casas, *De Thesauris*, f. 54v).

19. We cannot, therefore, share the position of those who see a simple continuity on this point throughout the history of the church and who voice such praise for a principle that, to be sure, contains values, but that harbors dangerous ambiguities as well and entails the abandonment of a defense of freedom in matters of religion. Quite perceptively, the "minority" at Vatican II maintained that the proposal in question, which would finally be approved by the Council, meant breaking with interpretations endorsed by the church for centuries in this area.

20. To that danger — which despite the best intentions ends in distortion — numerous studies on the question succumb. This is also the reason for the long list, in so many categories of writers, of the defenders of religious freedom and champions of peaceful evangelization, along with the so frequent assertion that there is great agreement among Vitoria, Las Casas, and even, according to Losada, Sepúlveda. This is the case with Carro, who has produced a great number of works on these questions (see V. Carro, *La teología y los teólogos-juristas*; idem, "Postulados teológico-jurídicos").

21. Later, Báñez (d. 1604), who, to be sure, prefers peaceful means of evangelization in principle, and who points out the risks of obliging an audience to listen to preaching, makes a curious proposal: The Indians may be constrained to hear the preaching of the gospel *once only*, "in order that, if they wish to believe, they may believe. But if they do not wish to believe, they

must be permitted to go their way with impunity" (*De Fide, Spe et Charitate* [Salamanca, 1586], 616; quoted by R. Hernández, "Doctrina americanista de Domingo Báñez," 251).

22. The text continues with the incisive observation that not even Muhammad obliged persons to embrace his religion, but only terrorized and subjected them — just as do those Christians who defend acts of war against the Indians.

23. Las Casas approves no pressure, direct or indirect (see *Apología*, f. 206v). Losada is correct, then, when he says that Las Casas, with his thesis on evangelization, "represents something authentically new" (Losada, "Fray Bartolomé de Las Casas, miembro insigne de la escuela de derecho internacional de Salamanca: Su obra inédita 'Apología,' " 232).

24. Francisco Suárez (d. 1617), like the great initiators of the Salamancan school, approves the use of force only under certain conditions. While far from maintaining Sepúlveda's positions, Suárez nevertheless yields in the matter of the historical times or moments, to which we have previously alluded, and goes so far as to say that coercion was legitimate even in the first centuries: "Although in the first times of the church this form of coercion was not usual, it was not because it would not have been licit, but because the church at that time was still without the temporal power to oppose the enemies of the faith. Our Lord Jesus Christ wished first to conquer the world by the strength of the word and miracles, that the power and truth of his teaching might be more evident" (Francisco Suárez, *De Fide Catholica*, tractate 1, disputation 18, sect. 1, no. 2 [in Suárez, *Opera*, vol. 12]; quoted in J. Höffner, *La ética colonial*, 419). This text, as in the case of Sepúlveda, has the merit of a clear-sighted grasp of the opportunities afforded by a position of power.

25. Among them we must count his close friend Bartolomé Carranza (see L. Pereña, *Misión de España en América*, 25–27; J. I. Tellechea, "Las Casas y Carranza: Fé y utopía," 406–7) and A. Salmerón (see Höffner, *La ética colonial*, 415).

26. Quoted in Parish, *Las Casas en México*, Appendix 1. Along the same lines, Zumárraga criticizes the wars undertaken in Peru during those years. For Zumárraga, see Enrique Dussel, *El episcopado latinoamericano y la liberación de los pobres (1504–1620)*, 289–309.

27. Las Casas speaks of it in the *Brevísima relación de la destrucción de las Indias*, O.E. 5:156b–157a. See Pérez Fernández, "Dos apologías de Las Casas," 133–34. He calls that experience the third "breach" between conquest and peaceful evangelization. (The first would be that of Pedro de Córdoba in 1513, the second a project of Las Casas's in Nicaragua.) Hanke, in his classic *La lucha por la justicia* (202–5), recalls later attempts at a peaceful evangelization with explicit or implicit reference to Lascasian ideas.

28. One must add to the list a close collaborator of Las Casas in Peru, a Dominican, Domingo de Santo Tomás.

29. The subject has been broadly studied, though never entirely clarified. M. Bataillon (*Estudios sobre Bartolomé de Las Casas*, 181–243) has questioned Remesal's version (A. Remesal, *Historia general de las Indias Occidentales*), which he regards as fictionalized. Along that line we also have André Saint-

Lu's detailed work, *La Vera Paz: Esprit evangélique et colonisation.* B. Biermann, "Bartolomé de Las Casas und Verapaz," adopts a somewhat different focus. See the recent balance sheet drawn up by J. A. Barreda, "Encuentro de dos absolutos: El hombre y el evangelio," 133–67. Parish promises new material on this episode in her forthcoming *Las Casas: The Untold Story.*

30. The text reads as follows: "And today, in all the Indies, there is no greater knowledge of God, or devotion to any idol or god of heaven or earth, nor has there been for a hundred years among these people, than in New Spain, where religious have gone, this least corner of the Indies" (*Brevísima relación*, 1542, *O.E.* 5:175b).

31. Saint-Lu, *La Vera Paz*, 450.

32. A particularly striking attitude, if we keep in mind the sixteenth-century climate with regard to religious freedom. R. Queraltó Moreno, "Fundamentación filosófica," 191, is correct about this. For that climate, the reader may consult J. I. Tellechea's fine study, *El arzobispo Carranza y su tiempo*, concerning a personage whom Las Casas valiantly defended before the Inquisition (see his texts from Carranza's judicial process: Tellechea, *El arzobispo Carranza*, 2:49–62). Kamen shows the complexity, not always bereft of a certain latitudinarianism, of the situation in Spain in this area (H. Kamen, "Toleration and Dissent in Sixteenth Century Spain: The Alternative Tradition").

33. Much has been written, despite our scant sources, about the Valladolid disputation. See Hanke, *La lucha por la justicia*, 312–62; and, with new documentation, idem, *All Mankind Is One*; V. Beltrán de Heredia, "El Maestro Domingo de Soto"; S. Zavala, "Aspectos Formales de la controversia entre Sepúlveda y Las Casas, en Valladolid, a mediados del siglo XVI." Among more recent studies, see the excellent article, already cited, of V. Abril Castelló, "La bipolarización"; J. González Rodríguez, "Planteamiento oficial de la crisis: La Junta de Valladolid y la suspensión de las conquistas"; idem, "Los amigos franciscanos de Sepúlveda." The reader may also consult Losada, *Fray Bartolomé de Las Casas a la luz de la moderna crítica histórica*; the author is an expert on Ginés de Sepúlveda and his enthusiastic defender. Dussel rightly points out that "theologically, the Valladolid disputation . . . is the most important discussion to be conducted in Europe on the ontological status, in the light of faith, of the nature of the human being and of the Third World cultures"; and he adds that only in our century has the question been posed once more (Dussel, "Introducción General," 284).

34. Andrés Marcos, another fervent Sepulvedist, regards this argument as the one having the most "probatory force" among the four presented by Ginés de Sepúlveda (see Teodoro Andrés Marcos, *Los imperialismos de Juan Ginés de Sepúlveda*, 123). Nor was Sepúlveda alone in adducing this "justification." Cerezo is correct when he writes that this motive, "when all was said and done, constituted the irrefragable and decisive argument for the justice of the American conquest. This is the case not only for authors like Sepúlveda, who found in this line of reasoning precisely the apposite foundation for their insistence on the barbarity of those aborigines and the reduction of their condition to that of 'barely human,' *vix homines*, but more generally, for

the sixteenth-century Spanish scholastics almost across the board" (P. Cerezo de Diego, *Alonso de Veracruz y el derecho de gentes*, 330).

35. But, as we shall see below, Las Casas rejects wholesale the "legitimate titles" advanced by Vitoria in justification of Spanish domination in the Indies (see Las Casas, *Apología*, ff. 237v–238v; see below, our chapter 12).

36. Actually the subject of this *relección* is not precisely the Indians themselves, but rather any rights that others might have *over* the Indians.

37. On the relationship between natural law and the Law of Nations in Vitoria, see Urdanoz, in T. Urdanoz, ed., *Obras* of Francisco de Vitoria, 585–88.

38. Carro attempts to explain this subtle analysis of violations of the natural law in terms of a motivating cause that would be variously legitimate or illegitimate depending on conditions. But he is forced to recognize that Vitoria ends by accepting, along another route, what he has previously rejected. With the satisfaction typical of an author accustomed to conceptual ideas and distinctions, Carro declares: "Here is how Vitoria concedes by reason of *sociability* what he has denied by reason of *sin*. Sin, as sin, confers no right of intervention; but these *crimes*, which include wrongful harm, are indeed the cause of a right — the right of legitimate defense" (Carro, *La teología y los teólogos-juristas*, 2:166; emphasis added in first two instances). Here is the very thing Vitoria has previously denied, but which he now accepts along another route: the proposition that war is justifiable in defense of humanity (way of sociability), even when the prince who intervenes has not been offended directly.

Bataillon, less at home in scholastic disquisitions, says — despite his evident sympathy for the great Spanish theologian — that he cannot escape a sense of uneasiness with "the maneuver that enables him to change his fifth *illegitimate* title like a glove and transform it into his fifth *legitimate* title" (*Estudios sobre Bartolomé de Las Casas*, 23; emphasis in the original). Even though we recognize the formal differences in the two arguments, we readers of Vitoria share Bataillon's discomfort.

39. Sepúlveda was aware of this. In his *Demócrates Segundo*, he explicitly indicates his disagreement with the Salamancan master (57). In the acrimonious correspondence he maintained with Melchior Cano, the point is equally plain. Cano points it out to him and appeals to this disagreement as a reason why the *Demócrates* ought not to be published. "After the abundant dissertation presented on the matter by that illustrious doctor, the worthy and reverend Francisco de Vitoria, which contradicts your views," Cano writes to Sepúlveda, "it was quite clear to us that we ought to question your opinion. After all, we now had very important considerations against it" (*Joannis Genesii Sepulvedae Cordubensis Opera*; Cano's letter is on 34–45). In his reply, the Cordovan declares that both Cajetan and Vitoria were partly right and partly wrong. He supports his rebuttal with references to Augustine, Ambrose, Gregory, Thomas, and Scotus (*Sepulvedae Opera*, 64–65).

40. See Andrés Marcos, *Los imperialismos de Juan Ginés de Sepúlveda*; idem, *Vitoria y Carlos V en la soberanía hispanoamericana*.

41. The agreement (in reference to the point already mentioned) with Sepúlveda's ideas is one of the reasons for which L. A. Getino has rejected

Vitoria's authorship of the controversial fragment (see Urdanoz, ed., *Obras* of Francisco de Vitoria, 997).

42. We shall analyze other aspects of this fragment in a later chapter (see below, our chapter 12). The text of the fragment is found on pp. 1039–59 of Vitoria, *Obras*. Our references to a different sequence of page numbers indicate the *De Temperantia* proper — the *relección* reproduced in the *Obras*.

43. "A defense of the innocent is licit even when they do not ask it" (Vitoria, *Obras*, 1051; CHP, 110). In the *De Indis* he maintains, likewise, that this defense would be legitimate even though "all barbarians should consent to such laws and sacrifices and not wish to be defended by the Spaniards in this matter" (94).

44. Commenting on the Secunda Secundae, q. 10, a. 8, Vitoria claims that unbelievers "may be obliged to observe the natural law. The Emperor may also defend someone not his subject, lest that person be put to death unjustly. As Scripture says: He delivers those being led to death. And thus the Emperor would justly wage war upon the Turks whenever they permit the slaying of innocents in their land" (*Comentario a la Secunda–secundae de Santo Tomás*, 1:194; also CHP, 124).

45. This difference was observed by M. Martínez ("Las Casas–Vitoria y la bula 'Sublimis Deus,'" 25). We shall return to this text of Vitoria in the chapter we devote to the ideas of the Salamancan master (our chapter 12).

46. Vitoria does not permit the consumption of human flesh even in case of extreme necessity. His successor at Salamanca, Andrés Vega, will introduce nuances into this doctrine (see Urdanoz, ed., *Obras* of Francisco de Vitoria, 1001).

47. Further on, summarizing his arguments, he will enunciate the present one as follows: "The second cause you have alleged is the deterrence of the abominable crime of the consumption of human flesh, by which nature is offended in a special manner, and further, the avoidance of the worship of demons in place of God, which is what most provokes the divine wrath, especially in this monstrous rite of the immolation of human victims" (*Demócrates*, 84).

48. This is the case with Andrés Marcos, who writes: "Those reading the Sepulvedian text calmly, in depth, and in a comparative view, will not have their minds empty of doubts as to whether Sepúlveda holds the mere worship of idols as sufficient cause for the exercise of force against those unbelievers, in a case in which they do not yield to peaceful subjugation. This we must grant" (Andrés Marcos, "Ideología del Democrates Secundus," xxviii–xxxix). But the truth is that Sepúlveda explicitly undertakes to empty our mind of such doubts, sparing us the time and effort that Andrés Marcos seems to require. In the *Apología* (GS), Sepúlveda writes: "In recalling, through these testimonials, the fact that idolatry, whether *per se* or *per accidens* (that is, by reason of the sacrifice of human victims), has been cause for a just war of extermination, we see quite plainly that idolatry offers, *per se*, adequate cause for a just war to be waged on the idolaters" (*Apología* [GS], 62).

49. In the *Apología* (GS), 65, Sepúlveda states: "These barbarians are

known to slay many thousands of innocents every year on the impious altars of the demons. (It is known that in New Spain alone they were accustomed to immolate more than twenty thousand each year.)"

50. See Losada, *Juan Ginés de Sepúlveda a través de su "Epistolario,"* 233–66.

51. This assertion is incompatible with his attempt in the *Apología* (GS) to refute Cajetan's celebrated classification of unbelievers, on which we have already commented. Sepúlveda writes: "Cajetan's position to the effect that unbelievers may not be lawfully and rightfully conquered by Christians must be understood in the sense that this may not be for mere reason of their unbelief. He is not referring to the case in which they were also idolaters or violators of the natural law in some other way" (*Apología* [GS], 63).

52. Democrates' interlocutor, Leopoldo, summarily defines the purpose and cause in question here: "...the deliverance from grave and wrongful harm of so very many innocent mortals, whom the barbarians have annually sacrificed, for it has been demonstrated that all human beings are obliged in virtue of divine law, if it is possible to them, to deliver any person from such acts of wrongful harm" (ibid., 84). Sepúlveda repeats the argument in another work, again with reference to the Indies (see his "El Reino y los deberes del rey," in *Tratados políticos de Juan Ginés de Sepúlveda,* 35–36).

53. Losada, incredulous that Friar Bartolomé could claim to be ignorant of the *Democrates,* wonders: "Really? When that book was the fundamental bone of contention between the two? Or is this not rather a stratagem on Las Casas's part — a ploy to win greater freedom to accuse his adversary of saying what he actually had not said?" (in Las Casas, *Apología* [1975], 119 n. 7; and in Las Casas, *Obras Completas,* 9:670). It is difficult to answer a question about someone's intentions. One thing is clear, however: the *Democrates* is more vulnerable, theologically speaking (especially in view of the methodology employed, that of the dialogue), than the summary (the *Apología*) made of it by Sepúlveda himself, to which Las Casas is replying. An acquaintance with the dialogue, then, would have facilitated Bartolomé's task of refutation. Besides, his opponent commits certain slips of language in the *Democrates* (e.g., the insulting terms he uses to speak of the Indians) that no polemicist would have allowed to pass with impunity. Thus, Losada's supposition seems to us to lack foundation.

54. Concluding the first chapter of his *Apología,* Las Casas writes: "This *Apología* will be divided into two parts. In the *first part* I shall demonstrate that the Reverend Doctor Sepúlveda, with his partisans, errs in the matter of *right and law* in all that he utters against the Indians; at the same time, I shall reply adequately to all of his arguments and authorities, the latter of which he violently eviscerates of their genuine meaning. In the *second part* I shall demonstrate how gravely Sepúlveda and his partisans err in the *facts* they adduce in support of their cause, to the serious detriment of their souls" (Las Casas, *Apología,* ff. 13–13v; emphasis added).

55. Soto writes: "Meanwhile, they fall into no fault and thus deserve no punishment. That they have some manner of excuse before *human beings* are concerned, though not before *God,* is plain from the probable opinion of Aristotle in the first book of the *Topics,* which wiser persons hold" (*O.E.* 5:306b;

emphasis added). This distinction is already suggested in Las Casas, apropos of idolatry and cannibalism, ten years earlier. In defense of the Indians, he says: "They have been slandered as idolaters, as if, even were they to be such, they might be punished by *human judgment,* rather than by the *divine* alone, since they have offended God alone" (*Octavo remedio,* 1542, *O.E.* 5:81b; emphasis added).

56. At one moment in his argumentation, as we know, Las Casas appeals to Cajetan, whose theological authority, and explicit opposition to war on the dwellers of the Indies, he greatly respected. Bartolomé says with admiration: "Our Lord Cardinal Cajetan has outstripped all others, theologians and jurists alike, in setting this matter straight." (In the *Historia de las Indias,* he says that on this question Cajetan "enlightened the blindness that had reigned until then"; *H.I.,* bk. 3, ch. 38, *O.E.* 2:264b.) Elsewhere Bartolomé adds significantly: "This opinion of Cajetan is likewise approved by that most learned man, Friar Francisco de Vitoria, in the *Relección de Indias,* under the fifth title" (*Apología,* ff. 182v, 183). This is one of the three mentions made by Las Casas of the master of Salamanca in this book. Indeed, on this concrete point, where Vitoria rejects the fifth illegitimate title, the two theologians are in agreement, as we have said.

57. A postulate that Sepúlveda did not accept. For him, "the Church and the Vicar of Christ" may rightfully oblige non-Christians to observe the natural law (see *Demócrates,* 46).

58. The first five cases are: (1) "When unbelievers unjustly hold realms of which previously, as well as unjustly, they have despoiled Christians." (2) When pagans "practice idolatry in provinces that in another time had been under Christian jurisdiction." (3) When "unbelievers are blasphemers of Christ...out of hatred and contempt for Christian truth." (4) When pagans "place obstacles in the way of the propagation of the faith, directly and intentionally, and not merely incidentally (*per se,* not *per accidens*)." (5) When "unbelievers invade our provinces under arms." Las Casas amply demonstrates that none of these cases obtains among the Indians (*Apología,* ff. 76–125v).

59. Losada rightly says: "This 'sixth case' can well be said to constitute the authentic nucleus of the *Apología,* since it is here that Las Casas replies to his adversary's weightiest argument" (Losada, in Sepúlveda, *Apología* [1975], 247 n. 1).

60. Las Casas never denies that such things have occurred in the Indies, but he observes that they are not as frequent as some claim (see, e.g., *Tratado comprobatorio,* 1552, *O.E.* 5:400b). Furthermore, he always expressed his revulsion for such practices. Apropos of cannibalism among the Caribs, he writes: "This is very cruel and beastly. I know not whether the Caribs of these lands that are infected with it can overcome it, since *if everything is true* that we hear, this is not something minor with them, but a major practice" (*A.H.,* ch. 205, *O.E.* 4:245a; emphasis added). One thing, however, is sure: reports were exaggerated (see J. P. Helminen, "¿Eran caníbales los caribes? Fray Bartolomé de Las Casas y el canibalismo").

61. Soto summarizes Las Casas's position thus: "The sixth: In order to

deliver innocents, not for the reason *quod unicuique mandatum est de proximo suo* ['each of us is enjoined responsibility for neighbor'], nor for their sins against the natural law, but because innocents are committed by divine law to the care of the church" (*O.E.* 5:302b; see also 306a).

62. In his summary Domingo de Soto presents Las Casas's use of this argument as follows. "Of two evils, one must choose the lesser; and that the Indians slay certain innocent persons in order to devour them, while this is even more seriously perverted than merely to slay them in sacrifice, is an incomparably lesser evil than those consequent on war. In war, even apart from the concomitant acts of plunder and rapine, far more innocent persons die than are the few whom one claims to deliver. Over and above this, these wars place the faith in ill repute and hatred with unbelievers, which is an even greater evil" (*Aquí se contiene*, 1552, *O.E.* 5:306a).

63. Saint-Lu, a fine Lascasian scholar, asserts in an interesting article ("Acerca de algunas 'contradicciones' lascasianas," 5–6) that the opposition between our author's assertions with respect to the number of victims of human sacrifice in his *Apología* and in his *Apologética historia* is to be explained by "tactical reasons." In the latter work, Saint-Lu explains, Bartolomé speaks of the "multitude of persons they offer to their gods each year in sacrifice" (*A.H.,* ch. 189, *O.E.* 4:188b). In the former, on the other hand, Las Casas's concern is to minimize the number of persons immolated (see f. 139v). Saint-Lu may seem to be right about this at first glance, but everything depends on the numerical scope we assign to the term, "multitude" (*muchedumbre*). If we look at the context of the sentence quoted from the *Apologética historia*, we find that when Bartolomé speaks of other peoples who offered such sacrifices, the highest figures he gives are in the area of "three hundred persons" slain in these "sacrilegious sacrifices." But among the Aztecs the figure was higher, he says. In the *Apología*, he admits that it may be a matter of "thirty, a hundred, or a thousand." But a thousand victims is surely a "multitude," by any reckoning. What Las Casas denies is that there were twenty thousand victims annually — Sepúlveda's figure. In making these observations, of course, we are prescinding from the repugnance Las Casas feels for the sacrifice of even a single human victim. We must not forget that the purpose of the present line of reasoning is to prevent a war that would cause the death of an immensely higher number of innocent persons.

64. It is interesting to observe that Motolinía, Las Casas's relentless enemy, agrees with him in this comparative estimate: "The greed of our Spaniards has done more to destroy and depopulate this land than all of the sacrifices, wars, and murders there have been in the times of their unbelief, with all of those who were sacrificed everywhere, who were many" (Motolinía, *Historia de los indios de la Nueva España*, tractate 3, ch. 11, pp. 350–51).

65. See A. Pagden, *The Fall of Natural Man*, 80–82.

66. This bold assertion is also found in the *Apologética historia*: "And if there were anything of more worth than human beings, as are angels, to offer them in sacrifice to God would have been a small matter, were they sacrificeable" (*A.H.,* ch. 183, *O.E.* 4:169a).

67. Las Casas considers that his experience in the Indies has helped him

to perceive this more clearly: "By seeing the care with which the Indians of these isles, especially here on Hispaniola and in Cuba, gave this part of the fruits they gathered as firstfruits, and spent them in this fashion in offering, I began to notice that the obligation to offer sacrifice to God was an obligation of natural law. This I had *previously read, but never seen*" (*A.H.*, ch. 166, *O.E.* 4:121b; emphasis added). Bartolomé's contact with the native world affords him an understanding of these religious customs from the inside.

68. In the *Apologética historia*, the identical principle is presented: "True, the offering of sacrifice to God is an obligation in natural law; still, the things in which, or of which, sacrifice should be offered is not of natural law, but rather are left to the decision of individuals, or of the whole community, whether by law or by commandment: or in default of these, each individual person has license to offer what he or she would wish; and thus the things in which, or of which, sacrifice is to be made or offered is a matter of positive law and not of natural right or law" (*A.H.*, ch. 143, *O.E.* 4:34a).

69. A century later, this will also be the effort, in her own fashion, of the extraordinary Sister Juana Inés de la Cruz. In an excellent study of Sor Juana, Marie-Cécile Bennasy-Berling presents the theme of one of her works as follows: "This nun has the immense merit of attempting to see human sacrifice *with the eyes of the Indians*. In her *Hymn of Praise for the Scepter of Joseph*, the character Idolatry becomes willing to offer traditional sacrifices to the Christian God, but not to renounce the sacrifices themselves. Sor Juana realized perfectly clearly that it was even more difficult to change religious customs than it was to switch the actual object of worship. Furthermore, Idolatry's logic is implacable: as we have seen, she desires to offer to the Divinity the best possible sacrifice. The poor arguments mounted by Nature and Natural Law encounter insurmountable obstacles. It will then fall to Faith to give the absolutely adequate response and expound the doctrine of the Mass — a sacrifice not only human, but superhuman. This time, Idolatry is vanquished on her own ground and declares herself satisfied" (Marie-Cécile Bennasy-Berling, *Humanismo y religión en Sor Juana Inés de la Cruz,* 322; emphasis added). We must add that this author's observations concerning Las Casas's position on this point are less accurate; see pp. 316–17.

70. Las Casas goes so far as to say that despite "their blindness and error" polities that "have ordained by law or by custom that human beings be sacrificed to the gods at certain times or on certain festival days had a loftier and more noble concept and estimation of their gods" (*A.H.*, ch. 183, *O.E.* 4:169a; see also *A.H.*, ch. 184, *O.E.* 4:173a).

71. Las Casas tries to get everything out of this biblical example that he can. The influence of Jewish customs in pagan nations is a frequent theme in the patristic era, but here the bold insinuation is that human sacrifice is of biblical origin. "It is not beyond the realm of possibility," he writes, "that the custom of immolating human beings had reached all peoples through the report that the almighty God of the Jews had ordered his beloved servant Abraham to sacrifice his own son to him, as well as that an illustrious chieftain of that same Jewish people, after having won a victory, had sacrificed

his only daughter to God, which he surely would not have done had he not known that this would be altogether pleasing to God" (*Apología*, 166).

72. The case of Jephthah ("illustrious chieftain") is also cited in the Eleventh Reply to Sepúlveda. That this example was important to him is evident from the fact that the final version (*O.E.* 5:337b–338a) develops this Reply at greater length than does the first redaction (found in Las Casas's *Tratado de Indias y el doctor Sepúlveda*, 244–45). He recalls that Jephthah is eulogized by St. Paul (see Heb. 11:32); and after all, since the vow that Jephthah made appears to have been pleasing to God, "it is easy to understand why unbelievers should think that the offering of human beings to God would be something due and agreeable to God" (*O.E.* 5:338a). In passing, Bartolomé calls Sepúlveda's attention to a passage from Augustine and his composition on the Book of Judges (ch. 49), where the bishop of Hippo does not condemn Jephthah.

73. Indignant, Sepúlveda will express his disgust with these statements of Las Casas: "This assertion that unbelievers are under no obligation to believe the preachers of the faith of Christ is impious and heretical. It expressly contradicts this: 'Go into the whole world and proclaim the good news to all creation. The man who believes in it and accepts baptism will be saved; the man who refuses to believe in it will be condemned' (Mark 16:15). But God condemns no one for omitting something that there is no obligation to perform." And the Cordovan humanist adds a strange argument: "After all, the reason why evangelizers may go in the company of soldiers and wicked persons, who have their minds more on robbery than on anything else, provides no argument against what I say, since a war that is just *per se* does not cease to be such because soldiers have a bad intention,... and thus preaching loses none of its holiness by reason of the company of the soldiers" (Sepúlveda, *Proposiciones temerarias*, 554). Pity that the Indians did not know this!

74. To those who maintained that it was enough to have the soldiers admonish the Indians to abandon their sins before making war on them, Las Casas addresses an elementary question: "What language will be spoken by these messengers to make themselves understood by the Indians? Latin, Greek, or perhaps Spanish or Arabic? The Indians know none of these tongues. Unless," he says ironically, "we might think the soldiers to be so holy that Christ will grant them the gift of tongues" (*Apología*, ff. 149–149v). The language obstacle obviously does not figure among the difficulties that Sepúlveda sees in an antecedent admonition. His attention is riveted on the Indians' stubbornness in their false religion.

75. Also Alonso de Veracruz, who will later be so close to Las Casas. In his *De Dominio Infidelium et Iusto Bello* he presents, among what he calls the "justifying causes" for the Conquista, solidarity with any victims of human sacrifice and cannibalism. Veracruz speaks in the conditional, like his master, Vitoria, but advances his argument convinced of its solidity. See *Writings of Alonso de la Veracruz*, nos. 824–39.

76. Soto — taking his distance from Vitoria — presents certain reservations in the argument from the defense of the innocent (the victims of human sacrifice) as a justification for war against the Indians. See Höffner, *La ética*

colonial, 441, with a note referring to a text of Soto taken from Beltrán de Heredia, *Los manuscritos del Maestro Fray Francisco de Vitoria,* 238.

77. It will be worth our while to observe that on the point in question Cano follows the line traced by Vitoria. He insists that it is a matter of a right of intervention on the basis of charity, not of justice. It is done in order to defend, and not to attack. See Pereña, *Misión de España en América,* 83.

78. See P. Duviols, *La lutte contre les religions autochtones dans le Pérou colonial,* 23.

79. The great Spanish historian Maravall approves Las Casas's attitude toward human sacrifice, but regards it as the result of a cultural relativism and even of a certain secularization on the part of Las Casas (J. A. Maravall, "Utopía y primitivismo," 340–42). Actually, however, the principal motive for Bartolomé's position is his evangelizing perspective.

80. Later, the Congregation for the Propagation of the Faith will lay down guidelines very close to those of Las Casas. See E. Hoornaert, "Las Casas o Sepúlveda," 862 n. 29.

81. Actually, the entire *Apologética historia* consists in an effort to adopt this viewpoint on the various aspects of the life of the natives of the Indies. This is the meaning of the observations that have won Las Casas such praise from contemporary historians as a forerunner of modern anthropology (see Hanke, *Estudios sobre Fray Bartolomé de Las Casas,* 207–30; A. M. Salas, "El padre Las Casas, su concepción del ser humano y el cambio cultural"). As we know, Las Casas employs Aristotelian categories to demonstrate the level of civilization of the inhabitants of the Indies. In an allusion to this, Pagden, concluding the chapter (significantly entitled, "A Program for a Comparative Ethnology") that he devotes to our author, writes: "The *Apologética historia,* in particular, . . . in the novelty of its form — not to reappear until the beginning of the eighteenth century — as well as in its main hypotheses, . . . is the first grand attempt to apply the categories of sixteenth-century Aristotelian anthropology to a substantial complex of empirical data" (Pagden, *The Fall of Natural Man,* 145). Las Casas's purpose was to show that the Indians had attained high levels of civilization and that consequently their achievements ought to be respected, and wars against them renounced.

82. Urdanoz, "Las Casas y Francisco de Vitoria," 262.

83. This celebrated and ambiguous distinction was first proposed by C. M. Curci, a Jesuit at the time, in his article "Il Congresso Cattolico di Malines e le libertà moderne," published anonymously (as was then the custom) in *Civiltà Cattolica* in 1863. (The manuscript, bearing the author's signature, rests in the periodical's archives.) Basically the same distinction is found in a slightly later text from the pen of the bishop of Orleans, F. Dupanloup, *La convention du 15 septembre et l'encyclique du 8 décembre,* 1865, being an able response to the papacy's harshest reproach of modern freedoms: the encyclical *Quanta Cura* and the famous *Syllabus of Errors* of Pius IX.

84. True, Thomas does not distinguish between thesis and hypothesis. He has no need to do so. The historical situation of his time corresponds to the thesis, the ideal.

85. John Courtney Murray and P. Pavan, whose influence on the doc-

ument with which we are dealing was decisive, succeeded in having this outlook prevail at the Council. See Murray, "La Déclaration sur la Liberté religieuse"; Gutiérrez, "Tres comentarios a la declaración sobre libertad religiosa."

86. Indeed, it is significant that the first patristic citation in the conciliar document should be from Lactantius.

87. If Urdanoz sees a contradiction between Las Casas's desire for the conversion of the Indians to Christianity and his defense of religious freedom, it is because he overlooks the importance of dialogue in evangelization. Both were very much emphasized by Las Casas and by the Council document.

88. As a reciprocal aid, Vatican II's Pastoral Constitution *Gaudium et Spes* presents the dialogue between church and world (nos. 40–45).

Conclusion to Part Two

1. Apparently that judgment had been suggested to him by a "religious person, prudent, educated, and experienced," who had written him that he knew "for certain that the greatest miracle of God in those lands is that the Indians believe, and receive our faith when they see the works of our Christian people" (*H.I.*, bk. 3, ch. 11, *O.E.* 2:197a).

Introduction to Part Three

1. This was the great dream of this restless and original man. The project of R. Lulio (or Llull) was the creation of a universal Christendom; see the old but still useful study of E. Longpré, "Lulle"; B. Perera, "La teología española desde mediados del s. XIII hasta las primeras manifestaciones del humanismo," for the historical context; and the short but interesting article of Abdelwahab Meddeb, "La religión del otro: Ibn'Arabi/Ramón Llull." The interesting study of R. de Sugranyes de Franch, "Bartolomé de Las Casas ¿discípulo de Raimundo Lulio?" broaches the theme that interests us.

2. On some historical aspects of this point, see the interesting article of L. Hanke, "The Theological Significance of the Discovery of America."

3. This is present in Gerónimo Mendieta in Mexico, Francisco de la Cruz in Peru, and other authors of the period. On de la Cruz see M. Bataillon, *Estudios sobre Bartolomé de Las Casas*, 353–67; this controversial friar is the subject of a recent and innovative study by V. Abril Castelló, "Francisco de la Cruz, utopía lascasista y la Contrareforma virreinal inquisitorial." The author will soon publish an extensive study on this Dominican. H. Urbano is also preparing a study of de la Cruz. José de Acosta rightly rejects the Jewish origin of the Indians (see *Historia natural y moral de las Indias*, bk. 1, ch. 23, in *Obras*, 36–37); Guamán Poma does the same (*Primer nueva corónica y buen gobierno*, 60); to the absence of laws and letters, noted by Acosta, he adds the lack of a beard. This hypothesis was, moreover, present in North America; see L. Hanke, appendix 1 to "Were the Indians Descended from the Lost Ten Tribes of Israel?" his doctoral thesis (Harvard, 1936). On this point see John L.

Phelan, *El Reino milenario de los Franciscanos en el Nuevo Mundo*, 41–47, which also provides an interesting bibliography on the question.

4. Citing letters of Portuguese Jesuit missionaries in Brazil, Las Casas mentions this thesis without comment (see *H.I.*, bk. 1, ch. 174, *O.E.* 1:465a). Armas Medina alludes to the role that this hypothesis played in the evangelization of Peru (*Cristianización del Perú*, 76). It is found, for example, in Juan Santa Cruz Pachacuti in his *Relación de Antiguedades deste Reyno del Pirú* (1613). Guamán Poma echoes this theory, but he attributes this supposed first evangelizing work not to Thomas but (according to another existing tradition, alluded to by, for example, Palacios Rubios, *De las islas del mar océano*, 6) to the apostle Bartholomew (1:93–94). Guamán's intention may be to discredit the motive of evangelization as a justification for the European presence, given that Christianity had already been preached; but he thereby falls into the trap of considering the Indians apostates (see the lines that follow in the text). On this theme and its presence in other authors see the interesting observations of Raquel Chang Rodríguez, "Santo Tomás en los Andes."

5. "El sacrificio humano en la Apologética Historia," 335.

6. This was the urgent concern of Las Casas, as has been pointed out by E. Ruiz Maldonado, "La justicia en la obra de Las Casas," 11–31.

Chapter 7: Conscience in God's Sight

1. Here was a clear theological victory for the defender of the Indians. See V. Abril Castelló, "Bartolomé de Las Casas y la escuela de Salamanca." This change of attitude, occurring in the second half of the sixteenth century, also finds expression in José de Acosta (whose experience in the Indies, furthermore, plays an important role in his reflections). Acosta acknowledges the argument to have been advanced by illustrious theologians and recognizes in theory that "the defense of the innocent is just cause for a war to be waged upon homicidal barbarians." With wise prudence, however, and from experience, he points out that "in actual confrontation with the reality [of the Indies, this motive] will be seen to be inadequate." And he explains: "First, the succor must be afforded with minimal injury to the aggressor: accordingly, the barbarians may not be stripped of their dominion or their lives when they can be restrained through fear or through limited subjugation. Second, it is absurd to claim to be defending those whose more extensive mortality is occasioned by the defense itself." Acosta then adds, strongly denouncing the events of the Indies: "Countless testimonials make it plain that an incomparably greater number have died in the wars waged on the Indians than in any act of tyranny on the barbarians' part. How many Indians have been sacrificed and slaughtered in the havoc wrought by the Spanish sword? Wherefore, morally speaking, rarely, if ever, can a defense of the innocent be alleged as a just cause for waging war on the Indians" (*De Procuranda Indorum Salute*, 1, II, ch. 6, pp. 295–97). We find the same argument in Las Casas. The concrete reality of the Indies leads both theologians to reject the pretext of saving the innocent as an argument for waging the wars. But as we have

seen, the Dominican's reasoning is more far-reaching, as he tries to get to the root of the problem.

2. See the classic and careful work of O. Lottin, *Psychologie et Morale aux XIIme et XIIme siècles,* vol. 2, chs. 5, 6.

3. See chapter 6, above.

4. "To inquire whether a will that refuses to conform with erroneous reason is evil is the same as to ask whether an erroneous conscience obliges" (Thomas Aquinas, *Summa Theologiae,* I–II, q. 19, a. 5, c.).

5. "But this opinion is illogical. In indifferent matters, the will that departs from erroneous reason or erroneous conscience is evil by reason of its object, on which depends the goodness or evil of the will — not, I grant, on the object regarded in itself, according to its nature, but inasmuch as, *per accidens,* reason represents it as an evil to be done or to be avoided" (ibid.).

6. For Thomas, a right conscience obliges *simpliciter,* or absolutely; while an erroneous conscience obliges only inasmuch as it subsists in us *secundum quid* (that is, on the hypothesis of its persistence in us).

7. This is Thomas's position in the *Sentences* and the *De Veritate.* His position is akin to the one maintained by St. Bonaventure in his *In II Sententiarum,* dist. 39, art. 1, 9, 3.

8. Lottin, *Psychologie et Morale,* 388–91. Lottin thinks the distinction plays a decisive role in Thomas's thought. This is likewise the opinion of E. d'Arcy, *Conscience and Its Right to Freedom,* 109.

9. In other words, an erroneous conscience obliges insofar as the subject has not been freed from ignorance and consequently has recognized the truth. See Thomas's *De Veritate,* q. 17, a. 4.

10. Thomas frequently refers to this principle, which he borrows from Denis the Pseudo-Areopagite: "Bonum ex integra causa; malum ex quocumque defectu." That is, in order to be good, a thing must be entirely good, whereas even a single defect will make it evil.

11. Lottin doubts that Thomas Aquinas had any intention of treating of the question of the goodness or evil of the act that proceeds from an erroneous conscience: "St. Thomas wishes to say only one thing, nor can he say anything else: An erroneous conscience frequently excuses its subject from any guilt" (Lottin, *Psychologie et Morale,* 406). Lecler (*Histoire de la tolérance,* 1:121 n. 112) limits himself to registering the fact. D'Arcy, on the other hand, openly criticizes this vagueness on the part of Aquinas, who, according to him, "failed to carry his own principle to its logical conclusion" (d'Arcy, *Conscience and Its Right to Freedom,* 113–26; here, 113). J. M. Alonso is indignant with this criticism of Thomas, but contributes nothing new to the debate; see his *Derechos de la conciencia errónea y otros derechos,* 201–84. Colavechio has made a detailed historical study of the question. After a consideration of the various prevailing interpretations of this point of Thomas's teaching, he concludes that, while Thomas does not assert that an act performed in accordance with an erroneous conscience is good, neither does he "deny this assertion; indeed, it is in the logic of his doctrine as a whole. He denies the existence of indifferent acts *in concreto;* thus, if an act is not evil, it must be good. In an earlier article, Aquinas writes that an evil can receive the *ratio*

boni due to reason's understanding it as something good" (X. Colavechio, *Erroneous Conscience and Obligations,* 101; the study on St. Thomas will be found on 67–115). This is likewise the position of de Finance, who writes: "If the act is represented as good, one must necessarily conclude — so long as the error is involuntary and innocent — that the subject *acts well* in performing it. However, St. Thomas does not say this, at least in his theological works (for fear of shocking?)....St. Thomas's teaching on indifferent acts called for a bolder response" (Joseph de Finance, *Ethique Générale,* 346). L. Janssens, in a recent article, after acknowledging Thomas's silence about any goodness of the acts in question, suggests that — in accord with Thomas's own guidelines — the distinction may be applied here between, on the one hand, good and evil and, on the other, correct and incorrect. The Dionysian principle of integrity (see our n. 10, above) would be valid for the second pair, but not for the first. When I perform an act in conformity with an erroneous conscience, "my morally incorrect act is morally good" ("A Moral Understanding of Some Arguments of Saint Thomas," 359–60).

12. Some theologians of the time even expressed fear that heretics might take advantage of Thomas's teaching to defend their error. At the close of the thirteenth century, Franciscan Mateo d'Aquasparta writes that in terms of Thomas's theory "heretics would be acting correctly in doing what they regarded as obligatory, as well as the Jews when they killed Christ — all of which is obviously absurd" (cited by J. Lecler, *Histoire de la tolérance,* 1:123).

13. Sertillanges — without taking a position on the absence of an explicit pronouncement by Thomas — goes a step beyond the Angelic Doctor and considers that to follow an erroneous conscience is, according to Thomas's actual principles, virtuous and meritorious. "Many have said," he writes, "that there is only excuse from guilt here. But nothing, philosophically, justifies this middle position. Inasmuch as conscience represents law *for us,* to follow an erroneous conscience is to orientate oneself toward that law *formally,* although not *materially,* and this movement can be neither neutral nor culpable" (A. Sertillanges, *La philosophie morale de Saint Thomas d'Aquin,* 392; emphasis in the original).

14. Ruiz de Santiago does not directly deal with the debated question that we have just recalled; nevertheless, his article is interesting for its analysis of Thomas's last treatment of the matter (in his commentary on the Letter to the Romans) and shows the importance of the assertion that conscience obliges, in all circumstances, in the area of respect for the ideas of others ("Conciencia errónea y reflexión moral"; see also L. J. Elders, "St. Thomas Aquinas' Doctrine of Conscience").

15. See B. Olivier, "Les droits de la conscience: Le problème de la conscience errante," in *Tolérance et communauté humaine,* 174. The author is among those who emphasize that Thomas did not explicitly resolve the question of the goodness of acts performed according to an erroneous conscience (ibid., 173 n. 6).

16. "St. Thomas goes so far as to see an unethical act in the violation of a pontifical constitution of which one is ignorant: 'All are under obligation to

know in some way this constitution of the Pope' (Quodl., I, a. 19)" (Lecler, *Histoire de la tolérance,* 1:122).

17. Thomas writes: "Ignorance of the law is no excuse from sin, unless the ignorance is invincible, as in the case of the insane or feeble-minded" (Quodl. 3, a. 27, ad 2). For him, then, only in these extreme personal cases might there be an invincible ignorance of the law.

18. Like all of the other theologians of his time, Thomas thought that "the gospel had been sufficiently promulgated in the world that everyone of good will could know its prescriptions" (Lecler, *Histoire de la tolérance,* 1:122).

19. On the other hand, let us emphasize, there can be no good faith or invincible ignorance on the part of the Spaniards in their harassment of the Indians. Las Casas specifies that, since Montesino's sermon in 1511, the character of these acts and the responsibility of those who commit them is plain (see *Tratado de las doce dudas,* 1564, *O.E.* 5:498b).

20. This is also Losada's interpretation (Losada, ed., *Apología* [1975], "Introducción," 35). Always on the lookout for possible contradictions in Las Casas, Losada thinks he sees one here. Actually, these distinctions and refinements protected Bartolomé from the imputation of heresy and withdrew him from the stern gaze of the inquisitorial eye.

21. Actually, the Reformation entailed a different religious situation from the one that prevailed in the Middle Ages and marked the beginning of the long, hard story of religious freedom. See Lecler, *Histoire de la tolérance;* Gustavo Gutiérrez, "Freedom and Salvation: A Political Problem."

22. In a brief passage that seems to indicate the points to be dealt with in the second session, which was never held, the following questions head the list: "Whether for the sin of idolatry, in order to avenge the offense to God, it would be licit to make war on and punish those who worship idols"; and "whether, if in these lands it is customary to devour human flesh,... it would be licit, in order to deliver innocent persons from this oppression,... to make war on them" (*Tratado de las doce dudas,* 145). Thus, the matter must have remained without resolution after the first confrontation.

23. In a later text, Sepúlveda will write caustically: "This, then, is the impious error of someone who either knows little of theology, or is puffed up and insolent, or has a very poor sense of the Catholic faith: to say that to sacrifice human beings to false gods is not against the law of nature, when it is idolatry and homicide. It seems not to have come to his notice that the precepts of the Decalogue are all natural laws, and that anyone who acts against any of them acts against the law of nature, as all theologians agree" (*Proposiciones temerarias,* 549).

24. "And I declare" — Las Casas continues sharply — "that they will never be under obligation to believe any preacher of our holy faith if these preachers are accompanied by tyrannical persons, men of war, robbers and killers, as the Doctor would seek to introduce" (*Aquí se contiene,* 1552, *O.E.* 5:334a). Sepúlveda will be scandalized and will label Las Casas's declaration "impious and heretical" (*Proposiciones temerarias,* 554).

25. Las Casas continues: "And by some of [these arguments] certain barbarians changed the minds of the Romans themselves about forbidding

human sacrifice, as Plutarch recounts on page 465 of his *Problemas*. And even the Romans, seeing themselves defeated and in sore distress at the hands of Hannibal, in order to placate gods they esteemed to have grown angry with them, sacrificed in the Circus a Frank of each sex and a Greek of each sex, as Plutarch says in the same place, along with Livy" (*Aquí se contiene, O.E.* 5:334b). The mention of the Romans is not casual: Sepúlveda had appealed to their high level of civilization as an argument against human sacrifice. Indeed, the humanist had much admiration for the Roman world, whose great classical writers he sought to imitate with his elegant Latin prose. (See Sepúlveda's letters to various friends in his *Epistolario,* which we have cited.)

26. We find this position echoed in Juan de la Peña. This Salamancan scholar accepts in principle the thesis that war may be waged out of solidarity with the victims of human sacrifices and concretely refers to the Caribs of the Indies (Juan de la Peña, *De Bello,* 1:219). But he lays down an important restriction, which reveals Las Casas's influence on certain great representatives of the so-called second-generation Salamanca school. One must proceed with caution, says de la Peña, "since there could be *invincible ignorance* of this sin of idolatry, if they were not to be idolaters for other reasons, or be accused of idolatry. The reason is that it is no easy matter to see by natural reason that it is sinful to immolate human beings to God, who is the Lord of life and death and the Supreme Good. Nor is it to be wondered at that someone should mistakenly think that the Supreme Good, which is God, ought to be offered in sacrifice the *supreme good* of this world, *human life.*" Thus, the question of invincible ignorance does arise in the matter of human sacrifice: natural reason does not dictate an evident conclusion. The expressions of Juan de la Peña are almost literally those of Bartolomé. The Salamancan is specific: "In such a case, therefore, culpable error will lie mainly in the misconception that the idol is a god — not that it ought to be sacrificed to and offered human being's lives" (ibid., 1:223; emphasis added). The question now arises: If there can be invincible ignorance in the matter of human sacrifice, can such sacrifice be forbidden by the natural law? Apparently not, if we follow Thomas Aquinas's teaching. De la Peña does not expatiate. Obviously we do not find in him Las Casas's forthright thesis that the matter of sacrifices offered to God falls within the orbit of positive law alone. The two thinkers' practical conclusions coincide, however: de la Peña declares the wars waged on the Mexicans by reason of their human sacrifices to be unjust.

27. The oversight was real. Sepúlveda gives proof of this when he maintains, years later, that "the erroneous conscience is improperly said to oblige; [but] this is the property of a just law" (*Proposiciones temerarias,* 553) — which betrays an ignorance of the subject as it is presented in scholasticism.

28. Las Casas's citation reads as follows: "...Quia conscientia recta ligat simpliciter et per se, erronea vero per accidens et secundum quid: in quantum scilicet apprehenditur ut bonum quod malum est. Unde si fiat, peccatum non evitatur, si autem non fiat, peccatum incurritur, secundum sanctum Thomam, I. 2e, q. 19, ar. 5 et 6; et 2 Sententiarum, distinctione 39, q. 3, ar. 3, passim, and elsewhere" (*O.E.* 5:337). (... "Because a right conscience binds simply and *per se,* but an erroneous one *per accidens* and *secundum quid,* that is, insofar as

something evil is apprehended as good. If it is done, then, sin is not avoided; while if it is not done, sin is committed, according to St. Thomas....")

The passage from the *Commentary on the Sentences* reads as follows: "*Conscientia enim recta obligat simpliciter et per se,* hoc enim quod est per ipsam dictatum est in se bonum, et ex judicio rationis bonum apparet; unde si non fiat, malum est, et si fiat, bonum est. Sed *conscientia erronea non obligat nisi per accidens et secundum quid:* si enim dictet aliquid esse faciendum, illud fieri in se consideratum non est bonum necessarium ad salutem, sed *apprehenditur ut bonum.* Et ideo cum non liget nisi secundum quod est bonum, non obligatur voluntas per se ad hoc, sed per accidens, scilicet ratione apprehensionis, qua judicatur bonum. Et ideo *si fiat* aliquid quod est secundum se malum, quod errans ratio judicat bonum, *peccatum non evitatur;* si autem *non fiat, peccatum incurritur*" (emphasis added).

29. Elsewhere he observes: "On the third proposition, [in which] the Chiapan says that he knows not the judgment of God upon idolaters who sacrifice innocent persons to a false God: This is heresy.... For a Christian, let alone a theologian, to say he knows not the judgment of God upon the idolatrous heathen when he is under obligation to know it, as the Bishop of Chiapa has been, is express heresy, to say that he knows not God's judgment upon heathen, since it is *de fide catholica* that heathen who do not believe are by that very fact judged and *condemned* by God" (*Proposiciones temerarias,* 564; emphasis added). This passage belongs to the second part of the document *Proposiciones temerarias,* which is dated 1571 — after Las Casas's death, then, and two years before Sepúlveda's.

30. Juan Antonio Llorente, *Histoire critique de l'Inquisition d'Espagne,* 433–34, indicates that Las Casas was denounced to the Inquisition for a work in which he "sought to prove that monarchs have no power of disposition over the goods and liberty of their American subjects, nor the right to subject them to other rulers... in a feudal regime or in that of the *encomienda.*" The book was denounced because it contradicted "what St. Peter and St. Paul taught concerning slaves' and vassals' submission to their lords." Llorente adds: "The author was sorely aggrieved at the prospect of being haled into Court. The Council did not issue him a summons, however, but only required he 'remit the work and manuscript,' which he did in 1552." The book in question is said to have been published later, outside Spain. Wagner and Parish (*The Life and Writings of Bartolomé de Las Casas,* 187–90) show that it is unclear what treatise of Las Casas is being alluded to. However, the characteristics cited seem to point to the *Erudita et Elegans Explicatio.* These authors further suggest that it may have been Sepúlveda who denounced Bartolomé to the Inquisition, precisely in the document that we have cited a number of times in the last several notes, called *Proposiciones temerarias....* The charges made against Las Casas in that document indeed resemble those to which Llorente refers.

31. This assertion comes from a text entitled "Declaration of How the Excuses for the Errors in the Book of the Bishop of Chiapas Are Inadequate and Irrelevant," found in the document called *Proposiciones temerarias* in A. M. Fabié, *Vida y escritos de Fray Bartolomé de Las Casas,* 567–69 (see Wagner and

Parish, *The Life and Writings of Bartolomé de Las Casas,* 189 n. 14, where it is suggested that Las Casas may have been formally denounced to the Inquisition). The declaration is of Sepúlveda's own authorship, as can be seen from its reference ("The example *I* used of when it is preached, [to be found in] the Acts of the Inquisition...": p. 568; emphasis added) to the first part of the *Proposiciones temerarias* (554), which is surely from his pen.

32. This frequently happens in polemical discussions. Replies and rebuttals necessarily attend more to the adversary's arguments than would a text composed independently of the controversy. Augustine of Hippo is a classic case of this in church history. Las Casas's style is heavily polemical, and this explains his manner of argumentation, his emphases, and his silences in different writings dealing with the same subject. See Saint-Lu, "Acerca de algunas 'contradicciones' lascasianas."

33. J. Friede, *Bartolomé de las Casas: Precursor,* 110.

34. The extensive treatment accorded by the *Apologética historia* to the question of human sacrifice, as well as the considerations in the *Apología* devoted to the *right* to offer the same (which we have summarized above), are an indication of this. Losada sums up Las Casas's position: "If Christians use violent means to impose their will on the Indians, it would be better for the Indians to keep to their traditional religion. Indeed, in such a case, it is the pagan Indians who are on the right path, and Christians who behave in this way might well learn from them" (Losada, ed., *Apología* [1975], "Introducción," 34). The wording is Losada's, but in placing them within quotation marks in his "Introducción" (as well as in other articles that he has written on the subject), Losada gives the impression that he is quoting Las Casas. The style Losada adopts — as well as the summaries from his own pen that he inserts into the actual text of Las Casas (in his 1975 edition) — readily lead the reader to think that some of the editor's writing is that of Las Casas. It seems to us that this is what has happened with Hanke's citation in *All Mankind Is One,* 94, which Hanke attributes to Fray Bartolomé. Happily, Losada's interpolations have been eliminated from the edition of Las Casas's works that he himself has published (Losada, ed., *Obras Completas* of Las Casas, v. 9).

Chapter 8: Salvific Will and Human History

1. For a statement of the issue and a good bibliography see B. Willens, "La necesidad de la Iglesia para la salvación," *Concilium,* no. 1 (January 1965): 114–27; in the same issue, J. Ratzinger, "Salus extra Ecclesiam nulla est." For a brief presentation of the evolution of the concept see Gustavo Gutiérrez, *A Theology of Liberation,* 83–86.

2. We have Francis Xavier's letter to a confrere in Rome (January 15, 1544): "Many are the Christians missing in these lands for want of persons committing themselves to the pious and holy work [of converting them]. Often I feel the urge to go to the scholars who busy themselves with matters concerning these regions and cry like one gone mad, especially at the University of Paris, to talk to those at the Sorbonne who have more education than willingness to adopt an attitude that would make that education bear fruit.

536 _____ *Notes to Pages 218–225*

How many souls are lost to glory and go to hell by their negligence! They study letters. Would that they studied the accounting that God our Lord will require of them and the talent they have received. Would that they were moved to take means and practice spiritual exercises that would bring them to know and feel in their souls the divine will, conforming themselves more to that will than to their own affections, and say: 'Domine, ecce adsum, quid me vis facere? Mitte me quo vis; et si expedit, etiam ad indos' " ("Here I am, Lord! What do you want me to do? Send me wherever you want to — even to the Indians, if that is the right thing"; cited in A. Arbeola, "Francisco Javier en el diálogo teológico sobre la justificación de los infieles"). Xavier's missionary practice, however, will move him to introduce certain nuances into his position.

3. Summarizing the chapters of Las Casas's book that have not survived, Antonio de Remesal says that they contain a demonstration to the effect that "no nation in the entire world has been altogether excluded and thrust aside from such a great grace and favor of the divine mercy so that some, at least a few, or many, of that nation should not be predestined to eternal life" (*Historia general de las Indias Occidentales*, 1:209a).

4. Fearing that a letter carried by "a reverend and saintly person" of the Franciscan order failed to reach its addressee, he says that this would aggravate "the lamentable, miserable lot of these Indian people, so deprived of the divine succor, when the Son of God has shed *all his blood for them*" (*Carta a un personaje*, 1535, O.E. 5:59b; emphasis added).

5. In the same sense, among numerous other texts, see *Tratado sobre los indios que se han hecho esclavos*, 1552, O.E. 5:262b, 290b. Las Casas invokes the argument persistently; see *De Thesauris* (1563): the Indians cannot accept a faith offered them amid abuse, amid the death of their children, and amid the condemnation to which those who "die in infidelity" are destined (ibid., 170v).

6. We must not think, however, that Bartolomé de las Casas is here justifying the "sale of the faith" that he so often denounced. Employing a paradoxical language charged with irony, our friar is only asserting that, even under the regime of the *encomienda* — which he rejects — it would be a matter of the most elementary justice to teach the gospel to those who had performed the toil required of them.

7. For the relationship between gratuity and justice, see Gutiérrez, *On Job*.

8. The text goes on: "Where, without great labors, without an uneconomical expenditure of wealth (but rather with great influx of the same), and with unimaginable happiness, might [one] see the knowledge, worship, and magnification of God to be more highly exalted and widely diffused among unbelieving people in any times since those of the Apostles?"

9. Las Casas takes very seriously this "favor" (*merced*) that the king ought to grant his subjects. Here is another text to the same effect (his final reason for urging the abolition of the *encomiendas*): "The twentieth and last reason that we give is that Your Majesty will be doing all the Spaniards in the Indies, and all in Spain, incredible, inestimable favors. These are:

their delivery from enormous sins of tyranny, robbery, violence, and homicide, which they commit daily by oppressing and robbing and slaying those people, and thereby from the impossible restitution to which they thereby become obliged, nor consequently will the whole of Spain be more sullied and infected than it already has been through its communication and sharing, in so many different ways, of wealth gained by robbery" (*Octavo remedio*, 1542, *O.E.* 5:117a).

10. Christians, by the fact of being Christians, know biblical revelation and its commandments. Thus their sins are more grave than the sins of those lacking this understanding. Being a Christian entails great responsibility. "Christians," writes Las Casas, "sin more, and more gravely, regardless of the kind of sin, than do unbelievers" (*H.I.*, bk. 2, ch. 63, *O.E.* 2:157a). What we have here is not the furious invective alleged to have been lodged by Las Casas against Christians involved in the Indies. Even apart from an elementary common sense, what we have here is an echo of the first chapters of Paul's Letter to the Romans apropos of the situation of gentiles and Jews vis-à-vis the law of God.

11. Hanke, for example, says in his Introduction to the *De Unico:* "For those who have read Las Casas's vigorous fulminations and frightful epithets in his *Brevísima relación de la destrucción de las Indias,* or in the *Historia de las Indias,* the moderate language and eloquent exhortations of the present work will be an agreeable surprise. It could appear that, here, he is making a special effort to practice what he has preached. Rarely does he mention the Indies. He develops his argument on a higher level and considers only universal truths" (Lewis Hanke, "Introducción a la primera edición," in *Bartolomé de Las Casas: Del único modo,* xxii). Friede, for his part, criticizes Hanke for failing to take it into account that *De Unico* belongs to what Friede calls Las Casas's "preaching stage," that is, to the "idealistic stage in the Lascasian struggle on behalf of justice" (*Bartolomé de las Casas: Precursor,* 79 n. 6). Actually, however, Friede's appraisal of Las Casas's work is not very different from Hanke's: for the Colombian historian, that work is "an example of this literary, theoretical, abstract tendency" (ibid.).

Both judgments seem to us to be excessive. They mistake the sense and context of Las Casas's book. As we have already observed, according to Helen Parish, the controversial and very concrete Enriquillo episode exerted an important influence in its redaction. Furthermore, Bartolomé de Las Casas employs the ideas present in this work — regarded as "moderate" in its language and "idealistic" — as one of his most powerful weapons in the battle against the treatment accorded to the natives of the Indies.

12. "Why," he asks them, "instead of sending sheep to convert wolves, do you send ravenous, tyrannical, cruel wolves, to tear, destroy, scandalize, and scatter the sheep?" (*Carta al Consejo*, 1531, *O.E.* 5:49a). Just above, recalling the enormous responsibility they bear with regard to the dwellers of the Indies, he has told them that "not even the Emperor, who has appointed them to this charge and granted them ecclesiastical and military dignities, would escape the punishment they would earn by any dereliction of duty on their part" (*O.E.* 5:45a, b). As we see, the Dominican friar minces no words.

13. For example, in the closing pages of the *Historia de las Indias*, with reference to occurrences of the second decade of the sixteenth century in which he had participated through his initiatives with the Court, Las Casas recounts that the king summoned his councilors to learn their opinion on the matter. "There was a great deal of disputing," he says, "and many observations made upon the justice, injury, harm, and destruction of these Indian people. This may have been owing to the great ignorance that at that time reigned in all of the Councils, for the most part, concerning this material, as they were ignorant of the principles and rule of the natural and divine law that they were under obligation to know. Or perhaps it was owing to the influence of some of those whose interests they were protecting, and which would founder in case the Indians were set free" (*H.I.*, bk. 3, ch. 155, *O.E.* 2:548a; see also *O.E.* 2:549b). A few chapters further on, apropos of the employment of the Indians in the harvesting of pearls along the coast of Cumaná, he writes: "Many times have I demanded the Council provide a remedy by royal order, to no avail. But the main fault and the greatest sin of the Council is that it seems to issue its orders only for form's sake. Lest an order in behalf of the Indians be complied with, no rigorous punishment is meted out to those who ignore it" (*H.I.*, bk. 3, ch. 166, *O.E.* 2:579a). Norms are not just unless they are applied.

14. This entire letter to the Council of the Indies (1531), whose importance we have already observed, focuses on the salvation of the Indians — as well as on another matter, of the utmost urgency: the salvation of those responsible for what is occurring in these lands.

15. Memorial from Hispaniola, one of whose authors would be Las Casas (*DII* 11:244). The same notion appears in the Recommendation ("Parecer," 1536), signed by Juan Zumárraga, composed in response to the "doubts" presented by Viceroy Antonio de Mendoza regarding Indian slavery. The text has been published by Parish, *Las Casas en México: Historia y obras desconocidas*, Appendix 1. "Our King of the Spains" — reads the "Parecer" — "is obliged, under pain of salvation, to employ a watchful, intensive diligence and to order the entire temporal regime in these regions toward the following: that the faith of Jesus Christ be preached and made known to these Indian tribes inhabiting this new, huge world, by suitable ministers." We have another text of this same tenor in the *Doce dudas*, 1564, *O.E.* 5:524a.

16. This demographic plunge resulted in a switch in the original selection of places for the erection of episcopal sees. The depopulation means, says Las Casas with irony (and a touch of poetry), that "in the episcopal sees that the Pope had erected and indicated, there was no longer anyone to convert or preach to but the birds and the trees. At this point the said Catholic King once more informed and besought the Pope that the locales indicated for the churches were no longer ready and suitable for them to be built there" (*H.I.*, bk. 2, ch. 1, 171a).

17. Las Casas specifies that "the effect of gold mining" is "to have destroyed and slain the innumerable Indian neighbors of this isle and of all of these isles" (*H.I.*, bk. 3, ch. 2, *O.E.* 2:173b)

18. Las Casas goes on: "The bishops' ignorance is evidenced here as well. They were blindly undertaking to keep the Indians mining gold regardless of

all else. Instead, they ought to have been on the watch not to bind themselves to something that might be unjust and wicked. Surely they were unaware of this possibility. The very terms of the undertaking ought to have made them suspicious (the Indians were to 'mine gold,' and 'perform service') — unless they imagined that mining gold would be like plucking ripe fruit from trees!" (*H.I.*, bk. 3, ch. 2, *O.E.* 2:174a).

19. Las Casas was long convinced that his sovereigns had been poorly informed by their functionaries, but he kept up the hope that over the years things would change. Of Charles V he says: "He is beginning to understand the criminal, treasonable acts being committed among these tribes and territories, against God's will and his" (*Brevísima relación*, 1542, *O.E.* 5:176a). The course of events will make him more critical toward the kings.

20. See also *Octavo remedio*, 1542, *O.E.* 5:84a. In another context, but with the same attitude, he recounts the atrocities committed by the Portuguese, under the direction of Infante Henrique himself, son and heir of the king of Portugal, against the black African population. Las Casas denounces the encouragement of these adventures motivated by the condition of gold and power at this time, and points to the Portuguese Infante as the guilty one. "Thus it happened," he writes, "on these voyages, in the case of the Infante and the Portuguese. He claimed to be acting out of zeal for the service of God and the attraction of unbelievers to a knowledge of God. But he had no care for the proper means and, as I believe, surely offended rather than served God, by defaming faith in God and making the Christian religion to stink in the nostrils of those unbelievers. Every soul seeming to receive the faith was actually, perhaps (and not merely perhaps), submitting to baptism out of fear alone and under constraint, so that what [the Infante and the rest of the Portuguese] were actually doing was dispatching many souls to hell." Las Casas unflinchingly points to the Portuguese Crown Prince as the one responsible for all of this: "And that it was he who was at fault, and the one guilty for all of this, is plain to see. After all, he was the one who sent them and commanded them,...approving everything. It was said that no injury was inflicted. But there certainly was" (*H.I.*, bk. 1, ch. 24, *O.E.* 1:91a, b).

21. See Pérez Fernández, "El 'tiempo dorado' de la primera evangelización de América."

22. Las Casas sees a proof of this in the fact that this wealth disappears in Spain: "No fortune that comes from the Indies...makes a profit or thrives. It vanishes as dust before the wind, or as salt spilt in water. Nor did the Holy Spirit fail to foretell this in Proverbs: 'Those who plunder others abide in poverty'" (f. 136v; the reference is to Proverbs 11:24: "One man is lavish yet grows still richer; another is too sparing, yet is the poorer"). On a number of occasions Bartolomé declares the gold of the Indies to be plunging Spain into poverty (see *H.I.*, bk. 3, ch. 90, *O.E.* 2:387b).

23. "In terms precisely of the royal culpability, Friar Bartolomé replies to the Peruvian colonists' twelve doubts or concerns with a synthetic view of the situation that will dictate a simple, either/or choice, and he will set this choice before Philip. Either the King will save Spain or let it go to ruin; and

in the process, either lose his soul or save it" (J. Denglos, "Tratado de las doce dudas de Fray Bartolomé de Las Casas [diciembre 1563]").

24. The passages we quote on these last pages are all from the Providence version. They are absent from the *Doce dudas* as previously known (as presented in the BAE edition).

25. Here is another energetic denunciation of the mistreatment of the Indians and the justifications brought forward: "You can readily guess, from how they neglect God's commands, that the riches they *honor* most are not that of God but that of *gold*, silver, and other things out of which one makes a pile of money.... For this kind of man brings cruel war to bear on those who never harmed him, people he never knew before, of that we are sure, people who never plotted evil against him. He kills, he slaughters human beings — never mind their sex or age — with a sword, with a spear, off with their heads! One stroke head from neck, and plunges the souls of his wretched victims into instant hellfire. Disgusting! Conquerors steal others' wives, force them into adultery.... As if this is not enough, preachers fanatic for the spread of faith in Christianity... malign the natives a million ways, even to the point of perjury, calling them dogs, idolaters, accomplices in rotten crimes, stupid morons, unfit, incapable of Christian faith and moral life. The things they then do to these people under the pretext of a lie — a false, a wicked, a heretical lie, a deadly detestable lie — might then seem just, or at least pardonable. 'But I am [Yahweh], I am not blind, says the Lord!'... Do you call this doing no harm to widows and orphans as the divine command enjoins?... Do you call them holy, these marauders, holy as God is holy, as God wishes Christians to be?" (*De Unico*, 164–165v; *The Only Way*, 133–34; emphasis added). Lofty are the Christian demands presented by the Dominican.

Chapter 9: A Heaven for Indians

1. See J. M. González Ruiz, "Extra Ecclesiam nulla salus a la luz de la teología paulina"; J. Ratzinger, "Salus extra Ecclesiam nulla est."

2. Fulgentius of Ruespe writes: "He who lives not in the bosom of the Catholic Church — be he pagan, Jew, heretic, or schismatic — can have no part in eternal life, but will go to 'that everlasting fire prepared for the devil and his angels' (Matt. 25:41), unless he enter it before dying." The text had much authority in Christian antiquity, as it was attributed to Augustine himself.

3. This also explains Boniface VIII's bull *Unam Sanctam* (1302, Denzinger, no. 469) and especially the Council of Florence, which adopts verbatim the text of Fulgentius that we cite in our note 2, just above (Denz. 714). Ratzinger, "Salus extra Ecclesiam nulla est," makes an interesting effort to interpret both magisterial documents in their immediate historical framework.

4. Thomas Aquinas, *De Veritate*, q. 14, a. 11, ad 1. The hypothesis is absent from the *Summa Theologiae* (written ten years later), which has led some to speak of a change of position on Thomas's part. It is clear, however, that he returns to the subject in some way in his *Commentary on the Letter to the*

Romans, which came after the *Summa.* L. Capéran, in his classic *Le problème du salut des infidèles,* 1:199, maintains therefore that Thomas remained faithful to the ideas presented in the *De Veritate.*

5. See Capéran, *Problème du salut des infidèles;* S. Harent, "Infidèles," in *Dictionnaire de Théologie Catholique;* Angel Santos Hernández, *Salvación y paganismo.*

6. See Capéran, *Problème du salut des infidèles,* 221; Santos Hernández, *Salvación y paganismo,* 29.

7. Cited by Harent, "Infidèles," col. 1749. The text is from Vives's commentaries on Augustine's *The City of God.*

8. Contemporary theology, while attending to other elements as well, has reemphasized love as the route of salvation. See Yves M.-J. Congar, *Vaste monde ma paroisse,* 110–83. Along these lines, Josef Ratzinger has said, in the article already cited: "We may say that the response we find in the New Testament is this: The one who possesses love, possesses all. He is safe, and no evil can befall him." But the fullness of this attitude requires a self-opening "to the gift of the Lord's love," which is "what Saint Paul calls faith." *Agape* and *pistis* are the Christian's basic dispositions. The one having them "possesses the essence of Christianity, and will be saved." The church is a "means of salvation" to the extent that it helps in the creation and living of these two dispositions. The church is "the little flock, the stepping stones by means of which God wills to save all persons. The church is not the entirety of this, but does represent it." We should not be surprised, then, at its small proportions in a framework of world history. Its mission resembles that of Simon of Cyrene: "to help the Lord carry the cross of redemption." The church is made up of those who live "for others."

9. T. Urdanoz ("Necesidad de la fe," 403 n. 2) observes that the edition was expurgated by the Inquisition and that this passage is not found in the *Obras Completas,* published in Valencia in 1782.

10. The example of Cornelius, who was justified before he was a Christian (see Acts 10:1–33), is frequently adduced in favor of this thesis.

11. See especially Urdanoz, "Necesidad de la fe," who levels a severe criticism against this thesis of Vitoria. This author even asserts that the Salamancan master seems to have perceived the flimsy foundations of this position, so that he attempted to erase its traces. This, he thinks, led him to withdraw the fourth part of his *relección* on *La obligación de convertirse a Dios al llegar al uso de la razón* (see "Necesidad de la fe," 408); unless he never actually wrote a fourth part (see Urdanoz himself in his "Introducción" to this *relección* in Francisco Vitoria, *Obras,* 1298). We have various examples of such intellectual scruples in the life of the great theologian. Here the reader may consult Capéran, *Problème du salut des infidèles;* Santos Hernández, who regards Vitoria's distinction as "unfounded and illogical" (*Salvación y paganismo,* 301); and Harent, "Infidèles."

12. In support of his second legitimate title (the right of Christians to evangelize), he will say that the Indians "are not only in sin, but also outside the state of salvation. Christians have the competency to correct them and set

them on the way to salvation; indeed, it seems that they are obliged to do so" (Vitoria, *Obras*, 715; CHP, 87).

13. "Vitoria maintained [in his course *De Fide*] that without explicit faith and the revelation of Jesus Christ, indeed without any supernatural faith at all, unbelievers can obtain grace and justification, but not eternal salvation" (Urdanoz, in Vitoria, *Obras*, 1299).

14. According to Urdanoz (in Vitoria, *Obras*, 1215), Vitoria was the first to exploit this hypothesis of Thomas Aquinas.

15. In the *De Indis* (Vitoria, *Obras*, 691–92; CHP, 61), however, which came several years later, he seems to suggest a more affirmative position on the possibility of the salvation of unbelievers.

16. This distinction was not altogether clear in terms of the Council of Trent. It was asserted gradually, not without a certain amount of disagreement as to the necessity of the means (see Harent, "Infidèles," 1760).

17. "I would prefer," Soto writes, "not to admit an invincible, inculpable ignorance of an explicit faith anywhere than accept that a person in the state of grace has need of something else in order to obtain salvation, to the point that he cannot die before having received a special revelation. But to deny the possibility of invincible ignorance would be to reject a universally held position. Therefore we conclude, saving a better opinion, that persons in invincible ignorance of the gospel can, without explicit faith and, by means of implicit faith alone, obtain salvation and grace" (cited by Capéran, *Problème du salut des infidèles*, 262). Let us notice, however, that the invincible ignorance in question is invincible ignorance of the gospel, not of truths of a natural order or demands of natural law. With respect to these, according to scholasticism, no invincible ignorance is possible. Here let us observe once more what we have said about Bartolomé de Las Casas's position on human sacrifices.

18. See Urdanoz, "Necesidad de fe"; Capéran, *Problème du salut des infidèles;* Santos Hernández, *Salvación y paganismo;* and Harent, "Infidèles."

19. See Harent, "Infidèles," from which we have also taken the texts cited. This author denies that Vega, theologian at the Council of Trent, slipped into a naturalistic position (1750, 1754), which some writers say he did. See also, for Vega, the other authors we have cited on these matters.

20. Cited in Capéran, *Problème du salut des infidèles*, 260. "In sum," writes Urdanoz with regard to Cano, "for first salvation an embryonic faith suffices, while for second salvation the fullness of revelation or knowledge of the gospel, as a means of divine institution, is required" (Urdanoz, "Necesidad de fe," 536).

21. Urdanoz says, trenchantly and straight out, that the opinion of both of these theologians present at Trent "altogether clearly is at odds with the teachings of the Council. But they had to retreat in the face of bitter criticism on the part of a powerful and tenacious adversary, Melchior Cano, to whom falls the glory of having brought it about that among the theologians of Salamanca such novelties were definitively abandoned" (Urdanoz, "Necesidad de fe," 529). But the truth is that none of them thought that salvation was possible without grace (possible by a merely natural act). They did believe that

supernatural assistance could not be lacking to persons invincibly ignorant of Christian truths.

22. Queraltó Moreno says that such a rigid soteriological position on the part of Las Casas would be out of the question — indeed he also cites a text of Las Casas that he regards as mitigating this rigorism — inasmuch as "not even Ginés de Sepúlveda himself affiliated himself with this extremist theory: the Cordovan accepted the salvation of unbelievers who would comply with natural laws and rights" (R. J. Queraltó Moreno, *El pensamiento filosófico-político de Bartolomé de Las Casas,* 380).

23. This letter, dated 1554, is reproduced in A. Losada, *Epistolario,* 233–37.

24. In that work, he says in his letter, "I have touched on this question in passing" (ibid., 224).

25. And thus absent as well from the edition of the *Demócrates* published by M. Menéndez Pelayo in 1892 (see A. Losada, "Introducción" to the *Demócrates,* xxvi–xxxii). T. Andrés Marcos believes, rightly, that this long digression on the salvation of pagans is somewhat out of place (cited by Losada, in the *Demócrates,* 47 n. 44). Very probably the passage was added after the Valladolid disputation.

26. The objectant is referring to the second part of the document, *Proposiciones temerarias,* 564, dated 1571, shortly before Sepúlveda's death. In a surely earlier text he had said, in justification of the subjugation, that "all infidels have need [of preaching], since none of them can be saved without faith in Christ" (Letter [Hanke], 383).

27. "For fourteen hundred years — at least as far as I know — there has been no trace of this thesis in either the Holy Fathers or the scholastic doctors. All of them unanimously deny that anyone can be saved without explicit faith in Christ." According to this, the problem arises (and this is historically incorrect) with the Indies. In this case, his experience in the Indies did not show him the need to nuance, at least, what the dominant theology of his time maintained.

28. "Especially," he continues, "because I claim to have a special attachment to the Indians' cause."

29. Acosta's criticism is not directed only against Soto and Vega, but includes Vitoria's distinction between a "first" and "second" salvation as well. Indeed, it seems to him, not without reason, that Vitoria, while thereupon at once attaching the possibility of salvation to explicit faith in Christ, in some sense opens the door to the positions of Soto and Vega.

30. This would mean that they had been taught the faith. In the Indians' case this seems impossible without a miracle. "What shall we do," he writes, "with the countless thousands of persons who have not possibly heard the gospel? Shall we judge that *none* of them can be saved? Far from it! But without a miracle, they cannot have been instructed in the faith!"

31. All of the texts quoted come from the *De Procuranda Indorum Salute,* bk. 5, chs. 3, 4; emphasis added. Acosta may have taken his rigoristic position partly because of his reaction to the theses maintained by Francisco de la Cruz (in whose proceedings at the hands of the Inquisition in Lima he participated), which he connects too closely with that of the great theologians

he mentions. Jesuit historian F. Mateos is correct when he says that, on this point, "perhaps...his pen got a little bit out of control" (F. Mateos, "Ecos de América en Trento," 587).

32. Denzinger, no. 1646. "Indeed, faith requires it to be maintained that outside the Roman Catholic Church no one can be saved; that it is the sole ark of salvation; that anyone who has not entered it will perish in the flood. Nevertheless, it must also be held as certain that those who suffer invincible ignorance of the true religion are guilty of no fault in the eyes of the Lord. Now, who will be so arrogant as to claim to be able to indicate the boundaries of this ignorance, seeing the reason and variety of peoples, regions, characters, and so many other circumstances? Truly, once freed from these corporeal bands, when we see God as he is (1 John 3:2), we shall surely understand how closely and beautifully connected are the divine mercy and justice" (Denzinger, no. 1637).

33. Paul VI uses the image of concentric circles around the church. The first, the wider circle, "whose limits are further than we can see, merges with the horizon, and are the boundaries that bind humanity as such to the world." Its values are appreciated, the necessity is recognized of a dialogue with it concerning salvation (*Ecclesiam Suam*, no. 101; see also nos. 102–9). The second and third circles embrace, respectively, the non-Christian religions and the other Christian churches. In both, the presence of God's salvific activity is recognized (see nos. 110–16).

34. "Nor does divine Providence deny the help necessary for salvation to those who, without blame on their part, have not yet arrived at an explicit knowledge of God, but who strive to live a good life, thanks to His grace" (*Lumen Gentium*, no. 16).

35. According to Thomas Aquinas, in whom Las Casas takes his inspiration in this matter (see *Tratado comprobatorio*, 1552, *O.E.* 5:352b), predestination is a part of divine providence, and the latter is respectful of human freedom (see *Summa Theologiae*, Prima Pars, q. 23). Thomas's concept is very different from the "double predestination" that we find, for example, in Calvin. "By predestination," writes this theologian, "God has ordered some to salvation and has assigned others to eternal damnation." God would have created the latter "to be instruments of His wrath, and examples of His severity. In order to cause them to arrive at their end, either He deprives them of the opportunity to hear the Word, or by the preaching of the Word He blinds and hardens them still more" (*Institutes of the Christian Religion*, bk. 3, ch. 21, no. 5; ch. 24, no. 12). On the function of the doctrine of predestination in Calvin's theology, see E. Fuchs, *La morale selon Calvin*, 26–39.

36. One of his sources on these points is the *De Vocatione Omnium Gentium*, a book attributed at that time to Ambrose of Milan. This work contains a considerably broader doctrine on the matter of the salvation of unbelievers.

37. In defense of the Caribs (even on the supposition that they practiced cannibalism), he says that we "must not look on them with contempt, inasmuch as divine Providence may have predestined *many of them*, and very many, that it intends ultimately to save" (*A.H.*, ch. 205, *O.E.* 4:245b; emphasis added). Even in this case, seemingly extreme.

38. Theology has always posed itself the question of the moment of the Incarnation. *Cur Tam Sero?* ("Why So Late?") asked Diognetus in the third century. Why at this time and not another? As we might expect, there was no definitive answer to the question. The most that could be done was to adduce reasons of "appropriateness," which reflected a particular way of understanding human history.

39. Gonzalo Fernández de Oviedo, *Historia general y natural de las Indias,* 111b. He continues with the following contemptuous reflections on the inhabitants of these lands. "These Indians for the most part are anything but willing to listen to the Catholic faith. It is like banging on cold iron to imagine that they could become Christians in the foreseeable future. And this is what they have gotten into their heads — or rather skulls, since they do not have heads as other people, but such thick, hard skulls that the best procedure for Christians to follow in doing battle with them when it comes to hand-to-hand combat is not to strike them on the head, or you will break your sword. And just as they have a heavy skull, so they have a beastly, recalcitrant understanding" (ibid.).

40. "Whence it necessarily follows," he declares, "that they are endowed with a good understanding. And Gonzalo [F]ernández de Oviedo was altogether confused on this point: he never dealt with the Indians nor concerned himself for a single moment with anything that had to do with the Indians, except to send them and use them as if they had been animals" (*H.I.,* bk. 3, ch. 145, *O.E.* 2:526b).

41. "As for the lies the Indians told Christians, and still tell where they have not yet been crushed and subjugated, the reason for these is the harassment, horrible servitude, and cruel tyranny with which whey are afflicted and mistreated." By their lies they defend themselves from their oppressors, since "otherwise, without lying and pretending, in order to content them and to placate their constant, implacable fury, they cannot escape a thousand other afflictions, sufferings, and abuses" (ibid., *O.E.* 2:527a).

42. "And here they also have experience of the numberless lies of the Spaniards, who have never kept faith with them when making a promise, nor ever told them the truth. The Indians have striking ways of putting things in speech." Then, by way of exemplifying one of these striking ways, Bartolomé recounts the following stinging anecdote, which turns the Iberians' accusation back on themselves: "Upon some Spaniards' asking the Indians if they were Christians, one of them responded, 'Yes, sir, I'm a little bit Christian; I can lie some now. Some day I'll be able to lie a lot; then I'll be a lot Christian.'" These "bad examples have miserably defamed and sullied our faith and Christian religion," comments Friar Bartolomé.

43. "As for many of them having committed suicide, he is correct. But that this has been for their amusement, obviously this is wishful thinking on his part. As I have said, the fact that they have stabbed themselves in the heart with poisoned arrows and those around them as well — thereby manifesting [their oppressors'] horrible, insufferable, abominable cruelty and tyranny — the fact that a people so mild and patient, whose suffering surely exceeds that of all other mortals, [has done so] has been in order to emerge from [that

suffering] and escape it. They have chosen to slay themselves as the lesser evil." And he adds: "By way of proof, let Oviedo answer whether he has ever heard that, before the Spaniards came into these lands and oppressed these people, and perpetrated such impieties upon and among them, any had 'slain themselves for amusement' " (ibid., *O.E.* 2:527a–b). On the frightful subject of the Indians' suicide (something unknown by them before contact with the Europeans, as Friar Bartolomé has just recalled), a contemporary historian says that it was actually a way of repelling the European oppressor. It was "a collective hunger strike, a sit-down strike, a revolutionary strike. It was even more; it was a biological strike required by nature, even without the knowledge of those whose laws of the rhythm of life were broken by the imposition of vice, one's own or another's" (Fernando Ortiz, *Historia de la arqueología indocubana,* quoted by J. Oliva del Coll, *La resistencia indígena ante la Conquista,* 39).

44. Oviedo, *Historia general y natural,* 168–69. (The texts that we quote from this author are faithfully reproduced by Las Casas, *H.I.,* bk. 3, ch. 143, *O.E.* 2:522b, 523a.) The Indians' death as their punishment from God is an important idea for Oviedo, as can be seen from another text: "In the third book of this Natural History" — in which Oviedo treats of the conquest of Hispaniola — "some causes have been expressed for the disappearance and death of the Indians of this isle of Hispaniola, and some of the same material has been repeated further on as well, in the first chapter of the fourth book, in speaking of the quality of these Indians. And for a better understanding of the fact that this blame and punishment is principally founded on the transgressions and abominable customs and rites of this people, something about them and their defects will be said in this fifth book" (Oviedo, *Historia general y natural,* 111a).

45. He reminds his adversary that many other peoples were idolaters and even "ate human flesh," but were not on that account "scorned by God," nor did the apostles and their successors "conceive any loathing for them or, like Señor Oviedo, despair of their conversion and salvation" (*H.I.,* bk. 3, ch. 143, *O.E.* 2:523b).

46. In his foreword to the *Historia de las Indias,* for example, Bartolomé writes with pride: "By God's grace, in the things of the faith what nation, generally speaking, will easily be seen to take precedence over Spain?" (1:13a). Then in sorrowful tones he will say that one of the reasons for his having written his history is "to deliver *my* Spanish nation from the most grave and pernicious error and deception" of a failure to accord the Indians' human dignity due acknowledgment (1:15b; emphasis added).

47. Las Casas recounts: A Franciscan friar was seeking to persuade Cacique Hatuey to become a Christian before he died. The latter asked "why one must be like the Christians, who were wicked. The Father replied, 'Because those who die Christian go to heaven, ever to behold the face of God, and take their ease and enjoyment.' [Hatuey] inquired once more whether Christians went to heaven: the Father said yes, those who were good did. The other finally said he had no wish to go there, since they [the Christians] went there, and were there. This occurred at a moment when it had been decided to burn

him alive, so then they extended him over a slow fire and burned him alive" (*H.I.*, bk. 2, ch. 25, *O.E.* 2:236a).

48. See below, our chapter 13.

49. On this parable see Gustavo Gutiérrez, *The God of Life*, 114–15.

50. "Impassioned with truth," Latourelle calls him (R. Latourelle, *Théologie de la Révélation*, 136).

51. Tertullian, *Apologeticum*, ch. 46, nos. 2–4.

52. Ibid., ch. 17, nos. 1–4 (pp. 107, 109; emphasis added).

53. Ibid., ch. 47, no. 2 (p. 255).

54. On Tertullian's doctrine in this and related matters, the reader may consult G. Guignebert, *Tertullien: Etude de ses sentiments à l'égard de l'empire et de la société civile*; P. Monceaux, *Histoire littéraire de l'Afrique chrétienne*, vol. 1/1; J. M. Horms, "Etude sur la pensée politique de Tertullien"; E. T. Menil, "Tertullian and Pliny's Persecution of Christians."

55. *De Institutionibus Divinis*, ch. 4, nos. 6, 9. The Alexandrian school had insisted: As the Law had led the Jews, philosophy was leading the pagans to Christ. According to Capéran, "No one has emphasized more insistently than Lactantius the means employed by God to supply all persons (at the heart of paganism itself) a kind of independent revelation" (L. Capéran, *Le problème du salut des infidèles: Essai historique*, 74).

56. "Where no preacher has come, the sound and bruit of his voice have always arrived, as in the past the rumor of the miracles wrought in Egypt came to the ears of all nations: witness Rahab the courtesan" (St. Ambrose, *In Rom.*, ch. 10, nos. 17–18, *PL* 18:146b).

57. Ibid., ch. 2, no. 16, *PL* 17:68–69. See other texts in this sense in Capéran, *Problème du salut des infidèles*, vol. 1.

58. *Epist.* 93, 5, 5; *Retract.* 2, 5.

59. This short but extremely interesting work has been the object of a complexity of interpretations. It seems to us that, in the first chapters (the core of the composition), he offers a balanced, broad doctrine on the question of salvation, based on an exegesis of the gospel text, "Many are called but few are chosen."

60. The Council of Trent, whose concern was with the Protestant Reform, did not take up new challenges, nor did it keep account of other problems of human nature and evangelization posed in the Indies. Spanish authorities undertook initiatives with Rome to obtain a papal brief dispensing bishops of the Indies from assisting at the Council. Nevertheless, the bishop of Popayán, Juan del Valle, set out for Trent with the intent of arousing interest in these matters there. However, he died en route. The Indian peoples of the New World were unable to rap on the Council doors. See P. de Leturia, "Perchè la nascente Chiesa ispano-americana non fu rappresentata a Trento"; Mateos, "Ecos de América en Trento" (echos of America at Trent were actually very faint, despite the presence, which Mateos demonstrates, of various individuals who were familiar with the Indies); C. Bayle travels in the opposite direction and inquires into the echos — numerous, this time — of Trent in America: "El concilio de Trento en las Indias españolas."

61. Lamennais, *Essai sur l'indifférence*, 3:29, 62, 256–57.

62. Ibid., 4:59.

63. Ibid., _O.E._ 2:483–84. Here Lamennais appeals to the testimony of Church Fathers Irenaeus and Justin and of course to Tertullian's celebrated text on the "soul naturally Christian" (Lamennais, _Essai sur l'indifférence,_ 4:460ff.).

64. Lamennais, _Essai sur l'indifférence,_ 4:498–99. For Lamennais, Christianity perfects and fulfills all of the virtues familiar to universal tradition. Lacordaire perceived clearly the consequences of those ideas on the manner of interpreting the church's mission; see _Considérations sur le système philosophique de M. de Lamennais._ About the Lamennais work, see L. Le Guillou, _L'évolution de la pensée religieuse de Félicité Lamennais._

65. Santos Hernández criticizes Lamennais's attempt to conclude "that salvation can be attained by human beings _equally,_ within the Catholic Church as without,...by following the salvific truths of universal reason" (Santos Hernández, _Salvación y paganismo,_ 486; emphasis in the original.

66. _Bull. Rom. cont.,_ 8:53.

67. In his first encyclical, Pius VIII (d. 1830) censures the defenders of freedom of conscience, calling them "the sophists of this century, who pretend that the _door of salvation_ is open to all religions alike, thereby heaping the same praise on both truth and error." For the entire passage, see Artaud de Montor, _Histoire du pontificat du Pape Pie VIII,_ 67–68.

68. Gregory XVI, _Mirari Vos,_ no. 697.

69. This is what the bishops and theologians of the so-called Coetus Internationalis Patrum ("International Group of [Council] Fathers") maintained. In a long document distributed at the beginning of Vatican II's fourth session, they conclude that that attitude leads to two errors in the preparatory schema on religions freedom: a purely juridical focus on the problem (forgetting the doctrinal aspects at stake) and a rejection of the competency of civil authority (apropos of the duty of rulers, which we have already seen) in the area of the protection and service of religious truth.

70. The text seems to have been redacted by Yves M.-J. Congar, within the terms of the _quaesitum_ approved in the conciliar aula on September 21, 1965.

71. This sentence was the fruit of a compromise. It entered the text, without explanation, in the fifth preparatory schema.

72. See Gutiérrez, "Tres comentarios a la declaración sobre la libertad religiosa."

73. Message of John Paul II to the Twenty-Fifth World Day for Peace (December 8, 1991), nos. 7, 8; emphasis in the original.

Introduction to Part Four

1. Las Casas reports this episode in his _Historia,_ chs. 134–37. M. Giménez Fernández, _Bartolomé de Las Casas: Capellán,_ 309–16, thinks that the royal preachers' initiative had no practical consequences of any importance.

2. Höffner observes that, unlike in the case of the wars, none of the Spanish scholastics "forthrightly raised his voice against [Indian] slavery or the _encomiendas,_ as, for example, Las Casas did" (J. Höffner, _La ética colonial,_ 482).

Chapter 10: The Trouble Is in the System

1. See the draft of his letter to Domingo de Soto. There, as a criterion for "distinguishing . . . among the various reports" being sent to the king from the Indies, he proposes "a consideration of the motives of each of them," and of the identity of the "promoters" [*movedores*] of these dispatches. The purpose will be to learn whether they are sending them "to deliver captives, . . . or to flay persons alive — or should we say," he adds drastically, "to kick the dirt over the flaying victim's blood to cover it up" (in M. Bataillon, *Estudios sobre Bartolomé de Las Casas*, 262).

2. See, among other works, those of Lewis Hanke, J. Manzano, and J. Pérez de Tudela. One of the main sources is Las Casas's *Historia de las Indias*. The basic elements in his version are corroborated by other documents of the era.

3. The work containing the passage is Thomas Aquinas's *De Regimine Principum*, which, beginning with bk. 2, ch. 5, is in fact from the pen of Tolomeo de Luca.

4. On the contrary, says Licentiate Gregorio, "seeing that these Indians are very vicious, and infected with serious vices, and are a slothful people having no inclination to or application of virtue or goodness, justly may Your Highness hold them in servitude as You do."

5. Gregorio must deal with a difficulty: The Indians have been proclaimed free by Queen Isabella, in the face of Columbus's first attempts to enslave them. Unintimidated, Gregorio interprets this intervention as follows. "Her intention has always been to declare that they are not servants who might be sold or who might own no property. But in her disposition and order that they serve Christians, she has sought to place them in a qualified servitude like the one at hand, which suited them, since complete freedom worked to their detriment." They could not be sold and bought, but they could indeed be made to toil like slaves, which, after all, was what was important. That "detrimental" complete freedom will constitute precisely the objective of Bartolomé's strivings.

6. Bartolomé de Las Casas summarizes, without transcribing them literally as he does in the case of Licentiate Gregorio, Bernardo de Mesa's ideas. Friar Bartolomé's rebuttal of Mesa's theses is lengthy and it will not be to our purpose to detail it here. For us the only important thing is that his rebuttal opens with a declaration that his confrere has credited only the slanders of the Antillean colonists: Mesa himself "had never seen a single Indian" (*H.I.*, bk. 3, ch. 10, *O.E.* 2:191b). Bartolomé's critique of Licentiate Gregorio is more brief, as he refers to his (foregoing) criticism of Mesa.

7. Matías de Paz, *Del dominio de los Reyes sobre los indios*, 223.

8. Ibid. (emphasis added). For now, let us leave aside the clause "once converted to the faith." In his commentary on these passages, Friar Bartolomé will say that Paz "has condemned the manner in which the Indians are being used: [he condemns] a 'distribution' as despotic and appropriate only with slaves — which is indeed what this distribution was — and consequently he has condemned this very distribution" (*H.I.*, bk. 3, ch. 8, *O.E.* 2:188a).

9. Ibid.; emphasis added.

10. As legal scholar García Gallo says: "The Burgos *Junta* has the effect rather of consolidating the earlier system than of introducing substantial changes in Indian policy" (A. García Gallo, "Génesis y desarrollo del Derecho Indiano," xxxvi).

11. The reader may consult the text of the Burgos Laws, in R. Altamira's authorized edition: "El texto de las leyes de Burgos de 1512," and in *Libro Anual*, 1974, 183–200. Shortly after, in Valladolid (July 1513), due to the intervention of Friar Pedro de Córdoba, certain points were added and specified which "in substance modified nothing," according to Pérez de Tudela, "Significado histórico," xxxvi.

12. At this early moment in the colonization of the Indies, Las Casas believes that the false information dispatched to the Court by interested parties was decisive for the handing down of these norms. And so he says, "They were not the King's laws" (*H.I.*, bk. 3, ch. 13, *O.E.* 2:201b). His attitude toward the royal responsibility will change when he deems that his sovereigns have this excuse no longer. In the matter of the *encomiendas*, however, he will persist in his assertion that the powerful in the Indies have always played a decisive role in the position of the Crown (see *Doce dudas*, 1564, *O.E.* 5:313–15). In Bartolomé's eyes, from the outset Nicolás de Ovando went beyond his royal mandate (see *Octavo remedio*, 1542, *O.E.* 5:100a).

13. Las Casas continues: "... not realizing that the root of the mortal plague that was slaying the Indians and preventing them from being taught about and coming to know their true God, was that the Spaniards had them in distribution" (*H.I.*, bk. 3, ch. 13, *O.E.* 2:201a).

14. And Bartolomé goes on the counterattack, writing apropos of the allegation that the Indians have vices: "Would that it had pleased God that the Spaniards did not have worse ones — apart from the faith, which for that matter they defamed among [the Indians] by their wicked lives and utterly corrupt example and offended God more through these [vices] and through their sloth than did the Indians they were so falsely and perniciously maligning" (*H.I.*, bk. 3, ch. 14, *O.E.* 2:204a).

15. The Prologue to the Burgos Laws referred to the ordinances that the sovereigns and the high officials of the Indies had issued in seeming behalf of a knowledge of the faith. Las Casas does not beat around the bush. He writes: "The ordinances of the second Admiral, Don Diego Colón, and the officials were handed down to no other purpose than that of furthering the tyrannical slavery that had been sown and had taken root, in which these unfortunate people were daily destroyed without anyone commiserating with them or their perdition, but looking only to the loss of temporal profit their deaths involved" (*H.I.*, bk. 3, ch. 14, *O.E.* 2:203b).

16. "We have already said above and do certify," he declares, "that in the places so indicated there was by that time no more real intent to teach these people the things of faith or of their salvation than if they had been dogs or cats." And he adds sorrowfully that, since neither did the few religious present there "have this care, the Indians were left without any spiritual remedy." Las Casas likewise points to the responsibility of the Council in this. "Let us notice another thing here: the blindness of the King's Councilors and

of the theologians who joined them in their deliberations — all the more inasmuch that they never stopped to notice that what they assumed as true was nothing but a wicked lie, namely, that the Spaniards had any care for the instruction of Indians" (ibid., *O.E.* 2:203b–204a).

17. The Council's responsibility becomes more serious still. Bartolomé de Las Casas shows that, entirely apart from the favors they received from the colonists, the members of the Council received huge benefits from the king based on the dispositions to which they themselves had contributed. One of the principal beneficiaries here was Juan de Fonseca, bishop of Palencia. "This Lord Bishop," writes Las Casas, "had eight hundred Indians — two hundred on each of these four islands, Hispaniola, Cuba, San Juan, and Jamaica. Secretary López Concillos had twelve hundred, we had heard." And so it went, although to a lesser degree with others, or frequently merely as the superior of those actually holding Indians (as we see, an *encomienda* or distribution is transferable), but this, Bartolomé observes, "has never occurred to Licentiate Santiago or Doctor Palacios Rubios." Las Casas ends on this painful, perceptive note, which shows the cruelty of the situation: "And so the sorrowful Indians, with their anguish, toil, and sweat, were part of the salaries paid" (*H.I.*, bk. 3, ch. 19, *O.E.* 2:216–17). The natives have been transformed into money and currency. These data, which the Dominican furnishes — as with so much else of the same kind that appears as one goes on studying the texts of the time — are corroborated by an "act of distribution made in 1514 by Rodrigo de Albuquerque and Treasurer Miguel de Pasamonte" (see *DII* 1:5–236). Pérez de Tudela's comment on the Burgos Laws is correct and in historical perspective: "Surely the circumstances and the debate from which they arose can be interpreted only in the general framework of daring experimental attempts to resolve the all but unheard-of problem of meshing two societies that had lived apart for centuries. But what strikes us in the concrete outcome is the consecration in the Court of that flux that we have described as gradual depravation; and the implacable Las Casas, who could sniff putrefaction a mile off, knew very well what he was saying when he indicted the Council as lying and treacherous" (Pérez de Tudela, "Significado histórico," xxxvii).

18. The judgment of contemporary historians is also critical of the laws examined. Zavala holds it that these maintained the *encomiendas* "in their condition of labor camps" and concludes from this that "the Burgos stage, on legal terrain, was not very favorable to the Indians" (S. Zavala, *La encomienda indiana*, 23, 24). Altamira thinks these laws were a "notorious rout of the Dominicans" ("Texto de las leyes de Burgos," 67–68). "Utter failure for Montesino's Dominicans," Arranz calls them, and furthermore considers that, after Burgos, "the *encomienda* is finally confirmed and consolidated" (F. Arranz, "Alonso del Espinar, O.F.M," 646). This is not to deny that there was one point or another, formally, at least, that sought to limit abuses (serious enough to be acknowledged as such in the mentality of the time) against the Indians (for example, Law XXIV prohibits the scourging of the Indians and calling them "dogs," which is saying, incidentally, that this is what was done). Perhaps it is on this account that Friede actually speaks of a prona-

tive mentality on the part of the Crown in these dispositions (see J. Friede, *Bartolomé de Las Casas: Precursor,* 34). However, the overall historical judgment must be negative, because the Laws maintain the structural causes of those abuses. In view of all of this, it is evident that what is so frequently said of this period does not apply to the Burgos Laws: The laws are good, it is only that they are not observed (on this notion, see B. Keen, "The White Legend Revisited," 341–42).

19. Here is the text: "The remedy, my Lords, for this isle and the others around it is altogether clear and has been most carefully thought out here. Everyone knows it, and it is: that the Indians be set free, and withdrawn from the power of the Christians, since they are still suffering cruel tyranny, which is what has so completely devastated these islands, and that they be moved to villages of their own choosing, so that they may in some degree live together and take their rest, without having to pay any tribute, since they have already paid tribute to overflowing, with their sweat" (*O.E.* 5:54b).

20. A good summary of this Lascasian treatise will be found in J. A. de la Torre, *El uso alternativo del derecho,* 138–44.

21. Even Acosta acknowledges evangelization to be "a task and charge that the *encomenderos* themselves rarely understand" and adds that in failing to fulfill this obligation they "commit a serious crime, for which the punishment is eternal damnation" (José de Acosta, *De Procuranda Indorum Salute,* bk. 3, ch. 12, p. 473).

22. This being the case, continues Las Casas in the document he addresses to the emperor, anyone who would place someone in this kind of danger "would beyond any doubt commit a great mortal sin, since no one has the right to place another at risk of bodily death — and still less that of the soul" (*O.E.* 5:89b). This is what occurs when the *encomiendas* are bestowed, and it would be well for the emperor to keep it in mind.

23. The classic work on the subject is, as we know, Zavala's monumental *La encomienda indiana.*

24. See John Paul II, "Inaugural Discourse at Puebla" (III, 3), and Puebla Final Document, nos. 1136, 1160, 1264.

25. No one today questions the center-stage role played by Las Casas in the working out of the New Laws (nor indeed did his contemporaries doubt that contribution). Some have tried to deny it because otherwise they would have to admit two things that they were determined to deny in Las Casas: his effective practical sense (they would rather disqualify him as a dreamer in comparison with the achievements of hundreds of his contemporaries, more mincing in their denunciations), and an accomplishment of which Spain can be proud today. But there are still those who regard the New Laws as unrealistic and inapplicable in their day. See I. Pérez Fernández's documented article, "Fray Bartolomé de Las Casas en torno a las leyes nuevas de Indias." Helen Parish has announced (in a personal communication) the discovery of a document that would endorse the Lascasian inspiration of these laws. Isacio Pérez is working on this text.

26. See below, our chapter 11.

27. See the text of the New Laws in J. de la Peña, *De Bello Contra Insu-*

lanos, 102–19. It is interesting to consult I. Pérez Fernández's article, "Primera edición desconocida de las 'Leyes Nuevas' de 1542: Promovidas por Fray Bartolomé de Las Casas."

28. Las Casas harbors few illusions regarding the repercussions in the Indies of the legal norms now in force. Years before he had written: "The King's letters have little effect here, other than those that serve one's own interests" (*Carta a un personaje,* 1535, *O.E.* 5:67a). The power-holders in the Indies observed them if they did not run counter to their privileges. Nevertheless, Las Casas now fought for new laws at the same time as he looks for mechanisms to make them operative.

29. See Enrique Dussel, *El episcopado latinoamericano y la liberación de los pobres (1504–1620),* 60, which has a list of the bishops appointed at this time (61).

30. Shortly before he had declined the offer of the episcopal see of Cuzco (see A. de Remesal, *Historia general de las Indias Occidentales,* 2:108). The see of Chiapa enabled him, among other things, to encourage the Verapaz experiment and to keep in closer contact with Spain, across the waters (see the documented study by Helen Parish, *Las Casas, Obispo,* especially xxxi–xl). On the other hand, it is not beyond the realm of possibility that this nomination was offered to him to distance him from the Court.

31. Charles V, in his *Provisión* issued from Mechlin, October 20, 1545, decrees, with respect to ch. 30 of the New Laws: "We have agreed to revoke this law and to issue upon it this my Provision in the said consideration, whereby do we revoke and render null, void, and without effect the said chapter and law heretofore incorporated, and reduce the whole to that point and state in which it stood previously, at the moment when the said law was handed down" (in E. Schäffer, *El Consejo Real y Supremo de las Indias,* 2:280).

32. We have already stated that the New Laws failed to satisfy all of Las Casas's aspirations. Pérez de Tudela calls the outcome a "partial triumph" and consequently a "partial failure" (Pérez de Tudela, "Significado histórico," cli). To this Pérez Fernández answers that in a dynamic, historical perspective, one should rather have to speak of an "almost complete triumph, and minimal failure" (Pérez Fernández, "Bartolomé de Las Casas en torno a las leyes nuevas," 455). Pérez Fernández cites with satisfaction Las Casas's dogged efforts in behalf of the application of the laws that had not been revoked or palliated and invokes these efforts in support of his positive judgment (see, e.g., his "El 'tiempo dorado' de la primera evangelización de América," 288–90).

33. To this purpose, Bartolomé sets forth the *modus procedendi* in detail. The respective viceroys will receive "documents with unfilled blanks," by which the *encomenderos* will be apprised of the royal desire to "consult them, or be informed that it will be to his service to speak with them. Thus, now one and the next day another, each will set sail, while still another is handed the royal order, in such a way that within two or three months half of them, or even all, will have left for Spain, each without knowing of the others' departure. Once they have arrived at Court, Your Majesty will communicate Your proposal to them, [one by one,] until all have come [to Spain] and left

these lands — at which point they will be told that it is not Your wish that they return to the Indies" (*O.E.* 5:127b, 131ab, 132b). It would be difficult to be more precise! The letter is considered to have been signed by Friar Rodrigo de Ladrada as well. The date of its composition is disputed: Pérez de Tudela (in his edition of Las Casas's *opuscula*, *O.E.* 5:xiii) and Pérez Fernández (*Inventario*, 314) think it was written in 1542. Wagner and Parish, in their *The Life and Writings of Bartolomé de Las Casas*, agree, but think that it might have to be dated shortly after the turn of the year 1553. Friede dates it 1544: in this case, the text he calls the "ultra-characteristic document of the Lascasian policy" (Friede, *Bartolomé de Las Casas: Precursor*, 147 n. 7) would have been sent *after* the promulgation of the New Laws, and thus, according to the Colombian historian, would have had no effect on them.

34. It is often pointed out, for example, that this is the moment at which a third stage in the life of Bartolomé de Las Casas begins. Friede even labels it a "new conversion" (Friede, *Bartolomé de Las Casas: Precursor*, 161), reckoning the "first conversion" as the one Bartolomé undergoes in 1514, as is often done (a conclusion that we have not followed), and the second at the end of the 1530s (others place it at the moment when he decides to become a Dominican).

35. V. Abril Castelló ("La bipolarización") thinks that the Valladolid disputation with Sepúlveda (1550–51) played a decisive role. He does not mean to deny that the ideas set forth in the Twelfth Reply, whose interest is underscored by the brilliant article just cited, had not been ruminating for some years. We shall return to this point in chapter 13.

36. One of them was held in Valladolid in 1550. The occasion was the arrival in Spain in the hands of Jerónimo de Aliaga of a tempting proposal from the *encomenderos* of Peru. Participating in the meeting were experts from this viceroyalty, Dominican Tomás de San Martín, Pedro de la Gasca, and Las Casas, all of whom opposed the perpetuity. Also assisting was Vasco de Quiroga, who voted in favor.

37. As we have already observed, the representatives of the *encomenderos* of Peru had an important role in this matter. See M. Goldwert, "La lucha por la perpetuidad"; L. Pereña, "La pretensión a la perpetuidad de las encomiendas del Perú"; H. Someda, "Fray Bartolomé de Las Casas y el problema de la perpetuidad de la encomienda en el Perú"; M. Belaúnde Guinassi, *La encomienda en el Perú*. H. López Martínez, *Diego Centeno y la rebelión de los encomenderos*, and especially, Efraín Trelles, *Lucas Martínez Vegazo: Funcionamiento de una encomienda peruana inicial*, have described the Peruvian experience of this particular moment.

38. The idea of the perpetuity of the *encomienda* was actually mooted at the time of the Hieronymites of Hispaniola (see Zavala, *La encomienda indiana*, 29). See a series of dispatches favorable to the perpetuity dating from 1545 in *Carta Magna de los indios: Fuentes constitucionales* (1534–1609), 215–49.

39. The worst enemies of the evangelization of the Indians are those theoretically in charge of it: the *encomenderos*. Far from encouraging the work of evangelization, they actually refuse to admit friars onto their estates, Las Casas reports. They know that the situation of the natives there will spark a

"call for justice" on the Fathers' part. This is the reason why the *encomenderos* prevent them from entering, threaten them with death, and, in order to seem to be doing their duty, will "take some idiot cleric, give him a hundred or a hundred and fifty *castellanos* [and let *him* on their property, instead, to 'evangelize the Indians'] — precisely the type who, apart from the abominations he commits in openly selling the sacraments and a thousand other examples, will be the one who plunders [the Indians] the most cruelly, afflicting, frightening, and oppressing them in the name and office of a Father! 'Now, would it be a falsehood, Father,' asks Bartolomé in all feigned innocence, 'or a big sin, to call these *comenderos* by their true, actual name — 'tyrants'?" (*Carta a Carranza,* 1555, *O.E.* 5:436b). Las Casas often applies the appellation "tyrant" to the conquistadors and *encomenderos.*

40. Besides offering a gift of money, the two friars propose a series of reforms of the system of the *encomienda* (for example, not handing over any more Indian land to the Spaniards). Goldwert puts it this way: "The caciques of Peru, guided by two humanitarian reforms, are asking and are willing to pay for a genuine revolution" (Goldwert, "La lucha por la perpetuidad," 358). J.-B. Lassègue gives the context and shows the scope of the memorandum in question in his "En torno al Memorial del obispo fray Bartolomé de Las Casas y de fray Domingo de Santo Tomás (hacia 1560): Apuntes, sondeos, cuestiones."

41. Las Casas discusses this author's ideas in his disputation with Sepúlveda. His first contact seems to have been indirect. In the *Historia de las Indias* he mentions him in passing, and in a rather ironical tone, apropos of a disciple of his, the arrogant "doctor of Paris in theology," Don Carlos de Aragón, who happened to be in Hispaniola representing the bishop-elect of Concepción and la Vega. Many times, Bartolomé recounts, this "most solemn preacher" cited his master, "Joannes Maioris [John Major], in the pulpit, and in doing so lifted his zucchetto, saying with great reverence, 'This is what that fine Joannes Maioris says'" (*H.I.,* bk. 3, ch. 35, *O.E.* 2:258a–b). In the *Apología* Las Casas mentions this same fact in another tone. This time he specifies that one of the things this Don Carlos did was annul "a marriage between an Indian woman and Spanish man on the sole grounds that, being an Indian, she must be stupid and without the use of reason" (*Apología,* folio 237v). A more direct allusion is to be found in the *Tratado comprobatorio* (1552), where Las Casas refers to Major's key text on the subject of the Indies (his commentary on the second book of Peter Lombard's *Sentences,* d. 44, q. 3; see *Tratado comprobatorio, O.E.* 5:382).

42. "The first to occupy those lands," he writes, "has the legal right to govern the people who dwell there, since they are slaves by nature, as is clear. In the first book of the *Politics,* chapters the third and the fourth, the Philosopher says that there is no doubt but that some persons are by nature slaves and others free, and that this is most certainly to the advantage of the former. It is altogether just that some should command and others obey. And thus in empire, which is, as it were, connatural, one must command and accordingly dominate, and another obey" (quoted in P. Leturia, "Maior y Vitoria ante la conquista," 72).

43. The Teutonic knights had already used the "natural slaves" argument to justify the actions they undertook against the Lithuanian pagans. Paulus Vladimiri protested this (see Stanislas Belch, *Paulus Vladimiri and His Doctrine*).

44. The list of those who thought in this way would be immense. See the comprehensive treatments, Zavala, *Servidumbre natural y libertad cristiana según los tratadistas españoles de los siglos XVI y XVII*; J. Z. Vázquez, *La imagen del indio en el español del siglo XVI*; Hanke, *Aristotle and the American Indians;* idem, *All Mankind Is One*; A. Pagden, *The Fall of Natural Man.* In a sense favorable to Fernández de Oviedo, who is regarded as a detractor of the Indians, see G. Soria, *Fernández de Oviedo e il problema dell' indio.* C. del Arenal, "La teoría de la servidumbre natural en el pensamiento español de los siglos XVI and XVII," reviews the positions of the Spanish theologians of this era with a tendency, at times somewhat forced, to look for points of agreement among them. L. Gómez Canedo, "¿Hombres o bestias?" maintains that calling the Indians "beasts" or comparing them with animals (what he calls the "animalistic theory") does not mean doubting their ontological human condition; but he cannot deny (this is his conclusion) that they were regarded by many as inferior beings. And that is the question, of course.

45. See J. Comas, "La realidad del trato dado a los indígenas de América entre los siglos XV y XX." This concrete side of the question always concerned Las Casas, above and beyond the theoretical aspects, who maintained that on this level the Indians were treated like animals and called beasts and dogs (see *H.I.*, bk. 3, chs. 87 and 402, *O.E.* 2:375b, 394b; see also Bartolomé de Las Casas, *De Unico*, 136v–137, as well as the *Carta a un personaje*, 1535, *O.E.* 5:62b, and the *Doce dudas*, 1564, *O.E.* 5:485b).

46. Those of Mexico, in particular, were always very close to him and knew how to requite him generously (see Hanke, *Aristotle and the American Indians*, 76). Bartolomé was alert to the practical implications of the Sepulvedian theses, whose material, he said, is "to the taste of and agreeable to all those who desire and seek to become wealthy" by the "sweat, anguish, and even death of others" (*Aquí se contiene*, 1552, *O.E.* 5:294b).

47. In his *Politics*, bk. 1, especially chs. 3, 5. It would not be to our purpose to enter into the debate over Aristotle's exact position. See Bataillon, "Las Casas frente al pensamiento aristotélico sobre la esclavitud." One should also look at Thomas Aquinas's questionable commentary on these Aristotelian texts (see J. Höffner, *La ética colonial*, 90–91).

48. There is a discussion about whether or not by the expression *natura servus* we are to understand something essential, equivalent to *slaves* by nature. Hanke thinks that Sepúlveda's interpretation of Aristotle leads to an affirmative response. R. Quirk ("Some Notes on a Controversial Controversy") and J. A. Fernández-Santamaría ("Juan Ginés de Sepúlveda and the Indians") do not think so. It will be of no interest here to examine that question: in any case the human inferiority of the Indians is asserted, and this was enough for the practical effects sought by the argumentation. That is how Las Casas understood it, nor does he embark upon disquisitions upon

how to translate the Latin expression used by the Cordovan humanist. The way in which the latter refers to the dwellers of the Indies is sufficiently clear.

49. In his eighth objection he explicitly refers to Fernández de Oviedo (see *O.E.* 5:314a).

50. This last sentence is not found in the manuscript that Losada calls "A," and which he regards as chronologically the last (A. Losada, in his "Introducción" to the *Demócrates segundo*). That Sepúlveda would have eliminated this sentence in the final version does not change his basic opinion much. Some pages further on he writes: "Compare now these endowments of prudence, invention, magnanimity, temperance, humanity, and religion with those of these little persons in whom traces of humanity can scarcely be found" (Losada, "Introducción," 35). Several lines later he says that the Indians are "such cowards and so timid that they can scarcely abide the hostile presence of our [soldiers]" (Losada, "Introducción," 35). Therefore, the suppression of the comparison with monkeys in the text on which Losada's edition is based indicates no variation in his fundamental position.

51. This is the case with Losada in his various works and especially with Andrés Marcos (to whom Losada frequently refers). See T. Andrés Marcos, *Los imperialismos de Juan Ginés de Sepúlveda,* which acknowledges, nevertheless, that the argument for the existence of two classes of human beings "is most difficult to establish" (Andrés Marcos, *Los imperialismos,* 217).

52. Sepúlveda's partisans adduce the following text as proof of the humanist's moderation: "I maintain not that the barbarians ought to be reduced to slavery, but only that they ought to be subjected to our command. I do not maintain that we ought to deprive them of their goods, but only subject them, without committing against them acts of any injustice whatever. I do not maintain that we ought to abuse our dominion, but only that it is noble, gracious, and useful for them. Thus, first we ought to snatch from them their pagan customs and, afterwards, affably thrust them to the adoption of the Natural Law and, with this magnificent preparation for accepting the doctrine of Christ, draw them with apostolic mildness and words of charity to the Christian Religion" (Letter to Francisco Argote, n.d., in Losada, *Juan Ginés de Sepúlveda a través de su "Epistolario,"* 193). The text surely seems to attenuate assertions contained in the *Democrates* and the *Apología* (GS). But we already know that subjugation and the use of force meant something concrete in the Indies. Thus, even if we take this as Sepúlveda's final position, Las Casas's observations maintain their validity.

53. The contempt of Europeans for the population of the Indies was a very widespread phenomenon. Hugo Grotius (d. 1645), regarded as one of the founders of modern international law, shows himself a partisan of Innocent IV's harsh theses upon the infidels. By contrast with what Vitoria, Vásquez, and Molina say, in Grotius's mind a war to be waged on "barbarians" is "natural," since they are "wild animals rather than men," and "delinquent with regard to nature." They are often adherents of vicious religions representing a threat to humanity (see Höffner, *Etica colonial,* 366–67). Hanke cites testimonials of English missionaries and thinkers in North America (see Hanke, "Pope Paul III and the American Indians," 68 n. 11; idem,

Aristotle and the American Indians, 99–101). These examples and many others demonstrate that the Spanish and Portuguese mentality with respect to the Indians is part of a broader European context.

54. Vasco de Quiroga, "Información en derecho," 358. With an appeal to one of his favorite authors, John Gerson (d. 1428) — who in this case follows Aristotle closely — declares that the Indians have none of the forms of government that he considers good. Rather they have the three he labels "bad": tyranny, oligarchy, and democracy. "They have them all," Quiroga says. "None is missing, if I am not mistaken, and some have neither good [forms of government] nor bad" (Quiroga, "Información en derecho," 360).

55. Quiroga, "Información en derecho," 346, 367, 385. The occasion for this work is the royal order of 1534 abolishing the prohibition of enslaving the Indians. Quiroga does not question the principle of the lawfulness of slavery, but its application to the Indians (see P. Castañeda Delgado, *Don Vasco de Quiroga y su Información en Derecho,* 64–88).

56. These correspond to those barbarians to whom "Aristotle alludes when he writes that they may legitimately be hunted like animals and tamed by force." The reference is to the second class of human beings, in Major's and Sepúlveda's classification. In that category fall, he says, "the Caribs, Chunchos, Chiriguanas, Moxos, Iscaingas,... some of the Brazilian peoples, and those of almost the whole of Florida" (Acosta, *De Procuranda Indorum Salute,* bk. 3, ch. 12, p. 67). As we readily see, we are far from the "altogether rare" and exceptional cases of which Las Casas speaks (see below, in this same chapter).

57. The passages we cite are from Acosta's *De Procuranda Indorum Salute,* bk. 3, ch. 12, pp. 63–71. In Brazil, Manoel da Nóbrega, after a time of favorable regard of the Indians, severely questions their human capacities. The characters in his *Diálogo da conversão do gentio* call the Indians a "people without judgment," and doubt whether they are "human beings as are we" (cited in O. Beozzo, "O diálogo da conversão do gentio").

58. See ibid., bk. 2, ch. 5, pp. 283–85. Ordinarily a champion of decent treatment, he sometimes considers it important to use a heavy hand ("Reach for the rod, if need be.... If he balks, thrust him not with the sword in anger: prick him moderately," lest he return "to the vacuous traditions of his forebears" (ibid., bk. 1, ch. 7, pp. 141, 192). At the same time, Acosta firmly believes in the Indian's capacity for education. On these aspects of Acosta's book the reader may consult M. L. Rivera de Tuesta, *José de Acosta: Un humanista reformista,* 100–105; C. Braciero, "La promoción y evangelización del indio en el plan de José de Acosta."

59. As neither was there in Friar Jacobo de Testero (closer to Las Casas's positions), who as early as 1533 rebuts the thesis of natural servants, apropos of the attacks mounted by Domingo de Betanzos (see Parish, *Las Casas en México,* n. 59).

60. And they continued to be influential for a long time to come, although certain categories change. F. Barreda Laos, a liberal thinker with a mind open to the ideas of modernity, in his *Vida intelectual del Virreinato del Perú,* includes a chapter, very well informed for the time, on the dispute between

Las Casas and Sepúlveda. He praises the former for his defense of the Indian, but reproaches him for what he calls his "theological sociology," which "marches in the diametrically opposite direction from our scientific sociology" (Barreda Laos, *Vida intelectual,* 78). Las Casas's "sociology" starts with heaven and comes down to earth, while the modern version moves from earth to heaven. In this perspective, obviously, Barreda's judgment of the Indian will be very different from Las Casas's. The Indians, he writes, "have created for themselves a special morality, a system adapted to their vices, into which they enter with fanatic fervor.... Altruism? They have never heard of it. That sentiment... died amid the frosts of the Andean plateaus. Native communities exist and thrive because they offer the Indian an opportunity for a more comfortable, carefree, and routine life — not for love of sociability." The communities will disappear as the Indian becomes educated. Barreda believes in modern progress and sees no way to free the Indians from their vices but by extirpating "vicious, wicked institutions like these communities" (Barreda Laos, *Vida intelectual,* 47–48).

61. In the *Historia de las Indias,* confronted with Bishop Juan Cabedo's (or Quevedo) appeal to Aristotle in support of the thesis that some persons are born natural slaves, cleric (at the time) Las Casas had replied with annoyance: "The Philosopher was a gentile and is burning in hell. His doctrine is to be used to the extent that it is consonant with our holy faith and the practice of the Christian religion." The latter sentence represents a sound principle of theological methodology and is also found in the passage from the *Apología* upon which we are commenting. In the *Historia,* he adds — uncoupling Christianity from any particular culture as such — "Our Christian religion is equally adaptable to all of the nations of the world and accepts all of them equally" (*H.I.,* bk. 3, ch. 139, *O.E.* 2:536a). This is the fashion in which he addresses the relationship between the Christian faith and native cultures — one delivered from an ethnocentric outlook. (Let us note that the bishop of Darién is a more complex personage than we might think from the citation we make of him here. See the whole of Las Casas's account [*H.I.,* bk. 3, chs. 138–39, *O.E.* 2:532b–37a]; and Pérez de Tudela, "Significado histórico," xcvi–xcvii.) Today we have begun to call it "inculturation."

62. See H. Mechoulan, "A propos de la notion de barbare chez Las Casas," 179.

63. With irony Las Casas tells his adversary that his arguments ought to be applied to himself. "It seems to me," he writes, "that Sepúlveda must think that there are more prudent persons in Spain than he: thus, he will see that he is under obligation to submit to them, in conformity with the eternal law" (*Apología,* 36). Bartolomé is alluding to the fact that the Cordovan has appealed to the "eternal law" in requiring the Indians to submit to the Spaniards.

64. On this last point, see the suggestive articles of distinguished historians J. L. Abellán ("Los orígenes del mito del buen salvaje: Fray Bartolomé de Las Casas y su antropología utópica") and J. A. Maravall ("Utopía y primitivismo," especially 343–57). The latter actually calls Bartolomé "a Rousseau *avant la lettre*" (350).

65. The historical roots of this conception, of course, are very old. Accordingly, perhaps indeed we have found another area of convergence with the friar from Seville.

66. On the other hand, for Rousseau the human being's natural state is more than a historical stage of the past. It is a criterion of judgment upon and reconstruction of present society, by way of a recovery of the natural human values of equality and liberty. This is why the *social contract* is not at odds with what is set down in the *Discourse on the Origin of Inequality* (see E. Cassirer, *La philosophie des lumières,* 260–73; E. Bréhier, *Histoire de la Philosophie,* vol. 2: *La philosophie moderne,* 468–80).

67. Rather, the Indians could rightly and reasonably say that they have seen customs in the Iberians that would lead them to look upon the Spaniards as "most barbarous" — not of the second class, but "of the first, being so savage, rough, cruel, and abominable" (*A.H.,* ch. 264, *O.E.* 4:436b).

68. As the nineteenth century dawns, Alexander von Humboldt writes of Mexico that the natives very quickly lost their priests, their most cultivated echelons, and watched the destruction of many of their works of art and architecture. And Humboldt wonders, in the face of this beheading: "How can one judge from these miserable remains of what was once a mighty people a level of culture that had been in the making from the twelfth century to the sixteenth century, let alone judge the intellectual progress of which these people are capable? Suppose there were to be nothing left of the French nation, or the German, one day but the rural poor. Could it be seen, from their physiognomies, that they belonged to the peoples that produced such as Descartes...as Leibniz?" (Alexander von Humboldt, *Ensayo político sobre el Reino de la Nueva España,* quoted in Alejandro Lipschutz, *El problema racial en la conquista de América,* 231–32; this latter work is important for the point with which we are dealing).

69. Friede, "Las Casas y el movimiento indigenista en España y América en la primera mitad del siglo XVI"; idem, *Bartolomé de Las Casas: Precursor;* see also Dussel, "Núcleo simbólico lascasiano."

Chapter 11: Persons and Poor

1. We shall cite these texts in the version presented by Helen Parish in her translation of them in her enlightening *Las Casas en México.* The author has had the kindness to furnish us with the manuscript of this interesting work — definitive in so many respects — accompanied by valuable notes, as well as by a transcription and translation of numerous documents, some of which have never before been published. Las Casas reproduces the passages from *Sublimis Deus* and *Pastorale Officium* in his *De Unico* (they were added, according to Parish in her introduction to *The Only Way* and in her Textual Appendix 2, when the second version was composed in Mexico in 1539) and in his *Apología.* He also quotes a portion of the former of these two papal documents in his *Doce dudas,* 1564 (*O.E.* 5:490b).

2. Minaya was in Mexico, Nicaragua, and Peru. His memorandum to Philip II has been published in its entirety in V. Beltrán de Heredia, "Nuevos

datos acerca del P. Bernardino Minaya y del licenciado Calvo de Padilla, compañeros de Las Casas." Previously, lengthy extracts had been presented by Lewis Hanke in his classic article, "El Papa Paulo III y los indios de América." Friar Bernardino recounts that he first tried to win to the cause of "the capacity of the Indians to enter Christianity" Cardinal García de Loaysa, president of the Council of the Indies, but that the latter had replied that "he was deceived, that the Indians were no more than parrots."

3. Minaya does not speak of this letter in his memorandum, nor does he mention Las Casas, but his identity as the messenger who brought the document was known to old Dominican historians (see Dávila Padilla, *Historia de la provincia de Santiago de México*, 1596, ch. 43; and A. Remesal, *Historia general de las Indias Occidentales*). We have in addition a text of Minaya himself in which the matter is mentioned: a dedication in Latin to Cardinal Tomás Badia (a Dominican), which is reproduced and translated in Parish, *Las Casas en México*, Appendix 6; G. López de Lara, *Ideas tempranas*, 226–27, also has a translation of this dedication.

4. Doctor Bernal Díaz de Luco (a member of the Council of the Indies) introduced him to the empress, who gave him certain letters of introduction to be presented in Rome, one of them addressed to the pope, which refers to Minaya, although — curiously — it does not mention him by name. Parish presents these unpublished documents in Appendix 5 of *Las Casas en México*. Díaz de Luco's mediation is significant, as it is a matter of someone with whom Las Casas corresponded. On one occasion in Rome, through Cardinal Tomás Badia, Friar Bernardino managed to meet with Paul III. On his return to Spain, Emperor Charles V, unhappy with these texts and with his dispatch to the Indies, had Minaya detained for two years in prison or under house arrest, on the pretext of having him preach to the inmates of Valladolid Prison (see Hanke, "El Papa Paulo III y los indios," 77). De la Hera publishes the queen's letter to the provincial of the Dominicans requesting this enclaustration of Minaya in a minutely detailed article on the subject (A. De la Hera, "El derecho de los indios"). The change in the queen's attitude has always attracted attention: plausible reasons have been advanced to explain it (an initiative on the part of Cardinal García de Loaysa, especially); even so, it seems to us, some further specifications are needed.

5. De la Hera had already remarked on this agreement of ideas in an annotation. According to him, the contract and agreement obtained by Bartolomé from Alonso Maldonado in 1537 contains the great themes found in the documents of Paul III: "capacity for the faith and the need to instruct them in it, liberty, possession of their goods — the three ideas that *Sublimis Deus* will definitively consecrate in the field of doctrine. There is even mention, just as there will be in Paul III's *Pastorale Officium*, of severe penalties to be incurred by anyone who might contravene *Sublimis Deus*. We have an interesting parallelism, then, between the implementation of the Lascasian ideas in the Indies and that which the disciple of the future bishop of Chiapa expounds in Rome" (De la Hera, "El derecho de los indios," 110).

6. We have the Latin text and a Spanish translation of this letter in A. Lobato Casado, "El obispo Garcés O.P. y la Bula *Sublimis Deus*."

7. Parish recognizes the importance of Bishop Garcés's letter in Minaya's initiative, but tempers her appreciation with the reminder that it does not reject the Conquista as a means of conversion, nor does it mention the slavery and oppression of the Indians. Furthermore, in 1531 Garcés approved the violent conquest of New Galicia, which Zumárraga condemned. To all appearances, Garcés later changed his mind; but these things are not as neatly rejected in the letter as we might desire (see Parish, *Las Casas en México*, ch. 1 and n. 12). Las Casas speaks little of Garcés. When he does, his tone is favorable, but he does not mention the basic differences he has with the future bishop of Tlaxcala. Here is how he presents him in the *Historia de las Indias:* "Master in Theology, outstanding preacher, and quite remarkable in Latin, to the point where Master Antoño de Nebrija, seeing his skill and expertness in the Latin language, is said to have cried, 'Me oportet minui, hunc autem crescere!'" ("He must increase, while I must decrease"; *H.I.*, bk. 3, ch. 118, *O.E.* 2:457a).

8. Furthermore, Parish gives us two unpublished petitions of Minaya to Charles V. In them, the restless friar defends the Indians, while criticizing Dominicans Vicente de Santa María and Domingo de Betanzos for their contemptuous opinion of them and for urging their subjection to slavery (Parish, *Las Casas en México*, Appendices 3, 4).

9. Parish holds that the first four chapters of Bartolomé's work were not lost, as has long been thought, but that Las Casas transferred them to some other book of his. One of these, she says, is the *Apología* (see Parish, *The Only Way*, "Textual Appendices"). The date of the redaction of this Lascasian work has been much disputed. To cite only a recent opinion: I. Pérez Fernández (*Inventario*, 201) and J. A. Barreda (*Ideología y pastoral misionera*, 25–27) think that we are dealing with a writing composed around 1524–26, when Las Casas was a Dominican student. Both accept later interpolations, of course. But Parish rejects the idea that what we have here is an early text redacted as a university dissertation (see Parish, *Las Casas en México*, n. 40b): rather it would be a book written over the years of his missionary labor and defense of the Indian.

10. See Parish, *Las Casas en México*, ch. 3.

11. Parish thinks (as does De la Hera, "El derecho de los indios") that this document was composed first as a papal brief beginning with the words *Veritas ipsa*, and that it was then raised to the status of a bull, with an introduction added (hence its date of June 2, after the publication of the other documents, when actually it must have been redacted first). This led to a double designation (*Veritas Ipsa*, which never existed as a bull, and *Sublimis Deus*) and has confused certain historians, who speak of two bulls (e.g., Hanke, "El Papa Paulo III y los indios," 66–67). On this document, besides Parish one may consult Hanke, De la Hera, C. Seco Caro ("De la bula *Sublimis Deus* [1–VI-1537] a la constitución *Gaudium et Spes* del concilio Vaticano II"), and López de Lara, *Ideas tempranas*, 225–307. Helen Parish's critical edition provides interesting data on the history of the text; see *Las Casas en México*, 34–39.

12. Las Casas recalls that in an effort to justify the exactions levied on the Indians many in these lands attribute, "falsely, to the Indian nations that they

were so far removed from the regimen of human beings that they were unable to govern themselves, but had need of tutors" (*De Unico*, 137). In the same sense, Bishop Julián Garcés, in elegant Latin, wrote to the pope: "Who would be so impudent, prideful, and shameless as to dare to assert that they have no capacity for the faith whom we see to be most capable in the mechanical arts and who indeed, when reduced to the service of our [Spaniards], we know by experience are of good disposition, loyal, and able? And, Most Blessed Father," says Garcés, in frank opposition to those who discredit the Indians, "should Your Holiness ever hear any religious man to wander from a like opinion, however he may appear to gleam with the eminent rectitude of his life or with his dignity, grant him not on that account any authority in this whatsoever, but be very sure that he certainly has shed little or no sweat to convert them and consider that he has little endeavored to learn their language or investigate their talent, since those who, with Christian love, have toiled for them declare that it is not in vain that the nets of charity have been hurled upon them" (in Lobato Casado, "El obispo Garcés," 786–87). This was Minaya's claim as well in his letters to Charles V and in the dedication he wrote to Cardinal Badia, cited above.

13. See, e.g., the letter addressed to the king by eleven Franciscans working in Mexico (July 31, 1533) on the servitude and shackles of the Indians (see M. Martínez, "Las Casas–Vitoria y la bula *Sublimis Deus*," 26).

14. The antislavery law of August 2, 1530, was the result of a meeting held in 1529 under the presidency of Cardinal Juan de Tavera. The king acknowledges that in the past the Crown has permitted Indian slavery; but now, in view of the harm that "has always followed on a daily basis, owing to the unbridled greed of the conquistadors and other persons," the king decrees that no Indian may be held as a slave (Konetzke, *Colección de documentos*, vol. 1, no. 68, pp. 134–36, gives the text of this royal decree). Years later Tavera would be the addressee of the brief *Pastorale Officium*, authorizing him to excommunicate anyone who subjects the Indians to servitude. It is possible that a memorandum dispatched from Hispaniola (in *DII* 11:243–49), one of whose authors, according to Parish, was Las Casas (in Pérez Fernández, *Inventario*, 220), exerted an influence in the matter. On the basis of this text, as well as other contributions, Parish regards Las Casas as indeed having had an important influence on the issuing of the antislavery decree (see Parish, "Introduction: Las Casas's Spirituality").

15. Even earlier, the king had decreed for New Spain that free Indians might not be subjected to slavery and shackled. But he accepted, of course, the slavery and shackling of those who were "held with just title" (see the royal orders of November 9, 1528, in Konetzke, *Colección de documentos*, vol. 1, no. 44, p. 87; no. 57, p. 109).

16. King Charles revokes his provision of four years before because great problems had flowed from it in his Indian territories. Having asked the opinion of the Council of the Indies, the king reestablishes slavery and once more authorizes that Indian slaves be shackled "with irons of our mark." Finally, he orders that "the content of this letter come to the notice of all and no one be able to claim ignorance" (Konetzke, *Colección de documentos*, 1:153–59).

17. Besides having obtained the revocation, García de Loaysa authorized new slave-hunting expeditions. We have already made reference to Minaya's testimony concerning the poor opinion the cardinal had of the Indians (see above, n. 2). This position was based on, among other things, the report we have already mentioned from Friar Domingo de Betanzos, in which the Indians' capacity to receive the Christian faith is denied in strong terms. On Betanzos and his controversial text see M. Cuevas, *Historia de la Iglesia en México,* 1:229–32, which furnishes interesting documents in this regard (Cuevas declares Betanzos "innocent," 229), as well as the more detailed study by D. Ulloa, *Los predicadores divididos.* But the Dominican friar retracted that opinion on his deathbed (1546; see the text of the retractation in Las Casas, *Tratado de Indias y el doctor Sepúlveda,* 184–92). For his part, García de Loaysa always maintained a rigid posture on the matter of the Indies. In the *Historia de las Indias,* Las Casas eulogizes Friar Domingo de Mendoza, brother of the archbishop of Seville (although he signs his name differently, having adopted his mother's surname, a frequent custom of the age). This religious had taken the initiative of dispatching a group of Dominican friars to Hispaniola in 1510. Las Casas says of Friar Domingo, using moderate language, but not dissimulating the contrast between the two brothers: "That brother of this Lord [García de Loaysa], God led by different paths and ways and raised him by more certain and secure degrees" (*H.I.,* bk. 3, ch. 54, *O.E.* 2:132b–133a).

18. This sentence is missing from some transcriptions of the bull, but it belongs to it according to the best versions (see De la Hera, "El derecho de los indios," 161–62, which studies the matter). It is contained in the version presented by Las Casas, thus representing one more proof of Bartolomé's fidelity in transcribing documents.

19. In Lobato Casado, "El obispo Garcés," 791–92. This "compensation" is a frequently recurring concept of the era.

20. Minaya says that the cardinal of Seville felt this as a "slap in the face" (in Beltrán de Heredia, "Nuevos datos," 492). Juan de Tavera, on his side, saw it as support for his antislavery position.

21. Cuevas speaks of the "truly satanic persecution undertaken against the native races, a persecution which, had it been completed to the taste of its perpetrators, would have pulled up by the root all of that recently planted, but already luxuriant, vineyard of the Lord and the whole of American civilization. It would have been a perpetual dishonor for Spain and for the sixteenth century" (Cuevas, *Historia de la Iglesia en México,* 1:226). The author therefore thinks that, first, the activity of the Dominicans on Hispaniola and, then, "the social campaign that the church crowned with the bull *Sublimis Deus*" (and the other texts cited) restrained that persecution.

22. This decentralization was still being requested from Latin America on the eve of Vatican Council II for a series of aspects of the daily life of the church (see Bishop José Dammert's incisive "Aplicación de la legislación canónica en América Latina").

23. See in recent times, for example, the rejection in certain Catholic circles of Leo XIII's encyclical *Rerum Novarum* and of documents like those of

Medellín; or the curtain of silence drawn in these same sectors over John Paul II's encyclical *On Human Labor.*

24. Parish (*Las Casas en México*) and Hanke ("El Papa Paulo III y los indios," 79–80; the English-language version of this article presents a facsimile of the papal document) quote the brief in Latin in its entirety (De la Hera gives only part of it). Parish, furthermore, provides a translation, which we follow — with slight modifications — in these pages. The text is signed in the environs of Nice. Here indeed was where the pope was sojourning while he attempted to reconcile Charles V and Francis I, whose quarrel was harmful to the Catholic Church in the face of the Turkish threat and Protestant dissidence. In these circumstances, the political situation led the pope to make concessions, including political ones, to Charles V — without neglecting to obtain certain personal benefits (see Hanke, "El Papa Paulo III y los indios," 83–84). Far more importantly, the Indians might now hope for better times. Indeed the kings signed a peace treaty one day before the date (June 18) under which the *Non Indecens* was published.

25. Parish, *Las Casas en México,* ch. 4. For his part, Beltrán de Heredia, who devotes no special attention to the point, asserts that Charles V obtained "a revocatory brief of *all* promulgations working to the prejudice of his rights overseas" (Beltrán de Heredia, "Nuevos datos," 1:480; emphasis added).

26. De la Hera, "El derecho de los indios," 173–77.

27. The text is based on a norm that, according to Hanke, is a "model law of the colonial period" in defense of the royal prerogatives: "Should any bulls or briefs come to our Indies bearing upon the Governance of those provinces, Patronage and Royal Jurisdiction, Matters of Indulgences, vacant Sees, or spoliums, or any other [bulls or briefs], of whatsoever quality; and should it not appear that they have been presented in our Council of the Indies and passed by the same: We order the Viceroys, Presidents, and Auditors of the Royal Audiencia to recover them, in the original, from the power of whatsoever persons may have them; and having besought in their regard His Holiness to proceed first in this manner, that [such a brief] be dispatched in the first instance to us, to our said Council; and if the latter approve their execution, let them be executed; and if [such briefs] be held for inappropriate, that he oblige the suspension of their execution; [and] let our Most Holy Father be besought concerning them" — says the king, on the strength of the success of his recent action — "that, being better informed, he order their revocation; and meanwhile let the Council provide that they not be executed, nor use made of them" (quoted in Hanke, "El Papa Paulo III y los indios," 78–79).

28. The pope granted that privilege with the bull *Universalis Ecclesiae* of July 28, 1508, upon the insistent demand of King Ferdinand. In 1505 the king wrote to Julius II: "It is needful that Your Holiness grant all the said patronate in perpetuity to me and my successors" (cited in Hanke, "El Papa Paulo III y los indios," 68; but his reference to *DII* does not correspond). Ferdinand pressured the pope to obtain the bull. Cuevas writes in this regard: "The Reverend Father Leturia, zealous advocate of the Patronage though he is, has revealed to us that, in order to obtain it from the rigid Julius II, the

means employed by King Don Fernando the 'Catholic' were a less than edi-
fying obstinancy, and even not very Catholic threats. In other words, that the
Patronage had a cradle or dawning very like its setting" (Cuevas, *Historia de
la Iglesia en México*, 2:48).

29. Letter cited in Cuevas, *Historia de la Iglesia en México*, 1:228; emphasis
added. Knowing that, "before the said *briefs* and *bulls* were taken from him,
[Minaya] had had many copies of them made and had widely distributed
them, so that some of them might have reached those provinces and provoked scandal," the king — obsessed with bulls — ordered the viceroy to
conduct an investigation. Finally he directed him to send them "to our Council of the Indies" and serve notice of "the said revocation to the prelates,
priors, and guardians of the orders who reside in that land" (Cuevas, *Historia de la Iglesia en México*, 1:228; emphasis added). Hanke reproduces certain
paragraphs in his "El Papa Paulo III y los indios," 81; De la Hera alludes to
these important texts of Charles V, but does not present or comment on them.

30. He was not alone in this opinion. The original of the controversial
brief *Non Indecens*, which is preserved in the Archivo General de Indias,
bears the following label: "Paul III: Brief by which His Holiness *revokes any
others whatsoever* that may have been issued previously to the prejudice of
His Majesty and the disturbance of the good governance of the Indies and
islands" (cited by Parish, *Las Casas en México*, Appendices, n. 41; emphasis
added) — once again a plural reference, seemingly referring to other briefs.
Parish observes, however — causing more headaches for the interpreters —
that the label of a copy of the brief in question (certified on August 29, 1538,
by the bishop of Cádiz, Antonio de Aguila, and a notary apostolic) refers to
the revocation "of *a* brief," in the singular: "Authorized [penned over: 'notarized'] copy of Pope Paul III's Brief of Revocation [of the] Year 1538 of *a Brief*
that he himself had given in which is disturbed the peaceful estate and good
governance of the Indies" (Parish, *Las Casas en México*, Appendices, n. 41;
emphasis added).

31. From the Spanish translation by Helen Parish (*Las Casas en México*,
Appendix 15; emphasis added), with some modifications.

32. An echo of the tribulations of these texts: the absence of *Sublimis Deus*
from the classic *bullaria*, or collections of papal bulls (see Pérez Fernández,
Inventario, 268).

33. Juan de la Peña, *De Bello*, 1:193. Elsewhere he appeals to Paul III's bull
in order to establish that the Indians are not deprived of dominion over their
possessions. Domingo de Soto cites and gives the essential content of *Sublimis
Deus*, summarizing what Las Casas said in Valladolid (see *O.E.* 5:308a). We
shall speak of Vitoria's silence on the matter in our following chapter.

34. In A. Utz and M. Boeglin, eds., *La doctrine sociale de l'Eglise*, 1:398–403,
404–13, 422–27, 449.

35. Letter to Domingo de Soto, in M. Bataillon, *Estudios sobre Bartolomé de
Las Casas*, 262.

36. Indeed, those who claim to serve their country with falsehoods "are
offenders of God, disloyal to their king, and enemies of the Spanish nation,

since they perniciously deceive it," Las Casas argues in the foreword to his replies to Sepúlveda (*O.E.* 5:319a).

37. Las Casas indicates, for example, that the conquistadors won to their cause Don Juan Cabedo, whom we have just mentioned, by manifesting generosity towards him. "It was also presumed," he says, "that Diego de Velázquez had greased his palm, by helping outfit him for the journey, . . . hoping that at Court he might be able to help him in his dealings with the new king, who was Emperor" (*H.I.,* bk. 3, ch. 147, *O.E.* 2:530b–531a). Conquistadors and *encomenderos* will continue to use the "palm greasing" method to defend their privileges against the criticisms of the missionaries and some honest civil officials.

38. We refer to an injunction dated October 19, 1545 — too soon for Las Casas to have learned of the revocation (decreed on October 10 of the same year), but not too soon for him to have felt it coming. The text has been published and studied by F. Cantù, "Esigenze di giustizia e politica coloniale: Una 'petición' inedita di Las Casas all'audiencia de los Confines." Fourteen years later, C. Sempat ("Fray Bartolomé de Las Casas obispo: La condición miserable de las naciones indianas y el derecho de la Iglesia") likewise reproduces the document, not knowing that it has been published, but providing interesting data on it in his commentary.

39. Bishop Marroquín withdrew his signature the day after the presentation of the petition. His friendship with Las Casas, once very close, had cooled and was broken off. See, on this difficult and painful relationship, C. Sáenz de Santamaría, *El licenciado don Francisco Marroquín: Primer obispo de Guatemala,* 41–47, 57–69; for another version of the facts, Martínez, "El Padre Las Casas y el obispo Marroquín," and Parish, *Las Casas en México.* For the martyred bishop Antonio de Valdivieso, see J. Alvarez Lobo's recent *Cartas del obispo Valdivieso,* which, besides containing precious texts of this great friend of Las Casas, carries an introduction by the compiler and a foreword by Bishop Pedro Casaldáliga.

40. P. Castañeda Delgado, "La condición miserable de indio," 245.

41. We cite the bishops' petition according to the text presented in Cantù, "Esigenze di giustizia," 158–62. The unreferenced passages in quotation marks are taken from this source.

42. On the Protectorate, see C. Bayle, *El protector de Indios;* the work we have cited of Enrique Dussel, *El episcopado hispanoamericano;* and M. Olmedo, *Jerónimo de Loaysa, O.P.: Pacificador de españoles y protector de indios,* 119–40. On the missionaries as protectors of the Indians in Peru, see Pablo Nguyen Thai Hop, "Los dominicos en la defensa del hombre andino."

43. Castañeda Delgado, "Condición miserable del indio," 263. The author further asserts that the term "miserable" is applied to the Indian only in official texts, as in an ordinance of Philip II in 1563. But there "the Indians are regarded as miserable because of the status as gentiles in which they find themselves" (Castañeda Delgado, "Condición miserable del indio," 264–65). The author further notes that "the theologians of the sixteenth century do not treat the question" (289), although there is something in Soto's rich *Declaración de la causa de los pobres,* written to defend the right of the poor

to beg alms (see F. Moreno's observations in his "Historia, ética e Iglesia en América Latina," 32–34). Cantù suggests that the theme's late appearance in the Indies may be due to the slant that Las Casas stamped on the petition, demanding that the Indians be transferred to the jurisdiction of the church.

44. "...Since the poor and miserable have all the privileges of the Church," says Palacios Rubios — the jurist we have already met — in his *Commentaria et repetitio rubricae et capituli, per vestras, de donationibus*, 389 (cited by Cantù, "Potere vescovile,..." 539).

45. An institution that, for that matter, and despite its good intentions, did not always function in favor of the Indians. See Castañeda Delgado, "Condición miserable del indio," 276.

46. This is why we have thought it important to cite this important text, which we owe to the sharp scholarly eye of Francesca Cantù. Elsewhere, Cantù adds: "The question of the Indians' falling under ecclesiastical jurisdiction will not be explicitly taken up by Las Casas again, although — as a consequence of that demand — he will be the object of more or less veiled threats of denunciation for the crime of lèse-majesté" (Cantù, "Bartolomé de Las Casas nel quadro del suo tempo," 75).

47. The date of 1546 is given by Pérez Fernández (*Inventario*, 470) and by Parish (*Las Casas en México*, chs. 5–8). In a study antedating those cited, R. Marcus ("La Quaestio theologalis inédita de Las Casas," 4–5) without going into detail had indicated a similar date. B. Biermann ("Las Casas und Carranza") and F. Zubillaga ("Quaestio theologalis: Escrito inédito del Padre Bartolomé de Las Casas") and, recently, A. Larios and A. García (Introduction to Las Casas's *Obras Completas*) indicate a later date, some time in the last years of Las Casas's life. But we must observe that behind the question of date is the matter of the meaning of this treatise. The last authors mentioned relate it to the controversial sentence passed on Carranza, in which Bartolomé took a forthright and generous position. Parish and Pérez Fernández, on the other hand — and correctly, it seems to us — think that the writing is wholly and entirely on matters of the Indies.

48. The treatise has just been published in vol. 12 of Las Casas's *Obras Completas*. Parish and H. Weidman have a text, which has been ready for some time, that will be published in *Las Casas en México*.

49. In a text that Parish holds was written with Prince Philip in mind, he says: "Let the Catholic prince, then, who hopes for the Lord's assistance in gaining victories, beware of attempting to usurp, personally or through his judges, the authority and jurisdiction belonging to the priesthood and to the ecclesiastical dignity or spiritual authority. Otherwise" — the text goes on, proclaiming three deaths — "he must be removed from the temple [excommunicated], slain by the sword of anathema, and, furthermore, smitten with the detestable leprosy of mortal sin, by which he is eternally separated from God's grace and heavenly glory" (*De Exemptione*, folio 105v). A severe warning.

50. On the conception that Las Casas had of the episcopal ministry, see Parish's classic *Las Casas, obispo*, and Cantù, "Per un rinnovamento della con-

scienza pastorale del cinquecento: Il vescovo Bartolomé de Las Casas ed il problema indiano."

51. This has already been pointed out by Cantù, who relates the unpublished text she has made known to us to the second corollary of the *Tratado sobre la esclavitud de los indios* and the *De Exemptione* (Cantù, "Esigenze di giustizia," 154).

52. In some extremely interesting pages, Parish has clarified the role that this treatise plays in the battle being waged by the bishop of Chiapa on the eve of his return to Spain. It was part of the strategy of his response to the abrogation of substantial parts of the New Laws and the will that prevailed in the Indies to ignore the others. These considerations enable us to perceive the scope of this writing, which Parish does not hesitate to call "a secret weapon and a challenge to the King" (see Parish, *Las Casas en México*, chs. 5–8, and the Introduction to the edition of Las Casas's treatise).

53. Pérez Fernández calls it the "black legend" against Las Casas. After having been censured as "anti-Spanish," says the great scholar of Las Casas, now he is presented as "antiblack." Two of Pérez Fernández's most recent works are intended to set the matter straight: *Fray Bartolomé de Las Casas: Brevísima relación de la destrucción de Africa* (hereafter, *Destrucción de Africa*), and *Bartolomé de Las Casas ¿contra los negros?* (hereafter, *¿Contra los negros?*). Another important Lascasist, Helen Parish, is also working on the question and will soon publish her findings.

54. Indeed, this occasioned in the church the appearance of religious orders for the ransom of slaves.

55. F. Pijper, "The Christian Church and Slavery in the Middle Ages," albeit with something of an apologetical slant, gives interesting indications in the matter. See also H. Cazelles, D. Richon, and G. Marsot, "Esclavage"; and C. Verlinden's important *L'esclavage dans l'Europe médiévale*.

56. "In the state of innocence, there would have been no domination of this kind, of one human being over another" (*ST*, I, q. 96, a. 4, c.; see also II–II, q. 47, a. 3, ad 2).

57. Adducing this baseless motive, the rulers of Portugal each obtain a papal bull empowering them to mount their levies in Africa and legitimating their forays. See the exceedingly lengthy study by Benedictine C. M. De Witte, "Les bulles pontificales et l'expansion portugaise au XV siècle."

58. It is estimated that, at the end of the fifteenth century in Spain, especially in Andalusia, "there were some 100,000 black slaves" (J. Muñoz, "La sociedad estamental," 640).

59. "It is a fact that all of the Spanish scholastics approved slavery, as long as it was based on recognized titles" (J. Höffner, *La ética colonial*, 460).

60. Those who reject Indian slavery — among whom is surely Las Casas — will make themselves heard in Rome and will obtain the bull *Sublimis Deus*. Nothing of the kind, unfortunately, will occur in the case of the Africans. The Puebla General Conference of the Latin American Episcopate recognizes this: "Unfortunately, the problem of the African slaves did not attract sufficient evangelizing and liberation-oriented attention from the

Church" (Puebla Final Document, no. 8. See the observations of F. Mires, *La colonización de las almas*, 219–20.

61. Slavery was practiced in the African interior as well, with the victims frequently the booty of war. But as Las Casas will perceptively remark later, the Portuguese could not escape the fact that their own greed for black slaves occasioned the waging of unjust wars on the part of Africans in order to capture slaves and sell them to the Europeans. For this reason, he concludes, "It is a perilous business and a precarious profit in which any Christian ought to be very well advised and full of dread when entering upon a contract or doing business with an unbeliever" (*H.I.*, bk. 1, ch. 24, *O.E.* 1:86a).

62. "Carta del maestro fray Francisco de Vitoria al padre Bernardino de Vique acerca de los esclavos con que trafican los portugueses y sobre el proceder de los escribanos." See Höffner, *La ética colonial*, 461–62; A. Pagden, *The Fall of Natural Man*, 33.

63. Ginés de Sepúlveda, for his part, has these and other reasons for finding black slavery justified. See his *Del Reino y los deberes del rey*, reproduced by A. Losada in *Tratados políticos de Juan Ginés de Sepúlveda*; on this point, 107–8.

64. One of the first voices is that of Dominican Alonso de Montúfar, archbishop of México, who, in a letter to the king of Spain in 1560, said that "the captivity of the blacks is as unjust as that of the Indians" (in F. Paso y Troncoso, *Epistolario de Nueva España*, 9:53, 55; quoted in R. Konetzke, *América Latina*, vol. 2: *La época colonial*, 70).

65. Mercado enunciates severe criticisms in his celebrated *Suma de tratos y contratos* (1571; there are modern editions). On this author, see L. Sastre, "Teoría esclavista de Tomás Mercado."

66. So thinks Höffner, who knows Molina's work well (he devotes a number of pages to it in his *Etica colonial española*, 463–75).

67. But the work was limited in scope — as well as in its consequences, being proscribed by the Index of Forbidden Books in Rome (not, however, for its position on slavery).

68. On these and other points of the history of the Catholic position on slavery, see J. F. Maxwell, *Slavery and the Catholic Church*; J. Dutilleul, "Esclavage"; and the recent work by I. Gutiérrez, "La Iglesia y los negros."

69. The work has been published recently under the title *Un tratado sobre la esclavitud*. It addresses the question of the justice of slavery in bk. 1, ch. 17. First, Molina says that, owing to his own perplexity on the matter, he had wondered "whether he would pass over it in silence," but that he has decided to leave "the determination of its justice to the doctors." His caution is dictated partly by the opinion of Jesuits in Angola and Brazil: he consults L. Brandon, rector of a boarding school in Luanda, and receives the answer that many of them buy "these slaves for our service without any scruple" (Luis de Molina, *Un tratado sobre la esclavitud*, 142–44).

70. By way of an explanation for this position, E. Cárdenas appeals to a text from the Colombian bishops on the occasion of the fourth centenary of the birth of Peter Claver, which declares: "There are saints and prophets who do not experience situations as systems of thought, but as existential realities" (E. Cárdenas, "La Etica cristiana y la esclavitud de los negros," 256).

71. The composition is preserved in the Archivo General de Indias under the designation Audiencia de Santo Domingo, legajo ("dossier") 527. (The text was kindly furnished to us by Francisco Moreno, who will soon publish an article about it.) A. Valtierra has published extracts from the document in the collection of works by various authors, *Los grupos afroamericanos*, 9–28. In Havana, Jaca met French Capuchin Epifano de Borgoña, or de Moirans, who in turn wrote a text against slavery entitled, *Siervos libres o la justa defensa de la libertad natural de los esclavos*. (Both memoranda have been published in J. T. López, *Dos defensores de los esclavos negros en el s. XVII*).

72. Earlier, in the fifteenth century, Eugene IV already calls for, for example, the liberation of the inhabitants of the Canary Islands, "recently converted to the true Catholic faith" (the bull *Dudum Nostras* of 1435; in A. Utz and M. Boeglin, *La doctrine sociale de l'Eglise*, 415). Pius II, in 1462, reasserts this demand and calls by the name of a "crime" what evil Christians do in reducing "recently baptized adults to slavery" (quoted in Maxwell, *Slavery and the Catholic Church*, 51–52). The provincial councils held in the Indies (Lima, Mexico City, and elsewhere) speak of a decent treatment to be accorded the blacks, but place no interdict on the supposed justice of their slavery.

73. Gregory XVI (apostolic letter of 1839; in Utz and Boeglin, *La doctrine sociale de l'Eglise*, 423–27). "All of those practices" are abominated "as absolutely unworthy of the name of Christian."

74. Especially in his letter to the bishops of Brazil (1888) on the occasion of the abolition of slavery (see the text in Utz and Boeglin, *La doctrine sociale de l'Eglise*, 429–57). We have referred to all of these texts apropos of their mention of Paul III's pronouncements on the situation in the Indies.

75. Theologians as well, Catholics and Protestant alike, of various European countries.

76. See David B. Davis, *The Problem of Slavery in Western Culture*, 114–21. As the author says, slavery has "the curious ability to generate dualisms of thought, or to adapt itself to them" (119). Indeed, at the very moment when the Europe of those years is becoming open to modern thought and liberal ideas, the cruel, infamous traffic in black slaves is carried on in a way and to a degree never before known. And justifications are put forth.

77. See M. Giménez Fernández, *Bartolomé de Las Casas: Capellán*, 551. See also A. Gutiérrez, "La primitiva organización indiana," 237. The disposition in question was abrogated, promulgated anew in 1504, and ratified in 1513.

78. See the chronologically ordered data drawn up by Pérez Fernández, *¿Contra los negros?* 71–77. See also the old but still useful work of J. A. Saco, *Historia de la esclavitud en la raza africana y en el Nuevo Mundo*, especially vols. 1, 2, 3; W. Philips, *Historia de la esclavitud en España*, especially 183–234.

79. L. Rivera, then, is correct when he says that Las Casas did not identify "slavery with blackness" (L. Rivera, "Libertad y servidumbre en la conquista española de América," 58).

80. "Item. He begs to be permitted the favor that the said citizens may freely import black slaves, as a remedy will thereby be provided: and they will mine a great quantity of gold, the Indians will be relieved of their toil,

and many other advantages will accrue" (*DII* 13:57; the memorandum is undated, but E. Rodríguez Demorizi, *Los dominicos y las encomiendas*, 18 n. 11, thinks it was written in 1510).

81. See Pérez Fernández, *¿Contra los negros?* 77, 80–81.

82. In May 1517, the Hieronymites request of Cardinal Cisneros that they "be allowed to bring . . . in *bozal* blacks," that is, slaves who had not been living in Spain, but directly from Africa, concretely, from Guinea (see Pérez Fernández, *¿Contra los negros?* 84); Las Casas's requests were for slaves from Spain. Mere months before, Cisneros had opposed sending slaves to the Indies, not out of any opposition to slavery, however, but only because he regarded it to be unsuitable for the governance of the Indies: Africans, he thought, "become much like the Indians and do evil and cause harm as in past times has been seen by experience" (Giménez Fernández, *Bartolomé de Las Casas: Capellán,* 554).

83. Pérez Fernández gives several examples (*¿Contra los negros?* 85–89; see also Giménez Fernández, *Bartolomé de Las Casas: Capellán,* 549–69).

84. *DII* 11:151. Some lines further on we read: "In such a way that these slaves are not given them that they may eventually purchase them, but as their actual property, for themselves and their children and decendants, whom they may sell and do with as they will, as their owners" (152). The *parecer* is dated 1517.

85. *Carta a los dominicos, DII* 11:214. The text goes on: "And even to those who have none of their own at present, let Your Highness send them some, to be sold to them on credit over a stipulated term" (214).

86. The matter also figures in the documents concerned with the contract for the Cumaná experiment of these same years.

87. See the petition he presents to Charles V, in Parish, *Las Casas, obispo,* p. 9, para. 22.

88. Perhaps one reason for so limiting the number of black slaves was Las Casas's conviction that the Indians were also frequently mistreated by the blacks. The Europeans and the Africans were better acquainted with each other, having been together in Spain, and at first constituted a mistrustful minority vis-à-vis the Indians. It is understandable, then, that the Spaniards should have more confidence in black slaves than in the natives and that they should often make them their stewards or foremen. Bartolomé indicates various cases of this kind (see *Octavo remedio*, 1542, *O.E.* 5:92a; *Carta a Carranza*, 1555, 5:435a–436a; and other references in Pérez Fernández, *¿Contra los negros?* 148). *Carta de franciscanos y dominicos,* 1519, *DII* 7:422, may also be consulted.

89. What he does do is submit a denunciation of the cruelties suffered by Indians and blacks in the pearl fishing, which must have led to the prohibition prescribed by Law XXV of the New Laws inspired by Las Casas. (There is an echo of this in the *Brevísima relación,* 163a–b; see Pérez Fernández, *¿Contra los negros?* 151–53.) As we know, there is an interesting kinship, and the same denunciatory force, between this text of Las Casas and one of Acosta, which was censured and which the Jesuit therefore eliminated from the pub-

lication of his *De Procuranda Indorum Salute*. (It is found, of course, in the CHP edition, 529–31.)

90. Pérez Fernández, *Cronología*, 718. In *¿Contra los negros?* 191–92, Pérez goes so far as to say that the Dominican went to Lisbon expressly to obtain this information. Be that as it may, it is interesting to recall that he shortly thereafter obtains from the Council of the Indies the emancipation of black slave Pedro de Carmona, personally posting his bond (Giménez Fernández had already called attention to the matter in *Bartolomé de Las Casas: Capellán*, 567–69).

91. We are referring to Gomes Eanes de Zarara's *Crónica dos feitos da Guiné*, and García de Resende's *Crónica del D. João II de Portugal*, both published in 1545; as well as to Fernão Lopes de Castañeda's *Historia do descubrimiento e conquista de India pelos portugueses* (1547), and later, João de Barros, *Décadas da Asia* (1552).

92. They are chapters 17–27 of the first book of the *Historia*. As Pérez Fernández says, they are a quasi-autonomous unit within the book. The chapters in question seem to have been written around 1554 at the latest (Pérez Fernández, *¿Contra los negros?* 196; in the *Destrucción de Africa* [35] he had dated them 1556), nor do they begin each with a synopsis, with which Las Casas was accustomed to open the respective chapters of his other compositions and which we find with the other chapters of the first book of the *Historia*.

93. See above, our chapter 2.

94. Applying the reasons that might conceivably have justified the wars the Portuguese waged in Africa, he denies that such justification is at hand: These "were only cruel wars, slaughters, captive-hunting forays, entailing the total destruction and annihilation of so many villages of people who had been living peacefully in their homes. [These wars] have been the sure damnation of many souls, who now have helplessly perished for all eternity, who never had attacked them, never done them any injury, or waged war on them, never insulted or prejudiced the faith, or ever considered throwing up obstacles to its propagation, and who held their lands in all confidence because they had never despoiled us of ours" (*H.I.*, bk. 1, ch. 25, *O.E.* 1:96b). As we see, these are the same terms as he employs in speaking of the Indies. Pérez Fernández is right to compare these chapters on Africa with the *Brevísima* that denounces what is happening in the new world.

95. The texts in question, written in 1560 (see Pérez Fernández, *¿Contra los negros?* 188), belong to bk. 3 of the *Historia de las Indias*. On the other hand, the change in Las Casas occurs in earlier years — around 1553, thinks André-Vincent ("Sur la date et la portée du 'repentir' de Las Casas," 243); between 1545 and 1547, says the ever meticulous Pérez Fernández (*¿Contra los negros?* 189). Both recognize the authenticity of the document discovered by A. Milhou ("Las Casas frente a las reivindicaciones de los colonos de la isla Española"), in which Baltazar García, recommended by Las Casas in 1555, asks to be allowed to establish himself on Hispaniola and mentions black slaves. But for various reasons, both deny that the discovery of the document settles the matter, since García's text may have been unknown to Las Casas.

96. Bartolomé says: "This instruction, to the effect that permission was

granted to bring black slaves to this land, was originally issued by [*dio primero*] cleric Casas." The expression *dio primero* has been curiously interpreted — against all historical and literal evidence — as meaning that Bartolomé had been *the first to make* the petition he now reproves. Surely it is obvious, especially in view of the context, that that declaration is part of his retraction: what he has held *in the past* ("primero") is not his view today.

97. In 1542 he made a distinction between the Indies and Africa to the effect that the wars are not justified in the former as, apparently, they might be in Africa (see *Octavo remedio*, 1542, *O.E.* 5:121b).

98. In saying he "returns" to the subject, we do not mean that ch. 129 was necessarily written after ch. 102.

99. Six decades after 1492. This is one of Pérez's arguments for saying that Las Casas himself dates his change on these matters before this year (see Pérez Fernández, *¿Contra los negros?* 196).

100. Even Losada, always reticent with Las Casas, says this: *Fray Bartolomé de Las Casas a la luz de la moderna crítica histórica*, 211–12.

101. J. L. Borges, as is known, in the opening lines of his *Historia universal de la infamia*, 17, makes a quick allusion to Las Casas's recommendation in 1516 that black slaves replace the Indians, without apprising his readers of Bartolomé's later retraction. Considering, on the one hand, Borges's enormous erudition and, on the other, his paradoxical, sly spirit, one cannot rule out the possibility that he wishes to leave an example — ironically, one of his own — of how contributions are actually made to the "history of slander." One really is tempted to imagine him today contemplating with an amused regard and mischievous smile those who so seriously and solemnly — without verifying the data — cite that initial passage of his book and continue to write, totally unaware, that history!

102. We also find in Las Casas a concern for the condition of poverty in which some Spaniards, old colonists of the Indies, live. They are old conquistadors, "which," says Bartolomé, is the most infamous title they could have, but today "they suffer very great need and live lives of tribulation and anguish." He therefore petitions the king that "those who have much be deprived that more may accrue to those who lack even . . . maize." Transfer the wealth from the rich *encomenderos* to the Spanish poor. Incidentally, this will make it unnecessary for the latter, in their desperation, to pillage Indian villages (*Informe sobre el licenciado Cerrato, O.E.* 5:425b; Parish and Pérez Fernández think that the text is from 1553). Surprised by this request, Bataillon comments: "It is touching to find the real Las Casas in these writings, to discover him to be different from the person of principle or of resentment, to whom he has so often been reduced" (Bataillon, *Estudios sobre Bartolomé de Las Casas*, 286). But the authentic Las Casas is the person who always sought to bring his principles down to incarnation in flesh and blood, in concrete situations. What we are seeing is Bartolomé somehow extending to the Iberians the gospel definition of poor, of which he has become aware in his commitment to, first, the Indians, and then to the blacks. At the same time, we have already remarked how much Las Casas appreciated the poor farm-workers of Spain.

103. This is recognized, for example, by the black historian of slavery in North America, J. H. Franklin (*From Slavery to Freedom*, 36).

104. Discourse of February 22, 1992; emphasis added. Thus, John Paul II endorses the need and appropriateness of something that so many have been proposing for some time: the inclusion of a penitential act in the commemoration of the fifth centenary on our continent.

Chapter 12: A Fact Looking for Justification

1. Among these are Vicente Valverde, who accompanied Pizarro and then was named bishop of Cusco, along with Jerónimo de Loaisa, first arch-bishop of Lima. On the work of these two and other Dominican friars in Peru in defense of the Indians, see P. Nguyen Thai Hop's documented study, "Los dominicos en la defensa del hombre andino." For their influence on the first catechisms used in Peru, see J. Castillo, "Catecismos peruanos del siglo XVI," 262–66.

2. Let us mention only a few of these works (among the more theological approaches): Luis G. A. Getino, *El maestro Fr. Francisco de Vitoria: Su vida, su doctrina e influencia;* V. Beltrán de Heredia, *Francisco de Vitoria;* Venancio Carro, *La teología y los teólogos-juristas;* idem, *España en América, sin leyendas;* Juan Manzano y Manzano, *La Incorporación de las Indias a la Corona de Castilla;* T. Urdanoz, "Introducciones" in Francisco de Vitoria, *Obras;* R. Hernández, *Derechos humanos en Francisco de Vitoria;* idem, numerous articles that we have cited throughout this book.

3. Apropos of the bishop of Chiapa's discussions with Sepúlveda in Val-ladolid and the alleged official withdrawal of the latter's teaching authority after that debate, Urdanoz, for example, writes: "It was the definitive triumph of Vitoria's principles and the humanitarian system of Las Casas, who *applied* them to practice" (Urdanoz, in Vitoria, *Obras,* 59; emphasis added). There are those who observe furthermore that Friar Bartolomé made that application with certain deficiencies. Urdanoz himself asserts that although "in his en-semble of ideas and theoretical principles, he maintains a substantial identity with Vitoria and his disciples," in Las Casas's "recklessness and impetuos-ity are found the causes of many of his accidental shortcomings and deviant views" (Urdanoz, in Vitoria, *Obras,* 512). Similar declarations are to be had in Carro, *La teología y los teólogos-juristas,* and other researchers. See the list of opinions on relations between Las Casas and Vitoria drawn up by I. Pérez Fernández, "Cronología comparada."

4. M. Bataillon, *Estudios sobre Bartolomé de Las Casas,* 21, 338.

5. This has been the tack taken by certain great scholars of Vitoria. The latter's authority is transformed, says Carla Forti, "Las Casas's passport to a place among the glories of Spain" ("Letture di Bartolomé," 29–30).

6. On the historical context, see P. Chaunu, *Conquête et exploitation des nouveaux mondes;* and on the cultural framework of the sixteenth century, see F. Moreno, "Teología moral y contexto histórico-cultural." Vitoria is recognized as a person who was open to the humanism of the age.

7. In an article to whose central thesis we should apply many a nuance,

Matiello correctly indicates that Vitoria shifts a question usually posed "on an individual and abstract level" (that of the baptism of children of unbelievers) to that of a "cultural and historical" perspective (the barbarian peoples who, as the Salamancan puts it, "have come under the power of the Spaniards") (C. Matiello, "Francisco de Vitoria ¿Un precursor de la teología de la liberación?" 276).

8. Urdanoz observes (in Vitoria, *Obras,* 494) — and this, he thinks, has passed unobserved on the part of the specialists on Vitoria — that the Dominican addresses only the first of these parts in his *relección,* even though it would have been more appropriate for the third to respond directly to the theological question initially posed. The CHP edition therefore tries to keep all three parts in account by splicing together various Vitorian texts from other writings.

9. "It does not belong to legal experts to make a decision in this matter, or at any rate not to them alone. As I shall presently explain, since the barbarians in question are not subject to human law, their affairs are not subject to examination in terms of human laws, but in terms of the divine laws, in which the jurists are not adequately qualified to determine such questions by themselves" (Vitoria, *Obras,* 649; CHP, 11).

10. True, the Salamancan was staying in Paris when the Burgos Conference was taking place (in which Matías de Paz participated). But he could have had word of it. Furthermore, another meeting of theologians is known to have taken place in the Convent of St. Stephen in Salamanca around 1517 (Las Casas reports this in *H.I.,* bk. 3, ch. 99, *O.E.* 2:409b–410a), six years before Vitoria's arrival at the famous Dominican cloister. Moreover, when he was teaching in the College of St. Gregory in Valladolid (between 1523 and 1526), this was a "favorite place of the Court and the royal councilors, especially those of the Council of the Indies" presided over by Dominican García de Loaysa (R. di Agostino Iannarone, "Génesis del pensamiento colonial en Francisco de Vitoria," xxi).

11. Even Urdanoz (in Vitoria, *Obras,* 449) acknowledges that it is somewhat difficult to admit that he was unacquainted with, for example, the lectures of John Major, who was a famous professor in Paris and who in 1510 published his commentary on Book II of Peter Lombard's *Sentences* (with a second edition in 1519, when Vitoria was still in Paris); or that he means he had not seen Cajetan's *Commentary on the Secunda Secundae of the Summa Theologiae* (printed in 1517), which he later cites a number of times. This last might be explained by the fact that Cajetan does not speak expressly of the Indians, although he clearly alludes to them, to the point that Las Casas can say that this work shed a great deal of light on the matter of the Indies. We should add Matías de Paz and other noted Dominicans, among them even Domingo de Soto, who some years earlier, in 1535, had presented his *relección De Dominio,* in which he deals with the question of the Indies.

12. He believes, therefore, that if he succeeds in focusing the point as it ought to be considered, he will have wrought "a work of great value" (Vitoria, *Obras,* 650; CHP, 11).

13. The term "title" will be used in discussions of the time to refer to an allegedly legitimate motive for the Spanish presence in the Indies.

14. The notion has old roots in Vitoria. Some years before, in 1535, he said, in a *Commentary on the Summa Theologiae* of Thomas Aquinas: "With reference to these Indians, no one may legitimately strip them of their lands, since for that matter no Christian prince is placed over them, nor is even the Pope their superior in temporal matters, unless they are baptized — inasmuch as the Pope is placed only over those who are Christians or who have been, as have heretics" (Vitoria, *In II–II,* q. 62, a. 1, n. 28; in Vitoria, *De Justitia,* 1:82).

15. See Vitoria, *De Potestate Ecclesiae Prior* (given in 1532). Abril declares that that thesis constitutes an "absolutely substantial and absolutely decisive" contribution, since it means an acknowledgment, from the lofty theological chair of Salamanca, of the status of the native nations as "juridical persons" (V. Abril Castelló, "Vitoria–Las Casas, confrontación y proyección," 165).

16. Manzano, perhaps thinking of the "demonstration" (which he lauds) that Viceroy Toledo will later make of the illegitimacy of the Inca sovereignty, seeks to weaken this point of departure of Vitoria's (Manzano, *La incorporación de las Indias a la corona de Castilla,* 267–69). Therefore he presents the assertion as if it had been formulated in the conditional, when in actuality, for the Salamancan, it appears in his conclusion as certain: "They were authentic sovereigns, publicly and privately." It is mistaken, then, to say that in this case Vitoria's argumentation "hangs by a thread" (Manzano, *Incorporación de las Indias,* 267) — which Toledo snipped. It is correct to maintain that the matter of the legitimacy of the dominion of the Inca sovereigns is decisive in the ratiocination of the Salamancan master throughout his *relección;* but by this very fact, an examination of the question ought to take fully into account the importance of the initial thesis of native sovereignty.

17. Manzano holds it that Vitoria was "under an obligation to call the attention of the responsible authorities to the obvious error into which they had fallen in basing the rights of the discoverer nation on something this flimsy, this unsuitable; but it was not honest or legitimate of him to leave the problem in the state in which it was, without a solution for the future." Nor could that solution consist in anything other than finding the *authentic* titles to the domination already in place. This is how the Salamancan master views the issue. "Even if only to the King," Manzano continues, "who was genuinely in good faith, he found himself under obligation to point to the route to be followed, to enable him to discern the potential genuine, authentic titles on which to found a new, solid, and unassailable position" (Manzano, *Incorporación de las Indias,* 71). This author is correct. This seems to have been Vitoria's conviction and intention. He announces it from the outset. And at all events this was the result. We should only like to add that the effort to establish that "solid and unassailable position" ended, in the concrete and despite all intentions, in a justification of the wars being waged against the Indians and of the domination being exercised over them.

18. Urdanoz cannot avoid a criticism of Vitoria's concessions on this point, and he comments: "The weight of the prevailing medieval conception

was very heavy, and it was not easy for him to escape all of it" (Urdanoz, in Vitoria, *Obras*, 229).

19. Vitoria explains his statement: "I say that he has the broadest authority because in whatever is necessary for the spiritual end, so long as it is necessary, the Pope has the authority to do not only all that temporal princes can, but furthermore to depose and install princes, divide realms, and the like" (Vitoria, *Obras*, 305–6). He will later appeal to this vast papal authority when returning to the point and making it one of the legitimate titles of Spanish dominion over the Indies.

20. John Major, a Parisian professor of whose thought Vitoria cannot have been ignorant, as early as the turn of the sixteenth century had also lodged a powerful criticism of the concept of a universal temporal sovereignty on the part of the Roman pontiff.

21. Vitoria's position regarding papal authority, in this and other areas, alienated him from Roman theologians and jurists. Pope Sixtus V (d. 1590) therefore sought to place Vitoria's works on the Index of Forbidden Books, since in his judgment these works "placed excessive restrictions on papal authority" (L. A. Getino, Introduction to *Relecciones internacionalistas del Padre Maestro Francisco de Vitoria*, 34). The question acquired new urgency during Rome's polemics with King James I of England at the beginning of the seventeenth century (see L. Pereña, "El texto de la relectio de Indis," in Vitoria, *De indis* [CHP], cxli; idem, "La tesis de la paz dinámica," in Vitoria, *De jure belli* [CHP], 81–82).

22. Vitoria seems not to have known the writings of John of Paris, but he must have had some echo of him, since in Paris he lived in the same convent as this illustrious medieval theologian.

23. Urdanoz holds that in his *De Potestate Ecclesiae* Vitoria "exaggerated such indirect power" (Urdanoz, "Las Casas y Francisco de Vitoria," 256). Thus an author such as Bellarmine (the most important theoretician of an indirect power) senses a great distance between himself and Vitoria (see J. Lecler, *L'Eglise et la souveraineté de l'etat*, 101).

24. See above, our chapters 5, 6.

25. On Vitoria's imprecisions and rectifications with reference to the Law of Nations as part of natural law or of positive law, as well as for the context of this discussion, see Urdanoz, in Vitoria, *Obras*, 551–65; A. Osuna, "De la idea del sacro imperio al derecho internacional: El pensamiento político de Francisco de Vitoria," especially 42–48; and the critical observations, based on Thomas Aquinas, of M. Villey, "Saint Thomas d'Aquin et Vitoria"; the last-named author thinks that the theoretical differences between the two are owing to the fact that Thomas works from a "primacy of the status of speculative life," while Vitoria seeks to be "at the service of order, of morality, of peace, and of the king of Spain" (Villey, "Saint Thomas d'Aquin et Vitoria," 94).

26. "It is legitimate for Spaniards to engage in trade with [the inhabitants of the Indies], provided it be without prejudice to their native country," Vitoria writes, "importing the products they lack and removing gold, silver, or other things in which they abound. Nor may their princes legitimately

prevent their subjects from engaging in trade with Spaniards, just as neither, correlatively, may the princes of the Spaniards prohibit the latter from engaging in trade with the former" (Vitoria, *Obras*, 708; CHP, 80). In an interesting study in which he eulogizes the Salamancan master for having opened new routes in the social theory of economic value, Demetrio Iparraguirre makes a perceptive remark that helps us to understand the political context of the Vitorian doctrine: "What is to be gathered from this is that Vitoria had appreciated, as had no one else, the need to concede the greatest possible facility to financial transactions, that indispensable condition of economic progress. The economic vitality of the capitalism of those years was fighting to open a path through the age-old barriers that barred its way" (Demetrio Iparraguirre, *Francisco de Vitoria: Una teoría social del valor económico*, 40). Vitoria perceives these dynamics. But what Iparraguirre fails to keep in account is that this "vitality of capitalism" meant, in the concrete, economic progress for the European powers, along with new forms of exploitation and spoliation for the poor, colonized peoples of other continents. In the same vein, Urdanoz assures us that "in his view of the relations and rights of free communication, Vitoria has...established the explicit principles of *economic neo-liberalism and of free trade on a world scale*" (Urdanoz, "Síntesis teológico-jurídica de la doctrina de Vitoria," xcl; emphasis in the original).

27. This special commission from the pope to the Spanish Crown was (see above, our chapter 3) one of Las Casas's war horses. Bartolomé, like Vitoria, was a person of his time. But unlike the latter, Las Casas will never deduce from this mandate the right to wage war on the Indians: on the contrary, he will invoke it to denounce the injustice of such wars.

28. One can justify the Vitorian assertion with an appeal to a realistic attitude toward irreversible facts, but this does not spare us the distaste we feel in reading these lines of the Salamancan. Despite what he has told us in commencing his *relección*, here he betrays a juridical and canonical outlook that weighs overly much in the balance. A *legitimate* title for waging war and exercising domination must not rest on something devoid of reason and of Christian authenticity. Manoel da Nóbrega, a missionary in Brazil and an alumnus of Salamanca, advances a reason for the use of force: he asks himself what the advantage of forcible conversions would be, and he replies with unsettling resignation: For the parents, little enough, "but the children, grandchildren, and so on, could come to be Christians" (Manoel da Nóbrega, *O diálogo da conversão do gentio*, quoted in O. Beozzo, "O diálogo da conversão do gentio"). By contrast, Friar Domingo de Betanzos, a great missionary who sometimes used harsh expressions with regard to the Indians — which he retracted shortly before he died — writes his confrere García de Loaysa on the matter of forcible conversions: "And that Your Mercy may appreciate what I have to say, one must know that the whole manner of converting these people, from the beginning until today, has always been more violent than voluntary, which is altogether contrary to the doctrine and gospel of our Redeemer" (letter of December 3, 1540; quoted in Getino, Introduction to *Relecciones internacionalistas de Vitoria*, 543). Nor did Las Casas express himself differently.

29. Apropos of the Spaniards' third title for waging war (where an infidel prince were to attempt to have any Christian converts among his subjects return to idolatry), Vitoria applies, for example, his basic principle. He says that this motive is justified, as one might expect, "not only by *title of religion*, but *of human friendship and society* as well. After all, by the very fact of any barbarians having been converted to the Christian religion, they have become allies and friends of the Christians" (Vitoria, *Obras,* 719; CHP, 91–92; emphasis in the original).

30. Vitoria's style, observes Bataillon (*Estudios sobre Bartolomé de Las Casas,* 23), provides persons like Sarmiento de Gamboa, a close associate of Viceroy Toledo, with a pretext for using his arguments "to legitimate the new sovereignty." It is not enough then to say, as Getino does — along with numerous scholars of the Salamancan — that "the legitimate titles under analysis have a purely conditional validity for Vitoria" (Getino, Introduction to *Relecciones internacionalistas de Vitoria,* 165). That would open up the possibility, as indeed eventuated, of an attempt to justify the wars *already* fought in the Indies by saying that the conditions were fulfilled. Sepúlveda did not make this mistake. Porras Barrenechea is correct then when he declares: "The chroniclers of the Toledan era mount a reaction that we could call anti-Lascasist and in part Vitorian" (R. Porras Barrenechea, "El pensamiento de Vitoria en el Perú," 479).

31. The examples indicated by Vitoria here are not very appropriate. His ignorance of the facts of the Indies does not help. One of these facts is that of the alliance struck by the Spaniards with the Tlazcaltecas against the Aztecs (a result of the hermeneutic and manipulative capacity of Cortés, Todorov would say; T. Todorov, *La conquête d'Amérique,* 51–131). When Cortés's intrigues become known (he later became Marquis of Valle for his exploits; "misdeeds," Las Casas will call them), the case turns against the line of reasoning being appealed to (see Las Casas's version of the facts, *H.I.,* bk. 3, ch. 123, *O.E.* 2:467–71). Vitoria's other example does not concern the Indies, but the Roman empire, which he says won the right of war through its alliances. He bases himself on the authority of St. Augustine and St. Thomas. The case is energetically rejected by Las Casas, omitting any mention of Vitoria, owing to the imperial domination it implies. Thus he speaks of "the tyrannies whereby the Romans had acquired" the imperial dignity; as for unjust wars, he says that it was precisely through these that the Romans "disturbed and plundered the world" (*Treinta proposiciones,* 1552, *O.E.* 5:253a, 254a). Domingo de Soto as well, who was so close to Vitoria, rejects this example and shows that "the common interpretation of this passage from St. Augustine is mistaken: he did not declare God to have given the Romans the empire as a reward for their virtues...since it cannot be doubted that they conquered the peoples rather by force than by right of law" (quoted by Manuel Martínez, "Las Casas on the Conquest of America," 327–28). Melchior Cano agrees with Soto in this judgment (cited by Martínez, "Las Casas on the Conquest," 327–28).

32. In this last text we make an option for Urdanoz's reading (based on the first and last versions of the manuscript), which reads *amentibus,* a term

Vitoria uses a number of times in this paragraph. This is also the version, based on the Palencia manuscript, furnished by R. Hernández in his *Doctrina sobre los indios,* 59. The CHP reads, in this case only, *adolescentibus,* on the basis of other manuscripts, but accepts the word *amentes* in the context.

33. Vitoria repeats, at this moment, that he is not advancing an argument of which he is certain: "This proposition remains (as I have said) without firm affirmation."

34. One cannot help but wonder, however, whether those who "have no suitable laws, nor magistrates, and who are not even sufficiently capable to govern a family" (Vitoria, *Obras,* 725; CHP, 97) can really be "legitimate rulers."

35. On this subject, speaking of Vitoria and Soto, Brufau explains that "persons of their time failed to perceive situations that, as they had been accepted for centuries, were regarded by their contemporaries as acceptable" (J. Brufau, "Francisco de Vitoria y Domingo de Soto," 57).

36. Text reproduced in *De indis* (CHP), 119–20.

37. Not that this prevents some from comparing them. On the point that we are addressing, Menéndez Pidal holds: "Vitoria arrives at a position closer to Sepúlveda's than to Las Casas's" (R. Menéndez Pidal, *El P. Las Casas y Vitoria: Con otros temas de los siglos XVI y XVII,* 26). Truyol says about the eighth Vitorian title: "This, several decades later, would be Sepúlveda's viewpoint"; but he rightly observes that Vitoria is less categorical (A. Truyol, "De la notion traditionnelle du droit des gens à la notion moderne de droit international public," 88–89).

38. For this reason, Abril holds that in his defense of the Indian Vitoria "stopped halfway" (Abril Castelló, "Vitoria–Las Casas, confrontación y proyección," 166).

39. Some of his sympathizers even appeal to this title in order to bestow on Vitoria the doubtful honor of having anticipated — "with great realism" — the foundation of colonization. That motive "is precisely one of those of greatest novelty, the one that, in modern international law and in the practice of nations, has been forthrightly recognized as the basic title of colonization" (Urdanoz, "Las Casas y Vitoria," 293). Here is the "right" of colonization and its "justification" defended by the great European powers. Commenting on this motive advanced by Vitoria the same author had written: The Indians' "inferior condition of civilization and wild state alone give rise to a *title of protection and tutelage*" (Urdanoz, in Vitoria, *Obras,* 523). For our part, we think that the importance of Vitoria's contribution to international law lies elsewhere.

40. It seems significant to us that Alonso de Veracruz, whose reflection takes place in the warm recesses of the school of Salamanca and who (otherwise) follows Vitoria's illegitimate and legitimate titles step by step in his own exposition, explicitly rejects the last motive adduced by his master. He speaks of the point in the seventh conclusion of the tenth doubt (of his *De Dominio Infidelium et Iusto Bello*), a work which ran into censorship problems. He inquires whether the emperor could have declared a just war on the Indians. The Augustinian rejects the title based on the judgment that they are

"children and incompetents, of little intelligence and prudence." It is not true that they have no right of legitimate dominion over their property and may be deprived of the same. Aristotle's text on natural slaves does not apply to them. Then he details the reasons for which the dwellers of the Indies must not be regarded as inferior beings, bringing out instead their human values (*Writings of Alonso de la Veracruz,* Doubt 10, nos. 708–19). Cerezo de Diego comments that, on this point, "Veracruz shows himself superior to Vitoria himself" and explains why the latter held the position that he did: "In his personal ignorance of American reality, as he lacked the necessary elements on which to base a personal opinion, he saw himself constrained to echo the testimonials that arrived from the New World" (P. Cerezo de Diego, *Alonso de Veracruz y el derecho de gentes,* 288).

41. Here Vitoria attempts to complete his consideration of the matter dealt with in "the earlier *relección*" (the *De Indis*). Rebutting Luther, he maintains that "it is licit for Christians to serve under arms and make war" (Vitoria, *Obras,* 814, 816; CHP, 97, 101). Vitoria's European historical context, we must not forget, is constituted by the cruel confrontation with the Turks. H. G. Justenthoven (*Francisco de Vitoria zu Krieg und Frieden*) has recalled the interest and currency of the Vitorian theory of war.

42. This is not to say, as we have already observed, that Vitoria had broken with the last residue of medievalism and with the ideal of a Christian *orbis terrarum* to champion merely an international community. Urdanoz is right when he maintains that both conceptions coexist in the theologian of law (see Urdanoz, in Vitoria, *Obras,* 626–28). It could not have been otherwise.

43. On the economic and political context of the age, see F. Mauro, *Le XVIe siècle européen: Aspects économiques;* and more concretely, José Larraz, *La época del mercantilismo en Castilla (1500–1700).*

44. It is in these Vitorian reflections that Hugo Grotius takes his inspiration in his celebrated *De Jure Belli et Pacis,* published in 1625.

45. In this position Alonso de la Veracruz follows Vitoria's position very closely. The right to engage in trade and the situation of the dwellers of the Indies who have received the faith (see *Writings of Alonso de la Veracruz,* Doubt 10, nos. 913–29) merge in the following conclusion: "Now the Catholic Emperor is seen to have a just dominion, independently of law and of the justice of a principle. But now no doubt is legitimate" (no. 930).

46. Concerning this last text of Vitoria, Martínez writes: "With all due respect, *aliunde,* to the great master of Salamanca, I confess that I have been unable to read without pain and a sense of scandal an assertion like the foregoing, which would suit the mouth of some *parvenu* in a defense of his interests by hook or by crook, or of a landowner concerned only with fattening his income, more than of a theologian of Vitoria's stature" (Martínez, "Las Casas–Vitoria y la bula *Sublimis Deus,*" 41).

47. Or shortly before, in the second half of that year. For the date, see Urdanoz, in Vitoria, *Obras,* 995.

48. The text was found in 1929 by Beltrán de Heredia (*Ideas del maestro Fray Francisco de Vitoria*).

49. See Martínez, "Las Casas–Vitoria y la bula," 42. The author is severe

in his criticism of the *De Indis*. "We can only conclude," he writes, "that it was equally serviceable for tranquilizing and lulling governors' consciences and preventing their punitive action against the outrages and violence of the Conquista" (44).

50. Martínez, "Las Casas–Vitoria y la bula," 43. The Vitorian passage upon which the author bases his statement does not exactly say that. It is limited to a denial that unbelief justifies war and says: "Just as a Christian prince who has just cause to wage war against another Christian prince does not immediately thereby acquire [*non statim consequitur*] the right to deprive him of his realm, so neither in the present case is it licit in a war against the barbarians immediately [*statim*] to deprive them of their domains and their possessions" (Vitoria, *Obras,* 1053; CHP, 112). Martínez's reading calls attention to a curious ambiguity in the meaning of the word *statim* as used (twice, here) by Vitoria. The use of the word in its proper, *temporal* sense (rather than simply with the transferred meaning of "by that very fact") would seem to limit the scope merely of *this* argument in favor of the war in question and suggest that Vitoria already has other motives in mind that he regards it as legitimate to invoke in favor of Spanish dominion. The context of the fragment is plain in this respect; besides, the seventh conclusion asserts it, shortly before, apropos of the title of human sacrifice and cannibalism: "Other reasons may be present for waging war on the barbarians, namely: an unwillingness to receive preachers of the faith; the assassination of these preachers once they have been received; and other just causes for war" (Vitoria, *Obras,* 1052–53; CHP, 111–12). But the Salamancan declares that it will not be to his purposes to develop these points now. He will do so in the *De Indis* and without beating around the bush.

A second argument Martínez brings forward is equally vulnerable. He claims that the *De Indis* approves a declaration of war by reason of obstacles thrown in the way of a preaching of the gospel, while the fragment *De Temperantia,* he says, forbids the use of force in making anyone a Christian. But, as we have seen in our chapter 5, there is a distinction to be made here, and a classic one, compatible with the theology of the time. It is one thing to *force someone to accept faith,* which would contravene the freedom that acceptance requires, and quite another to *eliminate* by violence *impediments* to the free acceptance of faith. As a good scholastic, Vitoria knew this distinction well.

51. One of the restrictions presented by Vitoria (on a war and a dominion that he justifies, however) may have attracted the notice of the royal councilors in the matter of the Indies. It is the restriction in which, in something of an abstract manner, he asserts that if a Christian prince has dominion over a pagan people, he must be attentive to the good of his subjects. "Whence it follows," he writes, "that if it would be better for that republic that gold not leave the country, the prince would proceed ill were he to permit it" (Vitoria, *Obras,* 1054; CHP, 113). It is possible that the world "gold" sounded like "Indies" to sensitive ears and that they saw in the Master's annotation a criticism of what was occurring in that time in those lands. This is an interesting point in the fragment. Beltrán de Heredia thinks that this allusion to a "stumbling block" was a bit of a scandal, and that therefore the text was

withdrawn — out of a "discreet reserve," he says, "to avoid conflict" (Beltrán de Heredia, *Ideas del maestro Fray Francisco de Vitoria*, 22).

52. This is the opinion of Beltrán de Heredia (*Ideas de Vitoria*, 82–83), J. Höffner (*La ética colonial*, 318), and Martínez ("Las Casas–Vitoria y la bula," 43). Urdanoz rejects this interpretation, and doubts that Vitoria ever "came to read this selection" (in Vitoria, *Obras*, 505). We are in the area of suppositions and lack conclusive evidence. Let us only say that due to the veneration he feels for Charles V, Urdanoz tends to minimize the concerns produced at Court by the discussions on the subject of the Indies. Apropos of a brief visit of the "Spanish Caesar" to Salamanca in 1534, on which occasion he must have met Vitoria, Urdanoz writes: "Each personage had the opportunity to make the other's acquaintance, and doubtless a burst of understanding crossed between the two great souls" (Urdanoz, in Vitoria, *Obras*, 42–43). It is difficult to know, surely. Besides, matters like these are usually less idyllic.

53. And below, he adds: "Inasmuch as our sovereigns, Isabella and Ferdinand, who were the first to occupy those regions, have been most Christian, and the Emperor Charles V is most just and most religious, it is not to be believed that they would have neglected to subject to the closest verification and scrutiny anything that might concern the security of their state and conscience, most of all in a matter of such importance" (Vitoria, *Obras*, 643; CHP, 5).

54. The first time that this occurs is in connection with Las Casas's own petition in 1541 that the matter of the preparation of the Indians for baptism be examined by Vitoria and other Salamancan theologians (see *Memorial al rey*, 1543, *O.E.* 5:203b). There are various other mentions, always with high expressions of praise for the Master's qualities; however, in the most extensive of his allusions, which we shall presently see, he manifests a critical attitude. Vitoria, on the other hand, never cites Las Casas.

55. Vitoria and Las Casas seem not to have become personally acquainted or to have corresponded. So maintains, among others, Pérez Fernández, in his "Cronología comparada," 557. Yet this is surprising. Las Casas's intellectual curiosity ought to have led him to make his confrere's acquaintance during the years of his residence in Spain from 1540 onward. (On earlier occasions when Las Casas had been in Spain, Vitoria had been in Paris.) Unless the reading of the *De Indis* (perhaps around 1540–41) had already suggested to him he take his distance from the Vitorian position.

56. See the text in the *De Indis* (CHP), 152–53. Faithful to his interpretation to the effect that the fragment belonging to the *De Temperantia* constituted a daring statement — so that it later had to be excised — Martínez comments: "Thus, when mere months later, on November 18, 1539, the king's severe letter arrived in the hands of St. Stephen's prior, enjoining upon him the recovery and dispatch to the Council of the sermons and lectures in question, ... far from finding anything against this in Master Vitoria's *De Indis*, he would have been able to find only support there" (Martínez, "Las Casas–Vitoria y la bula," 34; emphasis added). The author reiterates this judgment in *Las Casas and the Conquest*, 333.

57. Relations between Vitoria and Charles V have sparked impassioned

investigations, especially on the part of those unwilling to accept the annoyance provoked in lofty circles by the discussion in Salamanca of matters concerning the Indies, not excluding a resentment of Vitoria's opinions. Among them are Urdanoz (see his introductions in Vitoria, *Obras,* 55–57, 506); and of course T. Andrés Marcos in his various writings.

58. So says Hernández, "Francisco de Vitoria en la crisis de su tiempo," 61. The prohibition of debate on the justice of the presence of the Spanish Crown was no obstacle to Charles V's later expression of his appreciation for the person of the Salamancan master, for example, his request (at Las Casas's instance) that he give his opinion on the procedure to be followed in the baptism of adults in the Indies. The document issued by the Salamancans in response — Domingo de Soto and Andrés Vega also signed it — brings no novelties to the field of theology, but has the merit of establishing a clear, correct conclusion. That conclusion is expressed in these terms: "These barbarian unbelievers are not to be baptized unless they have been sufficiently instructed, not only in matters of faith, but of Christian customs as well, at least in that which is necessary for eternal salvation, in order that thus they may understand what they have received, show it reverence, and profess it in baptism, and be willing to live and persevere in the Christian faith and religion" (in *Libro Anual,* 207; a translation of the original Latin to be found in *De indis* [CHP], 157–64). It is a conclusion that shows respect for personal freedom and for the time required for a mature acceptance of baptism. It is a valid pastoral norm not only for the "unbelievers" of that time, but for many "believers" of our own, as well!

59. Beltrán de Heredia, who found and published this letter, gives it a date of November 8, 1534 (see Beltrán de Heredia, *Ideas de Vitoria,* 11 n. 1). Numerous scholars follow his indication. Urdanoz rejects this date and proposes instead the year 1545 (in Vitoria, *Obras,* 57, 505–6 n. 30), followed by Carro, *España en América,* 134 (who puts instead 1544, perhaps a typographical error). This is also the opinion of Pérez Fernández, "Cronología comparada," 554. This latter dating seems to us to be better founded.

60. As we have noted, we take this letter as being from 1545, but we should like to specify that the following observations take only the text of the letter into account and are valid even if it is assigned the date of 1534. What seems to us to be lacking in foundation is to maintain that this private missive, known only by its addressee, is the manifesto — early though the text may be — that launches a new approach to matters of the Indies (which is what Pereña maintains in his "Proceso histórico de las fuentes," 11).

61. Vitoria had health problems at this time, which obliged him to take extended absences from teaching. He died in 1546.

62. Finally, with great honesty, he attacks the "composition" (an arrangement whereby wrongs are pardoned in exchange for an alms, when the restitution of something unlawfully taken is no longer possible). Vitoria does not accept it, even though it comes from Rome and his rejection earns him the accusation that he is contradicting the pope. And thus we have yet another obstacle to expressing an opinion on matters of the Indies. (We have taken the letter to M. de Arcos from Beltrán de Heredia, *Ideas de Vitoria,* 9–11;

the text is reproduced in numerous works on Vitoria; see, e.g., *De indis* [CHP], 137–39.)

63. It is always painful, considering Vitoria's human and theological quality, to recall the objective ambiguity of his thinking when it comes to the Indies. It cannot be hidden, however. A. Milhou rightly refuses to admit the accusation of duplicity lodged with Vitoria, but admits that one may speak of an "ambiguity of Vitoria's" (A. Milhou, "Las Casas à l'âge d'or du prophetisme," 105 n. 54). Abril values Vitoria's contribution and scientific rigor, although he judges that Vitoria's hypotheses "cover over genuine doubts and information vacuums," as well as a "fear of compromising himself" in the face of possible reprisals "on the part of the established powers" (V. Abril Castelló, "Vitoria–Las Casas, confrontación y proyección," 172). "His practical failings," says Hernández, "are the fruit of circumstances": he knew the reality of the Indies only by hearsay, which "fully excuses the ambiguities and rescues the appearances of skepticism in the conditions he imposes on princes" (Hernández, "Las hipótesis de Francisco de Vitoria," 380–81). "Caution or theoretical prudence," lest he be himself compromised in matters in which he was not very familiar, says Pérez Fernández ("Cronología comparada," 568 n. 52).

64. Given the Salamancan's indubitable probity, if the letter in question, in which he demonstrates a knowledge of facts that made his blood run cold, were to be from 1534, it becomes more difficult to understand the hypothetical nature and almost distant tone of his *relecciones* on the issues of the Indies.

65. Abril Castelló ("Vitoria–Las Casas, confrontación y proyección") has made a valuable comparison of the ideas of Vitoria and Las Casas, insisting on the consequences of Bartolomé's radicalizations of some of his theses following his debate with Sepúlveda. We shall return to this point in a later chapter.

66. The latitude in question is explained precisely by the Master's style. Someone like Carro recognizes this, pointing out that "after setting forth the various solutions" Vitoria "rather leave[s] us up in the air, not knowing which he prefers, and flirting with indifference. This method," Carro adds critically, "which is fine for stimulating young hearts and minds, is not always the best for the solid solutions required by theological science" (Carro, *La teología y los teólogos-juristas*, 2:250).

67. Owing to this spectrum of possibilities, some have sought to compare, and others to contrast, Vitoria and Sepúlveda. The same thing occurs with the closeness or distance between Vitoria and Las Casas. Or there are cases like that of Losada (an acute historian to whom we owe valuable editions of the works of Sepúlveda and Las Casas), who seems to have evolved from a great diffidence in Las Casas's regard (explainable by his sympathy for Sepúlveda, on whom he is a noted expert) toward a higher esteem for our Friar's work. Losada betrays the latter attitude when, curiously, he narrows the gap between Las Casas and Sepúlveda. In that operation, Vitoria's positions between the two, which partly coincide sometimes with the one, sometimes with the other, serve him as a bridge (saving the obvious differences) for

seeking forced convergences between these two most bitter adversaries (see, e.g., his otherwise interesting *Fray Bartolomé de Las Casas a la luz de la moderna crítica histórica;* the same idea is found in several of his articles, "Juan Ginés de Sepúlveda: Su polémica con Fray Bartolomé de Las Casas," or in the notes to his translations of the works of Sepúlveda and Las Casas).

68. Pérez de Tudela ("Significado histórico," cxxxix) is on the mark when he writes with reference to Vitoria's doctrine: "In abandoning this conception, in which justice does not ignore but neither assigns a primacy to the cession of charity, Vitoria is as it were the anointed seer of a progressive humanity on the point of extending its dominion across the planet." The author adds that "Friar Bartolomé has assumed for good and all the role of the defense attorney of the Indian, whose humanity is historically the most underdeveloped"; and he concludes with an assertion of the complementarity of the two positions.

69. Carro presents Vitoria's theses as universal, immutable postulates (see Carro, *La teología y los teólogos-juristas,* vol. 2). That they were indeed; but, as Pérez de Tudela says with good judgment: "One need only imagine what the exercise of those presumed natural rights would have meant on the part of Moroccans on Spanish territory in order to understand the inconsistency of such titles as abstract postulation" (Pérez de Tudela, "Significado histórico," cxxxix, n. 361; emphasis added). This is something that Bartolomé always kept in account.

70. This is the case with Carro, who reproaches Las Casas with his "ignorance of the 'way of sociability' "; this would be one of his failings. Carro, who did so much to defend Las Casas from his most headlong, bitter adversaries, always judges Bartolomé's ideas in the light of the doctrine of Vitoria, "the Spanish Socrates," as he likes to say, since, according to him, "Las Casas has no ideas of his own" (Carro, *La teología y los teólogos-juristas,* 2:153, 456). On the question of sociability, Bataillon insightfully observes: "The reader should keep in mind the paradox that the demand of the sociability of peoples is utilized, according to this 'way,' not to found a right of contact with the natives of America, but a *right to make war on them* on the occasion of this contact" (Bataillon, *Estudios sobre Bartolomé de Las Casas,* 21; emphasis in the original). True, but there is no paradox. The matter is more serious and has profound causes, as we have observed.

71. J. Friede, *Bartolomé de Las Casas: Precursor,* 88–89.

72. Pérez Fernández, "Cronología comparada," 567 n. 52.

73. He has concerned himself with it in many writings, asserts the friar from Seville (see *H.I.,* bk. 1, ch. 173, *O.E.* 1:461a). Otherwise, as Lassègue says, a purely formal universality and equality would serve "to exploit the Indies and what we now call the Third World" (J.-B. Lassègue, *La larga marcha,* 233; see also the fine indication of J. A. de la Torre, *El uso alternativo del derecho,* 81).

74. See C. Barcia Trelles, *Francisco de Vitoria et l'école moderne du droit international.*

Introduction to Part Five

1. This judgment of Peru is vigorously reiterated in *Memorial al rey* (1542, *O.E.* 5:123–33).

2. A. de Remesal recounts the episode (*Historia general de las Indias Occidentales*, 2:108). Furthermore, Las Casas himself alludes to it in a letter to the future Philip II when he describes his diocese of Chiapa as "that most wretched land, which I wished to accept although Your Highness was offering me another, better one" (1545, *O.E.* 5:232a). See Helen Rand Parish, *Las Casas as a Bishop*, xi–xiv.

3. See the data on this figure and his request to Las Casas, with a letter from Vega that would confirm his status as author of the petition, adduced by M. Bataillon, in "Les 'douze questions' péruviennes résolues par Las Casas." However, Wagner has since maintained that the doubts were proposed rather by Domingo de Santo Tomás (Wagner and Parish, *The Life and Writings of Bartolomé de Las Casas*, 295).

4. So he says explicitly in concluding the *Doce dudas* (Providence version, folio 226v). "The most bruising of Las Casas's treatises" is Giménez Fernández's description of this work (H. Giménez Fernández, "Las Casas y el Perú," 368).

5. Letter of Las Casas to Domingo de Soto in Bataillon, *Estudios sobre Bartolomé de Las Casas*, 261.

6. This is one of the reasons for his violent, repeated opposition to the grants made to German bankers and colonists in Venezuelan lands (see *Carta al Consejo*, 1531, *O.E.* 5:50a).

7. This view legitimated the wars being undertaken against the Indians, as it would later do with the horrendous "uprooting of idolatry." For the case of Peru, see the important works of P. Duviols, *La lutte contre les religions autochtones dans le Pérou colonial*, and *Cultura Andina y Repressión*.

Chapter 13: Rights of the Indian Nations

1. See above, our chapter 2.

2. We call it his *Confesionario* for simplicity's sake and because this is what it is usually called, although, as A. Gutiérrez observes in his "El 'confesionario' de Bartolomé de Las Casas," the Lascasian text does not fall in the category of the classic handbooks for hearing confessions. Rather it treats of how a confessor should deal with the specific "case of conscience" posed by the duty of restitution.

3. See N. Jung, "Restitution."

4. See above, our chapter 1. Matías de Paz did the same in Spain (see above, our chapter 4).

5. Francesca Cantù has written an excellent article on the evolution of the teaching on restitution in Las Casas: "Evoluzione e significato."

6. The composition is present in the bull of the crusade renegotiated in the time of Ferdinand V by Royal Treasurer Miguel de Pasamonte. In the *Memorial* that we have cited (as well as in certain later texts), Las Casas details

his proposal: essentially, it consisted in spending the money from the "composition" for his reform projects for the Indies. Giménez Fernández (*Bartolomé de Las Casas: Capellán*) studies this point in detail.

7. The writing seeks to respond to the pastoral needs of his diocese (see *O.E.* 5:235a), a concern already present in his *Proclama a los feligreses de Chiapa,* 1545, *O.E.* 5:215–18. Las Casas took the precaution of having it approved by leading Salamancan theologians, despite which Ginés de Sepúlveda calls it a "libelous tract against our rulers and nation" (*O.E.* 5:317a–b).

8. A telling argument in the religious and cultural context of the time. See D. Ramos Pérez's lucid analysis, "La etapa lascasiana de la presión de las conciencias."

9. Las Casas lauds the Dominican, Franciscan, and Augustinian friars for their denial of absolution to the Spaniards who held Indian slaves. See his *Tratado sobre los indios que se han hecho esclavos,* 1552, *O.E.* 5:289a.

10. Let us see a remark by Las Casas, simple enough, but which cannot be read without recalling situations still prevailing among us: "The Indians almost never ask justice for themselves, however afflicted they may be, or if they ever do, they obtain it either not at all or with great difficulty. The reason," he specifies, "is that the Indians do not know how to read and write, nor do they know the Spanish language, and the Spaniards make no account of them, in fact they contemn them, and thus do not listen to them" (*Solicitud al Consejo de Indias,* concerning the Indians of Peru, 1555? *O.E.* 5:453b). Nor do they listen to them today.

11. Various meetings and decisions of bishops will echo the proposal: for example, "Los avisos breves para todos los confesores de estos reinos del Perú," approved by the Second Provincial Council of Lima, under the presidency of Jerónimo de Loaisa (commented on by B. Lopétegui, "Apuros en los confesionarios"). See also the texts on restitution promulgated by the synods of Santafé de Bogotá and Popayán, reproduced in *Carta Magna de los indios* (constitutional sources, 1534–1609), 137–49.

12. See the research by G. Lohmann on the effect of these Lascasian ideas in Peru: for example, in his "La restitución por conquistadores y encomenderos: Un aspecto de la incidencia lascasiana en el Perú." Cantù adduces an unpublished text confirming both Las Casas's notion on the matter as well as the repercussions of this notion in Peru: "Caso propuesto para salir de cierta duda" (Cantù, "Evoluzione e significato," 312–19). Lassègue has studied an interesting case of restitution in Chicama Valley in which two great friends of Las Casas in Peru participated, Tomás de San Martín and Domingo de Santo Tomás: J.-B. Lassègue, "Luchas en torno a la restitución y utopía de la justicia." In light of these cases, as well as of the repercussions mentioned in the foregoing note, it becomes difficult to assert that Bartolomé's battle had no practical consequences in his time.

13. Near the end of his work, he writes: "All of the gold and silver and whatever other precious objects the Spaniards have found, from the discovery up until today, except what the natives have bestowed upon them voluntarily before their ill requital at the hands of the Spaniards or have handed over to them by way of commutation, have been the object of theft and robbery,

and accordingly are subject to restitution" (*De Thesauris*, 130). A. Losada and J.-B. Lassègue are preparing a critical edition of this important treatise of Las Casas to be published as volume 11/1 of the *Obras Completas*.

14. Las Casas is thought to have written a treatise in Latin, *De Restitutione*, which we do not have (see *H.I.*, bk. 3, ch. 153, *O.E.* 2:545a). I. Pérez believes that this writing has been incorporated into the *De Thesauris* (I. Pérez Fernández, *Inventario*, 715).

15. To the king he writes: "All of the Indians of the Indies who until this day have dealt with and assaulted Christians have been waging a just war against them by reason of the great affliction, violence, tyranny, and unjust war with which the Christians have oppressed, slain, and destroyed them" (*Memorial*, 1543, 191a; here is an important Lascasian text in which our earlier point concerning restitution occupies a central place).

16. See the observations on this point by C. Castillo, "La conversión de las naciones indias," 71. Las Casas also speaks of the right to "natural defense" in the *Memorial* just cited (*O.E.* 5:181b).

17. It cannot be alleged, he says, as "certain persons ignorant of fact and of law" allege, that the sovereign of Hispaniola was the king of Castile: "Never have the natural rulers and lords of this isle recognized the king of Castile as their superior" (ibid.). We shall examine this thesis in detail in this chapter.

18. The "just war" doctrine has old roots in theological thought. It finds a major expression in Thomas Aquinas, who also treats of "just vengeance" (*ST*, II–II, q. 108), to which Las Casas likewise alludes, and was adopted once more in terms of the problems of the age by Vitoria in his *De Jure Belli*. But Las Casas does not treat the matter in systematic form, for example, with regard to tyrannicide, a prevailing theme in the discussions of the era. Vitoria, however, does so in the *relección* we have cited.

19. "The king and queen of Castile and León are authentic sovereigns, enjoying universal domain and empire, over many rulers, and to them belongs *de jure* all that high empire and universal jurisdiction over all the Indies by the authority, grant, and donation of the said Holy Apostolic See, and thus by divine authority. And this and nothing else is the juridical and substantial foundation whereon is founded and settled all their title" (*O.E.* 5:253a–b).

20. "Compatible with this sovereign, imperial, and universal principality and domain of the king and queen of Castile in the Indies is the administration, principality, jurisdiction, rights, and dominion that the native rulers and sovereigns of the same have over their subject peoples, that they be ruled, whether politically or royally, as the universal and supreme lordship of the emperors that they had of old over kings was compatible [with the authority of the latter]" (ibid.).

21. Nevertheless, this is what T. Urdanoz (along with a number of others) insistently declares in his "Las Casas and Francisco de Vitoria." The opposite is maintained by García Villoslada, who has no special sympathy for Las Casas and regards it as evident that Bartolomé does not defend any theocratic (or "hierocratic," as this author prefers to say) positions, nor the direct power of the pope in temporal matters (R. García Villoslada, "Sentido de la conquista y evangelización," 408–12).

22. This was the Ostian's position. See above, our chapter 4.

23. See above, our chapter 3.

24. A comment on the book by Palacios Rubios, a defender of theocratic positions, is interesting in this regard. Palacios asserts the jurisdiction of the pope "over all the infidels of the world." Las Casas notes in the margin: "Within the Church, this is true, and every creature, that is, Catholic and baptized" (*De las islas del mar océano,* 101). That is, the pope has power only over the baptized.

25. On the other hand, the theory of direct power assigned to the pope the condition of both spiritual and temporal sovereign, in his capacity as successor of Christ, King of the universe. The temporal sword (as it was called, with reference to the two swords of the gospel text; see Luke 22:38) was delegated by the pope to the emperor, but the commission was only that: a commission. It is important to note that this was not the only thesis in the Middle Ages; however, thanks to certain popes (Gregory VII, Innocent III, and Boniface VIII, among others), it acquired citizenship papers in Rome. It was defended by important jurists and theologians, and the reaction of other scholars was not long in coming. Thomas Aquinas laid the foundations for a distinction between the temporal and the spiritual; after him, others undertook to develop theories that ascribed to the pope only an indirect power (with a view to the spiritual) or directive (solely through the conscience of Christians) in temporal matters. This power, being a mere consequence of religious power, is limited to certain cases. Both positions likewise denied the pope the authority, as a temporal monarch, to enthrone and depose princes. For the history of these ideas, see G. Glez, "Pouvoir du Pape dans l'ordre temporel." (This author makes an interesting, and laudatory, reference to Las Casas's *Tratado comprobatorio,* which we are studying; col. 2754.) See also J. Lecler, *L'Eglise et la souveraineté de l'etat,* and Yves M.-J. Congar's excellent "Eglise et Etat," which clearly distinguishes between an indirective and a directive power. Admittedly, however, the vocabulary sometimes fluctuates. For example, Lecler and Congar, who hold basically the same position, express it in different language: Lecler speaks of "indirect" power, and Congar calls it "directive."

26. This thirteenth-century Dominican theologian is an extremely interesting personage. His thought lies along the lines of directive power, as we have defined it. Las Casas's reserve may stem from the fact that at one time John of Paris was associated with the royalist outlook (favorable to the power of the king), and was regarded as standing close to Ockham.

27. In the sixteenth of the *Treinta proposiciones,* he says: "The Roman Pontiff, Vicar of Jesus Christ, by divine authority, whose are all realms of heaven and earth, was able propitiously, licitly, and justly to invest the Sovereigns of Castile..." (*O.E.* 5:253a). The "whose" (*cuyos*) obviously refers to the divine authority, not to that of the vicar of Christ.

28. Urdanoz repeatedly appeals to it for his theocratic interpretation of Las Casas's thought (see his "Las Casas y Francisco de Vitoria," 255–57). One of the few Lascasian passages that approach it elsewhere is found in the *Quaestio Theologalis* (folios 100–100v), a work written to defend the jurisdiction of the church from encroachments of civil power (and which would date

from 1546, about the time of the *Tratado comprobatorio*). In it, besides, he reiterates the principle that church power is ordained for a spiritual end. Thus, vis-à-vis the text to which we have just alluded, A. Larios and A. García del Moral emphatically observe: "Las Casas is no theocrat" (in Las Casas, *Obras Completas,* 12:403–4 nn. 22, 27).

29. We have seen something of this in our foregoing chapter.

30. In the *De Indis* (see above, our chapter 12), Vitoria states in this perspective: "Although the Pope is not a temporal lord, as we have said before, nevertheless he has power in temporal matters with a view to the spiritual" ("in ordine ad spiritualia"; *Obras,* 716; CHP, 88). Basically he is repeating what he has maintained in *De Potestate Ecclesiae* (*Obras,* 305).

31. In a fine study of the point in Vitoria (in which he indicates his sources precisely), Beltrán de Heredia considers that for the Salamancan master (keeping the *De Indis* in account as well) "this power is so ample (as it goes beyond the position of many canonists) that, in virtue of it, the pope can do and dispose not only what secular princes can, but actually depose the princes themselves and name others in their place, divide empires, and much else besides." The author immediately specifies: "Obviously this power, as it refers to extreme cases, is more theoretical than practical, and although logic imposes it, reality has its purview, which no discreet person would dare to infringe without measuring the consequences" (V. Beltrán de Heredia, "Doctrina de Vitoria sobre las relaciones entre Iglesia y Estado y fuentes de la misma," 88–89). The illustrious theologian's authority undoubtedly had an influence on the Lascasian text that we are discussing.

32. If the faith is oppressed, the pope, he says, adopting the thought of Soto, one of the best of his experts, "can move against his enemies not only spiritual weapons, but material ones as well, calling Christian princes to his assistance even under threat of deposition. In a word: The Church and the Pope have rights that any nation and its King may have against the enemy of the Fatherland, against another nation that tramples its rights under foot. Prudence will indicate the most appropriate path to take" (V. Carro, *La teología y los teólogos-juristas,* 2:46).

33. Both theologians were influenced by another Spanish Dominican, Cardinal Juan de Torquemada (not to be confused with Tomás). Las Casas does not cite him in these treatises; he does so in another context in the so-called *Quaestio Theologalis,* 98.

34. He agrees with them as well that the pope had the faculty to grant the evangelizing charge only to the Spanish rulers, so that no other nation might intervene. For the Spaniards of the age, this concept of a certain "missionary monopoly" seemed self-evident.

35. This indicates that the scope of Bartolomé's mention of Innocent IV and the Ostian, whom he also severely criticizes once more (see *O.E.* 5:338a, 389a), is limited when he speaks of the temporal consequences of the pope's religious mission (see *O.E.* 5:371b).

36. See Yves M.-J. Congar, "Eglise et Etat," 401–2.

37. See G. Gutiérrez, "Las cosas nuevas de hoy: Una relectura de la Rerum Novarum."

38. See Mariano Cuevas, *Documentos inéditos del s. XVI para la historia de México,* 176–80, and in Bartolomé de Las Casas, *De Regia Potestate* (CHP), 168–72. I. Pérez Fernández does not pronounce explicitly, but he seems to accept this attribution (see his *Inventario,* 274). The texts that we shall cite on the following pages without references are taken from *Inventario;* emphasis is added.

39. For García Villoslada, a universal sovereignty of the Spanish Crown postulated by Las Casas is "pure fantasy." García asks: "Will an imperial power limited to the sending of missionaries not be utterly superfluous and meaningless?" ("Sentido de la conquista y evangelización," 411). From his viewpoint, he is not incorrect.

40. This thesis is opposed, moreover, to the one that argued: Given the donation, the rulers might dispose of the Indies at their good pleasure and for their own benefit — which would conclude to (among other things) a justification of war on the Indians.

41. It is a matter of a genuine pact between the pope and the Spanish sovereigns, on the strength of the final cause of evangelization as formulated in the bull. "With two precepts," he writes, "has the Pope obligated their Most Serene Highnesses. And the Sovereigns have accepted the said precepts, and by their own promise and *policitación,* made to the Vicar of Christ, to fulfill the said charge and office and care have obligated themselves, and have made themselves the debtors of the fulfillment, and consequently there has been celebrated between the Apostolic See and the sovereigns a certain pact" (*O.E.* 5:414a). *Policitación* meant a promise not yet accepted, the pact with a view to evangelization binds (ob-ligates) the rulers, with all of the consequences of such obligation. This will be specified by way of the juridical notion of the modal grant, which Las Casas employs.

42. See the interesting indications by J. A. de la Torre, *El uso alternativo del derecho,* 77–78, on the notion in law of a modal donation.

43. That is the reason for the difficulties experienced by some scholars in classifying Lascasian thought. See R. J. Queraltó Moreno, *El pensamiento filosófico-político de Bartolomé de Las Casas,* 103; Carla Forti, "Letture di Bartolomé," 49. Both consider the category "medieval" inadequate to characterize our friar's position.

44. Höffner had already made the observation. "One cannot help," he writes, "delighting in the agility with which Las Casas dismantles the edict of papal feudalization [Höffner's name for the donation] — the imposing exordium of his 'Propositions' — piece by piece, until finally nothing is left but a certain obligation on the part of the Indians converted to Christianity gratefully to acknowledge the king as Spain as their 'emperor' practically only honorifically" (J. Höffner, *Etica colonial,* 288).

45. Rejecting the name "discovery" for the subjection of the nations of the Indies, he writes: "And this occurs out of the ignorance of the members of the Council and the blind error in which they have ever walked in their notion that the Sovereigns of Castile had discovered those Indies through Admiral Columbus, so that they now had the right, by peace or war, evil or good, force or good pleasure, to subjugate and lord it over their peoples and dominions

as if they had been the lands of Africa" (*H.I.*, bk. 3, ch. 55, *O.E.* 2:303b). The reference to Africa is to the sanguinary procedures of the Portuguese slavers, who relied on an interpretation of the papal bulls they had received (see A. De Witte, "Les bulles pontificales et l'expansion portugaise au XVe siècle"). After this rejection, Las Casas reiterates the sole legitimate motive: "...the preaching of the gospel and the conversion of these people, and for that cause — not impelling but final," he specifies — "the Roman Church might interfere by granting them the said universal and sovereign or imperial dominion" (ibid.). We are familiar with the notion.

46. See above, our chapters 3, 5, 6.

47. This work is known to be part of a more extensive work that we do not have, but that, if we had it in our hands, would shed a great deal of light on this moment of the Lascasian thought.

48. The memorandum that we shall presently mention, then, is not the first text in which Bartolomé presents his thesis of the consent of the governed, as Urdanoz says ("Las Casas y Francisco de Vitoria," 252).

49. See K. Pennington, "Bartolomé de Las Casas and the Tradition of Medieval Law." Congar has sketched the influence of this maxim in the Middle Ages. He has also recalled the observation of certain historians with respect to its presence in the Dominican order, which could explain Las Casas's interest in the principle (see Congar, "Quod omnes tangit, ab omnibus tractari et approbari debet," especially 230–31).

50. Here is the complete text of the proposition: "All native [*naturales*] sovereigns and rulers, [all] cities, communities, and villages of those Indies are under obligation to acknowledge the sovereigns of Castile as universal and sovereign imperial rulers in the said manner, *after* having received of their own free will our holy faith and sacred baptism, and if *before* they receive it they do not do so or do not wish to do so, they may not be punished by any judge or justice" (*O.E.* 5:253; emphasis added).

51. This is clearly perceptible in the arguments he advances in defense of this distinction in his *Tratado comprobatorio* (see *O.E.* 5:403a–404a).

52. Those who maintained that the first step ought to be war appealed to this papal document.

53. As we see, Las Casas uses the expression, "human rights." They are founded on "reason and natural law and much more on the law of Christian charity" (*O.E.* 5:268b).

54. Losada translates, "...has its origin" instead of the future "nacerá" ("will be born," our own translation here). In his translation Poole writes "will be born." Abril observes that Losada reads the present tense *nascitur* where the text actually has the future, *nascetur* (V. Abril Castelló, "La bipolarización," 255).

55. Abril describes the process in these terms: "...in function of evangelization and to the extent that the latter wins its ultimate objectives" (ibid.).

56. Here is Sepúlveda's text: "To grant that they must subject themselves to the sovereigns of Castile along with their leading princes [only] after becoming Christians is to contradict all that has been said in order to avoid

war. After all, if the sovereigns of Castile have the right, as he says they do, to subject them in that manner after they have become Christians, then surely if they are unwilling to offer their obedience they may justly be forced to do so, and for this purpose war is necessary. Justly, then, have they been forced for lesser cause than the one we ourselves invoke" (*O.E.* 5:317a).

57. We refer to the first version of Las Casas's Twelfth Reply to Sepúlveda, published in Las Casas, *Tratado de Indias y el doctor Sepúlveda.* The text has been published, with a comparison of various manuscripts, by Abril Castelló, "Réplica que hizo el obispo de Chiapa contra el doctor Sepúlveda."

58. "But as to the second time, we have a heavier and more solid right" (Las Casas, *Tratado de Indias*). Here we have an echo of the old distinction between heathen and heretics, which we examine in our chapter 5. The severity that was regarded as admissible in dealing with heretics was rejected in the case of those who had never been Christians. We shall presently see the interest of recalling this to mind.

59. Abril Costelló, comparing both versions of Las Casas's Twelfth Reply, has called attention to this in an excellent, perceptive article that we have already cited: "La bipolarización." Thereby he has established the precise moment at which Las Casas rectifies his previous position.

60. This change in Las Casas's position had been noted by a number of authors: for example, Rumeu de Armas asserts: "With the passage of time, Las Casas's position becomes more rigid. He does not admit the obligation of the Indians to submit even after being converted, which can arise only from a spontaneous, free act," and he adds: "Along this one-way street he will finally advocate the wholesale withdrawal of the Spaniards" (A. Rumeu de Armas, *La política indigenista de Isabel la Católica*, 142; see also J. A. Maravall, "Utopía y primitivismo," 378). It is strange, then, that apropos of the Valladolid disputation Losada should assert that when it came to the use of force, Sepúlveda (and according to him Vitoria as well) differs from Las Casas only in what Las Casas calls the first stage: when the Indians have not yet adopted the Christian faith. All three agree, says Losada, as to the second moment: here, the wars are justified. As we see, no account is kept here either of Las Casas's rectification in the disputation that Losada is considering, or of his repetition (see the material to follow in our own text) in the *De Thesauris*, which Losada himself has translated and published. See Losada, "Juan Ginés de Sepúlveda: Su polémica con Fray Bartolomé de Las Casas," 575–76.

61. Abril speaks of "the revolution of the Twelfth Reply," and underscores the importance of this correction for the Sevillian friar's strategy (see Abril Castelló, "La bipolarización").

62. Here is the text: "The reason is that the choice of rulers and of who will govern free persons and peoples belongs to the very persons that are to be governed, by natural law and the Law of Nations, so that they themselves submit to the one elected by their own consent, which is an act of will that can in no way be forced (as we have said above), inasmuch as originally all human beings are born, and are, free" (*O.E.* 5:380a–381b). A bit further on he repeats the idea and even appeals to an old canonical tradition concerning the selection of bishops: "In full accord are the sacred Canons, founded on

the aforesaid natural reason, which provided that there be no bishops but by election of the clergy and petition of the people" (*O.E.* 5:381b; see Congar, "Quod omnes tangit").

63. Written in Latin "since it dealt with royal power," says Parish, in Pérez Fernández, *Inventario*, 605. Later Bartolomé will include it in a more extensive work: *De Regia Potestate*. Hence our allusion to *Principia Quaedam* will be brief.

64. The text goes on: "And with antecedent pact, agreement, and settlement between the king of Castile and the [Indian rulers], and the king of Castile's promise, confirmed by oath, [to secure and preserve] their superior good and to maintain and preserve their freedom and their dominion, dignities, rights, and ancient, reasonable, laws: they (I mean the rulers and peoples), promising and swearing to the sovereigns of Castile to acknowledge that loftier, supreme princely authority, and obedience to their just laws and commands" (*O.E.* 5:445a).

65. To their natural wealth, for example (see *O.E.* 5:445b).

66. "There is no reason, nor does Jesus Christ will it by his law, for the faith be announced to the Indians more dearly [i.e., at greater expense to the addressees] than it has been preached and announced to any nation in the world, including to us in Castile" (ibid.).

67. Todorov acknowledges that these outlooks express considerable sensitivity to the viewpoint of the "other," but he does not seem to situate well the roots and the place those perspectives have in the work of Las Casas. See T. Todorov, *La conquête de l'Amérique*, 191–99.

68. Pérez de Tudela comments: "The congruence between gospel and freedom, and the antinomy between gospel and war, was being carried to its ultimate consequences" (J. Pérez de Tudela, "Significado histórico," cxvi–cxvii).

69. Let us not forget that many persons of the time appealed to the *Inter Caetera* to justify wars and domination in the Indies. Las Casas erects this same document into a pillar of his own position, whose core theses will be adopted by some of the great professors of Salamanca (see Abril Castelló, "Bartolomé de Las Casas y la escuela de Salamanca," 511–12).

70. Among the treatises published by Las Casas in Seville (1552) are not only the *Treinta proposiciones* (of which some copies may nevertheless have circulated before being printed) and the *Tratado comprobatorio*, but also the *Aquí se contiene*, which presents the definitive version of the Lascasian replies. Let us note, besides, that among them is to be found the work entitled *Principia Quaedam*, which is the germinal version of his *De Regia Potestate*.

71. Wagner and Parish, *The Life and Writings of Bartolomé de Las Casas*, think it was redacted around 1552. L. Vicente Pereña, who published it in 1969, thinks it was written over the course of several years (between 1541 and 1566). Pérez Fernández, for his part, regards it as being from the years 1563–66. It will be the first book by Las Casas to be published outside Spain (in Frankfurt, in 1571). Certain doubts have arisen as to Las Casas's actual authorship of this treatise (see Pérez Fernández, *Inventario*, 722, which does not develop the issue; J. González Rodríguez, "Introducción" to vol. 12 of Las Casas, *Obras Completas*, "Dimensión histórica del *De Regia Potestate*," which

seems to us to be clearer in its presentation of prevailing doubts than in the solutions he proposes). Pereña, on the other hand, accepts the attribution to Las Casas as authentic (see Pereña Vicente, "Estudio preliminar" of his edition of the *De Regia Potestate,* cxiv–cxxi). In any event, no one doubts the Lascasian roots of the work.

72. See the historical framework Pereña Vicente presents in his "Estudio preliminar" of his edition of this treatise; and see González Rodríguez, who sets up an interesting parallel (along with certain divergences) between this treatise and the memorandum presented to the king by Las Casas and Domingo de Santo Tomás concerning the perpetuity of the *encomiendas* (González Rodríguez, "Introducción" to vol. 12 of Las Casas, *Obras Completas,* "Dimensión histórica del *De Regia Potestate,*" xliii).

73. Las Casas found precedents in medieval law that he could exploit in support of his great intuitions. Italian jurist Lucas de Penna is one of his best sources: he mentions him explicitly (not, however, adequately, according to Pereña, who thinks the *De Regia* takes many of its ideas from this author; see Pereña Vicente, "Estudio preliminar," cxlvii). As Carla Forti humorously observes, at least we must give Bartolomé credit, "in an age in which plagiarism was more the rule than the exception, with a fine nose and a sure critical eye, in spotting…the best lawyer of the fourteenth century" before de Pereña's works were printed (Forti, "Letture di Bartolomé," 41).

74. The distinction is similar to the philosophical one between potency and act, which he also employs in this work (see ibid., 127).

75. Clearly, of course, if the papal donation cannot be effective until the Indian nations accept it, this will be precisely because it has not been made by a "universal monarch" exercising a direct power in the political area.

76. "No possession has been juridically and rightly effected until now on the part of our sovereigns" (ibid., 117).

77. Strictly speaking, things were not the way they had been at the beginning. Throughout all of these years a destruction of the Indies had occurred, which Las Casas, and many others with him, denounces, and on whose account he posits the duty of restitution to those affected. In these pages this is called the third stage.

78. This is his basis for denying the invaders any right to seize the *huacas,* as we shall see in our chapter 15.

79. This is his name for the *De Thesauris* and the *Doce dudas* in his dedication to Philip II (Providence version, folios 136–136v). The similarity between the principles of this treatise and the conclusions of the *Memorial al Consejo,* 1565 (*O.E.* 5:538a–b), is common knowledge.

80. No more than anywhere else in the Indies, according to Las Casas, had Spanish domain been freely accepted. The Spaniards have been there "against the Indians' will," and the only reason the Indians have not driven them out was that "they were helpless to do so" (*O.E.* 5:482a).

81. The enunciation of eight principles enables Las Casas to respond to the list of "doubts" he has received. The first draft of these principles dates from 1536, and we have already cited this text (see above, our chapter 3, n. 9): "It appears to have been amplified with 'six truths' concerning Indian slaves

and peaceful conversion" originating with Juan de Zumárraga, but written by Las Casas, according to Parish, who has published it for the first time (in her *Las Casas en México: Historia y obras desconocidas*, Appendix 1; see also her observations in Pérez Fernández, *Inventario*, 254–58).

82. In the BAE text the sixth principle, likewise in Latin, is found in *O.E.* 5:495a–496a. In the Providence version, it is indicated that it has been written in that language "in order that scholars may see it, and, if it seems appropriate to them to do so, correct it" (folio 155).

83. This is what Francisco de Toledo will attempt to do (but in order to disqualify the legitimacy of the Incas) by convening the notables of Cuzco.

84. The sixth principle concludes (in the Providence version) with a reference to ch. 22 of the *De Thesauris*. In that work he had already presented his arguments from Scripture.

85. His name is Cristóbal Jiménez, identified thanks to a memorandum of Bartolomé de Vega (see J. Denglos, "Tratado de las doce dudas de Fray Bartolomé de Las Casas [diciembre 1563]: Le manuscrit de la John Carter Brown Library de Providence [USA]," 135 and n. 20).

86. Truth to tell, only in Peru were the concrete historical conditions present for a project of this style and scope to have any possibility of realization. In Peru, the legitimate succession of the native rulers was clearly known.

87. In his letter to Carranza, he has spoken of an acknowledgment to be made "with a single jewel" (1555, *O.E.* 5:445a).

Chapter 14: Two Deceptions

1. Dated March 16, 1571, the document is found in *Colección de documentos para la historia de España* 13:425–69. I. Pérez Fernández regards it as predated and is preparing a study on the question (personal communication to the author). Josyene Chinese has made an interesting transcription and critical reconstruction of the text, according to the manuscript in the Madrid National Library, and published it in the periodical *Historia y Cultura* (Lima) (1970): 97–152 (with a detailed explanation of the procedure she has followed in establishing the text, 97–104). This is the version of the *Parecer de Yucay* that we shall cite (with the word *Yucay* followed by Chinese's page number).

2. The authorship of this document, until recently called the *anónimo de Yucay* (the "Yucay Anonymous"), has been much discussed. Jiménez de la Espada initially attributed it to Pedro Gutiérrez Flores, a secular priest, the viceroy's confessor and chaplain (M. Jiménez de la Espada, *Tres relaciones de antigüedades peruanas*, xxviii). Vargas Ugarte agrees with him, although he admits the possibility that the author may have been Sarmiento de Gamboa (A. Vargas Ugarte, *Historia general del Perú*, vol. 2, *Virreynato [1551–1600]*, 191, 192 n. 10). For Bataillon (*Estudios sobre Bartolomé de Las Casas*, 317–19), the "almost sure" author is Father Jerónimo Ruiz del Portillo, first provincial of the Society of Jesus, who was also — before Pedro Gutiérrez — Toledo's confessor. Bataillon arrives at this conclusion by two routes, first of all by an analysis of the text: The author's "humble reference" to himself as a

" 'servant,' coupled with a certain liberty in judging 'the friars' generally, inclines one to think, rather than of a secular priest, of a religious who was not a friar — that is, of a Jesuit." The other route consists in checking into the traces of the presence of Ruiz de Portillo in the date line of the Yucay document. Vargas Ugarte has rejected this attribution (in his *Historia de la Compañía de Jesús en Perú;* and his *Estudios sobre Bartolomé de Las Casas,* 792 n. 10).

In a recent article that seems to lay the discussion to rest, Monique Mustapha thinks that the text in question must be from the pen of Dominican friar García de Toledo. Her basis for saying this is a letter from Francisco de Toledo to his protector, the powerful Cardinal Espinosa, in which he speaks of "a brief sketch" (*cuadernillo*) by that Friar on the tyranny that had reigned in Peru (Monique Mustapha, "Encore le 'Parecer de Yucay': Essai d'attribution"). This would mean returning to a second proposal that Jiménez de la Espada had made as well, in his "Primer siglo de la Universidad de Lima" (see S. Zavala, *El servicio personal de los indios en el Perú [extractos del s. XVI],* 259–60 n. 202). Mustapha's suggestion is gradually becoming more accepted among scholars. See, for example, Marianne Mahn-Lot, *Bartolomé de Las Casas et le droit des Indiens,* 218; L. Pereña, "La escuela de Salamanca y la duda indiana," 305; P. Borges, "Los misioneros ante la duda indiana," 604; G. Lohmann, "Propuestas de solución de juristas y políticos," 648 n. 27 (which declares Mustapha's solution to have been "authentically demonstrated"). However, V. Abril Castelló believes that García de Toledo's relationship with the text in question is less direct, and promises new specifications in a forthcoming article (personal communication to the author).

3. See above, our chapter 10.

4. Toledo corroborates the authenticity of this mandate, as well as that of the *Informaciones* (of which we shall speak later) in the letter to Cardinal Espinosa that we have mentioned in our n. 2, which is dated March 25, 1571. "I beseech Your Most Illustrious Lordship," writes the viceroy, "to have my Lords Doctor Velasco and Licentiate Ovando examine the *Información* that I have ordered brought to me concerning this matter — having done so in behalf of this realm through an appeal to the persons of greatest dignity and authority within it — along with the authenticated letter of description that I send His Majesty herewith in order to testify to this truth, *together with a brief sketch [cuadernillo] that I have ordered drawn up* by Friar García de Toledo on this matter, with which he has been at pains to familiarize himself most thoroughly" (in Mustapha, "Encore le 'Parecer de Yucay,' " 226; emphasis added; here is the passage to which Mustapha appeals for her position on the Dominican's authorship).

5. García de Toledo arrived in Peru with the viceroy and returned to Spain at the end of the latter's term of office. He was Toledo's cousin and was very attached to him. In another letter to Cardinal Espinosa, written earlier than the one just cited, the viceroy asked that his cousin be named Inquisitor of Lima, praising him in these terms: "I warrant Your Most Illustrious Lordship that I know no better religious or priest, nor one with more

experience [for this office], than Friar García de Toledo, prior of Alcalá, a Dominican, who came here in my company, unless it be to his detriment that he is my first cousin, of whom I have spoken with Your Lordship" (in Mustapha, "Encore le 'Parecer de Yucay,' " 220). Besides being his relative, the Dominican friar was one of the viceroy's counselors. His performance wins the following judgment on the part of Bartolomé de Hernández, Toledo's Jesuit confessor: "Another thing I wish to signify to Your Lordship, which seems to me to be no less important, at least for the time the Viceroy is here, is that he ought to be relieved of Friar García de Toledo, of whom I believe Your Lordship will have information from many others, and who as all agree does the Viceroy much harm with his advice in matters of government" (Letter to Juan de Ovando, president of the Council of the Indies, dated at Lima, April 19, 1572; reproduced in E. Lisson Chávez, *La Iglesia de España en el Perú,* vol. 2, no. 9, p. 608). For García de Toledo see J. M. Vargas, *En torno al Padre Bartolomé de Las Casas: El anónimo de Yucay,* 6–9.

6. How is this theological outlook to be reconciled with Teresa of Avila's esteem for the viceroy's cousin (she calls him his nephew), who had been her spiritual director? His bonds with the great Teresa have been recalled for us by Bishop José Dammert in a personal communication. See J. M. Vargas, *En torno al Padre Bartolomé* — which, however, does not question García de Toledo's authorship of the Yucay document. The question remains open.

7. As we know, the question is anything but a matter of merely theoretical or casual debate. The *Yucay Opinion* is under no illusions here.

8. García de Toledo repeats an assertion of Ginés de Sepúlveda here. The latter censures Las Casas for having recommended the enactment of the New Laws and thereby causing "great evils," Sepúlveda maintains, "which, if truth be told, had their origin in *one person,* and precisely the one who, whether through error, temerity, or a yen for novelty, is opposed to my teaching" (Ginés de Sepúlveda, *Apología,* 81; emphasis added). With this declaration Sepúlveda is seeking to isolate Las Casas and thereby disqualify his position on the matter of the Indies. The facts belie the claim: many were those who shared commitments and theses like those of Friar Bartolomé in these years.

9. Hanke rightly says: "The best example of the repercussions produced by Las Casas's theoretical writings on Spain's just title in America occurred in the high regions of Peru during the government of Viceroy Don Francisco de Toledo" (Lewis Hanke, *La lucha por la justicia,* 406).

10. With some disdain the author insinuates that theologians' opinions ought not to be kept much in account since they depend on how things are presented. "Very commonly," he writes, "scholars put their names to one thing today, and tomorrow to the opposite, condemning their former opinion, since they have been deceived in the facts. As we say, As the confession, so goes the absolution" (*Yucay,* 111).

11. The author of the *Yucay Opinion* demonstrates some knowledge of Las Casas's life when he says Bartolomé tried to reach Peru but did not succeed. He speaks of two attempts, but actually only one is known, the one thwarted by the shipwreck that left him in Nicaragua.

12. The extent of Las Casas's studies in Spain is under discussion.

Giménez Fernández thinks that Las Casas never received the Licentiate of Laws, and that Remesal's later statement to the effect that he did so in Salamanca is incorrect (M. Giménez Fernández, *Bartolomé de Las Casas: Capellán,* 384–85). Abril Castelló thinks the same ("Bartolomé de Las Casas y la escuela de Salamanca," 489–91). Helen Parish, however, seems to have found proof of Bartolomé's formal studies in law and the conferral on him of the degree of Licentiate in Canon Law by the University of Valladolid in 1519 (Helen Parish, "Introduction: Las Casas's Spirituality"). Parish will present this and other biographical points in her forthcoming *Las Casas: The Untold Story.*

13. The reference is doubtless to the partition of the New World between Spain and Portugal by Alexander VI, formalized in the Treaty of Tordesillas in 1494.

14. Bataillon, "Charles V, Las Casas et Vitoria," in idem, *Estudios sobre Bartolomé de Las Casas,* 335–51. To the number of the authors mentioned by Bataillon (García Gallo, Vargas Ugarte, Manzano, Armas de Medina, Pérez de Tudela), others must be added, for example, R. J. Queraltó Moreno, *El pensamiento filosófico-político de Bartolomé de Las Casas,* 186–87.

15. Bataillon, "Charles V, Las Casas et Vitoria," 344. But A. Flores Galindo (*Buscando un inca: Identidad y utopía en los Andes,* 37–38) has rightly observed that Bataillon (see the latter's *Estudios sobre Bartolomé de Las Casas,* 350–51) "goes beyond the anecdote," showing that if that rumor acquired a certain credibility it was because in Peru, unlike Mexico, the Inca monarchy enjoyed some practical reality.

16. As Basadre says with insight: "The personal importance of Vitoria, the gravity of the decision made by Charles V, and the relationship of all of this to the debate over the just titles would surely have afforded us a far more abundant and definitive documentation than that appealed to by García Gallo, had Vitoria's been the deciding voice in the continuation of the conquest and colonization of Peru" (Jorge Basadre, *La promesa de la vida peruana,* 82).

17. Of all of the authors mentioned, Manzano (J. Manzano y Manzano, *La incorporación de las Indias a la corona de Castilla*) has doubtless made the greatest effort — admirably but fruitlessly, as Bataillon recalls (see Bataillon, *Estudios sobre Bartolomé de Las Casas,* 337) — to establish this datum alleged by the *Parecer de Yucay.* Manzano takes very seriously what García de Toledo maintains concerning Charles V's promise to "return those provinces to their legitimate rulers as soon as they are *in a position to govern themselves* and, one must suppose, with their antecedent conversion to the Catholic faith" (Manzano, *Incorporación de las Indias,* 266; emphasis added). Let us begin by saying that the Spanish historian does not seem to notice that the truth of this statement would involve the emperor's embracing, in some way, the thesis of the inferiority of the Indians, who would be currently incapable of governing themselves — a position that Las Casas battled with all his might. Besides, and again in the supposition of the truth of Manzano's assertion (there is no clear documentary evidence of such a commitment), Charles V's alleged promise would be no more than a conditional statement of principle, without concrete scope. Even Ginés de Sepúlveda sometimes expresses himself in this

way. Friede is right, then, when he concludes as to Manzano's efforts that the latter "devotes a number of pages of his book — without utility, it seems to us — to an attempt to establish this alleged datum" (J. Friede, *Bartolomé de Las Casas: Precursor,* 201 n. 2).

18. See Bataillon, *Estudios sobre Bartolomé de Las Casas,* 344–51. Lucena discusses the matter clearly and in detail, arriving at conclusions similar to those of Bataillon (Manuel Lucena, "Crisis de la conciencia nacional: Las dudas de Carlos V"). Lucena divides the four testimonials from Peru into two pairs, those of 1567 (the memorandum by Lope García de Castro, president of the Royal Audiencia and governor of Peru, addressed to the archbishop of Lima, and a representation by Francisco Falcón, procurator general of the Indians of Peru, to the Second Council of Lima); and those dating from 1571–72 (the *Parecer de Yucay* and Sarmiento de Gamboa's version in the foreword to his *Historia Indica.* After examining them one by one, Lucena concludes: "A critical analysis of the testimonials that maintain the thesis of the Emperor's hesitation on the total or partial abandonment of the Indies demonstrates that they comport little credibility" (Lucena, "Crisis de la conciencia nacional," 184). Saint-Lu has taken up the question once more and concluded that it is little likely that Las Casas advised Charles V to abandon the Indies (A. Saint-Lu, "Las Casas et l'intention prêtée à Charles-Quint de renoncer aux Indes").

19. Bataillon, *Estudios sobre Bartolomé de Las Casas,* 350. As Lucena well says, as to whether some testimonial to the contrary might be found some day, "no historian can make predictions" (Lucena, "Crisis de la conciencia nacional," 185).

20. Bataillon, *Estudios sobre Bartolomé de Las Casas,* 350. A passage from Las Casas's *Historia de las Indias* seems to suggest the notion of an abandonment of these lands. It says that Charles V would have been ready, had this been the Council's advice, "even to give up his sovereignty over these Indies" (*H.I.,* bk. 3, ch. 14, *O.E.* 2:206a). The passage had already been pointed out by Menéndez Pidal, but Bataillon minimizes the import of this retrospective text (perhaps critical of Philip II), showing that the point figures in no Lascasian writing from the time of the alleged facts (see Bataillon, *Estudios sobre Bartolomé de Las Casas,* 18–21).

21. A. García Gallo (*Estudios del Derecho Indiano*) and Manzano are explicit here. Vargas Ugarte, for his part, surprised at the statements in the Yucay memorandum, comments enthusiastically: "Thus Charles V or Philip II is in a sense a precursor of the emancipation" (Vargas Ugarte, "Fray Francisco de Vitoria y el Derecho a la Conquista de América"; the article was published in 1932). The allusion to Philip II evinces the shock experienced by the illustrious historian on a first contact with the Yucay text.

22. R. Porras Barrenechea, *Los cronistas del Perú (1528–1650),* 365.

23. Bataillon, "Charles V, Las Casas et Vitoria," in idem, *Estudios sobre Bartolomé de Las Casas,* 338. See above, our chapter 12.

24. Toledo has come to Peru convinced that there would be many things to put in order. In the letter to Cardinal Espinosa in which he presents the *Yucay Parecer* he writes: "I hope in the mercy and power of God that, although

it be such a feeble instrument as I in which He will show his greater might, he will grant the spiritual and temporal means necessary to the security of this land and the great augmentation of the royal holdings" (cited in Mustapha, "Encore le 'Parecer de Yucay,'" 224).

25. For a comprehensive judgment on Toledo's work in Peru, see D. A. Brading, *The First America*, 128–46.

26. See B. Escandell Bonet, "Las adecuaciones estructurales: Establecimientos de la Inquisición en Indias," 713; D. Ramos Pérez, "La Junta Magna y la nueva politica," 438. On the dispositions of the *Junta* in the religious area, see Enrique Dussel, *El Episcopado latinoamericano y la liberación de los pobres (1504–1620)*, 81; P. Tineo, *Los Concilios Limenses in la Evangelización de Latinoamérica*, 211–29.

27. Pius V writes an affable letter to Toledo in which, among other things, he says: "It is also to be secured, insofar as possible, that such [the Indians] not be scandalized by the bad behavior of those who have come to those provinces from this part of the West" (dated August 18, 1568, and reproduced in the manuscript of a book from the first half of the seventeenth century in the Madrid National Library, "De Virreyes y Governadores del Pirú": *DII* 8:215).

28. Pérez Fernández (*Inventario*, 779–92) maintains that Las Casas (see his 1566 *Memorial* to the Council of the Indies) was the inspiration for the Junta of 1568 through cleric Luis Sánchez, the author of a memorandum to Cardinal Espinosa. The same author (*Bartolomé de Las Casas en el Perú*, 410–58) sketches a broad background for the assembly, always assuming that the idea comes from Las Casas, who has written a petition to King Philip at the same time as he sends him his two latest books. Bartolomé may perhaps be responsible for the idea of convoking the meeting but certainly not for its content. Actually, to judge from Toledo's activity in Peru, the *Junta* was held rather in an anti-Lascasian spirit. Besides, as we shall see, the Toledan campaign had the constant support of Espinosa and, especially, of Philip II.

29. "The year 1568, all-important and central in the reign of Philip II,... was also most important for and generative of the laws of the Indies and the organization of the American viceregencies" (P. de Leturia, "Felipe II y el pontificado en un momento culminante de la historia hispanoamericana," 61).

30. See A. Ybot León, *La Iglesia y los eclesiásticos españoles en la empresa de las Indias*, 1:283. According to Ramos, the recently appointed viceroy of Peru not only participated in some of the meetings, but, perhaps as "Espinosa's first consultant," submitted a memorandum recommending an agenda for the *Junta* to treat (Ramos Pérez, "La Junta Magna y la nueva politica," 438–39).

31. See de Leturia, "Felipe II y el pontificado," 63 n. 11.

32. "Instrucción del 28 de diciembre 1568," in Hanke, ed., *Los virreyes españoles en América durante el gobierno de la Casa de Austria*, vol. 1, *Perú*, 104. (The text had also been published in E. Lisson Chávez, *La Iglesia de España en el Perú*, vol. 2., no. 374, p. 450.)

33. In another Instruction to Toledo, dated only a few days before, Philip says with reference to an earlier communication of his to Peru: "In a letter

that we have ordered written to our viceroy and commissary of Peru, there is a chapter of the following tenor: We see what you say, that the friars and religious of these regions seek to interfere in the [secular affairs], and because they are prevented from doing so they voice their reproval from their pulpits, out of hand, and that We ought to command a remedy by writing to the prelates and provincials of the orders of those provinces. It does not seem to Us that We ought to have to do this: it is inappropriate in a number of respects. Instead, let these [friars and religious] be enjoined from the acts of which you write: You, the viceroy, will see to it that a remedy be applied, in communication with their prelates. And should this not suffice, you will have those responsible — such ones as you shall deem appropriate, and are scandalous and incorrigible — put on a ship and dispatched to these realms" ("Instrucción," in Hanke, ed., *Los virreyes españoles en América,* 81b). There is no need for the king to write the church authorities; the viceroy may take the appropriate measures.

34. Cited in S. Zavala, *La encomienda indiana,* 132. Pp. 123–33 are devoted to Valderrama's visit and his confrontation with the friars.

35. The *Junta* of 1568 had prescribed: "Let care be taken that nothing further be pronounced concerning the matter [of the rights of the Crown in the Indies]. Let care be taken that the superiors and provincials forbid their inferiors to speak of it" (quoted in M. Monica, *La gran controversia del siglo diez y seis, acerca del dominio español sobre América,* 234). See, in P. Tineo ("La evangelización del Perú en las instrucciones entregadas al virrey Toledo [1569–1581]"), a presentation of the guidelines that Toledo received.

36. In Mustapha, "Encore le 'Parecer de Yucay,' " 225–26. On this proposal by Toledo, see Manzano, *Incorporación de las Indias,* 241.

37. See Escandell, "Las adecuaciones estructurales," 714–16. Escandell observes the importance of the "counterreformist historical conjuncture" for the establishment of the Inquisition in the Indies. In that decision, he says, "the consequences of the ideological and religious war were regarded as more immediate and important than considerations of morality so frequently appealed to but thus far not taken into account" (715–16). "What was made public in the *Junta's* resolution was that His Majesty had established an Inquisitorial tribunal for those realms and another of burgesses of the Court and that the Viceroy should take both along with him. Everything else was secret, and in the proper place and proper time it would be [made public] what things committed to him the said Viceroy has executed" ("De Virreyes y Governadores del Pirú": *DII* 8:219).

38. Quoted in R. Levillier, *Don Francisco de Toledo,* 1:127. Just above, Levillier writes: "Shortly after entering into relations with the Orders and prelates of the Viceregency, he dealt with them on the suitability and manner of utilization of the Inquisition, informing them that in conformity with the resolution of the *Junta* of 1568 the king had created a Tribunal in Peru, by decree of January 25, 1569. He did not take this measure, he said, because there were heretics about, but rather to assure that there would be none" (ibid., 126–27). The silence to be imposed on the friars was part of that task and of the "ideological war" we mentioned in the foregoing note.

39. Manzano, *Incorporación de las Indias*, 241.

40. See Toledo's communiqué to the king from Potosí, March 20, 1573 (Archivo de Indias, Lima 29, bk. 5; quoted in Hanke, *La lucha por la justicia*, 408).

41. Letter of December 30, 1571 (Archivo de Indias, Lima 569, bk. 13, folio 341; quoted by Manzano in his *Incorporación de las Indias*, 248, a historian, it will be well to observe, who does not conceal his sympathy for the king and his viceroy). Hanke writes: "Toledo bitterly complained all through his tenure of the perverse, arbitrary conduct of the religious. They were bent on discovering the tyrannical and unjust aspects of all he sought to do, he complained, and they went so far as to hide the Indians from the royal tax gatherers when they considered the tributes demanded to be unjust. It is understandable, then, that the viceroy should earnestly desire the proscription of Las Casas's writings. With this object, he recovered all of them that he could find, thus withdrawing them from circulation, and besought the king not to permit others to be sent from Spain" (Hanke, *La lucha por la justicia*, 408). See also J. M. Barnadas, *Charcas: Orígenes históricos de una sociedad colonial*, 485.

42. Letter from Toledo to the king, dated September 24, 1572 (Archivo de Indias, Lima 28–B; quoted in Manzano, *Incorporación de las Indias*, 249; emphasis added). In the mother country, in November 1571, Philip II ordered the collection of "the books, treatises, and other papers...dealing with matters and business of the Indies that may remain and might be found of the said Bartolomé de Las Casas." Manzano writes: "It was a matter of completing in Spain the *cleanup* performed by Don Francisco de Toledo in Peru" (ibid., 254; emphasis added). This author attributes the proposal of this collection to Juan de Ovando, president of the Council of the Indies at the time.

43. Letter of March 20, 1574 (quoted in Levillier, *Gobernantes del Perú*, 5:405).

44. De Leturia, who spares the Junta of 1568 no praise (nor Philip II and Toledo either), nevertheless recognizes "its excessively centralizing and royalist orientation, including a mistrust and dislike of the immediate intervention of the Holy See in evangelization" (de Leturia, "Misiones Hispanoamericanas según la Junta de 1568" [1930], 230). It is true that the *Junta* had gone very far in this way. It approved the creation of a Patriarchate of the Indies (the title had existed, honorifically, since Ferdinand the Catholic). The patriarch was to reside in Madrid and from there conduct the ecclesiastical government of the Indies. Pius V regarded the project with scant sympathy; thus, Philip II left it unexecuted, hoping that with another pontiff more favorable winds would blow, but Rome never approved it. On the other hand, neither did Pius V succeed in obtaining from Philip II the presence in the Indies of an apostolic nuncio who would further in those lands the concerns manifested in his bull, *In Coena Domini* (see de Leturia, "Felipe II y el pontificado"; idem, "Misiones Hispanoamericanas según la Junta de 1568"; Monica, *La gran controversia*, 211–19; Ybot León, *Iglesia y los eclesiásticos españoles*, 2:1–21; Ramos Pérez, "La Junta Magna y la nueva politica," 440). Dussel comments: "The Roman attempt to establish a nunciature in America means an attempt to impose certain limits on the control of the Patronage over the Church, that is, it

was a critical, liberative measure" ("Introducción General" to *Historia general de la Iglesia en América Latina*, 265).

45. In a final report to the king concerning his work in Peru, Toledo recalls that on arriving he had found that friars and bishops were acting in these lands in disregard of the authority of the king and his functionaries. "As to the spiritual governance of that realm, Catholic Majesty, I found when I arrived there that the clerics and friars, bishops, and prelates of the orders were absolute lords of the entire spiritual area, and in the temporal they knew or held practically no superior." The viceroy sought to change the situation. "To remedy this and in conformity with what I had already ordered and deemed appropriate the first thing I did was to withdraw from the power of the said bishops and prelates the presentation and appointment of the clerics and catechists and to restore Your Majesty to the royal patronage that they had usurped." In this reestablishment of the king's authority, in the purest spirit of royalism, the viceroy continued what he had been expected to do. Thus, he boasts, he has ensured that in the future, "as Your Majesty and Your viceroys will have these reins in hand, they will hold them subject, and the obstacle that they have been posing to temporal governance with the freedom of their habit will be removed, in the form of words and works in which they are invested and that seemed to them that it was impossible to govern the realm without them and without their advice and opinion" ("Memorial que Don Francisco de Toledo dio al Rey Nuestro Señor del estado en que dejó las cosas del Perú después de haber sido virrey y capitán general por trece años, que comenzaron en 1569" [n.d., ca. 1581–82]; quoted in Hanke, *Los virreyes españoles en América*, 1:129–30).

46. This is the line taken by Philip II in a disposition of January 17, 1590 (incorporated into the Indies Laws as Law 46, title 14, bk. 1): "... Whereas it behooves religious not to burden themselves with matters foreign to their state and condition, let the prelates of the Indies be at pains that they not interfere in matters of government, nor permit this to their religious, and allow the governors to provide what seems appropriate to them; We shall regard the contrary as a disservice" (quoted in J. A. de La Torre, *El uso alternativo del derecho*, 40–41).

47. The question of native rule and Las Casas's unsettling theses regarding it occasioned excitement in Mexico as well. One of Cortés's companions complains to Charles V that this friar "calls us tyrannical conquerers and robbers, unworthy of the name of Christian, and says and declares that all that we have belongs to others, and that we must take it from our children and give it to those he indicates; and he causes scruples with regard to Your Majesty's rule, [saying] that we come to these regions illicitly." And yet, maintains this conquistador of long ago, it is clear that "Montezuma, the lord we find here, was not a legitimate lord" (letter of Ruy González of April 24, 1553, quoted in Manzano, *Incorporación de las Indias*, 242–43).

48. An instruction to Toledo in consequence of the Junta of 1568 refers to the caciques as "natural lords," but the reference is made in passing and has no important consequences for the matter concerning us (Instruction of December 19, 1568, quoted in Hanke, *Los virreyes españoles en América*, 1:83a).

Indeed, Toledo considered, rightly, that these allusions had been provoked by the scruples sown by Las Casas and that, further, they contradicted other dispositions of the Crown in the same text.

49. "We have no doubt," he writes, "that he knew the *Relección de Indis.* We readily gather this from certain questions in the reports he ordered delivered on his visit, as well as from a reference to a legitimate title very clearly expressed in the *Historia Indica* that he entrusted to Sarmiento de Gamboa." Levillier explains the reason for this interest: "Father Vitoria had insisted on the importance of the Indians being *genuine owners;* whether they were such and had *always* occupied the lands they possessed on the Spaniards' arrival; or were *not* such and had *not always* occupied the said lands, determined whether their title in this sense was *legitimate* or *illegitimate*" (Levillier, *Don Francisco de Toledo,* 1:197).

50. Manzano concludes his study of this matter with clear and revealing expressions: "In view of the facts evinced in Don Francisco de Toledo's *Informaciones,* we are in a far better position to appreciate the enormous difference between the postures of the illustrious master of San Esteban, Vitoria, and his confrere, Las Casas. The former has made no commitment whatever in the face of his adversaries with his simple 'supposition.' The latter, on the contrary, shows himself a deceitful troublemaker, an enemy of the Spanish cause, and therefore becomes the only target of the pitiless onslaughts of all elements of this revisionist sector. Vitoria, on the other hand, will enjoy the greatest respect on the part of them all" (Manzano, *La incorporación de las Indias,* 269). In "making no commitment whatever" he became deserving of greater respect.

51. "Deformations," Duviols rightly calls them (*La lutte contre les religions autochtones dans le Pérou colonial,* 46). Some of the viceroy's distinguished contemporaries thought the same. In a letter to Licentiate Ovando in 1572, Alonso de la Cerda, provincial of the Dominicans (later bishop of Honduras and then of Charcas; see Bataillon, "Les 'douze questions' péruviennes résolues par Las Casas," 229 n. 8), writes that the legitimacy of the Incas is "certain and well-known," and he says, of the *Informaciones* that they "have caused much laughter. They are less true than the Viceroy imagines" (quoted in Lisson Chávez, *Iglesia de España en el Perú,* vol. 2, no. 9, p. 625). The archbishop of Lima, Friar Jerónimo de Loaisa, "writing to the King under date of March 7, 1577, warned him plainly that they were not impartial and had been made by order of the Viceroy" (Vargas Ugarte, *Historia general del Perú,* 193).

52. Manzano, *La incorporación de las Indias,* 247.

53. The *Informaciones* have been published by Levillier in his *Don Francisco de Toledo,* vol. 2. The text quoted here is from p. 14.

54. Letter of March 1, 1572, ibid., 2:12.

55. Letter of Philip II to Toledo, dated December 30, 1571 (Archivo de Indias, Lima 569, bk. 3, folio 340v; quoted in Manzano, *La incorporación de las Indias,* 257).

56. Letter of Toledo (Archivo de Indias, Lima 29, bk. 1, f. 1v; quoted in Manzano, *La incorporación de las Indias,* 260 n. 50).

57. Pedro Sarmiento de Gamboa, *Historia de los Incas.* The texts that we shall cite are taken from the preface of this work. On historiographical aspects of this history see the book by R. Pietschmann, who discovered and published the manuscript, *La Historia Indica de Pedro Sarmiento de Gamboa.*

58. With all the clarity that could be desired, Sarmiento Gamboa presents the objective of his *Historia.* First he lays down a principle and then situates it polemically against those who deny the rights of the Crown. "But as among Christians it is unseemly to hold anything without good title, such as Your Majesty has to these regions, although it is the holiest and loftiest title that any ruler in the world has to his possessions, it has suffered detriment, as I have said above, in the minds of many scholars and other people for want of correct information." Then he lauds the viceroy for his visit to the territory of the viceregency, for his *Informaciones* respecting the "horrendous tyranny of the *Ingas,*" and for the dispositions he has decreed concerning the Indians, which make the latter "regard themselves as regenerated in all things and loudly call him their benefactor and protector, as they call Your Majesty, who has sent him, their Father." Next he specifies the reason for his book: "And in order that Your Majesty may with interest and much enjoyment be informed and others, adversaries, be plainly disabused, *I have been ordered* by Viceroy Don Francisco de Toledo, *whom I attend and serve* on this general visit, that I undertake this affair and record the history of the facts" (emphasis added). Porras Barrenechea's argument, then, does not seem very convincing, to the effect that Sarmiento de Gamboa was not "the spokesman of the opinions of Viceroy Toledo," on the basis of the "moral arrogance and innate spirit of rebellion and independence that was the life of this tireless adventurer and explorer" (Porras Barrenechea, *Los cronistas del Perú,* 362).

59. With reference to the Yucay document, Pietschmann writes: "Sarmiento seems to have drawn from this treatise, which mainly attacks the opinions of Bartolomé de Las Casas and his partisans, the concept that the discovery of the new world had been a providential reward bestowed on the King of Spain for his struggles against the Moors; and furthermore the statement that Charles V had come very close to abandoning his sovereign rights" (Pietschmann, *Historia Indica de Sarmiento de Gamboa,* 53–54).

60. In his enthusiasm to justify Spain's titles and to serve the viceroy, Sarmiento goes further than the *Informaciones.* The latter contain no reference to such customs. Levillier says that the questionnaire in the *Informaciones* contained "nineteen questions of which some are connected with Father Vitoria's principles, as they regarded idolatry, human sacrifice, cannibalism, and sins against nature. However, these points involved no revelations of interest, since it was already well known at the time, through chroniclers and conquistadors, that the Incas practiced idolatry and human sacrifice, just as it was known that *they were not cannibals, nor regarded sodomy with indifference* in the lands of their jurisdiction. And as this information was authentic, it constituted affirmative replies to the former two questions, and negative to the latter two, with the witnesses making the reservation that tribes foreign to the Incas had had these sinful usages" (Levillier, *Don Francisco de Toledo,* 1:275–76; emphasis added). The *Informaciones,* then, emphatically deny

what Sarmiento maintains. Obviously Sarmiento's interest in making these assertions is to align himself more closely with Vitoria's theses (for this latter concern on Sarmiento's part, see Pietschmann, *Historia Indica de Sarmiento de Gamboa*, 54 n. 102).

61. The reference is to Antonino of Florence and Pope Innocent IV, important doctrinal authorities in the discussions of the age. Although we may speak of points of agreement with Vitoria on the point at issue (with the nuances that we have seen), in others (for example, regarding the power of the pope in temporal matters) there are great differences.

62. Porras Barrenechea also observes Vitoria's importance in the Peru of this time. He says that his notions "on the motives for a just war had a special echo in Peru, in the era of Viceroy Toledo and in the doctrinal work of the jurists and historians that so influenced Toledo's political and legislative activity," especially the thesis that "it was licit to make war on and subject peoples" who "might seek to return to idolatry, ... had tyrannical laws, practiced cannibalism or human sacrifices and other abominable sins and crimes" (Porras Barrenechea, "El pensamiento de Vitoria en el Perú," 480).

63. From Vitoria as well Sarmiento de Gamboa may have taken the argument of love for neighbor in order to base the Spanish presence in the Indies. In the fifth legitimate title, the Salamancan master declares that the Spanish rulers may prohibit the Indians their abominable customs, as is clear, he says, from the fact that "God has enjoined upon each a care of his neighbor, and they are all our neighbors" (Francisco Vitoria, *De Indis; Obras*, 720–21; CHP, 93). But that which in Vitoria — due to his ignorance of the concrete reality of the Indies — was aseptic theological ratiocination, in Sarmiento is cynical opportunism.

64. In view of the forthright declaration of objectives presented in this preface, it is difficult to maintain, as does Porras Barrenechea, that Sarmiento writes "with love for the Inca past," a love Porras sees as manifested as well in the author's elegant prose (Porras Barrenechea, *Los cronistas del Perú*, 365). What is happening is that the great historian is paying less attention to the cause at whose service Sarmiento places his work (and its concrete repercussions on the life and death of the Indians of the time) than to the historiographical contributions of the *Historia Indica*.

65. They insist, furthermore, that "it is right that it be understood that in the first conquest we Spaniards do no battle with any natural lord of this land, but with Atabaliba, who was a tyrant and had tyrannically usurped the succession from his brother, Inca Guascar."

66. "Memorial del Cabildo del Cuzco sobre el derecho del Rey de España a los Reinos del Perú" (October 24, 1572), reproduced as an appendix in the edition that we cite of José de Acosta, *De Procuranda Indorum Salute*, 1:676–85. True, the *encomienda* begins, slowly, to lose ground in these years (with the increasing importance, on the other hand, of the corregidor's offices instituted by García de Castro in 1565). But Toledo's viceregency is an era of transition and, as Hampe has recalled, actually a time of an increase in the economic power and social influence of the *encomenderos* (see T. Hampe, "La encomienda en el Perú en el siglo XVI [Ensayo bibliográfico]," 175–76).

67. Toledo's campaign was doubtless hampered by the danger to his policy represented by the Taqui-ongoy politico-religious movement, which came into being only a few years before the viceroy's arrival. On this interesting movement, see Luis Millones, "Un movimiento nativista del siglo XVI: El Taki-ongoy"; Alfred Métraux, *Religions et magies indiennes d'Amérique du Sud;* M. Curatola, "Mito y milenarismo en los Andes: Del Taki Onqoy a Incarri"; S. Stern, "El Taki Onqoy y la sociedad andina"; also the important analysis presented on this topic by M. Hernández et al. in *Entre el mito y la historia,* ch. 4; and most especially, the documents and studies collected by L. Millones in *El retorno de las huacas.*

68. Levillier, *Don Francisco de Toledo,* 1:285. See also D. A. Brading, "The Incas and the Renaissance: The Royal Commentaries of Inca Garcilaso," 1.

69. "Hard battles were fought in the sixteenth century for control of the past. History supplied an ideological arsenal of arguments and information to support political rights and particular interests in the present" (Brading, "The Incas and the Renaissance"). There are examples of this in Latin America today. A document from the Peruvian bishops reports the following testimony of the native peoples of the Andean South: "Our history is very great. Our grandparents have told us something, but we do not know everything. They took our land and tried to take our knowledge as well. The mighty did not want us to know how things were in the beginning. We shall strike to regain our land and our history" (Peruvian Bishops of the Andean South, "La tierra: Don de Dios, derecho del pueblo," 11).

70. See, for example, Nathan Wachtel, *La vision des vaincus,* as well as Josefina Oliva de Coll, *La resistencia indígena ante la Conquista.* G. Delran attempts a history of the native Peruvian *campesinos* in terms of their own struggles: *Historia rural del Perú.* Likewise see the Aztec, Maya, and Inca texts collected by M. León Portilla in his *El reverso de la Conquista.* Flores Galindo's important work, *Buscando un inca: Identidad y utopía,* is more complex and tries to identify the causes and the content of the utopia that came to be conceptualized by a people for whom the Conquista was a cataclysm. See also M. Burga, *Nacimiento de una utopía,* and the considerations of J. Ansión, "De la utopía andina a la construcción nacional," 33–41.

71. Hanke has called attention to a certain freedom of expression that prevailed in the Indies and in Spain on these subjects in the sixteenth century (Hanke, *La lucha por la justicia,* 79–93). Toledo (with the support of Philip II) proposes to put an end to this situation, which is a legitimate motive for pride on Spain's part.

72. Cieza de León, *Crónica del Perú,* 66. F. Cantù has observed that in the manuscript she discovered in the Vatican Library certain corrections have been entered in Cieza de León's hand. In some cases these represent what the historian calls "certain interventions of self-censorship" (Cieza de León, *Crónica del Perú,* xxvii); concretely, in the text that we have cited, certain expressions are suppressed that make the judgment more severe. Here is the first redaction of the text cited: "It is no small occasion for grief to contemplate that it was the pagan, idolatrous Incas who had had a fine, *wise,* and orderly government, and could maintain their lands and so many and such

great realms, while we Christians had destroyed such great realms *with our greed,* so that wherever Christians had passed, conquering and discovering, nothing now remains but a universal *all-consuming* conflagration *of burning pitch"* (folio 29v; in Cieza de León, *Crónica del Perú,* xxviii, 66; emphasis added). See also the texts of various origin that Lohmann Villena presents, concluding his study with the following declaration. "A more profound investigation into documentary stores as yet scantily explored will enable us to glean an additional quota of testimonials abounding in the concepts and expressions that we have registered throughout the present work;...but it will not be overbold to assert that the series collected here evinces the spread of a critical spirit that succeeded in impregnating various social groups, and that at all events a concern for Las Casas's burning questions, which he asked with such peerless ardor and truly inexhaustible perseverance, was very far from being that of a little cluster of persons" (G. Lohmann Villena, "Exponentes del movimiento criticista en el Perú," 153).

73. Let us specify that in this case there was indeed a connection. We do not know how close a friendship existed between Las Casas and Cieza, but we do have Cieza's indication in his testament that the second and third parts of the *Crónica del Perú* had been sent to the bishop of Chiapa (see M. Marticorena, "Cieza de León y su muerte en 1554: Documentos"; F. Pease, "Introducción," in Cieza, *Crónica del Perú [Primera Parte],* xvii–xix).

74. Manzano, *La incorporación de las Indias,* 268–69.

75. Rather naively, Monica declares that Toledo's work in Peru resolved the difficulties arising with Antón de Montesino's sermon and put an end to the controversy of the Indies (see Monica, *Gran controversia del siglo diez y seis,* 283–87).

76. L. G. Lumbreras, *De los orígenes del Estado en el Perú;* E. Guillén, "La conquista del Perú de los Incas (1531–1572)," 12–14; and the important work of María Rostworowski de Diez Canseco, *Historia del Tahuantinsuyu.*

77. Indeed liberation and evangelization were to be achieved through domination. An ordinance of the Council of the Indies of September 24, 1571, says: "...that thus the said Indians may understand the favor we desire to bestow, and know that Our Lord's having placed them under our protection and shelter has been for their good, and to withdraw them from the tyranny and servitude in which they lived of old" (quoted in Manzano, *La incorporación de las Indias,* 265 n. 61).

78. Acosta, *De Procuranda Indorum Salute,* bk. 3, ch. 3, pp. 399–401. Among the historians of this century let us simply cite the judgment of three distinguished Hispanicists on this topic. De la Riva Agüero, after speaking of the idealistic view of the Incas presented by Valera and Garcilaso, says: "But Toledo's *Informaciones* go to the other extreme and calumniate them, or at least systematically denigrate them, hiding their virtues and good points and treating as matters of certainty distasteful things that are actually vague" (J. de la Riva Agüero, *La Historia en el Perú,* 185). Vargas Ugarte is less negative. But in spite of the admiration he feels for Toledo ("with a little more humanity and sense of adaptation he would have been perfect"; *Historia general del Perú,* 2:268), he also indicates the doubtful status of the data collected,

on the basis of the attitude of the Indians who supplied the information. He writes, "For all their scant perspicacity, some of them at least must have noticed what was afoot with the posing of these few questions, and for this reason as well as owing to the uniformity of the questions the replies were almost of the same tenor — a frequent phenomenon in meetings of this kind" (ibid., 2:193). Porras Barrenechea, however, does not think so. For him, Toledo (that "great lover of the history of Peru and its most determined protector"; *Los cronistas del Perú*, 37) has the great merit of having promoted these *Informaciones*. He does not deny the political reasons (which of course are evident) that motivated them, but he believes that they do not affect their historical truth. "The political theses," he maintains, "are the circumstantial, ephemeral element in the *Informaciones*, owing to the inevitable influence of considerations of state at the time, but their substance is history" (ibid., 38).

79. In the Providence version, the idea is developed (still with reference to the Inca): "...who, although he were to be or have been a tyrant, at least had not and has not destroyed and extirpated the tribes he subjected, as we have done throughout those Indies, and laid waste more than four thousand leagues of land" (*Doce dudas*, Providence version, folio 215v).

80. The text continues: "...thus in their souls as in their land holdings; since indeed, they know not what is fitting for them, or for the administration of their lands either, or the good order and governance of their possessions; so that for this reason they were many times deceived" (quoted in Levillier, *Don Francisco de Toledo*, 2:9–10).

81. The *Yucay Opinion* says: "I am simply astounded that there should be individuals under heaven who with all good intent seek to endow these Indians with titles and things that neither are theirs, because God has not wished to give them to them, nor are appropriate for them" (*Yucay*, 134–35). Instead, they are appropriate for others.

82. "Memorial que don Francisco de Toledo dio al Rey Nuestro señor del estado en que dejó las cosas del Perú después de haber sido virrey y capitán general por trece años, que comenzaron in 1569" (n.d., ca. 1581–82), in Hanke, *Los virreyes españoles en América*, 1:140a. Monica approves this depreciatory attitude on the part of the viceroy, and most highly. He too thinks that the Indians had to be made human beings first and Christians later. The "Memorial" quoted here "anticipated by two centuries French scientist Lapérouse, whose opinions are taken into very weighty consideration as representative of the eighteenth-century Age of Enlightenment" (Monica, *Gran controversia del siglo diez y seis*, 248; Lapérouse, after visiting the Franciscan foundations in California in 1781, declared that the first task was to "convert these people into citizens"). This "Memorial" was not alone in its "anticipation": the same attitude is to be found in a number of texts of the time. Bartolomé de Hernández, whose text on García de Toledo's bad influence on the viceroy we have cited, likewise holds that "in order to be made Christians," the Indians "must first be human beings in a political society." After all, "until now this policy has not been in force, but they have been living as savages in jungles" (quoted in Lisson Chávez, *La Iglesia de España en el Perú*, vol. 2, p. 602). José de Acosta also maintains: "First, care must be taken that the

barbarians learn to be human beings, then to be Christians"; this criterion is "so important that on it depends the whole business of the salvation or sure ruin of souls" (Acosta, *De Procuranda Indorum Salute,* bk. 3, ch. 19, p. 539). For other references see Borges, *Misión y civilización en América,* 4–13. As this author specifies elsewhere, "human Indian" means "civilized Indian" (Borges, "Evangelización y civilización en América," 232). And civilized, in this case, means, we would add, that the Indians live "under our management," or "in the manner in which Spaniard Christians live," as Charles V put it (quoted in Borges, "Evangelización y civilización en América," 237).

83. Here is another text from the same memorandum in which Toledo describes the life of the Indians: "The government the Indians had before I personally visited them was the same as, and very little more political than, the one they had in the time of the tyranny of the Incas....They dwelt in the mountains and worst jungles, avoiding doing so in public, open places. There each lived with the freedom he would. As for law, since they could not be indoctrinated, and in everything else: vices, drunkenness, dancing, and carousing, at great risk to their lives and health. They died like beasts and were buried in the fields as such. They spent their time eating, drinking, and sleeping, without anyone voluntarily doing any work" (in Hanke, *Los virreyes españoles en América,* 1:138a–b).

84. Viceroy Count de Nieva said the Indians were "like children, without the prudence to control themselves" (quoted in Levillier, *Gobernantes del Perú,* 1:444).

85. Letter to Hanke (in Hanke, *Los virreyes españoles en América,* 1:75a). A contemporary of Toledo, and one of his successors in the viceregency of Peru, was of a very similar opinion. García de Hurtado writes to the king, expressing a very categorical judgment: "With the changes, reductions, the work in the mines, so many sudden displacements, and the employment of them all in personal services, the Indians today are so disoriented and destroyed that, lest they be entirely so, it will be in order to apply some remedy in the form of provisions and new ordinances, as I am doing, as time and need shall dictate, inasmuch as, while some of those of Don Francisco de Toledo sound very salutary to the Indians, they are altogether destructive and venomous" (in Hanke, *Los virreyes españoles en América,* 1:75a).

86. The execution of Túpac Amaru I caused a great malaise. Opposed to it, for example, were the provincials of the religious orders working in Peru. "All begged the Viceroy on their knees to bestow on them the favor of granting the Inga his life and sending him to Spain" (Reginaldo de Lizárraga, *Descripción breve de toda la tierra del Perú, Tucumán, Río de la Plata, Chile,* quoted in Ramos Pérez, "La nueva situación dramática de finales del s. XVI," 721–23). Guamán Poma presents events as follows: "Don Sebastian de Lartaún, bishop of the city of Cuzco, fell on his knees before Viceroy Don Francisco de Toledo and begged for the life of Topa Amaro Inga. Together with him, all the priests and canons and conquistadors and neighbors and leading Indians of this realm made the same request. And they offered a great quantity of silver to His Majesty for the Inca's life" (Guamán Poma, *Primer nueva corónica y buen gobierno,* 450). Levillier (*Gobernantes del Perú,* 1:301–59) made a great

effort, without winning a consensus of historians (see Vargas Ugarte, *Historia general del Perú*, 2:224), to demonstrate the justice of Toledo's decision to proceed with the execution. This measure and other aspects of the work of the viceroy gained him the enmity of Garcilaso, of whom Levillier says he treated Toledo "as if he desired to subject him to a Chinese torture with his judgments, and indeed his revenge was most effective for centuries. Talent in the service of hatred is a mighty thing" (Levillier, *Gobernantes del Perú*, 2:xxvii). Without, of course, adopting the Argentinian historian's expressions, let us observe that, in his opposition to Toledo, Garcilaso appeals to the figure of the king by way of contrast. He is the inventor of the famous scene in which Philip II is supposed to have reproached Toledo for the beheading of Túpac Amaru I. No documentary proof exists for this, and there is nothing to indicate that there was any serious disagreement between the king and his representative in Peru. On the contrary, despite the ill will provoked in so many by Toledo's authoritarian, harsh character, occasioning many complaints against him, Philip II always supported him against his adversaries, for example, against the members of the Council of the Indies who a number of times asked for his removal (see E. Schaffer, *El Consejo Real y Supremo de las Indias*, 2:50–52). On Garcilaso's complex personality see M. Hernández's fine study, *Memoria de un bien perdido*.

87. Viceroy Toledo was well acquainted with the *encomienda* system. The Order of Alcántara, to which he belonged, had *encomiendas* in Spain (of a different kind, it is true, from those of the Indies). In a letter to the king toward the end of his tenure in Peru, Toledo, who frequently expresses a concern about compensation for his services, requests the grant of an *encomienda* in Peru. "I hold Your Majesty under petition," he writes, with good practical sense, "to bestow upon me the favor of confirming and approving my services in this land with deeds, as You have made and do make me so great with words;...and inasmuch as we presently have an offer here on the part of Doña Francisca de Guzmán to vacate her distribution of Indians, named Andaguailas, the income from which is seventeen thousand pesos, I petition Your Majesty to be pleased to grant me, without new title of ownership, the grace of its benefit for twenty years, with an option on my part to abandon it in favor of anyone I may name for the completion of the said term" ("Exposición de D. Francisco de Toledo, virrey del Perú, pidiendo a Felipe II que se sirva premiar sus servicios," in *Colección de documentos para la historia de España*, 13:556–57).

88. See E. Guillén, "La conquista del Perú de los Incas." On other forms of native resistance, see J. Tord and C. Lazo, "Economía y sociedad en el Perú colonial: Movimiento social."

89. Guamán Poma, *Primer nueva corónica y buen gobierno*, 459, 391.

90. According to an Andean tradition, the head of Túpac Amaru, impaled on a pike and displayed on the parade ground in Cuzco, began to grow beautiful — to gain new life in some way. Burga thinks that this is a sign of resurrection, which "may be the remote origin of the Myth of Inkarrí" (M. Burga, *Nacimiento de una utopía*, 120).

91. Toledo was always proud of the measure he had taken against Túpac

Amaru I. Thanks to it, he thought, he had pacified the territory of his Peruvian viceregency. In the memorandum in which he presents a report of his work, he writes: "The province of Vilcabamba was placed under Your Majesty's obedience and subjection: with a stronghold peopled by Spaniards and with a governor, and with the decapitation of the Inga — found alive and eliminated as an idol, as they considered dead Ingas there and to which the natives offered worship — all those of the kingdom were pacified" ("Memorial," in Hanke, *Los virreyes españoles en América,* 1:133b). The episode of the death of Túpac Amaru I is full of incidents. In a letter to the king, the president of the Audiencia of Charcas, L. Armendáriz, writes that the interpreter used in the affair was first imprisoned and then garroted — in prison, and not in public — by order of Toledo, "lest the Viceroy be accused in connection with the trials he conducted against the Ingas, in which the interpreter was one Gonzalo Jiménez, were he to make a retractation on his deathbed, as it was publicly said he intended to do" (quoted in Barnadas, *Charcas: Orígenes históricos,* 486).

92. Hanke says that he took with him on that expedition José de Acosta and lawyers Juan de Matienzo and Juan Polo de Ondegardo (see Hanke and Millares, *Cuerpo de documentos,* lviii).

93. Friar Reginaldo de Lizárraga (ordained a bishop by Toribio de Mogrovejo, archbishop of Lima), author of a *Parecer* in which he justifies war against the Araucanos and their subjection to slavery, was present at the Junta convened by Toledo. Lizárraga sketches the facts as follows. To the viceroy's question whether it was permissible to bestow the Chiriguan Indians as slaves, "he was answered by President Quiñones and Doctor Barros, the judge, that by no manner of means might he do so, since they had seen in the realm of Guatemala, where they had been judges, an order of the Emperor of glorious memory, in which he commanded that by no mean, might any Indians, even had they rebelled against his royal service or made war on him or his subjects or because they consumed human flesh or had other most enormous vices or had wrought irreparable harm to his lands and vassals, when taken as prisoners of war be bestowed as slaves. As this was the case, the Viceroy may not contravene what is ordered by his prince. To which the Viceroy responded that he had not seen that order, nor was there report of it in other realms than in those of Mexico and Guatemala. After this declaration by the Viceroy, all were of the opinion that he could sentence them as slaves" ("Parecer acerca de si contra los indios de Arauca es justa la guerra ques se les hace y si pueden dar por esclavos 1599," in Hanke and Millares, *Cuerpo de documentos,* 300). Vargas Ugarte (*Historia general del Perú,* 2:236) gives a somewhat different version from Lizárraga's, but does not indicate his sources.

94. See Hanke and Millares, *Cuerpo de documentos,* lix.

95. See the *Pareceres,* on both sides of the issue, published in Hanke and Millares, *Cuerpo de documentos.*

96. As Lohmann rightly says, this document is "the most finished expression of the ideology that drove Toledo's administration" (Lohmann, "Propuestas de solución," 648).

97. We can say that the document prolongs what Pereña calls "a kind

of theology of repression," which, he says, "the first conquerors of Peru set afoot" (Pereña, "Francisco de Vitoria: Conciencia de América," 96).

Chapter 15: Christ Did Not Die for Gold

1. Toledo had a great concern for the mines of Peru and issued numerous regulations in their regard. In a memorandum in which he recounts the exploits of his administration, the viceroy points with pride to his work regarding the important mercury and silver mines of Huamanga and Huancavelica, as well as those of Cuzco and Potosí (in Lewis Hanke, *Los virreyes españoles en América*, 145b–148b).

2. Further on he writes: "...by way of compensation for their toils and expenses in conquering for him the Kingdoms of Spain" (*Yucay*, 140).

3. "I hope, in Our Lord," Toledo writes to the king, "that He will grant His Majesty His light, to understand and zealously to further a business in which so many souls can be dispatched to heaven, and in which so much gold and silver is accustomed to be mined from the earth, whereby His Majesty may the better preserve his realms and defend the Catholic Church" ("Memorial del virrey Toledo a S. M. en que hace relación de todos sus servicios" [1578?], quoted in Hanke, *Los virreyes españoles en América*, 123b).

4. In undated letter of Domingo de Santo Tomás to Las Casas, the former forcefully asserts the right of the Indians to work for their own profit the mines they have discovered, "since," he says, "it is their land" (in *DII* 7:380–81).

5. The author manifests a downright enthusiasm for the wealth of Peru. The text we have just cited goes on: "And not here and there, either; all these mountains are full of it, and the earth in the houses and fields is everywhere mingled with gold dust" (*Yucay*, 141).

6. For reasons difficult to understand, respected historian M. Bataillon (*Estudios sobre Bartolomé de Las Casas*, 329) describes as a "pleasant parable" this contemptuous manner of speaking of the Indians and this incredible interpretation of the motives for evangelization.

7. José de Acosta, *Historia natural y moral de las Indias*, bk. 4, ch. 2, p. 90b; emphasis added.

8. M. Bataillon writes with regard to the parable of the *Parecer de Yucay:* "We must not think that his metaphor is a creation *ex nihilo* of the imagination of Padre Portillo....Acosta is expounding a providentialistic schema of the spiritual conquest of the New World that keeps close analogies with that of Portillo....In the extensive chapters he devotes to the precious metals of the New World, especially of Potosí, he essentially adopts Padre Portillo's explanation, although with greater discretion he places less emphasis on the hideousness of the ugly daughter. In adopting this parable, the author does not cite the author by name: he refers to him as a 'wise person'" (Bataillon, "El Parecer de Yucay," in *Estudios sobre Bartolomé de Las Casas*, 330–31). Let us recall that for Bataillon the author of the *Parecer* is Jesuit Jerónimo Ruiz del Portillo. His references to him consequently allude to the Yucay text.

9. Acosta severely criticizes at various moments the havoc wrought by

greed. Thus, in another passage, which was censured and which the Jesuit therefore suppressed in the edition of his work published during his lifetime, he wrote: "If there is any calamity to be lamented and wept for with abundant tears throughout these Indies,… it is the avarice and insatiable greed afflicting all, from the first to the last, from the priest to the prophet. The more gold and silver is transported from these treasure-troves to Europe, the less souls make their way to heaven. This, I think, is the scourge of these regions, this the caterpillar, this the ravenous locust, this the blight" (Acosta, *De Procuranda Indorum Salute,* bk. 1, ch. 12, p. 191). The text cited is reduced in the Biblioteca de Autores Católicos edition to the following: "After all, if there is any calamity to be wept for in this matter, it is greed. And what evils will the accursed thirst for gold not produce?" (Acosta, *De Procuranda Indorum Salute* [BAC], 419b).

10. Nor is this a mere premonition: Witness what actually occurred on the large islands of the Antilles that "in another time," he adds, "teemed with a population swimming in an abundance of gold, and that now are all but desert and wild." It made for a harsh experience.

11. Alonso de Ercilla, in his celebrated poem "La Araucana" ("The Araucan Woman"), likewise testifies to this fact. Here is one text:

> An infant in poverty, in Valdivia,
> All but deprived of estate,
> Will one day have fifty thousand vassals,
> Offering him twelve marks of gold a day.
> This, and so much more, was not enough —
> Thus, hunger kept him there:
> Greed sparked all this war,
> And the utter perdition of this land. (Canto III)

12. Acosta, *De Procuranda Indorum Salute,* bk. 3, ch. 18, pp. 527–37.

13. Domingo de Santo Tomás thinks that this attitude extended as well to the person of the Indians: "One thing alone I wish to say of the past,… and it is that ever since this land has been discovered, no more respect has been had for this wretched people — indeed, less — than for brute beasts, as they are stripped of their lands, robbed, and slain. It has been thought that everything in this land is there for anyone to take and that the Indians are lazy animals, whom the first to stumble upon them — these articles without an owner — may claim them as property" ("Carta a S. M. en el Consejo de Indias," July 1, 1550, quoted in E. Lisson Chávez, *La Iglesia de España en el Perú,* vol. 1, no. 4, p. 191).

14. This theme is likewise present in the *Doce dudas.*

15. Under the inspiration of Domingo de Santo Tomás, the Second Council of Lima had likewise asserted: "It has been denounced to this Synod that many of ours, oblivious not only of their religion, but of their human condition as well, carried off by a diabolical greed and seeking to take possession of the gold and silver buried with the bodies, destroy sepulchers, to the great scandal of the Indians, and exhume the corpses, which they then leave to ravening dogs and vultures." The text threatens with excommunication those who so behave (Second Council of Lima, Canon 113, quoted in A. Vargas

Ugarte, *Concilios Limenses*, 1:215–16). This disposition is opposed by the Yucay document, which is careful not to mention it.

16. García de Toledo says: "After all, these caciques and wealthy persons, who have buried these treasures with them when they died, after having supported their children, in life have left each what each has desired, and to those who have desired nothing have managed to leave something as well (even though they were not obliged to distribute their goods, nor did their children inherit by civil law, as they were not obliged by it, but only by natural law; nor has [natural law] obliged them to do more than beget and rear their children until these should reach an age at which they might support themselves and prosper)" (*Yucay*, 148).

17. We observe, in this case, the order of the transcription of the Yucay memorandum found in the *Colección de documentos para la historia de España*, which places the paragraph on which we are about to comment at the end of the text.

18. The expression "to have in some manner imitated our Lord Jesus Christ" is a variant presented by J. Chinese (see *Yucay*, 144 n. 520). Furthermore, this is the reading given in the *Colección de documentos* version, 469.

19. Guamán Poma, *Primer nueva corónica y buen gobierno*, 2:372. According to Titu Cusi Yupanqui, his father Manco Inca excoriated the Spaniards for their "importunity and exaggerated greed," telling them that they were worse than the *supay* (the devil), whose paths they tread because "he seeks no gold or silver, . . . and you seek it and wish to dig it out by force where there is none" (Titu Cusi Yupanqui, *Relación de la Conquista del Perú*, 64). See also the text that comes from the native informants of Sahagún, in Mexico, reproduced by León Portilla, *La visión de los vencidos*, 88.

20. Jesús Lara (*Tragedia del fin de Atawalpa*) has published this ancient text in the version that he regards as being closest to the original. This is the "Chayanta" text, which may be the same as the one used for presentation on stage in Potosí in 1555 (see *Teatro quechua colonial: Antología*, 521–24).

21. At the close, another personage rises up, called Spain. Pizarro falls dead, and Spain declares:

> Ay, unbridled sinner,
> Envenomed by gold! . . .
> Ay, Pizarro, Pizarro,
> What an abject traitor art thou!
> Heart born for pillage!

Lipschutz comments that this text expresses "the deep conviction that the *true* Spain is with them, is on their side" (A. Lipschutz, *El problema racial en la conquista de América*, 114).

22. Bataillon, "El Parecer de Yucay," in *Estudios sobre Bartolomé de Las Casas*, 273. The Yucay memorandum is one of the most important sources of inspiration of the book by Menéndez Pidal, *El Padre Las Casas: Su doble personalidad*, an anti-Lascasian diatribe that every serious historian has rejected out of hand; see, e.g., M. Giménez Fernández, "Sobre Bartolomé de Las Casas," in Bataillon, *Estudios sobre Bartolomé de Las Casas*, 14–42; Hanke,

"Ramón Menéndez Pidal vs. Bartolomé de Las Casas." See also the opinion of the moderate Venancio Carro (*Carta abierta a D. Ramón Menéndez Pidal: Anotaciones a su conferencia sobre Las Casas*) on the first writings of the prolific Spaniard; and then of the book itself (Carro, "La obra de Menéndez Pidal sobre Las Casas"). Only serious misinformation on the subject and short-sighted motivations could permit anyone to cite Menéndez Pidal's work as a serious basis for a knowledge of the work of Bartolomé de Las Casas. We think that that book (which is certainly no credit to its author, the illustrious philologist) deserves no further lines of commentary or refutation than the already copious ones it has received (perhaps it is for this reason that Espasa-Calpe, publisher of Menéndez Pidal's *Obras Completas,* has had the good judgment not to include his writing on Las Casas in that collection; see I. Pérez Fernández, *La última generación española de denigradores del padre Las Casas,* 24).

23. See above, our chapter 10.

24. Unless otherwise indicated, the texts that follow are taken from the pages devoted to this seventh reason (*O.E.* 5:84a–91b; emphasis added).

25. Maravall recalls the role of "fabled wealth" (*auri fames*) in the mentality of the Renaissance and maintains that "Las Casas demonstrated a knowledge of the psychology of the modern or Renaissance person" in making the observations that we are presenting. According to the fine historian, "Each epoch has its sin.... In the sixteenth century, it is that of greed." This is what Bartolomé mercilessly denounces (J. A. Maravall, "Utopía y primitivismo," 336–37).

26. Guamán Poma, *Primer nueva corónica y buen gobierno,* 2:367.

27. P. Castañeda Delgado and A. García del Moral are on the mark when they note that the editions of the Vulgate that Las Casas had at hand read, in Jeremiah 7:9 and 11:3, "the plural, *Baalim* (*baales,* 'lords,' 'masters'), instead of the singular with the first-person possessive suffix (*Baalí,* 'my ruler,' 'my master')." For his own part, Las Casas makes an option for the singular, and the editors of the *De Unico* comment: "With a critical sense that supplies for the deficiencies of the tools with which he worked, Las Casas in the exposition he offers inclines to the singular to designate *Baalí,* that imperious force which through passion dominates and enslaves the human being." They likewise point out that the Vulgate of John Paul II has simply "Baal" and thus avoids the confusion mentioned (Bartolomé de Las Casas, *Obras completas,* 2:416 n. 45).

28. The word "mammon" surely comes from the Aramaic radical *'MM,* which means "that in which one trusts." This indicates money with a certain pejorative accent; "unjust wealth" is the expression Luke uses (Luke 16:9, 11).

29. The term "to serve" (in Greek: *doulein*) has a ritual flavor: God is served. Therefore the text of Matthew speaks of the possibility, and peril, of serving wealth, serving Mammon, as God.

30. In Luke, the Pharisees, who refuse to accept these teachings of Jesus, are called "friends of money" (Luke 16:14). Jesus will respond to their ridicule with one of his most severe parables, that of the poor Lazarus and the anonymous "rich" person (*dives,* in the Latin Vulgate; see Luke 16:19–31).

31. In the _Historia de las Indias,_ apropos of the expeditions of Juan de Grijalva, he says ironically that for those who launched them, greed was "the principle of their gospel and the topic of their sermons." They were only interested whether there would be gold, so that the Indians understood that that was "their end and ultimate desire and cause of their coming to these lands" (_H.I.,_ bk. 3, ch. 109, _O.E._ 2:437b). Elsewhere he relates that on one occasion an interpreter told the Indians that the Europeans came from heaven and were going in quest of gold; and Las Casas comments insightfully: "rather disproportionate — coming from heaven and going in quest of gold" (_H.I.,_ bk. 1, ch. 54, _O.E._ 1:183b–184a).

32. _Carta de franciscanos y dominicos,_ 1519, _DII_ 7:427. Las Casas relates this anecdote at length, with certain slight variants and gives the name of the cacique in question: Hatuey (_H.I.,_ bk. 3, ch. 21, _O.E._ 2:224a–b).

33. Not otherwise did a great adversary of Las Casas's, Franciscan Motolinía, think. Describing the ten plagues razing the Indies, he declares the sixth to consist of "the gold mines." Working in these, the Indians who "have died cannot be numbered," and this due to the fact that "the gold of this land was as another golden calf, worshiped as a god, since they came from Castile to worship by undergoing toil and risk" (Motolinía, _Historia de los indios de la Nueva España,_ 120).

34. A little-known letter (October 8, 1524) of Pedrarias to the king of Spain well illustrates this immoderate lust for wealth. He informs him of his forays and gives him some good news, unfortunately accompanied by a bit of bad: "Rich mines have been discovered along the seacoast to the north, although for now there can be no gold mining because all of the Indians have fallen ill with smallpox, and great mortality has occurred among them. Praise to God that they are beginning to recover." Only for this was it worthwhile for them to live. (Helen Parish furnishes the text of this important letter in her _Las Casas en México,_ Appendix 8.) In less cynical tones, a similar attitude is expressed in a letter from the Hieronymites to the king in 1519 on the occasion of the epidemic of smallpox that devastated Hispaniola in those years (cited in D. Ramos Pérez, "¿Genocidio en la Española?" 49).

35. Castillo rightly emphasizes Las Casas's call for a conversion to Christ by way of a solidarity with the victims of the idolatry of gold, with those who are in "the same condition of suffering [as] Christ" (C. Castillo, "La conversión de las naciones indias," 83; see also 81–84; see what we have said above, in our chapter 2).

36. In a frequently cited text Domingo de Santo Tomás denounces with matchless energy the idolatry of those whom "for fear of lying I dare not call Christians": "It will be four years ago that, in order to make away with and destroy this land, a mouth of hell was discovered into which there enter, every year ever since, a great quantity of people whom the Spaniards' _greed_ sacrifices to their _god:_ certain silver mines called Potosí" (Domingo de Santo Tomás, "Carta a S. M. en el Consejo," July 1, 1550, quoted in Lisson Chávez, _La Iglesia de España en el Perú,_ vol. 1, no. 4, pp. 192, 195). We are dealing, it is clear, with an early text that comes from a fine expert on Peru; at the beginning of his letter he says with simplicity: "I shall say nothing that I

have not seen with my own eyes in this land" (Domingo de Santo Tomás, "Carta a S. M. en el Consejo," quoted in Lisson Chávez, *La Iglesia de España en el Perú,* vol. 1, no. 4, p. 190).

37. In Bataillon, *Estudios sobre Bartolomé de Las Casas,* 262.

38. Speaking of Hispaniola, he says: "In this land all were caught up in a passion to take the gold out of the mines, and [to have] the other labors performed that were to be undertaken for the sake of the mining (since that was the entire purpose of the Spaniards and of all their measures), and consequently the decimation and death of the Indians was needed" (*H.I.,* bk. 3, ch. 40, *O.E.* 2:99b).

39. As is known, Guamán Poma presents himself as a relative on his father's side with the Yarovilcas of Allauca Huánuco, who had preceded the Incas, and as the grandchild of Topa Inga Yupanqui on his mother's side. The publication of the so-called "Expediente Prado Tello" has confirmed, at any rate, Guamán Poma's local social rank, as the documents that have just appeared attribute to him the title of *cacique* or *curaca* (see Guamán Poma, *Y no hay remedio*).

40. Discovery and publication by R. Pietschmann.

41. On questions of language in Guamán, see the suggestive article by J. C. Godenzi, "Formas de tratamiento en el discurso de Guamán Poma."

42. As Adorno so well says: "There is a certain irony in the fact that he treats of European authors and researchers with the same indifference that they themselves had evidenced with regard to their autochthonous informants and assistants, who were condemned to oblivion, while he identifies his own native informants by name and ethnic origin" (Rolena Adorno, "El arte de la persuasión: El Padre de las Casas y Fray Luis de Granada en la obra de Waman Poma de Ayala," 103).

43. Together with Titu Cusi Yupanqui and Juan Santa Cruz Pachacuti, but with greater force and breadth than they, Guamán represents the voice "that speaks for the natives, presenting himself as their authentic interlocutor with the Spaniards and conquerors." One of his expressions is the chapter, "His Majesty Inquires, the Author Replies," which is in the form of a dialogue between Guamán and the king of Spain (A. Maguiña, "Guamán Poma y la evangelización," 201). On these chroniclers, see Raquel Chang Rodríguez, *La apropiación del signo: Tres cronistas indígenas del Perú.*

44. On Guamán's pictorial language, see the detailed study by Mercedes López-Baralt, *Icono y Conquista: Guamán Poma de Ayala.*

45. In this new focus Ossío's studies have been a landmark (see J. Ossío, "Guamán Poma: Nueva Corónica o Carta al rey: Un intento de aproximación a las categorías del pensamiento andino"). For Marzal, this contribution shows that Guamán "wrote not a mediocre history, but a different history" (M. Marzal, *Historia de la antropología indigenista: México y Perú,* 275). See also the important works of Rolena Adorno, *Guamán Poma: Writing and Resistance in Colonial Peru;* and her *Cronista y Príncipe: La obra de don Felipe Guamán Poma de Ayala.* See also F. Pease, the important "Prólogo" to Guamán Poma's *Primer nueva corónica y buen gobierno.*

46. Perceptively, Burga points out that the Indian chronicler "becomes the

transmitter of three voices, or three different reports." The first would be his own voice, that of an elderly, misunderstood person in search of recognition; the second comes from the local Ayacuchana nobility, to which he belonged; the third "makes a furtive appearance" and corresponds to the version of Cuzco nobility as descended from the Incas (M. Burga, *Nacimiento de una utopía*, 258). With the first voice, it would have to be said that frequently, rather than an "I," it is a "we" who speak.

47. The fact that at the same time Guamán Poma pursues other, lesser objectives — the assertion of his own family, a contradictory mistrust of the Incas, and striking out at some of his enemies — is no obstacle to a perception of what he ultimately seeks, through the manner in which he orders the historical data and how he orders his discourse.

48. Macera notes correctly: "Results aside, the mere fact that someone could have dared so much is surprising. Nothing of this could have occurred to Guamán Poma overnight. The day he accepted his fate, his must have then been an almost mystical or religious experience, an experience that sustained him throughout all the coming years, since perhaps at some moments he caught a glimpse of the totality of the historical, geographical, and moral universe he was building" (P. Macera, "Introducción," in Guamán Poma, *Y no hay remedio*, 70).

49. Guamán Poma, *Primer nueva corónica y buen gobierno*, 902. Elsewhere he says that "the first priest was Jesus Christ and he was the poorest" (550). A poor life, like the one he says he has taken up, is the appropriate life for one who is to proclaim the gospel. Hence his harsh criticism of priests who seek to grow wealthy at the expense of the Indians (526).

50. Ibid., 1100.

51. Ibid., 1109. This is his life responsibility, and so he specifies with concern: "Before growing old and dying, he wished to finish [his task] and give an account and report to God and to His Majesty" (ibid., 1109). Trigo maintains that there is also in Guamán "an evangelizing proposition, and that this proposition constitutes his guiding light" (Pedro Trigo, "El evangelio en la crónica indígena de Guamán Poma," 1).

52. See Guamán Poma, *Primer nueva corónica y buen gobierno*, 1094.

53. Ibid., 903. Further on, he writes: "And thus he became so poor, and to mingle among them for thirty years, although all of the Spaniards and other principal toadies, who devour the poor, told the author that the poor could do no business but that the rich, who had silver and gold, could by bribing him" (ibid., 1110).

54. Ibid.

55. Ibid. With human and Christian sensitivity, Guamán Poma does not forget that justice is due to all: "the head cacique, and the poor Indian or the Spaniard. Before God and justice, they are equal" (ibid., 502).

56. Ibid., 1105.

57. Ibid.

58. Ibid., 530.

59. Bishop Prado Tello interprets this expression thus: "Rather than a resigned complaint, this phrase contains strains of the ideal of someone ready

to fight for truth and justice" (Elías Prado Tello, "Presentación," in Guamán Poma, *Y no hay remedio*).

60. Guamán Poma, *Primer nueva corónica y buen gobierno*, 908. Elsewhere: "And so, my God, where are you? You hear me not when I ask a remedy for your poor, and I go harshly remedied" (1104).

61. Ibid., 1106. Here is another echo of Matthew 25:31–46. The "works of mercy" are the special expression of that service to the poor, a Christian notion that Guamán reinterprets in the light of the Andean theme of reciprocity and interchange (see Maguiña's annotations, in his "Guamán Poma y la evangelización," 205).

62. Guamán Poma, *Primer nueva corónica y buen gobierno*, 94.

63. Ibid., 1081.

64. Macera recalls that according to some of his enemies Guamán Poma was known as Lazarus. There are two Lazaruses in the gospels — the one that Jesus raised (in the Gospel of John) and the poor Lazarus in the parable recorded by Luke. It seems to us that our author would tend to identify more with the second than with the first (which in the long run is to identify oneself with the poor Jesus), since on so many occasions he proclaims himself a poor one, personally opposed to the wealthy persons he encounters (as Luke's text opposes Lazarus and the rich person). But the other possibility is not to be dismissed, which would tend to identify him with Jesus raised, as Macera observes. This author also observes that there may be a christological suggestion in his declaration that he was at the service of Cristóbal de la Cruz (see *Primer nueva corónica y buen gobierno*, 1108), a name meaning "bearer of Christ crucified" (Macera, "Introducción," in Guamán Poma, *Y no hay remedio*, 73).

65. That relationship has been carefully studied by Rolena Adorno in various works. This enables her to assert that "thus, even at a distance of twenty, or perhaps forty, years from Las Casas's death, . . . [his] ideas enjoyed a second wave of vitality, among the members of the native Andean population" (Adorno, "Las otras fuentes de Guamán Poma: Sus lecturas castellanas," 147).

66. Las Casas's works were confiscated in the viceroyalty of Peru in 1573.

67. For Guamán Poma, Indians, Spaniards, and blacks are "legitimate owners" of their respective lands (*Primer nueva corónica y buen gobierno*, 915).

68. "All unbelievers . . . have and hold just domain over their things" (*Doce dudas*, 1564, *O.E.* 5:48a). Adorno details the parallel in her "Otras fuentes," 145–46.

69. Adorno ("Otras fuentes," 146 n. 10) even identifies Cajetan with the "Cato of Rome" who figures in one of Guamán's sketches (*Primer nueva corónica y buen gobierno*, 916).

70. There are two other points of identification that it will be worthwhile to point out. One is the criticism of the *encomiendas* and *encomenderos*. Despite the fact that by Guamán's time they no longer carried the weight they had sixty or seventy years before, they were still causing havoc among the Indians (see *Primer nueva corónica y buen gobierno*, 547–59). The other point of convergence seems minor, but is actually significant: At one moment, Guamán proposes the presence of a papal legate, a second person of the pope, in

the Indies (see *Primer nueva corónica y buen gobierno,* 473, 1032). Las Casas had done so in the letter he writes jointly with Bishop Valdivieso to Prince Philip. Apropos of the Audiencia's proposal to dispatch a metropolitan justice, they write: "We should wish that he were to be more than a metropolitan, and that there were to be a legate of the Pope [here] — of whom there is more need than of anything else" when it comes to putting order into the church of the Indies (1545; *O.E.* 5:226b).

71. The topic appears extremely frequently in Guamán's work (see, e.g., *Primer nueva corónica y buen gobierno,* 526, 559, 1087).

72. Ibid., 949.

73. See Adorno, "El proyecto de Huamán Poma para el Perú: La resonancia de las obras de Las Casas en la de Huamán Poma"; and a more recent article, in which she summarizes all of these questions in breadth, idem, "Colonial Reform? Guamán Poma's Empire of the Four Parts of the World."

74. Guamán Poma, *Primer nueva corónica y buen gobierno,* 948.

75. Ibid., 949.

76. Adorno, "Proyecto de Huamán Poma."

77. See Gustavo Gutiérrez, *Entre las calandrias: Un ensayo sobre José María Arguedas,* 50–55.

78. See above, introduction to our Part Two.

79. Guamán Poma, *Primer nueva corónica y buen gobierno,* 376.

80. It was not necessary to appeal to a direct knowledge of Las Casas's texts. His theses lived on in the Peru of the time. But neither can we dismiss the possibility that Guamán may have read the *Tratado de las doce dudas,* which circulated widely in these lands.

81. See Adorno, "El arte de la persuasión"; idem, *Cronista y Príncipe,* 103–12. According to Adorno, Luis de Granada had an influence on the homiletic style frequently adopted by Guamán, especially in his twenty forewords, which are like short sermons and exhort "Christian readers" to emend their lives and be just with the Indians. Likewise in some examples found in the *Primer nueva corónica y buen gobierno.* At the same time, he supplies him with arguments for the recognition of the human and religious values of the non-Christians.

82. A letter of Friar Luis to Carranza (who was often concerned with questions of the Indies) has survived in which he warns the cardinal of the intrigues being contrived against both by Inquisitor Fernando de Valdés (in Fray Luis de Granada, *Obras,* 14:440–41). The bearer of this letter was Juan de la Peña, one of the Salamancan theologians closest to the Lascasian ideas. On the other hand, Friar Luis studied in the Convent of St. Gregory in Valladolid, which, in its time, was one of the providers of missionaries to the Indies.

83. In *Sermones del venerable Padre Maestro Fr. Luis de Granada,* 13:80 (quoted in A. García del Moral and A. Larios, "Introducción" to Las Casas, *Obras Completas,* 1:408).

84. Viceroy Toledo was not off course, then — from his viewpoint — in undertaking his campaign against Las Casas.

85. See J. Dammert, "Presencia de Las Casas en la Emancipación y la República," in J.-B. Lassègue, *La larga marcha,* 404–7.

Conclusion: And They Said They Would See It . . .

1. Bishop Leónidas Proaño, a bishop identified with the Indians for many reasons and without a doubt one of the great figures of the contemporary Latin American church, constantly warned of this danger today as well.

2. An important Lascasian echo can be found in the Instruction issued in 1659, to missionaries departing for China, by the Sacred Congregation for the Propagation of the Faith (founded in 1622): "Do not devote your zeal or propose any argument toward persuading these peoples to change their rites, their habits, and their customs, unless these be plainly contrary to religion and morality. Nothing could be more absurd than to transport, to the Chinese, France, Spain, Italy, or any other country of Europe. Carry to these peoples not your countries, but the faith. Make no attempt to supplant the usages of these peoples with European usages, and strive to adapt yourselves to the former" (quoted in: Pontifical Commission for Justice and Peace, *La Iglesia frente al racismo,* no. 6).

3. Medellín Document on Peace, no. 22.

4. See John Paul II's discourse on the island of Gorea (Africa), in 1992, begging forgiveness for Christians' participation in the ignominious traffic in slaves, many of whom were carried to the Indies.

5. Puebla Final Document, part 4, ch. 1, "A Preferential Option for the Poor," no. 1147.

6. See the interesting indications of Catalina Romero, "Evangelización: Una nueva relación social." See also the various works appearing in *La nueva evangelización: Reflexiones, experiencias y testimonios desde el Perú;* and in *Quinto centenario y nueva evangelización.*

7. M. D. Chenu, "Prophètes et théologiens dans l'Eglise: Parole de Dieu," *Masses Ouvrières,* no. 200 (October 1963): 59–70.

Appendix 1: The Demographic Question

1. A. Rosenblat, *La población indígena.*

2. W. Borah and S. F. Cook, *The Aboriginal Population of Central Mexico on the Eve of the Spanish Conquest;* idem, *Essays in Population History: Mexico and Caribbean.*

3. In W. M. Denevan, ed., *The Native Population of the Americas in 1492,* 1–12, 289–92. See also N. Sánchez Albornoz, *La población de América Latina: Desde los tiempos precolombinos al año 2000;* idem, "The Population of Colonial Spanish America"; and the more recent article of E. J. A. Maeder, "La población americana después de la conquista."

4. A. Gutiérrez, "La primitiva organización indiana," 243. According to this estimate, six million belonged to the Inca empire.

5. M. Lucena, "La estructura uniforme de Iberoamérica como región," 378.

6. L. N. McAlister, *Spain and Portugal,* 130–32.

7. This was also Las Casas's figure (see *H.I.,* bk. 3, ch. 2, *O.E.* 2:173b).

8. S. Moya, *Después de Colón,* 181–89.

9. And this in spite of the fact that, very early, Indians of the "useless" islands (that is, lacking in economic interest) were transported to replace those who were dying on Hispaniola. For this, and the situation of Hispaniola in general in these years, see E. Rodríguez Demorizi, *Los dominicos y las encomiendas;* on the point mentioned, see 39–45. Likewise for the historical context of the island, see D. Ramos Pérez, "La etapa de los gobernadores generales."

10. Speaking of San Juan, Puerto Rico, Acosta says: "In a short time, a densely populated island became completely uninhabited by any of its natives" (José Acosta, *De Procuranda Indorum Salute,* bk. 1, ch. 13, p. 195).

11. See N. D. Cook, *Demographic Collapse: Indian Peru 1520–1620,* 114, 247–55. Las Casas's figures were more moderate, but were also terrible. In 1563, he asserted that by then Peru had lost half or two-thirds of the population it had had around 1520 (see *Doce dudas,* 1564, *O.E.* 5:530a).

12. "And thus, procreation ceased among them," says Las Casas (*Octavo remedio,* 1542, *O.E.* 5:103b).

13. F. Guerra, "El efecto demográfico de las epidemias tras el descubrimiento de América."

14. The epidemic reached Mexico and Guatemala, facilitating the invasion of these lands (see C. O. Sauer, *The Early Spanish Main,* 204).

15. Guerra compares the depopulation of the Indies to that experienced in Europe owing to the plague of 1348, which "reached an overall mortality that has been estimated at 60,000,000 dead" (Guerra, "Efecto demográfico de las epidemias," 42).

16. Las Casas seems no longer to be reproached for the figures he gives; now he is criticized for not having correctly indicated the causes of the depopulation, whose enormous dimensions are now beginning to be accepted.

17. Twenty million, he says in *Aquí se contiene,* 1552, *O.E.* 5:334a.

18. Commenting on the studies of Borah and Cook, historian Chaunu wrote in 1964: "The catastrophe of the conquest, this dramatic collision of two worlds similar in numerical population but unequally endowed, was as great as Las Casas denounces it to be" (P. Chaunu, "La population de l'Amérique indienne [nouvelles recherches]," 117).

Appendix 2: A New Document of Las Casas

1. I. Pérez has since published a longer analysis and a transcription of the Lascasian text: "Hallazgo de un nuevo documento básico de Fray Bartolomé de Las Casas," *Studium* (April 1993): 459–504. H. Parish presents new data in her forthcoming *The Royal File on the Administration of the Indians.*

Bibliography

Abbreviations Used in Bibliography

AAFV   *Anuario de la Asociación Francisco de Vitoria* (Madrid)

Actas Simposio Etica
      Actas del Primer Simposio sobre la Etica en la Conquista de América (1492–1573). Salamanca: Ayuntamiento y Diputación Provincial, 1984

AEA   *Anuario de Estudios Americanos* (Seville)

AFP   *Archivum Fratrum Praedicatorum* (Rome)

AGI   *Archivo General de Indias* (Seville)

AHR   *American Historical Review*

AI   *Archivo Iberoamericano* (Madrid)

ANDE   *Anuario de Historia del Derecho Español* (Madrid)

Autour de Las Casas
      Autour de Las Casas: Actes du Colloque du Ve Centenaire. Paris: Tallandier, 1987

BAC   Biblioteca de Autores Católicos

BAE   Biblioteca de Autores Españoles

BLCHI   *Bartolomé de Las Casas (1474–1974) e Historia de la Iglesia en América Latina.* Barcelona: Nova Terra, 1976

BRAH   *Boletín de la Real Academia de Historia* (Madrid)

CA   *Cuadernos Americanos* (Mexico City)

CELAM   Consejo Episcopal Latinoamericano

CEP   Centro de Estudios y Publicaciones (Lima)

CH   Cultura Hispánica (Madrid)

CHP   Corpus Hispanorum de Pace

CSIC   Consejo Superior de Investigaciones Científicas (Madrid)

CT   *Ciencia Tomista* (Salamanca)

DEI   Departamento Ecuménico de Investigaciones (San José, Costa Rica)

DII   *Colección de documentos inéditos relativos al descubrimiento, conquista y organización de las antiguas posesiones españolas de América y Oceanía, sacados de los archivos del reino y muy especialmente del de Indias.* 42 vols. Madrid, 1864–84

Doctrina   *Doctrina Christiana y Catecismo.* Madrid: CSIC, 1986

Dominicos (1986)
> *Los dominicos y el nuevo mundo: Actas del I Congreso Internacional.* Madrid: Deimos, 1987

Dominicos (1989)
> *Los dominicos y el nuevo mundo: Actas del II Congreso Internacional.* Salamanca: Editorial San Esteban, 1990

DTC   *Dictionnaire de Théologie Catholique.* Paris: Librairie Letouzey et Ané

Estudios Lascasianos
> *Estudios Lascasianos: IV Centenario de la muerte de Bartolomé de Las Casas* (1566–1966). Seville: Escuela de Estudios Hispanoamericanos, 1966

Estudios sobre Las Casas
> *Estudios sobre Fray Bartolomé de Las Casas.* Seville: Anales de la Universidad Hispalense, 1974

Etica en la conquista
> *La ética en la conquista de América.* Madrid: CSIC, 1984

FCE   Fondo de Cultura Económica (Mexico City)

First Images
> *First Images of America: The Impact of the New World on the Old.* 2 vols. Berkeley: University of California Press, 1976

Franciscanos (1985)
> *Actas del I Congreso Internacional sobre los franciscanos en el nuevo mundo (siglo XVI).* Madrid: Deimos, 1986

Franciscanos (1987)
> *Actas del II Congreso Internacional sobre los franciscanos en el nuevo mundo (siglo XVI).* In Archivo Iberoamericano 48, nos. 189–92 (January–December 1988)

HAHR   *Hispanic American Historical Review* (Durham, N.C.)

HBA   *Historiografía y Bibliografía Americanista* (Seville)

HM   *Historia Mexicana*

HTR   *Harvard Theological Review* (Cambridge, Mass.)

IAA   *Ibero-Amerikanisches Archiv* (n.s.) (Berlin)

IBC   Instituto Bartolomé de Las Casas (Lima)

I diritti   *I diritti dell'uomo e la pace nel pensiero di Francisco de Vitoria e Bartolome de Las Casas.* Massimo-Milano: Università S. Tommaso (Angelicum), 1988

IEP   Instituto de Estudios Políticos (Madrid)

JGS   *Jahrbuch für Geschichte von Staat* (Wirtschaft und Gesellschaft Lateinamerikas) (Cologne)

LA   *Libro Anual* (1974). Mexico City: Instituto Superior de Estudios Eclesiásticos, 1975

Las Casas et la politique
> *Las Casas et la politique des droits de l'homme.* Aix-en-Provence: Institut d'Etudes Politiques–ICH, 1976

Las Casas in History
> *Bartolomé de Las Casas in History.* J. Friede and B. Keen, eds. Dekalb: Northern Illinois University Press, 1971

Le Supplément
> *Las Casas et Vitoria, le Supplément* 160 (March 1987)

NRT   *Nouvelle Revue Théologique* (Louvain)

NZMR   *Neue Zeitschrift für Missionswissenschaft und Religionswissenschaft* (Münster)

PL   *Patrologia Latina*

Política Indigenista
> *Estudios sobre Política Indigenista Española en América* (Valladolid)

PUF   Presses Universitaires de France (Paris)

REB   *Revista Eclesiástica Brasileira* (Petrópolis, Brazil)

RHA   *Revista de Historia de América* (Mexico City)

RI   *Revista de Indias*

UNAM   Universidad Autónoma de México

ZMR   *Zeitschrift für Missionswissenschaft und Religionswissenschaft* (Münster)

Works of Bartolomé de Las Casas

Principal Collections

Obras escogidas. Ed. J. Pérez de Tudela. 5 vols. Madrid: BAE, 1957–58 (cited as *O.E.*).
> Vols. 1–2: *Historia de las Indias* (cited as *H.I.*).
>
> Vols. 3–4: *Apologética historia* (cited as *A.H.*).
>
> Vol. 5: *Opúsculos, cartas y memoriales.*
>
> These works are cited by volume, page, and column. For volumes 1–4 the book and chapter are also provided to facilitate consultation of other editions of Las Casas's works. For volume 5 the name and date of the work are also included.

Obras completas. Madrid: Alianza Editorial.
> Vol. 2: *De unico vocationis modo* (1990).
>
> Vols. 6, 7, 8: *Apologética historia* (1992).
>
> Vol. 9: *Apología* (1989).
>
> Vol. 10: *Tratados de 1552* (1992).
>
> Vol. 11.2: *Doce dudas* (Providence version, 1992).
>
> Vol. 12: *De Regia Potestate y Quaestio Theologalis* (1990).
>
> Vol. 14: *Diario del primer y tercer viaje de Cristóbal Colón* (1989).

Tratados. 2 vols. Mexico City: FCE, 1965.

Other Works by Las Casas

Apologética historia sumaria. Ed. E. O'Gorman. Mexico City: UNAM, 1967.

Brevísima relación de la destrucción de las Indias. Ed. I. Pérez Fernández. Madrid: Tecnos, 1992.

Carta a Domingo de Soto. In M. Bataillon, *Estudios sobre Bartolomé de Las Casas.* Barcelona: Península, 1976.

Caso propuesto para salir de cierta duda (between 1550 and 1560). Published by F. Cantù in *Critica Storica* 12 (1975): 312–19.

Conclusiones Sumarias sobre el remedio de las Indias. (Madrid: Biblioteca Nacional, 1992).

De Thesauris. Madrid: CSIC, 1958.

De Unico. See above under *Obras completas* (vol. 2).

La exención o la damnación (also called *Quaestio theologalis*). Ed. H. Parish and H. E. Weidman. In H. Parish, *Las Casas en México,* forthcoming.

Historia de las Indias. Ed. A. Millares and L. Hanke. 3 vols. Mexico City: FCE, 1951.

In Defense of Indians. Translation of the *Apología.* Trans. S. Poole. De Kalb: Northern Illinois University Press, 1974.

The Only Way (De unico vocationis modo). Ed. H. Parish. Trans. F. Sullivan. New York: Paulist Press, 1992. (Full title of the Paulist book: *Bartolomé de las Casas: The Only Way.*)

Petición al emperador Carlos V (1543). In H. Parish, *Las Casas as a Bishop,* 3–7. Washington, D.C.: Library of Congress, 1980.

Representación a la Audiencia de los Confines (1545). Published by F. Cantù in *IAA* 3, no. 2 (1977): 156–62.

Sobre el título del dominio del Rey de España sobre las personas y tierras de los indios (1554). In M. Cuevas, ed., *Documentos inéditos del siglo XVI para la historia de México,* 176–80. Mexico City, 1914. Also in B. Las Casas, *De Regia Potestate,* 168–72. Madrid: CSIC, 1969.

Tratado de Indias y el doctor Sepúlveda. Caracas: Biblioteca de la Academia Nacional de Historia, 1962.

Studies

Abellán, J. L. *Historia crítica del pensamiento español: La Edad de Oro.* Vol. 2. Madrid: Espasa-Calpe, 1979.

———. "Los orígenes españoles del mito del buen salvaje: Fray Bartolomé de Las Casas y su antropología utópica." *RI* 36, nos. 145–46 (July–December 1976): 157–79.

Abril Castelló, V. "Bartolomé de Las Casas, abogado defensor del pueblo indio." *Doctrina,* 79–116.

———. "Bartolomé de Las Casas, el último comunero (mito y realidad de las utopías políticas lascasianas)." *Las Casas et la politique,* 92–123.

———. "Bartolomé de Las Casas en 1976: Balance y perspectivas de un centenario." *Arbor* (Madrid) 93, no. 361 (January 1976): 27–46.

———. "Bartolomé de Las Casas y la escuela de Salamanca." In J. Pérez de Mesa, ed., *De Bello Contra Insulanos,* 489–518. Madrid: CSIC, 1982.

———. "Bartolomé de Las Casas y la segunda generación de la escuela de Salamanca." *Revista de Filosofía* (Madrid), 2d series, no. 4 (1983): 5–19.

————. "La bipolarización Sepúlveda–Las Casas y sus consecuencias: La revolución de la duodécima réplica." *Etica en la conquista,* 229–88.

————. "El comunerismo lascasiano y las libertades políticas del indio americano." *Revista de Filosofía* (Madrid), 2d series, no. 7 (July–December 1984): 215–23.

————. "Francisco de la Cruz, la utopía lascasista y la contrareforma virreinal inquisitorial." *Cuadernos para la historia de la evangelización* (Cusco), no. 3 (1988): 9–67.

————. "¿Las Casas, comunero? El sacro imperio hispánico y las comunidades indoamericanas de base." *Revista de la Facultad de Derecho, Universidad Complutense* (Madrid), no. 17 (1973): 485–527.

————. "La obligación política en Francisco Suárez." *AAFV* 18 (1971–72): 77–105.

————. "La operación 'desarrollo de los pueblos' y sus precedentes en el pensamiento político clásico español." *AAFV* 17 (1969–70): 91–117.

————. "Réplica que hizo el obispo de Chiapa contra el doctor Sepúlveda." In B. de Las Casas, *De Regia Potestate,* 293–319.

————. "Vitoria–Las Casas, confrontación y proyección: Impacto en Las Casas de su enfrentamiento con Vitoria en 1550–1552." *I diritti,* 155–72.

Acosta, J. de. *De Procuranda Indorum Salute, ed. crítica.* Madrid: CSIC (CHP), 1984.

————. *Historia natural y moral de las Indias.* Mexico: FCE, 1962.

————. *Obras del Padre José de Acosta.* Madrid: BAE, 1954.

Acuña, R. *De Debellandis Indis: Un tratado desconocido.* Mexico City: UNAM, 1988.

Adorno, R. "El arte de la persuasión: El Padre de Las Casas y Fray Luis de Granada en la obra de Waman Poma de Ayala." *Escritura, Teoría y Crítica literaria,* no. 8 (1979): 167–89.

————. "Bartolomé de Las Casas y Domingo de Santo Tomás en la obra de Felipe Waman Puma." *Revista Iberoamericana,* nos. 120–21 (1982): 673–79.

————. *Colonial Reform or Utopia? Guamán Poma's Empire of the Four Parts of the World.* In preparation.

————. *Cronista y Príncipe: La obra de don Felipe Guamán Poma de Ayala.* Lima: Universidad Católica, 1989.

————. *Guamán Poma: Writing and Resistance in Colonial Peru.* Austin: University of Texas Press, 1986.

————. "Las otras fuentes de Guamán Poma: Sus lecturas castellanas." *Histórica* 2, no. 2 (December 1978): 137–58.

————. "El proyecto de Huamán Poma para el Perú: La resonancia de las obras de Las Casas en la de Huamán Poma." *Actas del Congreso sobre Bartolomé de Las Casas.* Lima, 1992.

Agostino Iannarone, R. di. "Génesis del pensamiento colonial en Francisco de Vitoria." In F. de Vitoria, *De Indis* (CHP), xxxi–xli.

Aguayo, R. *Don Vasco de Quiroga: Taumaturgo de la organización social.* Mexico City: Ediciones Oasis, 1970.

Almandoz Garmantía, J. A. *Fray Alonso de Vera Cruz, O.E.S.A. y la encomienda indiana en la historia eclesiástica novohispana (1522–1556).* Madrid, 1971–77.

Alonso, J. M. *Derechos de la conciencia errónea y otros derechos.* Madrid: Coculsa, 1964.

Alonso Cortés, N. "Fray Bartolomé de Las Casas en Valladolid." *RI* 1, no. 2 (1940): 105–11.

Altamira, R. "El texto de las leyes de Burgos de 1512." *LA,* 183–200.

Alvarez Lobo, J. *Cartas del obispo Valdivieso: La defensa de los pueblos de América (1547–1554).* Prologue by P. Casaldáliga. Cusco: CERA Bartolomé de Las Casas, 1992.

Alvarez López, E. "El saber de la naturaleza en el Padre Las Casas." *BRAH* 132, no. 2 (1953): 201–29.

Andreotti, R. "La teoría del 'bellum iustum', J. G. de Sepúlveda, antagonista di Las Casas." *I diritti*, 173–79.

Andrés, M. *La teología española en el siglo XVI*. Vol. 2. Madrid: BAC, 1976.

Andrés Marcos, T. "Ideología del Democrates Secundus." In J. G. de Sepúlveda, *Demócrates Segundo*, xxxv–xliv.

———. *Los imperialismos de Juan Ginés de Sepúlveda en su Democrates Alter.* Madrid: IEP, 1947.

———. *Vitoria y Carlos V en la soberanía hispano-americana*. 2d ed. Salamanca, 1946.

André-Vincent, P. *Bartolomé de Las Casas, prophète du nouveau monde.* Paris: Tallandier, 1980.

———. "La concrétisation de la notion classique de droit naturel à travers l'oeuvre de Las Casas." *Las Casas et la politique*, 203–13.

———. *Derecho de los indios y desarrollo en Hispanoamérica.* Madrid: CH, 1975.

———. "L'intuition fondamentale de Las Casas et la doctrine de Saint Thomas." *NRT* 96, no. 9 (November 1974): 944–52.

———. "Le prophétisme de Barthélemy de Las Casas." *NRT* 101, no. 4 (July–August 1979): 541–60.

———. "Le prophétisme évangélique de Barthélemy de Las Casas." *Autour de Las Casas*, 107–15.

———. "Sur la date et la portée du 'repentir' de Las Casas." *Autour de Las Casas*, 242–43.

Ansión, J. "De la utopía andina a la construcción nacional" *Páginas* 13, no. 94 (December 1988): 33–41.

Arbeola, A. "Francisco Javier en el diálogo teológico sobre la justificación de los infieles." *Revista Española de Teología* 21, cuad. 20 (1961): 167–94.

Arena, C. R. "Bartolomé de las Casas: An Early American Agrarian Reformer." *RHA* 61–62 (January–December 1966): 121–31.

Arenal, C. del. "La teoría de la servidumbre natural en el pensamiento español de los siglos XVI y XVII." *HBA* 19–20 (1975–76): 67–24.

Armas Medina, F. de. *Cristianización del Perú, 1532–1600.* Seville: Escuela de Estudios Hispano-Americanos, 1953.

Arquillere, H. X. *L'augustinisme politique.* 2d ed. Paris: Vrin, 1972.

Arranz Márquez, L. "Alonso del Espinar, O.F.M., y las leyes de Burgos de 1512–1513." *Franciscanos* (1985), 633–51.

Artaud de Montor. *Histoire du pontificat du Pape Pie VIII.* Paris, 1844.

Asturias, M. A. "Un inédito: Las Casas obispo de Dios." *Studi di Letteratura Ispanoamericana* 7 (1976): 137–45.

Avalle-Arce, J. B. "Las hipérboles del Padre Las Casas." *Revista de la Facultad de Humanidades* (Potosí) 2, no. 1 (1960): 33–55.

Aznar Gil, F. "La libertad religiosa del indio en autores franciscanos del siglo XVI." *AI* 48, nos. 189–92 (January–December 1988): 391–39.

Baciero, C. "Libertad natural y esclavitud natural en la escuela de Salamanca." *I diritti*, 181–89.

Bahr, H. E. "Martín Lutero y Las Casas: Las dos reformas del siglo XVI." *Revista de DDHH Justicia y Paz* 4, nos. 3–4 (July–December 1989): 79–84.

Ballesteros Gaibrois, M. *En el centenario del Padre Las Casas, revisión de una polémica.* Madrid: Fundación Universitaria Española, 1974.

Baptiste, V. *Bartolomé de las Casas and Thomas More's Utopia: Connections and Similarities.* Culver City, Calif.: Labyrinthos, 1990.

Barcia Trelles, C. *Francisco de Vitoria et l'école moderne du droit international.* Paris: Hachette, 1928.

———. "Francisco Suárez (1548–1617): Les théologiens espagnols du XVI siècle et l'école moderne du droit international." *Académie de Droit International, recueil des cours* (The Hague) 43 (1933): 430–501.

Barnadas, J. M. *Charcas: Orígenes históricos de una sociedad colonial.* La Paz: CIPCA, 1973.

———. "Una contribución a la historia del lascasismo." *BLCHI,* 91–119.

Barreda, J. A. "Aproximación histórica." Las Casas, *Obras completas,* 2:i–xvi.

———. "Diritto naturale e pedagogia della fede in Bartolomé de Las Casas." *I diritti,* 191–203.

———. "El encuentro de dos absolutos: El hombre y el Evangelio." *Studium* 32, fasc. 1 (1992): 123–61.

———. *Ideología y pastoral misionera en Bartolomé de las Casas, OP.* Madrid: Instituto Pontificio de Teología, 1981.

———. "Primera anunciación y bautismo en la obra de Bartolomé de Las Casas." *Dominicos* (1989), 113–36.

Barreda Laos, F. *Vida intelectual del virreinato del Perú.* Buenos Aires: Talleres Gráficos Argentinos, 1937.

Basadre, J. *La promesa de la vida peruana.* Lima: Mejía Baca, 1958.

Bataillon, M. "Les 'douze questions' péruviennes résolues par Las Casas." *Hommage à Lucien Febvre,* 221–30. Paris, 1954.

———. *Erasmo y España: Estudios sobre la historia espiritual del siglo XVI.* 2d ed. Mexico City and Buenos Aires: FCE, 1966.

———. *Estudios sobre Bartolomé de Las Casas.* Barcelona: Península, 1976.

———. "Las Casas, ¿un profeta?" *Revista de Occidente* (Madrid), no. 141 (December 1974): 279–91.

———. *Las Casas et la défense des Indiens.* Paris: Julliard, 1971.

———. "Las Casas face à la pensée d'Aristote sur l'esclavage." *Actes du XVI colloque international de Tours,* 403–20. Paris, 1976.

———. "Las Casas frente al pensamiento aristotélico sobre la esclavitud." *Casa de las Américas* 19, no. 109 (July–August 1978): 32–44.

———. "Zumárraga, reformador del clero seglar (una carta inédita del primer obispo de México)." *HM* (1953–54): 1–10.

Batiffol, P. *La paix constantinienne et le catholicisme.* 3d ed. Paris: Gabalda, 1924.

Bayle, C. "El Concilio de Trento en las Indias Españolas." *El Concilio de Trento,* 475–502. Madrid: Razón y Fe, 1945.

———. *El protector de indios.* Seville: Escuela de Estudios Hispano-Americanos de la Universidad de Sevilla, 1945.

Beauchot, M. "La aplicación del derecho natural a los Indios, según Bartolomé de Las Casas." *Evangelización y Teología en América (siglo XVI).* Pamplona: Universidad de Navarra, 1990.

———. "El primer planteamiento teológico jurídico sobre la conquista de América: John Maior." *CT* 103 (1976): 213–30.

Becker, J. *La Política española en las Indias.* Madrid, 1920.

Belaúnde Guinassi, M. *La encomienda en el Perú.* Lima: Ed. Mercurio Peruano, 1945.

Belch, S. *Paulus Vladimiri and His Doctrine.* The Hague: Mouton, 1965.

Bell, Aubrey F. *Juan Ginés de Sepúlveda.* Oxford: Oxford University Press, 1925.

Beltrán de Heredia, V. "Colección de dictámenes inéditos del maestro Fray Francisco de Vitoria." *CT* 43 (1931): 27–50, 169–80; also in *AAFV* 3 (1932): 17–41.

————. *Las corrientes de espiritualidad durante las primeras décadas del siglo XVI.* Salamanca: Biblioteca de Teólogos Españoles, 1941.

————. "Doctrina de Vitoria sobre las relaciones entre Iglesia y Estado y fuentes de la misma." *Miscelánea Beltrán de Heredia* (Salamanca) 2 (1972): 73–91.

————. *Domingo de Soto: Estudio biográfico documentado.* Salamanca: Biblioteca de Teólogos Españoles, 1960.

————. *Francisco de Vitoria.* Barcelona: Labor, 1939.

————. *Ideas del maestro Fray Francisco de Vitoria anteriores a las relecciones "De Indis," acerca de la colonización de América según documentos inéditos.* Salamanca, 1930; also in *AAFV* 2 (1931): 23–51.

————. "El maestro Domingo de Soto en la controversia de Las Casas con Sepúlveda." *CT* 47 (1932): 35–49, 177–93.

————. *Los manuscritos del Maestro Fray Francisco de Vitoria.* Madrid, 1928.

————. "Nuevos datos acerca del P. Bernardino Minaya y del licenciado Calvo de Padilla, compañeros de Las Casas." *Miscelánea Beltrán de Heredia* (Salamanca) 1 (1971): 469–96.

————. "Un precursor del Maestro Vitoria: El P. Matías de Paz O.P. y su tratado 'De Dominio Regum Hispaniae super Indos.'" *CT* 40 (1929): 173–90; also in *Miscelánea Beltrán de Heredia* (Salamanca) 1 (1971): 607–25.

Benito, J. A. "La promoción del indio en los concilios y sínodos americanos (1551–1622): Aportación dominicana." *Dominicos* (1989), 785–822.

Bennasy-Berling, M. C. *Humanismo y religión en Sor Juana Inés de la Cruz.* Mexico City: UNAM, 1983.

Benson, R. L. "Medieval Canonistic Origins of the Debate on the Lawfulness of the Spanish Conquest." *First Images.*

Benzoni, J. *La historia del Mundo Nuevo.* Lima: Universidad de San Marcos, 1967.

Beozzo, O. "O diálogo da conversão do gentio: A evangelização entre a persuasão e a força." *Actas del Congreso Internacional sobre Bartolomé de Las Casas.* Lima, 1992.

Bevenot, M. "St. Thomas and the Erroneous Conscience." *Thomistica Morum Principia,* 107–13. Rome: Officium Libri Catholici, 1960–61.

Biermann, B. "Bartolomé de las Casas und Verapaz." *Las Casas in History,* 443–86.

————. "Las Casas — ein Geisteskranker?" *ZMR* (July 1964): 176–91.

————. "Lascasiana, Unedierte Dokumente von Fray Bartolomé de las Casas." *AFP* 27 (1957): 337–58.

————. "Las Casas und Bartolomé Carranza." *AFP* 32 (1963): 339–53.

————. *Las Casas und Seine Sendung.* Mainz: Matthias-Grunewald-Verlag, 1968.

————. "Das Requerimiento in der Spanischen Conquista." *NZMR* 6 (1950): 94–114.

————. "Vasco de Quiroga y su tratado de Debellandis Indis." *HM* 72/18, no. 4 (April–June 1969): 615–22.

————. "Zwei Briefe von Fray Bartolome de Las Casas (1534–1535)." *AFP* 4 (1934): 187–220.

Borah, W. N. "The Mixing of Populations." *First Images,* 707–22.

Borah, W. N., and S. F. Cook. *The Aboriginal Population of Central Mexico on the Eve of the Spanish Conquest.* Berkeley and Los Angeles: University of California Press, 1963.

————. *Essays in Population History.* 3 vols. Berkeley: University of California Press, 1971–79.

Borges, J. L. *Historia universal de la infamia.* Buenos Aires: Emece, 1954.

Borges, P. "Actitudes de los misioneros ante la duda indiana." *Etica en la conquista,* 597–630.

———. "Un drama lascasiano: Franciscanos y dominicos en la actuación de Montesinos de 1511 a 1512." *Franciscanos* (1987), 755–80.

———. "Evangelización y civilización en América." *Doctrina,* 227–62.

———. *Métodos misionales de la cristianización de América.* Madrid: CSIC, 1960.

———. *Misión y civilización en América.* Madrid: Alhambra, 1987.

———. "La Santa Sede y América en el siglo XVI." *Estudios Americanos* 21, no. 107 (1961): 141–68.

Boria, R. *Fray Pedro de Córdoba (1482–1521).* Tucumán, 1982.

Bowser, F. *The African in Colonial Peru, 1524–1650.* Stanford, Calif.: Stanford University Press, 1974.

Braciero, C. "La promoción y evangelización del indio en el plan de José de Acosta." *Doctrina,* 117–62.

Brading, D. A. *The First America: The Spanish Monarchy, Creole Patriots, and the Liberal State (1492–1867).* Cambridge: Cambridge University Press, 1991.

———. "The Incas and the Renaissance: The Royal Commentaries of Inca Garcilaso." *Journal of Latin American Studies* 18, pt. 1 (May 1986): 1–23.

———. "The Two Cities: St. Augustine and the Spanish Conquest of America." *Revista Portuguesa de Filosofia* (Braga) 44, no. 1 (1988): 1–28.

Brady, R. L. "The Role of Las Casas in the Emergence of Negro Slavery in the New World." *RHA* 61–62 (January–December 1966): 43–55.

Braudel, F. *El Mediterráneo y el mundo mediterráneo en la época de Felipe II.* Mexico City: FCE, 1953.

Bravo, Ma. C. "Polo de Ondegardo y Guamán Poma, dos mentalidades ante un problema: La condición del Indígena en el Perú del siglo XVI." *Homenaje a Gonzalo Fernández de Oviedo,* 2:275–84. Madrid: CSIC, 1983.

Bréhier, E. *Histoire de la Philosophie.* Vol. 2: *La Philosophie moderne.* Paris: Presses Universitaires, 1941.

Brezzi, P. *Cristianesimo e imperio romano.* Rome, 1942.

Brice, A. F. "Simón Bolívar y Fray Bartolomé de Las Casas ante sus críticos." *Boletín Histórico* (Caracas), no. 19 (January 1969): 5–88.

Briere, Y. de la. *Le droit de juste guerre.* Paris, 1938.

Brion, M. *Bartolomé de Las Casas: Padre de los indios.* Buenos Aires: Ed. Futuro, 1945.

Brogle, G. de. "Notes et mélanges: Autour du problème des 'droits de la conscience erronée.'" *Recherches de Science Religieuse* 53 (1965): 234–50.

Brown, R. McAfee. *Bartolomé de Las Casas: A Man for the Next Five Hundred Years.* In preparation.

Brufau Prats, J. "La aportación de Domingo de Soto a la doctrina de los derechos del hombre y las posiciones de Bartolomé de Las Casas." *Las Casas et la politique,* 188–202.

———. *La escuela de Salamanca ante el descubrimiento del nuevo mundo.* Salamanca: Editorial San Esteban, 1989.

———. "Francisco de Vitoria y Domingo de Soto: Proyección de su doctrina en la evangelización de América." *Dominicos* (1989), 43–60.

———. "Poder político y los problemas planteados por la conquista de América." *El pensamiento político de Domingo de Soto y su concepción del poder,* 188–222. Salamanca: Universidad de Salamanca, 1960.

———. "La primera generación de la escuela de Salamanca: Soto, Cano, Covarrubias." *Actas Simposio Etica,* 223–38.

Bryant, S. V. "Vieira e Las Casas em face do indianismo." *Revista Trimestral do Instituto Histórico e Geográfico Brasileiro,* no. 290 (January–March 1971).

Burga, M. *Nacimiento de una utopía.* Lima: Instituto de Apoyo Agrario, 1988.

Burrus, E. "Alonso de la Veracruz's Defense of the American Indians (1553–54)." *Heythrop Journal,* no. 3 (1963): 224–53.

———. "Las Casas and Veracruz: Their Defence of the American Indians Compared." *NZMR* 22, no. 3 (1966): 201–12.

Cabrera Leiva, G. "Bartolomé de Las Casas: Champion of Humans Rights." *Americas* 31, no. 4 (April 1979): 31–36.

Calderone, S. *Costantino e il cattolicesimo.* Florence, 1962.

Cantù, F. "Bartolomé de Las Casas nel quadro del suo tempo." *I diritti,* 63–79.

———. "La dialectique de Las Casas et l'histoire." *Le Supplément,* 5–28.

———. "Esigenze di giustizia e politica coloniale: Una 'peticion' inedita di Las Casas all'audiencia de los Confines." *IAA* 3, no. 2 (1977): 135–65.

———. "Evoluzione e significato della dottrina della restituzione in Bartolomé de Las Casas." *Critica Storica* (December 1975): 231–319.

———. "Italia, documentos lascasianos." *HBA* 19–20 (1975–76): 3–31.

———. "Per un rinnovamento della conscienza pastorale del cinquecento: Il vescovo Bartolomé de Las Casas ed il problema indiano." *Annuario dell' Istituto Storico Italiano* (Rome) 25–26 (1973–74): 1–118.

———. "Potere vescovile...." *Annuario dell' Istituto Storico Italiano* 29–30 (1979): 533–64.

Capéran, L. *Le problème du salut des infidèles: Essai historique.* Toulouse: Grand Séminaire, 1934.

Carabes Pedroza, J. "Don Vasco de Quiroga." *Medellín* 13, no. 50 (June 1987): 257–88.

Carbonell, D. "En torno al Padre Las Casas con don Ramón Menéndez Pidal." *Duquesne Hispanic Review* (Pittsburgh) 2 (1963): 107–13.

Cárdenas, E. "La ética cristiana y la esclavitud de los negros." *Theologica Xaveriana,* no. 55 (April–June 1980): 227–56.

Carlos V. "Carta a Francisco de Vitoria." In F. de Vitoria, *De Indis* (CHP), 154–55.

———. "Carta al Prior de S. Esteban de Salamanca." In F. de Vitoria, *De Indis* (CHP), 152–53.

Carlyle, R. W. *A History of Mediaeval Political Theory in the West.* Vol. 5. New York: Barnes and Noble, 1950.

Carrasco Calvo, S. "Herejes e infieles en la obra de Santo Tomás." *Tommaso D'Aquino nella storia del pensiero.* Vol. 2: *Del Medievo ad oggi,* 27–34. Rome and Naples: Edizioni dominicane italiane, 1974.

Carreño, A. "Una guerra sine dolo et fraude: El Padre Las Casas y la lucha por la dignidad del indio en el siglo XVI." *CA* 193, no. 2 (March–April 1974): 119–39.

Carro, V. "Bartolomé de Las Casas y la lucha entre dos culturas: Cristianismo y paganismo." *Anales de la Real Academia de Ciencias Morales y Políticas* (Madrid) 18 (1966): 205–72.

———. "Bartolomé de Las Casas y las controversias teológico-jurídicas de las Indias." *BRAH* 132 (April–June 1953): 231–64.

———. *Carta abierta a Don Ramón Menéndez Pidal: Anotaciones a su conferencia sobre Las Casas (23–IX-1962).* Madrid: Imp. Juan Bravo, 1962.

———. *La comunitas orbis y las rutas del derecho internacional según Francisco de Vitoria.* Palencia and Madrid: Imprenta Merino, 1962.

———. *España en América, sin leyendas.* Madrid: Librería OPE, 1963.

———. "Introducción especial a los dos primeros libros de la obra 'de Iustitia et Iure,' Domingo de Soto." In Domingo de Soto, *De la justicia y el derecho,* lxvii–lxx. Madrid: IEP, 1967.

———. "Introducción general a la obra de Domingo de Soto." In Domingo de Soto, *De la justicia y el derecho,* xiv–lxii. Madrid: IEP, 1967.

———. *El maestro Fr. Pedro de Soto O.P. (confesor de Carlos V) y las controversias político-ideológicas en el s. XVI.* Salamanca: Convento S. Esteban, 1951.

———. "La obra de Menéndez Pidal sobre Las Casas." *CT* 92 (January–March 1965): 22–35.

———. "Los postulados teológico-jurídicos de Bartolomé de las Casas: Sus aciertos, sus olvidos y sus fallos ante los maestros Francisco de Vitoria y Domingo de Soto." *Estudios Lascasianos: IV Centenario de la muerte de Bartolomé de Las Casas* (1566–1966), 109–246. Seville: Escuela de Estudios Hispanoamericanos, 1966.

———. *La teología y los teólogos-juristas españoles ante la conquista de América.* Madrid: Escuela Estudios Hispanoamericanos de Sevilla, 1944.

Cassirer, E. *La philosophie des lumières.* Paris: Fayard, 1970.

Castaldo, A. "Les 'Questions Péruviennes' de Bartolomé de Las Casas." *Las Casas et la politique,* 53–87.

Castañeda Delgado, P. "La condición miserable del indio y sus privilegios." *AEA* 28 (1971): 245–335.

———. *Don Vasco de Quiroga y su "información en derecho."* Madrid: José Porrúa, 1974.

———. "La ética de la conquista en el momento del descubrimiento de América." *Actas Simposio Etica,* 37–75.

———. "Los franciscanos y el Regio Vicariato." *AI* 48, nos. 189–92 (January–December 1988): 317–68.

———. "Los métodos misionales en América ¿Evangelización pura o coacción?" *Estudios sobre Las Casas,* 123–89.

———. *La teocracia pontifical y la conquista de América.* Vitoria: Ed. Eset, 1968.

Castañeda, P., and J. Marchena. "Dominicos en la jerarquía de la Iglesia en Indias." *Dominicos* (1986), 715–38.

Castaño, J. "I diritto internazionale da Francisco de Vitoria a oggi." *I diritti,* 103–19.

Castelo Branco, M. J. de F. "A negação do sujeito na empresa colonial (por uma antropologia filosófica latinoamericana)." *REB* 47, fasc. 187 (September 1987): 601–36.

Castiglioni, L. "Bartolomé de las Casas, el gran precursor de Medellín y Puebla." *El Colombiano* (August 10, 1979): 3.

Castillo, C. *Acerca de la conversión según Bartolomé de Las Casas en la obra Historia de las Indias.* Lima, 1991.

———. "La conversión en las naciones indias." *Debates en Sociología* (Lima) 16: 57–124.

———. "El problema de los indios: Bartolomé de Las Casas." *Páginas* 14, no. 99 (October 1989): 51–67.

Castillo, J. *Catecismos peruanos del siglo XVI.* Cuernavaca, Mexico: CIDOC, 1966.

———. *La catequesis en el Perú.* Bogotá: CELAM, 1987.

Castro, A. "Fray Bartolomé de Las Casas en Oxford." *Memorias del Colegio Nacional V* (Mexico City), no. 1 (1962): 50–51.

———. *Fray Bartolomé de Las Casas o Casaus, Mélanges à la mémoire de Jean Sarrailh,* 1:211–44. Paris: Centre de Recherches de l'Institut d'Etudes Hispaniques, 1966.

Castro, A. de. "Parecer cerca de dar los yndios perpetuos del Perú a los encomenderos." In J. de la Peña, *De Bello Contra Insulanos,* 593–98. Madrid: CSIC, 1982.

Les Catholiques libéraux au XIXe siècle. Grenoble: Presses Universitaires, 1974.

Cazelles, H., D. Richon, and G. Marsot. "Esclavage." *Catholicisme,* 4:414–24. Paris: Letouzey et Ané, 1954.

Cerezo de Diego, P. *Alonso de Veracruz y el derecho de gentes.* Mexico City: Porrúa, 1985.

———. "Influencia de la Escuela de Salamanca en el pensamiento universitario americano." *Etica en la conquista,* 551–96.

———. "El pensamiento americano de un discípulo de Vitoria: Alonso de Veracruz." *I diritti,* 255–72.

Chacón y Calvo, J. M. *Cartas censorias de la conquista.* Havana, 1938.

———. *Cedulario Cubano: Los orígenes de la colonización (1493–1512),* vol. 1. Barcelona.

———. "La experiencia del indio ¿Un antecedente a las doctrinas de Vitoria?" *AAFV* 5 (1933): 203–25.

Chang Rodríguez, R. *La apropiación del signo: Tres cronistas indígenas del Perú.* Tempe, Ariz.: Center for Latin American Studies, 1988.

———. "Santo Tomás en los Andes." *Revista Iberoamericana,* no. 53 (1987): 559–67.

Chaunu, P. *Conquête et exploitation des nouveaux mondes (XVI siecle).* Paris: Nouvelle Clio, 1969.

———. *L'Espagne de Charles-Quint.* 2 vols. Paris: Peninsula, 1973.

———. "Francisco de Vitoria, Las Casas et la querelle des justes titres." *Bibliothèque d'humanisme et renaissance* (Geneva) 29, no. 2 (1967): 485–94.

———. "Las Casas et la première crise structurelle de la colonisation espagnole (1515–1523)." *Revue Historique* (Paris) 229 (January–March 1963): 59–102.

———. "La légende noire antihispanique." *Revue de Psychologie des Peuples* (1964): 188–223.

———. "La population de l'Amérique indienne (nouvelles recherches)." *Revue Historique* (Paris) 232 (1964): 111–18.

Chenu, M. D. "Prophètes et théologiens dans l'Eglise: Parole de Dieu." *Masses Ouvrières* (Paris), no. 200 (October 1963): 59–70.

Choy, E. "De Santiago matamoros a Santiago mata-indios." *Revista del Museo Nacional* 27 (1958): 195–272.

Cieza de León. *Crónica del Perú.* 3 vols. Lima: Universidad Católica, 1984–87.

Cioranescu, A. "La Historia de las Indias y la prohibición de editarla." *AEA* 23 (1966): 363–76.

———. *Primera biografía de Cristóbal Colón, Fernando Colón y Bartolomé de Las Casas.* Tenerife: Aula de Cultura de Tenerife, 1960.

Cisneros, L. J. "La primera gramática de la lengua general del Perú." *Boletín del Instituto Riva Agüero* 1951–1952 (Lima) 1 (1953): 197–264.

Colavechio, X. *Erroneous Conscience and Obligations.* Washington, D.C.: Catholic University of America Press, 1961.

Colon, C. [Christopher Columbus.] *La carta de Colón anunciando el descubrimiento del nuevo mundo.* Ed. C. Sanz. Madrid: Gráfica Yagues, 1961.

———. *Textos y documentos completos: Relaciones de viajes, cartas y memoriales.* Ed. Consuelo Varela. Madrid: Alianza Editorial, 1984.

Comas, J. "La 'cristianización' y 'educación' del indio desde 1492 a nuestros días." *América Indígena* (Mexico City) 11, no. 3 (July 1951): 219–34.

———. "Los detractores del protector universal de indios y la realidad histórica." *Ensayos sobre indigenismo,* 201–24. Mexico City: Instituto Indigenista Interamericano, 1953.

———. "Fray Bartolomé, la esclavitud y el racismo." *CA* 205, no. 2 (March–April 1976): 145–52.

————. "Las Casas, Menéndez Pidal y el indigenismo." *América Indígena* (Mexico City) 28, no. 2 (April 1968): 437–60.

————. "La realidad del trato dado a los indígenas de América entre los siglos XV y XX." *América Indígena* (Mexico City) 11 (1951): 323–70.

Condorelli, M. *I fondamenti giuridici della tolleranza religiosa nell' elaborazione canonistica dei secoli XII–XIV.* Milan: Giuffrè, 1960.

Congar, Y. "Eglise et Etat." *Sainte Eglise: Etudes et approches ecclésiologiques,* 393–410. Paris: Du Cerf, 1963.

————. "Quod omnes tangit, ab omnibus tractari et approbari debet" *Rev. hist. du droit fr. et étr.* (1958): 210–59.

————. *Vaste monde ma paroisse.* Paris: Témoignage Chrétien, 1959.

Cook, N. D. *Demographic Collapse: Indian Peru 1520–1620.* Cambridge: Latin American Studies, 1981.

Córdoba, P. de. "Carta al rey." *DII* 11:216–24.

————. *Doctrina cristiana para instrucción de los indios: México 1544 y 1548.* Ed. M. Medina. Salamanca: Editorial San Esteban, 1987.

————. *Doctrina cristiana para instrucción y información de los indios por manera de historia.* Ed. E. Rodríguez Demorizi. Ciudad Trujillo: Ed. Facsimil, 1945.

Coste, R. "Le droit de guerre à travers Saint Thomas, Vitoria et Las Casas." *Las Casas et la politique,* 183–87.

Crosby, A. W. *The Columbian Exchange: Biological and Cultural Consequences of 1492.* Westport, Conn.: Greenwood Press, 1975.

Cruz, S. "El Padre Las Casas y la literatura de independencia en México." *AEA* 24 (1967): 1621–39.

Cueva, A. "Historia, ideología y lucha de clases (a propósito del 'asunto' Las Casas)." *Plural,* no. 70 (July 77): 25–33.

Cuevas, M. *Documentos inéditos del siglo XVI para la historia de México.* Mexico City: Porrúa, 1975.

————. *Historia de la Iglesia en México.* 5 vols. Tlalpán (Santa Julia, El Paso), 1921–28.

Curatola, M. "Mito y milenarismo en los andes: Del Taki Onqoy a Inkarri." *Allpanchis,* no. 10 (1977): 65–92.

Curci, C. M. "Il congresso cattolico di Malines e le libertà moderne." *Civiltà Cattolica,* series 5, vol. 8, fasc. 326 (October 17, 1863): 129–49.

Dammert, J. "Aplicación de la legislación canónica en América Latina." *Revista Española de Derecho Canónico* 17, no. 50 (1962): 513–23.

————. "Presencia de Las Casas en la Emancipación y en la República." In J. B. Lassègue, *La Larga Marcha de Las Casas: Textos,* 404–7. Lima: CEP, 1974.

D'Arcy, E. *Conscience and Its Right to Freedom.* London: Sheed and Ward, 1979.

Davies, N. *Human Sacrifice in History and Today.* New York: William Morrow and Company, 1981.

Dávila Padilla, A. *Historia de la fundación y discurso de la provincia de Santiago de México de la Orden de Predicadores (1596).* 3d. ed. Prologue by A. Millares. Facsimile of the 2d ed. of Brussels, 1624. Mexico City, 1955.

Davis, David B. *The Problem of Slavery in Western Culture.* Ithaca, N.Y.: Cornell University Press, 1966.

Dawson, C. *The Making of Europe.* London: Sheed and Ward, 1932.

De Almeida, R. "Francisco de Vitoria e a renovação da teologia portuguesa no século XVI." *I diritti,* 293–307.

Dejo, J. "Guamán Poma de Ayala y la lógica andina de la conciliación." *Apuntes* (Lima) 26 (1990): 77–92.

D'Elia, F. "Studi lascasiani dell'ultimo ventennio: Bibliografia essenziale ragionata." *I diritti*, 309–21.

Delran, G. *Historia rural del Perú*. Cusco: CERA Las Casas, 1978.

Denevan, W. M., ed. *The Native Population of the Americas in 1492*. Madison: University of Wisconsin Press, 1976.

Denglos, J. "Tratado de las doce dudas de Fray Bartolomé de Las Casas (diciembre 1563): Le manuscrit de la John Carter Brown Library de Providence (USA)." *Autour de Las Casas*, 129–47.

Denzinger, H. *Enchiridion Symbolorum*. Barcelona: Herder, 1955.

Deschamps, P. "1513–1880 cimarrones y palenques: La insurgencia de los esclavos abona el camino hacia la libertad." *Bohemia* 81, no. 34 (August 25, 1989): 61–65.

"De virreyes y gobernadores del Pirú." *DII* 8:212–93.

De Witte, C. "Les bulles pontificales et l'expansion portugaise au XVe siècle." *Revue d'histoire Ecclésiastique* 58 (1953): 683–718.

Diez Alegría, J. M. *La libertad religiosa*. Barcelona: Instituto de Estudios Sociales, 1965.

Diez de Medina, F. "Una polémica que dura cuatro siglos: El Padre Las Casas y el último libro de Don Ramón Menéndez Pidal." *Cuadernos* (Mexico City), no. 80 (January 1964): 8–12.

Domingo de Santo Tomás. "Carta a S.M. en el Consejo de Indias." *La Iglesia de España...* 1, no. 4, 190–206.

———. *Gramática o arte de la lengua general de los indios de los reinos del Perú*. Valladolid, 1560.

Dupanloup, F. *La convention du 15 septembre et l'encyclique du 8 décembre*. Paris, 1865.

Durand, J. "El inca, hombre en prisma." *Studi di Letteratura Ispanoamericana* (Milan) 1 (1967): 41–57.

Dussel, E. *El episcopado hispanoamericano: Institución misionera en defensa del indio (1504–1620)*. Cuernavaca, Mexico, 1969–71.

———. *El episcopado latinoamericano y la liberación de los pobres (1504–1620)*. Mexico City: Centro de Reflexión Teológica, 1979.

———. "Introducción General." *Historia general de la Iglesia en América Latina*. 1:1. Salamanca: CEHILA-Sígueme, 1983.

———. "Núcleo simbólico lascasiano como profecía crítica al imperialismo europeo." *BLCHI*, 11–17.

———. "El pan de la celebración, signo comunitario." *Concilium* 172 (1982): 250–58.

———. "Sobre la historia de la teología en América Latina." *Desintegración de la Cristiandad Colonial y Liberación*. Salamanca: Sígueme, 1978.

Dutilleul, J. "Esclavage." *DTC* 5:457–520.

Duviols, P. *La lutte contre les religions autochtones dans le Pérou colonial*. Lima: Instituto Francés de Estudios Andinos, 1971.

Echegaray, H. "Derechos del pobre, derechos de Dios." *Anunciar el Reino*, 54–60. Lima: CEP, 1981.

Egaña, A. de. *La teoría del regio vicariato español en Indias*. Rome: Universidad Gregoriana, 1958.

Ehler, S. E., and J. B. Morral, eds. *Church and State through the Centuries*. London, 1954.

Elders, L. J. "St. Thomas Aquinas' Doctrine of Conscience." *Studi Tomistici* (Vatican City) 30 (1987): 125–34.

Elliot, J. H. *The Old World and the New, 1494–1650*. Cambridge: Cambridge University Press, 1970.

Enzensberger, H. "Las Casas a través de escritores alemanes." *Humboldt* 91: 34–40.

Escandell Bonet, B. "Las adecuaciones estructurales: Establecimiento de la Inquisición en Indias." *Historia de la Inquisición en España y América*, 713–30. Madrid: BAC, 1984.

———. *Estudios Cisnerianos*. Alcalá de Henares: Universidad, 1990.

Esponera, A. "El punto de partida de la hermenéutica bíblica de Bartolomé de Las Casas (1559–1564)." *Actas del VI Simposio de Teología Histórica* (1990): 379–98.

Esponera, A., and J.-B. Lassègue. *El corte en la roca (Memorias de los dominicos en América [siglos XVI–XX])*. Cusco: CERA Bartolomé de Las Casas, 1991.

Esteva Fabregat, C. "La conquista española ante la Etica india." *Actas Simposio Etica*, 393–415.

Fabié, A. M. *El Padre Fray Bartolomé de Las Casas*. Madrid: Ateneo de Madrid, 1892.

———. *Vida y escritos de Fray Bartolomé de Las Casas, obispo de Chiapas*. 2 vols. Madrid, 1879.

Fernández, L. "Nuevos documentos de Fray Bartolomé de Las Casas en Valladolid 1550–1557." *Dominicos* (1986), 365–84.

Fernández de Oviedo, G. *Historia general y natural de las Indias*. Ed. J. Pérez de Tudela. Madrid: BAE, 1959.

Fernández Santa Maria, J. A. "Juan Ginés de Sepúlveda on the Nature of the American Indians." *The Americas* (Washington, D.C.) 31, no. 1 (July 1974): 34–451.

———. *The State, War and Peace: Spanish Political Thought in the Renaissance*. London: Cambridge University Press, 1977.

Figueiredo Lustosa, O. de. "A contestação de um profeta: Bartolomeu de Las Casas (1474–1566)." *REB* 34, fasc. 136 (December 1974): 806–23.

———. "Notas para um Centenario: Bartolomeu de Las Casas O.P. (1474–1575)." *Revista de Historia*, no. 102 (1975): 717–29.

Finance, J. de. *Ethique générale*. Rome: Pontifizia Università Gregoriana, 1988.

Flores Galindo, A. *Buscando un inca: Identidad y utopía en los andes*. Lima: Instituto de Apoyo Agrario, 1987.

Fluck, M. R. "Evangelização no Brasil colónia séculos XVI–XVII." *Estudos Teológicos* 31, no. 2 (1990): 151–61.

Flynn, G. "Padre Las Casas: Literature and the Just War." *RHA* 61–62 (January–December 1966): 57–62.

Forti, C. "Letture di Bartolomé de Las Casas: Uno specchio della conscienza e della falsa conscienza dell'Occidente attraverso quattro secoli." *Critica Storica* 26, no. 1 (1989): 3–52.

Franklin, J. H. *From Slavery to Freedom: A History of Negro Americans*. New York: Alfred A. Knopf, 1974.

Friede, J. *Bartolomé de las Casas: Precursor del anticolonialismo: Su lucha y su derrota*. Mexico City: Siglo XXI, 1974.

———. "La censura española del siglo XVI y los libros de historia de América." *RHA* 47 (1959): 45–94.

———. "Los franciscanos en el nuevo reino de Granada y el movimiento indigenista del siglo XVI." *Bulletin Hispanique* (Bordeaux) 60, no. 1 (1958): 5–29.

———. "Fray Bartolomé de Las Casas, exponente del movimiento indigenista español del siglo XVI." *RI* 12, no. 51 (1953): 25–55.

———. "Las Casas y el movimiento indigenista en España y América, en la primera mitad del siglo XVI." *RHA* 34 (1952): 339–411.

———. *Vida y luchas de Don Juan del Valle, primer obispo de Popayán y protector de Indios.* Popayán, Colombia: Universidad, 1961.

Frutos Valiente, F. "Doctrina de Vitoria sobre la realeza de Jesucristo." *AAFV* 3 (1930–31): 89–103.

Fuchs, E. *La morale selon Calvin.* Paris: Du Cerf, 1986.

Gallegos, R. *El hombre y el mundo de los teólogos españoles de los siglos de oro.* Mexico City: Editorial Sytlo, 1946.

Galmes, L. *Bartolomé de Las Casas: Defensor de los derechos humanos.* Madrid: BAE, 1982.

———. "Bartolomé de Las Casas y su visión crítica de la 'Empresa de Indias.'" *I diritti,* 353–68.

Garcés, J. "Carta a Paulo III." *Dominicos* (1986), 769–92.

García, R. "La conversión a los indios del clérigo Bartolomé de Las Casas." *Didascalia* (Argentina) 404 (May 1987): 4–22.

García Del Moral, A. "Estructura y significación teológicas." Las Casas, *Obras completas,* 2:xliii–lxxv.

García Gallo, A. *Estudios de historia del derecho indiano.* Madrid, 1972.

———. "Génesis y desarrollo del derecho indiano: Recopilación de leyes de los Reinos de las Indias." *Estudios Histórico-Jurídicos.* Mexico City: Escuela Libre de Derecho and Porrúa, 1967.

———. "Las Indias en el reinado de Felipe II: La solución al problema de los justos títulos." *AAFV* 13 (1960–61): 95–136.

———. *Las Casas, jurista.* Madrid: Instituto de España, 1975.

———. *Los orígenes de la administración territorial de las Indias.* Madrid: CSIC, 1944.

García Icazbalceta, J. *Don Fray Juan de Zumárraga, primer obispo y arzobispo de México (1881).* Vols. 1–4. Ed. R. Aguayo Spencer and A. Castro Leal. Mexico City: Porrúa, 1947.

García-Pelayo, M. "Juan Ginés de Sepúlveda y los Problemas Jurídicos de la Conquista de América." In J. G. de Sepúlveda, *Tratado sobre las justas causas de la guerra contra los indios.* Mexico City: FCE, 1941.

García Villoslada, R. "Sentido de la conquista y evangelización de América según las bulas de Alejandro VI (1493)." *Anthologica Annua* 24–25 (1977–78): 381–452.

———. "Un teólogo olvidado: Juan Maior." *Estudios Eclesiásticos* (Mexico City), no. 15 (1936): 83–118.

———. *La Universidad de París durante los estudios de Francisco de Vitoria.* Rome: Universidad Gregoriana, 1938.

García y García, A. "La promoción humana del indio en los concilios y sínodos del siglo XVI." *I diritti,* 369–78.

———. "El sentido de las primeras denuncias." *Etica en la conquista,* 67–115.

Garibay, A. M. "Todavía Fray Bartolomé de Las Casas." *Lectura* (Mexico City), no. 1 (1964): 18–23.

Gasteazoro, C. M. "El ciclo de Pedrarias." *Historia general de España y América,* 7:261–73. Madrid: Rialp, 1982.

Gerbi, A. *Il Mito del Perú.* Milan: Franco Angelli, 1988.

———. *Viejas polémicas sobre el Nuevo Mundo.* Lima: Banca de Crédito, 1946.

Getino, L. A. "Introducción." *Relecciones internacionalistas del Padre Maestro Francisco de Vitoria.* Vol. 1. Madrid, 1933.

———. *El maestro Fray Francisco de Vitoria: Su vida, su doctrina e influencia.* Madrid: Imprenta Católica, 1930.

Gil-Bermejo García, J. "Fray Bartolomé de Las Casas y el 'Quijote.'" *Estudios Lascasianos: IV Centenario de la muerte de Bartolomé de Las Casas* (1566–1966), 351–61. Seville: Escuela de Estudios Hispanoamericanos, 1966.

Giménez Caballero, E. "Epistolario lascasiano." *Espa* 1 (La Asunción) (1963): 9–16.

Giménez Fernández, M. "Actualidad de las tesis lascasianas." *Facultad de Letras* (Seville) (1966): 445–74.

———. *Bartolomé de Las Casas: Capellán de S.M. Carlos I, poblador de Cumaná (1517– 1523).* Seville: Escuela de Estudios Hispanoamericanos, 1960.

———. *Bartolomé de Las Casas: Delegado de Cisneros para la reformación de las Indias.* Seville: Escuela de Estudios Hispanoamericanos, CSIC, 1953.

———. "Bartolomé de Las Casas en 1552." Prologue to *Los Tratados del Padre Las Casas*, 1:xxi–lxxxvii. Mexico City: FCE, 1965.

———. "Fray Bartolomé de Las Casas: A Biographical Sketch." *Las Casas in History*, 67–126.

———. "Influencia del criticismo lascasiano en la política indiana de Carlos V." *AAFV* 13 (1960–61): 67–94.

———. "La juventud en Sevilla de Bartolomé de Las Casas (1474–1502)." *Miscelánea de estudios dedicados a Fernando Ortiz* (Havana) 2 (1956): 669–717.

———. "Las Casas y el Perú: Ensayo crítico acerca de las noticias y juicios que respecto al descubrimiento y conquista del Perú formula en sus escritos Fray Bartolomé de Las Casas." *Documenta* (Lima) 2, no. 1 (1951): 343–77.

———. *Más sobre las Bulas Alejandrinas de 1493.* Seville, 1953.

———. *Nuevas consideraciones sobre la historia, sentido y valor de las bulas alejandrinas de 1493 referentes a las Indias.* Seville: Escuela de Estudios Hispanoamericanos, 1944.

———. "Sobre Bartolomé de Las Casas." *Anales de la Universidad Hispalense* (Seville) 24 (1964): 1–66.

———. "Ultimos días de Bartolomé de Las Casas." *Miscellanea Paul Rivet Octogenario Dicata* (Mexico City) 2 (1958): 701–15.

Glez, G. "Pouvoir du Pape dans l'ordre temporel." *DTC* 12, cols. 2670–72.

Godenzi, J. C. "Formas de tratamiento en el discurso de Guamán Poma." *Lexis* 15, no. 2 (1991): 179–93.

Goldwert. "La lucha por la perpetuidad de las encomiendas en el Perú virreinal, 1550–1600." *Histórica* (Lima) 22 (1955–56): 336–60.

Gómara, F. López de. *Historia general de las Indias.* Madrid, 1852.

Gómez Canedo, L. "Bartolomé de Las Casas y sus amigos franciscanos." *Libro Jubilar de Emeterio S. Santovenia*, 75–84. Havana, 1957.

———. "La cuestión de la racionalidad de los indios en el siglo XVI (nuevo examen crítico)." *Actas y Memorias del XXXVI Congreso Internacional de Americanistas* 4 (Seville) (1966): 157–65.

———. "Evangelización y política indigenista: Ideas y actitudes franciscanas en el siglo XVI." *Política Indigenista* 2 (1977): 21–46.

———. "¿Hombres o Bestias? (Nuevo examen crítico de un viejo tópico)." *Estudios de Historia Novohispana* (Mexico City) 1 (1967): 29–51.

Gómez Moreira, J. A. *Conquista y conciencia cristiana: El pensamiento jurídico-teológico de don Vasco de Quiroga.* Quito and Mexico City: Abya-Yala-CENAMI, 1990.

González Dorado, A. "Evangelización integral y comunidades amerindias." *Medellín* 13, no. 50 (June 1987): 145–212.

González Rodríguez, J. "Los amigos franciscanos de Sepúlveda." *Franciscanos* (1987), 873–93.

————. "Dimensión histórica del 'De Regia Potestate.' " Las Casas, *Obras completas,* 12:xli–lix.

————. "Fray Bernardino de Arévalo en la Junta de Valladolid (1550–51) a través del epistolario de Juan Ginés de Sepúlveda." *Franciscanos* (1985), 699–717.

————. "Juan Ginés de Sepúlveda, ¿Antihumanista?" *RI* 41, no. 163–64 (January–June 1981): 265–68.

————. "La Junta de Valladolid convocada por el Emperador." *Etica en la conquista,* 199–227.

————. "La libertad del indio en el Democrates Alter." *Revista Quinto Centenario* (Madrid), no. 13 (1987): 197–208.

————. "Planteamiento oficial de la crisis: La Junta de Valladolid y la suspensión de las conquistas (1549–1556)." *Actas Simposio Etica,* 269–84.

————. "Sobre naturaleza e historia en Las Casas." *RI* 39, nos. 155–58 (1979): 329–36.

González Ruiz, J. M. "Extra ecclesiam nulla salus a la luz de la teología paulina." *Selecciones de Teología* (Barcelona), no. 4 (1962): 282–84.

González Vigil, R. *Comentario al Inca Garcilaso.* Lima: Banco Central de Reserva, 1990.

Granada, Fray L. de. *Obras.* Ed. J. Cuervo. Vol. 14. Madrid, 1906.

Grisel, E. "The Beginnings of International Law and General Public Law Doctrine: Francisco de Vitoria's De Indis Prior." *First Images,* 305–25.

Los grupos afroamericanos: Aproximaciones y pastoral. Bogotá: CELAM, 1980.

Guamán Poma de Ayala, F. *El primer nueva corónica y buen gobierno.* Ed. J. Murra and R. Adorno. 3 vols. Mexico City: Siglo XXI, 1980.

Guerra, F. "El efecto demográfico de las epidemias tras el descubrimiento de América." *RI* 46, no. 177 (1986): 41–58.

————. "The Problem of Syphilis." *First Images,* 845–51.

Guignebert, G. *Tertullien: Etude de ses sentiments à l'égard de l'empire et de la société civile.* Paris, 1901.

Guillén, C. "Un padrón de conversos sevillanos (1510)." *Bulletin Hispanique* (Bordeaux) 65, nos. 1–2 (1963): 49–98.

Guillén, E. "La conquista del Perú de los Incas (1531–1572)." *Historia del Perú.* Vol. 4. Lima: Mejía Baca, 1980.

Gutiérrez, A. "La primitiva organización indiana." *Historia de Iberoamérica,* 201–306. Madrid: Cátedra, 1990.

Gutiérrez, G. "Las Cosas nuevas de hoy: Una relectura de la Rerum Novarum." *Páginas* 16, no. 110 (August 1991).

————. *El Dios de la Vida.* Lima: CEP-IBC, 1989. Eng. trans.: *The God of Life.* Maryknoll, N.Y.: Orbis Books, 1991.

————. *Entre las calandrias: Un ensayo sobre José María Arguedas.* Lima: CEP-IBC, 1990.

————. "Freedom and Salvation: A Political Problem." In G. Gutiérrez and R. Shaull, *Liberation and Change,* 1–94. Atlanta: John Knox Press, 1977.

————. *Hablar de Dios desde el sufrimiento del inocente: Una reflexión sobre el libro de Job.* Lima: CEP-IBC, 1986. Eng. trans.: *On Job: God-Talk and the Suffering of the Innocent.* Maryknoll, N.Y.: Orbis Books, 1987.

————. *Teología de la liberación.* 7th ed. Lima: CEP, 1990. Eng. trans.: *A Theology of Liberation.* Rev. ed. Maryknoll, N.Y.: Orbis Books, 1988.

————. "Tres comentarios a la declaración sobre la libertad religiosa." *IDOC* (Rome), no. 13 (1966).

Gutiérrez Azopardo, I. "La Iglesia y los negros." *Historia de la Iglesia en Hispanoamérica y Filipinas,* 321–37. Madrid: BAC, 1992.

Gutiérrez Nieto, J. I. "La idea de libertad en Castilla durante el Renacimiento." *América y la España del siglo XVI,* 11–26. Madrid: CSIC, 1983.

Gutiérrez Rodríguez, A. "El 'Confesionario' de Bartolomé de Las Casas." *CT* 102, no. 333 (1975): 249–78.

Hampe, T. "La encomienda en el Perú en el siglo XVI (Ensayo bibliográfico)." *Histórica* 6, no. 2 (December 1982).

———. "Fray Domingo de Santo Tomás y la encomienda de indios en el Perú (1540–1570)." *Dominicos* (1989), 355–80.

Hanke, L. *All Mankind Is One: A Study of the Disputation between Bartolomé de Las Casas and Juan Ginés de Sepúlveda in 1550 on the Intellectual and Religious Capacity of the American Indians.* Dekalb: Northern Illinois University Press, 1974.

———. *All the Peoples of the World Are Men: The Disputation between Bartolomé de Las Casas and Juan Ginés de Sepúlveda in 1550 on the Intellectual and Religious Capacity of the American Indians.* Minneapolis: University of Minnesota Press, 1970.

———. *Aristotle and the American Indians: A Study in Race Prejudice in the Modern World.* London: Hollis & Carter; Chicago: Henry Regnery Co., 1959.

———. *Bartolomé de Las Casas: Letrado y propagandista.* Bogotá: Tercer Mundo, 1965.

———. "¿Cómo debería celebrarse el medio milenio del descubrimiento de América?" *Conferencia, José Gil Fortoul.* Caracas, 1981.

———. "¿Cómo deberíamos conmemorar en 1974 la vida de Bartolomé de Las Casas?" *CA* 194, no. 3 (May–June 1974): 131–42.

———. "¿Cómo Estudiar la Historia del Derecho Indiano?" *Revista Chilena de Historia del Derecho,* no. 7 (1978): 121–30.

———. "Don Ramón Menéndez Pidal and Fray Bartolomé de Las Casas." *Documenta* (Lima), no. 4 (1965): 345–58.

———. *Estudios sobre Fray B. de Las Casas y sobre la lucha por la justicia en la conquista española de América.* Caracas: Biblioteca de la Universidad Central de Venezuela, 1968.

———. Introduction to Las Casas, *Del único modo de atraer a todos los pueblos a la verdadera religión,* xv–xliv. Mexico City: FCE, 1942.

———. "Las Casas historiador." Introduction to *Historia de las Indias.* Mexico City and Buenos Aires: FCE, 1961.

———. *La lucha por la justicia en la conquista de América.* Buenos Aires: Editorial Sudamericana, 1949.

———. "A Modest Proposal for a Moratorium on Grand Generalizations: Some Thoughts on the Black Legend." *HAHR* (February 1971): 112–27.

———. "More Heat and Some Light on the Spanish Struggle for Justice in the Conquest of America." *HAHR* 64, no. 3 (1964): 293–340.

———. "Una palabra." *Fray Bartolomé de Las Casas en Hispanoamérica: Primer Simposio Internacional de Lascasistas,* 263–70. Chiapas, Mexico: Gobierno Constitucional del Estado de Chiapas, 1975.

———. "El Papa Paulo III y los indios de América." *Estudios sobre Las Casas y sobre la lucha por la justicia,* 59–88.

———. "Paranoia, Polemics and Polarization: Some Comments on the Four-Hundredth Anniversary of the Death of Bartolomé de Las Casas." *Ibero-Americana Pragensia* 5 (1971): 83–92.

———. "Pope Paul III and the American Indians." *HTR* 30 (1937): 65–102.

———. "Ramón Menéndez Pidal vs. Bartolomé de Las Casas." *Política* (Caracas), no. 33 (April 1964): 21–40.

———. "The 'Requerimiento' and Its Interpreters." *RHA* 1 (1938): 25–34.

————. *The Spanish Struggle for Justice in the Conquest of America.* Boston: Little Brown, 1965.

————. "The Theological Significance of the Discovery of America." *First Images,* 363–89.

————. *Los virreyes españoles en América durante el gobierno de la Casa de Austria.* Madrid: BAE, 1978.

————. "Was Bartolomé de Las Casas a Scholar?" *Miscelánea de Estudios Dedicados a Fernando Ortiz.* Havana, 1956.

————. "Were the Indians Descended from the Lost Ten Tribes of Israel?" Appendix to Hanke's unpublished doctoral dissertation.

Hanke, L., and F. M. Giménez. *Bartolomé de Las Casas (1474–1566): Bibliografía crítica y cuerpo de materiales para el estudio de su vida, escritos, actuación y polémicas que suscitaron durante cuatro siglos.* Santiago de Chile: Fondo Histórico y Bibliográfico "José Toribio de Mendoza," 1954.

Hanke, L., and C. A. Millares. *Cuerpo de documentos del siglo XVI sobre los derechos de España en las Indias y en las Filipinas.* Mexico: FCE, 1943.

Harent, S. "Infidèles." *DTC* 7:1726–1930.

Hauben, J. P. "White Legend against Black: Nationalism and Enlightenment in a Spanish Context." *Americas* 34, no. 1 (July 1977): 1–19.

Helminen, J. P. "¿Eran caníbales los caribes? Fray Bartolomé de Las Casas y el canibalismo." *RHA* 105 (January–June 1988): 147–58.

Hemming, J. *The Conquest of the Incas.* San Diego: Harcourt Brace Jovanovich, 1970.

Henkel, W. "Le missioni e la legislazione coloniale alla luce della prasi e della dottrina di Fray Bartolome de Las Casas." *I diritti,* 379–88.

Henríquez Ureña, P. *Las corrientes literarias en la América Hispana.* 2d ed. Mexico City and Buenos Aires, 1954.

Hernáez, F. J. *Colección de bulas, breves y otros documentos relativos a la Iglesia de América y Filipinas.* 2d ed. Brussels: Alfredo Vromant, 1879.

Hernández, M. *Memoria del bien perdido.* Madrid: Colección Encuentros, 1991.

Hernández, M., et al. *Entre el mito y la historia.* Lima: Ediciones Psicoanalíticas Imago, 1987.

Hernández, R. *Derechos humanos en Francisco de Vitoria: Antología.* Salamanca: Editorial San Esteban, 1984.

————. "Doctrina americanista de Domingo Báñez." *CT* 116, no. 379 (May–August 1989): 235–69.

————. "Domingo Báñez, continuador de Francisco de Vitoria en la doctrina internacionalista sobre las Indias." *Dominicos* (1989), 61–92.

————. "La escuela dominicana de Salamanca ante el descubrimiento de América." *Dominicos* (1986), 101–32.

————. "Francisco de Vitoria en la crisis de su tiempo." *I diritti,* 31–62.

————. "Francisco de Vitoria y Bartolomé de Las Casas." *Actas del Congreso sobre Bartolomé de Las Casas.* Lima, 1992.

————. "Las hipótesis de Francisco de Vitoria." *Etica en la conquista,* 345–81.

————. "Las Casas en contra de la guerra." *CT* 111 (May–August 1984): 279–305.

————. "Las Casas y Sepúlveda frente a frente." *CT* 102, no. 333 (1975): 209–47.

————. *El obispo dominico de Panamá, Fray Tomas de Berlanga.* In preparation.

————. "Personalidad de Francisco de Vitoria." *CT* 114, no. 372 (January–April 1987): 37–69.

————. "Pobreza y evangelismo de los dominicos en Indias." *CT* 114, no. 3 (September–December 1987): 437–58.

————. "Presupuestos de Francisco de Vitoria a su doctrina indiana." *CT* 111 (1984): 61–86.

Hernández Sánchez-Barba, M. "Actitud del conquistador ante la ética de la conquista." *Etica de la conquista.*

Hilton, R. "El Padre Las Casas, el castellano y las lenguas indígenas." *Cuadernos Hispanoamericanos,* no. 331 (January 1978): 123–28.

Höffner, J. *La ética colonial española del Siglo de Oro: Cristianismo y dignidad humana.* Madrid: CH, 1957.

Hoornaert, E. "Las Casas entre o direito corporativo e o direito internacional." *REB* 49, fasc. 196 (December 1989): 899–912.

———. "¿Las Casas ou Sepúlveda?" *REB* 30, fasc. 120 (December 1970): 850–70.

Horms, J. M. "Etude sur la pensée politique de Tertullien." *Revue Hist. Phil. Rel.* 38 (1958): 1–38.

Hourbon, L. "Evangéliser la Caraïbe: Régime de conquête ou régime de droit?" *Les rendez-vous de Saint-Domingue.* Paris: Centurion, 1991.

Huerga, A. "La antropología indiana: Colón, Las Casas, Acosta." *I diritti,* 389–408.

———. "La antropología indiana de Cristóbal Colón." *Horizontes* 29, no. 58 (April 1986): 5–20.

———. "Bartolomé de Las Casas, dominico." *Communio* (Seville) 7, fasc. 1 (1974): 5–31.

———. "Las culturas de los indios en el idearium del Padre Las Casas." *Horizontes* 19, no. 38 (April 1976): 81–95.

———. "El humanismo profético de Bartolomé de Las Casas." *Horizontes* 28, no. 55 (October 1984): 31–48.

———. "La instalación de la Iglesia en el Nuevo Mundo." *Angelicum* 63, no. 1 (1986): 227–56.

Iparraguirre, D. *Francisco de Vitoria: Una teoría social del valor económico.* Bilbao: Universidad de Deusto, 1957.

Jaca, F. J. de. "Resolución sobre la libertad de los negros y sus originarios en el estado de paganos y después ya cristianos." *AGI:* 527.

Janssens, L. "A Moral Understanding of Some Arguments of Saint Thomas." *Ephemerides Theologicae Lovanienses* 63, fasc. 4 (December 1987): 354–60.

Jarlot, G. "Domingo de Soto devant les problèmes moraux de la conquête américaine." *Gregorianum* 44 (1963): 80–87.

Jiménez de la Espada, M. "Primer siglo de la Universidad de Lima." *Revista Crítica de Historia y Literatura Españolas, Portuguesas e Hispanoamericanas* (Madrid) 1, nos. 9–12 (1896).

———. *Tres relaciones de antigüedades peruanas.* Madrid, 1879.

Joblin, J. "Las Casas et les perspectives présentes du droit international." *I diritti,* 409–19.

Joroshaeva, F. "Bartolomé de Las Casas y Motolinía." *Historia y Sociedad* (Mexico City) (spring 1966): 85–95.

Journet, C. *L'Eglise du Verbe incarné.* Vol. 1. Paris: Desclée, 1941.

Juan de la Cruz. *Obras completas.* Madrid: Editorial de Espiritualidad, 1988.

Jung, N. "Restitution." *DTC* 13/2, cols. 2466–2501.

Junquera, C. "Pervivencia de las religiones africanas en el Perú." *IAA* 10, no. 2 (1984): 175–88.

Justenhoven, H. G. *Francisco de Vitoria zu Krieg und Frieden.* Cologne: J. P. Bachem Verlag, 1991.

Kamen, H. "Toleration and Dissent in Sixteenth Century Spain: The Alternative Tradition." *Sixteenth-Century Journal* 19, no. 1 (1988): 3–23.

Keen, B. "Approaches to Las Casas, 1535–1970." *Las Casas in History,* 3–63.

———. "The Black Legend Revisited: Assumptions and Realities." *HAHR* 49 (November 1969): 703–19.

————. "The White Legend Revisited: A Reply to Professor Hanke's Modest Proposal." *HAHR* (May 1971): 336–55.

Klein, H. *African Slavery in Latin America and the Caribbean.* New York: Oxford University Press, 1986.

Konetzke, R. *América Latina II: La época colonial.* Mexico City: Siglo XXI, 1972.

————. *Colección de documentos para la historia de la formación social de Hispanoamérica, 1493–1810.* 4 vols. Vol. 2: *La época colonial.* Madrid: CSIC, 1958–62.

————. "Ramón Menéndez Pidal und der Streit um Las Casas." *Romanische Forschungen* (Frankfurt) (1964): 447–53.

Krasic, S. "Un contemporáneo adversario di Las Casas: Il domenicano Vincenzo Paletin di Korcula." *I diritti,* 421–30.

Lacordaire, E. de. *Considérations sur le système philosophique de M. de Lamennais.* Paris, 1834.

Lactancio. "De Institutionibus Divinis." *PL* 6.

————. "Epitome Divinarum Institutionum." *PL* 6.

La Hera, A. de. "El derecho de los indios a la libertad y a la fe; la bula 'Sublimis Deus' y los problemas indianos que la motivaron." *ANDE* 35 (1956): 89–181.

————. "La ética de la conquista de América en el pensamiento europeo anterior a Vitoria." *Actas Simposio Etica,* 104–30.

————. "El regio vicariato de Indias en las bulas de 1493." *ANDE* 27–29 (1957–58): 317–49.

Lamennais, Félicité. *Essai sur l'indifférence.* Paris, 1823.

Lara, J. *Tragedia del fin de Atawualpa.* Cochabamba, Bolivia: Imprenta Universitaria, 1957.

Larios, A., and A. García. "Introducción." Las Casas, *Obras completas,* 12:229–61.

Larraz, J. *La época del mercantilismo en Castilla (1500–1700).* Madrid, 1943.

Lassègue, J.-B. "De quelques sources et de leur interprétation, dans la pensée de Fray Bartolomé de Las Casas." *I diritti,* 431–38.

————. "Exigences de l'Evangile et droit des Indiens dans l'administration du 'sacrement' des christs crucifiés aux Indes." *Autour de Las Casas,* 116–20.

————. *La larga marcha de Las Casas.* Lima: CEP, 1974.

————. "Luchas en torno a la restitución y utopía de la justicia: Domingo de Santo Tomás en la fundación, administración y en los pleitos en torno a la doctrina de Chicama, convento de Trujillo (1548–1569)." Forthcoming.

————. "En torno al memorial del obispo Fray Bartolomé de Las Casas y de Fray Domingo de Santo Tomás (hacia 1560): Apuntes, sondeos, cuestiones." *Evangelización y teología en el Perú: Luces y sombras en el siglo XVI,* 149–78. Lima: CEP-IBC, 1991.

Latourelle, R. *Théologie de la révélation.* Bruges: Desclée de Brouwer, 1962.

Lavalle, Bernard. "Planteamientos casianos y reivindicaciones criollas en el siglo XVII." *Histórica* (Lima) 4, no. 2 (December 1980): 197–220.

Lecler, J. *L'Eglise et la souveraineté de l'état.* Paris: Flammarion, 1946.

————. *Histoire de la tolérance.* 2 vols. Paris: Aubier, 1955.

Ledesma C., J. M. "Comentarios en torno a las bulas concedidas por el Papa Alejandro VI a los Reyes Católicos a raíz del descubrimiento de América." *Horizontes* 18, no. 36 (April 1975): 25–45.

Le Guillou, L. *L'évolution de la pensée religieuse de Félicité de Lamennais.* Paris: Armand Colin, 1966.

Leonard, I. *Books of the Brave: Being an Account of Books and of Men in the Spanish Conquest and Settlement of the 16th-Century New World.* Cambridge, Mass.: Harvard University Press, 1949.

León Portilla, M. *Crónicas indígenas: Visión de los vencidos.* Madrid: Historia 16, 1985.

———. "Las Casas en la conciencia indígena del siglo XVI: La carta a Felipe II de los principales de México, en 1556." *Homenaje a E. O'Gorman: Conciencia y autenticidad históricas.* Mexico City: UNAM, 1968.

———. *El reverso de la conquista.* 6th ed. Mexico City: Joaquín Mortiz, 1978.

———. *Visión de los vencidos.* Mexico City: UNAM, 1969.

Le Roy, L. F. "Bartolomé de Las Casas, solo en la pelea." *Universidad de La Habana,* no. 202 (1975): 119–33.

Leturia, P. de. "Autenticidad e integridad de la encíclica del Papa León XII sobre la revolución hispanoamericana." *RHA* 34 (December 1952): 413–41.

———. "Felipe II y el pontificado en un momento culminante de la historia hispanoamericana." *Relaciones entre la Santa Sede e Hispanoamérica,* 1:59–94. Rome and Caracas: Universidad Gregoriana, 1959.

———. "Maior y Vitoria ante la conquista de América." *Estudios Eclesiásticos* (Madrid), no. 11 (1932): 44–83.

———. "Misiones Hispanoamericanas según la Junta de 1568." *Relaciones entre la Santa Sede e Hispanoamérica,* vol. 1. Rome and Caracas: Universidad Gregoriana, 1959.

———. "Perchè la nascente Chiesa ispano-americana non fu rappresentata a Trento." *Il Concilio de Trento I.* Rome, 1942.

Levene, R. "Bartolomé de Las Casas y la doctrina de la libertad." *Boletín de la Junta de Historia y Numismática Americana* (Buenos Aires) 1 (1924): 111–24.

Levillier, R. *Don Francisco de Toledo, supremo organizador del Perú: Su obra (1515–1582).* 3 vols. Madrid: Espasa-Calpe, 1935–42.

———. *Gobernantes del Perú: Cartas y papeles del Archivo de Indias.* Madrid: Sucesores de Rivadeneyra, 1922.

———. *Los Incas.* Seville: Escuela de Estudios Hispanoamericanos, 1956.

———. "Una nueva imagen de Las Casas y el arte crítico de Menéndez Pidal." *RI* 23, nos. 91–92 (1963): 111–22.

———. *Ordenanzas de don Francisco de Toledo, virrey del Perú 1569–1581.* Madrid: J. Pueyo, 1929.

———. *Organización de la Iglesia y órdenes religiosas en el virreinato del Perú en el s. XVI: Documentos del Archivo de Indias.* Madrid: Sucesores de Rivadeneyra, 1919.

Leyes de Burgos (1512). Burgos, 1991.

Libro Anual (1974). Mexico City: Instituto Superior de Estudios Eclesiásticos, 1975.

Lipschutz, A. "La merma demográfica en el siglo XVI." *Desarrollo latinoamericano* (Colombia) 2, no. 8 (September 1968): 51–58.

———. *El problema racial en la conquista de América.* Mexico City: Siglo XXI, 1975.

Lizárraga, R. de. *Descripción breve de toda la tierra del Perú, Tucumán, Rio de la Plata, Chile.* Buenos Aires, 1914.

Llaguno, J. "500 años de evangelización de México." Minutes of the consultation held under the auspices of the Episcopal Commission for Native Americans, under the presidency of Bishop J. Llaguno. *Estudios Indígenas,* no. 3 (October 1987).

———. *La personalidad jurídica del indio y el III Concilio Provincial Mexicano.* Mexico City: Editorial Porrúa, 1963.

Llinares, J. A. "Evangelización liberadora según Bartolomé de Las Casas." *CT* 102, nos. 331–32 (April–September 1975): 185–208.

Llorente, J. A. *Colección de las obras del venerable obispo de Chiapa, Don Bartolomé de Las Casas, defensor de la libertad de los indios americanos.* 2 vols. Paris: Casa de Rosa, 1822.

———. *Histoire critique de l'inquisition d'Espagne.* 2d ed. Vol. 2. Paris: Trouttel et Wurtz, 1818.

Lobato Casado, A. "El obispo Garcés O.P. y la bula Sublimis Deus." *Dominicos* (1986), 739–96.

Lo Grasso. *Ecclesia et Status: Fontes selecti.* Rome, 1952.

Lohmann Villena, G. "Los dominicos en la vida cultural y académica del Perú en el siglo XVI." *Dominicos* (1989), 403, 432.

———. "Exponentes del movimiento criticista en el Perú." *Las Casas et la politique,* 45–52.

———. "Las Leyes Nuevas y sus consecuencias en el Perú." *Historia general de España y América,* 7:417–35. Madrid: Rialp, 1982.

———. "El memorial del racionero Villareal al virrey Toledo." *Histórica* (Lima) 5, no. 1 (1981): 21–43.

———. "Propuestas de solución de juristas y políticos en América." *Etica en la conquista,* 631–58.

———. "La proyección en las Indias de las doctrinas de Vitoria y Las Casas: De la teoría a la praxis." *I diritti,* 133–51.

———. "La restitución por conquistadores y encomenderos: Un aspecto de la incidencia lascasiana en el Perú." *AEA* 23 (1966): 21–89.

———. "Tras el surco de Las Casas en el Perú." *Estudios sobre Las Casas,* 327–51.

Longpré, E. "Llulle, Raymond." *DTC* 9, cols. 1072–1141.

Lopétegui, B. "Apuros en los confesionarios." *Missionalia Hispánica* 2, no. 4 (1945): 571–84.

Lopétegui, L. "Influjos de Fray Domingo de Soto O.P. en el pensamiento misional del Padre José de Acosta S.I." *Estudios Eclesiásticos,* no. 36 (1961): 57–72.

López, J. T. *Dos defensores de los esclavos negros en el s. XVII.* Caracas: Universidad Católica Andrés Bello, 1982.

López-Baralt, M. *Icono y conquista: Guamán Poma de Ayala.* Madrid: Hiperión, 1988.

López de Lara. *Ideas tempranas de la política social en Indias: Apología de los indios, Bula de la libertad.* Mexico City: Editorial Jus, 1977.

López Martínez, H. *Diego Centeno y la rebelión de los encomenderos.* Lima, 1970.

Losada, A. "Bartolomé de Las Casas y la bula 'Inter Caetera.'" *Communio* (Seville) 7, no. 1 (1974).

———. "Fray Bartolomé de Las Casas, miembro insigne de la escuela de derecho internacional de Salamanca: Su obra inédita 'Apología.'" *Fray Bartolomé de Las Casas en Hispanoamérica: Primer Simposio Internacional de Lascasistas,* 219–62. Chiapas, Mexico: Gobierno Constitucional del Estado de Chiapas, 1975.

———. *Fray Bartolomé de las Casas a la luz de la moderna crítica histórica.* Madrid: Tecnos, 1970.

———. "La huella americana del humanista franciscano Antonio de Guevara." *Franciscanos* (1987), 807–18.

———. "Introducción." *Ginés de Sepúlveda, Demócrates segundo o de las justas causas de la guerra contra los indios.* Madrid: CSIC, 1951.

———. "Juan Ginés de Sepúlveda: Su polémica con Fray Bartolomé de Las Casas." *Cuadernos de Investigación Histórica* (Madrid), no. 2 (1978): 551–89.

———. *Juan Ginés de Sepúlveda a través de su "Epistolario."* Madrid: CSCI, 1973.

———. "Observaciones sobre 'La Apología' de Fray Bartolomé de Las Casas (respuesta a una consulta)." *CA* 211, no. 3 (May–June 1977): 152–60.

————. "La polémica entre Sepúlveda y Las Casas y su impacto en la creación del moderno derecho internacional." *Cuadernos del Instituto Matías Romero de Estudios Diplomáticos* (Mexico City), no. 8 (1982): 7–45.

————. "Ponencia sobre Bartolomé de Las Casas." *Las Casas et la politique*, 22–24.

————. "Sepúlveda–Las Casas–Vitoria: Más coincidencias que divergencias." *I diritti*, 439–62.

————. "Sobre la huella de Las Casas: El P. Lebret, pionero de los tiempos modernos." *Dominicos* (1986), 351–64.

————. "Los Tesoros del Perú y la Apología contra Sepúlveda, obras inéditas de Fray Bartolomé de Las Casas." *BRAH* 131 (1953): i–xxviii.

————. *Tratados políticos de Juan Ginés de Sepúlveda.* Madrid: IEP, 1963.

Lottin, O. *Psychologie et morale aux XIIme et XIIIme siècles.* Vol. 2. Louvain: Abbaye du Mont César, 1948.

Lubac, H. de. *Corpus mysticum: L'eucharistie et l'Eglise au moyen âge.* Paris: Aubier, 1949.

Lucena, M. "Crisis de la conciencia nacional: Las dudas de Carlos V." *Etica en la conquista*, 163–98.

————. "La estructura uniforme de Iberoamérica como región." *Historia de Iberoamérica*, 323–419. Madrid: Cátedra, 1990.

Lumbreras, L. G. *De los orígenes del Estado en el Perú.* Lima: Milla Batres, 1972.

MacCormack, S. "'The Heart Has Its Reasons': Predicaments of Missionary Christianity in Early Colonial Perú." *HAHR* 65, no. 3 (1985): 443–66.

————. "Pachacuti: Miracles, Punishments, and Last Judgment: Visionary Past and Prophetic Future in Early Colonial Peru." *AHR* 89: 960–1006.

Macera, P. "Introducción." *Guamán Poma: Y no hay remedio*, 25–80. Lima: Centro de Investigación y Promoción Amazónico, 1991.

MacNutt, F. *Bartholomew de Las Casas: His Life, His Apostolate, and His Writings.* New York and London: Putnam's Sons, 1909.

Maeder, E. "La población americana después de la conquista." *América y España: Encuentro de dos mundos*, 116–29. Buenos Aires: Angel Estrada, 1988.

Maguiña, A. "Guamán Poma y la evangelización." *Evangelización y teología en el Perú: Luces y sombras en el siglo XVI*, 199–211. Lima: CEP-IBC, 1991.

Mahn-Lot, M. "Bartolomé de Las Casas, évêque de Chiapa: Un saint ou un politicien?" *Mélanges de la Casa de Velázquez* (Paris) 13 (1977): 161–76.

————. "Bartolomé de las Casas, homme de l'Evangile et homme politique." *Mélanges de la Bibliothèque Espagnole*, 205–11. Paris, 1977–78; Madrid: Ministerio de Asuntos Exteriores, 1982.

————. *Bartolomé de Las Casas et le droit des Indiens.* Paris: Payot, 1982.

————. *La conquête de l'Amérique espagnole.* Paris: PUF, 1974.

————. "Controverses autour de Bartolomé de Las Casas." *Annales* (Paris) (July–August 1966): 875–85.

————. "Droit des Indiens et devoir de restitution selon Las Casas." *Las Casas et la politique*, 81–91.

————. "Espagne et indigénisme au Nouveau Monde." *Revue d'Histoire* (1978): 86–98.

————. "La 'liberté' de l'Indien d'Amérique aux XVI et XVII siècles et la politique de regroupement." *Revue Historique* (Paris) 285 (1990).

————. "L'oidor Tomás López: Divergences et convergences avec les positions de Las Casas." *IAA* 3, no. 2 (1977): 167–76.

————. "Transculturation et évangélisation dans le Pérou du XVI S.: Notes sur Domingo de Santo Tomas, disciple de Las Casas, méthodologie de l'histoire et sciences humaines." *Mélanges en l'honneur de F. Braudel*, 353–65. Paris: Privat, 1973.

———, ed. *Barthélemy de Las Casas: L'évangile et la force.* Paris: du Cerf, 1964.

Malley, F. "De Las Casas à Gustavo Gutiérrez et Leonardo Boff." *Echanges,* no. 195 (September 1985): 8–18.

Manrique, J. A. "Las Casas y el arte indígena." *Revista de la Universidad de México* 20 (June 1966): 11–14.

Manrique, N. "Historia y utopía en los Andes." *Márgenes* 4, no. 8 (December 1991): 21–33.

Manzano y Manzano, J. *Fray Bartolomé de Las Casas ante la Junta de Valladolid de 1542.* Madrid: CH, 1948.

———. *Historia de las recopilaciones de Indias.* Madrid: CH, 1950.

———. *La incorporación de las Indias a la corona de Castilla.* Madrid: CH, 1948.

Maravall, J. A. *Las Comunidades de Castilla: Una primera revolución moderna.* Madrid: Revista de Occidente, 1963.

———. "La corriente democrática medieval en España y la fórmula 'Quod Omnes Tangit.'" *Estudios de Historia del Pensamiento Español,* 163–77. Madrid: CH, 1983.

———. "El descubrimiento de América en la historia del pensamiento político." *Estudios de Historia del Pensamiento Español,* 393–426. Madrid: CH, 1984.

———. "Utopía y primitivismo en el pensamiento de Las Casas." *Revista de Occidente* (Madrid), no. 141 (December 1974): 311–88.

Marcus, R. "Bartolomé de Las Casas–Sepúlveda." *IAA* 3, no. 2 (1977): 231–32.

———. "Bartolomé de las Casas, un discepolo di Savonarola." *Terra Ameriga: Associazione Italiane Studi Americanisti* (Genova), no. 41 (December 1980): 39–43.

———. "La conquête de Cholula: Conflit d'interprétations." *IAA* 3, no. 2 (1977): 193–213.

———. "Droit de guerre et devoir de réparation selon Bartolomé de Las Casas: Les Cultures ibériques en devenir." *Essais à la mémoire de Marcel Bataillon,* 549–65. Paris, 1979.

———. "Las Casas pérouaniste." *Cahiers du Monde Hispanique et Luso-Brésilien* (Toulouse), no. 7 (1966): 25–41.

———. "Le mythe littéraire de Las Casas." *Revue de Littérature Comparée* (Paris) (1978): 390–415.

———. "El primer decenio de Las Casas en el nuevo mundo." *IAA* 3, no. 2 (1977): 87–122.

———. "La 'Quaestio Theologalis' inédite de Las Casas." *Communio* (Seville) 7, no. 1 (1974): 67–83.

———. "La transformación literaria de Las Casas en Hispanoamérica." *AEA* 23 (1966): 247–65.

Mariátegui, J. C. *Peruanicemos al Perú.* Lima: Amauta, 1970.

Markus, G. *Bartolomé de Las Casas: The Gospel of Liberation.* Dublin: Veritas/St. Paul Publications, 1988.

Marticorena, M. "Cieza de León en Sevilla y su muerte en 1554." *AEA* 12 (1955): 615–74.

Martin, C. "L'Empereur Constantin fut-il un chrétien sincère?" *NRT* 78, no. 9 (November 1956): 952–54.

Martínez, M. "De la sensibilidad estética del Padre Las Casas." *RI* 26, nos. 105–6 (1966): 497–505.

———. *Fray Bartolomé de Las Casas, el gran calumniado.* Madrid: Imprenta La Rafa, 1955.

——. *Fray Bartolomé de Las Casas, padre de América.* Madrid: Rafa, 1958.

——. *Fray Bartolomé y sus contemporáneos.* Mexico City: Librería Parroquial, 1980.

——. "Las Casas, historiador. I. Valor Histórico de 'La Destrucción de las Indias.' " *CT* 79, no. 244 (July–September 1952): 441–68.

——. "Las Casas on the Conquest of America." *Las Casas in History,* 309–49.

——. "Las Casas–Vitoria y la bula 'Sublimis Deus.' " *Estudios sobre Las Casas,* 25–51.

——. "El obispo Marroquín y el franciscano Motolinía, enemigos de Las Casas." *BRAH* 132 (1953): 173–99.

——. "El Padre Las Casas, promotor de la evangelización de América." *AEA* 23 (1966): 91–108.

——. "El P. Las Casas y el obispo Marroquín." *CT* (January 1973): 299–307.

Martínez Paredes, D. "Fray Bartolomé de las Casas motivo de controversia." *Boletín Bibliográfico de la Secretaría de Hacienda y Crédito Público* (Mexico City), no. 263 (1963): 11–14.

Martín Rivera, J. de. "El sermón de Fray Antonio de Montesinos." *LA,* 111–17.

Marzal, M. *Historia de la antropología indigenista: México y Perú.* Lima: PUC, 1981.

Mateos, E. "El mito de Las Casas." *Razón y Fe* (February 1963): 191–98.

Mateos, F. "Ecos de América en Trento." *RI* 6, no. 22 (1945): 559–606.

Matiello, C. "Francisco de Vitoria ¿Un precursor de la teología de la liberación?" *Stromata* (Buenos Aires) 30, nos. 3–4 (July–September and October–December 1974): 257–93, 471–502.

Mauro, F. *Le XVIe siècle européen: Aspects économiques.* Paris: PUF, 1981.

Maxwell, J. F. *Slavery and the Catholic Church: The History of Catholic Teaching.* London: Brown and Son, 1975.

McAlister, L. *Spain and Portugal in the New World (1492–1700).* Minneapolis: University of Minnesota Press, 1984.

McFarlane, K. B. *Wycliffe and English Non-Conformity.* Harmondsworth, Middlesex: Penguin Books, 1972.

Mechoulan, H. *L'antihumanisme de Juan Ginés de Sepúlveda: Etude critique du Democrates Primus.* Paris: Mouton, 1974.

——. "A propos de la notion de barbare chez Las Casas." *Las Casas et la politique,* 176–82.

Meddeb, Abdelwahab. "La religión del otro: Ibn'Arabi/Ramon Llull." In T. Todorov, *Cruce de culturas y mestizaje cultural,* 131–44. Madrid: Ediciones Lucar, 1988.

Medina, M. A. *Una comunidad al servicio del indio: La obra de Fray Pedro de Córdoba, 1482–1521.* Madrid: Instituto Pontificio de Teología, 1983.

——. *Doctrina Cristiana para instrucción de los indios por Pedro de Córdoba. México 1544 y 1548.* Salamanca: Editorial San Esteban, 1987.

——. "Evangelización y colonización: Ideario y praxis de los dominicos americanos antes de las leyes nuevas." *I diritti,* 497–513.

——. "Métodos y medios de evangelización de los dominicos en América." *Dominicos* (1986), 157–208.

Mejía Sánchez, E. *Las Casas en México: Exposición bibliográfica conmemorativa del cuarto centenario de su muerte (1566–1966).* Mexico City: UNAM, 1967.

——. "Mier, defensor de Las Casas." *Boletín de la Biblioteca Nacional de México* 14, nos. 3–4 (1963): 57–84.

Melida y González-Monteagudo, M. "El Padre Bartolomé de Las Casas y Valladolid." *Política Indigenista* 1 (1977): 9–27.

Mendiburo, M. *Diccionario Histórico-Biográfico del Perú.* Lima, 1874–90.

Menéndez Pidal, R. *El Padre Las Casas: Su doble personalidad.* Madrid: Espasa-Calpe, 1963.

———. *El Padre Las Casas y Vitoria.* Madrid, 1958.

Meneses, T. L., ed. *Teatro quechua colonial.* Lima: Edubanco, 1983.

Menil, E. T. "Tertullian and Pliny's Persecution of Christians." *American Journal of Philosophy* (1918): 124–35.

Merino, J. "Fundamentos de la teoría política del Padre Las Casas." *CT* 102, no. 333 (1975): 279–323.

Merino, M. "¿Cuándo y dónde se ordenó Bartolomé de Las Casas?" *Missionalia Hispánica* (Madrid) 1, nos. 1–2 (1944): 356–60.

Merino Brito, E. G. "Fray Bartolomé de Las Casas y la guerra justa." *Revista de la Biblioteca Nacional "Jose Martí"* (Havana), year 57, 3a época, 8, no. 4 (October–December 1966): 5–17.

Mesa, C. "La enseñanza del catecismo en el Nuevo Reino de Granada." *Medellín* 13, no. 50 (June 1987): 213–56.

Métraux, A. *Religions et magies indiennes d'Amérique du Sud.* Paris: Gallimard, 1967.

Milhou, A. *Colón y su mentalidad mesiánica en el ambiente franciscano español.* Valladolid: Universidad de Valladolid, 1983.

———. "El concepto de 'destrucción' en el evangelismo milenario franciscano." *Franciscanos* (1987), 297–315.

———. "De Jerusalén a la tierra prometida del nuevo mundo: El tema mesiánico del centro del mundo." *Iglesia, religión y sociedad en la historia latinoamericana (1492–1945),* 31–56. Budapest: Segued, 1989.

———. "De la destruction de l'Espagne à la destruction des Indes: Histoire sacrée et combats idéologiques." *Etudes sur l'impact culturel du Nouveau Monde.* Paris: Ed. L'Harmattan, 1981.

———. "Du pillage au rêve édénique: Sur les aspirations millénaristes des 'soldados pobres' du Pérou (1542–1578)." *Caravelle,* no. 46 (1986): 7–20.

———. "El labrador casado." *Estudios de Historia Social,* nos. 36–37 (June 1986): 433–61.

———. "Las Casas, prophétisme et millénarisme." *Etudes* (Paris) 376, no. 3 (March 1992): 393–404.

———. "Las Casas à l'âge d'or du prophétisme." *Autour de Las Casas,* 77–105.

———. "Las Casas et la richesse." *Etudes d'Histoire et de Littérature Ibéro-Américaines* (Paris) (1973): 111–54.

———. "Las Casas frente a la esclavización de los caribes." *Hommage à Noël Salomon,* 607–24. Barcelona, 1979.

———. "Las Casas frente a las reivindicaciones de los colonos de la isla Española (1554–1561)." *HBA* 19–20 (1975–76): 1–56.

———. "Pobreza, oro y tesoros: De los franciscanos espirituales a Colón." *Cuadernos Colombinos* 11 (1983): 113–44.

———. "Prophétisme et critique du système seigneurial et des valeurs aristocratiques chez Las Casas." *Mélanges de la Bibliothèque Espagnole,* 231–51. Paris, 1977–78; Madrid: Ministerio de Asuntos Exteriores, 1982.

———. "Radicalisme chrétien et utopie politique." *Las Casas et la politique,* 166–76.

———. "Sufficientia." *Mélanges de la Casa de Velázquez* (Paris) (1981): 105–45.

Millones, L. "Un movimiento nativista del siglo XVI: El Taki-Onqoy." *Revista Peruana de Cultura* (Lima), no. 3 (1964): 134–40.

———. *El retorno de las huacas: Estudios y documentos del siglo XVI.* Lima: Instituto de Estudios Peruanos-Sociedad Peruana de Psicoanálisis, 1990.

———. "Taki Onqoy." *Cielo Abierto* (Lima) 10, no. 28 (1984): 9–15.

Minaya, B. "Memorial." *Miscelánea Beltrán de Heredia* (Salamanca) 1 (1971): 490–92.

Mires, F. *La colonización de las almas*. San José, Costa Rica: Colección Universitaria, 1987.

———. *En nombre de la cruz: Discusiones teológicas y políticas frente al holocausto de los indios (período de conquista)*. San José, Costa Rica: DEI, 1989.

Monachino, V. "L'impiego della forza politica al servizio della religione nel pensiero di S. Agostino." *Nova Historia* (1959): 13–38.

Monceaux, P. *Histoire littéraire*. Vol. 1. Paris: Leroux, 1901.

Monica, M. *La gran controversia del siglo diez y seis, acerca del dominio español sobre América*. Madrid: CH, 1952.

Monner, M. *Race Mixture in the History of Latin America*. Boston: Little Brown and Company, 1967.

Montoya, R. "La utopía andina." *Márgenes* 4, no. 8 (December 1991): 35–73.

Mora, S. de. "Apéndice documental." *HBA* 19–20 (1975–76): 23–31.

Morales, F. "Las Casas y la leyenda negra." *Mundo Hispánico* (Madrid) 28, no. 322 (January 1975): 51–54.

More, T. *L'Utopie de Thomas More*. Ed. A. Prévost. Paris: Mame, 1978.

Moreno, F. "Historia, ética e Iglesia en América Latina." *Páginas* 19, no. 99 (October 1989): 27–38.

———. "Teología moral y contexto histórico-cultural." *Evangelización y teología en el Perú: Luces y sombras en el siglo XVI*, 215–30. Lima: CEP-IBC, 1991.

Morino, C. *Chiesa e stato nella dottrina di S. Ambroggio*. Rome: Idea, 1963.

Motolinía, T. *Historia de los indios de la Nueva España*. Madrid: Castadia, 1985.

Moya, F. *Después de Colón: Trabajo, sociedad y política en la economía del oro*. Madrid: Alianza Editorial, 1987.

Moya, R. "Las autoridades supremas de la Orden y la evangelización de América." *Dominicos* (1986), 855–70.

Muldoon, J. "John Wyclif and the Rights of the Infidels: The Requerimiento Reexamined." *The Americas* (Washington, D.C.) 36, no. 3 (January 1980): 301–16.

Muñoz, J. "La sociedad estamental." *Historia general de España y América*, 7:623–44. Madrid: Rialp, 1982.

Murillo Rubiera, F. "Bartolomé de Las Casas y los orígenes del derecho de gentes." *Las Casas et la politique*, 131–32.

Murra, J. *Formaciones económicas y políticas del mundo andino*. Lima: Instituto de Estudios Peruanos, 1975.

Murray, J. C. "La déclaration sur la liberté religieuse." *NRT* (January 1966): 41–67.

Murúa, M. de. *Historia general del Perú: Origen y descendencia de los Incas*. 2 vols. Madrid: CSIC, 1962–64.

Mustapha, M. "L'après-lascasisme au Pérou chez les Pères de la Compagnie de Jésus: Acosta." *IAA* 11, no. 3 (1985): 267–81.

———. "Encore le 'Parecer de Yucay': Essai d'attribution." *IAA* 3, no. 2 (1977): 215–29.

Nari, M. "Desestructuración del mundo indígena." *RHA* 104 (July–December 1987): 7–18.

Nguyen Thai Hop, P. "Los dominicos en la defensa del hombre andino." *Evangelización y teología en el Perú: Luces y sombras en el siglo XVI*, 17–47. Lima: CEP-IBC, 1991.

La nueva evangelización: Reflexiones, experiencias y testimonios desde el Perú. Lima: IBC-CEP, 1992.

O'Gorman, E. *Cuatro historiadores de Indias del s. XVI: Pedro Mártir de Anglería, Gonzalo Fernández de Oviedo y Valdez, Bartolomé de Las Casas y Joseph de Acosta*. Mexico City: Secretaría de Educación Pública, 1972.

———. "Génesis, elaboración, estructura y contenido de la apologética." In Bartolomé de Las Casas, *Apologética historia sumaria*, xv–lxxix.

———. "La idea antropológica del Padre Las Casas, edad media y modernidad." *HM* 14, no. 3 (1967): 309–19.

———. *La idea del descubrimiento de América: Historia de esa interpretación y crítica de sus fundamentos*. Mexico City: UNAM, 1951.

———. *La invención de América*. Mexico City: FCE, 1958; Mexico City: UNAM, 1977.

———, ed. *La utopía de Tomás Moro*. Mexico City: Alcancia, 1937.

Olaechea, J. B. "El clero indígena." In P. Borges, ed., *Historia de la Iglesia en Hispanoamérica y Filipinas*, 1:261–79. Madrid: BAC, 1992.

Oliva del Coll, J. *La resistencia indígena ante la Conquista*. Mexico City: Siglo XXI, 1974.

Olivier, B. "Les droits de la conscience: Le problème de la conscience errante." *Tolérance et communauté humaine*, 163–90. Tournai: Casterman, 1952.

Olmedo, M. "El arzobispo Loaysa, organizador de la Iglesia del Perú: 1543–1579." *Dominicos* (1986), 797–808.

———. "La instrucción de Jerónimo de Loaysa para doctrinar a los indios en los dos primeros concilios limenses (1545–1567)." *Dominicos* (1989), 301–54.

———. *Jerónimo de Loaysa, O.P.: Pacificador de españoles y protector de indios*. Granada: Universidad de Granada, 1990.

Oltra Perales, E. "Fray Toribio Motolinía fundador de Puebla de los Angeles y profeta de la justicia." *Nuevo Mundo* (Argentina), nos. 17–20 (1979–80): 297–327.

O'Malley, J. "The Discovery of America and Reform Thought at the Papal Court in the Early Cinquecento." *First Images*, 185–209.

Ortiz, F. *Historia de la arqueología Indocubana*. Havana, 1935.

———. "La leyenda negra contra Fray Bartolomé." *CA* 65, no. 5 (September–October 1952): 46–84; and 217, no. 2 (March–April 1978): 84–116.

Ossío, J. "Guamán Poma: Nueva corónica o carta al Rey: Un intento de aproximación a las categorías del pensamiento andino." *Ideología mesiánica del mundo Andino*. Lima: Edición de Ignacio Prado, 1973.

Osuna F. L., A. "De la idea del sacro imperio al derecho internacional." *El pensamiento político de Francisco de Vitoria*. Salamanca: Instituto Teológico de San Esteban.

———. "El tratado de 'Las doce dudas' como testamento doctrinal de Bartolomé de Las Casas." *CT* 102, no. 333 (1975): 325–78.

Otte, E. "Un episodio desconocido de la vida de los cronistas de Indias, Bartolomé de Las Casas y Gonzalo Fernández de Oviedo." *IAA* 3, no. 2 (1977): 123–33.

———. "Los jerónimos y el tráfico humano en el Caribe: Una rectificación." *AEA* 32 (1975): 187–204.

Pacaut, M. *La théocratie, l'Eglise et le pouvoir au Moyen-Age*. Paris: Aubier, 1957.

Pagden, A. "Cannibalismo e contagio: Sull' importanza dell' antropofagia nell' Europa preindustriale." *Quaderni Storici* (Bologna) 50 (1982): 533–50.

———. *The Fall of Natural Man: The American Indian and the Origins of Comparative Ethnology*. London and New York: Cambridge University Press, 1982.

———. "The 'School of Salamanca' and the 'Affair of the Indies.'" *History of Universities of England* 1 (1981): 1–112.

Palacios Rubios, J. *De las islas del mar océano*. Ed. A. Millares and S. Zavala. Mexico City: FCE, 1954.

Paniagua Herrera, J. "Ramón Menéndez Pidal y su Bartolomé de Las Casas." *La Querella de la Palabra* (Mexico City) (1967): 27–34.

Parish, Helen Rand. "Introduction: Las Casas's Spirituality — The Three Crises." In *Bartolomé de las Casas: The Only Way*. New York: Paulist Press, 1991.

———. "Introduction: The Secret Story of Las Casas and the New Laws." *Las Casas's Pro-Indian Tracts*. Vol. 1: *New Laws to Halt Dissemination*. Kansas City: Sheed & Ward, 1994.

———. *Las Casas: The Untold Story*. Berkeley: University of California Press, in preparation.

———. *Las Casas as a Bishop: A New Interpretation Based on His Holograph Petition in the Hans P. Kraus Collection of Hispanic American Manuscripts*. Washington, D.C.: Library of Congress, 1980.

———. *Las Casas en México: Historia y obras desconocidas*. Mexico City: FCE, 1992.

———, ed. *The Only Way*. (Full title: *Bartolomé de las Casas: The Only Way*.) New York: Paulist Press, 1992.

Parish, H., and H. Weidman. "The Correct Birthdate of Bartolomé de Las Casas." *HAHR* 56, no. 3 (August 1976): 385–403.

Parry, J. H. "A Secular Sense of Responsibility." *First Images*, 287–304.

Paso y Troncoso, F. *Epistolario de Nueva España 1505–1818*. 16 vols. Mexico City: Antigua Librería Robredo, 1939–42.

Patiño, V. M. "La historia natural en la obra de Bartolomé de Las Casas." *RHA* 61–62 (January–December 1966): 167–86.

Paz, M. de. *Del dominio sobre los indios*. Mexico City: FCE, 1954.

Paz, O. "Ocultación y descubrimiento de Orozco." *Vuelta*, no. 119 (October 1986): 16–28.

Pease, F. "Introducción." *Cieza, Crónica del Perú*. Vol. 1. Lima: Universidad Católica, 1984.

———. "Prólogo." *Nueva corónica y buen gobierno*. 2 vols. Caracas: Biblioteca Ayacucho, 1980.

Peña, J. de la. *De Bello contra Insulanos: Intervención de España en América*. 2 vols. Madrid: CSIC, 1982.

Pena, L. "Presupuestos histórico-doctrinales de la teoría de Las Casas de la libertad." *Las Casas et la politique*, 153–65.

Peña, R. I. *Vitoria y Sepúlveda y el problema del Indio en la antigua gobernación de Tucumán*. Córdoba, Argentina, 1951.

Pennington, K. J., Jr. "Bartolomé de Las Casas and the Tradition of Medieval Law." *Church History* 39, no. 2 (1970): 149–61.

Pereña Vicente, L. "La escuela de Francisco de Vitoria en la promoción de la Paz." *I diritti*, 81–101.

———. "La escuela de Salamanca y la duda indiana." *Etica en la conquista*, 291–344.

———. "Estudio preliminar." In B. Las Casas, *De Regia Potestate*, xxi–clv. Madrid: CSIC, 1969.

———. "Fray Bartolomé de Las Casas, profeta de la liberación." *Arbor* (Madrid) 89, no. 347 (November 1974): 181–94.

———. "La Intervención de España en América." In J. de la Peña, *De Bello contra Insulanos*, 21–134. Madrid: CSIC, 1982.

———. *Misión de España en América 1540–1560*. Madrid: CSIC, 1956.

———. "La pretensión a la perpetuidad de las encomiendas del Perú." *Política Indigenista* 2 (1977): 427–69.

———. "Proceso histórico de las fuentes." *Carta Magna de los Indios*, 33–125. Madrid: CSIC, 1988.

———. "Respuestas universitarias a la duda indiana." *Actas Simposio Etica*, 177–99.

Pereña Vicente, L., and V. Abril, eds. "Declaración de motivos." *Derechos civiles y políticos*, 143–65. Madrid: Editora Nacional, 1974.

Perera, B. "La teología española desde mediados del siglo XIII hasta las primeras manifestaciones del humanismo." *Historia de la teología española*, 447–89. Madrid: Fundación Universitaria Española, 1983.

Pérez, J. *Isabel y Fernando: Los Reyes Católicos*. Madrid: Nerea, 1988.

——. "Las Casas Polémiste." *Mélanges de la Bibliothèque Espagnole*, 219–29. Paris, 1977–78; Madrid: Ministerio de Asuntos Exteriores, 1982.

——. *La révolution des comunidades de Castilla 1520–1521*. Bordeaux: Bibliothèque de l'école des hautes études hispaniques, 1970.

Pérez, J. M. *¿Estos no son hombres?* 2d ed. Santo Domingo: Fundación García Arévalo, 1988.

Pérez, V., and B. Escandell. *Historia de la Inquisición en España y América*. Vol. 2. Madrid: BAC, 1984.

Pérez Bustamante, C. "El lascasismo en 'La Araucana.'" *Revista de Estudios Politicos* (Madrid) 64, no. 64 (July–August 1952): 157–68.

Pérez de Tudela, J. "La gran reforma carolina de las Indias en 1542." *RI* 17, nos. 73–74 (July–December 1958): 463–509.

——. *El horizonte teologal en el ideario de Las Casas*. Madrid: Instituto de España, 1975.

——. "Ideas jurídicas y realizaciones políticas en la historia indiana." *AAFV* 13 (1960–61): 137–71.

——. *El Padre Las Casas desde nuestra época*. Santander: Publicaciones de la Universidad Internacional Menéndez Pelayo, 1966.

——. "Significado histórico de la vida y escritos del Padre las Casas: Estudio crítico preliminar." In Bartolomé de Las Casas, *Obras escogidas*, vol. 1: *Historia de las Indias*, i–clxxxviii. Madrid: BAE, 1957.

Pérez Fernández, I. "Acusaciones y reivindicaciones en las Indias y la Metrópoli." *Etica en la conquista*, 117–62.

——. "Análisis extrauniversitario de la conquista de América en los años 1534–1549." *Actas Simposio Etica*, 239–65.

——. *¿Bartolomé de Las Casas contra los negros?* Madrid: Editorial Mundo Negro, 1991.

——. *Bartolomé de Las Casas en el Perú*. Cusco: CERA Las Casas, 1988.

——. "¿'Casas' o 'Casaus'? revisión crítica del doble apellido utilizado por Fray Bartolomé, obispo de Chiapa." *Studium* (Madrid) 23 (1983): 403–46.

——. "Las conquistas de Indias fueron, en si mismas, injustas y antisignos de la evangelización." *Studium* (Madrid) 32, fasc. 1 (1992): 3–76.

——. "Cronología comparada de las intervenciones de las Casas y Vitoria en los asuntos de América." *I diritti*, 539–68.

——. *Cronología documentada de los viajes, estancias y actuaciones de Fray Bartolomé de las Casas*. Bayamón, P.R.: Centro de Estudios de los Dominicos del Caribe, 1984.

——. "De Las Casas a Marx." *Studium* 17 (1977): 345–64.

——. "Dos apologías de Las Casas contra Sepúlveda: La 'Apología en Romance' y la 'Apología en latín.'" *Studium* 17 (1977): 137–60.

——. "La fidelidad del Padre Las Casas a su carisma profético." *Studium* 16 (1976): 65–109.

——. *Fray Bartolomé de Las Casas*. Caleruega, Burgos: OPE, 1984.

——. "¿Fray Bartolomé de las Casas, 'desleal' a Zumárraga y Betanzos y 'defraudador de su proyecto' de viaje evangelizador a China? (incidente documentalmente resuelto)." *Escritos del Vedat* 10 (1980): 533–64.

———. *Fray Bartolomé de Las Casas, O.P., Brevísima relación de la destrucción de África.* Salamanca: Editorial San Esteban; Lima: IBC, 1989.

———. "Fray Bartolomé de las Casas ante el último guerrillero indio del Caribe." *Studium* (Madrid) 24 (1984): 499–533.

———. "Fray Bartolomé de Las Casas en torno a las 'Leyes Nuevas de Indias' (su promotor, inspirador y perfeccionador)." *CT* 102, no. 333 (1975): 379–457.

———. *Fray Toribio Motolinía, O.F.M., frente a Bartolomé de Las Casas, O.P.* Salamanca: Editorial San Esteban, 1989.

———. "Identificación del escrito 'Del bien y favor de los Indios' de Fray Bartolomé de las Casas." *Escritos del Vedat* 9 (1979): 247–302.

———. *Inventario documentado de los escritos de Fray Bartolomé de Las Casas.* Revised by Helen Rand Parish. Bayamón, P.R.: Centro de Estudios de los Dominicos del Caribe, 1981.

———. "Un nuevo autógrafo de Fray Bartolomé de Las Casas (de la Brevísima)." *Studium* 18 (1978): 115–23.

———. "Primera edición desconocida de las 'Leyes Nuevas,' de 1542, promovidas por Fray Bartolomé de las Casas." *Studium* (Madrid) 25 (1985): 399–421.

———. "El protector de los americanos y profeta de los españoles." *Studium* 16 (1976): 543–65.

———. "Sobre la fecha del primer libro de Fray Bartolomé de Las Casas." *Studium* 18 (1978): 125–43.

———. "Sobre la primera exageración acerca del nuevo mundo." *Studium* (Madrid) 23 (1983): 119–236.

———. "El 'tiempo dorado' de la primera evangelización de América, hechura del Padre Las Casas." *Dominicos* (1989), 137–56.

———. "Tres nuevos hallazgos fundamentales en torno a los tratados de Fray Bartolomé de Las Casas, impresos en Sevilla en 1552–1553." *Escritos del Vedat* 8 (1978): 180–200.

———. *La última generación española de denigradores del Padre Las Casas.* Madrid: Instituto Pontificio de Filosofía y Teología "Santo Tomas," 1991.

Pérez Mallaína, P. E. "Tierras por descubrir y ganar." *Historia de Iberoamérica,* 2:23–108. Madrid: Cátedra, 1990.

Pérez Prendes, J. M. "La solución legal de la 'duda Indiana.' " *Actas Simposio Etica,* 493–510.

Phelan, J. L. "El imperio cristiano de Las Casas, el imperio español de Sepúlveda y el imperio milenario de Mendieta." *Revista de Occidente* (Madrid), no. 141 (December 1974): 292–310.

———. *El reino milenario de los Franciscanos en el Nuevo Mundo.* Mexico City: UNAM, 1972.

Philips, W. *Historia de la esclavitud en España.* Madrid: Editorial Playor, 1990.

Pietschmann, R. *La "Historia Indica" de Pedro Sarmiento de Gamboa.* Lima: Universidad de San Marcos, 1964.

Pijper, F. "The Christian Church and Slavery in the Middle Ages." *AHR* 14, no. 4 (July 1909): 675–95.

Pikaza, X. "Religión pagana y conversión cristiana en el antiguo Perú: Presencia de La Merced en América." *Revista Estudios* (Madrid) (1991): 489–593.

Pollini, P. "Bartolomé de Las Casas y Juan Ginés de Sepúlveda." *Rivista di Filosofía Neo-Scolástica,* no. 74 (1982): 343–54.

Pontifical Commission for Justice and Peace. *La Iglesia frente al racismo.* Rome, 1988.

Poole, S. "Successors to Las Casas." *RHA* 61–62 (January–December 1966): 89–114.

Porras Barrenechea, R. *Los cronistas del Perú (1528–1650)*. Lima: Biblioteca Clásicos del Perú, 1986.

———. "El pensamiento de Vitoria en el Perú." *Mercurio Peruano* 27, no. 234 (1946): 465–90.

Post, G. "A Roman-Canonical Maxim, Quod Omnes Tangit." *Early Parliaments Studies in Medieval Legal Thought: Public Law and State,* 1100–1322. Princeton, N.J.: Princeton University Press, 1966.

Prado Tello, E. "Presentación." *Guamán Poma: Y no hay remedio.* Lima: Centro de Investigación y Promoción Amazónica, 1991.

Priem, H. J. *La historia del cristianismo en América Latina.* Salamanca: Sígueme, 1985.

Przybylski, B. "Le problème de la guerre juste selon St. Thomas et P. Wlodkowic." *Interpretation und Rezeption,* 823–36. Mainz: Mathias-Grunewald-Verlag, 1974.

Queraltó Moreno, R. J. "Fundamentación filosófica del derecho de libertad religiosa en el pensamiento de Bartolomé de Las Casas." *IAA* 3, no. 2 (1977): 177–92.

———. *El pensamiento filosófico-político de Bartolomé de Las Casas.* Seville: Escuela de Estudios Hispanoamericanos, 1976.

———. "Síntesis doctrinal del pensamiento de Bartolomé de Las Casas." *Autour de Las Casas,* 148–62.

"Quinientos años de evangelización: Significado y perspectivas." *Páginas* 12, no. 85 (August 1987): 4–16.

Quinoñero Gálvez, J. "El Padre Las Casas según su rostro." *Mundo Hispánico* (Madrid) 28, no. 322 (January 1975): 55–58.

Quintana, M. S. *Fray Bartolomé de Las Casas.* Buenos Aires: Poseidón, 1943.

Quinto centenario y nueva evangelización. Lima: CEP, 1992.

Quirk, R. E. "Some Notes on a Controversial Controversy: Juan G. de Sepúlveda and Natural Servitude." *HAHR* 34 (1954): 356–64.

Quiroga, V. de. *De Debellandis Indis: Un tratado desconocido.* Ed. R. Acuña. Mexico City: UNAM, 1988.

———. "Información en Derecho." *DII* 10:333–516.

Rahner, H. *Abendlandische Kirchen Freiheit.* Cologne, 1943.

Ramos Pérez, D. "La 'conversión' de Las Casas en Cuba: El clérigo y Diego Velásquez." *Estudios sobre Las Casas,* 247–57.

———. "El Criterio Historial Universalista de Juan Ginés de Sepúlveda." *J. G. de Sepúlveda y su crónica indiana,* 27–33. Valladolid: Sem. Americanista de la Universidad de Valladolid, 1976.

———. "La etapa de los gobernadores generales." *Historia general de España y América,* 7:122–121. Madrid: Rialp, 1982.

———. "La etapa lascasiana de la presión de las conciencias." *AEA* 24 (1967): 861–954.

———. "¿Genocidio en La Española? Algunas precisiones sobre la cuestión." *Doctrina,* 19–54.

———. "El hecho de la conquista de América." *Etica en la Conquista,* 17–63.

———. "La Junta Magna y la nueva política." *Historia de España y América,* 6:437–54. Madrid: Rialp, 1982.

———. "La nueva situación dramática de finales del s. XVI." In J. de Acosta, *De Procuranda Indorum Salute,* 697–734. Madrid: CSIC, 1984.

———. "El Padre Córdoba y Las Casas en el plan de conquista pacífica de Tierra Firme." *Boletín Americanista* (Barcelona) 1, no. 3 (1959): 175–210.

———. "Un paralelo seglar del Padre Las Casas: Juan de Ampies." *AEA* 34 (1977): 149–71.

———. "Sepúlveda, Cronista Indiano y los problemas de su Crónica." *J. G. de Sepúlveda y su crónica indiana,* 101–67.

———. "La solución de la Corona al problema de la conquista en la crisis de 1568: Las dos fórmulas derivadas." *Etica en la conquista,* 716–24.

Randles, W. G. L. *De la terre plate au globe terrestre: Une mutation Epistémologique rapide (1480–1520).* Paris: Armand Colin, 1980.

Ratzinger, J. *Salus extra Ecclesiam nulla est.* Rome: IDOC, 1963.

Rech, B. "Bartolomé de las Casas und Aristotles." *JGS* 22 (1985): 39–68.

———. "Las Casas und das Alten Testament." *JGS* (1981): 1–30.

———. "Las Casas und die Autoritäten Seiner Geschichtsschreibung." *JGS* 16 (1979): 13–52.

———. "Las Casas und die Kirchenväter." *JGS* 17 (1980): 26–43.

Regalado de Hurtado, L. "La relación de Titu Cusi Yupanqui, valor de un testimonio tardío." *Histórica* (Lima) 5 (1981): 527–38.

Regina, M. "Las Casas: The Philosophy of His History." *RHA* 61–62 (January–December 1966): 73–87.

Remesal, A. de. *Historia general de las Indias Occidentales.* 2 vols. Madrid: BAE, 1964.

Restrepo, F. "El Padre Las Casas: El libro del año 1963." *Boletín de la Academia Colombiana* 14, no. 51 (1964): 5–16.

Reyes Católicos. "Instrucción para el Gobernador (March 20, 1503)." *DII* 31:156–74.

———. "Instrucción secreta para el gobernador Fray Nicolás de Ovando (March 29, 1503)." *DII* 31:174–79.

Ricard, R. *La "conquête spirituelle" du Mexique.* Paris: Institut d'ethnologie, 1953.

Ríos, F. de los. *Religión y estado en la España del siglo XVI.* New York: Instituto de las Españas en los EE.UU.; Madrid: J. Molina, 1927.

Riva Agüero, J. de la. *La Historia en el Perú.* Lima: La Imprenta Nacional F. Barrionuevo, 1910.

Rivera de Tuesta, M. L. *José de Acosta: Un humanista reformista.* Lima, 1970.

Rivera Pagan, L. "Libertad y servidumbre en la conquista española de América." *Cuaderno de Teología* (Argentina) 10, no. 2 (1989): 41–67.

Rivière, J. *Saint Justin et les apologistes du second siècle.* Paris: Bloud, 1907.

Rodríguez, A. "La influencia de la universidad de Salamanca en Hispanoamérica, aportación de los dominicos." *Dominicos* (1986), 641–74.

Rodríguez, V. "Isabel La Católica y la libertad de los indios de América: Devolución de los esclavos." *Anthologica Annua* (Rome) 24–25 (1977–78): 645–80.

Rodríguez Cruz, A. M. "Juan de Lorenzana, universitario salmantino y catedrático de la universidad de San Marcos de Lima." *Dominicos* (1989), 381–402.

Rodríguez Demorizi, E. *Los dominicos y las encomiendas de indios de la isla Española.* Santo Domingo: Editora El Caribe, 1971.

Romero, C. "Evangelización: Una nueva relación social." *Páginas* 14, no. 99 (October 1989): 17–26.

Romero, J. "Las Casas and His Dominican Brethren's Fight for the Recognition of the Human Dignity of the Latin American Indian." *RHA* 61–62 (January–December 1966): 115–20.

Rosenblat, A. *La población de América en 1492: Viejos y nuevos cálculos.* Mexico City, 1967.

———. *La población indígena desde 1492 hasta la actualidad.* Buenos Aires, 1945.

Rostworowski, M. *Historia del Tawantinsuyo*. Lima: Instituto de Estudios Peruanos, 1988.

Rousseau, J. J. "Discours sur l'origine et les fondements de l'inégalité Parmi les hommes (1754)." *Oeuvres complètes de J. J. Rousseau*. Paris: Furne, 1835–36.

Rubio, V. "Una carta inédita de Fray Pedro de Córdoba, O.P." *Communio* (Seville) 13, no. 1 (1980): 411–25.

Ruiz de Lira, R. *Historia de América Latina: Hechos, documentos, polémica*. Madrid: Editorial Hernando, 1978.

Ruiz de Santiago, J. "Conciencia errónea y reflexión moral." *Tommaso d'Aquino nel suo VII Centenario, Congreso internazionale* (Rome-Naples) 5 (April 17–24, 1974): 521–26.

Ruiz Maldonado, E. "Bartolomé de Las Casas y la justicia en Indias." *CT* 101, nos. 2–3 (April–September 1974): 351–410.

———. *La justicia en la obra de Bartolomé de Las Casas: V Centenario de Bartolomé de Las Casas*, 11–33. Mexico City: ISEE, 1974.

———. "Tomás de Aquino, Bartolomé de Las Casas y la controversia de Indias." *Studium* 14 (1974): 518–42.

Rumeu de Armas, A. *La política indigenista de Isabel La Católica*. Valladolid: Instituto Isabel La Católica de Historia Eclesiástica, 1969.

Saco, J. A. *Historia de la esclavitud de los indios del Nuevo Mundo*. 2 vols. Havana: Cultural.

Sacoto, A. "Fray Bartolomé de Las Casas: Paladín de la justicia social." *CA* 202, no. 6 (November–December 1975): 136–48.

Saénz de Santa Maria, C. *El licenciado don Francisco Marroquín, primer obispo de Guatemala (1499–1563): Su vida, sus escritos*. Madrid: CH, 1964.

———. "El Padre Las Casas de don Ramon Menéndez Pidal." *Razón y Fe* (Madrid) (December 1963): 488–94.

———. "Remesal, la Verapaz y Fray Bartolomé de Las Casas." *AEA* 23 (1966): 329–49.

———. "La tradición lascasiana y los cronistas guatemaltecos: El caso del cronista Fray Antonio Remesal, O.P." *RI* 16, no. 64 (1956): 267–85.

Saint-Lu, A. "Acerca de algunas contradicciones lascasianas." *Estudios sobre Las Casas*, 11–17.

———. "Bartolomé de Las Casas, teórico y promotor de la conquista evangélica." *Communio* (Seville) 7, no. 1 (1974): 57–68.

———. *Condition coloniale et conscience créole au Guatemala (1524–1821)*. Paris: PUF, 1970.

———. "Los dominicos de Chiapas y Guatemala frente al confesionario las-casiano." *Antropología e Historia de Guatemala* 2, no. 1 (1979): 88–102.

———. "Fondaments et implications de l'indigénisme militant de Bartolomé de Las Casas." *JGS* 14 (1977): 47–56.

———. "Las Casas et la première crise du colonialisme moderne." *Las Casas et la politique*, 3–9.

———. "Las Casas et l'intention prêtée à Charles-Quint de renoncer aux Indes." *Le Supplément*, 49–58.

———. *Las Casas indigéniste: Etudes sur la vie et l'oeuvre du défenseur des Indiens*. Paris: L'Harmattan, 1982.

———. "Significación de la denuncia lascasiana." *Revista de Occidente* (Madrid), no. 141 (December 1974): 389–402.

———. *La Vera Paz: Esprit Evangélique et colonisation*. Paris: Centre de Recherches Hispaniques, Institut d'Etudes Hispaniques, 1968.

Salas, A. "El Padre Las Casas: Su concepción del ser humano y el cambio cultural." *Estudios sobre Las Casas,* 259–78.

———. *Tres Cronistas de Indias: Pedro Mártir de Anglería, Gonzalo Fernández de Oviedo, Fray Bartolomé de las Casas.* Mexico City: FCE, 1959.

Sánchez Albornoz, N. *La población de América Latina desde los tiempos precolombinos al año 2000.* Madrid: Alianza Editorial, 1973.

———. "The Population of Colonial Spanish America." *The Cambridge History of Latin America.* Ed. L. Bethell. New York: Cambridge University Press, 1984.

Sánchez Bella, I. *La organización financiera de las indias (s. XVI).* Seville: CSIC, 1968.

Sandoval, A. de. *Un tratado sobre la esclavitud.* Ed. E. Vila Vilar. Madrid: Alianza, 1987.

Santisteban Ochoa, J. "Fray Vicente Valverde: Protector de los indios y su obra." *Revista de Letras* (Cusco), no. 2 (1948): 117–25.

Santos Hernández, A. *Salvación y paganismo.* Santander: Sal Terrae, 1960.

Saranyana, J. I. "Principales tesis teológicas de la 'Doctrina cristiana' de Fray Pedro de Córdoba O.P." *Dominicos* (1986), 323–34.

———. "Teología académica y teología profética americanas (siglo XVI)." *Evangelización y teología en América (siglo XVI).* Pamplona: Universidad de Navarra, 1990.

Sarmiento de Gamboa. *Historia de los Incas.* Ed. A. Rosenblat. Buenos Aires: Emece, 1943.

Sastre Varaz, L. "Teoría esclavista de Tomás de Mercado." *Dominicos* (1989), 287–300.

Sauer, C. O. *The Early Spanish Main.* Berkeley: University of California Press, 1969.

Schäffer, E. *El Consejo Real y Supremo de las Indias.* 2 vols. Seville: Universidad de Sevilla, 1935; Seville: Escuela de Estudios Hispanoamericanos de Sevilla, 1947.

Schneider, R. *Bartolomé de Las Casas frente a Carlos V.* Madrid: Encuentro, 1979.

Schuster, E. J. "Juridical Contributions of Las Casas and Vitoria." *RHA* 61–62 (January–December 1966): 133–57.

Seco Caro, C. "De la bula 'Sublimis Deus' de Paulo III (I-VI-1537) a la constitución 'Gaudium et Spes' del Concilio Vaticano II (7–XII-1965)." *AEA* 24 (1967): 1821–41.

Sempat, C. "Fray Bartolomé de Las Casas obispo: La condición miserable de las naciones indianas y el derecho de la Iglesia (un escrito de 1545)." *Allpanchis* 1, nos. 35–36: 29–104.

Sepúlveda, J. G. *Apología.* Madrid: Editora Nacional, 1975.

———. *Demócrates segundo o De las justas causas de la guerra contra los indios.* Ed. and trans. Angel Losada. 2d ed. Madrid: CSIC, 1984.

———. *Epistolario (selección): Primera traducción castellana del texto original latino, introducción, notas e índices por Angel Losada.* Madrid: CH, 1966.

———. *Historia del Nuevo Mundo.* Madrid: Alianza Editorial, 1987.

———. *Joannis Genesii Sepulvedae Cordubensis Opera.* Madrid, 1780.

———. "Proposiciones temerarias, escandalosas y heréticas que notó el doctor Sepúlveda en el libro la conquista de Indias, que, Fray Bartolomé de las Casas, Obispo que fue de Chiapa, hizo imprimir 'sin licencia' en Sevilla, año de 1552, cuyo título comienza, aquí se contiene una disputa o controversia." In A. Fabié, *Vida y escritos de Fray Bartolomé de Las Casas,* 542–69.

———. *Tratados políticos.* Madrid: IEP, 1951.

———. Undated letter, included as the appendix to the unpublished thesis of L. Hanke (Harvard).

Serrano y Sanz, M. "Doctrinas psicológicas de Fray Bartolomé de Las Casas." *Revista de archivos, bibliotecas y museos* (Madrid) (1907): 59–79.

Sertillanges, A. *La philosophie morale de Saint Thomas d'Aquin.* Paris: Aubier, 1961.

Sierra, V. D. *El sentido misional de la conquista de América.* Madrid: Consejo de la Hispanidad, 1944.

Sierra Corella. *La Censura en España.* Madrid, 1947.

Sievernich, M. "Theologie der Befreiung im Interkulturellen Gesprach: Ein Historischer und Systematischer Blick auf das Grundanliegen." *Theologie und Philosophie* 61, no. 3 (1986): 336–58.

Silva, A. de. *Trent's Impact on the Portuguese Patronage Missions.* Lisbon: Centro de Estudios Ultramarinos, 1969.

Silva Tena, M. T. "Las Casas, biógrafo de sí mismo." *Anuario de México* (Mexico City) 4, no. 4 (April–June 1955): 523–43.

———. *Las Casas biógrafo de sus contemporáneos y de sí mismo en la "Historia de las Indias."* Mexico City: UNAM, Colegio de Historia, 1963.

———. "Retrato de Alonso de Hojeda por el Padre Las Casas." *Anuario de Historia* 4 (1964): 289–303.

———. "El sacrificio humano en la 'Apologética Historia.'" *Anuario de Historia* (Mexico City) 16, no. 63 (1967): 341–57.

———. "Tres vocaciones del Padre Las Casas." *Homenaje a E. O'Gorman: Conciencia y autenticidad históricas.* Mexico City: UNAM, 1968.

Slicher Van Bath, B. H. "The Calculation of the Population of the New Spain, Especially for the Period before 1570." *Boletín de Estudios Latinoamericanos y del Caribe* 24 (1978): 67–95.

Smith, R. *Un humanista al servicio del imperialismo: Juan Ginés de Sepúlveda (1490–1573).* Córdoba, Argentina: La Ley, 1942.

Someda, H. "Fray Bartolomé de Las Casas y el problema de la perpetuidad de la encomienda en el Perú." *Histórica* (Lima) 5 (1981): 263–94.

Soria, C. "Cristianismo, teología y política en Fray Bartolomé de Las Casas." *Las Casas et la politique,* 124–28.

———. "¿Fray Bartolomé de las Casas historiador, humanista o profeta?" *CT* 101 (1974): 411–30.

Soria, G. *Fernández de Oviedo e il problema dell' indio.* Rome: Bulzoni, 1989.

Soto, D. de. *De justitia et jure (De la justicia y del derecho).* 5 vols. Madrid: IEP, 1967–68.

———. *Deliberación en la causa de los pobres.* Madrid, 1965.

Specker, J. "Fray Bartolomé de Las Casas im Widerstreit der Meinungen." *NZMR* 22 (1966): 213–30.

Staffner, H. "Bartolomé de las Casas 1474–1566: A Great Champion of Liberation Theology." *Vidyajyoti* 53, no. 11 (November 1989): 601–10.

Stanley, J., and B. Stein. *La herencia colonial de América Latina.* Mexico City: Siglo XXI, 1970.

Stern, S. *Peru's Indian People and the Challenge of Spanish Conquest: Huamangato 1640.* Madison: University of Wisconsin Press, 1982.

———. "El Taki Onqoy y la sociedad andina (Huamanga, siglo XVI)." *Allpanchis,* no. 9 (1982): 49–77.

Sugranyes de Franch, R. de. "Bartolomé de Las Casas ¿discípulo de Raimundo Lulio?" *Etudes des Lettres* (Lausanne) 2 (1986): 3–17.

Szeminski, J. "Las generaciones del mundo según Don Felipe Guamán Poma de Ayala." *Histórica* (Lima) 7, no. 1 (July 1983).

Taviani, P. "La personalità e gli intenti di Cristoforo Colombo nella scoperta delle Americhe." *I diritti,* 15–30.

Tellechea, J. I. *El arzobispo Carranza y su tiempo.* 2 vols. Madrid: Guadarrama, 1968.
———. "Las Casas y Carranza: Fe y utopía." *Revista de Occidente* (Madrid), no. 141 (December 1974): 403–27.
Tertullian. *Ad Scapulam.* Turin: O. Tescari, 1951.
———. *Apologeticum.* Turin: O. Tescari, 1951.
Thomas Aquinas. *Opera omnia.* Rome: Leonina, 1897.
Tineo, P. *Los Concilios Limenses en la evangelización de Latinoamérica.* Pamplona: Universidad de Navarra, 1990.
———. "La evangelización del Perú en las instrucciones entregadas al virrey Toledo (1569–1581)." *Mercurio Peruano* 502 (April–June 1991): 9–23.
Titu Cusi Yupanqui. *Relación de la conquista del Perú.* Lima: Ediciones de la Biblioteca Universitaria, 1973.
Todorov, T. *La conquête de l'Amérique: La question de l'autre.* Paris: Seuil, 1982.
Tord, J., and C. Lazo. "Economía y sociedad en el Perú colonial: Movimiento social." *Historia del Perú,* 5:9–327. Lima: Mejía Baca, 1982.
Toro, I. D. "El concepto de destrucción en el pensamiento de las Casas, Cuestiones Teológicas." *Medellín* 16, no. 46 (1990): 155–76.
Torre, J. A. de la. *El uso alternativo del derecho.* Mexico City: Universidad Autónoma de Aguas Calientes, 1991.
Torre Villar, E. de la. "Los presentes de Moctezuma: Durero y otros testimonios." *Revista de Historia Americana y Argentina* (Mendoza) 1, nos. 1–2 (1956–57): 55–84.
Trelles, E. *Lucas Martínez Vegazo: Funcionamiento de una encomienda peruana inicial.* Lima: PUC, 1991.
Trigo, P. "El Evangelio en la crónica de Guamán Poma." *ITER, Revista de Teología* (Venezuela), no. 1 (January–June 1991): 113–40.
———. *Imperialismo mesiánico providente.* In preparation.
———. "Pachacuti mundo al revés: Crónica de la conquista." *ITER, Revista de Teología* (Venezuela), no. 2 (July–December 1990): 79–107.
Truyol Serra, A. "De la notion traditionnelle du droit des gens à la notion moderne de droit international public." *Le Supplément,* 84–91.
———. "F. Vitoria y H. Grocio: Cofundadores del derecho internacional." *CT* 111 (1984): 24–25.
———. "Sepúlveda en la discusión doctrinal sobre la conquista de América por los Españoles." *J. G. de Sepúlveda y su Crónica Indiana,* 16–25. Valladolid: Sem. Americanista de la Universidad de Valladolid, 1976.
———. "Vitoria en la perspectiva de nuestro tiempo." In F. de Vitoria, *De Indis* (CHP), cxlii–clviii.
Turchetti, M. "Religious Concord and Political Tolerance in Sixteenth and Seventeenth Century France." *Sixteenth Century Journal* 22, no. 1 (1991): 15–25.
Ulloa, D. *Los predicadores divididos (Los dominicos en Nueva España, siglo XVI).* Mexico City: El Colegio de México, 1977.
Urbano, E. "En nombre del dios Wiracocha…apuntes para la definición de un espacio simbólico prehispánico." *Allpanchis,* no. 32 (1988): 135–54.
Urdanoz, T. "Las Casas y Francisco de Vitoria." *Las Casas et la politique,* 235–302.
———. "La necesidad de la fe explícita para salvarse según los teólogos de la Escuela Salmantina." *CT* 59 (1940): 398–414, 529–53; 60 (1941): 109–34; 61 (1941): 83–107.
———. "Síntesis teológico-jurídica de la doctrina de Vitoria." In F. de Vitoria, *De Indis* (CHP), xliii–cxlii.
———, ed. *Obras* of Francisco de Vitoria. Madrid: BAC, 1960.

Utz, A., and M. Boeglin. *La doctrine sociale de l'Eglise à travers les siècles.* Vols. 1, 2, 3. Paris: Beauchesne, 1973.

Valenzuela Rodarte, A. "Menéndez Pidal y Fray Bartolomé." *Abside* (Mexico City) 17 (1963–64): 104–7.

Valtierra, A. "Los grupos afroamericanos." *Los grupos afroamericanos: Aproximaciones y pastoral,* 9–28. Bogotá: CELAM, 1980.

Vargas, J. M. *Bartolomé de Las Casas: Su personalidad histórica.* Quito and Santo Domingo, 1974.

———. *En torno al Padre Bartolomé de Las Casas: El anónimo de Yucay.* Quito: n.p., n.d.

Vargas Ugarte, A. *Concilios limenses (1551–1772).* Lima, 1951–54.

———. "Fray Francisco de Vitoria y el derecho a la conquista de América." *Boletín del Instituto de Investigaciones Históricas* (Buenos Aires), no. 9 (1930): 29–44.

———. *Historia de la Compañía de Jesús en el Perú.* Buenos Aires, 1963.

———. *Historia general del Perú.* Vol. 2: *Virreynato (1551–1600).* Lima: Carlos Milla Batres, 1966.

Vázquez, J. Z. *La imagen del indio en el español del siglo XVI.* Jalapa, Mexico: Universidad Veracruzana, 1962.

Vásquez Franco, G. *La conquista justificada: Los justos títulos de España en Indias.* Montevideo: Tauro, 1968.

Vega y Rodríguez, A. C. "El Padre Las Casas." *Religión y Cultura* (Madrid) 8, no. 31 (1963): 417–23.

Veracruz, A. de la. *The Writings of Alonso de la Veracruz.* Ed. E. J. Burrus. St. Louis: Jesuit Historical Institute and St. Louis University, 1968.

Vera Urbano, F. de. "Aportación de Santo Tomás a la doctrina de la libertad religiosa." *Revista Española de derecho canónico,* no. 31 (1975): 29–48.

Vereecke, L. "François de Vitoria (1484–1546) dans l'histoire de la théologie morale du XVI siècle." *I diritti,* 613–24.

Verlinden, C. *L'esclavage dans l'Europe médiévale.* Bruges: De Tempel, 1955.

———. "La population de l'Amérique précolombienne: Une question de méthodologie de l'histoire et sciences humaines." *Mélanges en l'honneur de Fernand Braudel,* 453–62. Paris, 1973.

Vermeersch, R. P. *La tolérance.* Paris, 1912.

Vicente, F. "Las órdenes religiosas pioneras de la defensa de la capacidad mental de los indios." *I diritti,* 625–38.

Vigil, Ralph. "Bartolomé de Las Casas, Judge Alonso de Zurita, and the Franciscans: A Collaborative Effort for the Spiritual Conquest of the Borderlands." *The Americas* (Washington, D.C.) 32, no. 2 (July 1981): 45–57.

Vilanova, E. *Historia de la teología cristiana.* Barcelona: Herder, 1989.

Villegas, J. "Providencialismo y denuncia en la 'Historia de las Indias' de Fray Bartolomé." *BLCHI,* 19–44.

Villey, A. "Saint Thomas d'Aquin et Vitoria." *Le Supplément,* 93–100.

Virt, G. "Conscience in Conflict?" In G. Zecha and P. Weingartner, eds., *Conscience: An Interdisciplinary View,* 165–200. Dordrecht, 1987.

Vitoria, F. "Carta al P. Miguel de Arcos." In Beltrán de Heredia, *Ideas del Maestro Fray Francisco de Vitoria.*

———. "Carta del maestro Fray Francisco de Vitoria al Padre Fray Bernardino de Vique acerca de los esclavos con que trafican los portugueses y sobre el proceder de los escribanos." *AAFF* 3 (1930): 38–40.

———. *Comentario a la secunda-secundae de Santo Tomás.* Ed. V. Beltrán de Heredia. 5 vols. Salamanca, 1932–52.

———. *De Indis.* See below under *Relectio de Indias o libertad de los indios.*

———. *Doctrina sobre los indios.* Ed. R. Hernández. Salamanca, 1989.

———. *Obras: Relecciones teológicas.* Ed. T. Urdanoz. Madrid: BAC, 1960.

———. *Relectio de Indias o libertad de los indios.* Ed. L. Pereña Vicente and J. M. Pérez Prendes. Madrid: CSIC (CHP), 1967.

———. *Relectio de Iure Belli.* Madrid: CSIC (CHP), 1981.

Wachtel, N. *La vision des vaincus: Les indiens du Pérou devant la conquête espagnole.* Paris: Gallimard, 1971.

Wagner, H., and H. R. Parish. *The Life and Writings of Bartolomé de las Casas.* Albuquerque: University of New Mexico Press, 1967.

Weckmann, L. *Las Bulas Alejandrinas de 1493 y la teoría política medieval.* Mexico City, 1949.

———. *La Herencia medieval de México.* 2 vols. Mexico City: Colegio de México, 1984.

———. *El pensamiento político medieval.* Mexico City: UNAM, 1950.

White, H. "The Noble Savage: Theme as Fetish." *First Images,* 121–35.

Wilder, A. "Francisco de Vitoria and the Defense of Human Life." *I diritti,* 651–80.

Willems, B. "La necesidad de la Iglesia para la salvación." *Concilium,* no. 1 (January 1965): 114–27.

Wolfel, D. J. "La curia romana y la corona de España en la defensa de los aborígenes canarios." *Anthropos: Revue Internationale d'Ethnologie et de linguistique* (Austria) 215 (1930): 1011–33.

Wynter, S. "New Seville and the Conversion Experience of Bartolomé de Las Casas." *Jamaica Journal* 17, no. 2 (May 1984): 25–32; no. 3 (August–October 1984): 46–55.

Yañez, A. *Las Bulas Alejandrinas de 1493 y la Teoría Política Medieval.* Mexico City, 1949.

———. *Fray Bartolomé de Las Casas, el conquistador conquistado.* Mexico City: Sur, 1974.

Ybot León, A. *La Iglesia y los eclesiásticos españoles en la empresa de Indias.* Barcelona: Salvat, 1954.

Yucay (García de Toledo). "Copia de Carta . . . donde se trata el verdadero y legítimo dominio de los Reyes de España sobre el Perú y se impugna la opinión del P. Fray Bartolomé de las Casas." Ed. J. Chinese. *Historia y Cultura* (Lima) (1970): 97–152. Also in *Colección de documentos inéditos para la historia de España.* Vol. 13. Madrid: Imprenta de la viuda Calero, 1849.

Zavala, S. "Aspectos formales de la controversia entre Sepúlveda y Las Casas, en Valladolid, a mediados del siglo XVI." *CA* 211, no. 248 (May–June 1977): 137–51.

———. *La defensa de los derechos del hombre en América Latina (Siglos XVI–XVII).* Brussels: UNESCO, 1945.

———. *Las doctrinas de Palacios Rubios y Matías de Paz.* Mexico City: FCE, 1954.

———. *La encomienda indiana.* 2d ed. Mexico City: Porrúa, 1973.

———. "En torno al tratado 'De Debellandis Indis' de Vasco de Quiroga." *HM* 72/18, no. 4 (April–June 1969): 623–26.

———. *La filosofía política en la conquista de América.* Mexico City: FCE, 1947.

———. *Ideario de Vasco de Quiroga.* Mexico City: FCE, 1941.

———. *Las instituciones jurídicas de la conquista de América.* 2d ed. Mexico City: Porrúa, 1971.

———. "Las Casas ante la doctrina de la servidumbre natural." *Revista de la Universidad de Buenos Aires* 2 (1944): 45–58.

———. "Las Casas ante la encomienda." *CA* 5, no. 17 (February 1974): 143–55.

———. "¿Las Casas esclavista?" *CA* 16, no. 2 (March–April 1944): 149–54.

————. *Por la senda hispana de la libertad.* Madrid: Mapfre, 1991.

————. *Recuerdo de Bartolomé de Las Casas.* Guadalajara: Lib. Font., 1966.

————. "Relectura de noticias sobre el botín de los conquistadores del Perú." *RHA* 97 (January–June 1984): 7–22.

————. *El servicio personal de los indios en el Perú (extractos del s. XVI).* Mexico City, 1978.

————. *Servidumbre natural y libertad cristiana según los tratadistas españoles de los siglos XVI y XVII.* Buenos Aires: Instituto de Investigaciones Históricas, 1944.

————. *Temas hispanoamericanos en su quinto centenario.* Mexico City: Porrúa, 1986.

Zea, L. *América en la historia.* Mexico City: FCE, 1957.

Zevallos, N. "Acerca de un discurso liberador: El sermón de Montesinos." *Páginas* 99 (1989): 41–49.

————. "El Padre José de Acosta." *Evangelización y Teología en el Perú: Luces y sombras en el siglo XVI,* 179–98. Lima: CEP-IBC, 1991.

Zubillaga, F. "Quaestio theologalis: Escrito inédito del Padre Bartolomé de Las Casas." *Estudios sobre Las Casas,* 279–381.

Zuidema, R. T. "Observaciones sobre el Taki Onqoy." *Historia y Cultura* (Lima), no. 1 (1965): 137ff.

Index

Abelard, Peter, 198, 201
Abril Costelló, V., 490 n. 15, 505 n. 17, 554 n. 35, 577 n. 15, 581 n. 38, 586 nn. 63, 65; 594 nn. 54, 55; 595 nn. 59, 61
Absolution, 33, 365, 589 n. 9
Acosta, José de, 322, 417, 436, 469 n. 16; on culpability of *encomenderos*, 552 n. 21; on the defense of the innocent as a reason for war, 529 n. 1; on gold and evangelization, 426–28; on greed, 616 n. 9; on Hispaniola in 1520, 475 n. 25; on Indians and education, 558 n. 58; on the inferiority of the Indians, 558 n. 56, 612 n. 82; on miracles and evangelization, 506 n. 20; overall view of Indians, 293–94; on salvation of unbelievers, 250–52, 543 nn. 27, 28, 29, 30, 31; on war and evangelization, 127, 131; works of, 503 n. 1
Acts of the Apostles, the, 65, 483 n. 8, 541 n. 10
Adorno, R., 451
Adrian of Utrecht, 38
Africa, 158; Las Casas's denunciation of Christians' cruelty in, 107; massacres in, 485 n. 13; Portuguese and, 103, 219, 494 n. 1, 496 n. 10, 539 n. 20. *See also* Slavery of Africans
Albornoz, Bartolomé de, 322, 329
Alexander of Hales, 51
Alexander VI, 68, 111, 601 n. 12; donation of Indies and, 64, 380; Ferdinand V and, 33; Las Casas on responsibility of, 72; *Memorial de denuncias* and, 71; *Memorial de remedios* and, 70; Sepúlveda and, 136, 311; testament of Isabella and, 70; Vitoria on, 372. See also *Inter Caetera*
Altitudo Divini Consilii, 309; context of, 302–4; overview of, 307–8; scholarly opinions on, 490 n. 12; use after "revocation," 312
Alvares Cabral, Pedro, 106
Ambrose of Milan, 146, 510 n. 45, 512 n. 61, 544 n. 36, 547 n. 56
Andrés, M., 469 n. 12

Andrés Marcos, T., 508 n. 28, 519 n. 34, 521 n. 48, 543 n. 25
Anthropology, 527 n. 81
Antonio of Florence, 609 n. 61
Apologética historia (Las Casas), 527 n. 81; on "barbarians," 295; on equality of all humans, 218–19; on human sacrifice, 173, 178–79, 525 n. 68; on Indian culture, 299; overall viewpoint of, 191, 194; purpose of, 276
Apología (Las Casas): attack on natural servitude, 291–92; on "barbarians," 295; documents from Paul III and, 307, 311; on human sacrifice, 154, 173, 175–78, 179–82; on *Inter Caetera*, 386; notion of erroneous conscience in, 198; outlook of, 91–92; plan of, 522 n. 54; on the temporal authority of the pope, 375; Thomas Aquinas and, 211; versions of, 515 n. 5
Apología (Sepúlveda): bibliographical data on, 508 n. 26; Las Casas's repudiation of, 522 n. 53; on salvation of unbelievers, 250
Aquí se contiene una disputa o controversia (Las Casas), 175
Arcos, Miguel de, 349
Arguedas, J. M., 450
Arianism, 142
Arias de Avila, Pedro. *See* Pedrarias
Aristotle, 500 n. 32, 522 n. 55, 558 n. 56; on "barbarians," 295; on natural servitude, 113, 291, 292, 296, 340, 556 nn. 47, 48; 559 n. 61, 582 n. 40; references to, at Burgos, 280–81; salvation of, 248; on slavery, 81, 320
Asia, 106, 107, 294
Atahualpa, 115, 116, 349, 419, 437, 486 n. 27, 501 n. 39
Athanasius, 142
Audiencia de los Confines, 317–19
Augustine, 164, 215, 239, 254, 508 n. 27, 526 n. 72, 535 n. 32; on belief and free will, 128; on conscience, 198; on faith and will, 142; on religious freedom, 143, 163, 511 nn. 55, 57;

669